THE PURSUIT OF LIBERTY

A History of the American People

VOLUME TWO   SINCE 1865

THIRD EDITION

R. Jackson Wilson
Smith College

James Gilbert
University of Maryland

Karen Ordahl Kupperman
New York University

Stephen Nissenbaum
University of Massachusetts

Donald M. Scott
The New School for Social Research

HarperCollins*College Publishers*

Executive Editor: Bruce Borland
Developmental Editor: Judith M. Anderson
Project Coordination and Text Design: Ruttle, Shaw & Wetherill, Inc.
Cover Designer: Kay Petronio
Cover Illustration: Painting by Jacob Lawrence: "The Library," 1960 National Museum
    of American Art, Smithsonian Institution; Gift of S. C. Johnson & Son, Inc.
Art Studio: Mapping Specialists Ltd.
Photo Researcher: Corrine Johns
Electronic Production Manager: Angel Gonzalez Jr.
Manufacturing Manager: Willie Lane
Electronic Page Makeup: Americomp
Printer and Binder: R.R. Donnelly & Sons Company
Cover Printer: The Lehigh Press, Inc.

For permission to use copyrighted material, grateful acknowledgment is made to the copyright holders on pp. C–1 and C–2, which are hereby made part of this copyright page.

The Pursuit of Liberty: A History of the American People,
Volume Two   Since 1865, Third Edition

Library of Congress Cataloging-in-Publication Data
The pursuit of liberty : a history of the American people / R. Jackson
Wilson . . . [et al.]. — 3rd ed.
    p.   cm.
    Includes bibliographical references (p.) and index.
    ISBN 0-673-46921-2 (pbk. : v. 1). — ISBN 0-673-46922-0 (pbk. : v. 2)
1. United States—History. I. Wilson, Raymond Jackson.
E178.1.P985 1996   95-35092
973—dc20   CIP

95 96 97 98   9 8 7 6 5 4 3 2 1

BRIEF CONTENTS

iii

DETAILED CONTENTS

27 AN ERA OF IDEOLOGIES   557

28 AMERICAN DIVERSITY 615

MAPS, TABLES, AND FIGURES

PREFACE

Some forty years ago, when the oldest of the authors of *The Pursuit of Liberty* was in the eighth grade, he had to take his first course on the history of the United States. His teacher was a legend in the school, a tough, slightly forbidding woman, who was determined that her students were going to learn something about the history of their country.

She gave her roomful of fourteen-year-olds a demanding task. They had to memorize 200 "facts" about American history, including their dates. When the final examination came, they had to write down their list of facts in the correct chronological order. You could choose any facts, as long as there were 200 of them and they were in chronological order. You might start with "1492—Columbus discovers America." Or you could begin with "1607—First English colony in America at Jamestown, Virginia." (In both cases, you would be a bit wrong. But that didn't matter. These "facts" were in the textbook, and the important thing was that you had learned them.)

Nowadays, of course, everything about learning history has changed. The authors' own children have come home from history classes in schools and colleges with their heads full of "concepts" instead of "facts." They don't think "1607—Jamestown" (or even "1587—Roanoke," which is closer to the truth). Instead, they are taught to talk about large and abstract matters like "The Confrontation of European and Native-American Cultures." They study grand processes such as "Industrialization, Immigration, and Urbanization." They seem to learn history in a more sophisticated and better way than memorizing some arbitrary list of 200 facts.

But there is a problem. Students who study American history today seem to know something in general, but nothing much in particular. They discuss abstractions and generalizations, but these are not connected with any firm grasp of relevant factual information. Have our best and most innovative teachers and professors simply replaced 200 facts with 20 vague concepts? The old problem was that history was a grab bag of names and dates and places. Students learned something in particular and nothing much in general. But the new problem, knowing the general but not the particular, is just as serious. Either way, studying history runs the risk of being a plain waste of time.

This dilemma is partly the result of the nature of history itself. There are large and general tendencies and there are particular facts. The difficult thing is to see how the two fit together. We tend to look at history the way we look at a painting. We focus on the foreground—the facts. Or we think about the background, about the general way the picture is structured and the kinds of claims it makes on our imagination. But when we study history, it is difficult to put the foreground and the background, the facts and the general concepts, together. We seem to choose between foreground and background, unable to see how each makes sense in terms of the other.

When most history textbooks try to bring specific facts and general concepts together, they do so by simply telling readers that this or that fact is an example of this or that general tendency. First comes a heading, something like "The Contact of European and Native American Cultures" or "Industrialization." Then comes a sentence or two of generalization. A little further on come the facts, such as "In 1607, an English colony was established at Jamestown, in Virginia," or "The first transcontinental railroad was completed in 1869."

Some important things are lost in this way of writing history. We are not asked to see or understand the relationship between fact and general concept at all. Did something called industrialization *cause* the first transcontinental railroad or did a host of facts, such as the building of that railroad, *cause* industrial development? Concrete facts and general concepts merely coexist in most textbooks, each of them inert and incapable of giving any sort of life to the other.

Perhaps worse, when students study history in textbooks of this sort, they get no sense of the human experience involved in either the specific events they find listed there or the generalizations they read and underline to study for next week's test. Most history textbooks contain no narrative, no stories, no accounts of the dramatic, sometimes triumphant, often shameful efforts and struggles of human beings. Human action is squeezed out of history and we are left with dead events and equally lifeless generalizations.

We have written *The Pursuit of Liberty* in the belief that we have found ways to solve these kinds of problems. We started with two convictions. First, we had to make it possible for students to see and understand the ways that specific sequences of human action were related to the general setting in which they took place. Second, historians ought not to keep a secret of the remarkably exciting and dramatic ways people actually acted in the past.

These two convictions have shaped our book and explain its unusual structure. Each chapter has two different parts. In the first, we tell the *story* of a very specific and concrete episode: a witchcraft hysteria in Salem Village, Massachusetts, in 1692, for example; or the massacre of a band of Native American Sioux people at Wounded Knee Creek in the Dakotas in 1890; or the rending struggle for custody of the infant known as Baby M in the 1980s. Episodes like these are the human material out of which history is made.

But history is more than stories. It involves coming to understand how the stories could have happened. To do this, we have to know something about the general context within which a specific episode took place. So the second part of each chapter is a discussion of the historical setting of the chapter's episode. The narrative of Salem witchcraft is followed by a discussion of new people and new patterns in the later seventeenth century; the Wounded Knee massacre by an examination of the westward expansion of European-American society into the territories of the Native Americans; the story of Baby M by a discussion of the tangled relationships between private morality and public politics that characterized American life in the 1980s.

And so we go through *The Pursuit of Liberty*, alternating between the specific and the general, between narrative and explanation. In the end we think our readers will have a much better grasp of the way history works, of the way that all the specific actions of people are shaped by the historical setting in which they take place. And we have faith, too, that some of our readers will learn the most important thing that history has to teach all of us: We all live in history, profoundly shaped by the society around us, by what it has been as well as by what it is now.

If this lesson is learned, then our readers will have learned what we already know, that learning history is a way of discovering our kinship with all those real people who have come before us, who have acted out their struggles, terrors, and occasional exaltations with the same anxiety and effort that go so deeply into all our lives. The past is inescapable, for everyone, whether one knows it or not. It is better to know it.

We have been gratified by the way teachers and students have responded to the first two editions of *The Pursuit of Liberty*. But along with many kind words have come criticisms and suggestions for change. In this third edition, we have done our best to respond to those criticisms we found valid, and to act on the suggestions we found useful. So this edition is more than a collaboration among the five of us. It is a larger collaboration with our readers and critics. Out of this larger collaboration have come a multitude of small but worthwhile changes and a number of large ones. All of the chapters have been carefully revised. But we have worked hardest throughout the book to continue to try to rescue American history from its traditional focus on the actions of politically important men of European descent, and to tell as well the legitimate history of women and all those "minorities" who have long been the true American majority. Our two chapters on the Jacksonian period, for example, have been completely reorganized and rewritten in ways that have allowed us to do even more justice to the story of the Native Americans' encounter with the relentless westward advance of European-American society.

Our coverage of the colonial period has been expanded from three chapters to four. But more than expanded coverage is involved. The episode for Chapter 2 has been entirely replaced with a story that focuses much more sharply on the complicated relationships in Virginia between Europeans and Native Americans. A new chapter has been added on the eighteenth century. Its episode tells the story of an English effort to dislodge the Spanish from their settlement at St. Augustine, Florida. But this is more than the story of a military encounter between European forces. It is a story in which African-American slaves, "runaway" slaves, and Native Americans take their important place in the action alongside the English and Spanish. The second half of this chapter is an exploration of the ways all these groups—and with them women and people from other European countries as well—were interacting to create distinctive and diverse societies, not just in the English colonies of the Atlantic coast, but all over North America.

We have added a new chapter on the period of Reconstruction that followed the Civil War. This chapter, whose episode focuses on the wrenching experience of African Americans on Edisto Island, South Carolina, has given us a chance to explore in much greater detail the long, difficult and often disappointed efforts of freed slaves to gain a decent measure of control over their own lives and destinies.

A new final chapter has been added to bring our history down to the present. Its episode centers on the police beating of Rodney King, the criminal trials of the white policemen involved, and the riots in Los Angeles that followed during the spring of 1992. The second half of the chapter is our attempt to grasp the significance and meaning of the startling diversity that characterizes the United States as it prepares to enter the twenty-first century.

R. Jackson Wilson

James Gilbert

Karen Ordahl Kupperman

Stephen Nissenbaum

Donald M. Scott

SUPPLEMENTS

FOR INSTRUCTORS

- **Instructor's Resource Manual.** Prepared by the authors of *The Pursuit of Liberty*, this manual includes lecture suggestions, audiovisual materials, test questions, and suggestions for enhancing student involvement.

- **Test Bank.** This test bank, prepared by Dona Brown of the University of Vermont contains over 2000 objective, conceptual, and essay questions with an emphasis on critical thinking and making connections. All questions are keyed to specific pages in *The Pursuit of Liberty*.

- **America Through the Eyes of Its People: A Collection of Primary Sources.** Prepared by Carol Brown of Oakland Community College, this one-volume collection of primary documents portrays the rich and varied tapestry of American life; contains documents by women, Native Americans, African Americans, Hispanics, and others who helped to shape the course of U.S. history. Designed to be duplicated by instructors for student use, the documents have accompanying student exercises.

- **Primary Sources in Gender in American History.** Prepared by Ellen Skinner of Pace University, this collection includes both classic and unique documents from diverse perspectives covering the history of women and gender in America. The book includes critical thinking questions, bibliography, and contextual headnotes and is available shrinkwrapped with *The Pursuit of Liberty* at a low cost.

- **Primary Sources in African American History.** Prepared by Roy Finkenbine of Hampton University, this compelling collection includes both social and political documents and covers the history of African Americans in America. The book includes critical-thinking questions, bibliography, and contextual headnotes and is available shrinkwrapped with *The Pursuit of Liberty* at a low cost.

- **American Impressions: A CD-ROM for U.S. History, Volume I.** This unique and ground-breaking CD-ROM for the U.S. History course is organized in a topical and thematic framework that allows in-depth coverage with a media-centered focus. Hundreds of photos, maps, works of art, graphics, and historical film clips are organized into narrated vignettes and interactive activities to create a tool for both professors and students. The first volume includes: "The Encounter Period," "Revolution to Republic," "A Century of Labor and Reform," and "The Struggle for Equality." A Guide for Instructors provides teaching tips and suggestions for using advanced media in the classroom. The CD-ROM is available in both Macintosh and Windows formats.

- **Visual Archives of American History, 2/e.** This two-sided video laserdisc explores history from the meeting of three cultures to the present. It is an encyclopedic chronology of U.S. history offering hundreds of photographs and illustrations, a variety of source and reference maps—several of which are animated—plus 50 minutes of video. For ease in planning lectures, a manual listing barcodes for scanning and frame numbers for all the material is available.

- **HarperCollins Comprehensive American History Transparency Set.** This vast collection of American history map transparencies will soon become a necessary teaching aid. This set includes over 200 map transparencies ranging from the first Native Americans to the end of the cold war, covering wars, social trends, elections, immigration, and demographics. Included are a reproducible set of student map exercises, teaching tips, and correlation charts. This fresh and extensive map package provides complete geographical coverage of American history.

- **Discovering American History Through Maps and Views.** Created by Gerald Danzer of the University of Illinois at Chicago, the recipient of the AHA's 1990 James Harvey Robinson Prize for his work in the development of map transparencies—this set of 140 four-color acetates is a unique instructional tool. It contains an introduction on teaching history through maps and a detailed commentary on each transparency. The collection includes cartographic and pictorial maps, views and photos, urban plans, building diagrams, and works of art.

- **A Guide to Teaching American History Through Film.** Written by Randy Roberts of Purdue University, this guide provides instructors with a creative and practical tool for stimulating classroom discussion. The sections include "American Films: A Historian's Perspective," a list of films, practical suggestions, and bibliography. The film listing is in narrative form, developing connections between each film and the topics being discussed.

- **Video Lecture Launchers.** Prepared by Mark Newman, University of Illinois at Chicago, these video lecture launchers (each 2 to 5 minutes in duration) cover key issues in American history from 1877 to the present. The launchers are accompanied by an Instructor's Manual.

- **"This Is America" Immigration Video.** Produced by the American Museum of Immigration, these two 20-minute videos tell the story of American immigrants, relating their personal stories and accomplishments. By showing how the richness of our culture is due to the contributions of millions of immigrant Americans, the videos make the point that America's strength lies in the ethnically and culturally diverse backgrounds of its citizens.

- **TestMaster Computerized Testing System.** This flexible, easy-to-master computer test bank includes all the test items in the printed test bank. The TestMaster software allows you to edit existing questions and add your own items. Tests can be printed in several different formats and can include figures such as graphs and tables. Available for IBM and Macintosh computers.

- **QuizMaster.** This new program enables you to design TestMaster generated tests that your students can take on a computer rather than in printed form. QuizMaster is available separately from TestMaster and can be obtained free through your sales representative.

- **Grades.** A grade-keeping and classroom management software program that maintains data for up to 200 students.

FOR STUDENTS

- **Study Guide and Practice Tests.** This two-volume study guide, created by Dona Brown of the University of Vermont, includes chapter outlines, significant themes and highlights, a glossary, learning enrichment ideas, sample test questions, exercises for identification and interpretation, and geography exercises based on maps in *The Pursuit of Liberty*.

- **Learning to Think Critically: Films and Myths About American History.** Randy Roberts and Robert May of Purdue University use well-known films such as *Gone with the Wind* and *Casablanca* to explore some common myths about America and its past. Many widely held assumptions about our country's past come from or are perpetuated by popular films. Which are true? Which are patently not true? And how does a student of history approach documents, sources, and textbooks with a critical and discerning eye? This short handbook subjects some popular beliefs to historical scrutiny in order to help students develop a method of inquiry for approaching the subject of history in general.

- **Mapping American History: Student Activities.** Written by Gerald Danzer of the University of Illinois at Chicago, this free map workbook for students features exercises designed to teach students to interpret and analyze cartographic materials as historical documents. The instructor is entitled to a free copy of the workbook for each copy of the text purchased from HarperCollins.

- **TimeLink Computer Atlas of American History.** This atlas, compiled by William Hamblin of Brigham Young University, is an introductory software tutorial and textbook companion. This Macintosh program presents the historical geography of the continental United States from colonial times to the settling of the West and the admission of the last continental state in 1912. The program covers territories in different time periods, provides quizzes, and includes a special Civil War module.

ACKNOWLEDGMENTS

We believe that everything that is said in *The Pursuit of Liberty* is true. Well, almost everything. But the book contains two unavoidable half-truths, both of them on the title page. Both are formulas that are imposed by the powerful conventions that govern the publication of books in our society. The first is the suggestion that an abstract corporate entity named HarperCollins College Publishers brought the book into existence. The second is that five individuals known as authors are responsible for all the words and ideas in the book. We would like to set the record straight on both these points.

The truth of the matter is that HarperCollins is not a corporate abstraction but a set of very specific people who have generously invested efforts, care, and talent in this book. Two of them, in particular, have been extremely helpful. Bruce Borland had the imagination and courage to set this third edition of *The Pursuit of Liberty* in motion. Judith Anderson brought to her editorial work seemingly inexhaustible reserves of intelligence, patience, and generosity of spirit. The book owes much to them.

The truth is, as well, that the writing of history is a collective enterprise. We owe an incalculable debt to generations of men and women who have labored to make the history of the American people comprehensible. We also owe a great deal to the people—many of them now mature men and women—who have been our students. We cannot repay them for all the history lessons they have given to us; we can only hope that some of their children may learn as much from our book as we have from them.

Newell G. Bringhurst
College of the Sequoias

John H. DeBerry
Somerset Community College

Ronald P. Formisano
University of Florida

Gerald J. Goodwin
University of Houston

James A. Hijiya
University of Massachusetts, Dartmouth

David Hudson
California State University, Fresno

Donald M. Jacobs
Northeastern University

Stephen J. Kneeshaw
College of Ozarks

Timothy Koerner
Oakland Community College

Jesus Luna
California State University, Fresno

Gerald W. McFarland
University of Massachusetts

Peter C. Mancall
University of Kansas

David Nasaw
City University of New York

Sheila Skemp
University of Mississippi

Ephraim Smith
California State University, Fresno

John Snetsinger
California Polytechnic University

Gary E. Thompson
Tulsa Junior College

Robert E. Weir
Bay Path College

In addition, we are most grateful to our consultants and critics whose thoughtful and constructive work contributed greatly to this edition. Their many helpful suggestions led to significant improvements in the final product.

The Pursuit of Liberty is also the product of some fine advice from other intelligent and dedicated people. Sometimes their suggestions have posed formidable tasks for us. Nonetheless, we are grateful to all our colleagues, particularly to: Katherine Abbott, Paul Francis Bourke, Dona Brown, Lawrence Foster, Ron Formisano, Paula Franklin, William Graebner, James Henretta, Marvin L. Jaegers, Stephen Kneeshaw, Gary Nissenbaum, Gregory Nobles, Thomas C. Parramore, Stephen Weisner, and Nancy Woloch.

ABOUT THE AUTHORS

R. JACKSON WILSON is Professor of History at Smith College. He is a graduate of the University of Missouri and received his Ph.D. from the University of Wisconsin. He has taught at an unusually wide range of institutions, including the University of Arizona, the University of Wisconsin, Columbia University, the University of Massachusetts, Hartford College for Women, Yale University, the University of Pennsylvania, and the Flinders University of South Australia. He has been a fellow of the Woodrow Wilson Foundation, the National Endowment for the Humanities, the Charles Warren Center, Harvard University, and the National Humanities Center. He is the author of *In Quest of Community: Social Philosophy in the United States* and *Figures of Speech: American Writers and the Literary Marketplace, from Benjamin Franklin to Emily Dickinson* (1989).

JAMES GILBERT is Professor of History at the University of Maryland. He is a graduate of Carleton College and received his Ph.D. from the University of Wisconsin. He has taught at Teachers College, Columbia University; Warwick University in Coventry, England, and the University of Paris. He has held Fulbright Professorships in Sydney, Australia, and Amsterdam, the Netherlands. His books include *Writers and Partisans* (1968), *Designing the Industrial State* (1972), *Work Without Salvation* (1978), *Another Chance: Postwar America* (1981), *A Cycle of Outrage: America's Reaction to the Juvenile Delinquent in the 1950s* (1986), and *Perfect Cities: Chicago's Utopias of 1893* (1991). He is currently finishing a book on American religion.

KAREN ORDAHL KUPPERMAN is Professor of History at New York University. She is a graduate of the University of Missouri and holds an M.A. from Harvard University and a Ph.D. from Cambridge University. She is the author of *Providence Island, 1630–1641: The Other Puritan Colony* (1993), *Roanoke, The Abandoned Colony* (1984), and *Settling with the Indians: The Meeting of English and Indian Cultures in America, 1580–1640* (1980). Her edited books include *America in European Consciousness* (1995), *Major Problems in American Colonial History* (1993), and *Captain John Smith: A Select Edition of His Writings* (1988).

In 1980, her essay "Apathy and Death in Early Jamestown" won the distinguished Binkley-Stevenson award of the Organization of American Historians. Her book, *Providence Island*, won the Albert J. Beveridge Award, given by the American Historical Association, for the best book in American History including Canada and Latin America. She has been a Mellon Faculty Fellow at Harvard, a fellow of the National Humanities Center, and a National Endowment for the Humanities Fellow at the John

Carter Brown Library. In 1995–1996 she is the Times-Mirror Foundation Visiting Research Professor at the Huntington Library, and Chair of the Council of the Institute of Early American History and Culture.

STEPHEN NISSENBAUM is Professor of History at the University of Massachusetts, Amherst, where he teaches cultural history. He is a graduate of Harvard College, holds an M.A. from Columbia University, and a Ph.D. from the University of Wisconsin. He has held fellowships from the National Endowment for the Humanities, the American Council of Learned Societies, and the American Antiquarian Society, and has been a fellow of the Charles Warren Center at Harvard. He has been the James Pinckney Harrison Professor of History at The College of William and Mary. He has served as president of his state humanities council, the Massachusetts Foundation for the Humanities. He is the author of *Sex, Diet, and Debility in Jacksonian America* (1988) and (with Paul Boyer) *Salem Possessed: The Social Origins of Witchcraft* (1974), which won the John H. Dunning prize awarded by the American Historical Association. He is currently writing a book about the history of Christmas in America.

DONALD M. SCOTT is a Professor of History at the Eugene Lang College of The New School for Social Research. He is a graduate of Harvard College and received his Ph.D. from the University of Wisconsin. He is the author of *From Office to Profession: The New England Ministry, 1750–1850* (1978), and is co-author of *America's Families: A Documentary History* (1982). He has been a fellow at the Davis Center for Historical Studies, Princeton University, and a National Endowment for the Humanities Fellow at the American Antiquarian Society. He is currently working on a book on democracy and knowledge in nineteenth-century America.

Reconstruction

THE EPISODE: *After four long years, the Civil War had once and for all determined that the American Republic could not be divided. But the society that had to be reunited was very different from the one that had split apart in 1861. The war had destroyed the institution of slavery. But the question of the place of the former slaves in American society, of the degree of "freedom" white America would grant them, remained very much an open question.*

There was no absence of possible and deeply conflicting answers to the question. The victorious Northerners were deeply divided over the matter. Most of them did not want to see blacks elevated to a position of civil and social equality—especially in the North. Even most abolitionists doubted that the former "bondsmen" were fully ready for freedom and envisioned a period of tutelage in the ways of freedom.

The defeated white Southerners—especially the former slaveowners—were much clearer in their answer. Whatever "system" was devised for the former slaves, they wanted it to be one that provided former masters with a dependent labor force and relegated blacks to a position of clear social subordination.

The newly freed blacks were no less clear in their answer than their former masters. They wanted "independence," freedom from anything that resembled the domination that ownership had entailed. And they wanted land.

Historians traditionally portrayed the newly freed blacks as relatively passive— bystanders or pawns—in a battle over Reconstruction fought out by ex-Confederates and northern Republicans. More recently, historians have pointed out that, on the contrary, the newly liberated blacks moved quickly—though by no means always suc-cessfully—to claim their newfound freedom and turn it to their own ends.

One place they did so was Edisto Island, off the coast of South Carolina. There in 1865 and early 1866, the issue of the place of the freedman in Southern society was immediately and fully joined, as all the parties—the freedmen, the former masters, and divided Northerners—fought to create their particular vision of a "reconstructed" South.

THE HISTORICAL SETTING: *Lincoln once said that the issue that the Civil War was fought over was union but that the cause was slavery. Similarly, the formal issue that dominated what historians have called Reconstruction (the period from 1865 to 1877) was "reunion." But what "caused" the process of reunification to take so long—it took more than twice as long as the war itself—and made it such a bitter and violent process was the question of the place the former slaves would occupy in the new and different South.*

The battle over the freedman was fought on two fronts. In Washington, between president and Congress, between moderate and Radical Republicans, and between Democrats and Republicans. But it was fought with greatest intensity in the South. The nature of the question itself—and, quite literally, the deadly seriousness with which it was taken—is sufficient to account for much of the intensity and violence of the battle. But it also took place under conditions that no Americans other than the southerners have ever faced—military occupation. "Reconstruction" took place, not simply within the context of a military defeat, but within a framework of conquest and an occupation that endured longer and with greater bitterness than the Allied occupation of Japan and Germany after World War II.

EDISTO ISLAND—LAND AND FREEDOM

Early on the morning of October 19, 1865, a small steamer carried General Oliver O. Howard from Savannah, Georgia, up the South Carolina coast to Edisto Island just twenty miles below Charleston. Veteran of the battles of Gettysburg and Atlanta and of Sherman's march to the sea, Howard was the Commissioner of the Bureau of Refugees, Freedmen, and Abandoned Lands (popularly known as the Freedmen's Bureau), the agency established in March of 1865 to aid the former slaves in their transition from slavery to freedom. He was on his way to Edisto, a settlement of nearly 4,500 blacks, almost all of whom were recently liberated former slaves, to explain recent changes in federal policy regarding "abandoned and confiscated lands."

In less than ten months, the freedmen on Edisto Island had transformed it from a war-torn, abandoned waste into a burgeoning community of independent farmers. Before the war one of the largest and most populous of the sea islands, Edisto early succumbed to the vicissitudes of war. In late 1861 most of the white owners fled the island to get away from the approaching Union forces. They and Confederate troops tried to take their slaves with them to the mainland, but the slaves resisted and fled to the periphery of the island, where they built huts and eked out a livelihood fishing and hunting. In early 1862 federal troops occupied the island and many of the slaves returned to their home plantations as squatters and as paid laborers on the plantations now run by Northern "supervisors." But in July 1862, the federal army abandoned Edisto, leaving more than 2000 acres of planted crops in the soil and evacuating the more than 2,000 former slave inhabitants. Then at the end of 1864, the war once again transformed Edisto Island.

As General William Tecumseh Sherman's army cut its sixty-mile swath across Georgia from Atlanta to Savannah, it produced another army, a refugee army made up of the tens of thousands of homeless, landless, impoverished former slaves who flocked to the Union forces as the army of their liberation. Something had to be done about the immediate problem of the refugees. A little more than three weeks after Sherman captured it, Secretary of War Edwin Stanton went to Savannah to survey the situation. At the suggestion of the Reverend James Lynch, a 26-year-old black minister from Baltimore who had gone to Savannah to work with the ex-slaves there, Stanton organized a meeting with Sherman, himself and his aides, and twenty black churchmen from the area. Sherman saw little point to the meeting, called to deal with what he referred to in a letter to his wife as "that Negro nonsense." To him, the meeting smacked of the poison politics of Washington. Besides, he resented sitting down almost as an equal with members of a race that he believed should never be "put on any equality with Whites"

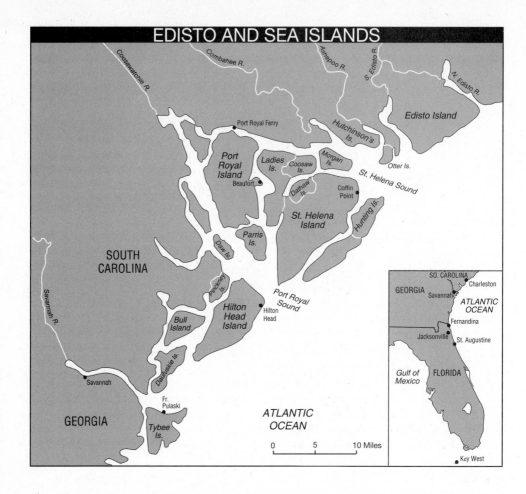

EDISTO AND SEA ISLANDS

at a meeting called to solicit *their* views about what they wanted from their new freedom.

Stanton conducted the meeting as a species of military or judicial board of inquiry. The churchmen were asked to select a spokesman and to answer a set of carefully selected, written questions. All but one of the twenty black leaders, ranging in age from 26 to 72, were from the Savannah area: five had been "free born," three were former slaves who had been freed at the death of their masters, three had purchased their own freedom before the war, and the remaining eight had remained slaves until "the army freed" them. They selected as their spokesman Garrison Frazier, aged 67, who had served as a minister for thirty-five years and in 1856 had "bought himself and his wife, paying $1,000 in gold and silver," as their spokesman. Stanton composed his questions as a catechism designed to determine the extent of the former slaves' understanding of the principles of American freedom. The churchmen prepared their answers with subtlety and care. They knew it was a test. They and Stanton knew full well that even strongly antislavery whites doubted whether "the poor, debased" former slaves were ready or even capable of freedom. They were determined to prove that there was enough "understanding and intelligence" among the former slaves to sustain freedom and prosper under it. After first eliciting a clear and subtle exposition of the acts of Congress and "President Lincoln's proclamation, touching the condition of the colored people in the Rebel States," Stanton moved directly to the key question. "State," he asked, "what you understand by Slavery and the freedom that was to be given by the President's proclamation." The answer came back clear and succinct. "Slavery is," Frazier asserted, "receiving by *irresistible power* the work of another man, and not by his *consent*," whereas "the freedom, promised by the proclamation, is taking us from under the yoke of bondage and placing us where we can reap the fruit of our own labor, take care of ourselves and assist the Government in maintaining our freedom." Stanton then posed the obvious follow-up: How, he asked, do "you think you can take care of yourselves, and how can you best assist the government in maintaining your freedom?"

The question was not quite so simple and innocent as it seemed. A good deal was riding on the answer. Few ideas were more deeply embedded in the white consciousness than the notion that the former slaves were "lazy," either, in the racist version, because of inborn racial characteristics, or, in the antislavery version, because slavery itself had made enslaved blacks that way. Unless carefully and gradually nurtured in the ways and responsibilities of freedom, such thinking went, the ex-slaves were destined to remain a "degraded" and "dependent" people. Moreover, most whites (North and South alike) envisioned the ex-slaves becoming a free, largely agricultural wage-labor force. The churchmen could have answered, "give us steady work and good wages and we will take care of ourselves." But they didn't. They knew what they wanted and Frazier stated it clearly and unmistakably: "The way we can best take care of ourselves is to have land, and turn it and till it by our own labor."

There was a good deal of meaning packed into this simple sentence. Freedom meant to the former slaves just what it meant to whites in North and South alike—independence, freedom from dependence upon and control by others. And just as did most free whites, especially in the South, the freedmen associated independence with the ownership of land, with possession of what was aptly called a "homestead." With a homestead, a man as the "head of household" who held title to the land could secure, protect, and provide for his family. With their own land to turn and till with their own hand, the former slaves hoped, black wives and children would no longer be forced to labor in the fields of whites. Wives might even be able to forswear fieldwork altogether to attend more fully to the tasks of nurture, child rearing, and the domestic production their families required. So that the key point shouldn't be lost, Frazier concluded simply, "We want to be placed on the land until we are able to buy it and make it our own."

After the meeting Stanton asked Sherman for his suggestions about what to do with the newly freed fugitives that had flocked to his army. Sherman came up with a surprising proposal: he suggested turning the confiscated and abandoned land in the Sea Islands off the coast of South Carolina and Georgia over to the refugees. Four days later, on January 16th, 1865, after much discussion and careful reworking of several drafts, Sherman issued Special Field Order No. 15. It was a revolutionary document. It set aside the Sea Islands and "the abandoned rice fields along the rivers for thirty miles back from the sea" from Charleston south to the St. Johns River in Florida, for the "settlement of the negroes now made free by the acts of war." According to the provisions of the Order, whenever "three respectable negroes, heads of families" selected a "locality clearly defined," a settlement would be established in which "themselves and such others as may choose to settle near them" would be given "a plot of not more than forty acres of tillable land."

As soon as Sherman issued Field Order No. 15, former inhabitants who had evacuated Edisto, landless inhabitants from nearby islands, and refugees who had followed Sherman's army into Savannah flocked to the island and its rich lands. By the fall of 1865, the island held more than 4,500 people, and nearly 550 households had managed to "establish a home on their own lands." Just as rapidly they put in their crops. "The crops on these lands," the Freedmen's Bureau agent on the Island reported, "look remarkably well considering the lateness of the season when they were planted. The cotton and the corn crop looks much better than those seen on either of the other sea islands. There are one thousand and three acres of excellent cotton planted, and nearly two thousand acres of corn, also nearly two hundred acres of rice besides many acres of vegetables." The freedmen of Edisto not only laid claim to land and put in their crops. They also, the Bureau agent reported, "feel it their duty as well as a privilege of establishing a simple form of Gov–among themselves." The inhabitants established a system of "selectmen and constables elected by the people." In addition, they had a "Constitution & laws of this Civil Gov . . . about ready" for submission to the deputy commissioner for his approval. The inhabitants also established the practice of holding a "general meeting" each Saturday in which they discussed "general issues" and read reports on local and national doings from a black newspaper, *The South Carolina Leader,* and other Republican newspapers.

Howard was not eager to meet with the freedmen of Edisto but considered it his "duty" to do so. Dubbed the "Christian General" because of his piety and dedication to "good works," Howard considered himself an "ardent friend of the Negro," one of their truest "champions" in the federal government. As did the freedmen themselves, he believed that the best policy for the former slaves was to settle them on homesteads of their own. The legislation that established the Freedmen's Bureau, in fact, contained a clause that extended to "the several insurrectionary states" the Sherman formula for settling freedmen on forty-acre homesteads carved out of lands "abandoned" by or "confiscated" from those who had supported the Insurrection. Howard had worked quickly to implement the land policy. On July 28, 1865, he issued a Circular (# 13) firmly enunciating the policy and ordered his assistant commissioners to survey the lands, settle freedmen and their families on specified plots, and provide them with formal, written "certificates" of possession. (By October 1865, freedmen occupied 16,000 acres on Edisto Island, and Howard's assistant commissioner for South Carolina and Georgia, General Rufus Saxton, had issued Circular 13 grants to 367 Edisto families.)

But now "the Christian General," friend and protector of the freedmen, was on his way to Edisto Island to inform the people there of a dramatic reversal of federal land policy. President Andrew Johnson had established a new policy to "restore" the once "abandoned" land to former owners who had been pardoned under the terms of an

WILLIAM TECUMSEH SHERMAN. More than any other general, Sherman understood that defeating the Confederacy demanded a "total" war, directed at the civilian population and the Confederate armies alike, that would destroy the enemy's capacity and will to fight. He conducted this "modern" form of warfare with devastating effectiveness in his march through Georgia and the Carolinas in late 1864.

amnesty proclamation Johnson had issued the previous May. Johnson, further, ordered Howard to withdraw Circular 13. The new policy even challenged the validity of land grants bestowed under Special Order No. 15. Howard's "hard task" was to tell the Edisto inhabitants that they would have to give up their farms and surrender their land to the very men who had fought the Union armies that had liberated the slaves.

General Howard and his entourage—consisting of his brother; Colonel John Alvord, an old abolitionist and head of the Freedmen's Savings Bank; and Colonel William Whaley, a lawyer and representative of the former owners who himself had owned one of the largest plantations on the island—did not know what awaited them on the island. Howard certainly expected to find anger and disappointment. But he also thought he could persuade the Edisto inhabitants to accept his proposal for working out a "just" solution to which freedmen and former owners could both agree. Howard had met with the former owners the night before. They all, but especially Whaley, impressed him as "gentlemen" of moderation who fully accepted the reality of slavery's demise and had genuine concern for the freedmen's welfare. Armed with this belief in the planters' good faith, he was sure that in the end he could convince the freedmen to adopt his formula by which the freedmen would "contract" with the owners for their labor. Under these "contracts," the Edisto farmers would agree to exchange a set amount of labor either for wages, a lease for land, or the opportunity to buy a parcel of land. A Board of Supervisors—made up of a representative of the planters, a representative for the freedmen, and an agent of the Freedmen's Bureau—would work out specific contracts, which were then subject to approval by the assistant commissioner of the Bureau or his designated agent.

Rumor had preceded him that Howard was coming to the Island to take away the freedmen's land. The more than 2,000 men, women, and children gathered in a large church in the center of the island to hear what the General had to say could not contain their anger and sense of betrayal. The hall was filled with "noise and confusion" and to Howard the eyes of his audience "flashed unpleasantly." The Edisto islanders called on their most powerful medium of expression as the crowd turned to "the Lord's Songs." The church rang out with the sorrowful sounds of the spirituals, "Wandering in the Wilderness of Sorrow and Gloom" and "Nobody Knows the Trouble I Seen." When Howard "endeavored as clearly and gently as [he] could to explain the wishes of the President as they were made known to me in an interview I had just before leaving Washington," he was met with anguished cries of "No! No!" One man, described by Howard as "very black, thick set and strong" cried out from the balcony, "Why, General Howard, why do you take away our lands? You take them from us who are true, always true to the government! You give them to our all-time enemies! That is not right!"

Finally, in desperation, Howard asked the assembly to select a committee to prepare a more formal response. He beseeched the group to be charitable toward their former owners. And he specified the condition of their tenure on the land under "our President's actions," explaining that they had "no absolute title but simply occup[ied] the homesteads." He urged the committee to come up with a way to "make the best possible terms with the holders of the titles." The next day the committee gave Howard its written response. "With painful Hearts" the committee informed Howard that the people of Edisto could not sign the kinds of contracts "you wished us to Sign." Instead, they went on

> General we want Homesteads; we were promised Homesteads by the government; If It does not carry out the promises Its agents made to us, If the government Having concluded to befriend Its late enemies and to neglect to observe the principles of common faith between Its self and us Its allies In the war you said was over, now takes away from them all right to the soil they stand upon save such as they can get by again working for *your* late and their *all time enemies*. If the government does so we are left In a more unpleasant condition than our former . . .
>
> We can only do one of three things   Step Into the public *road or the sea* or remain on [the land] working as In former time and subject to their will as then. We can not resist It In any way without being driven out homeless upon the road.
>
> You will see this Is not the condition of really freemen
>
> You ask us to forgive the land owners of our Island. *You* only lost your right arm In war and might forgive them. The man who tied me to a tree & gave me 39 lashes & who stripped and flogged my mother and sister & who will not let me stay In His empty Hut except I will do his planting and be satisfied with His price & who combines with others to keep away land from me well knowing I would not Have any thing to do with Him If I had land of my own—that man, I can not well forgive.

The former owners were confident. They sensed that momentum was on their side. They had the president squarely in their corner and understood Howard to have committed himself to the restoration of their lands. But they also knew they had pow-

BLACK REFUGEES CROSSING THE RAPPAHONNOCK RIVER, VIRGINIA, 1862. From early in the war, the incursion of Northern forces into the Confederacy produced a growing army of black refugees, as tens of thousands of slaves availed themselves of the opportunity warfare opened up to place themselves beyond slavery's grasp. Sherman issued Special Field Order No. 15 to resolve the "refugee problem" that surrounded his conquering army.

erful enemies in the North and realized that conditions remained volatile and unsettled. At the very moment, the Senate Judiciary Committee in Washington was considering a bill to extend the life and powers of the Freedmen's Bureau that contained a provision to validate the Sherman grants in the Sea Islands for the lifetime of the head of household currently on the land. The owners were determined to regain possession of the land and get a labor force bound to them by contract as quickly as possible. They believed that Howard had agreed that their "lands would be restored *first,* and the agreements with the freedmen "arranged *afterwards.*" They wanted the freedmen under contract to them or off the land by the beginning of the new year, and insisted that Captain A. P. Ketchum, the Freedmen's Bureau agent for Edisto, go with them to Edisto and tell the farmers that if they did not sign contracts by Jan. 1, 1866, they would be removed from the land.

The freedmen were no less determined. The Edisto farmers realized the severity of the blow to their hopes for land and feared they might in the end have to leave the land they now occupied. But they were not about to give up without a fight. They also knew they had two things going for them. They were *on* the land: they might not have clear titles but, some 4,500 strong, they in fact *occupied* Edisto Island. They wouldn't be easily dislodged. In fact, when one of the planters went to the island to try to claim his land, the inhabitants forced him to turn back. Panic-stricken, he told his fellow planters that "the Negros on that Island are armed and have announced their purpose to allow no white man on it." Second, the Edisto farmers possessed a new and very important kind of freedom: their labor was now theirs to give or withhold. As the churchmen had told Stanton and Sherman, they were free "to reap the fruit of our own labor." Above all else the planters wanted their land back, but they also wanted and needed the freedmen's labor. Cotton prices were very good and the planters were desperate to recoup from the personal economic devastation the war had visited upon them. Plantations with no one to work them would do the owners little good.

The Edisto freedmen had some important allies of their own. Their anguished plea for land and justice had clearly moved Howard. As he reported to his superior, Secretary of War Stanton, "They will submit with evident sorrow to the breaking of the promise of General Sherman's order. The greatest aversion is exhibited to making contracts, and they beg and plead for the privilege of renting or buying land on the island . . . I am convinced that something must be done to give these people and others the prospect of homesteads." And he replied to the Edisto committee that "You are right *in wanting homesteads* and will *surely be defended in the possession of every one* which you shall purchase or have already purchased." He made it clear that he would work to secure them lands *somewhere,* pointing out that "Congress must meet before any public lands can be had and before I can buy any for you." In the meantime, he urged them to "enter into contracts, leasing or for wages or purchase when possible for next year."

The Edisto committee knew that, in the end, men in Washington would determine their fate. They told Howard that they intended to petition Congress. Howard assured them that he "would see to it that [their petition] is not passed by without proper attention." They even appealed directly to President Johnson himself to prove himself "a true friend of the poor and Neglected race" by granting them the "protection and Equal Rights [and] with the privilege of purchasing A Homestead— A Homestead right here in the Heart of South Carolina." In their petitions to both, they based their claims on their loyalty, their standing as freemen, and the actions of the government itself:

> Here is where secession was born and Nurtured. Here is where we have toiled nearly all Our lives as slaves and were treated like dumb Driven cattle. This is our home, we have made These lands what they are. We were the only true and Loyal people that were found in posession of these Lands. We have been always ready to strike for Liberty and humanity yea to fight if needs be To preserve this glorious union. Shall we who Are freedmen and have been always true to this Union have the same rights as are enjoyed by Others? Have we broken any Laws of these United States? Have we forfieted our rights of property In Land? If not then are our rights as A free people and good citizens of these United States To be considered before the rights of those who were Found in rebellion against this good and just Government (and now being conquered) come (as they Seem) with penitent hearts and beg forgiveness for past offences and also ask if thier lands Cannot be restored to them. Are these rebellious Spirits to be reinstated in their *possessions* and we who have been abused and oppressed For many long years not to be allowed the Privilege of purchasing land But be subject To the will of these large Land owners? God Forbid.
>
> We have been encouraged by Government to take Up these lands in small tracts, receiving Certificates of the Same . . . We are ready to pay for this land When Government calls for it. And now after What has been done will the good and just government take from us all this right and make us Subject to the will of those who have cheated and oppressed us for many years. God Forbid!

Howard's subordinates in South Carolina were sympathetic to the Edisto farmers' plea for their homesteads. The assistant commissioner of the Bureau, General Saxton, in fact, was determined to resist restoration as long as possible in the hope that Congress would at least partially honor the Sherman grants on the island. Even though he considered it his "solemn duty" to secure "just" contracts between the former owners and the people of Edisto, Captain H. P. Ketchum, the Bureau agent responsible for Edisto, refused to issue any orders of restoration until a contract was secured and approved. And he refused to approve of any contract to which the freedmen did not freely and mutually agree. Saxton and Ketchum were not about to force the freedmen to sign contracts for "hire," nor would they try to force them off the island if they did refuse to sign. The road to "restoration" was proving a bit more rocky than the owners had reckoned.

A "somewhat discomposed" William Whaley confronted Ketchum directly over his failure to carry out his duties as the owners saw them. He threatened to "write the President immediately" and report that the agents of the Bureau were deliberately subverting Johnson's formally declared policy to restore abandoned land to its rightful owners. But Ketchum cleverly turned the tables on Whaley. Had the pardoned owners, he asked pointedly, in fact selected a person to represent them on the Board of Supervisors called for in Howard's Field Order laying out the procedures for the restoration of the lands? They had not. Whaley claimed that he understood Howard to have said that the lands would first be restored to the owners who would then work out an agreement with the freedmen. Ketchum warned Whaley that if he did "write the President" as he threatened, it would be clear to all that he would be making demonstrably false statements that "could not be substantiated." Whaley, seeming "better contented," backed down. (But, to cover himself and the Bureau in the event Whaley did go to the president, Ketchum sent Howard a detailed account of the meeting.)

GENERAL OLIVER OTIS HOWARD. A native of Maine and a graduate of West Point, Howard underwent religious conversion during a Methodist revival in 1853 at the age of 23. The experience shaped his sense of himself as a soldier in the Union cause and the antislavery cause and as commissioner of the Freedmen's Bureau. A wounded veteran of the battles of Fredericksburg and Gettysburg, he commanded one of Sherman's armies in the March to the Sea.

The owners moved quickly to recoup their position as reasonable men perfectly willing to work out a "just" arrangement with the inhabitants of Edisto Island. The next day, they informed Ketchum that they had selected Whaley as their representative on the Board of Supervisors. Shortly thereafter "the planters of Edisto Island" sent to Howard and Ketchum a formal resolution that declared their entire "willingness to comply with General Howard's order for the restoration of lands on Edisto Island." They avowed that it was their "intention to deal justly and generously with the freedmen with whom we may contract and to do all in our power to promote their physical welfare and moral improvement and to labor to give the greatest success to the system of free labor which has been inaugurated." The planters were in for another surprise. The Edisto freedmen selected a black man as their representative, Charles Branwell, a 40-year old minister "of intelligence and influence, one of those with whom the Secretary of War had a conference at Savannah." Whaley immediately sent Howard a telegram objecting to Branwell. He wanted to know if Howard had in mind only white men when he specified that "citizens" should be selected as the representatives on the supervisory boards. Howard agreed that such had been his intent. When it became clear that Ketchum considered Branwell a citizen and was unwilling to exclude him from the board without an explicit order from Howard, the "Edisto planters" were furious. Whaley "became quite violent," according to Ketchum's report to Howard, and "declared the Dred Scott decision the law of the land, and said he would rather have his plantation 'sunk' than submit to having a black man on the board." Ketchum urged Howard not to remove Branwell, a "fair and generous man" who would "do as much as any man can to bring about an understanding between the freedmen and former owners." In addition, removal would only deepen the "distrust of the people, which is almost universal on the island," making agreement between owners and freedmen almost impossible to achieve.

Howard agreed to let Branwell remain on the Edisto board. Branwell told the board that he did not think the Edisto farmers would agree to contract for *wages*, though he promised to try to get the farmers to consider the planters' proposals fairly. In early December Ketchum went with several of the planters to visit their respective plantations. Once again the farmers were adamant: they absolutely refused to make "simple contracts for service *with their former owners*," even though Branwell had succeeded in wresting more favorable terms from the former owners. This intransigence baffled some of the Bureau and other federal officials. It seemed to indicate an inability of "the colored people to appreciate this style of agreements." Formal, written contracts for wages were a standard feature of free Northern society. But the freedmen saw the matter very differently. They feared that such contractual arrangements, especially ones that bound them to the owners for a full year, would amount to a surrender of the very hard-won independence that to them was the essential difference between slavery and freedom. They were unwilling to agree to anything that threatened to resubject them to the control of their former masters. As one observer put it, the freedmen "consider the effect of this class of contracts as a practical return to slavery."

Once again the owners went over the head of the Freedmen's Bureau officials in South Carolina. The planters' Washington agent, Henry Trescot, complained to President Johnson that Saxton and Ketchum were deliberately thwarting government policy. He alleged that they had ordered Branwell to ask "the freedmen in Edisto" if they would be willing to purchase land from the owners if the government would help them "buy the land of the former owners." The very question, the owners argued, simply exacerbated the freedmen's stubbornness: so long as Bureau agents "encouraged" them to believe that there was a chance to hold on to the land, the Edisto inhabitants would continue to refuse to sign contracts with the owners. Moreover, Saxton's actions, Trescot told Johnson, had fostered such a "spirit of resistance among the freedmen" that General Daniel Sickles, the federal commander of the South Carolina military district, had been forced to send in troops to ensure "order." So long as Saxton "controls [the South Carolina] department of the Bureau," Trescot insisted, solving the impasse between the freedmen and the former owners would remain an "utter impossibility." The only solution was the immediate "removal of General Saxton."

The planters also tried to enlist General Sickles on their side. The owners sent him a long petition claiming that the agents of the Freedmen's Bureau were motivated by a "factious spirit of opposition to accommodation" and used their "pernicious influence" to prevent the freedmen from making contracts. The petition was a clever move. The planters knew of the rivalry between the army and the Freedmen's Bureau and knew that Sickles, who thought that Bureau agents in his military district should be under his command, resented Bureau disregard of his authority and interference with things he considered military affairs.

"Slave" quarters on an Edisto Island plantation after the white owners had fled but before the Union forces evacuated the island. The man in the foreground is clothed in a Union uniform.

The planters' petition, complete with five attached "documents," made two key points: (1) the planters had acted in full good faith; and (2) the Bureau agents, especially Captain Ketchum, had ignored the express orders of Johnson and Howard and were subverting clearly established and declared policy. Ketchum, the planters alleged, claimed that if the freedmen refused to contract at all, "the entire plan of settlement was thereby defeated" and "the whole matter must be referred back to General Howard for a decision." To the owners, this interpretation of Howard's order "gives the freedmen in possession a veto upon all proceedings for adjustment whatsoever." Clearly, the petitioners insisted, this was "not contemplated by General Howard . . . and would not be tolerated by him." They concluded that the "just and equitable settlement of General Howard" had been dangerously delayed by his agents in the field and was "in danger of being defeated altogether," and they invited Sickles to investigate the facts and take "such action" as he deemed proper. They knew full well what action they wanted Sickles to take. They conceded that Howard's order "contemplated the restoration of the lands in question as soon as contracts approved by the board should be made," but insisted that "the Freedmen were required to enter into such contracts before January 1, 1866 or else to leave the island." The petition was designed to lay the groundwork for Sickles to "forcibly remove" the freedmen if they persisted in their refusal to contract with the landowners. As they reminded him in their petition, Sickles had already acted "in regard to Edisto" when he sent a detachment there to counter the "hostile attitude of the Freedmen" that had denied "access to the island to the landowners."

General Sickles dispatched one of his key aides, Colonel Edwin Tremain, to "investigate and report on the petition of certain pardoned owners of land on Edisto Island." Tremain's findings were not exactly what the owners wanted nor, probably, what Sickles expected. He found wholly unsubstantiated the allegations "against the faithfulness and integrity of Ketchum" (who, Tremain assured Sickles, "voluntarily invited my inspection of all the documents on file in his office, . . . and desired me to express to General Sickles his gratification at being able to lay the whole matter fully and frankly before him.") In fact, Tremain found that Ketchum followed the letter and spirit of Howard's instructions scrupulously. The planters based their case against Ketchum on a document Ketchum had submitted to the Board of Supervisors asking it to consider the "subject of the freedmen's leasing and buying of lands, and if so upon what terms." They claimed that this action was calculated to foster the inhabitants' intransigence and thereby render accommodation "utterly impossible." Tremain found that this was not the case. Ketchum presented the proposition only to the board. Barnwell, instead of using it to prevent the "negroes from contracting," in fact agreed not to take the proposition to the freedmen and had "not yet done so." Even more to the point, Tremain reported that Howard's written orders expressly directed Ketchum to "ascertain if leases could be made and, if contracts for service could not be arranged, to execute, if possible, *leases* for the freedmen." Moreover, he pointed out that the purchase of land was expressly one of "the modes of settlement" Howard himself had proposed. Finally, Tremain found no basis for the claim that the freedmen had to contract by Jan. 1, 1866 or leave the island. On the contrary, Tremain cited Secretary of War Stanton's telegraph to Howard after his Edisto meeting stating that Stanton "did not understand your orders [from President Johnson] require you to disturb the freedmen in their possession at present, but only to ascertain whether a just and mutual agreement can be made between the pardoned owners and the freedmen, and, if it can, to carry it into effect." Tremain concluded from this that since no agreements had been reached and no new orders issued, there was no ground for imposing the Jan. 1, 1866 deadline on the freedmen.

Oddly enough, despite its full exoneration of Ketchum, Tremain's report to Sickles actually acknowledged the accuracy of the owners' assessment of the situation they faced. All Howard's instructions, "assumed that an agreement could be made with the freedmen by their former owners." But, "the real trouble," Tremain concluded, "is the freedmen will not make agreements with these gentlemen." The reason was really very simple. "Believing," as they did, "that assistance may possibly be afforded by the United States securing them in some manner the continued possession of the lands in question, it is not unnatural," Tremain pointed out, "that they should for present refuse to contract with parties, who—as the negroes believe—have no claim against them." After all, he went on, under the existing orders, "if the freedmen and pardoned owners agree, restoration follows; if they do not agree, restoration is in abeyance." In effect, the freedmen of Edisto were conducting a kind of strike. In the end, it came down to one question: "can an agreement be effected?"

Once again a delegation made its way across the sound to Edisto Island. Colonel Tremain, accompanied by Captain Ketchum, a few aides, and a "deputation of planters" headed by William Whaley set out to make one more effort to see if "some *agreement* might not be determined upon by which the pardoned owners would receive the services of the resident negroes, and the latter a just and remunerative compensation." The prospects for agreement were not entirely favorable. The pardoned owners had not been idle. "Time," as they pointed out to Sickles, "was all important." "If they did not effect their arrangements for labor at once, the crop for the ensuing year must be lost." Whaley "repaired" to Washington, where he secured a meeting with the president attended by General Howard. Whaley came away from the meeting, he told Tremain, with the "expressed intention of the President to restore immediately in case the freedmen were unwilling to contract or lease." Tremain sensed, he later reported, that the owners, armed with Johnson's assurances, didn't really want an agreement but would be "quite satisfied" if they came away from Edisto able to "show the unwillingness of the freedmen to do either."

The pardoned owners urged Tremain to summon the Edisto inhabitants to a general meeting and inform them straight out that the government "required them to contract" by a set time or "leave the island." Tremain bluntly told the planters that in fact he had no authority to tell the freedmen that they were *required* to contract or leave the island. He pointed out that a meeting such as they proposed could only serve to inflame matters. He advised, instead, that the owners go to their estates and "*converse* with the freedmen" and "attempt an agreement of some kind with the resident negros there."

The party learned that on the next day the Edisto farmers were to hold their weekly public meeting. It might be "advisable" for them to attend. When the delegation of white men arrived the meeting had been in progress for over an hour. It continued, "orderly and attentive" for two additional hours. Ketchum asked permission to address the meeting and explained that the "planters present wished to confer with them on matters of great interest to both." Ketchum knew how angry the freedmen were and that their distrust of the former owners ran deep. He was apprehensive about how the assemblage would react to the planters' attempt to persuade them to contract or lease.

Adopting the pose of a stern but kindly father, he pointed out that while the government "demanded that the colored people should be treated like men," it was equally "their duty to be considerate and respectful." He advised them to be "business-like and patient" with their former owners, to resist being "carried away by personal prejudice" and warned them to follow "individual judgement" and not let themselves be "led astray" by some who "would claim to be leaders."

Ketchum then introduced Tremain. He spoke very briefly, stressing that the government "desired" them to make agreements with the owners. It could be in their best interest to do so, he said, if some "mutual understanding" could be achieved. He then told them that "their enemies" claimed that the freedmen were lazy and did not want to "earn their bread by the sweat of their brow" and asked them who "proposed to work and who did not." The count, he reported to Sickles, was unanimous: "all expected to work for a living." He then introduced Whaley, who, according to Tremain, spoke "in excellent and considerate terms." The freedmen listened closely without interrupting. Whaley assured them that the planters were willing to do whatever was "fair and reasonable" in arranging contracts or leases, all of which would be for a year. He closed by offering the freedmen a bit of advice. He stated unequivocally that the former owners had "unquestionable titles" to the land and would soon return to them. The people of Edisto would be well advised to come to terms with Whaley and his colleagues.

Tremain then asked the chairman of the meeting if some of their "own leading speakers" would give their views. The speakers were clear about what they did and

This photograph, taken after the "liberation" of the slaves but probably before 1864 when the freedmen set up individual farmsteads, depicts a "domestic" scene—"wash day—" on Edisto Island. It appears carefully composed but nonetheless reflects the division of work roles of men and women among the freedmen. The women are shown at work at the household tasks that were their province, but the men are bystanders. (The boy with the man at the left of the picture reflects the status of the father as "head" of household.)

did not want. They wanted to "secure for themselves a *home, . . . somewhere.*" Above
all else, they wished to "*own lands* and to have some security for this result before
working again under their former masters." All were opposed to the year contract system. Before the meeting closed, Tremain asked the assembly to select a committee to
meet with him, Ketchum, and the owners later that evening. The committee that had
written Howard and petitioned the Congress and the president reassembled. But before it met with the visitors to the island, the committee conducted a session with its
constituents.

Tremain asked the chair of the committee, Henry Bram, to reply for the committee to the proposals that the owners had presented to the general meeting earlier in the
day. Again Bram repeated the simple plea that the churchmen had made to Stanton and
Sherman and that the committee had sent to Howard, the president, and to Congress.
Their desire was to "acquire land" because only land could "secure their liberty." They
of course would prefer land near their old homes, but, if necessary they would go elsewhere. They did not expect "large possessions," but simply a "little plot of ground"
upon which as a freedman one could establish a "home for his family from which no
one would have a right to eject him, and in the possession of which he would be secured by the laws of the land." The committee pointed out that most of the families on
the island had "a little money and wished to buy."

Then the committee made a surprise move that for the moment at least caught the
"deputation of planters" off guard. They proposed that the planters "*sell to the freedmen,
or to each head of a family, a plot of ground from one to five acres in size,* as might be determined by direct agreement or by decree of the Supervisory Board." The freedmen were
perfectly willing to "pay a reasonable price." What was a reasonable price? the owners
wanted to know. The committee could not give a specific number but suggested that
"tax evaluation" might be taken as a suitable basis. The owners immediately objected,

The freedmen, as well as their
northern supporters, put great stock
in education. As soon as the Sea
Islands fell under Union control,
northern freedmen's aid societies
sent northern "missionaries"—the
majority of whom were unmarried
young women from New England—
south to set up and conduct schools.
The Penn School, shown in this
photo, was sent in prefabricated
sections to St. Helena Island by the
Pennsylvania Freedmen's Relief
Association.

suggesting that such a figure was for tax purposes and did not represent a fair sale price. At this point, Captain Ketchum suggested that tax evaluation "might not always be inappropriate" since the planters themselves had used tax evaluations when they claimed estates worth less than $20,000 and thereby made themselves eligible for the general pardons that gave them the claim to have their lands restored. At this point, Tremain asked the committee if the people would be willing to contract "for service" with "their former masters" if the owners would agree to sell them a plot of ground from one-half to five acres. The response was immediate. If "the planters would sell them *even one acre*, they would then make agreements for service." Tremain turned to Whaley, the planters' representative, for his response. "I am not authorized to consider them," Whaley replied. His instructions "contemplated only *contracts or leases*" and he had "nothing to say on the subject of sales." When Tremain asked the other planters for their response, they repeated Whaley's answer. There was little more to say so, the meeting adjourned.

Whaley's silence spoke volumes. The pardoned owners feared that even selling small parcels of land to just a few freedmen would make the others even more reluctant to engage as hired laborers. Besides, it was increasingly clear that there was little chance that they would have to concede on the land question. Time now seemed clearly on their side. And it was. On Jan. 9, General Saxton, the freedmen's strongest advocate, was removed from office. Less than two weeks later the Senate Judiciary Committee eliminated from the Freedmen's Bureau Bill the provision that would have given the holders of Sherman grants lifetime title to the land. General James Beecher (brother of Harriet Beecher Stowe, commander of a black regiment in the war, and military officer under Sickles in charge of the Sea Islands) moved quickly to settle the confused matter of "so called land titles." A large number of the Edisto farmers held "certificates" from Saxton but many did not and many of those who did held certificates to lands other than those they had cultivated. Beecher ordered that "such parties and such parties alone" who held duly authenticated certificates to accurately surveyed lands that they had actually occupied and cultivated "should not be disturbed in possession" of the land. He ordered all others "removed from the plantations" if they persisted in their "refusal to contract."

With great bitterness and reluctance a large number of Edisto farmers signed a contract for lease or hire. In the winter months of 1866 there weren't many places they could go where conditions would be any better. By mid-summer of 1866, a Bureau official reported, Edisto Island was settled and orderly and the freedmen "will make enough during the present year to comfortably clothe them and support them until they have time to make contracts for the ensuing years." But the freedmen of Edisto Island had not surrendered their hope for land. Many still refused to contract, even if it meant expulsion from Edisto. They had learned that under a new act of Congress some land for homesteading had been opened up in Florida. "The freedmen are much exercised about the Homestead Act," Saxton's successor, General R. K. Scott, reported to Howard, "and are holding meetings in each District to devise ways and means of migration." In January of 1867 a large party of Edisto inhabitants led by Henry Bram left Edisto for St. Johns River in Florida to establish homesteads on the "abundance of Government land" that had been set aside for "freedmen and refugees." "Persons," Bram wrote General Scott, "are anxious to take up this opportunity as they are pressed daily to leave their present quarters or make a contract which they are opposed to do." The freedmen suffered defeat at Edisto Island, but the dream "to have land and turn and till it" endured.

Reunion and Reconstruction

When the Confederate armies lay down their arms in unconditional surrender in April of 1865, the nation faced two distinct but intertwined tasks. One task was reunion, or "restoration" as Andrew Johnson preferred to call it, "binding the nation's wounds" and returning the seceded states to full and equal participation in all the political processes of the nation. Normal political and governmental operations had to be restored on the local and state levels. With the collapse and surrender of the Confederacy, civilian authority in many areas simply evaporated as occupying northern forces became the major source of law and order. Procedures had to be established for electing members from the "insurrectionary" states to the national Congress in Washington. But what should be the terms of these "restorations," and who would determine them? The terms of surrender had ensured that ordinary Confederate soldiers would not be held as prisoners or treated as traitors. But what about officers, Confederate officials, and the planters who had supported secession and rebellion— what should be their role in restored governments and in the national polity?

The nation also faced another, even more troublesome task—namely, the task of "reconstructing" the defeated South, of determining what kind of society would replace the slave-based society that the war had irrevocably destroyed. As a Memphis, Tennessee newspaper put it in 1865, "the events of the past five years have produced an entire revolution in the social system of the entire Southern country." There were no clear or settled answers to the question, "What shall we do with the Negro," which General Oliver Howard asked when he took over command of the Freedmen's Bureau. And no question was more controversial or more bitterly contested. But one thing was clear—as General Howard and the Edisto planters such as William Whaley quickly learned. The freedmen and their former owners had very different and essentially incompatible ideas about what they wanted to replace the old master-slave relationship.

By the summer of 1865 most slaveholders had relinquished their slave property. But they still held on to the attitudes that had justified holding blacks in bondage. Even though many masters had trusted *individual* slaves with important tasks and responsibilities, they nonetheless considered blacks as a whole to be childlike people, whom they had fed, clothed, housed, and cared for. And most had convinced themselves that their own slaves were loyal and happy, content with the lot to which their race had consigned them. The former masters thus had great difficulty even imagining blacks as anything but a dependent and subservient people. Masters were perplexed, angered, and even hurt when their slaves (often led by personal or house servants, who had been considered most loyal) left them, refused to work, or stole tools and food.

As the reality of the death of slavery sunk in, the former masters were determined that whatever replaced it would come as close as possible to the control and subordination of blacks that had characterized slavery. Slavery had been, first and foremost, a labor system. The former owners, above all else, wanted whatever "free labor" system replaced it to provide them with a labor force that they could depend on and control. But slavery was also a social system and a system of race relations and control. In early 1865, one black soldier saw his former master among a group of Confederate prisoners. "Hello massa," he shouted, "bottom rail on top dis time." The former masters were determined to do all in their power to see that this reversal did not become a permanent state of affairs. After all, even William Whaley, whom whites and blacks alike had accounted a "good master," went into a rage when told that a black man would serve as his equal on the Edisto Island Board of Supervisors. The former owners were no less determined to exclude the freedmen from civil equality and participation in the polity and thereby maintain white supremacy and return the freedmen to a position of social inferiority and subordination.

The response of the ex-slaves to their new status varied. In some places—particularly in the rice country of South Carolina—accumulated anger and bitterness burst forth in open defiance and occasional violence. Former slaves on the Middleton plantation near Charleston burned the main house and broke open the grave vaults in the family cemetery and scattered the bones. The cook on a plantation in Florida on which "never before" had there been "a word of impudence from any of our black folk," bluntly told her mistress that "if she want dinner she kin cook it herself." In Charleston and Richmond, emancipation brought outpourings of jubilation. In Charleston

thousands of blacks turned out for a huge parade, complete with soldiers, bands, tradesmen with their tools, and a contingent of children bearing a banner that declared "We Know No Master but Ourselves." At the center of the celebration was a mock funeral with a coffin blazoned with the motto, "Slavery Is Dead."

In more remote, rural areas the initial response was more confused. Word of emancipation penetrated many places slowly and often in a garbled way. A few slaves wondered if emancipation meant that they now belonged to Lincoln. When slavery ended, there was nothing definite to take its place. The freedmen possessed a number of agricultural and other skills, but they were a people suddenly released from bondage, with few personal possessions and no money, property, or housing. It was not at all clear what they should do, where they should go, or how they could feed, clothe, and shelter themselves. Some set off for places from which they had been sold, hoping to reunite with their families. Others stayed where they were, working for their former masters or for nearby planters. Others, essentially refugees of war, roamed about and flocked to Union encampments in search of food, shelter, and protection.

In spite of all the confusion and uncertainty, as the Edisto people made clear, the ex-slaves possessed a clear and definite idea of the difference between slavery and freedom. One former slave put it to his former master this way: "If I cannot do like a white man I am not free. I see how the poor white people do. I ought to do so too, or else I am a slave." But, above all else, it was "independence"—the condition that from the American Revolution on white Americans had most associated with liberty—that the former slaves saw as the essential hallmark of their newfound freedom. They often asserted their desire for independence—for freedom from the control and dependence on masters that had defined their lives under slavery—in subtle ways. A rural and agricultural population tied to land and place, most were reluctant to leave areas they regarded as home. But, refusing to stay in quarters that reminded them of their previous situation, they often moved to huts scattered around their

FREED AFRICAN AMERICANS IN RICHMOND, VIRGINIA.   A major problem after the war was the future of the former slaves. Slavery ended without a clear sense of what was to take its place. All over the South, freed men and women drifted to the cities in search of work or simply to test their newfound freedom.

former master's lands. Some moved to a neighboring planter's land to demonstrate that the tie to their former master had indeed been broken. For many, simply the act of moving, whatever the distance, was a gesture of liberation, a deliberate exercise of the choice and freedom that had been denied them under slavery.

Many blacks, as the Edisto planters learned to their frustration, firmly resisted contracting for their labor, a refusal many whites condemned as a sign of laziness and irresponsibility. But many freedmen were suspicious of anything that seemed to bind them and their labor to any white man. Possession of their labor had been one of the essential marks of their enslavement. Indeed, many thought themselves justified in taking food, tools, and mules from their former masters as payment morally due them for their previous labor. But land was probably the most important token of freedom—a parcel of land that was their own. Again and again, blacks during Reconstruction pleaded for land, "forty acres and a mule," that would enable them to establish their independence and set up households where husbands and wives could work for themselves and rear

and protect their children. Even when they suffered a defeat as on Edisto Island, they continued to seek out ways to get a parcel of land—by moving on, saving bit by bit until they could purchase some when and if economic and political conditions changed, banding together to buy a large enough tract to set up a small black community.

LINCOLN'S PLAN FOR RECONSTRUCTION

Lincoln had begun to plan for the aftermath of war well before the end of the fighting. He hoped to restore political relations as quickly and with as little animosity as possible. On December 8, 1863, he issued the Proclamation of Amnesty and Reconstruction as a kind of companion piece to his earlier Emancipation Proclamation. Drawing on his constitutional authority to grant pardons for federal offenses, he offered "full pardon" and the restoration of all property "except slaves" that might have been abandoned or confiscated during the war to anyone who had engaged in rebel-

"THE FREEDMEN'S BUREAU."   The Freedmen's Bureau was controversial in the North as well as the South. Democrats condemned it as a tool of "radicals" designed to promote "Negro equality," and some conservative Republicans attacked it as the cause of much of the racial strife in the South. Here, *Harper's Weekly,* a highly influential northern publication, counters these attacks, showing the Bureau "agent," here depicted as a black man, as an agent of peace.

lion but was now willing to swear an oath of loyalty to the United States, the Constitution, and to all acts freeing the slaves. (High civil and military officials of the Confederacy were excluded). Once 10 percent of the number voting in the 1860 election had taken the oath of allegiance, a state government could be established, which the "national Executive" would recognize. (Lincoln took care to point out that only the houses of Congress could authorize seating members from such reconstructed states.) Once a state government was established, it was required to call a constitutional convention or amend its prewar constitution to formally abolish slavery. No provision was made for the enfranchisement of former slaves. Since blacks had not been eligible to vote in 1860, under the terms of Lincoln's proclamation they were excluded from the suffrage.

The Republican leaders in Congress wanted a much tougher procedure than that contained in

Lincoln's proclamation. They wanted to guarantee what they considered true loyalty to the Union. In July 1864, Congress passed the Wade-Davis Bill, which Lincoln "pocket-vetoed." (An outright veto likely would have been overridden, so Lincoln, who ten days before the bill would become law without his signature, had simply ignored the bill thereby killing it since Congress had adjourned before the ten days were up.) The bill required action by 50 percent of the eligible electorate. More important, it contained provisions for an ironclad oath—a pledge of past as well as future loyalty—which was designed to bar all former secessionists and Confederate officeholders from political participation. The Wade-Davis Bill did not provide for black suffrage, though some Republicans had tried to have such a provision included in the bill.

Lincoln was not unmindful of the troubling question of the freedmen, nor was he unaware of the tricky relationship between race and the politics of reunion. But just as he had initially subordinated slavery to the task of preserving the Union, he now placed highest priority on reestablishing normal political relations. In some ways, in fact, just as was the Emancipation Proclamation, his Proclamation of Amnesty and Reconstruction was a wartime measure. It was issued in late 1863, after the victories of Gettysburg and Vicksburg and the capture of Memphis. With large parts of five Confederate states under Union control, some form of "loyal" civil government was highly desirable. In addition, such generous and nonpunitive terms might induce lukewarm supporters of the Confederacy to abandon the cause. Moreover, Lincoln thought reconstruction could be best achieved if the question of the freedmen was separated from the process of political reunion: if the ordinary political machinery was reestablished, the nation would be better able to work out what the freedman's place in American society should be.

Although Lincoln worked hard for the passage of the Thirteenth Amendment abolishing slavery, he had always been reluctant to push for civil and social equality for blacks, partly because of his awareness of the depth of American racism and partly because he shared some of that prejudice. Still, at the time of his death, he had begun to work on the problem of the freedmen and on the politics of that problem. When Louisiana in 1864 drew up its constitution under the provisions of Lincoln's proclamation, he wrote the governor "a private letter" urging Louisiana to consider giving the vote to "some of the colored people," especially "the very intelligent and those who have fought gallantly in our ranks." On March 3, 1865, he signed a bill creating the Freedmen's Bureau. The bill gave federal protection and aid to ex-slaves and contained a limited provision for giving them land, a provision that looked forward to the possible establishment of a landholding black yeomanry. In his "last speech," delivered on April 11, 1865, just three days before his assassination, Lincoln declared that he would "prefer that [the vote] were conferred on the very intelligent and those who serve our cause as soldiers" and promised to deliver "some new announcement" on Reconstruction very soon. John Wilkes Booth made certain that no such announcement was ever made.

─≍═◈═≍─

PRESIDENTIAL RECONSTRUCTION UNDER JOHNSON

Lincoln's successor, Andrew Johnson, fully intended to carry out the policy Lincoln had begun. He, too, hoped to restore normal political institutions and relations as quickly as possible. There was considerable support, especially in the country at large, for such an approach. Declaring that "we want true Union and concord in the quickest possible time," the *Springfield Republican*, an important Massachusetts newspaper, called for an end to the "reproaches and invectives" that prolonged "the spirit and the evils of the war after the war itself has terminated." But at the same time, there was equally strong sentiment in the North, and especially among both moderate and Radical Republicans in Congress, that the terms of "restoration" not deprive the Union of its hard-won victory. They wanted the "errant states" returned to the Union, but only if they absolutely repudiated secession and if the freedom and basic civil rights of the freedmen were guaranteed. Furthermore, they wanted arrangements that would grant those southerners who had opposed secession dominant power and for the time, at least, exclude ex-Confederate leaders from the political process. Andrew Johnson came to the presidency with some important credentials. Like Lincoln he was a self-taught man of humble origins and great ambition, who used politics as a road to power and standing. He had held office almost continuously for more than thirty years, including two terms as governor of Tennessee, and a term as U.S. Senator. From 1862 until his election as vice president, he served as military governor of Tennessee. His Unionist credentials

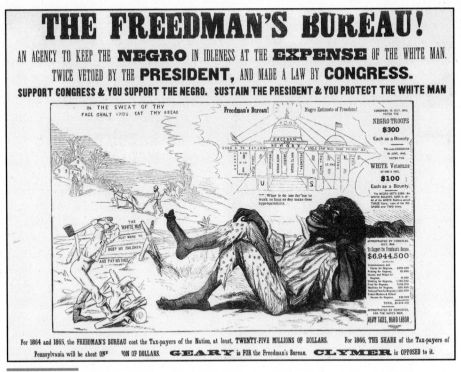

From well before the Civil War, the Democratic party had based much of its electoral appeal on race, presenting itself as the champion of "the white man." As this broadside from 1866 demonstrates, the Democrats continued during Reconstruction to play "the race card" at every opportunity.

were impeccable. In political terms, he seemed to have the support of two important, but not always compatible, constituencies. A former Democrat and strong southern Unionist, he could draw support from Union Democrats and southern Whigs. But, initially, he also had the support even of some Radical Republicans, some of whom thought he was preferable to the seemingly more moderate Lincoln. He loathed the old planter gentry as "a cheap, purse-proud set" nowhere near the moral equal of "the man who earns his bread by the sweat of his brow," and declared again and again during the war that "treason is a crime and must be made odious."

But Johnson also took office with some severe disadvantages. Some Republicans regarded him with suspicion as a former Democrat and a southerner who had once held slaves. In addition, many Republicans in Congress considered reconstruction a legislative rather than an execu-

tive responsibility. Johnson also lacked the political power Lincoln had amassed through his adroit dispensing of favors and patronage. Even more important, Johnson lacked the stature—the legitimacy—Lincoln had acquired as the head of state who had seen the Union through to victory and the first president since Andrew Jackson to win reelection. Even with all these assets, Lincoln had run into stiff opposition to his approach to Reconstruction. But Johnson's greatest weakness was more personal. He lacked Lincoln's understanding of the politics of governing—when to follow and when to lead "popular opinion," when to consult and when to keep his own counsel, the need for flexibility and compromise, the crucial importance of timing. Johnson was a loner, proud and suspicious, who rarely consulted others. His most loyal supporter in the cabinet, Secretary of the Navy Gideon Welles, even conceded that Johnson "has no confidants and seeks none."

ANDREW JOHNSON. When Tennessee seceded in June 1861, Johnson—alone among Southern senators—refused to resign and join the Confederacy. Lincoln quickly appointed him military governor of Tennessee. His staunch Unionism and effectiveness in restoring civilian rule there made him a logical choice as Lincoln's running mate in 1864.

Rigid and intolerant of opposing views, he was quick to equate disagreement with enmity and treachery.

So Johnson charged ahead. Congress was not in session when he took office, and he proceeded to carry out his own plan for Reconstruction by executive action, without consulting the Republican leaders of Congress. Here, too, he partly followed Lincoln's example. Lincoln had jailed opponents to the war, ended slavery in the Confederate states, and instituted a draft—all by executive action. He had launched Reconstruction by proclamation and vetoed the Wade-Davis Bill because he opposed its more stringent conditions and thought Reconstruction was properly an executive function. Johnson issued his own Amnesty Proclamation. He renewed the promise of amnesty to most ex-Confederates, but did make one major modification in Lincoln's policy. He expanded the number of categories of persons to be exempted from general amnesty and re-

quired people with more than $20,000 in taxable property to seek individual presidential pardons. In addition, he set three conditions for a rebel state's reentry into the political system: the state had to nullify its ordinance of secession, accept the Thirteenth Amendment, and repudiate all Confederate debts.

Johnson moved quickly to restore the Confederate states to the Union. He granted recognition to the governments in Arkansas, Tennessee and Louisiana sponsored by Lincoln under his 1863 proclamation, named the loyal government established in western Virginia as the legitimate government of the whole state, and named a provisional governor of North Carolina and directed the calling of a convention to draw up a new constitution. By July of 1865, he had appointed provisional governors for the remaining six states of the old Confederacy with similar injunctions to hold conventions to establish constitutions that would meet the conditions of his Amnesty Proclamation of May 29. Johnson, arguing like Lincoln that there had been no legal basis for secession, insisted that the states had never legally been out of the Union and hence retained the power to set their own rules on who could vote. He also assured southern leaders that Congress was constitutionally bound to accept these governments. Under the leadership of many ex-Confederates, the South moved quickly. When Congress came back into session in December, it was presented with a fait accompli: all but Texas had set up state governments filled with many former slaveholders and Confederate leaders and had sent senators and representatives to Washington to claim their seats in the new Congress.

Johnson and most white southerners thought political reconstruction was substantially complete. Johnson's major goal was political reunion. He also had a more personal, political agenda. His amnesty procedures were designed to restore the southern states to local control. (Though he used executive authority to achieve this, Johnson remained loyal to his lifelong democratic commitment—his middle name was Jackson—to states' rights and local autonomy.) But he wanted that control in the hands of southerners who had been if not always antisecession Unionists, at least reluctant Confederates. Even more importantly, he wanted the new political alignment to once and for all break the old "slavocracy's" domination of southern politics. He expected these new leaders—and leaders from the old elite who could regain political standing only through Johnson's individual pardon—to provide crucial political support for his own ambition to win the presidency on his own in 1868.

Johnson's decision to rescind General Sherman's Special Field Order No. 15 was part of this political strategy. But it also reflected his vision of what a reconstructed South should look like. Johnson had been antislavery, less out of regard for the black slaves than out of hatred of the planters' power. As he once put it, "Damn the Negroes! I'm fighting these traitorous aristocrats, their masters." He even once declared that he wished "to God that every head of family in the United States had one slave to take the drudgery and menial service off his family." The "new south" he envisioned remained a "white man's" society. Under his proclamations for instituting new governments only white men who had taken oaths of allegiance could participate in the political process. Moreover, he believed that only the states themselves, not Congress and certainly not the executive branch, had the power to define the franchise. He insisted that "white men alone must manage the South" and in his State of the Union address in 1867 went so far as to declare that blacks possessed "less capacity for government than any other race."

BLACK CODES

As soon as the ex-slaveholders found themselves regaining local power, they moved rapidly to reestablish their economic and social dominion, to return the freedmen to a position of social subordination and keep them as a cheap source of plantation labor. In fact, even before regaining formal power, some whites had resorted to violence to try to keep the newly freed blacks in a subordinate position. In May of 1866 in Mem-

phis and in July in New Orleans white mobs aided by some police killed dozens of blacks. Mississippi, South Carolina, and Alabama enacted Black Codes (the other states followed in early 1866), designed to erect state controls that would clearly and carefully define the place of the former slaves in post–Civil War southern society. The codes were multifaceted. Some permitted freedmen to hold property, enter into contracts, contract legal marriages, and sue in the courts. But they also restricted rights. No codes, of course, permitted black voting, and all prohibited freedmen from serving on juries and prohibited intermarriage. (Most northern states also prohibited these things as well.) Other codes restricted blacks to agricultural labor or positions as "servants," forbade carrying firearms, and imposed curfews on them. But it was in the area of labor that the codes were most restrictive. As William Trescot, the agent who pleaded the Edisto planters' cause in Washington, put it, "This question of the control of labor underlies every other question of state interest." The most severe labor codes were passed in Mississippi and South Carolina. Such codes required freedmen to sign annual contracts. In Louisiana and Florida, the contracts extended to "all the members of the family able to work." (As freedmen moved off large estates and onto homesteads, black women had withdrawn from the kinds of field labor they had done under slavery.) If freedmen broke their contracts, they lost all back wages and were subject to arrest by any white man. Vagrancy laws were passed, under which unemployed blacks who could not pay their fines for vagrancy could be bound out to work for anyone who paid their fine.

To many in the North, the new South that Johnson's Reconstruction had ushered in seemed frighteningly similar to the old South. Most of the ex-Confederates seemed right back in power. They filled the state legislatures. And the former vice president of the Confederacy, Alexander Stephens, six former cabinet members, nine generals, and more than fifty members of the Confederate legislature had been elected to the national

Congress by the reconstructed states. Moreover, the Black Codes seemed to have reestablished slavery under another name. As the *Chicago Tribune* thundered, "We tell the white men of Mississippi that the men of the North will convert the state of Mississippi into a frog pond before they will allow any such laws to disgrace one foot of soil over which the flag of freedom waves."

Northerners were divided over what they wanted out of Reconstruction, and few were eager to grant equality to blacks. (Twelve northern states still refused to give the franchise to blacks.) Still, they had opposed slavery, fought and won a war that had come about partly because of slavery, and they did not want to see it restored under some new guise. But most upsetting of all, those who had led the rebellion—those responsible for the terrible war—refused to acknowledge defeat. Mississippi and Texas rejected the Thirteenth Amendment, South Carolina refused to nullify its ordinance of secession, and members of the old slavocracy demanded seats in Congress. In Louisiana a government filled with conservative Unionists, Democrats, and former secessionists was elected on a platform that proclaimed the state government to be a structure "for the exclusive benefit of the white race." It seemed as if Reconstruction was about to deprive the North of the victory for which so many of its men had died.

When the new Congress returned to Washington, it refused to seat the senators and representatives from the former Confederate states. Even moderate Republicans were deeply disturbed at the apparent turn of events. They opposed the Radicals' call for the enfranchisement of the freedmen, fearing that if the party embraced the measure it would lose crucial support in the North. They were alarmed by the repressiveness of many of the newly installed regimes. As Senator Lyman Trumbull of Illinois, a leading moderate, put it, unless there was "some legislation by the nation for his protection," the ex-slave stood in danger of being "abused and virtually reenslaved." The Republicans set up a Joint Committee on Reconstruction, headed by a moderate

and dominated by moderates even though it contained the strong-willed Radical Republican, Representative Thaddeus Stevens of Pennsylvania. (The most vociferous Radical in the Senate, Charles Sumner of Massachusetts, who desperately wanted to be on the committee, was excluded as too "ultra.") Army officers, officials from the Freedmen's Bureau, some freedmen and southern Unionists testified before the committee about a rising tide of antiblack hostility and neo-Confederate, anti-North sentiment.

CONGRESSIONAL RECONSTRUCTION

Moderates like Lyman Trumbull and Senator John Sherman of Ohio did not want to throw out the governments organized under Johnson. But they did want to give some protection to the freedmen. Lyman Trumbull, perhaps the most influential man in Congress, introduced two bills early in 1866. The first was a measure to extend the life and expand the scope of the Freedmen's Bureau by giving it funding of its own and extending jurisdiction of its agents to cases involving actions against blacks. It authorized Bureau agents to punish officials who denied blacks the "civil rights belonging to white persons." But to the bitter disappointment of the Edisto farmers the final version of the bill dropped an earlier provision that would have extended at least temporarily their possession of land granted to them under Sherman's special order. Trumbull's second measure was a civil rights Bill. The bill was designed to give legislative substance to the Thirteenth Amendment. It declared all people born in the United States (except Native Americans) citizens and specified that without regard to race they all possessed equal rights to make contracts, to sue in the courts, and to "full and equal benefit of all laws . . . for the security of persons and property." In potentially its most radical feature, it made civil rights a federal responsibility by giving federal officials the authority to bring suits in federal courts against violations. Trumbull (as were most other moderates) was certain he had Johnson's support. He had met with Johnson in late December and believed that "the President wishes no issue with Congress and if our friends would be reasonable we would all get along harmoniously." The moderates considered both bills the height of "reasonableness."

Johnson—to the horror of Congress and the glee of Democrats and southern leaders "restored" to power under Johnson's procedures—vetoed both bills. (Both were later resubmitted and passed over his veto.) In his veto messages, Johnson not only condemned the specific measures, he also challenged the bills' constitutional legitimacy. The Freedmen's Bureau bill, he declared in a statement that challenged the authority of the then-sitting Congress to pass *any* Reconstruction legislation, was unconstitutional because it was passed by a Congress that con-

THADDEUS STEVENS. Like Lincoln, a former Whig who played an important role in founding the Republican party, Stevens was a Republican congressman from Pennsylvania. During the war he served as chairman of the powerful House Ways and Means Committee, and after the war he became the leader of the radical Republicans in the House and one of the leading advocates of the distribution of confiscated lands to the freedmen.

tained no members from the "eleven states which are to be mainly affected by its provisions." He condemned the Civil Rights Bill as an unconstitutional violation of states' rights and an unconstitutional "stride towards centralization and the concentration of all legislative powers in the national government."

The moderates countered with the Fourteenth Amendment, a complex measure designed to give some basic protection to the ex-slaves in a form that the moderates hoped the South would accept. The amendment contained the basic features of the Civil Rights Act. By constitutional amendment it declared all "persons born or naturalized in the United States" to be citizens (and thereby nullified the Dred Scott decision) and prohibited any state from depriving "any person of life, liberty, or property, without due process of law." But it also reduced the political power of the old southern elite by barring from public office anyone who had ever sworn fidelity to the Constitution and then participated in rebellion. The Radicals tried to get a black suffrage clause included in the amendment. The rights of the freedmen was not the Republicans' only concern. Johnson's Reconstruction plan threatened them with the loss of their political power, and many Republicans were more concerned with holding on to political power than with the rights of blacks. With the end of slavery, southern representation in the House of Representatives would be increased by about twenty seats, since for purposes of apportionment a slave had been counted as only three-fifths of a person. Republicans, especially the Radicals, feared that the exclusion of southern blacks from the vote would ensure the election of unreconstructed rebels, who would join with pro-southern Democrats to drive the Republicans from power. But the moderates resisted the radical demand for a suffrage clause. Instead, the amendment only threatened to reduce southern representation if blacks were not permitted to vote. Nor did it contain any provision for the confiscation or redistribution of lands—the measure to which Stevens was most committed. It was clear, however, that the Republican Congress would not accept any state back into the Union that did not ratify the amendment.

President and Congress were now at complete loggerheads. Johnson denounced the amendment and even urged southerners to reject it. He decided to take the issue of Reconstruction directly to the voters in the upcoming congressional elections. Contrary to custom, Johnson went on the political hustings, denouncing the Republican Congress and further polarizing the issue. Johnson was confident that popular opinion would rally to him. "The right of each state to control its own affairs," was an idea cherished in all parts of the country. Johnson was also certain that few northern whites really supported the expansion of black civil rights. When he asked an election rally, "What does the veto mean?" a supporter shouted back, "It is keeping the nigger down." These were the issues, moreover, by which he hoped to build his own electoral base of a coalition of Democrats, conservative and moderate Republicans, and southern Unionists. But he miscalculated. He underestimated the impact of southern actions—especially the violence against the former slaves and the defiant rhetoric of many restored southern officeholders—on northern opinion. Northern willingness to "forgive" only went so far. Not far below the surface was deep and residual northern anger over the terrible war that they thought the South had visited on the country. Johnson's campaign was a disaster, and the voters overwhelmingly repudiated his policies. The Republicans, now increasingly under the influence of Sumner and Stevens, won more than two-thirds of the seats in both houses, enough to override any presidential veto.

Most of the members of the newly constituted southern legislatures were firmly opposed to the Fourteenth Amendment, which would remove many of their members from office. But white southerners were also angry and felt a deep sense of betrayal. Many had complied with Lincoln's and Johnson's requirements in good faith—a number had condemned the outbreak of violence against blacks and the harshest measures of the restored legislatures—only to have new and harsher conditions imposed on them in what seemed like an all-

too-familiar resurgence of Yankee tyranny. Amid fiery denunciations of the fanatical South-hating Republicans, all the southern states except Tennessee, which was eager to have its congressional delegation seated, rejected the Fourteenth Amendment, further infuriating the Republicans in Congress. "The last one of the sinful ten has flung back into our teeth the magnanimous offer of a generous nation" was how Representative James Garfield of Ohio saw it. It was now two years after the end of the fighting, and North and South were further from reconciliation than ever. In his last major speech, Lincoln had pleaded for Americans "to bind up the nation's wounds"; two years of Reconstruction politics had only poured salt on them.

⟶≡●≡⟵

RADICAL RECONSTRUCTION

An aroused Republican Congress came to Washington in December 1866 determined to impose a new style of Reconstruction on a dismayed and angered South. The Republicans moved quickly to consolidate their power and to ensure that neither the courts nor the president thwarted their will. When the Supreme Court issued a ruling that seemed to challenge the validity of the military courts of the Freedmen's Bureau, they reduced the size of the Court, depriving Johnson of the chance to make any appointments to it. When in 1868 the Court seemed about to challenge the Reconstruction Acts the Radicals had passed, they took jurisdiction over such matters away from the Court. But it was Johnson's power that the Republicans were most determined to check. The election had given them the votes to nullify his veto power. The Republicans were equally determined to nullify his use of executive authority, especially his powers as commander in chief (the powers Lincoln had used so effectively during the war to bypass Congress). They enacted legislation that required all military orders, including those of Johnson, to go through General-in-Chief Ulysses S. Grant. The Republicans were also worried that Johnson would try to use federal patronage to create a political machine that would be loyal to him. To thwart this possibility, they passed the Tenure of Office Act, which was designed to prevent Johnson from firing people opposed to his policies.

Radicals, convinced that Johnson would use all means at his disposal to thwart Reconstruction policies passed even over his veto, opened up a campaign to impeach him and remove him from office. They argued that a public official could be removed for "grave misuse of his powers, or any mischievous nonuse of them—for any conduct which harms the public or perils its welfare." Moderates, believing that a president could be removed from office only if he did something that would be indictable as a crime if he were a private citizen, succeeded in blocking two initial attempts to launch impeachment proceedings against Johnson.

CHARLES SUMNER. A senator from Massachusetts, Sumner was the best known advocate of Radical Reconstruction in the Senate. A powerful orator, he was less effective as a legislative leader than Stevens and was often outmaneuvered by moderates.

In early 1867, the Radicals succeeded in passing a resolution calling for an impeachment investigation, but the House Judiciary Committee, dominated by moderates, declined to act. For a time, Johnson seemed to relent in his efforts to subvert congressional Reconstruction policy and let it be known that his administration would implement the laws Congress had passed. But after Congress adjourned in August, Johnson suspended Secretary of War Stanton (who actively supported the Radicals) and enlisted Ulysses S. Grant as interim secretary. Then, against Grant's wishes, Johnson removed from their commands Generals Philip Sheridan and Daniel Sickles, effective administrators and clear supporters of congressional policy, leading some moderates to change their minds and endorse impeachment. By a 5 to 4 margin, the House Judiciary Committee recommended to the full House that Johnson be impeached for "usurpation of power." The fall elections brought more conservative members into the House, which failed to vote on the measure.

But the impeachment issue was by no means dead. Under the provisions of the Tenure of Office Act, the Senate had to agree before Stanton could be removed from office. Technically, he was only suspended until the Senate acted. When the Senate refused to concur, Grant stepped aside and Stanton returned to his office. Johnson retaliated on February 21, 1868, and ordered Stanton removed, whereupon Stanton barricaded himself in his office. This apparently blatent violation of the Tenure of Office Act pushed many moderates to support impeachment and on February 24 the House voted by 126 to 47 to impeach Johnson. Under the Constitution, the House votes articles of impeachment—the equivalent of an indictment in criminal law—and the Senate acts as the court that conducts the trial on the charges. For eleven weeks an enthralled public watched the Senate proceedings. In the end, despite the complex legal issues as to what constituted legitimate grounds for removing a president from office, what was on trial was Johnson's unrelenting attempt to thwart Republican Reconstruction. But some moderates who deplored

Johnson's actions were equally fearful of setting a precedent under which a two-thirds majority of Congress could remove a president who opposed congressional policies, thereby perhaps permanently undermining the balance of powers that lay at the heart of the American constitutional system. Johnson, finally realizing the precariousness of his position, moderated his own behavior. He stopped publically denouncing Congress and promised moderates that he would enforce all the Reconstruction Acts. On May 16, 1868, the Senate finally voted. Seven Republicans and twelve Democrats voted against impeachment. By one vote impeachment failed to secure the two-thirds majority needed for conviction.

In the spring and early summer of 1867, the Republican Congress passed a series of Reconstruction Acts that envisioned a political structure and society very different from that being "restored" under Johnson's mode of reconstruction. Lincoln and Johnson had argued that since secession itself was illegal, the Confederate states had never really been out of the Union. But the Radicals insisted that by rebelling, the states had forfeited their statehood, committing "state-suicide," as Sumner called it. Radicals pushed for a far-reaching plan that would disenfranchise ex-Confederates for a long time, confiscate land for homesteads for the freedmen, and establish a system of federally supported schools. But they settled for a considerably less radical plan that declared the Johnson governments illegal and divided the conquered South into five military districts. The commander of each district, with the aid of the army, was required to prepare the states for readmission by registering all adult black males and all adult white males not disenfranchised by the Fourteenth Amendment. This new electorate would then elect delegates to conventions that were required to draw up state constitutions that guaranteed the vote to blacks and ratified the Fourteenth Amendment. Once the constitution was ratified by popular vote, elections could be held and the state's representatives would be readmitted to Congress. Ironically, by putting the word *male* into the Constitution for the first

time, the Fourteenth Amendment erected a constitutional barrier to opening the franchise to women. It is doubly ironic—though not surprising—that while requiring the black vote in a reconstructed South, the Republicans still resisted extending the requirement to the North. Fearing an adverse reaction in the 1868 elections, moderate Republicans resisted the Radicals' call for a constitutional amendment prohibiting the denial of the right to vote "on account of race, color, or previous condition of servitude." In fact, it was not until the Republicans began to lose power in the North in 1870 that they passed the Fifteenth Amendment, granting suffrage to black males in the North and South.

"Radical," or Republican, Reconstruction might not have taken such radical steps as barring the old political elite from power for a generation or laying the economic foundations for the development of an independent black yeomanry. From one perspective, in fact, the term "radical" is something of a misnomer. Those denominated "Radicals" from whom the label derived never gained clear control of Congress and never succeeded in passing their most radical social measures. Nonetheless, Republican Reconstruction did amount to a very real *political* revolution. It brought black voters into the center of the political process and, for a time, gave them very real political power in a way and to a degree that would have been simply unimaginable to most northern or southern whites even two years earlier. By September of 1867, the military supervisors had registered approximately 725,000 black and 650,000 white voters. (Between 100,000 and 175,000 white voters were probably disenfranchised. Over 25 percent of the eligible white voters failed to register either out of apathy or as a protest against the whole new system.) Moreover, blacks constituted a majority of the voters in five states.

The freedmen greeted the franchise with almost as much enthusiasm as they had emancipation itself. All over the South black voters mobilized almost as rapidly as freedmen had flocked to Edisto Island when Sherman's Special Field Order No. 15 was issued. Every institution—but especially the black churches—lent itself to polit-

"AND NOT THIS MAN?"   This woodcut by Thomas Nast was designed to enlist northern support for the franchise for blacks. It evokes the idea that blacks used to claim equal rights from the Revolution through World War II, the idea that as defenders willing to die for the nation, they deserved the freedom for which they had fought.

ical organization. Political notices were read at "churches, societies, leagues, clubs, picnics and all other gatherings." Branches of the Union League (founded in the North as a club to rally support to the Union cause) sprung up everywhere as a major instrument for political education and voter mobilization. One startled observer declared, "You never saw a people more excited on the subject of politics than are the negroes of the south. They are perfectly wild." In areas free of violence and intimidation (see below) voter turnout often reached nearly 90 percent.

THE REPUBLICAN COALITION IN THE SOUTH

The first step in the making of Radical Reconstruction in the South was the mobilization of a Republican coalition that could dominate the writing of the new constitutions and secure control of state and local government. The coalition was composed of three key groups. Certainly

the largest group consisted of the newly enfranchised blacks. Throughout the whole period, they were the electoral backbone of the Republican party in the South, constituting from 60 to 85 percent of the Republican vote. But blacks were a majority of the population in only three states—South Carolina, Mississippi, and Louisiana. They were one-quarter of the population in three states, and between 40 and 47 percent in the remaining four states of the old Confederacy. Thus, even with some (short-lived) disenfranchisement of whites, Republican power required varying degrees of white electoral support. This support came from two groups. The smallest component of the Republican coalition—in no place did it make up more than 2 percent of the electorate—consisted of northerners, dubbed "carpetbaggers" by resentful southerners who portrayed them as lowly, grasping, and greedy men, little better than "maggots feeding on Southern misfortune." In fact, the "carpetbaggers," the majority of whom were veterans of the Union army, were a well-educated, middle-class group of ambitious men in their twenties and thirties that included teachers, agents of the Freedmen's bureau, and investors in many cotton plantations. Although they constituted a minuscule portion of the electorate, they held a widely disproportionate number of the key public offices in the Reconstruction governments: they made up nearly 18 percent of the delegates to the constitutional conventions, and sixty of them served in Congress during Reconstruction.

The second group of whites in the Republican coalition consisted of southern whites, dubbed "scalawags" and condemned as "lepers" by many of their countrymen. There were, in general, two quite different groups of scalawags. A number came from the ranks of the former southern Whigs and Unionists who had opposed secession and were often of considerable local prominence and political experience. The largest group of southern white supporters of Republicans were those from the up-country regions, where there had been few slaves and where resentment of the planter aristocracy that had largely controlled antebellum politics was deepest. These up-country Republicans had been Union loyalists during the war and were often the most vehement in demands that the "rebels" be barred from office and their lands confiscated. To them, Republican Reconstruction, initially at least, represented the opportunity to once and for all bring "the reign of the would be aristocracy" to a "close."

The Republican coalition was a fragile and vulnerable one, made up of not always compatible groups with different interests, ideas, and priorities. For the more prominent and wealthy former Whigs and southern Unionists in the coalition, adherence to the Republican party was often perceived as an avenue to political power. Such men hoped to become the leaders of a new South built by securing the support of the freed blacks and the whites who resented the old planter and Confederate leadership as the agents who had brought war and destruction on the South. But the interests and wishes of such leaders were often at odds with those of the whites from the hill country, where slavery had been less of a presence. But most unstable of all was the biracial character of the Republican coalition. The newly freed slaves and poorer whites had a number of interests in common—the need for education and basic welfare, access to land and credit, limitations on the power of economic elites. But race cut deep, especially when economic conditions seemed to put whites and blacks in competition for scarce and dwindling resources. In the prolonged and deepening "hard times" that plagued much of the rural South in the decades following the Civil War, racial antagonism only intensified. At the same time as blacks struggled to gain access to land, an increasing number of poor whites found themselves *losing* land, a loss that made the Democrats' call for restoring the South as a "white man's country" all the more powerful.

As soon as registration was complete, the states elected delegates to the constitutional conventions. Less than half the registered whites but more than 80 percent of registered blacks cast ballots for delegates. Nearly 18 percent of the delegates were carpetbaggers. These delegates, typically in their thirties, were well-educated professionals who often chaired the key committees and drafted the key provisions of the new constitutions. Southern whites made up the largest group of delegates, the majority of whom were farmers, artisans, and merchants from the up-country who had little previous political experience. Blacks constituted a large block of 265 delegates overall, about half of whom had been born in slavery. At least 80, thirty of whom had spent most of their lives in the North, had been born free. At least 40 of the black delegates had served in the Union armies. In most states, the black delegates were relegated to minor roles, but in South Carolina and Louisiana experienced free-born delegates played a major role in shaping the final document.

As soon as the new constitutions were drafted, the battles for ratification were joined. In

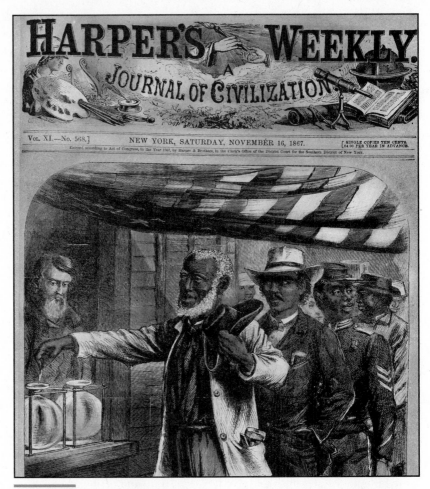

"THE FIRST VOTE."   To the former slaves the vote was as much a measure of freedom as the possession of land. This idealized depiction of "the first vote" by Nast is careful to represent the new black voters not as poor, uneducated farmers and agricultural laborers but as solid citizens no different from white voters, as artisans, as veterans, and as well-appointed gentleman. But by 1874, Nast and *Harpers* had retreated from their support of blacks and depicted black legislators in the southern states as corrupt, illiterate buffoons.

many places, conservatives worked strenuously to defeat ratification. They were sure that in the presidential election coming up in 1868 northern whites would turn against the Republican attempt to force "Negro rule" on the South. If the Democrats prevailed, perhaps things could be reversed and self-rule without black suffrage restored. In many places, the antiratification forces resorted to intimidation and violence, using a new terrorist organization, the Ku Klux Klan, to keep blacks away from the polls. But their major tactic was a voter boycott. Ratification required a majority of *registered* voters. There was little chance of getting more votes against ratification than for it, but if enough whites stayed away from the polls ratification would not win the majority it needed. The tactic succeeded in defeating ratification in Alabama: the vote was 70,812 to 1,005 in favor of ratification, but only 43 percent of the registered voters cast ballots. The Republicans in Congress retaliated by passing an additional Reconstruction Act that changed the requirements for ratification: henceforth it would only require a majority of those actually voting. By July of 1867, six states had ratified their constitutions by majorities ranging from 51 percent to 72 percent in South Carolina and had elected Republican governors and legislatures. It took until 1869 for Texas, Mississippi, and Virginia to complete the process that established—for a time at least—Republican rule in each of the states of the old Confederacy.

The North finally had reconstructed states it could accept as legitimate, full-fledged members of the Union. But to many white southerners these governments were never legitimate, and they were determined to do whatever it took to undermine them. To them, Republican Reconstruction was an unmitigated nightmare, and it left a century-long legacy of bitterness. There was, first, the tyranny—the imposition by military force of governments and rulers that they themselves would never have chosen. Moreover, it was an imposition by *outsiders*, by conquerors. Not only was Republican Reconstruction the act of a national government from which southerners had been excluded, it also turned local government *in* the South over to "invaders" from the North. It was a long-standing American axiom that government rested on the consent of the governed, and the majority of white southerners had certainly never consented to the kinds of governments that military Reconstruction forced on them. In fact, of course, in several of the states a majority of *all* Southerners—that is, of blacks and whites—had consented to them. But to most white southerners, the greatest of the horrors of Republican Reconstruction was that it subjected them to "Negro rule," a rule they condemned as wholly incompetent and corrupt.

The charge of "Negro rule" had a kind of truth to it. The Reconstruction governments did bring blacks into the political process and give them real political power: nearly 80 percent of Republican voters were blacks, freedmen were elected and appointed to local and national office—fourteen were elected to the House of Representatives and two were elected to the U.S. Senate—and the governments passed legislation to meet the demands and needs of the newly empowered black constituency. Indeed, it was precisely this *fact* of black political power that rendered these governments so illegitimate in the eyes of most southern whites. White supremacy was not an idea they were about to surrender. But at the same time, the conservative portrait of "Negro rule" was also largely a mythic creation, designed to delegitimize these governments not only in the eyes of white southerners but in northern eyes as well. Although black suffrage was essential for keeping these regimes in power, their electoral base, especially in the beginning, extended beyond the ex-slaves. Many former Whigs, southern Union men, and antisecessionists initially allied themselves with the new Republican governments. Many whites in nonslaveholding regions who had always resented the rule of the planter elite, voted for and participated in the Reconstruction governments. Moreover, only 6 percent of the congressmen elected during Reconstruction were blacks, who never held more than 20 percent of the local offices. In no state did blacks dominate or control the government. There was not a single elected black governor, and only in South Carolina was there ever a black legislative majority. Moreover, the range of ability, education, and competence among black officeholders was not wildly different from the range among most white officeholders in the North or South. Opponents of the Reconstruction governments castigated the carpetbaggers as "too depraved, dissolute, dishonest, and degraded to get" even "the lowest places" in their home states. But, in fact, they were more highly educated, competent, and probably more idealistic than the officeholders in most states in the Union. The Reconstruction governments certainly contained corruption, but they were no more corrupt than their lily-white counterparts before or after the war.

The Reconstruction governments were in many ways reform governments. Their constitutions were more advanced than many in the North. They not only established universal manhood suffrage, but also mandated public school systems for both races. Many of the constitutions called for the expansion of governmental responsibility for social warfare. The South Carolina constitution—the most far-reaching—for example, called for an integrated school system, abolished imprisonment for debt, provided for public support for "the aged, infirm, and helpless poor" (persons whom under slavery, masters had been responsible for), and called for "the division and sale of unoccupied lands among the power classes." The Reconstruction governments spent comparatively little time trying to achieve social equality between whites and blacks. Instead, they concentrated on such things as public education and eliminating the undemocratic features of the antebellum political system, by which the planter elite had maintained its dominion—things that benefited poor whites as well as the freedmen.

REDEEMING THE STATES

In standard political terms, there was much about the Reconstruction governments for the former slaveholders and old planter elite to oppose. They redistributed power and advocated programs that were often against the old elites' perceived interests. Moreover, the burden for paying for schools and welfare fell most heavily on them. But such considerations were not the ultimate source of opposition. Their opponents considered these governments to be wholly illegitimate—an outrage. Illiterate black field hands who could vote while former planters could not, blacks who held office, uppity ex-slaves who mocked their former masters, black soldiers who now patrolled whites—all these things in the eyes of the former slaveholders turned Republican Reconstruction into "Black Reconstruction." "Negro rule" became the galling symbol of all the horrors of Radi-

cal Reconstruction, of all they had lost, of the defeat they had suffered and the degradation they now felt.

The opposition struck back against the hated Reconstruction governments with all the means at their disposal. They were determined to regain control of politics and government and "redeem" the South by purging it once and for all of the twin specter of Yankee dominion and "Negro rule." They appealed to white supremacy to draw support of the poorer whites away from the Republicans. For the most part they relied on the ballot box for victory, but in many areas they used intimidation and violence against blacks and their allies to so reduce the black vote as to grant them electoral victory.

At the center of the resort to violence and intimidation were secret organizations like the Ku Klux Klan, which served as a kind of guerrilla force to restore white supremacy. In the words of Eric Foner, a leading historian of Reconstruction, the Klan and similar organizations, such as the Knights of the White Camellia and the White Legions, sought "to destroy the Republican Party's infrastructure, undermine the Reconstruction state, reestablish control over the black labor force, and restore racial subordination in every aspect of Southern life." Democrats—and many subsequent scholars—asserted that Klan violence and terrorism stemmed largely from the racial hatreds of poor whites, that violence was not something the "better sort" condoned. To be sure, a number of southern whites were appalled by the violence (though very few condemned it in public). But in areas of its greatest strength, the Klan drew members from across the social spectrum. Moreover, its leadership (which did not always participate directly in the overt violence itself) came from "respectable gentlemen." And many other "leading men" lent tacit support to the institution so long as it served their political and social purposes.

The Klan directed some of its terror against black schools and churches. In some areas, the Klan "enforced" labor contracts by whipping blacks who challenged or "disobeyed" their employers. Often "prosperous" blacks and those in positions considered too "elevated" for blacks were assaulted. But black officeholders and leaders were the major target of Klan violence. (Scalawags were also frequent targets.) More than thirty of the blacks who served in the constitutional conventions in 1867 were attacked and seven were murdered. In Arkansas, more than 200 political murders, including the assassination of a Republican congressman, took place in 1868 alone.

"TWO MEMBERS OF THE KU KLUX KLAN IN THEIR DISGUISES." The Ku Klux Klan began as a secret, relatively harmless fraternal order, but by early 1868 it had become a terrorist organization, filled with Confederate veterans and led by more than two dozen generals and colonels. Its hoods and robes, ostensibly intended to keep their identities secret, were thought to play on the alleged "superstition" of blacks and to add to the terror of the Klan.

The Klan's greatest strength was in areas of the Piedmont, where blacks were a minority or only a bare majority and where the population was evenly divided between Democrats and Republicans. (In the early and mid 1870s paramilitary "White Legions" operated extensively in Louisiana, Texas, Arkansas, and Alabama.) The Klan was largely absent from low-country South Carolina and Georgia, but was very active in a number of counties around Atlanta and in western Alabama and was deeply entrenched in the central Piedmont regions of North and South Carolina. In Jackson County, Florida, more than 150 people were killed; in Spartanburg County, South Carolina, the Klan whipped hundreds of Republicans and destroyed their livestock and farm property; and in Union County, where almost the entire white population belonged to the Klan, eleven blacks were killed and several hundred whipped.

By itself the campaign of violence did not bring about the "redemption" of the South. But its importance should not be underestimated. It seriously crippled the Republican infrastructure by decimating its leadership and intimidating others out of taking their places. It kept large numbers of black voters from the polls—in districts with the greatest Klan presence, the black vote was often reduced to almost nothing. (In the Klan-dominated counties of Georgia in 1868, for example, only a little over 100 out of more than 9,000 registered black voters cast ballots; in a group of 21 parishes in Louisiana, a Republican vote that had reached more than 26,000 was reduced to 500.) The violence undermined the Republicans in yet another way. Even in power (both locally and nationally) it seemed unable to protect its supporters. Only in Arkansas and Tennessee did Republican governors successfully use state force to combat the Klan. The campaign of terror alarmed northern Republicans. Two "force bills" and a Ku Klux Klan Act were passed by Congress, and in 1871 President Ulysses S. Grant initiated federal prosecutions in Mississippi. In South Carolina, Grant placed a few counties under martial law. These measures succeeded for a time in cutting down on violence and reducing the power of the Klan, which had lost much of its force by 1872. But after that the laws were unevenly enforced and when the White Legions resorted again to violence in Louisiana, Mississippi, and Alabama the Republican administration in Washington only intervened in a few, particularly dramatic—and well-publicized—cases.

It did not take long for "redemption" to begin reclaiming southern states. In states like Tennessee, Virginia, and North Carolina, where white voters had a clear majority, the "redeemers" gained control by 1870. In fact, in Virginia and Tennessee, opposition Democrats had controlled the state legislature from the beginning. It did not take long to regain the governorships. After only one year of Republican rule, Georgia followed suit in 1871, through the combination of the Democrats' success in drawing white voters away from the Republicans and a significant reduction of black votes in Klan areas. (In Alabama, the Democrats won control in 1870, lost it in 1872, and regained it permanently in 1874.) The battles for redemption in the deep South where there were black majorities were prolonged, intense, and violent. The Democrats successfully used white supremacy, and the reduction of taxes (the social measures of the Republican governments fell most heavily on property owners, who were especially hard hit by a continuing agricultural depression) to pry whites away from the Republicans. In Texas, which they captured in 1873, the Democrats were aided by a massive migration of southern whites, which reduced the Republican coalition to a minority.

In Louisiana and Mississippi, the contest was especially intense and violent. In Louisiana, extensive violence—and considerable fraud on both sides—plagued every election from 1868 to 1876. The Democratic and Republican candidates in 1872 both claimed victory. The Democratic claimant, John McEnery, organized a militia and tried to take control of New Orleans police stations. In April of 1873, a clash between the largely black state militia (few whites were willing to serve under Republican administrations) and armed whites in upstate Louisiana left two white men and more than seventy blacks dead. In the fall of 1874, the White Legion tried to take over New Orleans and set McEnery up as governor. Some 3,500 Legionnaires overran the militia and police forces and captured city hall, the state house, and the arsenal. Only after the arrival of federal troops did they withdraw. In Mississippi conditions were not much different. As the 1875 Mississippi election approached, whites were determined to keep blacks and Republicans away from the polls, and the governor feared a bloodbath if he used black militia to oversee the elections. When he asked for federal help, the Grant administration refused, declaring that "the whole public are tired of these annual autumnal outbreaks in the South." The Democrats swept to power, aided by the White Legions, and Mississippi too joined the ranks of the redeemed.

In the end, redemption amounted to a stunningly successful counterrevolution. The "redeemer" governments didn't repeal everything the Reconstruction governments had tried to accomplish. The public school systems—perhaps the most lasting achievement of Republican Reconstruction—remained intact but with severely reduced funds. Fiscal, social welfare, and land policies that had been directed toward blacks and poorer whites were scaled back if not largely abandoned. But what redemption did overturn was the revolution in political power that had given blacks a very real—though by no means dominant—place in the political community and thus, for a time, established the framework within which they might achieve equal standing as "free men."

Blacks were not immediately excluded from the political process. And the pace and process of restoring "white rule" and white supremacy varied from place to place. Some black officeholding continued after redemption: a few remained in several legislatures and even in Congress, they retained seats on some city councils, and some enclaves of black power like the second

MEMBERS OF THE MISSISSIPPI STATE LEGISLATURE, 1874–1875. This official roster of the Mississippi Senate shows the membership of the last legislature before Mississippi was "redeemed" in 1876. Note the arrangement of the profiles and the relegation of the blacks to the bottom two rows. Note also the presence of one woman, Miss Adies Ball, a black woman who was the Senate postmistress.

congressional district in North Carolina and areas in the South Carolina backcountry persisted until near the end of the century. Similarly, black suffrage was not completely rolled back with redemption. But what was broken with remarkable haste was the *effectiveness* of black political participation as state after state moved to make the Fourteenth and Fifteenth amendments "dead letters on the statute book." Black officeholders found themselves increasingly isolated and their powers curtailed. Local offices in areas with large black electoral majorities were stripped of much of their authority, which was transferred to county commissioners or appointed officials. Districts were redrawn to dilute the black vote and city-wide rather than ward elections were instituted. Along with the border and former slave states of Delaware, Kentucky, and Maryland, the "redeemed" states instituted a series of measures—poll taxes, residency requirements, and, in some places, property qualifications—that re-

duced the black electorate. And finally, especially in the Deep South, the threat—and fact—of antiblack violence was used to return blacks to subordination.

The former slaves and their free black allies fought hard, even after "redemption," to preserve their schools and hold on to whatever land they had. Despite the turmoil, the fickleness and reversals of policy, and the violence and intimidation, they persisted in their quest for land and independence. Availing themselves of the small window of opportunity the Reconstruction governments—and the Fourteenth and Fifteenth Amendments—provided them, by the end of Reconstruction nearly 20 percent of the blacks in the South succeeded in securing at least a parcel of "land [to] turn and till by [their] own labor." But white unity, continuing intimidation, and the ever deepening indifference of the North isolated the ex-slaves politically and made their rights—and even, oftentimes, their hard-won land—ever more vulnerable.

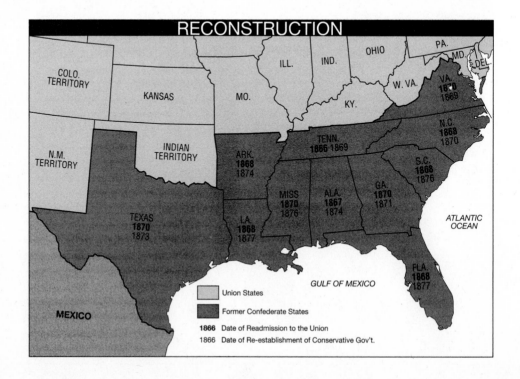

THE END OF RECONSTRUCTION

By 1876 only Louisiana, South Carolina, and Florida remained unredeemed. Even there the hold of Reconstruction was precarious, dependent on the continuing presence of federal troops. The election of 1876 removed this prop, largely because most northerners (at best minimally interested in the welfare of the ex-slaves) no longer cared very much about what was happening in the South. The Republican retreat from the politics of reconstruction really began with the passage of the Reconstruction Acts of 1867 and the election of General Ulysses S. Grant as president in 1868. In many ways, Grant's strong victory—he won 55 percent of the northern vote and carried every northern state but Oregon, New Jersey, and New York—represented an endorsement of Republican Reconstruction. But it also was believed to have finally "settled" the issue of Reconstruction—to have set the policies and procedures by which it would at long last be carried out—and opened the way for the nation and especially the North to return to the ordinary concerns of politics. (In fact, except for "force bills" and the Ku Klux Klan Act, no additional reconstruction measures were passed.) In his inaugural address of 1869, Ulysses S. Grant called for "peace," which most northerners took to mean relief from the turmoil of Reconstruction politics.

The election of 1872 indicated how rapidly northern concerns had shifted. It was not only the South that came out of the Civil War a changed society. A number of important changes—the development of a modern transportation system and mechanized agriculture, a series of technological innovations that underlay industrialization and the emergence of a wide-scale factory system—were well under way by the outbreak of war. (In fact, they were central in enabling the North to win the war.) But the war dramatically accelerated these changes. Moreover, it radically shifted the regional distribution of wealth, both by increasing the wealth in the North and because of the impoverishment that the war brought to the South. In 1860, southern whites had 95 percent *more* per capita wealth than northern whites: in 1870, northern whites had 44 percent more than southern whites. Production (both industrial and agricultural) had been about even on a per-capita basis at the outbreak of war: by 1870, it was nearly 60 percent greater in the North. And in 1870, the South contained only 12 percent of the overall national wealth. The North wanted to get back to business, and business didn't require paying any real attention to the South and what might be happening there.

In 1872, many liberal Republicans who had been staunch in their concern for black rights, including Charles Sumner, turned against the Republican party and supported the Democratic nominee, Horace Greeley, himself an old Whig-Republican, who focused his campaign largely on the corruption of the Grant administration. By the mid-1870s, northerners were more preoccupied with the politics of corruption and agrarian discontent, and with the problems of inflation, tariffs, and railroads, than with Reconstruction or, certainly, the fate of the former slaves.

The election of 1876 resulted in a bizarre deadlock between Rutherford B. Hayes, the Republican nominee, and his Democratic opponent, Samuel J. Tilden. In exchange for the disputed electoral votes of South Carolina, Florida, and Louisiana, Hayes, who had narrowly lost the popular vote to Tilden, promised to remove all remaining federal troops from the South, thus putting a symbolic end to the Reconstruction that in all essential respects had already come to an end. In his second inaugural address, Lincoln had linked the survival of the Union to the fate of the slaves. Slavery had ended and the mighty scourge of war was lifted, but twelve years of Reconstruction had made it clear that white Americans were far from ready to make good on the promise of emancipation.

-->=◎G=<-

CHRONOLOGY

1861   Planters flee Edisto Island; blacks remain and plant crops under Union supervision

1862   Union forces evacuate Edisto

1863   Lincoln issues the Emancipation Proclamation;

Lincoln issues the "Proclamation of Amnesty and Reconstruction"

1864   Congress passes Wade-Davis Bill; Lincoln vetoes it;

Sherman captures Atlanta and Charleston, South Carolina

1865   Sherman and Stanton meet with twenty black leaders in Charleston, South Carolina;

Sherman issues Field Order No. 15;

Blacks return to Edisto Island and establish family farms;

Freedmen's Bureau established; General O. O. Howard appointed commissioner;

Lincoln assassinated, Johnson becomes president;

Johnson issues his Amnesty Proclamation;

Thirteenth Amendment ratified;

Johnson rescinds special Field Order No. 15;

General Howard visits Edisto Island to explain Johnson's policy

1866   Johnson recognizes southern state governments established under his reconstruction plans;

Southern legislatures adopt "Black Codes";

Republican Congress refuses to seat members elected from the former Confederate states;

Johnson vetoes Freedmen's Bureau Bill and Civil Rights Act;

Congress passes Fourteenth Amendment;

Republicans win large majorities in both houses;

Republicans pass Civil Rights Bill and

Freedmen's Bureau Bill (without provision protecting black land titles) over Johnson's veto;

Ku Klux Klan established

1867   In continuing search for land, Henry Bram leads migration of Edisto inhabitants to Florida;

Congress passes set of Reconstruction Acts, establishing Military Reconstruction;

Congress passes Tenure of Office Act

1868   Arkansas, Alabama, Florida, Louisiana, North Carolina, South Carolina are readmitted to Union and elect representatives to Congress under provisions of Military Reconstruction;

Fourteenth Amendment ratified;

Violence against blacks in the South escalates;

Johnson impeached, not convicted;

Ulysses S. Grant (Republican) elected president

1869   Congress passes Fifteenth Amendment granting vote to adult black males

1869–1871   Tennessee, North Carolina, Virginia "redeemed"

1870   Congress passes two "force bills" and the Ku Klux Klan Bill in response to antiblack violence

1872   Grant reelected president

1872–1874   Texas, Alabama, Arkansas, Georgia "redeemed";

White Legions established in Louisiana, Texas, Arkansas, and Alabama

1875   Grant refuses to send federal troops to oversee Mississippi election

1876   Rutherford B. Hayes (Republican) elected president;

Federal troops withdrawn from the South, Reconstruction officially ends

1877   Louisiana and Florida "redeemed"

SUGGESTIONS FOR FURTHER READING

EDISTO ISLAND: LAND AND FREEDOM

Willie Lee Rose, *Rehearsal for Reconstruction* (1964), is the classic study of Reconstruction during the Civil War in the Sea Islands and contains important material concerning Edisto Island. William S. McFeely, *Yankee Stepfather: General O. O. Howard and the Freedmen* (1994), devotes a chapter to Edisto. Vincent Harding, *There Is a River: The Black Struggle for Freedom in America* (1981), Edward Magdol, *A Right to the Land: Essays on the Freedmen's Community* (1977), and Eric Foner, *Reconstruction: America's Unfinished Revolution* (1988), also contain discussion of the struggle over Edisto Island. Ira Berlin, et al., "The Terrain of Freedom: The Struggle over the Meaning of Free Labor in the U. S. South," *History Workshop,* 22 (Autumn 1986), reprints the Edisto farmer's petitions to Howard and Johnson.

REUNION AND RECONSTRUCTION

The best, most comprehensive treatment of Reconstruction is Foner, *Reconstruction: America's Unfinished Revolution* (1988.) James McPherson, *Ordeal by Fire: The Civil War and Reconstruction* (1982), has a short but very useful discussion. John Hope Franklin, *Reconstruction After the Civil War* (1961), and Kenneth M. Stampp, *The Era of Reconstruction* (1965), are useful short, general accounts. W. E. B. du Bois, *Black Reconstruction* (1935), remains a classic, pathbreaking study. W. McKee Evans, *Ballots and Fence Rails* (1966), is a superb study of the politics of Reconstruction on the local level in North Carolina. Lawanda Cox and John Cox, *Politics, Principle, and Prejudice* (1965), and William Gillette, *The Right to Vote* (1969), treat race and politics in this period. Eric McKitrick, *Andrew Johnson and Reconstruction* (1966), is a thorough study of early presidential Reconstruction. Hans Trefousse, *Andrew Johnson* (1991), is a useful recent biography. Dan T. Carter, *When the War Was Over: the Failure of Self-Reconstruction in the South, 1865–1867* (1985), is a provocative and highly suggestive study of the early years of Reconstruction. William S. McFeely, *Grant* (1981), is the best study of Grant's presidency. The

same author's *Yankee Stepfather: General O. O. Howard and the Freedmen* (1968), is a useful study of the Freedmen's Bureau. James L. Roark, *Masters Without Slaves: Southern Planters in the Civil War and Reconstruction*, is a superb study of a complex subject. Michael Perman, *The Road to Redemption* (1984), is a solid study of the overall subject of redemption. Allen Trelease, *White Terror* (1967), remains the best treatment of the role of the Ku Klux Klan and white terrorism in defeating Reconstruction. C. Vann Woodward, *Reunion and Reaction* (1951), and William Gillette, *Retreat from Reconstruction* (1980), describe the end of Reconstruction.

The story of blacks in Reconstruction is explored in a number of works. Especially valuable for setting the Civil War context for postwar developments is Ira Berlin, et al., *Slaves No More: Three Essays on Emancipation and the Civil War* (1992). Among the most notable studies of the freedmen during Reconstruction are Joel Williamson, *After Slavery* (1966), and Leon Litwack, *Been in the Storm So Long* (1979), and Thomas Holt, *Black Over White* (1977). Ronald E. Butchart, *Northern Schools, Southern Blacks, and Reconstruction: Freedmen's Education, 1862–1875* (1980), is a solid study of the important topic of the freedmen's quest for education. Other important books on Reconstruction and its impact on white and black southerners alike are Paul D. Escott, *Many Excellent People* (1985), and Stephen Hahn, *The Roots of Southern Populism* (1983). Morgan Kousser and James McPherson, eds., *Region, Race, and Reconstruction* (1982), is a valuable collection of essays.

Rupert S. Holland, ed., *The Letters and Diary of Laura M. Towne* (1970), is a superb collection of letters from a young woman who went to the South Carolina Sea Islands to teach the ex-slaves. Though they deal with the period of the Civil War, the four volumes in *Freedom: A Documentary History of Emancipation*, edited by Ira Berlin, et al., *The Destruction of Slavery* (1986), *The Black Military Experience* (1983), *The Wartime Genesis of Free Labor: the Lower South* (1991), and *The Wartime Genesis of Free Labor: the Upper South* (1993), are invaluable.

The Politics
of Restoration

THE EPISODE: In 1876, the United States passed through the most unusual presidential election in its history. What made the election unique was not the candidates. Republican Rutherford B. Hayes and Democrat Samuel J. Tilden were not remarkable men. The issue turned on disputed election returns from three states—Louisiana, Florida, and South Carolina—the only states where federal troops still enforced Republican "Reconstruction" measures designed to protect the voting rights of African Americans.

The Constitution was extremely vague about how electoral votes should be counted. It said only that the members of the electoral college in each state should send their votes to Washington. Then "the President of the Senate shall . . . open the certificates and the votes shall then be counted." What the Constitution did not say was exactly who should count the votes, or who should choose between competing votes when more than one set of men claimed they had been chosen as electors by the voters of their state. The Democratic candidate, Tilden, had won a clear majority of the popular vote. But Republicans realized that if they could get the electoral votes of all three disputed states, Hayes would win the electoral balloting by a bare margin of one.

THE HISTORICAL SETTING: In normal political times, the way the disputed election was settled would not have been of such urgent importance. But the 1870s were not

normal times. The Civil War had ended just eleven years before, and most of the nation's political leaders had taken part in that struggle. The contest between Republicans and Democrats still evoked extremely bitter memories. The fundamental issue in 1876 and 1877 was not who would be president, but how Reconstruction would be ended and national politics restored to the "normal" practices of the pre–Civil War period.

The twin political outcome was the end of Reconstruction and the restoration of competition between two very evenly matched political parties. But, for a generation after 1876, the parties tried to win elections by avoiding clear stands on issues. This had three important results: a shift of power to Congress; a failure to confront problems resulting from profound social and economic change; and the rise of protest movements that attempted to bypass an inert political structure.

This chapter—the first of four that deal with the last quarter of the nineteenth century—establishes a political framework. The three subsequent chapters will analyze the impact of the climax of the industrial revolution, the expansion of European-American society into the far western territories of Native Americans, and deep changes in the lives of women and their families. Many basic features of modern American society were taking shape during these twenty-five years; looking at the period from four distinct angles can help us understand the world we inherited from our great-great-grandparents.

THE ELECTION OF 1876

More than half a century ago, the novelist Thomas Wolfe thought back to the political times of his own father. It was a dull and vague past, that world of the 1870s and 1880s, a world of forgotten men, in which even the presidents had been a dreary lot: "Garfield, Arthur, Harrison, and Hayes . . . for me they were the lost Americans: their gravely bewhiskered faces mixed, melted, swam together. And they were lost. For who was Garfield, martyred man? Who had heard the casual and familiar tones of Chester Arthur? And where was Harrison? Where was Hayes? Which had the whiskers, which had the burnsides: which was which?"

The problem for Thomas Wolfe was not just one of time. Abraham Lincoln's career lay further back in the past, but Lincoln could never have seemed lost. Or Andrew Jackson or George Washington either. The fog that settled over the political history of the 1870s and 1880s was a fog of dullness and sameness, with no personalities, no drama, no profound causes won and lost. No Washingtons, Jacksons, or Lincolns.

Thomas Wolfe was a novelist, not a historian. But the historians have echoed his judgment. They have called the politics of the late nineteenth century "the politics of complacency," or "the politics of inertia." They have defined it as a period of "uncertainty" or "drift." Little wonder that the bewhiskered faces mix, melt, and swim together.

But the odd fact is that this period of American political history began with an election that was extremely tense and dramatic. From election day in November 1876 down to the dawn of March 2—less than two days before a new president had to be inaugurated—no one could be sure who would be sworn into office. It was even possible that no one would be, and that a new election might have to be held. Another possibility was that two men would claim the presidency and that the question might have to be settled by force of arms. Except for the crisis of secession following Lincoln's election in 1860, no four months of American political history have seemed more dramatic to the participants than that winter of 1876–1877.

At the end of election day, November 7, 1876, everything seemed over. In Ohio, the Republican candidate, Rutherford B. Hayes, passed the evening with a few friends and supporters in his home. The telegrams that came in made it clear he had lost. His wife, Lucy, tried to hide her disappointment. But she lost heart and went upstairs to bed, saying she had a headache. Sometime before 1:00 A.M., Hayes joined her, and they talked for a while the talk of losers: about how defeat was really a good thing, since it meant that their personal lives would be quiet and easy. Their sadness, they told each other, was not that Hayes had lost but that the "poor colored people" of the South would now be abandoned to an administration of Democrats dominated by the ex-rebels of the South. "This said," Hayes wrote in his diary, "we soon fell into a refreshing sleep and the affair seemed over."

In New York, the home of the Democratic candidate, Samuel J. Tilden, it had rained in the afternoon. But by nightfall, bonfires of celebration lit up the wet streets. At the Democratic party's headquarters, the telegrams came in from state after state, promising victory. There was no doubt that Tilden had received a clear majority of the popular vote.

But the leaders of both parties understood perfectly well that presidents of the United States were not elected by the votes of the people. They were chosen by the members of the electoral college. The professional politicians all knew the formula. If the Democrats could win the electoral votes of all the old slave states and carry Tilden's own New York, then they only needed to win any two out of three promising states in the North: Indiana, Connecticut, and New Jersey.

By midnight, the Western Union code machines had dotted and dashed the messages into party headquarters: the Democrats had almost the whole South. They had New York by more than they had dared hope for. And they had won in all three of the other northern states they had needed. Now, even if two southern states still under federal military occupation—South Carolina and Louisiana—were taken from them, they still had won. Tilden's campaign manager, New York Congressman Abram S. Hewitt, stepped onto the wet pavement just before midnight and bought a copy of the leading Republican newspaper, the *New York Tribune*. The headline was short and to the point: TILDEN ELECTED.

At Republican national headquarters in the Fifth Avenue Hotel, everyone except for one clerk had already gone home. A little before midnight, Republican Daniel Sickles, a Union general who had lost a leg at Gettysburg, stumped in, to find only a few gaslights still burning and the clerk putting away the records of defeat. Sickles studied the telegrams. They seemed at first to confirm what the party's chairman, Zach Chandler, had decided an hour or so before, when he gave up and went to his room with a bottle of consoling whiskey.

But Sickles was one of those Republican leaders for whom politics was deeply associated with the war. It was not just because of the Confederacy that men like Sickles had lost legs or arms or had suffered in prison camps. The Democratic party had also been their enemy. Sickles would surrender only when the enemy's victory was absolutely certain. As he shuffled the telegrams, they seemed to hold out one tiny hope. If Hayes could claim Louisiana, South Carolina, *and* Florida, then he would have exactly the 185 electoral votes needed to win the presidency. And all three of these states still had lame-duck Republican governors, who just might be able to "deliver" the necessary electoral votes.

Sickles believed—as every loyal Republican did—that the vote in these three southern states had been determined by force and fraud on both sides. Federal marshals and Republican election officials had done whatever they could to throw these states to Hayes. Democratic crowds and local officials had done whatever they could to keep African-American voters from the polls. If force and fraud were going to prevail on one side or the other, there might still be time to make sure that these states cast their official electoral votes for Hayes.

HAYES CAMPAIGN POSTER. This engraving, done by the nation's most successful illustrating firm, Currier & Ives, is filled with the political symbolism of the day. The eagle is taken from the Great Seal of the United States. The slogan, "Liberty and Union," is meant to recall the Northern cause in the Civil War. The stars appear as they did on military uniforms during the war. And the horn of plenty at the center suggests that Hayes will bring renewed prosperity. In the midst of it all is Hayes, looking candidly at the voter with an expression meant to convey an incorruptible honesty.

But if these three states were going to be saved, the Republican election officials had to be warned to be alert. Sickles, on no authority, drafted telegrams to the three Republican governors: WITH YOUR STATE SURE FOR HAYES, HE IS ELECTED. HOLD YOUR STATE. He signed the name of Zach Chandler, who was asleep upstairs. But did he dare send the telegrams? Just then, Chester A. Arthur, a New York Republican officeholder, wandered in and offered to share responsibility for the decision. Sickles sent the telegrams and Arthur went home to a sick wife. Then Sickles also left.

For the next few hours, only a handful of Republican leaders were still awake, and still clinging to their slender hope. William Chandler, a New Hampshire senator, was on a night train from his home state to New York. About dawn, he walked into the party headquarters in the Fifth Avenue Hotel, to find only the solitary clerk, who gave him the news of Hayes's apparent defeat. Another wakeful Republican was a newspaper editor, John Reid, who had been at work all night on the dawn edition of *The New York Times*. Reid had been a prisoner during the war, at a Confederate camp of horror known as Libby Prison, in Virginia. Like Sickles, he did not forget. And like Sickles, he regarded the Democrats as the party of slavery and rebellion. Reid's determination had kept the *Times* from conceding the election to Tilden. The paper's morning edition bravely said: RESULTS STILL UNCERTAIN.

Now Reid rushed into the Fifth Avenue Hotel with a bit of news he thought might be important. He had just received a telegram from Democratic headquarters asking exactly what the *Times* thought the electoral count would be. If the Democrats themselves were not completely certain of the outcome, maybe there still was a chance to pull the election out for Hayes.

At party headquarters, Reid met William Chandler. Reid told his story, and together the two men decided to go upstairs and try to rouse Zach Chandler. They had to beat on the door of his room for a long time, and when he finally appeared, he was in a nightshirt and thoroughly befuddled. Sleepily, and probably a little drunk, he told the two men to do whatever was "necessary." Back downstairs, Reid and William Chandler sent out more telegrams. The messages to South Carolina, Florida, and Louisiana were about the same as Sickles had sent earlier: CAN YOU HOLD YOUR STATE?

Some hours later, around mid-morning, Zach Chandler roused himself, dressed, and did his arithmetic. Leaving Florida, Louisiana, and South Carolina aside, Tilden had certainly carried sixteen states, with a total of 184 electoral votes, just one short of the necessary 185. Hayes had clearly won nineteen states, with a total of 166, 19 short of victory. Tilden's forces were claiming all 19 electoral votes from Louisiana, South Carolina, and Florida. (Even Hayes still believed that Tilden had surely won at least one of the three.) In the face of these facts, Zach Chandler did something audacious. He issued a brief and blunt statement saying, "Hayes has 185 votes and is elected."

The Democrats were astounded. Tilden had won a clear majority of the popular vote—about a quarter of a million more than Hayes, out of the 8 million votes cast. He had a sizable reported majority in Louisiana: around 9,000 votes. And he seemed to have won decisively in Florida. In South Carolina, things were closer. But Tilden could concede South Carolina if he had to and still win the presidency.

There was only one chance for the Republicans to snatch the election from Tilden and the Democrats. The small election boards that had to certify election results in South Carolina, Louisiana, and Florida were still controlled by Republicans. And the states had Republican governors. If those officials threw out enough Democratic votes, they might report a victory for Hayes.

As both sides quickly understood, the first step that had to be taken was to complete the official count of the votes in the three disputed states. In this process, the election boards had the legal right to challenge and exclude votes where there had been evidence of fraud or coercion of voters. This would mean days and days of taking testimony and reviewing sworn statements. And so both parties sent teams of "observers" to the three southern state capitals, to make certain that the election officials behaved fairly. It was in this stage of things that something quiet but remarkable began to happen.

As the Republican "observers" went south, they encountered something that surprised them. They found that the southern Democratic officials were thoroughly professional politicians, and not just fanatic ex-Confederates. And so two sets of men began to come together in New Orleans, Tallahassee, and Columbia (just as they had been doing in Congress increasingly for ten years). These were ex-officers of the Union

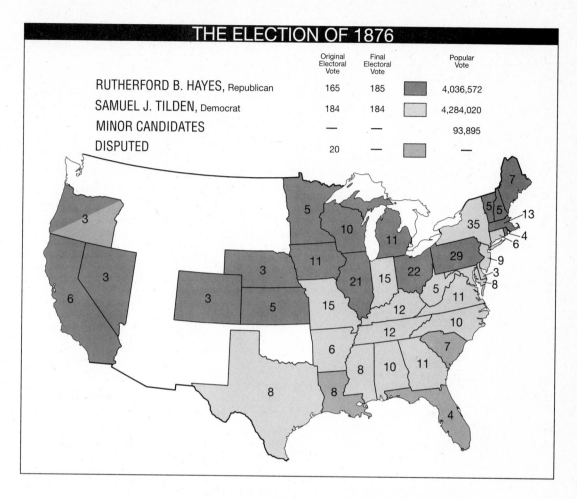

THE ELECTION OF 1876

	Original Electoral Vote	Final Electoral Vote		Popular Vote
RUTHERFORD B. HAYES, Republican	165	185		4,036,572
SAMUEL J. TILDEN, Democrat	184	184		4,284,020
MINOR CANDIDATES	—	—		93,895
DISPUTED	20	—		—

and of the Confederacy, men who remembered all the violence and the passion of the war, and in whom old hatreds could be roused by a careless remark or discourtesy. But now they could not afford to look backward, for they were politicians and lawyers as well as ex-generals and ex-colonels. This newer role demanded order, courtesy, and decorum—and above all a capacity for bargaining. And it was this professional side of their lives that began now to dominate the political maneuvering.

Former Union general James A. Garfield, now a Republican congressman from Ohio, was one of the Republican observers in Louisiana. He scratched into his diary the story of a day in November when a curious group of men took a day off from the political struggles to take a boat trip down the Mississippi. One member of the party was General William Tecumseh Sherman, who had been the most feared and hated of all Lincoln's commanders. The leader of the excursion was the Confederate general P. G. T. Beauregard, who had commanded southern troops at Shiloh, one of the bitterest battles of the war. Under Beauregard's courtly eye, the visiting Yankees marveled at the river's beauty, at the "vast plantations" and "great orange groves that made the shore beautiful with green and gold." Garfield, who had fought at Shiloh, talked with Beauregard: "He told me, quite fully, the history of the battle in which we were both engaged. It was curious to hear the history of the battle by the rebel commander."

The Democratic observers who went south met "reconciliation" of a different kind from Republican officials in Florida, Louisiana, and South Carolina. (At least they thought they did.) Various Democrats were met with apparent offers from the Republican members of electoral boards to *sell* their states' electoral votes to Tilden. Henry Watterson, a Kentucky Democrat observing in Louisiana, was visited by a man who claimed he had an offer from the two white and two black Republican members of the state's election board. They would sell the election for $250,000—$100,000 each for the two white members, and (as Watterson brutally put it) "$25,000 each for the two niggers."

Watterson apparently did not take the offer seriously. But other Democrats did. Soon coded telegrams were flying back and forth between the three Southern states and Tilden's mansion in New York. They never reached Tilden, or even his campaign manager, Abram Hewitt. Instead, they went to Tilden's nephew, William Pelton. One, sent by New York editor Manton Marble from Florida, was decoded by Pelton to read:

> HAVE JUST RECEIVED A PROPOSITION TO HAND OVER AT ANY HOUR REQUIRED TILDEN DECISION OF BOARD AND CERTIFICATE OF GOVERNOR FOR $200,000.

Pelton wired back, PROPOSITION TOO HIGH. Marble responded that he had another offer to help rig the vote for only HALF A HUNDRED BEST UNITED STATES DOCUMENTS—meaning $50,000.

All these "negotiations" failed. And the fact is that Marble and Pelton were probably being tricked into dealing with intermediaries who had no control over the votes anyway. As soon as Tilden found out about the telegrams, he put a stop to such dealings on Pelton's part. Marble and Pelton themselves explained that they were convinced they were only proposing to use the bribes to prevent the Republicans from "stealing" the election. On their side, the visiting Republican observers were offering federal jobs to election officials once their "duty" had been completed.

In the end, both sides concentrated their attention on the legal process of getting the votes counted and certified. No one said so, at least in public, but a kind of informal agreement was gradually being reached by the politicians: The election would be decided on the basis of a bundle of legal technicalities. It would be dealt with by lawyers and by politicians, using the quiet skills and devices of their trade. In all three southern capitals, the spirit of inducement, legality, and courtesy prevailed. One by one, and in peace, the Republican election boards turned their results over to Republican governors, to be certified and returned to the Republican president of the U. S. Senate. In each case, the result was the same: All nineteen disputed electoral votes in the South were recorded for Hayes. And in each state, Democratic officials refused to recognize the result and sent in contesting results: nineteen electoral votes and the presidency for Tilden.

But the first of many practical compromises had been made: Voters and officials in the three southern states had in effect agreed to leave the final solution in the hands of officials in Washington. During the month between the election and the official submission of the electoral votes of the states, there was no violence in the South, no mobs, no hangings or beatings of visiting Yankees, no challenges to the federal troops that were still posted in the three state capitals.

A curious villain now entered the scene: English grammar—more precisely, the passive voice. The Constitution contains no more cumbersome and creaking piece of machinery than the electoral college, an institution that never meets and exists only as an abstraction every four years. But the framers must have been in an especially wry frame of mind when they prescribed what was to be done with the electoral votes once they were cast. According to Article II and the Twelfth Amendment, the electoral votes "shall be transmitted to the seat of the government of the United States, directed to the President of the Senate" (who is normally the vice president). Then "the President of the Senate shall, in the presence of the Senate and House of Representatives, open all the certificates and the votes shall then be counted."

There it was, the insidious passive voice: "the votes shall then *be* counted." But counted by whom? By the president of the Senate? He was a loyal Republican. By the members of the House and Senate, sitting together? The Democrats outnumbered the Republicans in Congress as a whole. By each house separately? That could only produce an impasse, since the Democrats controlled the House and the Republicans the Senate.

The dilemma was acute. And it could not be resolved on any clear constitutional ground. But such puzzles provide a field day for professional politicians. Where the rules are not clear, outcomes can be determined by negotiation and compromise. The talents of bluff, swap, and deal now became paramount. The only question was, could some sort of compromise be reached before inauguration day? If not, the possibilities would become even more dizzying. President Grant might try to decide who had been elected, and somehow use the army to enforce his choice. The Democratic House might name Tilden president and the Republican Senate might name Hayes. Then whom would the army obey? For men who had lived through secession and Civil War, such possibilities, though remote, were real enough, especially when some politicians were publicly calling for 100,000 armed men to come to Washington to settle the matter in the streets.

At this point, the personalities and strategies of Hayes and Tilden themselves became crucial. Would either of them demand the presidency and exhort their followers to action, even if it meant using force of some sort?

On the face of it, Tilden was the least likely leader of any kind of aggressive movement. He was a soft-spoken lawyer (but a lawyer whose soft speech had won him a fortune of around $10 million), a scholarly bachelor who seemed to love the great library in his Gramercy Park mansion much more than the roughhouse of politics. Unlike many politicians in both parties, he was not a veteran of the Civil War. His quiet habits had been reinforced by a mild stroke he had suffered in 1875. The Republican chairman, Zach Chandler, had assembled a drawerful of signed statements by various nurses and doctors who had treated Tilden, statements that claimed that Tilden was "physically sexless." In a Victorian world where "manliness" was an obsession (at least among men), there could have been no more profound suspicion.

During the weeks after the election, Tilden played the role of lawyer and scholar. He spent a month doing detailed research on the history of presidential elections. He ignored the pleas of his supporters that he issue a strong statement claiming that he had won. He forbade any mass meetings in his name. He sent telegram after telegram in which the key word was "wait," or "delay," or even "procrastinate." Democratic leaders who came to him looking for instruction, advice, or practical wisdom on how to handle the crisis went away shaking their heads in disappointment.

Tilden gave his blessing to only one practical action. In Oregon, one of the Republican electors was also a local postmaster. But the Constitution forbade any federal officeholder from serving as an elector. So, working with the Democratic governor of Oregon, Tilden's campaign manager, Abram Hewitt, devised a scheme to replace the Republican elector with a Democrat: a hole card to use against the inside straight the Republicans were trying to put together in the South. For the rest, Tilden contented himself with quiet, legalistic preparations, making it clear that he wanted no hint of force, fraud, or a mobilized public opinion. The questions, he insisted, were all legal, not political. In this attitude, Tilden was consistent from beginning to end.

Hayes, on the other hand, was a man divided against himself. In many ways, he was quite different from Tilden. He was a lawyer and a man of some cultivation, but far from being scholarly. He was married and had several children. He had fought for the Union and had been seriously wounded. He was something of a self-made man and, though very well-to-do, had nothing approaching Tilden's fortune. Above all, Hayes was a man who was deeply committed to being decent and moral. And it was this commitment that established an initial division in his mind about what to do.

On one side, Hayes was convinced that a fair election, with African Americans permitted to vote in the South as the Fifteenth Amendment provided, would certainly have given him a victory. On the other side, however, he had felt all his life that politics

SAMUEL J. TILDEN. Tilden's face was hardly likely to inspire passionate support among his followers. It did suggest a capacity for worry or concern. But its most striking feature, given the fashion of the day, was what it lacked, for Tilden sported no beard, no moustache, not even elaborate sideburns. And even his hair was much more closely cut than most men's in the post–Civil War decades.

was a dirty business, full of fraud and deception. He had managed to avoid being "soiled," and his first reaction to his apparent defeat was to let the election go rather than risk getting involved in a sneaky strategy. His diary recorded his puzzlement.

> November 12—We shall, the fair-minded men of the country will, history will, hold that the Republicans were by fraud, violence, and intimidation, by a nullification of the Fifteenth Amendment, deprived of the victory which they fairly won. But we must, I now think, prepare ourselves to accept the inevitable.

> November 27—A fair election would have given us about forty electoral votes in the South. But we are not to allow our friends to defeat one outrage and fraud by another. There must be nothing crooked on our part. Let Mr. Tilden have the place by violence, intimidation, and fraud, rather than undertake to prevent it by means that will not bear the severest scrutiny.

As late as December 3, Hayes believed that Louisiana would probably be decided for Tilden. But he had gradually come to think more realistically. He was looking for a way to have Congress investigate the Louisiana vote, to throw out Democratic ballots: "Should not the whole case be gone into?" (But when Louisiana was finally certified as Republican, Hayes would decide that Congress had no right to investigate the vote in any state.)

Two days later, a group of Republicans who had been in New Orleans came to Columbus to assure Hayes that he had won Louisiana fairly, without bribery or trickery. The assurances were bland and pious, and Hayes was a little suspicious. He went around the room asking each man in turn to promise that the result had been "lawful" and "honest." Congratulations began to pour in by telegram and letter. Hayes began to feel more and more "presidential." He would act, he wrote in his diary, "as Washington would have acted under similar circumstances." From this point onward, he made it clear to his supporters that they were free to make strategies (honest ones, of course) and pursue them in a concerted effort to win the presidency by political means as well as legal. In contrast to Tilden, Hayes gave his party an important advantage. The question was, how could they use it?

Hayes's men began to work on a strategy. The lame-duck Congress whose authority would last until inauguration day in March, was divided. In the Senate, the Republican majority was 46 to 29. In the House, the Democrats held the majority: 181 Democrats, 107 Republicans, and 3 who called themselves independents. If 36 southern Democrats could somehow be persuaded to break with their party in the House and vote with the Republicans, then Hayes could become president with the consent of both houses of Congress.

On the surface, the idea was bizarre. Why would southern Democrats suddenly forsake the hatreds of a generation and help elect a Union general as their president? But against the apparent absurdity of such a notion, Hayes and his strategists could weigh a number of very tempting facts.

First, soon after the election stalemate became clear, Hayes began to be visited by southern politicians and journalists assuring him of their "good will." They claimed to represent large numbers of southern political and business leaders.

Second, a plain majority of Republicans had grown weary of Reconstruction and were convinced that it had ended in corruption and failure. Many southerners understood this perfectly well. So a congressman from Mississippi or Tennessee might well be ready to make "peace" with a changed Republican party.

Third, the southerners made it clear in everything they said and did that their main concern was to put an end to Reconstruction in the South: to get rid of the hated "carpetbagger" governments that still claimed to rule South Carolina and Louisiana; to see the federal soldiers taken out of the southern capitals and never returned; and to be free to "handle the color problem" their own way. This goal was much more important to them than the question of who had won the presidency.

Fourth, the Republicans remembered all too well that before the Civil War, the South had been anything but "solid" for the Democrats. There had been a vigorous opposition party there until 1850, led by the same sorts of urban, national-minded businessmen who had now become the backbone of the Republican party in the North. A tantalizing vision began to form in Hayes's mind: maybe a real Republican party could be built in at least some southern states, like Tennessee, Texas, and Arkansas.

But what did Hayes and his supporters have to offer to southern Democrats? The answers to this question provided the basis for one of the most famous attempted bargains in American history: the so-called Compromise of 1877.

The bargainers for Hayes were initially a group of journalists and newspaper publishers, headed by three men who were convinced that they might be real kingmakers: William Henry Smith, an old friend of Hayes and the head of the Western Associated Press; Confederate colonel and ex-Whig William Kellar, a Memphis publisher; and Henry Van Ness Boynton, who was the Washington correspondent of a Cincinnati newspaper. With Hayes's apparent blessing, these men began to cultivate contacts with southern politicians and to work out—or to think they were working out—a monumental deal.

On his side, Hayes would promise to order federal troops in the South to their barracks and keep them there, where they could no longer "interfere" with "local" affairs—especially the treatment of the former slaves. Hayes would recognize Democratic governors and legislatures in the "unredeemed" states of Louisiana and South Carolina. And he would appoint at least one southerner to his cabinet, as a sign of "reconciliation."

On their side, the southerners would quietly accept the Republican count of the contested ballots from Louisiana, Florida, and South Carolina, and they would "promise" that African Americans in the South would be given their political and civil rights as the Thirteenth, Fourteenth, and Fifteenth amendments required.

The difficulty with the deal, taken this far, was that it offered nothing to the southerners that Tilden would not also give them. He would recognize Democratic governments everywhere. He would appoint southerners to the cabinet. And Tilden would certainly hobble the federal troops in the South. (The issue had never been whether federal soldiers would be stationed in the South. The question was, would they play the role of an occupying army, or be "confined" to their forts and posts?)

Something more was needed, something Tilden would not give the southern Democrats, and Hayes would.

The southern politicians were talking a good deal about "internal improvements": federal money for reopening harbors that had been ruined during the war, or for repairing wrecked levees on the Mississippi that had left 28 million acres of prime cotton land exposed to floods. As southern Democrats saw it, the northern states had sucked at the federal treasury for sixteen years. Now, with the South back in the Union, would it get its share? Would the difference be made up? Would the old Confederate states be "reconstructed" in a way their white leaders wanted: with expensive road, harbor, and flood control projects paid for in Yankee dollars? The North had even built a railroad to the Pacific, with more than $100 million worth of federal government support—a sum greater than the total of all federal expenditures for transportation facilities from 1789 to 1860. Was it now to be the South's turn?

Here Hayes's strategists had a card worth playing. Tilden and the Democratic party were opposed to spending federal money for internal improvements—and had been since the days of Thomas Jefferson. The Republicans, on the other hand, had an impressive record of opening the federal treasury for improvements. And so Boynton, Kellar, and Smith began to propose that Hayes commit himself to a strong program of federal projects of construction and reconstruction in the South. This, they believed, would lure in the thirty-six Southern congressmen they needed.

The confidence of the negotiators was high because they had a specific project in mind: a southern railroad to the Pacific. It so happened that one of the most restless railroad promoters in the nation, Thomas Scott, vice president of the powerful Pennsylvania Railroad, had already secured a land grant of 16 million acres for building a rail line from Texas to the West Coast. Companies had already been formed to promote a system of branch lines connecting Fort Worth to New Orleans, Vicksburg, Memphis, and St. Louis. (In fact, William Kellar was an officer of one of these companies. And numerous southern Democratic politicians were officers and board members of the companies.)

Thomas Scott had built a huge reputation as a successful lobbyist. Hayes's journalist agents were awed by the possibility that they might set Scott's forces in motion, divide the Democrats, and make Hayes president with little further ado.

What Hayes understood but his negotiators did not was that the Republicans themselves were no more solid than the Democrats. President Grant had told his cabinet that he believed Tilden had won. A key Republican senator, Roscoe Conkling of New York, had never supported Hayes. And there were the Republican senators and congressmen from the South whose careers would be ruined if Hayes came in as a result of a bargain with the South. The Republican majority in the Senate was slender. If seven men refused to support Hayes, the Senate would be lost. Paradoxically, all the Republican efforts to win in the Democratic House would then be defeated in the Senate they supposedly controlled.

And so the bargainers bargained, and Hayes's forces worried about whether they could keep the Republican senators in line. But meanwhile, a quiet process had been going forward that would eventually decide who was to be president. During the first two weeks of December, both houses of Congress had passed motions to create special committees to study the problem of the election. From the House came four Democrats—including Tilden's campaign manager, Hewitt—and three Republicans. From the Senate came a committee of four Republicans and three Democrats.

From the middle of December to the middle of January the two committees hammered away at their problem, sometimes meeting together and sometimes separately. Their votes were usually along party lines, and it was clear to all of them that they would have to devise a scheme they could all support, or no scheme at all.

What gradually emerged from these committee meetings was the idea of handing the question of the election over to a special body, an electoral commission. The committees proposed plan after plan, but what finally won their approval was a cumbersome idea that would, in effect, leave the decision up to one man whose identity could only be guessed at. On January 15, the committees agreed to propose an Electoral Commission made up of five members of the House, five senators, and five Supreme Court justices. The House, clearly, would send three Democrats and two Republicans. The Senate would balance off with three Republicans and two Democrats. The committees chose two Supreme Court justices whose past records were clearly Republican and two others with equally clear Democratic loyalties. These four justices were to agree on which remaining member of the Court was to be the fifteenth member of the commission—the deciding vote.

Perhaps the most important feature of the proposal was that the commission's findings would be final unless *both* houses of Congress rejected them. In effect, the House and Senate were about to surrender their separate powers over the decision. Hayes was upset. Tilden was as close to anger as he came during the entire crisis. But the members of Congress were calm. The politicians in Congress, professionals all, understood that whoever became president now would come in with the weakest possible mandate. The system of power would tilt away from the presidency and back toward Congress, where it had firmly rested during the generation before the Civil War. Control over budgets, patronage appointments, and policy would lie with the senators and the congressmen, not with either Tilden or Hayes. It had simply become more important to the professional politicians to name *a* president peacefully than to name any one man.

For the professionals in Congress, the important thing was to be able to pursue political interests in an atmosphere of compromise and customary horse-trading. To win this, they were prepared to leave the question of the presidency to fate. (At one point, the House and Senate committees had strongly favored letting the fifteenth member of the electoral commission be chosen by lot!)

This attitude became sharply clear when Hewitt went up to New York to explain the proposed electoral commission to Tilden. Tilden complained that it was a bit late in the day for the Democrats in Congress to consult him. Hewitt's reply was short, but it spoke volumes about the way the leaders of both political parties had begun to look at the presidency: "They do not consult you," he said. "They are public men with their own responsibilities."

Of course, each side could still hope to win, even if the question had been handed over to fate. And the Democrats probably had more cause for hope at this stage. Everyone supposed that the fifteenth member of the electoral commission, with the deciding vote, would be Supreme Court Justice David Davis, who called himself an independent but leaned toward the Democratic side. Then, just as the electoral commission was being passed by Congress, came astounding news from Illinois, Davis's home state. The Illinois legislature had just elected him to the Senate. He would resign from the Court and so would not be available to serve on the electoral commission. (Ironically, Davis had been elected to the Senate with overwhelming Democratic support in Illinois. Neither Tilden nor his supporters had paid any attention, even though they knew that Davis, their best hope for the deciding vote, was a candidate for the Senate.)

Now the four justices did their duty. They named the least partisan of the remaining justices, Joseph Bradley of New Jersey. Bradley was a Republican, but he had a reputation for fairness.

The electoral commission was, in essence, a judicial body. It even held its sessions in the chamber normally occupied by the Supreme Court. Both parties hired the most talented and famous lawyers they could find. The lawyers presented arguments that lasted day after day on each of the disputed states.

A cynical observer might have supposed that everyone would simply vote along party lines—with the possible exception of Justice Bradley. But the commission could hardly afford to function that way, at least in public. The lawyers' arguments were learned. The galleries of the courtroom were crowded to overflowing with the rich, the famous, and the powerful. The commission's members kept an anxious watch over each other. Bradley kept a scrupulous silence.

The first state to be considered was Florida, and the first question was technical but all-important. Congress had left the commission itself to decide one key question: Could the commission investigate the actual voting in the contested states? Or were its powers confined to examining the procedures by which the *electoral* votes had been arrived at and certified? The Democrats, of course, wanted a full inquiry into what had happened in Florida, South Carolina, and Louisiana on election day. The Republicans wanted to examine only what had happened *after* the election.

On February 6 and 7, after four days of public arguments, the commission met in secret to decide the case of Florida. One by one the members read their opinions—for seven hours on the first day, and five more on the second. One after another, they voted on party lines, until the Republicans and Democrats each had seven votes. Finally, it was Bradley's turn. Garfield, who was a member of the commission, wrote in his diary, "All were intent, because B. held the casting vote. All were making a manifest effort to appear unconcerned."

Bradley made this crucial ruling: the commission could not investigate the actual voting. It could only determine whether all legal rules had been followed in the certifying and casting of a state's vote in the electoral college. Two days later, the commission ruled that Florida's Republicans had followed the technical rules, and that the votes of the state would go to Hayes.

There was less than a month to go before the scheduled inauguration of a new president. One by one, the commission took up the states in question. One by one, they decided each case for Hayes. Even the Democrats' Oregon ace in the hole failed. The commission simply ruled that Hayes was entitled to all three Oregon votes. Every vote was the same: eight for Hayes, seven for Tilden, with Justice Bradley casting every tie-breaking vote.

The game was up. But there were two political instincts still alive that made the players want to keep it going until the bitter end. One was the instinct of pure partisanship, best put by a Tilden adviser: "God damn them, they will beat us and elect Hayes, but we shall give them all the trouble we can."

The second and more practical instinct was southern. It was clear that Hayes would win. But it was equally clear that he would like to win gracefully and come into office on a wave of goodwill that was as truly national as possible. This opened a tactical possibility. If the Democratic House could delay by filibuster and adjournment until the very dawn of inauguration day, then Hayes would be kept on tenterhooks, practically imprisoned out in Ohio, unable to adopt the grand style of the president-elect, unable to make the fine speeches calling for national unity. Perhaps some practical concessions could still be won.

Now, *after* the decision had been made, the Democrats in the House began to reject the commission's findings. It could make no practical difference, for the Senate naturally voted to accept them all. But the House Democrats began a war of nerves, adjourning from day to day. In corridors and in the hotel suites of senators and congressmen around Washington, southern politicians and Hayes's spokesmen began to deal and trade.

Finally, on February 26, a conference took place of a type that Hayes's journalist-strategists had dreamed of in early January. At Wormsley's Hotel, five Ohioans close to Hayes met with four southerners who spoke for the Democratic parties of Louisiana and South Carolina. A curious bargain was struck. Hayes's people made general commitments on his behalf: that there would be a southerner in the cabinet and that the president would be "liberal"—that is, generous—on the question of internal improvements in the South. The southerners made promises that were equally vague, especially that the political and civil rights of the African Americans would be "protected," once the South was granted "home rule." Hayes's spokesmen then made it clear that they would return the army to its barracks and that they would allow the Republican governments in Louisiana and South Carolina to fall and would recognize Democratic governors there.

(The Texas and Pacific railroad scheme was not mentioned. Tom Scott had already presented his request for a subsidy to Congress, and the total bill was too high—a staggering $200 million. The plan died in committee, with two of Hayes's closest supporters voting against it. It would have to wait for a new Congress, where it had no real chance.)

Here was the most famous back-room deal in the political history of the United States. It was known for generations as the bargain that put an end to Reconstruction and preserved the political "stability" of the nation. But as a bargain, it was meaningless. Hayes had already decided to confine the army to its barracks in the South. Indeed, Grant had already drawn up an order making this last "magnanimous" gesture to the white South. Hayes had already decided on a southerner for the cabinet, and the politicians all knew it. The southern Democrats' promise to "protect" black rights could be believed by only the most absurdly naive—though Hayes stubbornly chose to believe it, since it was the only real alternative to thinking of himself as a traitor to the memory of Lincoln, the Union dead, and the crusade against slavery.

Then what were nine experienced, tough, and even cynical men doing in that room in Wormsley's Hotel? Why were they sealing a "bargain" that exchanged nothing for nothing? And why did their "deal" become monumentally famous overnight and for a century afterward?

The answer is that they were doing what their careers required. They were professional politicians all. Hayes's representatives hoped for future cooperation from southern Democrats in the House and Senate. To get it, the new administration had to keep up the appearance of being approachable and ready to compromise. The southern Democrats, on their side, needed to convince their supporters back home that they had not simply knuckled under, that they had shrewdly won last-minute concessions from the victorious Republicans. They had done their job and had, by a spectacular bluff, achieved "home rule" for the South. Or so they wanted it to appear, no matter what the realities were.

For the next five days, the Democrats in the House walked a tightrope. They put up enough opposition to delay the completion of the official count of the electoral

PHILADELPHIA CENTENNIAL. Somewhat ironically, the stalemated presidential election of 1876 occurred during the same year as the one hundredth anniversary of the Declaration of Independence. The center of national celebration was a great fair, or exposition, in Philadelphia, where independence had been declared. This crowd is waiting patiently in the rain for the door to open on the exposition's first day, watched over by the ever-present eagles that were a favorite patriotic symbol of the time.

votes to the last minute. But they moved along just fast enough to make it clear that the count could be finished on time. They manufactured an atmosphere of crisis that allowed their supporters to believe that they had held out to the last, used every weapon, fought every battle, and lost only to superior force. In fact, they held out until dawn on March 2, when Hayes was finally declared the winner. But the struggle, like the bargain at Wormsley's Hotel, was by now more show than reality. Hayes would become president. Reconstruction was ended. But the real victory was for party politics. What had been restored was not so much the Union, but a "normal" political practice, in which the arts of the professionals mattered much more than any ideological commitment to policies or programs.

Government in an Age of Industrial Capitalism

The political maneuvers and compromises of 1876 and 1877 preserved the Republican control of the presidency, which already had lasted for sixteen critical years. But now the party was openly committed to ending Reconstruction. Something profound had happened, something that would not only affect Grant's career and the 1876 election, but that would shape the history of American politics for a generation. The Republican party, which had begun as a movement with a strong sense of ideological mission, had become a typical American political party, less concerned with ideology and mission than with elections and offices. In fact, it had suddenly become a party that was difficult to distinguish from its Democratic opposition. For the next quarter of a century, the two parties would continue to struggle mightily for control of the presidency, Congress, and state governments. But the contest between them would be one that offered voters no significant choice between differing policies or programs.

Of course, the Republican party had always had its political side. Many of its leaders, including Lincoln, had been professional politicians, with careers that linked them to the Whig party of the 1840s. But during the Civil War and Reconstruction, the party professionals had driven to power with a definite program. They might differ among themselves in degree; some might be more radical than others. But there had been something to be radical *about*. After 1876, there was simply no Republican position on which any politician could have taken a radical stance, even if he had wanted to. And the Democratic party was no different.

The two parties became mirror images of each other. There were some differences during the 1870s and 1880s. The Democrats came to control a solid base in the South, the Republicans in the Middle West. Republicans appealed more to Protestant, native-born Americans, the Democrats to urban Catholic immigrants. The Republicans consistently nominated former Union officers as presidential candidates. The Democrats almost always ran governors of New York, certain that that state held the key to their political fortunes.

But underneath these differences lay a crucial sameness. Both parties habitually nominated a special kind of presidential candidate: a man of supposedly spotless "character" and record, who could promise the electorate "clean government." And this practice had a marked effect on the way political power was divided between the presidency and the Congress. The political wheelers and dealers in Congress weakened their own chances of becoming president (unless they might come in the side door, through the vice presidency). But, in return, they maintained control over the House and Senate, the party's organizational machinery, and the all-important system of patronage appointments.

Both parties were very conscious of the need for organization, from the ward and precinct level up to the Senate. Both were acutely sensitive to the need for money to mobilize more and more voters. Both succeeded in mustering larger voter turnouts than in the pre–Civil War period. At the presidential level, elections became desperate struggles for slim victories. Only one president between 1872 and 1896 won the office with a majority of the popular vote. And this forced both parties into a struggle for swing voters. Democrats and Republicans both tried to occupy a noncontroversial center on major issues at election time, so both had to avoid taking any position that might generate any sort of open division in party ranks.

--->==o==<---

THE POWERLESS PRESIDENTS

The net result of all these political factors was to make the presidency an office for men who did not control their own parties and had not been elected on any sort of program they might press through Congress, men whose position was almost that of a figurehead. They might have very strong personal character, as several of them did, but in political terms their situation was almost impossible. They entered office to find all the important positions in their administration already sold to win the nomination or the election, all the important legislation controlled by the Senate leadership, and Congress usually divided between a Democratic House and a Republican Senate.

Grave questions could hardly find their way onto the political stage, where the only issue seemed to be control of the government. National politics became a kind of serpent devouring itself, concerned not with economic and social issues, or even with serious questions of foreign policy and war, but only with the political process. Government had become its own object. A twentieth-century president, Calvin Coolidge, once remarked, "The business of America is business."

Any of his predecessors from the 1870s and 1880s could aptly have said that the politics of America was politics.

HAYES VERSUS HIS OWN PARTY

Soon after his election in 1876, Rutherford B. Hayes announced that he would not run for another term. This, taken together with the way he had won his office, made him almost powerless. When the Democrats got control of the Senate in 1878, the administration was even further weakened. Hayes did end Reconstruction—which the Democratic Congress would have done anyway, through its control over appropriations for the military. But for the rest, he confined himself to trying to make decent appointments and to institute a merit system of civil service in some of the federal departments, particularly in the astonishingly corrupt Post Office and Treasury.

In fact, Hayes's worst enemies turned out to be not Democrats but the Republican party leaders. The party was divided into the "Stalwarts," headed by Roscoe Conkling, and the "Half-Breeds," who were very much like the Stalwarts but wanted a few concessions to the small, good-government "Mugwump" wing of the party. The Half-Breeds were led by a curiously charismatic senator from Maine, James G. Blaine, whose career had been besmirched by the revelation of railroad fraud. Blaine had written several letters to a colleague in corruption named Mulligan, letters that often ended, "Burn this letter!"—an instruction that Mulligan did not obey. For Conkling and Blaine and their followers, Hayes's concerns for clean government and for appointments based on merit were the worst kind of nuisance.

The president vainly attempted to get an appropriation through Congress to fund the modest Civil Service Commission that had been created during the Grant administration. Finally, in frustration, Hayes removed two of Conkling's New York supporters, Alonzo B. Cornell and Chester A. Arthur, from their lucrative federal offices. Conkling fought back by persuading the Senate not to approve replacements for the two men. Hayes could do nothing but submit name after name, waiting for the Senate to turn each of them down, until finally even the senators grew weary and allowed two names to pass.

GARFIELD AND ARTHUR

When the Republicans met to choose a nominee in 1880, Conkling and his Stalwart faction supported Grant. Blaine and his Half-Breeds, with Mugwump help, were able to deny Grant the nomination for thirty-five ballots, until the convention finally turned to a noncontroversial dark horse, James A. Garfield, a man of pure character, a tried veteran of the House of Representatives from Ohio—and, of course, a former Union officer. The Stalwarts contented themselves with the vice presidential nomination for a model party professional, Chester A. Arthur. The Democrats chose to play dead—or to try to beat the Republicans at their own game. They made the uninspired choice of their own Union general, Winfield Scott Hancock, a man whose military record had created no political following. The result was a Republican victory but a narrow one, in which Garfield won 4,454,000 votes against 4,444,000 for Hancock.

Garfield was a study in rags to riches, a self-made man. He had been born in a log cabin—a real one—and had managed to become a teacher, then a lawyer and a politician. He had served in Congress since the war years and was apparently a man of honesty. His postmaster general, with Garfield's strong support, unearthed a major fraud in the postal service, and the stage seemed set for another struggle between a reasonably clean president and the barons of the Senate. But before the struggle could reach a climax, Garfield was assassinated. On July 2, 1881, after four months in office, he was shot by an obscure, ambitious, and clearly insane man named Charles Guiteau, who shouted as he shot: "I am a Stalwart, and Arthur is president!"

Garfield clung to life for three months before Arthur was indeed president. The new chief executive surprised everyone by continuing to press the fraud cases in the Post Office, and by making independent appointments, as though he were trying to live down a career as a consummate spoilsman of the Stalwart faction. He even got a modest civil service law, the Pendleton Act, through Congress in 1883. The law put only about one federal job out of ten on a merit system, but it did allow for future expansion of the number by executive order. (In fact, it put every future president in the position of being able to appoint supporters to non-civil-service jobs, and then, once they were in place, to extend the blanket of protection to them so they could not be removed. Through this process, by the 1940s a bare majority of federal jobs were brought under the Civil Service Act.)

GROVER CLEVELAND

Arthur made no one in his own party happy—not Stalwarts, Half-Breeds, or Mugwumps. The Republican convention of 1884 simply ignored him, and turned instead to the prince of the Half-Breeds, James G. Blaine. The Mugwumps announced they would not support Blaine if the Democrats were to nominate a "good-government" man, and the Democrats obliged them by choosing Grover Cleveland, a reform mayor of Buffalo and governor of New York. The resulting campaign was heavily financed on both sides, and consisted mainly of attacks on the personal character of the candidates. For his part, Blaine was vulnerable because of the Mulligan letters, and the Democrats could chant:

> Blaine! Blaine! James G. Blaine,
> Continental liar from the state of Maine!
> (Burn this letter!)

But Cleveland proved to have an unexpected weak spot. He had accepted responsibility for an illegitimate child in his youth, so his opponents could come back with a chant of their own:

> Ma! Ma! Where's my Pa?
> Gone to the White House, Ha! Ha! Ha!

In November, Cleveland got the better of the chanting contest. The election may in fact have been thrown to him at the last minute. Blaine, at a reception in New York City, was called on by a delegation of Protestant ministers. One of them made a brief speech, in which he accused the Democrats of being the party of "Rum, Romanism, and Rebellion." Blaine, who had a Catholic

GROVER CLEVELAND.   Grover Cleveland, shown here in a studio photograph, was a shortish, heavy man whose political reputation was built entirely on an honest willingness to say no—to both corrupt party organizations like Tammany Hall and small appropriations meant to relieve farmers ruined by drought. The photographer managed to capture some of Cleveland's determination, along with the conventional brave stare into the distance.

mother, either did not hear the remark or chose to ignore it. But when it became public, he was stuck with it. And this slender bit of chance may have moved enough immigrant and Catholic voters in New York City to swing the election to Cleveland. Almost 10 million men voted, and Cleveland received only about 20,000 more votes than Blaine. New York State could have given either man the necessary electoral votes for a victory.

Grover Cleveland believed staunchly in laissez faire—the notion that governments should not "interfere" in social and economic affairs. The government, he thought, should be a minimal institution, whose main purposes were maintaining law and order and conducting foreign policy. He

once vetoed a relief bill to aid farmers who had been stricken by drought, with the observation that "the people should support the government, but the government should never support the people." He even did what no president before him had done: he actually *read* the applications that Union veterans submitted to Congress when they asked for special relief and pension legislation. He vetoed hundreds of such requests—to the fury of the congressmen whose constituents' loyalty was heavily dependent on their ability to deliver such government favors. Congress responded with a bill granting general pensions to *all* disabled veterans—no matter when or how their disability had come about. Cleveland provoked an even more serious storm by vetoing this act.

The president's laissez-faire attitude even extended to one of the sleeping giants of American politics, the tariff. For twenty years or more, the country had had a high Republican tariff, and a system had been worked out for buying support from agricultural states by putting their products—sugar or wool, for example—on the protected list along with manufactured goods. But Cleveland, in the middle of his administration, went to Congress to ask for substantial reductions in tariffs. He was, among other things, embarrassed by a large surplus in the treasury, a surplus that made it clear no tariff was necessary for revenue. For him, the meaning of the surplus was plain and outweighed all the possible arguments for a high tariff: "It is a *condition* that confronts us," he said, "not a theory."

The Democrats in the House of Representatives managed to push through a bill making some reductions in tariff schedules, but the measure stalled. For the first time in years, the presidential contest coming up in 1888 would have a stateable, though minor, issue.

BENJAMIN HARRISON

The Democrats chose Cleveland again. The Republicans turned to Benjamin Harrison of Indiana, who was as unknown as Hayes and Garfield had been, and just as "respectable" and easy to identify with the cause of "clean government." He was the grandson of William Henry Harrison, who had been elected president in 1840.

But if the parties at least had one clear issue—high tariffs or low—the voters were not ready with a verdict. Cleveland won the popular vote, though by less than 100,000 out of 10 million. In fact, he was the only presidential candidate of the period to win a clear majority of the total popular vote. But he lost the election. The vote of the electoral college was 233 for Harrison, 168 for Cleveland.

Harrison rode into office on a very frail horse. But his Republican Congress behaved as though the party had won a decisive mandate for a great cause. They set out to write the highest protective tariff law in United States history, and they won. The resulting McKinley tariff—named for its sponsor in the House, William McKinley of Ohio—established a level of protection that satisfied every tariff lobby in the nation.

But the initiative had come almost entirely from Congress. Harrison himself was as hamstrung by his lack of control over his party as his predecessors in office had been. After he left office he complained, "When I came into power, I found that the party managers had taken it all to themselves. I could not name my own Cabinet. They had sold out every place to pay the election expenses." And if that were not enough, he was soon to face a Congress in which his party was crippled. When the results of the congressional elections of 1890 came in, the Republicans had won only 88 of the 323 seats in the House.

To some extent, the congressional elections of 1890 may have been a referendum on the McKinley tariff. If it was, the answer was clear: McKinley himself was defeated in his home district, and his political career seemed to be over. But the tariff itself was less the issue than it was the symbol of a range of issues that were struggling to the surface of American political life, issues that focused on the general problems of "monopoly" capitalism and the failure of governments to take any effective measures to control or regulate it. A few Democrats—even some who had supported the tariff where it protected economic interests in their home states—began to play on the problem of "monopoly" and to argue that the tariff was designed only to protect giant corporations from overseas competition. They hit a responsive chord. The electorate had become increasingly concerned and frustrated over the apparent inability of their political leaders to do anything about the power of corporations over American life.

CLEVELAND, AGAIN

In the presidential election of 1892, the Republicans ignored the danger signs and renominated Harrison. The Democrats countered with Cleveland. Once again, as in 1888, the two parties' platforms were almost identical—except for the tariff. The Republicans once more promised to maintain the kind of protection provided by the McKinley tariff. The Democrats promised tariff reductions. This time, the swing that had been clear in the congressional voting of 1890 bore fruit for the Democrats. Cleveland won almost twice as many electoral votes as Harrison, and almost a 10 percent edge in the popular voting. More important, the Democrats won majorities in both the House and the Senate. For the first time in a generation, they controlled both the executive and legislative branches of the federal government.

The result was disappointing to anyone who had voted for a significant change in policies. Cleveland stood more firmly than ever for his laissez-faire policies, his belief that the government should not "support" any of the people by intervening in their economic life in any significant way. Cleveland did try to push a lowering of the tariff rates through Congress, but even here he failed. The Democrats in Congress would give him only about a 10 percent reduction in the average duties that had been voted a few years earlier. On the surface, at least, the Democrats' surge to power had produced little or nothing in the way of an important shift in major government policies.

⋅→═◉═←⋅

THE RISE OF THE POPULIST PARTY

But there were straws in the political wind suggesting that some sort of challenge to the prevailing political order of things was building toward a climax. The new tariff included the first peacetime income tax in the history of the United States. The rates were mild—2 percent on all incomes over $4,000, a formula that meant a large majority of Americans would pay no tax at all. But the income tax had been a clear concession to a new and highly visible element in politics, a movement of protest demanding changes that

were, from the point of view of the normal politics of the preceding twenty years, almost revolutionary. The political challenge took its clearest form in the South and the West as an organized movement of farmers, and it finally resulted in the formation of a new political party.

The movement, whose roots went well back into the 1870s, focused on questions of policy on which the major parties had either taken a weak and tentative stand or no stand at all.

THE GRANGE

Farmers during the early 1870s—times of prosperity for most of them—had begun to organize themselves into local chapters of the National Grange of the Patrons of Husbandry. The word *grange* was from a medieval term for a building on a manor where grain was stored. In England, *grange* was a name sometimes given to the farmhouse and buildings of a well-off gentleman farmer. The Americans who first became Grangers, or Patrons of Husbandry, were adopting a terminology that suggested farming was in fact a gentleman's occupation. They met primarily for cultural and social purposes, and used a somewhat elaborate secret ritual.

But in 1873 the nation entered the most serious economic depression in its history, and farmers suffered even more than other Americans. They began to join the Grange in massive numbers—800,000 by 1875—and to redefine its purposes. They formed cooperative grain elevators, stores, milk-processing plants, even factories to make farm machinery and stoves— all in the hope of freeing themselves from the grip of what they clearly understood to be monopolies. Most of all, they turned to politics at the state level, to attack what they felt were the cruel and monopolistic practices of the railroads.

Beginning in 1871, then with even greater success after 1873, the Grangers were able to muster enough votes in the state legislatures of Wisconsin, Illinois, Iowa, and Minnesota to impose rate regulations on railroad companies. (These attempts at regulation were at first endorsed by federal courts, but then increasingly struck down as unconstitutional. (See pp. 102–106.)

The return of prosperity in the late 1870s reduced both the size and the effectiveness of the Granger movement. By 1880 it had lost 700,000 of its 800,000 members, and it would remain small and inconsequential after that.

THE ALLIANCE MOVEMENT

As the 1880s wore on, however, the farmers who raised staple crops—wheat and cotton especially—began to experience a steady and serious drop in the market price for their crops. They began to organize into farmers' alliances. In the plains states, they formed the National Farmers' Alliance. By 1890 the organization had a membership of over 3 million.

In the South, the rise of the Alliance movement created the possibility of the first large-scale collaboration between poor farmers, black and white. A society in which race had been the main way of maintaining social divisions seemed, for a time at least, to be dividing along lines of class and status, rather than along the "color line." African-American and white farmers joined parallel alliances, the Colored Farmers' Alliance and the Southern Farmers' Alliance. By the middle of the 1880s the two organizations had over 1 million members. And the movement continued to grow. By 1890 the Southern Farmers' Alliance claimed over 2 million members, and the Colored Farmers' Alliance more than 1 million. (Both claims were probably exaggerated. But even if the Colored Farmers' Alliance had only 250,000 or so active members, that was still an astonishing number, since these men faced harassment, threats, and even death.)

Never before in the history of the South had the pent-up frustrations of so many farmers found organized expression. And never before had political activism posed such an obvious threat to the established order of southern society. Tom Watson of Georgia, who was one of the most radical and eloquent white political leaders of the farmers' movement, summed up the situation of the farmers in a way that bluntly made class interest more important than race. "The crushing burdens which now oppress both races," he said, could only be overcome if blacks and whites alike took action to win "a similarity of remedy." Calling for "remedies" that would treat black and white people the same way was a serious departure from southern white traditions. But Georgia voters sent Watson to Congress in 1890, a definite sign that economic hardship might create a solidarity that cut across the lines of race.

The Alliance movement was much more political than the Grangers had been. The western group ran candidates under its own party label for state and national offices. In the South, the Alliances tried a different tactic: they attempted to gain control of the entrenched Democratic party. In fact, in 1890—the year the Republicans suffered their massive defeats in congressional elections—the Alliances managed to win varying degrees of control over eight legislatures in the South and four in the West. From the South came forty congressmen who had been endorsed by the Alliances against conservative Democrats.

During the next two years, the Alliance leaders planned an even more active challenge to the standing political order. They founded a new party, the People's, or Populist, party. In 1892, delegates representing the Alliances, the Knights of Labor, and other antimonopoly groups gathered at an exultant convention in Omaha to write a platform and nominate a candidate to oppose Cleveland and Harrison.

The Populist platform was a radical document, in the sense that it addressed political and economic questions that had been either kept offstage entirely or dealt with by the federal government in a hesitant and reluctant way. The Populists had three main concerns: public finance, monopoly, and the conduct of politics. They confronted these concerns much more directly than either Republicans or Democrats had been able or willing to do.

GRANGER POSTER.   This 1872 poster captured many of the ideas of the agricultural reform movement known as the Granger movement. Its main message is that the honest toil of the yeoman farmer is the basis of prosperity: "I pay for all" is the slogan at the center. But the agricultural reality depicted here belonged not to the 1870s so much as to the 1830s. All labor is being done by hand. There is not a single reaper in sight, no steam engine, no cotton gin, no railroad line. At the bottom is the dilapidated house of a farmer who failed not because of economic conditions but because of his own "Ignorance" and "Sloth."

CURRENCY AND CREDIT

For the Populists, public finance boiled down to two related questions: currency and credit. The federal government, under both Republicans and Democrats, had been pursuing policies that led to a restricted supply of currency, or "tight" money, and to equally restricted credit. Both currency and credit had been eased during the Civil War. The Lincoln administration had printed paper greenbacks—about $450 million worth. At the end of the war, some $400 million worth were still in circulation. The government had also built up a large debt by selling bonds. Most of the bonds were owned by national banks, which had been allowed to make loans to their customers in return for the bonds, to be held by the banks as their reserve to pay off depositors. These two inflationary policies had resulted in easy credit for most farmers and higher prices for their crops.

After the war, the federal government had decided to keep a limited amount of greenbacks in circulation but to back them with gold. This policy did not maintain a money supply large enough to feed the tremendous economic expansion of the postwar period. In fact, the volume of money in circulation actually was decreasing in proportion to the size of the economy. In addition, Congress in 1873—in what many Populists saw as the "Crime of '73"—had removed the silver dollar from the list of money to be coined.

No one had objected at the time, but over the next twenty years the idea took root that the solution to the currency problem was to increase the money supply through the free and unlimited coinage of silver. Cleveland and most Republicans were "sound money" men—committed to a "gold standard," the notion that every paper dollar in circulation could be "redeemed" for a dollar's worth of gold held by the government. And so the Populist plank demanding free and unlimited coinage of silver was a direct challenge to the dominant politicians of both major parties.

As for credit, the Populist platform of 1892 included a program that would have moved the federal government much further into the credit system. The party's leaders were acutely aware that rural areas were served by few and often insecure banks. The platform asked for government-run savings banks that would be operated by the Post Office. And it asked the federal government to create storage warehouses for grain and cotton, where farmers might keep their crops when the market price was low. The scheme would have allowed farmers to receive interest-free loans worth 80 percent of the current market price of the crops being held in storage. The farmers could then wait until prices rose to market the crops.

MONOPOLIES

The credit scheme was, when compared with policies then existing, a radical one. But the 1892 platform took an even more radical attitude toward the great monopolies the Populists thought were oppressing them. Corporate "combinations" of all sorts—pools, trusts, holding companies, and mergers—had become a major fact of American life. But Democratic and Republican politicians had responded very little to the growing uneasiness of many of their voters. In a few states, there had been attempts to regulate railroads. But the prevailing attitude of politicians had been one of benign neglect toward, or even support for, corporate growth and integration.

During the late 1880s some members of Congress had recognized the necessity of making at least a token gesture toward controlling corporations. The result had been two laws that seemed to discourage monopolistic practices—one by regulating them, the other by forbidding them.

The first was the Interstate Commerce Act of 1887. This law created the Interstate Commerce Commission, which was charged with regulating the railroad industry. The commission was, in theory, to make certain that all railroad rates were "reasonable." The railroads were forbidden to create market pools or to discriminate among shippers by giving a lower price to some than to others.

The second was the Sherman Antitrust Act of 1890. In its language, the act was an affirmation of the idea that the best economy was one in which there was pure competition. It forbade every "combination" that acted to "restrain trade"—reduce competition—in interstate commerce.

These two laws had seemed to move in the direction the Populists wanted. But in practice, both turned out to be virtually meaningless. It was clear by 1892 that neither was going to provide an effective check on the power of corporations. And so the Populists wrote their most radical plank to deal with the monopolies they believed oppressed them most: the railroads. They demanded, simply, government ownership of all railroad and telegraph companies. As a challenge to the power of other corporations, the platform proposed that the eight-hour workday be made standard in all industries—though this would have been a marked extension of federal power to regulate private businesses and industries.

Experience had taught the Populists that they had no hope but to try to win control over the political process itself. So their platform included demands for significant reforms to the system. They wanted the secret ballot in all elections. They asked for a system of initiative and referendum, through which voters could pass laws or repeal them. And they sought to break the stranglehold of the two major parties over the system by providing that senators be elected directly, instead of by state legislatures.

To run on this platform, the Populists nominated James B. Weaver, who had been a Democrat before the Civil War, then a Republican, now a Populist. In the election of 1892 Weaver won twenty-two electoral votes, and the Populists won over a million popular votes. About a dozen members of Congress now called themselves Populists.

-→=◦==◦=←-

DEFEAT OF THE POPULISTS

The stage seemed set for a mighty contest in 1896 to determine whether the People's party would gain full access to federal power for their reform challenge. The drama was intensified by a depression that began in 1893 and was in some ways the most serious the nation had ever experienced. Well over 100 railroads and 400 banks failed. Even more important, probably as many as 20 percent of the nation's workers were unemployed—in an era when no programs of relief or unemployment compensation existed. If the Populists could tap the discontent growing out of the depression and add it to the older and still smoldering complaints that had created their party, they might expect to play a profoundly important role in the future of American politics.

On their side, the Republicans had just as much reason to expect victory. The depression was, as usual, blamed on the current administration. The congressional elections of 1894 had seemed to confirm both Populist and Republican hopes. Taken all together, Populist candidates collected almost 1.5 million votes—a sharp increase over 1892. But the Republicans came out of the election in full control of the House of Representatives, something they had had only twice in the preceding twenty years.

McKINLEY VERSUS BRYAN

So the parties approached 1896: the Republicans confident, the Populists excited, the Democrats divided between those who wanted to nominate another eastern conservative (as the party had done for a generation) and those who wanted to move South or West, to tap the political energies the Populists had unleashed.

The Republicans nominated William McKinley, author of the McKinley tariff, who after losing his seat in Congress had become governor of Ohio. Behind McKinley stood the man who was, in effect, the head of the party, Marcus A. Hanna, who would manage to raise somewhere between $4 million and $15 million for the campaign. (No one probably will ever know the full amount, but it is clear that McKinley's run for the presidency was the first modern campaign in terms of the dollars spent. Standard Oil alone contributed $300,000—almost as much as the Democrats spent on their entire effort.) For a platform, Hanna and his party decided on even higher tariffs, solid support for the gold standard, and a vague promise of "prosperity." Nothing was said about the problem of the corporations, regulation of railroads, or the income tax.

At the Democratic convention in Chicago, there was nothing but confusion. The party was divided. On one side was a Cleveland faction that was predominantly eastern, favored gold, and rejected most of the Populist program. On the other side were southerners and westerners who demanded the endorsement of free silver and wanted the party to support at least some of the Populist program—the income tax, for example, or a stronger federal attempt to regulate railroads and corporations. This faction wanted, in effect, to repudiate Cleveland, who had led the party into all three presidential elections since 1884.

To settle the question of the Democrats' position on gold, a debate was arranged, with three men speaking for the gold standard and three for the coinage of silver, or "bimetallism." Surely none of the politicians expected the party to resolve such a problem with mere speeches to a noisy convention. But for once they were surprised. The final speaker for silver, William Jennings Bryan, gave such a masterly address that the convention, swept by something approaching

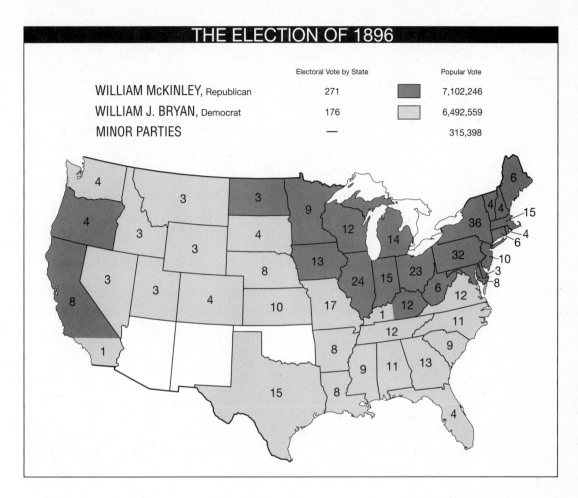

THE ELECTION OF 1896

	Electoral Vote by State		Popular Vote
WILLIAM McKINLEY, Republican	271		7,102,246
WILLIAM J. BRYAN, Democrat	176		6,492,559
MINOR PARTIES	—		315,398

political hysteria, nominated him for president the next day.

Bryan's strengths were his words and his voice. He could roll out sentences that schoolchildren would be forced to memorize for decades. He ended his address to the convention with a dramatic challenge to the Republicans, a challenge that attempted to identify free silver with the cause of the common man:

> If they dare to come out into the open and defend the gold standard as a good thing, we will fight them to the uttermost. Having behind us the producing masses of this nation and the world, supported by the commercial interests, the laboring interests and the toilers everywhere, we will answer their demand for a gold

standard by saying to them: "You shall not press down upon the brow of labor this crown of thorns; you shall not crucify mankind upon a Cross of Gold."

Bryan was a Nebraskan with only two terms in the House of Representatives to his political credit. But he had managed to steal the party and to steal, in the bargain, one of the main planks of the Populists. The Democrats also endorsed the income tax and railroad regulation. This created a painful dilemma for the Populists. Bryan was almost certain to win every state where a Populist would have had a chance against a traditional Democrat. They seemed to have no option but to endorse him and the principle of "fusion" with the Democrats. And so a majority of

MCKINLEY CAMPAIGNS (MORE OR LESS).   While his opponent Bryan traveled and spoke more than any candidate ever had before, William McKinley stayed home in Ohio, speaking occasionally from his own front porch to carefully chosen crowds. His was a cautious campaign in which the greatest risk was probably to put the candidate on a rug covering an unstable wicker basket that substituted for a speaker's "stump." But from the Republican point of view, it all worked splendidly.

Populists voted in their convention to accept Bryan as their candidate, preserving a fiction of independence by choosing Tom Watson of Georgia as their vice presidential nominee.

The Democrats' problem was, in part, lack of money—a problem Bryan attempted to offset by traveling almost 20,000 miles and making more than 600 speeches to audiences that finally totaled in the millions. (In this way, Bryan's cam-paign was as modern as McKinley's. But McKin-ley stayed at home and campaigned from his front porch. It would be some time yet before a candidate would conduct a race using *both* money and speeches on a grand scale.)

But money was only part of the Democrats' problem. Bryan defined the campaign almost from the beginning as a contest between rural and urban Americans. "Burn down your cities," he said, "and leave our farms, and your cities will spring up again as if by magic; but destroy our farms and grass will grow in the streets of every city in this country." The result was that Bryan won little support from urban workers, even from those who were unemployed or embittered. Hanna, on the other hand, had 120 million pamphlets printed in half a dozen languages, aimed specifically at the urban and heavily immigrant industrial workforce.

Bryan, to no one's surprise, carried the South. He also won much of the electoral vote of the Great Plains and the mining states of the Rockies—where the benefits of coining silver were obvious and direct. But he could not carry states where the Granger movement had been popular in the 1870s: Iowa, Wisconsin, Minnesota, or Illinois. He failed in California and

Oregon. And, most important, he did not win a single state north of the Ohio River and east of the Mississippi. The cities, including most industrial workers, went for McKinley, gold, high tariffs, and the Republican promise of "prosperity."

Twice more, in 1900 and 1908, Bryan would attempt to lead the Democrats to victory. But he would fail decisively. And with his failure would go the failure of the Populists as a party. They had staked their political future on Bryan and on "fusion," and it had failed. They had mounted a serious challenge to corporate power, to laissez faire, and to the political system. They had condemned a "conspiracy" between government and private wealth. (They had even, some of them, blamed "Jews," though they were no more anti-Semitic than the members of the two principal parties.) The Populists had won a victory of a

BRYAN CAMPAIGNS (MORE). William Jennings Bryan's strongest political weapon was his ability as a speaker. And his only real hope of victory was to use that skill as often as possible. He traveled and spoke tirelessly but nevertheless failed to carry most of the states he visited. Her in a rare photograph of him in 1896, he is talking to a crowd in Union Square in New York City.

kind: the Democratic party would never again be quite the same. But the victory had cost them their chance at national power over the long run.

In the wake of the Populists' defeat lay the remnants of another dreamlike possibility, the possibility of political unity among poor southern farmers, black and white. It was a dream that a clear majority of southern whites had always rejected, but one that thousands of whites and African Americans in the South had dared to believe in for the first time. Racism, however, not racial or social democracy, triumphed in the South in the 1890s.

As the Southern and the Colored Farmers' Alliances had grown in the 1880s, Democratic politicians had begun to put more and more restrictions on black voting rights. "Literacy" tests were one method used in many states. Another was the requirement that in order to vote, a man had to prove he had paid a per capita tax known as a poll tax—a flat dollar amount each year. But many blacks did pay the poll tax, and an increasing number every year were literate. So as the Populist movement neared its climax, the conservative Democratic establishment in the South responded with sterner measures.

Mississippi took the lead in 1890 with a provision that every voter had to be able not only to read but to "interpret" the state's constitution. And it was up to the supervisors at the polling place—who were always white—to decide whether the voter's "interpretation" was acceptable. Black college graduates were turned away, and watched while white men who could not read at all were allowed to vote. The Mississippi law became a model for other southern states. In states like South Carolina, black voting fell from about 70 percent of eligible voters in 1880 to about 10 percent in the election of 1896.

But white voters knew perfectly well that a strategy like this could be used to prevent poor whites from voting—especially if they were known to be Alliancemen or Populists. The question for the Democratic party regulars was how to devise a voting statute that would drive a wedge between blacks and whites and still get around the Fifteenth Amendment, which forbade any

state to deny a citizen the right to vote because he was black or had once been a slave. On this delicate question, Louisiana took the lead. In 1898 the state's Democratic party invited the defeated white Populists back into the fold with a voting-rights law built around the first "grandfather" clause. According to this law, if a man—literate or not—could prove that either of his grandfathers had ever voted, then he could vote. Since almost every black's grandfather had been a slave, the law clearly favored whites and denied all but a few blacks the vote.

The net effect of the threat that the Southern and the Colored Farmers' Alliances had posed to the political supremacy of the southern white elite was, in the end, that racism in the South became more intense and vicious. The white establishment rose up in full wrath against the threat. And many white Populists, embittered by failure and lured on by demagogic politicians, came out of the experience more deeply committed than ever to white "supremacy." It is no coincidence that the decade of Populist and Alliance agitation in the South was the same decade in which the ultimate expression of racism—lynching—reached terrifying heights. A mass lynching helped bring the Colored Farmers' Alliance to an end. In 1891 some black cotton pickers in western Tennessee carried out a strike during the picking season. Like all seasonal field workers, they had only one powerful weapon: to refuse to work during the short, crucial period when the crop was ready. For the white landowners of the area, this was the ultimate challenge to the system of racial exploitation that had replaced slavery, and they responded with great force. A "posse" was sworn in to hunt down the strikers. They resisted, and in the end fifteen blacks were hanged.

During the rest of the 1890s about 100 blacks were illegally hanged every year. (These were the *known* lynchings; many other blacks surely perished deep in woods or swamps, silently and without trace.) The victims were almost always male, and their bodies were often mutilated, before and after their deaths, as a warning to other African-American men to keep in their "place." Whatever promise of a new kind of social and racial democracy Populism had held, for the South or for the nation as a whole, it had failed. And the federal courts were making that failure even more ringing and definite.

⤙⟐⤚

RACE, CLASS, AND THE CONSTITUTION

From the 1870s to the end of the century, the federal judiciary became increasingly committed to maintaining social arrangements in which distinctions of class and race were becoming more obvious and extreme. This commitment was clearly expressed in two landmark Supreme Court decisions of 1895 and 1896. In the first, *Pollock* v. *Farmers' Loan and Trust Co.*, the justices struck down the primitive income tax Congress had passed as part of the tariff law of 1894. In the second, *Plessy* v. *Ferguson,* the Court gave its approval for the first time to legal racial segregation.

In *Pollock,* the income tax case, the judges were presented with an argument that the tax law violated a constitutional provision that all taxes be "apportioned" among the states according to their population. But the argument went much further, and pictured the income tax as an attempt on the part of the poor to "take" the property of the rich. The tax exempted all incomes under $4,000. This amounted, according to the argument, to a decision on the part of three-fourths of the people—who had elected the Congress but would pay no tax—to tax the other fourth. From this, the lawyers argued, would inevitably result "communism" and "anarchy." The opinion of the Supreme Court justices was less emotional, but they did reject the principle of the income tax outright—and so took away the one legislative success for which the Populists could claim credit.

The next year the Court took up what may have been the most radical potential of Populism in the South: the challenge to racism. In 1876, in *United States* v. *Reese,* the Court had already gone a long way toward nullifying the Fifteenth Amendment's guarantee of the right to vote. In that case, the justices had ruled that state restrictions on voting rights were valid as long as they did not clearly and *explicitly* base those restrictions on race or color or "previous condition of servitude"—meaning enslavement. Then, in *Williams* v. *Mississippi,* 1898, the Court upheld the Mississippi law of 1890 providing that voters must not only be able to read but to "interpret" the state constitution. The effect and purpose of the law was simple, and obvious to everyone: it was meant to prevent black men from voting. But the Court approved the law because it did not actually mention race or color.

Meanwhile, however, the Court had been preparing to take up a different kind of civil rights question. This one did not involve "political" rights like the right to vote or to serve on juries. Instead, it involved matters like education or seating in railroad cars and other public places. The issue was, did the Fourteenth Amendment's insistence that all citizens were entitled to the "equal protection of the laws" mean that states could not legally segregate schools or public accommodations such as trains or hotels or restaurants? If state legislatures were forbidden to use race or color as explicit tests of voting rights, could they make race or color an outright basis for legal segregation? This was the crucial issue in the landmark case of *Plessy* v. *Ferguson* (1896).

The case involved a Louisiana law that required railroads to provide "equal but separate accommodations for the white and colored races," and required "white and colored" passengers to sit only in the designated seats or cars. The question was simple. Did this state law deprive citizens—white or black—of the "equal protection of the laws"? Plessy, a man who had seven white great-grandparents and one who was an African American, had been arrested for refusing to leave a "white" railroad car.

In its decision, the Court made a distinction between "political" equality and "social" equality. The Fourteenth Amendment, clearly, required that the states respect "political" rights absolutely, without regard to race or color. But the

Constitution could not—in matters of race or any other area of ordinary human life—require "social" equality. In matters the court called "social," a state legislature was free to pass laws that enforced the "customs and traditions of the people." The court's majority had decided, firmly, that "legislation is powerless to eradicate racial instincts or to abolish distinctions based on physical differences. . . . If one race be inferior to the other socially, the Constitution of the United States cannot put them upon the same plane."

Justice John M. Harlan wrote a powerful dissent that captured almost perfectly the ideas that had once given the Republican party its sense of mission—the sense of mission the party had lost during the 1870s and 1880s. The Louisiana law, he said, was "cunningly devised to defeat legitimate results of the war." Like most white, northern Republicans, Harlan was openly racist. He was convinced that the "white race" was the "dominant race in this country," and would "continue to be so for all time." But he still held fast to the line that had once shaped the views of Lincoln and his party: that in the eyes of the *law* "the humblest is the peer of the most powerful":

> In view of the Constitution, in the eye of the law, there is in this country no superior, dominant, ruling class of citizens. There is no caste here. Our Constitution is color-blind and neither knows nor tolerates classes among citizens. . . . The arbitrary separation of citizens, on the basis of race . . . is a badge of servitude. . . . It cannot be justified upon any legal grounds.

A year later, the justices of the Supreme Court would decide that education, like seating arrangements on trains, was a "social" fact and not a "political" one. And so it would endorse segregated public schools as a proper way to prevent the "co-mingling of the two races upon terms unsatisfactory to either."

The message was clear. An act of Congress that attempted to make wealthier citizens pay an income tax that others did not pay had been struck down, amid wild talk about the dangers of "anarchy" and "communism." The right of the "dominant race" to segregate private and public facilities and schools had been judicially established. All this, combined with the clear failure of the Populists, seemed to make it certain that the United States could look forward only to a continuation of politics that accepted official racism and the privileges of wealth as fundamental principles of government.

But there were voices demanding change, demanding that economic and social and political privilege be spread more equally. During the two decades since Reconstruction had ended with the election of 1876, feminists were organizing and working for a greater measure of equality and participation. Socialist and labor leaders were listening to the complaints of workers, and held out hope that the future might be different. Native Americans on the Great Plains were resisting the destruction of their society and culture. And black leaders still spoke their eloquent dreams of a new day and a new kind of society. In the year of *Plessy* v. *Ferguson* an African-American college professor with the appropriate name of John Hope gave voice to the passion for equality in words that other oppressed Americans might have understood very well indeed:

> Rise, Brothers! Let your dissatisfaction break mountain-high against the walls of prejudice. Then we shall not have to plead for justice, nor on bended knee crave mercy; for we shall be men.

The major political parties and the court system had turned deaf ears to such voices. But the drama of American history often takes place outside politics and government, and this was emphatically the case during the period between the end of Reconstruction and the turn of the century. The next three chapters will examine the efforts of workers and immigrants to find their way to decent lives in a new industrial order; the efforts of Native Americans to maintain their culture and society against the white advance into the West; and the ways women of different classes and colors tried to come to terms with a society that hemmed them in behind John Hope's "walls of prejudice."

CHRONOLOGY

1876   Samuel J. Tilden (Democrat) wins majority of popular vote for president, apparently defeating Rutherford B. Hayes (Republican)

1877   President Ulysses S. Grant orders end of military Reconstruction in the last three former Confederate states;

Congress creates special commission to decide contested electoral votes in four states;

Congress accepts the judgment of the commission that Hayes should be inaugurated;

Supreme Court decides *Munn* v. *Illinois*

1878   Economic depression eases;

Granger movement begins to decline

1880   James A. Garfield (Republican) defeats Winfield Scott Hancock (Democrat) in presidential election

1881   Garfield assassinated by Charles Guiteau;

Chester A. Arthur becomes president

1883   Pendleton Act creates federal civil service system

1884   Grover Cleveland (Democrat) defeats James G. Blaine (Republican) in presidential election

1885   Farmers' Alliance movements begin to gain strength in South and West

1886   Supreme Court decides *Pollock* v. *Farmers' Loan and Trust*

1887   Interstate Commerce Act

1888   Benjamin Harrison (Republican) defeats Grover Cleveland (Democrat) in presidential election

1889   McKinley Tariff raises import duties

1890   Supreme Court decides *Chicago, Milwaukee, and St. Paul Railway Co.* v. *Minnesota;*

Farmers' Alliance movements claim several million members, black and white, in South and West;

Alliance candidates win many seats in state legislatures;

1890 (cont'd)   Democrats win landslide victory in congressional elections;

Mississippi enacts first "literacy" tests designed to exclude African-American voters;

Sherman Anti-Trust Act

1891   Mass lynching ends strike of black cotton workers in Tennessee

1892   Populist party founded;

Cleveland defeats Harrison and James B. Weaver (Populist) in presidential election;

Democrats gain control of both houses of Congress for first time since the Civil War;

Populist-supported candidates win approximately 10 percent of Congressional seats;

First peacetime income tax enacted;

Tariffs on imports reduced by about 10 percent

1893   Beginning of long and severe economic depression

1894   Populist candidates receive 1.5 million votes in congressional elections;

Republicans gain control of the House of Representatives

1895   Supreme Court decides United States v. *E. C. Knight* and *Pollock* v. *Farmers' Loan and Trust Co.*

1896   Supreme Court decides *Plessy* v. *Ferguson;*

Populist party endorses Democrat William Jennings Bryan for president;

Bryan defeated by William McKinley (Republican) in presidential election

1898   Louisiana enacts first "grandfather clause," designed to lure poor whites back to the Democratic party;

Supreme Court decides *Smyth* v. *Ames*

SUGGESTIONS FOR FURTHER READING

THE ELECTION OF 1876

The classic work on the Compromise of 1876–1877 was published in 1951 by C. Vann Woodward as *Reunion and Reaction: The Compromise of 1877 and the End of Reconstruction*. It should be read alongside the more northern-oriented work of K. I. Polakoff, *The Politics of Inertia: The Election of 1876 and the End of Reconstruction* (1973). A third important study is William Gillette, *Retreat from Reconstruction, 1869–1879* (1979). The lives of Tilden and Hayes can be studied in A. C. Flick, *Samuel Jones Tilden* (1939); Harry Barnard, *Rutherford B. Hayes and His America* (1964), and Kenneth E. Davidson, *The Presidency of Rutherford B. Hayes* (1972).

PARTIES AND PRESIDENCIES

Thoughtful overviews are Sean Cashman, *America in the Gilded Age* (1984), Morton Keller, *Affairs of State: Public Life in Late-Nineteenth-Century America* (1977), and Nell Irwin Painter, *Standing at Armageddon: the United States, 1877–1919* (1987). Good discussions of politics are also available in Robert Wiebe's influential *The Search for Order, 1877–1920* (1967); H. Wayne Morgan, *From Hayes to McKinley* (1969); R. Hal Williams, *Years of Decision: American Politics in the 1890s* (1978); Richard J. Jensen, *The Winning of the Midwest: Social and Political Conflict, 1888–1896* (1971), and Paul Kleppner, *The Third Electoral System, 1853–1892* (1979). The relationship between the parties and voters is nicely analyzed in Michael E. McGerr, *The Decline of Popular Politics* (1986). Useful studies of elite reformers in politics are John G. Sproat, *The Best Men: Liberal Reformers in the Gilded Age* (1968), and Gerald McFarland, *Mugwumps, Morals, and Politics, 1884–1920* (1975). Three good studies of the election of 1896 are Paul W. Glad, *McKinley, Bryan, and the People* (1964); Robert Durden, *The Climax of Populism: The Election of 1896* (1965); and Stanley Jones, *The Election of 1896* (1964).

POPULISM

Lawrence Goodwyn, *Democratic Promise: The Populist Movement in America* (1976), stresses the radical egalitarian side of the movement. A different view can be found in Stanley B. Parsons, *The Populist Context: Rural Versus Urban Power on a Great Plains Frontier* (1973), and Robert C. McMath, *Populist Vanguard: A History of the Southern Farmers' Alliance* (1975). Two important biographies of Populist leaders are Peter Argersinger, *Populism and Politics: Alfred Peffer and the People's Party* (1974), and C. Vann Woodward's beautifully written *Tom Watson* (1938). Steven Hahn's *The Roots of Southern Populism* (1983) is a superb book. An excellent state study is Scott G. McNall, *The Road to Rebellion: Class Formation and Kansas Populism* (1988). For the story of the disenfranchisement of blacks in the South, see J. Morgan Kousser, *The Shaping of Southern Politics: Suffrage Restriction and the Establishment of a One-Party South* (1974). But no student should miss a chance to read C. Vann Woodward's elegant little book, *The Strange Career of Jim Crow* (3rd ed., 1974).

The Climax of the Industrial Revolution

THE EPISODE: *In 1886, workers at the McCormick Harvester Works in Chicago went on strike. They managed to shut down the huge factory that manufactured machinery for reaping grain. But the McCormick family and management were determined to break not only the strike but the unions that had organized it. They brought in a force of armed detectives and tried to replace their union workers with strikebreaking "scabs."*

During the same spring, thousands of other Chicago workers organized a general strike, asking their employers for an eight-hour working day. These strikers were very attentive to what was happening at the Mc-Cormick company. A violent incident at the main gate of the McCormick factory provoked a workers' evening protest meeting at a square in Chicago known as The Haymarket. Again there was violence. Someone planted a bomb, which killed or wounded a number of policemen. The bombing set off a police riot, in which several civilians were killed and many others injured. Some public authorities in the city were convinced that they were facing a revolutionary conspiracy led by "foreign anarchists." They were determined to restore "order" and put down labor "unrest." Their efforts produced one of the most spectacular trials in American history, a trial that pitted the power of the state against those who had tried to organize workers to resist the system of industrial capitalism.

THE HISTORICAL SETTING: *This is the second of four chapters that focus on the period between the end of Reconstruction and the beginning of the twentieth century. In the preceding chapter, the political history of the period was established as a chronological framework. This chapter examines the nature of the climactic phase of the nineteenth-century industrial revolution and the ways it affected how Americans lived, worked, and came into conflict with each other.*

Many of the six main themes of this chapter had a direct bearing on what happened in the Haymarket episode: (1) a rapid introduction of heavy machine technology in agriculture, manufacturing, and transportation; (2) the growth of large corporations and the formation of trusts and other kinds of monopolies; (3) a rapid increase in immigration from areas of the world that had not supplied much of the American population before the Civil War; (4) increasing prejudice among Americans who thought of themselves as "natives" against "foreigners" of all sorts; (5) the rapid growth of cities, most of them with immigrant slums and racial ghettos; and (6) a heightening conflict between labor and capital. The political system that was described in the preceding chapter proved unable or unwilling to find ways of dealing with the problems produced by these deep and important changes.

THE HAYMARKET—STRIKE AND
VIOLENCE IN CHICAGO

April 15, 1885

My Dear Virginia,

We have had a week of trial and anxiety on the great subject of disturbances in our main factory—the serious labor troubles we have encountered—a great strike, and all the resulting derangement of our relations–old and pleasant as they were—with our workmen.

Trouble has come to hundreds of families in consequence; hatred and fierce passions have been aroused; and an injury has resulted to our good name.

It began with a few molders and went on, one force operating on another, until 1,200 men went out, part of them by intimidation and part of them led by ignorant and blind passion. It ended by our conceding the terms demanded.

What a sore heart I have carried these days!

Your Devoted Mother

This letter was written by a bewildered woman in her early seventies to her daughter. The writer, Nettie Fowler McCormick, was the widow of Cyrus Hall McCormick. An ambitious and ingenious Virginia farm boy, McCormick had made millions of dollars from the invention and manufacture of the reaper, a machine that harvested grain crops mechanically. He opened his Chicago factory, the McCormick Harvester Works, in the 1840s. It was the largest producer of harvesting machines in the world.

Nettie McCormick had always paid close attention to the family business. Now, just a year after her husband's death, a stable and profitable enterprise seemed to be falling to pieces before her eyes. At first, her husband had known all the original 23 workmen by name. He had worked alongside them in the little Chicago factory. Even when, after a few years, there were about 200 workers producing over 1,000 reapers a year, he could still name those who had been with the company for any length of time.

As the business grew, relations with the workers had become more difficult. During the Civil War, when labor had been scarce and prices had jumped every week, there had been many strikes or threats of strikes. McCormick had been forced to agree to one wage increase after another. But after the war ended, McCormick was able to cut wages in the plant five times in five years.

During the two decades after the Civil War, the McCormick company had grown rapidly. In 1884, when Cyrus McCormick died, the main factory covered dozens of acres. Its modern machinery, including two huge steam engines that supplied power for the whole factory, covered twelve acres of floor space. On these floors, about 1,300 men put in six 10-hour days a week. They turned 10 million feet of lumber and thousands of tons of iron into about 50,000 reapers a year. And these machines were making possible an agricultural miracle in the United States.

For the McCormicks, the result was money and status. In 1884 the company showed a profit of 71 percent. The family lived in a great mansion staffed with servants. They had invitations to the "best" Chicago homes, counted other wealthy people among their friends, sent their sons to Princeton, traveled luxuriously, and supported carefully selected philanthropies. Nettie Fowler McCormick had ample reason to be concerned about "our good name."

She had some reason to "carry a sore heart," too. The McCormick workers had always seemed content enough. Nine out of ten of them were Germans, Norwegians, or Swedes, and most lived in the neighborhoods just west of the factory—neighborhoods built by the McCormicks—with Swedish and German street names. All this made the strike of 1885 difficult for Nettie Fowler McCormick to understand. Perhaps her husband's death was part of the problem. But McCormick was still a family business. Her son, Cyrus McCormick II, had taken over the presidency, and other members of the family had always held important positions in the company. What had happened, then, to the McCormicks' "old and pleasant relations with our workmen"?

The problem had to lie, the McCormicks believed, with some small, misguided minority within the plant. And the most likely candidates for this role were clearly the iron molders. Ethnically, the molders were a distinct group. Almost all of them were Irish—"fighting Irish," as one plant official called them. And they had a tight, successful craft union, Molders Local No. 233. This union had been making trouble for the McCormicks for twenty years. There were only about ninety molders, but their operation was crucial to the manufacture of reapers. They could bring production to a complete standstill, and they had successfully used the power of this threat several times. Every time old Cyrus McCormick had tried to cut wages, the molders had been the first to resist.

⤝⟿⟿⟾⟾⤞

The strike of 1885 had its origins in a decision by the new young president of the company to cut wages again. In December 1884 he had announced a 10 percent pay cut throughout the workforce—except for the molders, who were to be cut by 15 percent. At first, there was quiet. Even the molders appeared to accept the reduction. But they were only biding their time until production reached its annual peak in the spring. In March 1885, the molders demanded that their former wages be restored to them. When McCormick refused, the molders went out on strike. And, to the McCormicks' alarm, some of the other workers followed them out.

Cyrus McCormick II was anxious to prove himself. To break the strike, he sent telegrams to McCormick salesmen all over the Midwest, asking them to send strikebreaking molders to Chicago. He even had these workers listed on the company payroll as "scabs"—a union term of insult for nonunion replacement workers. The replacement workers were housed inside the plant, in a barracks listed in the company's own records as "scab house."

But McCormick's efforts to break the strike did not work. The scabs could not be trusted. Early in April, these two revealing telegrams were sent from company headquarters to salesmen in Iowa and Illinois:

> To Tom Braden, Agent, Des Moines, Iowa: Out of the lot of men you sent us yesterday, but two of them showed up in Chicago. We find it not safe to ship these critters at our expense unless nailed up in a box car or chained.

> To J. F. Utley, Agent, Sterling, Illinois: The gentleman you sent to us as a molder did not remain over an hour or two until he packed his valise and skipped. We took special pains to get him into the Works by his riding with Mr. McCormick in his buggy. If you are able to do so, try and collect back his Rail Road fare.

Just a week after Cyrus McCormick had sneaked this unreliable scab into the plant, hidden in the president's own buggy, the strike reached a climax. On April 14, with the police scattered all over the city to patrol a local election, strikers attacked McCormick workers outside the plant. McCormick Harvester, like many other companies of the period, had hired a small private army of the Pinkerton "detective" agency to maintain peace. A wagon loaded with Pinkerton men and a case of Winchester repeating rifles tried to enter the plant gate. The strikers attacked the wagon and burned it, and the rifles disappeared into the crowd. The captain in charge of the few Chicago police still in the area did nothing. His name, O'Donnell, was as obviously Irish as that of any molder.

The violence only confirmed the McCormick family's opinion of the "fighting Irish" molders. If twenty years' experience was not enough, the Pinkerton agents' secret reports confirmed what the family had long suspected: They were the victims of an ethnic "conspiracy" between workers and the Chicago police force. Just after the violent episode of April 14, one Pinkerton man submitted this report:

> The assault on the Pinkerton police during the strike of last week was urged by Irishmen, who are employed at McCormick's as molders and helpers. These Irishmen are nearly all members of the Ancient Order of Hibernians [an Irish social fraternity] who have a bitter enmity against the agency.

To the Pinkertons, it seemed clear that the molders were actually supported by their fellow Irishmen on the police force:

> It looks somewhat strange that these men at McCormick's could have police protection. On each occasion, the police stood by during the assaults and made no effort to stop the outrage.

Once, during the strike, a group of molders had attacked a group of nonunion workers outside the plant gate. The police, according to Pinkerton reports, had this time not merely stood by but had actually chased and arrested the Pinkerton men who were trying to restrain the molders:

The police made the utmost speed in calling a patrol wagon, which followed the Pinkerton men and arrested them! The men who made the arrests were treated by the strikers in saloons, and from their talk and insinuations, the police urged the mob to more violence by saying the Pinkerton men were sons of bitches, no better than scabs, there to take the bread out of women and children's mouths.

After the molders' triumphant April 14 attack on the Pinkertons, Cyrus McCormick went looking for help and advice. He appealed first to the mayor, Carter Harrison. But Harrison remembered full well that the McCormicks had consistently opposed him in local politics. He politely advised the young industrialist to give in to the molders' demands. McCormick then turned to what he hoped would be a more sympathetic listener, old Philip Armour, head of a large meat-packing company and a veteran of many labor troubles. But even Armour told McCormick that the molders had won. There seemed to be no choice. McCormick offered to give back to the molders 5 percent out of their original 15 percent pay cut. But they refused this, and he ended by restoring the whole 15 percent.

To both Cyrus McCormick and his mother, their defeat at the hands of a few Irishmen was a painful mystery. But it was a mystery that had to be solved. Cyrus wrote to his mother as he mulled over the problem:

> The whole question of these labor troubles is vast and important and throws more new light on a department of our manufacturing interests which we have not hitherto studied with sufficient depth and understanding.

But to this twenty-five-year-old, who had only two years earlier been taken out of Princeton University to run the plant, "depth and understanding" were limited to one fact and one conclusion. The fact was that a handful of disaffected molders could bring the entire McCormick enterprise to a standstill. The conclusion was that such a situation must be avoided in the future by making the skills of the molders unnecessary. He wrote his mother:

> I do not think we will have a similar trouble again because we will take measures to prevent it. I do not think we will be troubled if we take proper steps to weed out the bad element among the men.

McCormick went to work at once to weed out the "bad element"—the offending Irish molders. He focused his efforts on a daring technological gamble. During the summer of 1885, the summer following the strike, the McCormick company bought a dozen new "pneumatic molding machines." They were supposed to perform mechanically most of the foundry tasks that the skilled molders had always done by hand. The machines were expensive, and they were experimental. No one knew whether they would work. McCormick hoped that they would enable the company to rid itself once and for all of the troublesome molders.

In August the McCormick foundry closed for two months so that the machines could be installed. But when the foundry reopened for fall production, the new machines were in place. Not one molder who had participated in the spring strike was back on the payroll.

McCormick seemed to have won a complete victory. All he had done was spend a vast sum of money on the new machinery. A few months after the machines went into operation, he wrote his mother triumphantly that the machines

are working even beyond our expectations and everybody is very much pleased with the result. Two men with one of these machines can do an average of about three days work in one. Add to this fact that we have only nine molders in the whole foundry (the rest are all laborers), and you can see what a great gain this will be to us.

But McCormick was being more optimistic than he should have been—probably to reassure his anxious mother. Actually, there were troubles with the machines. In October the McCormick company complained to the manufacturer that the castings turned out by the pneumatic molding device were too brittle to use. And in November, Cyrus McCormick was called home from a trip to New York because of a crisis in the foundry. He wrote in his diary for November 11: "Telegram from mother urging come home at once about molding machines—probably failure. Critical situation."

The machines were fixed, but even when they worked they seemed to require an endless amount of labor to keep them functioning. Before the machines were installed, the total wage bill in the foundry was about $3,000 a week. After the machines had

THE REAPER WORKS. This company picture of the McCormick plant exaggerated the factory's size a little. But it did suggest the strategic location of the city at the junction of railroad, lake, and river transportation. In the nineteenth century, smoke was a symbol of "progress" and a national blessing—the thicker and blacker, the better.

been in operation for about six months, foundry wages totaled $8,000 a week. Most of the labor was common, unskilled work. But gradually the company had to hire additional new molders to supervise the work. Economically, the machines were a complete failure.

Still, the new technology had broken the molders' union at McCormick. And the union was unhappy. The leader of the molders was a veteran union man named Myles McPadden. He devised a new scheme that was much more dangerous to the McCormicks than the old union, with its ninety members. If there was to be no molders' union, then McPadden would simply organize *all* the other workers in the plant into one union or another. The workers were discontented, so the time was ripe. By February 1886 he had succeeded in organizing every major group of workers in the plant. The skilled workers—blacksmiths, machinists, and so on—joined the Metalworkers Union. McPadden encouraged the others to join the Knights of Labor, a general, nationwide union. Only 300 of the 1,400 McCormick workers remained nonunion. The lines of a new strike battle were shaping up clearly.

During this time McCormick, too, was busy. After his frustrated attempt to enlist Mayor Harrison's help, McCormick had gone to some lengths to make peace with the powerful political leader of the city. In every election before 1885 the McCormicks had opposed Harrison. After that year they supported him. As a result, Captain O'Donnell, the Irish police official who had been sympathetic to the workers in the spring of 1885, was replaced. The new man in charge of the area where the works were located was Police Inspector John Bonfield.

Bonfield had a reputation as a tough antilabor cop. He had once beaten his way through a crowd of strikers, shouting a slogan for which he became famous: "Clubs today spare bullets tomorrow." If there was going to be trouble in 1886, McCormick could count on the police in a way he could not have just a year before.

In mid-February 1886 a union committee representing all three unions—the Knights of Labor, the Metalworkers, and the Molders—presented McCormick with a series of demands:

> First, that all wages of laboring men be advanced from $1.25 to $1.50 a day. Second, that all vise hands [metal workers] be advanced to $2.00 a day, and that blacksmith helpers be advanced to $1.75. Third, that the time the men spend in the water closet [the toilet] not be limited as heretofore. Fourth, that, inasmuch as the molding machines are a failure, the preference should be given the old hands. The scabs in the foundry must be discharged, and a pledge given that no man would be discharged for taking part in a strike.

The company offered to meet some of the demands, but not the fourth—which would have meant rehiring the members of the molders' union. The unions responded by calling a strike.

Before the strike was scheduled to begin, however, the company announced a lockout, a complete shutdown of the plant for an indefinite period of time. Union pickets started marching near the plant, but they were kept away by 400 city policemen, now under Bonfield's command. To show its gratitude, the company served free hot meals to the police, with Cyrus McCormick sometimes personally pouring the coffee.

After two weeks the works were reopened, but only to nonunion employees. There was a loyal holdover force of only 82 men. The company furnished them with pistols. McCormick hoped they would lead an enthusiastic rush for jobs, but only 161 men showed up the first day. The second day was not much better. Once again the company's agents scoured the region for workers. Gradually, the company's situation improved a little. McCormick was willing to sacrifice almost half a year's production in order to break the unions once and for all.

For the men on strike the situation was just as important. If they lost, their future at McCormick (or any other manufacturing plant in the city) was dim. As March turned into April, families got hungrier and tempers hotter. The explosion McCormick had avoided the year before by giving in to union demands now looked inevitable.

The situation at McCormick was complicated by the fact that during the spring of 1886 strikes were taking place all over Chicago. On May 1 all the unions in the city began a general strike for the eight-hour day, one of the largest and most heated labor actions in American history. The strike at McCormick merged with the more general agitation, involving thousands of skilled and unskilled workers from plants all over the city.

Then, on May 3, two days into the general strike for an eight-hour day, a lumber workers' union held a mass meeting to hear an address by August Spies, a radical journalist. The meeting took place on Black Road, just a short distance from the McCormick factory. Some McCormick men were at the meeting, even though none was a lumber worker. The McCormicks had been so desperate for workers that they had already granted the eight-hour day (with ten hours' pay) to their scab workers. So at 3:30, two hours before the former 5:30 closing, the bell at the plant rang, and the strikebreaking workers streamed out of the plant. The striking union men at the meeting watched the scabs leave the plant on their new short schedule.

Here were union men, on strike for an eight-hour day, watching scabs who were already working an eight-hour day. The sight proved too much. Several hundred men, some of them McCormick strikers and some of them lumber workers, mobbed the scabs leaving the plant, driving them back inside the gate. The strikers began to smash windows, unleashing anger that had been building for months. About 200 policemen, under Inspector Bonfield, were there. Suddenly, they began firing their revolvers into the crowd (forgetting Bonfield's slogan about using clubs to spare bullets). When the noise died away, two workers lay dead and several others had been wounded.

August Spies, who had been addressing the meeting, witnessed the violence. The next day, in the newspaper office where he worked, he heard that a mass meeting was scheduled at The Haymarket to protest the shootings at McCormick. A circular announcing the meeting was being printed in both German and English when Spies arrived at the paper. Spies agreed to address the meeting, but he insisted that one line in the circular be omitted. About 200 of the circulars had already been printed, but the line was removed from the rest. Few of the 20,000 circulars that were finally distributed on the streets of Chicago contained the words "Workingmen Arm Yourselves."

CHICAGO ANARCHISTS OF 1886.

Attention Workingmen!

GREAT

MASS-MEETING

TO-NIGHT, at 7.30 o'clock,

AT THE

HAYMARKET, Randolph St., Bet. Desplaines and Halsted.

Good Speakers will be present to denounce the latest atrocious act of the police, the shooting of our fellow-workmen yesterday afternoon.

Workingmen Arm Yourselves and Appear in Full Force!

THE EXECUTIVE COMMITTEE

THE CALL TO THE HAYMARKET. This poster was prepared to call a meeting to protest the shooting at the McCormick factory. August Spies insisted that the line calling on the workers to come to the square armed be omitted before the poster was circulated.

Spies was not, in the usual sense, a working man. He was thirty years old and the editor of the *Arbeiter-Zeitung*, a German-language newspaper with a radical viewpoint. He was also the business manager of an organization called the Socialist Publishing Society, an organization run by a small political party known as the Socialist Labor party.

From time to time Spies had been in trouble with the police. Only a year before, during the McCormick strike of 1885, he had angered the police by intervening in the case of a poor German servant girl who had been arrested by the police and held in jail for several days. When Spies and the girl's mother went to the jail, they discovered that the girl had been sexually molested repeatedly. Rather than keep quiet, Spies swore out a warrant for the police sergeant in charge of the jail. He lost the case for lack of evidence, but he became well known to the Chicago police.

Spies was, in short, a politically active radical who did not hesitate to condemn people in positions of authority. He was also a committed socialist politician. He hoped that the rally at The Haymarket would attract enough people to fill the square, which could hold about 20,000.

Spies reached The Haymarket late, at about 8:30 on the night of May 4. He must have felt disappointed. No meeting was in progress, and there were only about a thousand people scattered around the square. The other main speaker, a socialist named Albert R. Parsons, was nowhere in sight. Spies climbed on a wagon, sent someone to look for Parsons, and began his talk. He was a good speaker, and soon the small crowd became enthusiastic:

> The fight is going on. Now is the chance to strike for the oppressed classes. The oppressors want us to be content. They will kill us. The day is not far distant when we will resort to hanging these men. [Applause, and shouts of "Hang them" now came from the crowd.] McCormick is the man who created the row on Monday, and he must be held responsible for the murder of our brothers! [More shouts of "Hang him!"]

Spies went on in the same vein for about an hour, trying to rouse his working-class audience to anger and a sense of solidarity against their oppressors. Then someone announced that Albert R. Parsons had been found. Spies turned over his wagon rostrum to the second speaker.

The crowd had been waiting for Parsons, for he had a reputation as a spellbinder. Unlike Spies and many other Chicago socialists, he was a native-born American. Born in Alabama in 1848, Parsons came from a family whose ancestry went back to 1632 in New England. He was a self-trained printer in Texas before the Civil War. During the war he fought for the Confederacy in a Texas artillery company. After the war Parsons became converted to socialism and moved to Chicago, the center of working-class politics in the United States.

Like Spies, Parsons was not a worker at all but a political journalist. He edited a radical workingmen's paper called *The Alarm*. The Haymarket rally was just one more in a long series of political speeches for him. His speech was much like that of Spies but slightly stronger in tone:

> I am not here for the purpose of inciting anybody, but to speak out, to tell the facts as they exist, even though it shall cost me my life before morning. It behooves you, as you love your wife and children—if you don't want to see them perish with hunger, killed or cut down like dogs in the street—Americans, in the interest of your liberty and independence, to arm, to arm yourselves!

Here again there was applause from the crowd and shouts of "We'll do it! We're ready!"

What Parsons and Spies did not know was that the crowd was full of police detectives. Every few minutes one or another ran back to a nearby stationhouse to report what the speakers were saying. Waiting in the station were almost 200 policemen, fully armed, and under the command of none other than John Bonfield.

Parsons and Spies probably did not notice Mayor Carter Harrison in the crowd, either. Only the mayor's presence had kept Bonfield from breaking up the meeting. As Parsons finished, the mayor left; it was obvious to him that everything was peaceful. It was almost ten o'clock and rain was in the air. Most of the crowd, too, began to drift off as the third speaker, Samuel Fielden, began to speak.

Suddenly, 180 policemen (a group almost as large as the remaining crowd) marched into the square and up to the wagon where Fielden was speaking. One of the captains turned to the crowd and said: "In the name of the people of the State of Illinois, I command this meeting immediately and peaceably to disperse." After a moment the police captain repeated his order. The crowd was already starting to melt away (it

THE HAYMARKET TRAGEDY.
Newspapers and magazines had a field day with events in The Haymarket. This engraving was originally published with the title "Anarchist Riot." It shows the workers and their leaders as a wild-eyed mob, firing into the police ranks. And it pictures the police advance as resolute and orderly. In truth, there was no mob, and the police had no discipline.

was almost 10:30 by now). Fielden had stopped speaking and was climbing down from the wagon platform. "We are peaceable," Fielden said to Bonfield.

At that moment, without any warning, a dynamite bomb was thrown (it is not known from where or by whom). The fuse burned for a second or two after the bomb struck the ground. Then it went off with a deafening roar. Screams split the air as people ran in all directions. A number of policemen lay on the ground, one dead and the others wounded. Quickly, the police re-formed their ranks, and some of them began to fire into the crowd. Other policemen waded into the confusion swinging their clubs. The uproar lasted only a minute or two. Then suddenly the square was empty.

In addition to the dead policeman, seventy-three of his colleagues were wounded, six of whom died later. Four civilians were killed, and the official reports listed twelve as wounded. The twelve were those who had been too badly hurt to leave the square. Probably several times as many limped or struggled home and never became official statistics.

Like most such incidents, the Haymarket affair had been brief. And considering what could have happened, very few people were hurt. But it occurred on the heels of trouble at the McCormick plant, in the midst of the strike for an eight-hour day, with 80,000 Chicago workingmen off the job. Thus the Haymarket bomb touched off a near-panic in the city and much of the rest of the nation. Thousands of respectable citizens convinced themselves that a dangerous conspiracy of anarchists, socialists, and communists was at work to overthrow the government and carry out a bloody revolution. One of the leading business magazines of the day, *Bradstreet's*, spoke for thousands of Americans when it said of the Haymarket incident:

> This week's happenings at Chicago go to show that the threats of the anarchists against the existing order are not idle. In a time of disturbance, desperate men have a power for evil out of proportion to their numbers. They are desperate fanatics who are opposed to all laws. There is no room for anarchy in the political system of the United States.

THE HAYMARKET TRAGEDY: ANOTHER VIEW. This representation of what happened in Chicago in 1886 is probably more accurate than the one on page 92. It shows workers fleeing, none firing at the police. And it shows the bomb killing both workers and the policemen who were beating them with nightsticks.

Also important was the fact that many people had been frightened and angered by a recent flood of immigration from Europe to America—and many of the "anarchists" were also foreigners. Not only in Chicago but all over the nation, newspaper editorial writers and public speakers demanded the immediate arrest and conviction of the "alien radicals" who had conspired to murder honest policemen and subvert law and order. The result was a swift and efficient series of illegal raids by the Chicago police. They searched property without warrants. They imprisoned people without charging them and threatened potential witnesses. All in all, the authorities arrested and questioned about 200 "suspects"—probably none of whom had anything at all to do with the bombing.

In this heated atmosphere, fueled by journalists who whipped up unreasonable fears of an anarchist conspiracy, a grand jury met to determine whether indictments could be brought against anyone for the violence. It decided that although the specific person who threw the bomb could not be identified, anyone who urged violence was a "conspirator" and was as guilty of murder as the bomb thrower. On the basis of this decision, another grand jury met and indicted thirty-one persons on counts of murder. Of the thirty-one, eight were eventually tried, all of them political radicals. Most had not even been present at the Haymarket bombing.

The effect of the Haymarket affair had now become clear. What had begun weeks before as an ordinary strike at the McCormick works had been transformed into a crusade against political radicalism, most of which was said to be foreign in origin. Of the eight men on trial only Parsons and Samuel Fielden were not German or of German descent. The names of the other six would have been as natural in Berlin or Hamburg as in Chicago: August Spies, Michael Schwab, Adolph Fischer, George Engel, Louis Lingg, and Oscar Neebe.

In one way or another, all the defendants had some connection with the labor movement and with political agitation for revolution. Several of them were anarchists, though their ideas about anarchism were vague. They might as well have called themselves socialists, as several of them did at one time or another. In general, they were intellectuals. Their jobs were connected with radical journalism in either the English- or German-language press. They did not all know one another, but by the time their trial was over, most of them were probably genuine "comrades," a word they used more and more in the months ahead.

On the other side of the battle were all the forces of "law" and "order." True, some people agreed with Mayor Harrison that the Haymarket meeting had been peaceful, that the whole idea of a conspiracy was a false and legally incorrect notion. But most of Chicago society (including even many elements of the labor movement) favored a quick conviction and the hanging of all eight defendants. The judge who tried the case, the prosecuting attorney, most business leaders, almost all the local clergymen—almost everyone who had any influence in Chicago—were convinced even before the trial began that the defendants were guilty. Moreover, most of Chicago's leading citizens, and their counterparts in the rest of the country, agreed that the trial was a struggle to the death between American "republicanism" and foreign "anarchism." The entire established order of American society, with very few exceptions, was determined to make an example of the "conspirators."

⋆⟶⟹◯⟸⟵⋆

The Haymarket trial began June 21, 1886. The first three weeks of the seven-week trial were spent selecting a jury. Under Illinois law, the defense had the right to reject a total of 160 jurors on "peremptory" challenges—that is, without having to give reasons why a potential juror should be disqualified. As one prospective juror after another was called, it became clear that most of them were extremely prejudiced against the defendants. The defense attorneys quickly used up their 160 peremptory challenges. They then had to show cause for turning down a juror and depend on the judge, Joseph Gary, to rule fairly. Again and again, plainly biased jurors were accepted by the judge—whose own prejudice against the defendants became apparent as the process went on. The result was a jury composed of twelve citizens who obviously wished to hang the defendants.

In his opening statement, prosecuting attorney Julius Grinnell set the tone of the entire trial:

> Gentlemen, for the first time in the history of our country people are on trial for endeavoring to make anarchy the rule. I hope that while the youngest of us lives this will be the last and only time when such a trial shall take place. In the light of the 4th of May, we now know that the preachings of anarchy by these defendants, hourly and daily for years, have been sapping our institutions. Where they have cried murder, bloodshed, anarchy, and dynamite, they have meant what they said. The firing on Fort Sumter was a terrible thing to our country, but it was open warfare. I think it was nothing compared with this insidious, infamous plot to ruin our laws and our country.

It was obvious that this would not be an ordinary murder trial. The defendants would be judged by their words and their beliefs. A ninth "conspirator," Rudolph Schnaubelt, had fled. The prosecution would try to prove that he had thrown the bomb. The next step would be to convict the other eight of conspiracy, which would carry the same penalty as murder itself. And they would be convicted by the fact that they had made speeches and written newspaper articles urging "violent revolution." Day after day the prosecution offered evidence about the defendants' beliefs, their writings, and even pamphlets they had not written but supposedly helped to sell.

The prosecution had weak cases against the individual defendants. They did have some evidence that one, Lingg, had actually made some bombs. But Lingg was a stranger to most of the others, and he had not even been at Haymarket Square on May 4. Parsons, Spies, Fischer, and Schwab had all been there, but had left the square before the bomb was thrown. George Engel proved that he had been home drinking a glass of beer with his wife. In the end the prosecution's case rested on a theory of "general conspiracy to promote violence." No evidence of a single violent *act* was brought into court that could withstand even the mildest cross-examination by the frustrated defense attorneys.

After four weeks of testimony the jury retired. The jury members had been instructed by Judge Gary in such a way as to make conviction almost inevitable, and they needed only three hours to discuss the matter—and most of this time was spent talking about the fate of one defendant, the youngest, Oscar Neebe. After this short deliberation they filed solemnly back into the courtroom. It was ten o'clock, August 19, 1886, when the foreman read the verdict.

> We the jury find the defendants Spies, Schwab, Fielden, Parsons, Fischer, Engel, and Lingg guilty of murder in the manner and form as charged, and fix the penalty at death. We find Oscar Neebe guilty of murder in the manner and form as charged, and fix the penalty at imprisonment in the penitentiary for fifteen years.

Years later Judge Gary recalled that the verdict was received by the friends of social "order" with a roar of almost universal approval.

Before they were sentenced, each of the defendants made a speech to the court. Spies spoke for all of them when he said, in the German accent he had never lost:

> There was not a syllable said about anarchism at the Haymarket meeting. But "anarchism is on trial," foams Mr. Grinnell. If that is the case, your honor, very well; you may sentence me, for I am an anarchist. I believe that the state of classes—the state where one class dominates and lives upon the labor of another class—is doomed to die, to make room for a free society, voluntary association, or universal brotherhood, if you like. You may pronounce the sentence upon me, honorable judge, but let the world know that in A.D. 1886, in the state of Illinois, eight men were sentenced to death because they believed in a better future.

There were appeals, of course, first to state courts and then to the Supreme Court of the United States. One by one the appeals failed. Then there were pleas to the governor of Illinois for mercy, and the sentences of Fielden and Schwab were commuted to life. Lingg, the bomb maker, who was probably half mad, committed suicide—using dynamite set off by a fuse that he lit with his jail-cell candle. The other four condemned men—Engel, Spies, Parsons, and Fischer—were hanged on November 11. As the four stood on the scaffold, ropes around their necks and hoods over their heads, Spies broke the deep silence by shouting: "There will come a time when our silence will be more powerful than the voices you strangle today!"

"THE VOICES YOU STRANGLE TODAY."   On November 11, 1886, three months after one of the most unfair verdicts in American history, Albert Parsons, August Spies, George Engel, and Adolph Fischer were hanged by the state of Illinois. Victorian refinement required that the victims be put into robes to hide two things: that they were tightly tied up and that most people who are hanged lose muscular control and soil their clothing.

⤙═◯═⤚

Months before these hangings, things had returned to "normal" at the Mc-Cormick works. On May 7, 1886, three days after the Haymarket bombing, Cyrus McCormick was able to write in his diary: "A good force of men at the works today, and things are resuming their former appearance." He was about to take full advantage of the hysterical public outrage over what he called the "devilish plot" at Haymarket Square. The harvester factory quietly returned to a ten-hour workday. On Monday, May 10—less than a week after the bombing—McCormick made this satisfied note: "Things going smoothly. We returned to 5:30 closing hour today, instead of 3:30."

Factories, Workers, and a New Social Order

This chapter is about the creation of a new social and economic system in the United States: the system of industrial capitalism. In a sense, industry is as old as human society. People have always made things—tools, weapons, clothing, and so on. But beginning in the eighteenth century, their ability to make goods began to increase rapidly. This so-called industrial revolution originated in England and spread quickly to the rest of western Europe and to the United States. By the time of the Civil War, this revolution was well under way in North America, fed by inventions like the steam engine, the cotton gin, and the reaper. After the war, industrialization altered the basic patterns of life in the United States even more drastically.

Everything had to be changed, since every element of this new system had to hang together. Raw materials, like coal and iron for making steel, had to be found and developed. Cheap transportation, like railroads, had to be available to bring these materials to factories and to take finished products from them. Workers had to be hired to operate the factories. And agriculture had to be improved so that fewer and fewer people would be needed to grow more and more food. More and more machines were needed to provide a livelihood for more and more factory workers, who would in turn make still more machines. Nothing could happen at all unless everything else happened—and in the proper order. Every factory functioned as part of a chain of invention, materials, transportation, and workers.

The McCormick Harvester Company, for example, was only part of a complicated series of events and machines. The reapers made at the McCormick works enabled farmers on the Great Plains to produce unheard-of quantities of grain. Some of this grain was milled into flour for bread eaten by people like McCormick's molders. Other farm products fed cattle, which were slaughtered in big cities and processed at factories owned by men like Philip Armour.

The new transcontinental railroads were necessary to take the reapers west and bring the flour and beef east. Since there were not enough workers to lay the new rails, Irish and Chinese were encouraged to immigrate. The McCormick plant, too, was tended by more than a thousand immigrants. And it was German immigrants who were the main victims of the Haymarket riot. The city of Chicago itself was a new kind of city, built around railroads and factories—a great barracks for the workers at dozens of factories like the McCormick works.

The United States was transformed. It had once been a nation in which nine out of every ten people lived on farms or in rural communities. By the end of the nineteenth century, it was the world's most productive industrial nation, and one of the most urban. The landscape had been remade. The people had been changed, too. There had always been immigrants to the United States, but new industries attracted different types of immigrants in greater numbers. In the end, the daily lives and even the language of Americans were changed. New words like *telephone*, *subway*, *scab*, and *millionaire* became common speech. They signaled just how deep and complete the change had been.

⊰─◉═◉─⊱

TECHNOLOGICAL CHANGE

Few of the men and women who made or watched the industrial revolution understood its complexity. Most of them probably regarded it as a product of new types of machines. Certainly one of the most obvious changes of the nineteenth century was that many things that had once been done slowly by hand were now being done rapidly by machine. But technological change touched more than machinery. It transformed every sector of economic life, including the way food was produced.

AN AGRICULTURAL REVOLUTION

Agriculture was a prime example of the replacement of hand labor by machine power. The most striking introduction of new agricultural technology took place on the Great Plains. On these flat and treeless expanses, plowing, planting, and harvesting could be done on a scale that would have stunned colonial settlers and even most plantation owners of the Old South. But what happened on the plains was just an extreme version of what went on in all areas of American agriculture: the industrialization of the farm.

At first, the new machinery was fairly simple. McCormick's earliest reapers, built before the Civil War, were small. They were drawn by one horse and worked by one or two men. Another invention, a steel plow that could cut deeper and faster than the old iron plow, was a

further small step. But gradually the new technology gained force and speed. Reapers were soon equipped with automatic binders that could fasten grain into bunches mechanically. The single steel plow was soon modified into a multiple, or gang, plow that could cut several furrows at one time.

Soon other new machines appeared. One could plow and plant at the same time. Another, the "combine," added to the reaper a mechanical thresher, which could separate grain from stalks. A combine could move quickly through a wheat field, gathering wheat, separating the grain, and leaving behind only waste to be plowed under in the spring. The machine accomplished its work without a single human hand touching the earth, the wheat plants, or the grain.

During most of the nineteenth century, new machinery was still driven primarily by animals. Some steam engines were used, but the final mechanization of farms had to await the gasoline-driven tractor in the twentieth century. Still, even before the tractor, the life of the American farmer had been fundamentally altered by technology. Farming gradually came to resemble the running of factories, in which a product for sale was processed and made ready by machinery. Sooner or later, almost every step in all but a few kinds of agriculture was mechanized.

The result of the mechanical changes in agriculture was to double and redouble the volume and pace of food production. In 1840 it took more than three hours of human work time to produce a bushel of wheat. By the 1890s the time had been cut to ten minutes. In 1840 a bushel of corn required almost five hours of labor, from planting to final processing. By the 1890s the time had been cut to forty minutes.

The area of land under cultivation doubled between the Civil War and 1900. And the new lands were usually well adapted to the use of machinery. The net result of the agricultural revolution was an enormous abundance of food.

Hand in hand with the reduction of hours went a marked decrease in the number of farmers needed to produce food. Mechanization made it possible for a tiny minority of Americans to feed all the rest. Those who left farms were then free to work for the railroads and in oil fields, iron mines, factories, and offices—hurrying the process of industrialization along.

IMPROVING RAIL TRANSPORT

The agricultural revolution depended not only on new technology on the farms but also on new methods of carrying food from the farms to the cities—that is, railroads. It was railroads that brought Wyoming beef, Kansas wheat, and Louisiana rice to the table of a McCormick molder. Without the new railroad network built after the Civil War, the mechanization of agriculture would have had much less impact.

Railroads, like farms, benefited from new technological developments. The principle of the steam engine remained the same, but almost every other mechanical aspect of railroading changed drastically during the generation after Appomattox. The old railroads had used iron rails, small and dangerous wood-burning engines, and tiny, rickety coaches and freight cars.

The new lines used steel rails that would last for many years without cracking or rusting. Steel rails could support almost twenty times as much weight as iron, so larger engines and cars could be used. Freight cars increased in weight from 10 tons to over 100 tons. The typical pre–Civil War engine had weighed about 20 tons. By 1900 some locomotives weighed as much as 300 tons. The coal-burning locomotive became a giant source of power that could pull huge freights over the most difficult grades efficiently and safely.

Railroad mileage increased dramatically. In 1870—even after the completion of the first transcontinental line—there were only about 40,000 miles of track in the United States. By 1900 there were almost 200,000 miles. This total was greater than the entire railroad mileage of Europe, including Russia. Other inventions like the telegraph and the electric signal made it possible to control complicated traffic patterns and freight yards.

The trains and tracks of 1900 were as dramatically different from those of 1850 as today's

AN AGRICULTURAL VISTA. Even without steam engines or gasoline motors, giant commercial farms were able to harvest wheat fields with industrial efficiency. These machines, sometimes drawn by as many as thirty mules, cut and threshed the wheat, hauling the grain away and leaving a field of stubble at day's end. Here each machine is tended by only two men, plus a third to drive the mules.

jet plane is from the wobbly aircraft of the 1920s. Railroads were the new giants of the landscape, transforming the process of moving food, objects, and people from one place to another.

---◦≡◦⊙◦≡◦---

MANUFACTURING

Taken by themselves, the technological changes in agriculture and the railroads would have meant little. They were important only in their relation to other parts of the new industrial system. In this system, manufacturing was the crucial center.

By 1900—a little more than a century after George Washington had taken the presidential oath—the United States was the leading manufacturing nation in the world. Many factors made this possible. Americans found new beds of coal. They discovered iron ore in Michigan and Minnesota. They opened oil fields in Pennsylvania, the Ohio Valley, and the southern Great Plains. These raw materials and new energy sources fed the new factories of Pittsburgh, Chicago, and dozens of other cities. Mechanized agriculture made it possible for millions of people to move to cities to work in industrial plants. A high tariff kept down competition from foreign manufactured goods. Most important of all were the new machines and processes that enabled Americans to produce so much so quickly.

THE STEEL INDUSTRY

Steel was very close to the heart of the new economy. It is stronger than iron, more resistant to rust, and easier to shape or mold. People had been making small quantities of steel for centuries, but the process was slow and difficult, since it depended on hand labor. In the 1850s an Englishman, Henry Bessemer, invented a converter that could turn iron into steel by blowing a blast of hot air through the molten iron. The process was spectacular to watch, sending a bril-

liant shaft of sparks and smoke skyward. The economic results were just as startling. For the first time it became possible to produce steel cheaply and in massive quantities.

The combination of the Bessemer converter, the demand for steel from the railroads and other industries, and the discovery of additional sources of iron ore and coal created a new industry. In 1870 the United States produced only about 77,000 tons of steel. By 1900 production had risen to over 10 million tons a year—an increase of more than 1,300 percent. Pittsburgh became the first of the steel towns. But eventually, cities like Birmingham, Alabama, and Gary, Indiana—built almost entirely around the steel industry—sprang up in what had until then been open countryside.

OTHER INDUSTRIES

What happened in steel was repeated in dozens of other industries. The sewing machine and other inventions made it possible to manufacture shoes and clothing on a mass scale. Steam-powered mills using steel equipment could cut lumber, or grind wheat, or print newspapers with a speed and efficiency no one had dreamed of earlier.

Another new industry grew up based on electricity. The foremost American in this field was the versatile Thomas A. Edison. Throughout the late nineteenth century, a stream of inventions poured from his laboratories: the phonograph, the first practical electric light bulb, the storage battery, the dynamo, the electric voting machine, and the motion picture camera.

An industry also developed rapidly around the discovery of oil and new ways of refining it. Oil yielded kerosene for lamps and stoves. Heavier oils lubricated the motors of the new technology. Beginning around 1900, oil became important as a source of gasoline for the internal combustion engine (see Chapter 21). This vast new industry simply had not existed in 1800.

A revolution in communications began in 1876, on the hundredth anniversary of the Decla-

AN INDUSTRIAL VISTA. For millions of Americans, industrial growth was not a miracle but a misery. The steelworkers who lived in these crowded houses and walked along these dirt streets to the Pittsburgh mills often worked twelve hours a day, seven days a week.

ration of Independence. In that year a young inventor named Alexander Graham Bell exhibited the first working model of the telephone. At first, the telephone was purchased only by individuals who wanted to communicate between two specific locations, like a house and a factory or office. But soon there were enough phones in use to create the first telephone exchange. It was opened in New Haven, Connecticut, in 1878. Other cities and towns followed suit.

Soon cities began to link up with one another. The first intercity telephone line joined New York and Boston in 1884. New York and Chicago were connected in 1892. By 1915, when a line opened between New York and San Francisco, it was possible to place calls between any two major cities in the nation.

The magnitude of what was happening to the United States can be measured only in statistics. In 1869 the value of American manufactured goods was about $1.5 billion. By the end of the century the figure was more than $4.5 billion. In 1869 about 2 million workers ran American shops, mills, and factories, and the market value of the average person's yearly output was about $940. By 1900, when almost 5 million men and women worked in industry, the market value of their average yearly product had almost doubled, to nearly $1,800.

By the 1890s the United States had more steel, more rails, more electric trolleys, more telephones, and more electric lights than any other nation in the world. To accomplish all this, Americans mined more metal, cut more lumber, dug more iron ore, and pumped more oil than any other country.

—◦◉◦—

THE GROWTH OF "BIG BUSINESS"

Technology and manufacturing were crucial in making the United States an industrial nation. But new methods of organizing industry and business were also vital.

THE FACTORY SYSTEM

At the beginning of the Civil War, most Americans who worked in industry were employed in small mills or shops—a tailor shop, for example, or a blacksmith's or harnessmaker's. In 1870, when the revolution in industry was already under way, the average industrial plant still had only 8 employees. A median plant (one halfway between the largest and the smallest) had 30 workers. By 1914 the average plant had 28 workers, and the median 270. In 1870 no factory in America employed over 1,000 workers. By 1914 several had over 10,000 workers.

What was occurring, in other words, was a change that went beyond the technology of production. The change was nothing less than a parallel revolution. The factory was replacing the traditional small shop.

In a traditional shop (or in the home manufacture of items like cloth or soap), work centered on the person. Power was supplied mainly through human toil. The same worker was involved in all stages of production, from spinning thread, for example, to weaving the final cloth.

The idea behind a factory (first introduced in England in the late eighteenth century) is very different. Work in a factory centers on a machine. Power is mechanical, not human. Parts are nearly identical, and so they are interchangeable. Most important is the division of labor. Each worker specializes, performing only one step in a chain. He or she may never touch or see the raw material. He or she may never see or handle the final

product. The result is mass production—manufacturing large numbers of articles in standard shapes and sizes.

Factories are inevitably larger than shops. They cost more money to build and equip with machinery. And more capital is needed in order to enter and compete in almost any line of business. As the factory system grew, then, so did the size of companies.

CHANGES IN ORGANIZATION

Growth in turn demanded changes in the organization of business. Mass production required a sizable investment. This made it difficult for family firms to be truly competitive. So large corporations gradually replaced companies owned by one family or a few partners.

The corporation is an old idea, and the idea is as simple as it is old. If many people invest in an enterprise by buying stock in it, the company can grow much larger than if it is funded by only a few individuals. If the company fails, each investor has lost only the value of his or her stock. Individual investors cannot be held personally responsible for any of the corporation's debts.

Just as there had been a few American factories before the Civil War, so had there been corporations. But their number increased greatly after the war. The corporation became the standard way of organizing business, just as the factory became the characteristic method of organizing production.

Mass production required not only corporate investment, but that each firm market its product efficiently on a broad regional or national scale, instead of selling just locally. To remain in business, a corporation had to create effective distributing and selling divisions. It also had to buy raw materials on a large scale. Ideally, in fact, it would purchase its own source of materials—for example, a forest for a paper company, or an iron mine for a steel mill.

In other words, mass production made it profitable for a company to invest in all the stages of its industry, from original materials to final sales. Economists call this phenomenon "vertical integration." It involves a firm not only in manufacturing but in all the other stages and phases relating to the business. An oil company that owns wells, pipelines, and refineries and has its own sales force is fully integrated. It is freed from dependence on any other economic unit—except, of course, customers.

COMPETITION AND CONSOLIDATION

The new industrial order brought a new kind of competition into the American economy. Before the era of mass production, small shops and mills had catered to limited territories. They competed only where one territory bordered on another. But large corporations needed large markets to absorb their massive outputs. Thus a number of companies might find themselves competing for the same customers.

To win a big market, a corporation might advertise heavily. It might hire high-pressure salesmen and reward them with big commissions. But the most obvious way to win a market was to cut prices. A large company with efficient factories and lower production costs could force competitors into bankruptcy simply by lowering prices beyond the point where the smaller firms could stay in business.

In one industry after another, a few corporations gradually emerged as the leading firms. Each was too large, efficient, and powerful to be driven out of business by the others. Each was too small to be able to control the whole market. When this happened—and it happened sooner or later in most industries—the firm usually entered a period of intense competition. But most American businesses did not welcome such competition and tried to find ways to avoid it.

Railroads led the way. Railroad owners had witnessed the havoc and ruin that could be created when one railroad waged a price war with another. By a process of trial and error, the railroads worked out private agreements among themselves to control freight rates. Railroads also

developed a system of grouping their customers in "pools," with each line "entitled" to a certain share of the total market without direct competition. Gradually, too, the railroads had become consolidated into a few major lines, each one absorbing dozens of smaller companies. The Pennsylvania and New York Central railroads dominated the Northeast. The Southern Railway controlled much of the South. The Louisville and Nashville line was supreme in the Ohio Valley.

The agreements and consolidations of the railroads became the models for other businesses. Other industries soon copied what railroad leaders had learned and used the devices they had developed. Consolidation became the order of the day.

No matter what industry was involved, the process was the same. First, a few large, competing firms would emerge. A period of intense and costly competition would follow. Then firms would consolidate as a way of avoiding competition. During its period of rapid growth, the McCormick Harvester Company was competing with a handful of other large manufacturers of agricultural machinery. In the years after the Haymarket affair, however, the McCormicks began to realize that competition was wasteful and unnecessary. Early in the twentieth century, McCormick merged with its competition to form the huge International Harvester Company, which produced practically all the harvesting machinery manufactured in the United States.

A similar kind of "horizontal integration" occurred in the steel industry, which was dominated for almost half a century by a Scottish immigrant, Andrew Carnegie. Carnegie was a classic example of the rags-to-riches success story. At thirteen he came to America with his family and immediately went to work. At eighteen he was a telegraph clerk for the Pennsylvania Railroad. During the rapid railroad expansion of the Civil War years, Carnegie realized that iron and steel for rails and bridges were the key to the railroads' future, and that railroads, in turn, were the key to an expanding economy. He saved every cent and invested daringly but successfully. By 1872 he was able to build his own steel plant near Pittsburgh.

Carnegie's company grew with the industry. By 1890 he was producing almost a third of a million tons of steel. By 1900 this amount had nearly tripled. At the same time, Carnegie worked to achieve vertical integration. He bought iron ore deposits, steamers to transport ore on the Great Lakes, and railroad cars to carry it overland—in fact, everything he needed for making steel.

In the meantime, the process of competition had eliminated all but a few other steel companies. In 1892 the Carnegie company was reorganized to combine seven other corporations in which Carnegie had acquired a controlling interest. In 1901 the largest steel concerns in the nation were all merged into one great new corporation, the United States Steel Corporation. The power behind this consolidation was another dominant figure of the period, J. Pierpont Morgan, a New York banker and financier. Morgan spent nearly half a billion dollars to buy out Carnegie and set up this supercorporation. Like International Harvester, the giant company dominated its industry. It produced almost all of some forms of steel and three-fifths of the total steel made in the United States.

An even more stunning example of consolidation brought John D. Rockefeller into control of the oil industry. Rockefeller started out as a poor boy, like Carnegie. He too saved every cent he could (except for the 10 percent tithe he regularly gave to his Baptist church). Starting with one refinery in Cleveland, Rockefeller by 1872 had created the giant Standard Oil Company.

THE TRUST

Rockefeller also created a new device that made it even easier to consolidate an industry: the trust. A business trust is an arrangement in which several companies "sell" themselves to a single group of "trustees." The companies are paid for with shares in the new trust itself. Only paper changes hands, but the result is a single group of directors who control the operations of several companies.

Through the Standard Oil trust, the Rockefeller interests acquired almost total control of the oil industry. The trust could phase out "unnecessary" plants. It could take full advantage of mass production and distribution techniques to provide most of the kerosene that lighted American lamps and the oil that lubricated American machines. Rockefeller himself summed up the reasons for the trust:

> It has revolutionized the way of doing business all over the world. The time was ripe for it. It had to come, though all we saw at the moment was the need to save ourselves from wasteful conditions [of competition]. The day of combination is here to stay. Individualism has gone, never to return.

One by one, the main American industries passed from competition to consolidation. It might occur through giant corporations created by mergers, like International Harvester or United States Steel. Or it might result from the formation of trusts in various industries, from cottonseed oil to sugar to whiskey. By 1900 a few large concerns controlled almost all the major facilities of production and distribution in the United States.

THE COURTS AND THE CORPORATIONS

The Constitution did not mention corporations, or labor unions, or trusts. It had been drawn up by men who would hardly have been able to imagine the scale of Standard Oil or of Andrew Carnegie's steelworks, and certainly not the billion-dollar realities of the great railroad corporations. And the decisions of the courts affecting corporations during the pre–Civil War period had been about small bridge companies or shipping companies—or even incorporated colleges.

The question now was, how could the Constitution be adapted to the astonishing industrial and corporate developments of the second half of the nineteenth century? What powers did state

CAPITAL AND ITS CHAMPION. One of the favorite subjects for nineteenth-century cartoonists was the trust. Here Capital brings its newest gladiator to the edge of the ring to introduce the victor. The vanquished at the rear include the small dealer and the traveling salesman.

and local governments have to control and regulate the gigantic new enterprises of the period? How would the brief statement in the Constitution that the federal government had the power to regulate interstate commerce be interpreted in an industrial age?

When judges had to decide on the validity of state and local regulation of business, the new legal problem they had to come to terms with was the Fourteenth Amendment, which guaranteed that no state could take away any of the privileges of citizens of the United States. And it extended to the states an old provision—from the Fifth Amendment, in force since 1791—that no person could be deprived of life, liberty, or prop-

erty, without "due process of law." On the other hand, the courts had long recognized that state and local governments had general "police" powers to control the persons in their jurisdictions—including artificial "persons" like corporations. The question now was, did the Fourteenth Amendment protect corporations from the police powers of state and local governments?

This question was put to the Supreme Court very directly in what were known as the Slaughterhouse Cases, decided in 1873. A Louisiana law of 1867 had given one slaughterhouse a monopoly of business in New Orleans by simply ordering all competing meat processors to stop doing business in the city.

The Court ruled—by a bare majority—that Louisiana was in the right. The state had followed all the legal forms in creating the law, and so had satisfied the "due process" requirements of the Fourteenth Amendment. To be sure, the justices admitted, the complaining slaughterers had been deprived of the right to do business. But so long as the state had not violated any legal procedures, the law was a valid exercise of the police power. For the moment, the power of governments to intervene drastically in the conduct of business had been upheld.

RAILROAD CASES

The efforts of railroads to prevent state regulation of their rates had a similar outcome in the 1870s. In several Midwestern states, farmers' movements gained control of state legislatures and pushed through laws controlling the prices charged by railroads and grain elevator companies. The railroads went to court, and the question eventually reached the Supreme Court, in 1877, in the case of *Munn* v. *Illinois*.

The companies argued, in effect, that the states were depriving them of rights and property without due process of law. But the Court refused to go along. The justices made a distinction between types of property and ruled that a railroad or a grain elevator was a special kind of property, devoted to a "public use." This public use created a "public interest" in the property, so the railroads had to submit to being controlled by the public for the common good.

For the moment, the railroads had no option but to go back to the state legislatures to try to get the rate regulations repealed—which they were able to do in the long run. But there had been dissenting votes—four in the Slaughterhouse Cases. And in the next decade, seven new justices would be appointed. Gradually but certainly, the Court would work its way to a new vision of property rights and of the concept of due process of law.

In 1886, in the case of *Stone* v. *Farmers' Loan and Trust Co.*, the Court examined a Mississippi law that had set up a commission with the power to establish railroad rates and fares. The Court upheld the statute but added an important new caution—one that had been absent from the Slaughterhouse Cases and from *Munn* v. *Illinois*: the regulation must set rates that would allow the railroads to make a profit. The problem of regulation was coming to a clear focus on two questions: What was a fair profit for a corporation to expect on its property? And who was going to *decide* what was fair—the legislatures and their commissions? The railroads and other companies? The courts?

The answers came in 1890, in a complicated case known as *Chicago, Milwaukee, and St. Paul Railway Co.* v. *Minnesota*. Corporations, the Court now decided, were not only entitled to own their property, they were entitled to *use* it to make a profit. And state legislatures could not be allowed to decide what was reasonable. Due process of law required a judicial finding of the "reasonableness" of regulation.

In 1898 this opinion received a ringing confirmation in the case of *Smyth* v. *Ames*. The Court set aside a Nebraska law that had set railroad rates directly by enactment and not through any commission. The Court made a very lengthy examination of the company's records and found that the rates set by the legislature were "unreasonable" and so constituted a taking of property without due process of law. The Court had be-

come something new: a type of regulating agency in itself, which would review state and local regulations to determine whether they met the requirements of the "rule of reason."

FEDERAL REGULATION

The occasional efforts of Congress to control corporations and commerce met a similar fate. The Sherman Antitrust Act had outlawed all "combinations in restraint of trade." And if there was a "combination" that seemed clearly devoted to restraining competition, it was the Sugar Trust, a holding company that controlled more than 90 percent of all sugar refining in the United States. But when a federal suit against the company, E. C. Knight, reached the Supreme Court, the Sherman Act was sliced neatly in two. The Court, in *United States* v. *E. C. Knight* (1895), reached the conclusion that the company was not engaged in *commerce* at all, but in *manufacturing*. And since the Constitution did not give the federal government the power to regulate manufacturing, the company was not subject to federal power. Indeed, according to the Court, production of all kinds—in agriculture, mining, and manufacturing—was beyond the reach of congressional legislation.

The Interstate Commerce Act, Congress's second tentative exercise in regulation, was attacked in a slightly more piecemeal way, but the result was no less clear. In 1898, in *Cincinnati, New Orleans, and Texas Pacific Railway Co.* v. *Interstate Commerce Commission*, the Court ruled that the commission did not have the power to establish railroad rates. The justices had already found that rates on interstate shipments could not be controlled by the states. Now they were in effect deciding that such rates could not be set by any governmental authority. The force of the Interstate Commerce Act was reduced to two provisions: that the railroads publish their rate schedules, and that they charge all shippers the same prices. The commission itself was becoming, in the words of a dissenting justice, a "useless body for all practical purposes."

In all the important cases of the 1880s and 1890s, the Court had consistently ruled in favor of the arguments of corporations, and against the regulation of business by either federal or state governments. Later, many legal scholars and historians would come to call the decisions "conservative," even "reactionary." But there was nothing conservative about them. The Court was not protecting legal tradition against innovation. It was *making* innovations, and it was doing so not to protect the past but to sanction the present.

THE NEW AMERICANS

Industry has always needed people to do the work, and the new industrial order needed armies of them. The growth in agriculture, railroads, and industry demanded millions of people.

The American population kept pace with industrial growth. For every 100 people living in the United States in 1870, there were 126 in 1880, 158 in 1890, 190 in 1900, and 230 in 1910. In one generation, the population more than doubled, from about 40 million in 1870 to over 90 million forty years later.

These were the millions who moved into the Great Plains and the Rockies, bringing about the final defeat of the Native Americans. These were the millions who made or bought McCormick's harvesters, who built the railroads that carried his reapers into every flat corner of the country where grain could be planted and harvested by machine.

SHIFTING TRENDS IN IMMIGRATION

These millions, however, were not just more of the same kinds of Americans who had lived in the United States in preceding generations. Many of them were new people—with different languages, different religions, and different ways of life. Before the Civil War, the American "common man" was, most likely, born in America; he was white, Protestant, and a farmer. His parents or grandparents might have been immigrants,

but they would probably have come from England or Scotland. When they arrived here, they would have found the language, the ways of worshiping God, and the customs familiar and comfortable.

But the "common" men and women in 1900 were more likely to be Jews from Poland or Catholics from Italy. They lived in a great city and probably had a job in a factory or a business. Their English might be poor. Their memories of the "old country" would be at least as important to them as their hopes for the new. They represented a social revolution that had accompanied the revolutions in technology, industry, and business—the creation of an urban immigrant working class.

There have been immigrants in America for thousands of years, since people began to cross over from Asia into Alaska. In the hundred years following the American Revolution, the actual proportion of immigrants to the total population did not change much. Two other things happened instead. First, the nature of the immigrant population changed. Second, the immigrants (along with other Americans) began to congregate in great urban centers. These two changes made industrial cities like Chicago the gathering places for a new kind of American: the poor immigrant from a country where English was not spoken and where an Anglo-Saxon Protestant was unheard of.

In 1790, when the United States took its first census under the new Constitution, nine out of ten Americans (except for the black slaves in the South) had English or Scottish ancestors. This pattern changed somewhat with the immigration of the 1840s and 1850s—the "old immigration"—when large numbers of German, Scandinavian, and Irish immigrants began to arrive. Although their languages might be strange to American ears, most of the Germans and Scandinavians were at least Protestants. And although many native-born Americans resented the Catholicism of the Irish, these immigrants at least spoke English. In 1865 the United States had only about 200,000 inhabitants who had been born in

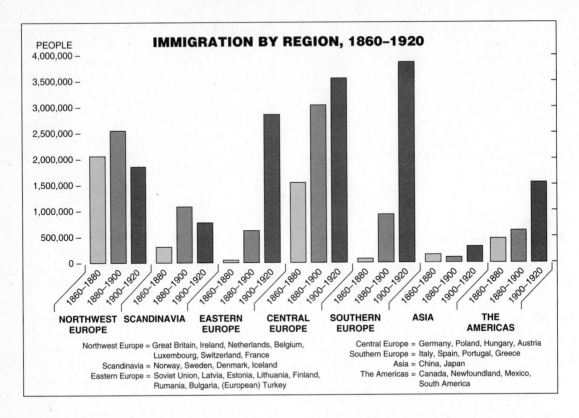

IMMIGRATION BY REGION, 1860–1920

Northwest Europe = Great Britain, Ireland, Netherlands, Belgium,
Luxembourg, Switzerland, France
Scandinavia = Norway, Sweden, Denmark, Iceland
Eastern Europe = Soviet Union, Latvia, Estonia, Lithuania, Finland,
Rumania, Bulgaria, (European) Turkey

Central Europe = Germany, Poland, Hungary, Austria
Southern Europe = Italy, Spain, Portugal, Greece
Asia = China, Japan
The Americas = Canada, Newfoundland, Mexico,
South America

southern or eastern Europe. They were easily absorbed in a total population of about 40 million.

By 1914 this picture had changed dramatically. A "new immigration"—mainly from Italy, Poland, Russia, and Austria-Hungary—flooded into the United States. Poverty drove many of these people from their home countries. Some men left to avoid the military draft, which discriminated against the poor. Jews wanted to escape the official anti-Semitism of Russia and Poland. Armenians fled from persecutions carried out by the Turkish government. The new immigrants were drawn to the United States by advertisements of cheap steamship transportation, by rumors of free land and golden opportunity, and by a massive propaganda campaign conducted by railroads anxious for workers and for customers to buy up their lands.

Immigration from southern and eastern Europe amounted to only a trickle in the 1860s and 1870s. But by the 1890s over half the immigrants

to America were from southern and eastern Europe. Between 1901 and 1910—the peak decade for immigration in the history of the United States—the proportion of new immigrants rose to over 75 percent, as over 6 million Italians, Russian Jews, Hungarians, and other immigrants from southern and eastern Europe poured into the country.

REACTION TO THE NEWCOMERS

The McCormick strike and the Haymarket affair occurred just as the new immigration was about to reach its peak. So the entire Haymarket affair fed off deep prejudices that had been aroused by the entry of Irish and Germans, and by the beginnings of the influx from eastern and southern Europe. Both the McCormick strike and the trial of the Haymarket Eight occurred in an atmosphere of fear and bigotry. The Pinkerton report on the "fighting Irish" molders and the newspaper hysteria about "foreign anarchists" make it clear that events in Chicago would probably have been different if they had not taken place at the time of this bewildering flood of immigrants.

The new immigrants were not only different in culture, language, and religion, they behaved in ways different from those who had preceded them. They moved into a society that was no longer predominantly agricultural and rural, but urban. So they did not fan out onto farms as many of the old immigrants had done. Instead, they followed the lead of millions of other Americans and settled into cities. Two-thirds of foreign-born residents in the United States lived in towns and cities by 1900.

Bewildered and often victimized in America, new immigrants clustered together in their own city neighborhoods, or "ghettos"—originally an Italian word for a segregated neighborhood of Jews. People from a particular European province or even a particular village would move into buildings on the same block, re-creating much of the culture of their Old World homes. As the new immigration swelled, so did antiforeign sentiment. Ghetto dwellers developed a reputation among native Americans for being clannish, dirty, superstitious, and generally undesirable. They were considered "strange," chattering in their old languages, and somehow "suited" only for city life. Actually, of course, they were no more "natural" city dwellers than were the English who had come to Virginia and Massachusetts in the seventeenth century. They were simply caught in a phase of the industrial revolution— the creation of an urban society.

Immigrants from Asia—almost all from China and Japan—were among the most ghetto-bound of the newcomers, rigidly segregated in "Chinatown" communities. And for generations, neither the Asian Americans nor native-born whites believed that they ever could or should become integrated into American life. Most of the Asian immigrants believed that Western civilization was a form of barbarism, something to be resisted in every possible way. Few American officials paid any attention to whether Asian-

American children attended public schools. No one thought it necessary for them to learn English. They were the victims of harassment, cruel jokes, and vicious cartoons. The state of California had special taxes for "foreign" miners. Murderous riots against the Chinese took place in every major western city during the 1870s and 1880s. The Asians' subtle and sophisticated way of cooking attracted some favorable attention, but even their food came into the American diet and language as "chop suey," an unkind culinary joke.

In California, especially, the Chinese immigrants were the objects of a double discrimination. Almost every American of European ancestry believed Asians were "racially inferior." But white workers also resented competition in the labor market, especially during times of economic depression and high unemployment. In the 1870s the California Workingman's party began to agitate for a law forbidding any person from China to hold a job. The effort succeeded. In 1879 a clause was added to the state constitution of California that forbade any employer even to hire Chinese workers. But no state had a constitutional right to forbid immigration. That was up to the national government. In 1882 an act of Congress put a ten-year prohibition on Chinese workers entering the United States as immigrants.

And so the new society that grew out of the industrial revolution was an intensely segregated society. As a result of the railroads and the rush of pioneers to the West, Native Americans were confined to their shrinking reservations. Blacks, Asians, and European immigrants in the towns and cities were just as confined to their ghettos. The very meaning of the word "American," as it was normally used, reflected these racial and ethnic segregations. Being an "American" meant, to most native-born white people, *not* being "colored," *not* being Catholic or Jewish, *not* having Slavic or Greek or Polish ways and words. The two most intensely debated questions of the day among "Americans"—that is, Protestant white people whose ancestry was British or northwest

OPEN-AIR RESTAURANT.   This pair of Chinese Americans have established their restaurant in a lumber camp in the West. Chinese cuisine made its way into the European-American diet only slowly in the nineteenth century. Guidebooks routinely described Chinese restaurants as the "haunts" of the Chinese themselves, and of the European-American poor, "outlaws," and African Americans. It never occurred to the authors of the guidebooks that poor people might not be quite as bigoted as the American-born middle class (and that they might have better taste in food as well).

European—were: What could be done to slow down or stop the "foreigners" from coming? Who among them (if any) had a chance to become "Americans"?

BECOMING "AMERICAN"

The goal of many—perhaps even most—of the new immigrants was to stay in the United States for a time, then return home with enough money to buy land or set up a shop. But the hope of some immigrants was still "assimilation"—to take on the traits of their new society so as to blend with it. But becoming an "American" was not an easy process for most European immigrants in the late nineteenth century.

Real assimilation meant, first, knowing the language. Many immigrant parents made enormous sacrifices to bring their families to a country where education was free and easily available. Mary Antin, a Jewish immigrant, remembered it this way:

Education was free. It was the one thing that my father was able to promise us when he sent for us; surer, safer than bread or shelter. On our second day in the country a little girl across the alley came and offered to conduct us to school. We five children between us had a few words of English by this time. We knew the word "school." We understood. This child, who had never seen us till yesterday, who was not much better dressed than we were, still was able to offer us the freedom of the schools of Boston! No application made; no questions asked; no examinations, rulings, exclusions; no fees.

Learning the language was only one step toward assimilation. Many immigrants joined some kind of voluntary association that brought them contacts with native-born Americans. In cities, the most obvious associations were political parties. They could provide favors, food, and jobs.

"Boss" Richard Croker of the Tammany Hall Democratic party organization in New York described the work of his "machine" as dealing with people who

> do not speak our language and do not know our laws, yet are the raw material with which we have to build up the state. [The Tammany organization] looks after them for the sake of their vote, grafts them upon the Republic, makes citizens of them, in short; and although you may not like our motives or our methods, what other agency is there by which so long a row could have been hoed so quickly or so well?

Another powerful influence on the new immigrants was those who had preceded them. Some of the earlier arrivals learned English and helped recruit workers from Europe. They sometimes even paid the newcomers' transportation and helped them settle in the cities. One popular name for such men was *padrone* (an Italian word meaning, roughly, "patron"). A padrone might be paid by an employer for supplying cheap labor, by a political machine for delivering immigrant votes, or by the immigrants themselves for favors. Often the padrones, who existed among almost every immigrant group, were ward leaders in political machines, serving as links between the newcomers and the city organizations.

URBANIZATION

In the ancient world, only two great cities—Rome and Alexandria—had populations of over half a million people. By the time of Christopher Columbus, Rome and Alexandria had long since declined. The only European cities to have reached a comparable size were London and Paris. At the time of the Haymarket affair, however, Chicago had already become a great city. In fact, by 1900 the United States had six cities with more than half a million inhabitants.

The process of urbanization was not confined to the United States. All the industrializing nations of western Europe experienced it too. The factory system demanded high concentrations of workers, and the agricultural revolution made it possible for millions of people to leave their farms—whether in Germany or in Maine.

The United States experienced three great migrations in the generation after the Civil War. One was from the East to the Great Plains and the Far West. Another was from Europe to America. The third was from the country to the city. Of the three, the movement from farm to city was the most extensive.

In 1800 only about 3 Americans out of every 100 lived in cities larger than 8,000. By 1900 this proportion had grown 1,000 percent; almost one-third of the nation lived in cities of over 8,000. In 1800 there had been only 6 cities larger than 8,000; by 1900 there were over 400.

This increase was not gradual and smooth. Most of it came in the half-century after the end of the Civil War. During this period, at least 15 million native-born Americans moved out of farming areas and into cities, and their number was swollen by an almost equal number of new immigrants who settled in cities instead of on farms. Statistics tell the story. Between 1870 and 1900 the total population of the United States increased by about 35 million people. During the same period the urban population increased by about 24 million. The cities had absorbed more than two-thirds of the total increase.

TECHNOLOGICAL FACTORS

A city is not just a collection of people in a small area. Like industry, modern cities were made possible by technological change. In the centuries

AN EARLY CHICAGO SKYSCRAPER. One of the breakthroughs of the nineteenth century was the steel-frame technique that made possible construction of skyscrapers, like this one in progress in Chicago in 1894. Once the frame was up, the walls could simply hang on the outside of the building, since they no longer had to support the structure.

before the industrial revolution, the size of a city had been determined mainly by the available transportation. It could not be too big, because a person had to be able to walk or travel by wagon or carriage to a marketplace or job and back home again. After about 1880, however, cities began to experience a transportation revolution. The introduction of electricity made it possible to replace slow and awkward horse-drawn transport with fast, clean trolleys, elevated trains, and subways. These improvements meant that people could live many miles from their place of work and still be part of a vast city.

Electricity also made it possible to light city streets effectively. Cleveland, in 1879, became the first city to have electric street lighting. Similarly, the introduction of the telephone in the 1880s meant that homes, offices, and factories could be tied together in an almost instantaneous communications network.

At first, city buildings themselves were a limiting factor. Even with the thickest walls, a

stone or brick building could not extend higher than fifteen stories. To build a structure even this high, builders had to reduce the size of windows, because glass could not support the weight. A second problem was that human legs could tolerate only so many flights of stairs. The first problem was solved by the invention of the skyscraper in the 1880s, pioneered by a Chicago architect, Louis Sullivan. Skyscraper construction, in which walls were hung on steel frames, made structures as tall as a hundred stories possible. Thus more people could be concentrated, level upon level, on smaller parcels of land. The second problem was solved at about the same time by the invention of the electric elevator, which made the tall buildings usable.

⊶═◉═⊷

THE INDUSTRIAL SYSTEM

The new industrial system, with its machines and its factories, had some obvious economic advantages. It could produce more goods, with less labor, and at a lower cost. There were some equally obvious disadvantages. The factories were dirty, noisy, and dangerous. And so were the cities where they were built. Factories could produce only standardized goods, lacking the mark of individual craftsmanship. They undercut the skilled worker's control over the pace and intensity of work. And they drove small producers, using simpler methods, out of business.

Many Americans—perhaps even a majority—were convinced that the advantages outweighed the disadvantages. In fact, most Americans seem to have believed that there was something almost inevitable about industrial "progress."

CONDITIONS OF LABOR

On the other hand, the new system did exploit and oppress many of those who worked in the factories and mills, on the railroads, in the mines, and on the farms. And they knew it. It took no sophisticated economic analysis for a man or woman who worked at a quickened pace from eight in the morning until six at night to under-

AN URBAN VISTA. This was a relatively prosperous, predominantly Jewish neighborhood in lower Manhattan at the end of the nineteenth century. The pedestrians and shoppers are comfortably dressed, and the pushcarts and storefronts offer a bewildering variety of goods and services, including a public bathhouse, an important institution in urban Jewish communities in central and eastern Europe.

stand fatigue. And seven out of ten Americans worked just such a sixty-hour, six-day week—collecting an average of about ten dollars a week in wages. For others, the situation was worse. In the steel industry, the norm was an eighty-four hour, seven-day week.

The average American worker at the end of the nineteenth century was earning about $450 a year. Everyone understood that a family needed about twice that much to live decently. In fact, about $600 a year was necessary to keep out of deep poverty. The difference, of course, had to be made up with the labor of children and, increasingly, women—all pooling miserable wages to try to put together a passable life.

In addition, the character of work itself was changing. In earlier times, the pace and nature of work had been adjusted primarily to people—to

their arms, hands, and tools. But in factories, machinery set the pace, and people had to follow. Skilled workers, especially, understood that the factory threatened their control over the tone and atmosphere of the workplace, and that industrial work tended always to become dull, routine, speeded, and intensely bossed.

Working men and women—and even some of the children—responded to these conditions with complaints, protest, and resistance. On the simplest level, they argued and complained in their factories, challenging their bosses' authority and control. They agreed silently among themselves to slow down their efforts, until the machines themselves had to be adjusted to a more relaxed pace. When they could, they quit jobs and moved on to other towns and other factories. They brought effective emotional pressure to bear on foremen, who often shared their ethnic and religious identifications. They managed to insist, in a dozen different ways and in the most desperate situations, on the simple dignity and independence of the working person.

Increasingly, however, it became clear that individual resistance and sabotage were not going to work, and that something more systematic and organized was necessary. And so working people began a generation-long quest for a method of action that would get results; one that would give them shorter hours, better pay, an increased degree of control over work itself, and perhaps even a larger voice in the way the new industrial society was shaped and managed.

EARLY ATTEMPTS TO ORGANIZE LABOR

One possibility was direct political action: entering party politics, either to support one of the major parties or to find labor candidates. Before the 1890s neither of the two principal parties was much interested in courting the support of organized groups of workers. So the most active workingmen experimented with parties of their own. In 1872 a National Labor Reform party tried to nominate a Supreme Court justice, David Davis, for president. But the candidate refused to run on their ticket. In 1876, labor leaders in the East helped to create a National Independent party, but their candidate won few votes, even among workers. A similar experiment in 1880 brought the same result. Just two years before Haymarket, an Anti-Monopoly party, created in part by labor leaders, was crushed.

With the Democratic and the Republican parties turning a deaf ear, and with third-party politics offering no hope, it was clear that the only possible path was to organize labor itself, not to engage directly in politics.

In 1866, on the initiative of an iron molder who belonged to the same kind of trade union that was so active in the McCormick strike, the National Labor Union was formed. Its leader, William Sylvis, conceived it as a reform union. It included temperance groups and women's suf-frage groups as well as trade union organizations. And it repudiated the traditional last resort of workers, the strike. This union made little or no headway and lasted only about seven years.

A much more promising organization was the Noble Order of the Knights of Labor, created in 1869 by a tailor in Philadelphia. Its plan was to organize all workers—skilled and unskilled, farm and factory, male and female, even black and white—in one grand union. In fact, the Knights specifically excluded only four types of people, whom they labeled "parasites": liquor dealers, bankers, professional gamblers, and lawyers. Like the National Labor Union, the Knights of Labor officially discouraged strikes and favored, instead, the education of workers and owners.

For a decade, the Knights grew slowly. Then leadership passed to an extraordinarily handsome and magnetic machinist from Pennsylvania, Terence V. Powderly. Powderly dropped an old rule making the Knights' ritual, rules, and membership a fraternal secret. In turn, the Catholic Church dropped its official opposition, and membership began to increase. Still, Powderly opposed strikes and talked as though he did not represent workers at all but men who were anxious to become small capitalists: "I shudder at the thought of a strike," he said. "We must give men the chance to become their own employers."

But it was a strike that skyrocketed the Knights to prominence and to a remarkable rise in membership. Some of the local assemblies decided to stage a "wildcat" strike against the Texas and Pacific Railroad in 1885. Surprisingly, the railroad met their demands. The word spread quickly along the railroad lines, and within a year the Knights suddenly had 700,000 members—a tripling of their rolls.

The Knights of Labor was not involved in the McCormick strike of 1886, and only indirectly in the Haymarket affair. But the organization was one of the principal victims of the public hysteria that followed the bombing and shooting in Chicago. Membership began to fall, and when the railroad assemblies were soundly beaten in a second strike against the Texas and Pacific in the

CHILD LABOR. Working-class families were usually unable to support themselves on a father's earnings, so others had to take jobs. In many ethnic communities, there was a much stronger prejudice against women working than against children, so boys and girls found themselves in mills and mines. (Often, though, working-class families had no choice but to put women *and* children to work.) One result was the haunting faces of children like this scratched and dazed boy, whose ten-hour-a-day job was to carry mats bigger than he was.

same year, the disaster was complete. By 1890, 600,000 men and women had deserted the Noble Order, and it was, for all practical purposes, dead.

Meanwhile, another type of labor organization was building, one that would eventually become the most successful and characteristic in American society. In 1881 a group of craft unions formed the Federation of Organized Trades and Labor Unions. The principles of this organization were clear from the outset. First, it was concerned with skilled workers, not with trying to organize the industrial "masses." Second, they would use the strike as a weapon—as a last resort. Third, they were concerned strictly with wages, hours, and working conditions—not with politics, social reform, or other kinds of "utopian" schemes.

Here was "unionism pure and simple," as the members liked to say. Under the leadership of an immigrant cigar maker, Samuel Gompers, and under a new name, the American Federation of Labor, the organization made steady gains. By the end of the century, it had half a million mem-

KNIGHTS OF LABOR. The Knights of Labor held out the hope, for a brief time, of racial integration in the labor movement. Here, at an 1886 annual convention of the Knights in Richmond, Virginia, an African-American delegate, Frank J. Farrell, has just finished introducing the visionary leader of the Knights, General Master Workman Terence Powderly. The artist has carefully shown the audience looking and gesturing enthusiastically toward Farrell, not Powderly.

bers (and a dozen years later, it would boast of 2 million).

STRIKES AND STRIKEBREAKERS

Large national unions were destined to be part of American life. But for most people, the "labor question" focused not so much on unions as on a series of spectacular outbreaks of violence that rocked a society that had never witnessed anything of the sort on such a scale. For a generation—from the 1870s until after the turn of the century—it seemed possible that American society might actually be divided between rich and poor, owners and workers, in an increasingly desperate class struggle. This was, in fact, the atmosphere that fed the hysteria of Haymarket. And it was an atmosphere that intensified in every decade.

In 1877, the first year of Rutherford B. Hayes's presidency, four large railroads in the East announced a 10 percent cut in wages. The result was a sudden strike that paralyzed rail traffic all over the country. Crowds of workers stopped trains and occupied railroad buildings and roundhouses. In Pittsburgh, especially, the strikers' control seemed to be almost complete. Finally, in July, a frightened Hayes administration sent troops to restore "order"—that is, to break the strike. There was resistance. Nervous soldiers fired. Angry workers burned. In Pittsburgh a three-mile-long fire destroyed 160 locomotives and hundreds of freight cars.

Nine years later came Haymarket, less violent and destructive, but just as frightening to those Americans who feared that "radicals" were out to promote "anarchy" or "communism."

Then, in 1892, six years after Haymarket, a Carnegie Steel plant at Homestead, Pennsylvania, was struck after the company announced pay cuts. The management asked the Pinkerton company to bring in several hundred armed "guards"—"goons" and "gun-thugs," the strikers called them. The Pinkerton men came on barges, down the river that ran next to the Homestead plant. The striking workers met them, as heavily armed. Someone fired, and before the guns had stopped several hours later, seven men were dead and many more wounded. In response, the governor of Pennsylvania sent in the entire state national guard, some 8,000 troops—as usual, to restore "order." The strike was broken. The men who had remained anonymous enough drifted back to work. The others simply drifted away.

Two years later, in Illinois, a similarly angry and violent strike occurred, bringing back memories of Haymarket on both sides. George Pullman, who held a monopoly on the manufacture of sleeping coaches and parlor cars, had built what he boasted was a model industrial town near Chicago. Workers lived in company houses, bought in company stores, attended churches built and controlled by the company, and—mostly—worked for the company.

Most of the Pullman workers were members of the militant American Railway Union, led by the greatest of American union leaders, Eugene Victor Debs. A confrontation was almost certain when, in response to a depression, Pullman announced a 25 percent cut in wages, but with no cuts in the rents of company houses or the prices in company stores. The workers struck, and Debs called on all 150,000 members of his union to refuse to move any train with a Pullman coach. Railroads everywhere fired any of Debs's men who refused to handle Pullmans. When this happened, the union called a strike against the offending railroad. In a few days, railroads from Chicago to the West, as well as many in the East, were paralyzed.

Once again, the solution was military. President Grover Cleveland sent federal troops into Chicago to "protect the mails," even though Illinois' governor John Peter Altgeld—who had par-

doned the surviving Haymarket defendants—objected. The strike collapsed. Debs went to prison. And Americans on both sides of the struggle seemed to have new evidence that industrial revolution might have more revolutionary consequences than they had at first imagined.

AMERICAN CULTURE, 1875–1900

Economically and socially, the most important facts about American society in the period following the Civil War were industrialization, urbanization, and immigration. These facts together brought about a change in the landscape that was almost brutally obvious—the crowded, dirty, smoky city, with its alien working class. But people very often did not or would not see or acknowledge what was most plain. In their art and architecture, their novels and magazines—in all the areas of their culture—native, white, middle-class Americans seemed determined to ignore the realities of their age.

At both the popular and the sophisticated level, middle-class culture seemed almost serene in its lack of awareness of industrial capitalism and its social consequences. To some extent, of course, the practice of ignoring, evading, or denying reality is a characteristic of culture in any society. But Americans in the 1870s and 1880s were abnormally, almost absurdly, consistent in their unwillingness to come to terms culturally with the actualities around them.

LITERATURE

This characteristic of American culture was not confined to the sentimental and quaint books and essays published for a middle-class, primarily female audience. It was evident in the most talented and sophisticated intellectuals, too. Henry James wrote great novels and stories, as great as any ever published in English. But they were about the elegant and complicated lives of wealthy Americans and were usually set in Europe. Even when one of James's heroes was a businessman, as in *The American* (1876), he appeared in the novel only after he had made his fortune and arrived in Europe in pursuit of "culture" and an aristocratic French bride.

Henry James was born to wealth, cultivated society, and European travel. Samuel Clemens was born in Missouri into a modestly well-to-do family and spent much of his life scratching for a living as a journalist. As "Mark Twain," he wrote about plain people. But his plain people were not immigrants or factory workers. And his settings were the small towns of the Mississippi, where boyish and innocent characters like Huckleberry Finn and Tom Sawyer had their "adventures." *Huckleberry Finn* (1885) was a great novel by almost any standard. But it was hardly a novel that confronted American social realities. Clemens lived in Hartford, Connecticut, a modern city; he was married to the daughter of a coal baron. But the closest he came to an examination of such matters was when he fantasized about the experience a technologically inventive "Yankee" might have if he suddenly woke up in medieval England, as in *A Connecticut Yankee in King Arthur's Court* (1889).

What was true of Mark Twain and Henry James was equally true of lesser talents. Even when novels were about businessmen—as in William Dean Howells's *The Rise of Silas Lapham* (1884)—the real subject seemed to be not business but high society and romance, and the action occurred after the fortune was acquired. Edward Bellamy's *Looking Backward* (1888), one of the most popular novels of the period, was a utopian romance about Boston in the year 2000. Bellamy's utopia was, in theory at least, highly industrialized, urbanized, and socialistic. And the response of middle-class readers was enthusiastic. But beneath its appearance of relevance to nineteenth-century realities, *Looking Backward* really described a small, pleasant Boston, from which the factories, the poor, and the immigrants had disappeared as though by magic.

In the 1890s, a few books did try to deal with the more sordid aspects of factory and slum life. Jacob Riis's *How the Other Half Lives* (1890) described a slum in vivid language that alarmed his primarily middle-class, native audience:

> Cherry Street. Be a little careful, please! The hall is dark and you might stumble over the children pitching pennies back there. Not that it would hurt them: kicks and cuffs are their daily diet. They have little else. Here where the hall turns and dives into utter darkness is a step, and another, another. A flight of stairs. You can feel your way, if you cannot see it. Close? Yes! What would you have? All the fresh air that ever enters these stairs comes from the hall-door that is forever slamming, and from the windows of dark bedrooms.

Stephen Crane's *Maggie: A Girl of the Streets* (1893) was a dark account of the way slum poverty turned innocent girls to sordid lives. But such books came only after decades of industrialization. And they created almost as much scandal as if they had been about sexual perversion. For the most part, native-born writers and other intellectuals provided no insight whatever into the lives and difficulties of the new, immigrant, urban working class.

On the level of popular culture, the picture was much the same. A revolution in printing technology had made inexpensive books and magazines easily available, and a flood of popular fiction poured off the new steam-driven presses. But most of the stories and books dealt with rural life or with the doings of chaste and sentimental small-town girls; or they had as their heroes idealized Western cowboys, romantic sailors, or heroic figures from ancient history.

A new type of popular fiction did emerge after the Civil War: the tale of business success. The most notable promoter of the rags-to-riches formula was a Harvard-educated former clergyman, Horatio Alger. His *Ragged Dick: Or, Street Life in New York* (1867) was a sensational bestseller. For the next thirty years Alger sold over 200 million copies of his stories, with titles like *Jed the Poor-House Boy* and *Struggling Upward*.

Superficially, at least, the Alger stories reflected important economic realities. But the

THE LURE OF SUCCESS. More than any popular writer of his time, Horatio Alger captured the essence of the dream of success that attracted many American youths from the countryside into the cities. This was the cover for one of Alger's many novels, *From Farm to Fortune*. It is a "before and after" depiction of the sudden rise of a farmer's son to urban wealth. He has exchanged his hunting rifle for a business document, but the artist is careful to suggest that the transition need not endanger the innocent virtue of a young man of good character.

reflection was indirect and distorted. Alger did not deal with the adult, business careers of his heroes. Instead, he wrote coy exercises in moralism, designed to show how Ragged Dick or Tattered Tom or Poorhouse Jed overcame orphanhood and poverty by saving the drowning daughter of a wealthy, sonless merchant. The books always ended just as their heroes were about to embark on adult careers in commerce. The reader was left to assume that, in their adult lives, Alger's heroes

would continue to thrive through a steady application of "pluck."

ART AND ARCHITECTURE

The practice of turning away from economic and social realities that was so central to the literature of the 1870s and 1880s was equally characteristic of the art and architecture of those decades. The greatest American artist of the period, James McNeill Whistler, painted mostly portraits and nocturnal landscapes. When Whistler did depict a scene of contemporary social or economic activity, the subject was more likely to be European than American.

Most artists confined themselves to painting scenes of nature, domestic life, or portraits of the wealthy in which the sources of wealth were carefully ignored. Winslow Homer, who probably was the second most talented American painter of the period, used his muscular and vivid style primarily on seascapes or on small New England village life. When Homer did paint men at work, they were almost always fishermen in aged, wooden boats—an ardently preindustrial subject.

Architecture was even more flagrantly systematic in denying the actualities of industrialism. The expanding society of the period required an enormous number of new buildings—campuses for colleges and universities; buildings for banks and corporations; homes and summer houses for new millionaires; railroad stations; and so on. But even the most talented architects were mired in a contest to restore ancient styles. The familiar, reliable Greek and Roman styles that had been so popular since the Revolution were pressed into service again. There was an astonishing revival of Gothic and Georgian, especially in campus architecture. And anyone could stare for days at the largest of the new railroad stations, with their Greek columns or baroque decorations, without gaining any clue as to what the function of the building actually was. In their buildings, as in their novels and paintings, Americans seemed more intent on disguising the industrial revolution than in celebrating it.

CHRONOLOGY

1866	William Sylvis founds National Labor Union
1867	Horatio Alger publishes *Ragged Dick, Or, Street Life in New York*
1869	Knights of Labor founded in Philadelphia
1870	Railway track mileage in United States reaches 40,000;
	Two decades of mob violence against Asian Americans begins
1872	John D. Rockefeller founds Standard Oil Company;
	Andrew Carnegie builds steel plant near Pittsburgh, Pennsylvania;
	National Labor party attempts to nominate Supreme Court Justice David Davis for president; he refuses
1876	Alexander Graham Bell exhibits working telephone;
	Eastern labor leaders form National Independent party;
	Henry James publishes *The American*
1877	Administration of Rutherford B. Hayes begins;
	Railroad strike paralyzes eastern lines; Hayes uses military to restore "order"
1878	First working telephone system installed in New Haven, Connecticut
1879	California constitution forbids employers to hire Chinese workers;
	Cleveland, Ohio, becomes first American city with electric lighting system
1880	"New" immigration from central, eastern, and southern Europe begins rapid acceleration;
	Terence Powderly assumes leadership of Knights of Labor;
	Labor leaders form Anti-Monopoly party
1881	Administration of James A. Garfield and Chester A. Arthur begins;
	Federation of Organized Trades and Labor Unions, forerunner of American Federation of Labor, founded
1882	Federal law places ten-year prohibition on immigration of Chinese workers into United States
1884	Chicago architect Louis Sullivan begins to pioneer "skyscraper" architecture;
	First intercity telephone line opened between New York and Boston;

1884 (cont'd)	McCormick Harvester Works shows 71 percent profit; cuts workers' wages 10 to 15 percent;
	William Dean Howells publishes *The Rise of Silas Lapham*
1885	Administration of Grover Cleveland begins;
	Strike at McCormick Works; 1884 pay cuts restored;
	McCormick installs new molding machinery;
	Knights of Labor hold successful strike against Texas and Pacific Railroad;
	Mark Twain publishes *Huckleberry Finn*
1886	McCormick workers join Metalworkers Union and Knights of Labor;
	Strike at McCormick, and general strike in Chicago for eight-hour day;
	Haymarket bombing and police riot;
	Four men hanged for Haymarket "conspiracy";
	Knights of Labor begins rapid decline after failed strike against Texas and Pacific railroad
1888	Edward Bellamy publishes *Looking Backward*
1889	Administration of William Henry Harrison begins;
	Mark Twain publishes *A Connecticut Yankee in King Arthur's Court*
1890	Jacob Riis publishes *How the Other Half Lives*
1892	Telephone connection completed between New York and Chicago;
	Strike at Carnegie steel plant at Homestead, Pennsylvania, broken up by National Guard troops
1893	Cleveland's second term begins;
	Beginning of severe economic depression;
	Stephen Crane publishes *Maggie, a Girl of the Streets*
1894	American Railway Union strike at Pullman Railway Car Company near Chicago; President Cleveland orders federal troops to Chicago; strike broken, and its leader, Eugene Victor Debs, imprisoned
1900	Railway track mileage in United States reaches 200,000;
	United States becomes world's leading manufacturing nation
1901	United States Steel Company founded

＊→◎←＊

SUGGESTIONS FOR FURTHER READING

THE McCORMICK STRIKE AND THE HAYMARKET BOMBING

The most recent study of the Haymarket affair is Paul Arvich, *The Haymarket Tragedy* (1984). But Henry David, *History of the Haymarket Affair* (1936), is still worth reading. The strike at the McCormick plant is discussed in Robert Ozanne, *A Century of Labor and Management Relations at McCormick and International Harvester* (1959).

TECHNOLOGICAL CHANGE

The most curious and interesting study of technological change during this phase of the industrial revolution is an aging book by Lewis Mumford, *Technics and Civilization* (1934). A breezier book is Roger Burlingame, *The Engines of Democracy* (1940). Matthew Josephson, *Edison* (1959), is a fine biographical study of one of the most important innovators of the period, as is Robert V. Bruce, *Bell: Alexander Graham Bell and the Conquest of Solitude* (1973). The best places to begin the study of railroads are Alfred Chandler, *The Railroads, the Nation's First Big Business* (1965), and Robert Fogel, *Railroads in American Economic Growth* (1964). Chandler stresses the significance of railroad development; Fogel casts doubt on it. See also Oscar Winther, *The Transportation Frontier: The Trans-Mississippi West, 1865–1890* (1964), and John F. Stover, *American Railroads* (1961). The best general book on agriculture in the Middle West is still Fred A. Shannon, *The Farmer's Last Frontier* (1963).

MANUFACTURING

A very useful survey is David Hounshell, *From the American System to Mass Production* (1984). The basic industries can be approached through these special studies: Peter Temin, *Iron and Steel in Nineteenth-Century America: An Economic Inquiry* (1964); J. F. Wall, *Andrew Carnegie* (1971); Harold Livesay, *Andrew Carnegie and the Rise of Big Business* (1975); Alfred D. Chandler, *Strategy and Structure: Chapters in the History of Industrial Enterprise* (1962); Ralph W. and Muriel E. Hidy, *Pioneering in Big Business, 1882–1911: A History of Standard Oil* (1955); and John Ingham, *Iron Barons: A Social Analysis of an American Urban Elite* (1978). Two

excellent studies of the technological impact of electricity are Andre Millard, *Edison and the Business of Innovation* (1990), and David E. Nye, *Electrifying America* (1990). A challenging analysis of the role of the corporation is Martin J. Sklar, *The Corporate Reconstruction of American Capitalism* (1988).

IMMIGRATION

A very readable introduction to the general problem of immigration is Philip Taylor, *The Distant Magnet: European Immigration to the U.S.A.* (1971). Humbert Nelli, *The Italians in Chicago, 1880–1930* (1970), and Thomas Kessner, *The Golden Door: Italian and Jewish Immigrant Mobility in New York City, 1880–1915* (1977), are two of the better studies of particular immigrant experiences. Josef Barton, *Peasants and Strangers* (1975), treats the experiences of Italians, Slovaks, and Romanians in an urban setting. Andrew Rolle, *The Italian Americans* (1980), is excellent, as is Helen Znaniecki Lopata, *Polish Americans* (1976). On Asian Americans, see Jack Chen, *The Chinese of America* (1980), William Peterson, *Japanese Americans* (1971), and Yusi Ichioka, *The Issei: The World of the First Japanese Immigrants, 1885–1924* (1988). Immigrant women are skillfully treated in Elizabeth Ewen, *Immigrant Women in the Land of Dollars* (1985), and Judith E. Smith, *Family Connections* (1985). Urban public education is the subject of Lawrence A. Cremin, *American Education: The Metropolitan Experience* (1988).

URBANIZATION

Howard P. Chudacoff and Judith E. Smith, *The Evolution of American Urban Society,* 4th ed. (1993), is a useful survey of the subject, as is David Goldfield and Blaine Brownell, *Urban America,* 2d ed. (1990). The transformation of Boston from a small center with a number of outlying towns into a major city is a model of what happened to American cities during this period. The process can be followed in Sam Bass Warner's fine book, *Streetcar Suburbs: The Process of Growth in Boston, 1870–1900* (1962). The same author's *The Urban Wilderness* (1972) is a good introduction to urban history. These general books are also extremely useful: Howard Chudacoff, *Evolution of American Urban Society* (1981); Zane Miller, *The Urbanization of America* (1973); Constance M. Green, *The*

Rise of Urban America (1965); and Raymond Mohl, *The New City: Urban America in the Industrial Age* (1985). Thomas L. Philpott, *The Slum and the Ghetto* (1978), provides an excellent treatment of black and immigrant life in Chicago. Martin Melosi, *Garbage and the Cities* (1982), is a fascinating and important book. An excellent study of urban politics is Jon C. Teaford, *The Unheralded Triumph: City Government in America, 1870–1900* (1984).

THE INDUSTRIAL SYSTEM

Two fine places to begin are Herbert Gutman's collection of essays, *Work, Culture and Society in Industrializing America* (1976), and David Montgomery, *Workers' Control* (1979). David Brody's study of the steelworkers, *Steelworkers in America: The Nonunion Era* (1960), is one of the best of the works on particular industries. The shaping of the Pullman world is sympathetically treated in Stanley Buder, *Pullman: An Experiment in Industrial Order and Community Planning, 1880–1930* (1967). A different view of the matter is Ray Ginger's very readable *The Bending Cross: A Biography of Eugene Victor Debs* (1969), which should be supplemented by the more recent study by Nick Salvatore, *Eugene V. Debs, Citizen and Socialist* (1982). A good brief survey is Joseph Rayback, *A History of American Labor* (1959). The contest between the industrial unions and the craft unions is detailed very nicely in Gerald N. Grob, *Workers and Utopia* (1961). Labor radicalism is discussed in John Laslett, *Labor and the Left* (1970). An excellent discussion of the social consequences of industrialism is Thomas J. Schlereth, *Victorian America: Transformations in Every-*

day Life (1991). Two other important books are Peter Shergold, *Working-Class Life* (1982), and Roy Rosenzweig, *Eight Hours for What We Will* (1983). For women as workers, see the Suggestions for Further Reading for Chapter 18.

AMERICAN CULTURE, 1875–1900

Gunther Barth, *City People* (1980), is a good introduction to the leisure-time activities of urban Americans during the period. Another very useful study is Robert V. Snyder, *The Voice of the City: Vaudeville and Popular Culture in New York City, 1880–1920* (1990). Perry Duis, *The Saloon* (1983), and John Kasson, *Amusing the Millions: Coney Island at the Turn of the Century* (1978), are also important. But the most brilliant study of popular culture in the period is David Nasaw's *Going Out: The Rise and Fall of Public Amusements* (1993). The leisure-time activities of women workers is very well treated in Kathy Peiss, *Cheap Amusements: Working Women and Leisure in Turn-of-the-Century New York* (1986). Henry F. May, *The End of American Innocence* (1959), contains a very readable survey of the cultural life of the last decades of the nineteenth century. On writers, a good introduction is Jay Martin, *Harvest of Change: American Literature, 1865–1914* (1967). One of the most interesting ways to approach the culture of the Gilded Age is through Lewis Mumford, *The Brown Decades: The Arts in America, 1865–1895* (1931). On art and architecture, see Oliver W. Larkin, *Art and Life in America* (1949), and John Burchard and Albert Bush-Brown, *The Architecture of America: A Social and Cultural History* (1966).

A New West

THE EPISODE: *A few days before the year 1890 ended, near the banks of a small creek deep in the Dakotas, occurred the last major armed struggle between Native Americans and the army of the United States. Some people called what happened that morning at Wounded Knee Creek a battle. Others called it a massacre. It was really some of both. Sioux warriors and the men of the United States Seventh Cavalry began shooting at the same time. That began what might be called a battle. But the Sioux had their women and children with them, and the cavalry rifles and cannon made no distinctions of age or sex. When the shooting finally stopped, only about half the Sioux dead were men, many of them unarmed. The other Sioux bodies were women and children. And some cavalrymen had lost discipline during the combat and pursued fleeing, unarmed Sioux of both sexes and cut them down with bullets or sabers. So Wounded Knee can fairly be called a massacre. But the exact word for it did not matter much to the people involved. What had really happened was the end of a long, sometimes heroic, and often tragic struggle by the Sioux people to maintain their civilization and culture against the advance of the European Americans.*

THE HISTORICAL SETTING: *The Sioux were only one of many Native-American groups who, during the closing decades of the nineteenth century, had their lands taken, their cultures severely damaged, and* their people herded onto reservations that were sometimes hundreds of miles from their original homelands. Whites were moving into the Pacific Coast, the Sierras, and the Rockies, and onto the Great Plains with explosive speed and energy. The lures were many: gold in California, Colorado, and Nevada; traces and rumors of gold and silver in other areas like the Dakotas' Black Hills; a cattle bonanza in the Southwest; seemingly endless stretches of farm and timber land that could be had for next to nothing under federal land policies designed to promote westward migration.*

The drama of Wounded Knee was a moment in the long and unhappy story of the systematic attempt of European Americans to destroy a civilization they did not understand and to take for their own uses the lands that had sustained it. The Native Americans had little chance to keep their cultures intact. One by one the western tribes were forced to choose between accepting a miserable half-life on the reservations or attempting a futile and usually deadly resistance.

This chapter is the third that deals with the last decades of the nineteenth century. It shows how the political system discussed in Chapter 15 did little to control westward expansion. It also shows that the industrial revolution, discussed in Chapter 16, had consequences that reached far beyond the manufacturing cities of the East and hastened the brutal suppression of Native American ways of life.

MASSACRE AT WOUNDED KNEE

There was a confusion about names—there almost always was when Native Americans were involved. Most whites called the tribes the Sioux. But they called themselves the Dakota. There was also more than one Indian name for what whites called Wounded Knee Creek, on the Pine Ridge Reservation in South Dakota. And some people called what had happened at Wounded Knee Creek a battle, but others called it a massacre. Even the man who rode out from reservation headquarters to Wounded Knee Creek on New Year's Day, 1891, had two names. One was a Native-American name, Ohiyesa. The other was a white man's name, Charles Eastman. He was a Sioux, but he had been educated in white schools in New England. In fact, he was a doctor of medicine—white medicine.

But there was no confusion about what Charles Eastman saw on that snowy morning:

> On the day following the Wounded Knee massacre, there was a blizzard. On the third day it cleared, and the ground was covered with fresh snow. We had feared that some of the wounded Indians had been left on the field, and a number of us volunteered to go and see.
>
> Fully three miles from the scene of the massacre, we found the body of a woman completely covered with a blanket of snow, and from this point on we found them scattered along as they had been hunted down and slaughtered. When we reached the spot where the Indian camp had stood, among the fragments of burned tents and other belongings, we saw the frozen bodies lying close together or piled one upon another. I counted eighty bodies of men, who were almost as helpless as the women and babes when the deadly gun fire began, for nearly all their guns had been taken from them.
>
> Although they had been lying in the snow and cold for two days and nights, a number had survived. Among them I found a baby of about a year old, warmly wrapped and entirely unhurt. Under a wagon, I discovered an old woman, totally blind and helpless.

Eastman began to load the few survivors into wagons to return to the agency (reservation headquarters), where he had set up a small hospital. Two groups of white men stayed behind at Wounded Knee. One was a troop of the U.S. Seventh Cavalry. The other was a group of about thirty white civilians who had agreed to bury the dead (at a charge to the government of two dollars a body). They found the body of the chief of the band, an old man named Big Foot, frozen half sitting, half lying down. Ill with pneumonia, he had been lying on a blanket on the frozen ground when the shooting had started.

It took until the next day to dig a big, open grave. Then the bodies were gathered. Under an unusually strong January sun, the gravediggers sweated; many worked in

CHIEF BIG FOOT.   The body of Big Foot, the leader of the Sioux band that was massacred at Wounded Knee, waits, frozen, for the burial party of whites shown in the background. He is wearing mostly white man's clothing. His frozen body is wrenched into a half-sitting position and is partially covered with the snow that fell after the massacre.

their shirtsleeves. They stacked 146 dead Sioux—128 men and women and 18 children—in the pit. A commercial photographer, representing the "North Western Photo Co." had made the long trip from Nebraska to get a "scoop." He persuaded a mixed group of cavalrymen and civilian gravediggers to pose in a half-circle around the open grave and the stiffened bodies of the Sioux dead. Then the men shoveled dirt into the grave, covering the bodies. When the diggers and the cavalry rode away, nothing was left at Wounded Knee but the fresh soil of the mass grave and the charred poles of the tepees that Big Foot's people had put up only a few days before.

Wounded Knee was the last and most tragic moment in a long and often ugly process: the conquest of the Sioux Indians. The conquerors were the white citizens and blue-coated soldiers of the United States. The process began before the Civil War. At that time the Sioux were a powerful tribe, probably numbering well over 20,000. They hunted on thousands of square miles of the plains west of the Missouri River.

The Sioux had resisted the invasion of white miners, farmers, and ranchers. They fought often, and they usually won. In the summer of 1876 they had won two astonishing victories. At Rosebud Creek, in what is now Montana, they had attacked a large column of cavalry and infantry and forced the soldiers into a retreat. Then, just a few days later, the Seventh Cavalry, with Colonel George Armstrong Custer commanding, attacked a large Sioux camp on the Little Bighorn River, just a few miles from the Rosebud. Custer divided his force, and the Sioux killed Custer as well as over 200 men of the Seventh, which was one of the most experienced cavalry units operating in the West.

But there were too many soldiers. Though the Sioux were never defeated, they finally had to surrender. In 1877, just a year after Custer's last stand, the great war chief Crazy Horse led many of his followers onto a reservation that had been recently set aside for the Sioux. Crazy Horse was murdered a short time later. Some of his people fled to Canada to join another outstanding Sioux leader, Sitting Bull. About 2,500 Sioux then tried to survive in Canada. But hunger and cold—and the fact that white people had slain most of the buffalo that were so essential to Sioux survival—finally drove them to the reservation. In 1881 Sitting Bull surrendered—"came in," as it was called. This was the end of a golden age for the Sioux, one that had lasted more than a century.

Before white Europeans had come to North America, the Sioux had lived very much like the Native Americans of the eastern seaboard. Their territory was not the open plains of the Dakotas but the woods and lakes of Minnesota and Wisconsin. There they had built permanent bark houses, used canoes, and hunted small game. They had also farmed. This life was disturbed by indirect contact with white civilization. The Sioux were driven out of their woodlands and onto the Great Plains by another tribe, the Ojibwas, who had come into contact with the French in Canada and had obtained guns in trade for furs. The guns gave the Ojibwas an overwhelming advantage, and the Sioux had had to retreat to the west and south, out onto the inhospitable Great Plains.

But what began as a painful retreat soon turned into a triumphant new life. Gradually, the Sioux themselves obtained guns. They also discovered another European import, the wild horses descended from the mounts the Spanish had brought into Mexico and the Southwest. Together, these European tools, the horse and the rifle, transformed the Sioux culture. For the first time, they could successfully hunt buffalo. The plains were transformed from a barren, hostile environment into a hunting paradise. The buffalo herds became a source of meat, clothing, and shelter. The old bark houses gave way to hide-covered tepees that could be moved from one hunting area to another. This nomadic life brought the Sioux into contact (and conflict) with other Plains tribes. Hunting and warfare became the central focus of the Sioux economy and culture. For men, status in the tribe became dependent on skill and bravery in hunts and skirmishes. To a Sioux man, the tools of the hunt—his ponies, his rifle, his bow and arrows—were everything. The rituals of hunting and warfare gave meaning to his life. Any work that was not part of hunting, like preparing hides or drying meat or gathering berries, belonged to women. By the early part of the nineteenth century, the new society the Sioux had built on the plains was confident and expanding. They hunted all the way from the Missouri River to the valleys of the Big Horn Mountains on the eastern edge of the Rockies.

But almost as soon as this civilization was established, it was challenged. The whites, with their cannon, their railroads and telegraphs, their plows and fences, and their reservations, eventually destroyed the Sioux way of life. The whites slaughtered buffalo by the thousands, until practically none were left. Then the whites insisted that the Sioux live again in permanent houses, on the reservations. Government rations of beef, flour, and beans were substituted for the hunt. It did not help much if an agent sometimes allowed the men to mount their horses and "hunt" their twice-monthly ration of cattle. Games like this could not replace the old life. The authority of warriors and chiefs had depended on their skill in violent and dangerous activities. Reservation life was, above all, peaceful. The white agents even forbade the most holy annual ritual of the Sioux, the Sun Dance. And they insisted, too, that the men of the tribe could have only one wife.

What was happening was simple and, from the Sioux point of view, tragic. They had been defeated by a much more powerful and complex society. Some of them—the ones the whites referred to as the "nonprogressives"—might resist in a few ways. They could reject the cotton shirts and trousers of the white man and continue to wear their traditional clothing. They could insist on keeping their hair in the traditional long braids. But resistance could not revive the old life. They had long ago accepted some of the white ways and tools. The horse and the rifle had been useful in the old life. But the government, with the "Great Father" president at its head, had plans for the Sioux that were utterly at odds with the old ways.

American policy was aimed at one long-range goal: to make each Native American family into a self-supporting farming unit. In the old life, the tribal band, not the family, had been the basic social unit. The band moved, hunted, ate, and worshiped together, and families tended to merge imperceptibly with the common life of the band. The white vision saw each family gathered in its own log house, wearing white people's clothes, huddled around its own, private fire (the white man's stove), and, preferably, worshiping the white God instead of the old Sioux god, Wakan Tanka. To well-intentioned reformers in the East, this meant raising the Indian to "civilization." To many whites in the West, it meant a final end to the Indian as a barrier to westward expansion.

For the Sioux, it all meant a divided world. Even those who wanted to cooperate most, the so-called "progressives," lived a double life. A man might put on white clothes, might plow and harvest, have only one wife, and send his children to white schools. But the old life was still alive in memory. George Sword, for example, was a progressive. He was even a member of the Indian police force the government agents used to help keep order. But George Sword's description of his religious beliefs captures the painful division of loyalty that existed in the minds of even the most "civilized" Sioux:

> When I believed that Wakan Tanka was right, I served him with all my powers. In war with the white people, I found their Wakan Tanka superior. I then took the name of Sword, and have served their Wakan Tanka according to the white people's manner.

I became chief of the United States Indian police, and held the office until there was no trouble between the Sioux and the white people. I joined the church and am a deacon in it and shall be until I die.

But all this Christianity and "progress" had not erased the old ways in George Sword. He was still a member of the Oglala band of the Dakota tribe, and his spirit might find itself in the Sioux's heaven, not the whites':

I still have my Wasicun [ceremonial pouch] and I am afraid to offend it, because the spirit of an Oglala may go to the spirit land of the Dakota.

This divided consciousness, unable to choose finally between the old and the new, the Native-American way and the European-American way, touched every area of life for the reservation Indians. To the whites who watched them, the Indians seemed almost like "children" in their confusion. In fact, the Sioux men, especially, had been deprived of their adult roles in the hunt and battle, so their maturity was at stake.

One of the whites' main hopes for destroying the old Sioux culture was to educate a new generation in white schools. They took numbers of Sioux children away from their parents and put them in distant boarding schools. The Sioux reaction was mixed. They could hope that this process would make their children's lives better. But there was the inevitable resentment, too, the feeling that their children had been, in effect, kidnapped by the whites.

Even when the white schools were close to home, the Sioux sent their children to them reluctantly. When a new school was opened at Pine Ridge, Sioux parents brought their children in on the first day, but they stayed outside the building, milling about, curious and frightened. Their fears were increased when the white teachers pulled down the shades so that no one could see what was happening inside. Suddenly, a gust of wind blew one of the blinds aside for a moment. The parents got a glimpse of something that filled them with horror. A white woman was holding one Sioux boy while another woman cut his hair. The whole meaning of the reservation experience came quickly into focus. In the old life, a Sioux male's long braids were a symbol of his manhood. Here were white women scissoring away, symbolically, the tribal badge of masculinity. The parents, alarmed and outraged, charged into the school and took their children out.

Only at odd moments and in ineffective ways did the Sioux resist the relentless white pressure on their old customs. The whites controlled the Indians' sources of food, blankets, fuel, housing. The whites even controlled the ownership of an Indian's individual plot of land. The Sioux, like other Native Americans, did not have a clearly defined concept of the private ownership of land. But they could see plainly that their survival depended on the mysterious white concept of land ownership. To lose the land would be to lose everything.

The deep conflict between Indian and white ways came to the surface in 1883, when a Senate investigating committee visited the Sioux. Sitting Bull, who had been one of the Sioux leaders at the battle of the Little Bighorn, came to testify. But the senators would not recognize Sitting Bull as chief. Sitting Bull got up and left, and all the Indians followed him out. But several of the progressive Indians returned to plead with the committee to use its influence with the Great Father to get better treatment for the Indians. Soon even Sitting Bull swallowed his hurt pride and returned to apologize.

Then Sitting Bull gave a remarkable account of what defeat had meant to the Sioux. They had been wealthy in their own terms, with land, ponies, and buffalo aplenty. In one lifetime the white man had reduced them to poverty.

> Whatever you wanted of me I have obeyed. The Great Father sent me word that whatever he had against me in the past had been forgiven and thrown aside, and I accepted his promises and came in. And he told me not to step aside from the white man's path, and I am doing my best to travel in that path. I sit here and look around me now, and I see my people starving. We want cattle to butcher. That is the way you live, and we want to live the same way. When the Great Father told me to live like his people, I told him to send me six teams of mules, because that is the way the white people make a living. I asked for a horse and buggy for my children; I was advised to follow the ways of the white man, and that is why I asked for those things.

Sitting Bull's ideas were a little confused, at least by white standards. But he summed up neatly the dilemma of the Sioux. He was still proud of himself and his tribal ways. He resented the whites' failure to understand this pride. But another side of him recognized defeat and was prepared to plead with the whites not for less civilization but for more. In Sitting Bull, and in almost all the other reservation Indians, pride, resentment, hunger, and begging were so intermixed that a meaningful pattern of life was almost impossible. The Sioux were gradually becoming "civilized." But anger was just below the surface. Some crucial event or idea was all that was needed to bring conflict with the whites back into the open, tip the scales one way or the other, and offer the Indians a clear choice between the old life and the new.

A new idea did come, and from an unpredictable direction. In the summer of 1889—about a dozen years after Crazy Horse had surrendered his band of "hostiles"—the Sioux began to hear rumors of an Indian Messiah (or savior) who had come to earth in the West. They had learned enough of Christianity on the reservation to understand the alien notion of a Messiah. If it were true that one had come to save the Indians from the whites, surely it was worth investigating.

The Messiah was said to be at the Paiute reservation at Walker Lake, Nevada. The Sioux selected important men to make the trip west. It was about a thousand miles away—farther than almost any of the Sioux had ever traveled. Pine Ridge Reservation sent eight men, including Kicking Bear, who was to become the most effective disciple of the new Messiah. One of the men from Rosebud was Short Bull. The Cheyenne River Reservation, with a smaller population than either Pine Ridge or Rosebud, sent one man.

The eleven Sioux started west by train. Railroads had by then penetrated all the major western areas, and Indians hopped freight cars with little or no opposition from the white railroad men. When the Sioux reached Wyoming, they found that other tribes—Cheyennes, Arapahoes, Bannocks, and Shoshones—had also sent wise men to seek the Messiah. The whole group then traveled south to Walker Lake. There the Paiutes gave them wagons to complete the pilgrimage. Soon they were in the presence of the Messiah.

WOVOKA. Wovoka, or Jackson Wilson, was the Paiute who apparently originated the Ghost Dance religion. His ideas were a blend of Native-American legends and Christianity. He asked his followers only to dance the Ghost Dance and to await the resurrection of their dead ancestors.

His Indian name was Wovoka, his white name Jackson Wilson. He was about thirty-five years old. He was Paiute, but he had grown up close to a white ranching family named Wilson, who gave him his English name. The Wilsons were a religious family. From them Wovoka had learned in some detail how Jesus had controlled the wind and the seas, how he had promised eternal life to his followers, and how other whites had crucified him. Wovoka was apparently the son of a Paiute shaman, or medicine man. One day in 1889, when he was ill (and perhaps delirious) with a high fever, there was an eclipse of the sun. This led him to believe that he had been taken up to heaven. After talking with God, he had been returned to earth to bring salvation to the Indians.

Wovoka's doctrines were a fairly straightforward Native-American version of some of the basic teachings of the New Testament. In a sermon to some visiting Cheyennes he summarized his new faith:

> You must not hurt anybody, or do harm to anyone. You must not fight. Do right always.

> Do not tell the white people about this. Jesus is now upon the earth. The dead are all alive again. I do not know when they will be here; maybe this fall or in the spring. When the time comes there will be no more sickness and everyone will be young again.

Wovoka was telling his disciples that the dead would be resurrected soon. The earth would tremble; a new earth would cover the old. But true believers need not be afraid, because they would soon enjoy perfect life, youth, and health. In the meantime, the Indians should live in peace with the whites.

> Do not refuse to work for the whites, and do not make any trouble with them until you leave them. When the earth shakes, do not be afraid, it will not hurt you. That is all. You will receive good words from me again some time. Do not tell lies.

Wovoka gave the visiting Cheyennes some clay for making the sacred red paint of the Paiutes. Symbols drawn with it were signs of their salvation. Then he advised them: "When you get home, you must make a dance to continue five days. You must all do it in the same way."

This was the "Ghost Dance" from which Wovoka's new religion soon took its name. During the five days it lasted, men and women sang, danced, and went into trances. During the dance they were supposed to be able to visit their departed relatives in heaven.

When Short Bull returned to South Dakota, he gave his version of the Ghost Dance religion to his excited Sioux audience. The tone was much more militant than Wovoka's. Short Bull promised punishment for those who refused to be converted—just as the Christian missionaries promised damnation for those who rejected *their* Messiah. He also promised victory over the hated and feared soldiers for those who wore holy shirts into battle. The shirts were supposed to protect wearers from the whites' bullets.

> If the soldiers surround you, three of you, on whom I have put holy shirts, will sing a song around them, then some of them will drop dead. Then the rest will start to run, but their horses will sink into the earth. The riders will jump from their horses, but they will sink into the earth also. Then you can do as you desire with them. Now, you must know this, that all the soldiers and that race will be dead. There will be only five thousand of them left living on the earth. The guns are the only things we are afraid of, but they belong to our father in heaven. He will see that they do no harm.

Short Bull was not the only one who brought back this interpretation from the visit to Wovoka. A militant version of the Ghost Dance faith emerged on all the Sioux reservations during the summer of 1890. The Sioux were offered a new ritual, the Ghost Dance, and a new faith, which held that the whites would soon be buried in the earth and the Indians would once again own the plains. There is no way of knowing how sincere Short Bull was. Nor is there any way of knowing whether Sitting Bull, who soon became a disciple of the Ghost Dance, really believed in the coming resurrection. Most of the Sioux probably rejected the Ghost Dance and decided to continue along the whites' "path." For many, though, the religion of Wovoka offered great hope for the return of the old life and the end of their humiliating captivity. There can be no doubt that large groups of Sioux did accept the Ghost Dance.

Agents on all the reservations tried to stop the dances, using Indian police. But time and again, the dancing Sioux refused to be intimidated. They threatened their own police with rifles, insulted the agents, and began to behave like the Sioux of the 1870s. The agents reacted in various ways. When the police failed to make the Sioux obey, some of the agents refused to issue rations to those Indians who were active Ghost Dancers. At least two of the agents asked for federal troops. One, a new agent at Pine Ridge, was so incompetent that the Indians named him "Young-Man-Afraid-of-Indians." White newspapermen, always hungry for a sensational story, began to write about "hostile" Sioux. And white settlers in the Dakotas began to demand protection from the government.

Finally, after a tug-of-war between the Department of the Interior and the Department of War in Washington, the government authorized the army to send infantry and cavalry onto the reservations. This move brought about the first real confrontation since 1876 between the Sioux and the dreaded "bluecoats" of the United States Army. On November 20, 1890, cavalry and infantry units occupied the Pine Ridge and Rosebud reservations. A few days later the entire Seventh Cavalry arrived at Pine Ridge. This had been Custer's unit, and it included many veterans of the Little Bighorn.

The effect on the Sioux of the appearance of the troops was overpowering. Instead of retreating to the outer edges of the reservations, most of the Indians at Pine Ridge and Rosebud immediately left their cabins and camps and gathered around the agency buildings. They pitched tepees in rambling confusion and hoped that they would not be suspected of any wrongdoing. It was as though the only way to be safe from the rifles and cannon of the army was to be right under the noses of the officers and agents.

Thus the arrival of the army segregated the Indians. Those who wanted "peace" with the whites had gathered at the agencies. Only the most militant of the Ghost Dancers, led by Kicking Bear and Short Bull, decided to hold out. They were gathered along the creeks not far from the Pine Ridge agency—at Medicine Root, Porcupine, and Wounded Knee.

About a week after the cavalry's arrival, several hundred of the militant Indians broke for open country. They plundered the farms of the peaceful Indians who had fled to the agencies, and they raided the agency cattle herds for beef. Then about 600 warriors and their families struck out for a low plateau at the northwest corner of Pine Ridge. This was known as the Stronghold. Here the Indians had grass, water, cattle, ponies in large numbers, and plenty of guns and ammunition. They announced that they intended to stay all winter, dancing, and then see what the spring might bring.

Fortunately, the officer in command at Pine Ridge decided to be cautious. He sent one messenger after another to the Stronghold, promising that there would be no punishment if the militants surrendered and returned to the agency. In turn, the Indians had to agree to give up the Ghost Dance and return the cattle and other things they had taken. The messengers were badly treated, but some of the men at the Stronghold wanted to surrender. It seemed clear that sooner or later the militants would disagree among themselves and the threat of uprising would be broken. The situation at Pine Ridge settled into a stalemate, with neither side ready to force a confrontation.

Now the scene of the action shifted north to Standing Rock Reservation, where Sitting Bull kept his camp. The nonprogressive Indians regarded Sitting Bull almost reverently. He was probably not as great a war chief as Crazy Horse had been, but Sitting Bull had held out against the whites longer than any other Sioux leader. And his people believed that he had extraordinary powers as a medicine man.

The agent at Standing Rock was James McLaughlin, a tough and experienced man. For years he had struggled to gain moral leadership of the Indians, and for years Sitting Bull had stood in his way. McLaughlin had been looking for a way to break Sitting Bull's hold over the nonprogressive Sioux at Standing Rock. When Sitting Bull took up the forbidden Ghost Dance, McLaughlin decided that arresting him would be

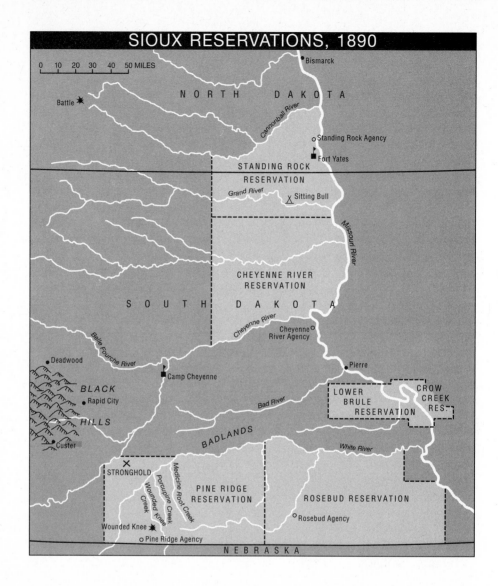

the best course. McLaughlin wanted to delay the arrest until winter, when the Indians spent a lot of time indoors to avoid the bitter cold. The agent also believed that the arrest should be made by the Sioux police, not by the cavalry units stationed near the agency at Fort Yates.

In November 1890, McLaughlin began to enlarge the force of Indian policemen that the Sioux called "metal breasts"—because of their badges. He ordered them to keep a close watch on Sitting Bull's camp and make certain that the old chief did not leave.

In mid-December McLaughlin learned that Sitting Bull had been invited to the Stronghold, where he would join the Pine Ridge and Rosebud Sioux under Short Bull and Kicking Bear. The agent was determined to stop Sitting Bull from taking his group to Pine Ridge. He knew that a stalemate had developed there, and he felt that Sitting Bull's presence might be enough to tip the scales toward open warfare between the Sioux and the cavalry. So McLaughlin ordered Sitting Bull's arrest. He commanded the Indian police, who were led by an experienced lieutenant, Bull Head, to sneak into Sitting Bull's camp at dawn on December 15. They were to arrest the chief and bring him into the agency.

Bull Head and the police met the order with mixed feelings. Most of them were progressives. They prayed to the white man's God before starting their mission. But the thought of Sitting Bull still brought back memories of the great days of the Sioux. One of the police, He Alone, whose white name was John Lone Man, later remembered how he felt when the orders were read and translated to the police. (The English here is the work of a relative of He Alone.)

> I'm simply expressing my viewpoint as one who had reformed from all the heathenish ways, formerly one of the loyal followers of Chief Sitting Bull. But ever since I was about ten years of age, I had participated in a good many buffalo hunts and fought under Sitting Bull. But the most important fight I took part in was the Custer fight. After this fight I still went with Sitting Bull's band to Canada. Even after Sitting Bull was returned to Standing Rock Reservation, I remained in his camp, where I tamed down somewhat. We all felt sad.

The police gathered in the early evening of December 14 and passed the night telling war stories. Then, just before dawn, Bull Head ordered He Alone and the thirty or so other police to get ready.

Sitting Bull's camp stood on the north bank of the Grand River. The police, circling from the east, crossed the river to cut off any possible escape southward toward Pine Ridge. Soon they could see Sitting Bull's log cabin. In front of it stood the very tall tepee that was the headquarters for the Ghost Dance. Sitting Bull's two wives, his son Crow Foot, and several other children and relatives lived in the cabin. Other tepees were ranged around it. The police paused for a moment, then crossed the river again. He Alone described what happened:

> We rode up as if we attacked the camp. We quickly dismounted, and while our officers went inside we all scattered around the cabin. It was still dark, and everybody was asleep, and only dogs greeted us.
>
> Bull Head knocked at the door, and the Chief answered, "*How, timahel hiyu you.* All right, come in."
>
> Bull Head said, "I come to arrest you. You are under arrest."
>
> Sitting Bull said, "How. Let me put on my clothes and go with you."
>
> When Sitting Bull started to go with the police, one of Sitting Bull's wives burst into a loud cry which drew attention. No sooner had this started, when several leaders were rapidly making their way toward Sitting Bull's cabin. Bear That Catches, particularly, came up close saying, "Now, here are the metal breasts just as we had expected. You think you are going to take him. You shall not do it."

By now the entire camp was awake and angry. The police might still have been able to arrest the sleepy Sitting Bull if Crow Foot, his seventeen-year-old son, had not intervened. Sitting Bull had been grooming Crow Foot to be a chief, filling his youthful

SITTING BULL: TWO VIEWS. The photograph on the left shows Sitting Bull dressed in the costume he wore in traveling circuses. His face is that of a brave warrior and leader of his people. His eyes are unflinching and his expression grave, but his costume is a theatrical white version of Indian dress. The second photograph, of Sitting Bull and his family and a white woman, was taken on the Dakota reservation, not in a white circus. It shows the other side of Sitting Bull's personality— confused and shy of the camera. This is a family that has been very nearly broken in spirit by defeat and reservation life.

head with tales of courage in battle. As He Alone described it, Crow Foot upset the delicate balance of fear and anger in the cabin:

> Just about this time, Crow Foot got up, moved by the wailing of his mother and the remarks of Bear That Catches, and said to Sitting Bull, "Well, you always called yourself a brave chief. Now you are allowing yourself to be taken by the metal breasts."
>
> Sitting Bull then changed his mind, and said, "*Ho ca mni kte sni yelo.* Then I will not go."
>
> Lieutenant Bull Head said to the chief, "Come now, do not listen to any one."
>
> I said to Sitting Bull, "Uncle [Native Americans often used words like Uncle and Father as terms of respect, not kinship], nobody is going to harm you. Please do not let others lead you into any trouble."
>
> But the chief's mind was made up not to go, so the three head officers laid their hands on him, pulling him outside. By this time, the whole camp was in commotion. Bear That Catches pulled out a gun from under his blanket and fired into Lieutenant Bull Head, wounding him. I ran up toward where they were holding the chief, when Bear That Catches raised his gun. He pointed and fired at me, but it snapped [misfired]. I jerked the gun away from his hands and laid him out. It was about this moment that Lieutenant Bull Head fired into Sitting Bull while still holding him, and Red Tomahawk followed with another shot which finished the chief.

There was more shooting, and soon Sitting Bull's followers ran for a line of trees. The police took shelter in Sitting Bull's cabin. The inner walls were hung with strips of brightly colored sheeting, sewn together and tacked to the walls. Suddenly, one of the policemen noticed a movement in a corner, behind the sheeting. He Alone raised the curtain:

> There stood Crow Foot, and as soon as he was exposed to view, he cried out, "My Uncles, do not kill me. I do not wish to die." Lieutenant Bull Head said, "Do what you like with him. He is the one that has caused this trouble." I do not remember who fired the shot that killed Crow Foot—several fired at once.

Just after Crow Foot was killed, the cavalry units from Fort Yates arrived. The remaining members of Sitting Bull's band scattered toward the south.

He Alone and the rest of the police went home filled with the contradictory feelings that were so much a part of reservation life. He Alone performed a Sioux ritual. He built a small shelter and dropped hot stones into water to create a steam bath "that I might cleanse myself for participating in a bloody fight with my fellow men." Then he burned all the clothes he had worn to Sitting Bull's camp. Next, He Alone set out to perform a white man's ritual:

> The next day, I took my family into the agency. I reported to Major McLaughlin. He laid his hand on my shoulders, and said, "He Alone is a man. I feel very proud of you for the way you have carried out your part in the fight with the Ghost Dancers." I was not very brave at that moment. His comment nearly set me acrying.

Four Indian policemen died at Sitting Bull's camp. Two more (including Lieutenant Bull Head) would soon be dead of their wounds. One of them, Shave Head, asked McLaughlin, "Did I do well, Father?" McLaughlin nodded. Shave Head went on:

> Then I will die in the faith of the white man, to which my five children already belong. Send for my wife, that we may be married by the Black Gown [priest] before I die.

Shave Head's wife came, but too late. The next day, the six dead police were buried. A squad of bluecoats fired honorary volleys over the graves, and "Taps" was blown.

At least eight of Sitting Bull's followers had died. Their bodies were left where they had fallen. Only Sitting Bull was buried. A few moments after the ceremonies for the Indian police, Sitting Bull's body, in a plain coffin, was lowered into a grave in the Fort Yates cemetery. The only people who watched were three officers, serving as official witnesses, and the four guardhouse gravediggers.

None of Sitting Bull's followers was present at his burial. Most of them—about 400—had fled south and west from the Grand River camp. The authorities at Standing Rock had a number of nightmarish ideas about what might happen next. The Standing Rock Ghost Dancers might join Chief Big Foot on the Cheyenne River, where the dance had been in full swing for weeks. On the other hand, the Sitting Bull group might strike out for the Stronghold, where Short Bull and Kicking Bear still held out. Or they might set Big Foot in motion toward the Stronghold too, with terrible results. News of the death of Sitting Bull, likely to spread like prairie fire, could ignite the entire Sioux reservation system.

Agent McLaughlin immediately sent friendly scouts to Sitting Bull's band. The scouts were able to persuade most of them to return to the Standing Rock Reservation. Others simply scattered and sooner or later went back to their homes around Grand River. The rest—fewer than a hundred—headed south to join Big Foot.

They reached a camp that was already nervous and confused. Big Foot had been a great chief. But he was old now, in his seventies, and his control over his band was slipping. The band's medicine man, Yellow Bird, was a fanatical Ghost Dancer. Many of the young braves were ready to bring about their hoped-for victory over the whites. There were about 200 in the band, and all of them were aware of mounting pressure from the white soldiers.

The War Department had ordered Big Foot's arrest, on the false theory that he was almost as large a source of potential trouble as Sitting Bull had been. An observation camp, Camp Cheyenne, had been established by the cavalry just a few miles up the Cheyenne River. Infantry units from the east were trying to cross the Missouri River, which was partially covered with winter ice.

For several days Big Foot wavered among various alternatives. At one point he was convinced by messengers from the cavalry to go to the Cheyenne River agency. But many of his young men wanted to go to the Stronghold instead. Big Foot had also been invited by the Pine Ridge chiefs to go there to help settle the "troubles." He had a great reputation as a diplomat, and he was offered a hundred ponies to heal the split between the "friendly" Sioux and the Ghost Dancers at Pine Ridge. Most of the time, however, Big Foot seemed to want only to stay put at his own camp and wait.

Finally, for reasons that are difficult to guess, Big Foot made his decision. He would go to Pine Ridge, make peace, and accept the gift of ponies. What he did not realize was that leaving his reservation when the whites were so frightened of a Sioux uprising would make him a fugitive "hostile" in the eyes of the military. Almost immediately, new orders went out for Big Foot's arrest. According to these orders, his band was to be disarmed and their horses taken. Then they were to be be marched to the railroad and sent to Omaha—far away from their own reservation lands. Big Foot never understood that this was the army's plan. He assumed that he was going to Pine Ridge on a mission of peace.

Big Foot's band left camp December 23, under the cover of night. As soon as the officers at Camp Cheyenne realized the old chief had gone, cavalry units started patrolling the line between Big Foot's camp and the Stronghold, looking for him. But the chief passed east of the patrols. The band moved very slowly, for Big Foot had caught pneumonia. He rode in a wagon without springs. Soon Big Foot was bleeding from his nose. And it was bitterly cold for the old man. At one point, in a pass through a steep bank along the Bad River, Big Foot's men had to dig out a road for the wagon. Big Foot managed to reach Porcupine Creek, only about thirty miles from the Pine Ridge agency, without being sighted by the army. He sent men ahead to tell the Sioux he was coming.

On December 28, five days after starting south, Big Foot's band was finally located by the Seventh Cavalry. When the Indians and cavalry met, there was a tense moment. The cavalry formed a skirmish line and brought up cannon. Big Foot's braves formed a battle line in front of his wagon. But then the cavalry commander came forward. He and Big Foot shook hands, and the chief accepted an escort—going, he thought, to Pine Ridge. Together, the cavalry and the Indians made their way to a trading post at Wounded Knee Creek.

The officer in charge had wisely not tried to disarm the Sioux, and he let them keep their horses for the trip. He even transferred Big Foot into an ambulance wagon. When the two groups reached Wounded Knee Creek, the Indians were issued rations. The rest of the Seventh Cavalry came from Pine Ridge to join the patrol. The Sioux pitched their tepees in a low hollow near a ravine that led into the creek. There were 102 men and 230 women and children. The soldiers, a total of about 500, camped on a rise just to the north. Armed sentries surrounded the Indians, but on the whole everything seemed peaceful enough.

Soon the Indians settled down and the cavalry—except for the ring of sentries around the Indian camp—went to sleep. Only a few officers, veterans of Custer's Little Bighorn disaster, stayed up late. They celebrated over a keg of whiskey someone had brought from the agency.

The next morning Colonel James Forsyth, commander of the Seventh Cavalry, asked all the men of Big Foot's group to gather in a council between the tepees and the cavalry encampment. The sentries remained in place. The rest of the cavalry units drew up, mounted, around the Sioux men and their camp. Forsyth asked the Indians for their weapons.

Big Foot tried diplomacy. From his ambulance bed he quietly advised his men to give up a few bad guns but to hide the good ones. Soon Forsyth sent twenty of the Sioux to the tepees to bring the guns. Meanwhile, however, the Sioux women (who understood the value of a weapon) had hidden the rifles that the Sioux had bought, stolen, or taken in battle. The Sioux returned to the council with only two old, broken cavalry carbines.

Forsyth heightened his search. He placed a line of troops between the Sioux braves and their camp and sent his own men into the tepees. But this search uncovered only thirty rifles, most of them old and useless. This left one other real possibility: some of the Sioux might be hiding rifles under the blankets they kept draped over their shoulders against the cold.

By now the situation was very delicate. Forsyth ordered Big Foot brought out on his blanket. The medicine man, Yellow Bird, was dancing around, chanting Ghost Dance songs, urging the young braves to be firm. In the tepees women were hastily packing, ready to flee.

Suddenly, one Sioux man, Black Coyote, pulled a rifle from his blanket and began to shout, holding the weapon over his head. He was probably deaf and—by the Indians' testimony—a little insane. Two soldiers grabbed him and struggled for the rifle. It went off, firing overhead. In what may have been a signal, Yellow Bird threw a handful of dust into the air. Several braves pulled rifles from their blankets and aimed at the cavalry. "By God, they have broken," an officer shouted. Some Sioux fired, and at about the same moment came the command to the cavalry: "Fire! Fire on them!"

No one could stop what happened next. Big Foot was quickly killed. Cavalry carbines ripped into the group of Sioux men. The bullets that did not find a Sioux body passed on across the ravine into the tepees. Women ran this way and that, followed by children. Some of the Sioux broke toward the creek, where they were cut down by waiting cavalrymen. Others ran into the ravine.

Corporal Paul Weinert manned one of the Seventh Cavalry's small, rapid-firing cannon on the hill. Like the other cavalrymen, he was surprised when the shooting started. But within a moment or two, he was caught up in the battle, pumping shots angrily wherever he saw moving Sioux:

> All of the Indians opened fire on us. Lieutenant Hawthorne ran toward me and was calling, when suddenly I heard him say, "Oh, my God!" and then I knew he had been hit. I said: "By God! I'll make 'em pay for that," and ran the gun into the opening of the ravine. They kept yelling for me to come back. Bullets were coming like hail from the Indians' Winchesters. I kept going in farther, and pretty soon everything was quiet at the other end of the line.

Corporal Weinert was a veteran soldier with a sophisticated weapon. The experience of Catching Spirit Elk, a Sioux who had surrendered his rifle, was almost the opposite of Weinert's:

> Then followed firing from all sides. I threw myself on the ground. I then jumped up to run toward the Indian camp, but was then and there shot down, being hit on my right leg, and soon after was shot again on the other leg. When the general firing ceased, I heard an interpreter calling out, saying the wounded would be kindly treated. I opened my eyes and looked about and saw the dead and wounded all around me.

Some officers did what they could to prevent women and children from being shot down. But the Sioux (at least those who still had weapons) were fast and accurate with their repeating rifles, so the soldiers sometimes fired at anything that moved. When the artillery on the hill opened up on the Indians in the ravine, the shells exploded on all without regard to age or sex. Apparently, too, some of the raging soldiers broke ranks and chased down fleeing Indians. These were the bodies Charles Eastman found miles away from Wounded Knee.

The battle lasted only a few minutes. About 150 braves rode out from Pine Ridge, too late and too few to help their comrades. The cavalry gathered their own dead (25) and wounded (39) and returned to the Pine Ridge agency. They took some of the wounded Sioux with them and left the rest on the field. There were at least 146 Indian dead—about half of them men. Some bodies were probably taken away during the next two days, before Eastman's party arrived to rescue the living and bury the rest. All in all, probably 200 Sioux and whites had died.

Wounded Knee was followed by a few small skirmishes. But soon Pine Ridge was pacified. The Stronghold Indians had given up while Big Foot's band was on the march. The Ghost Dance was over. Spring came and went, but the earth did not cover the white man, as Wovoka had promised. Paul Weinert, the cannoneer, received a Congressional Medal of Honor for his part in the action at the edge of the ravine. A small white church was later built at the Sioux mass grave, on what came to be called Cemetery Hill. In 1903, with the help of white missionaries, the Sioux put up their own small monument, burying Wounded Knee in the past:

BURYING THE DEAD AT WOUNDED KNEE.   Several days after the massacre, a party of white men went to Wounded Knee Creek to bury the Sioux dead. They were paid $2 a body, a total of a little less than $300, for their work. But they also got to pose, with some of the men of the Seventh Cavalry, for publicity photographs like this one.

This monument is erected by surviving relatives and other Oglala and Cheyenne River Sioux Indians in memory of the Chief Big Foot Massacre, Dec. 29, 1890.

Col. Forsyth in command of U.S. troops.

Big Foot was a great chief of the Sioux Indians. He often said, "I will stand in peace till my last day comes." He did many good and brave deeds for the white man and the red man.

Many innocent women and children who knew no wrong died here.

Last Frontiers

There is nothing unique about the history of the Sioux. It is true they resisted the whites longer and more fiercely than some other Native Americans, east or west. And they developed a more militant resistance to reservation life than some other Native Americans. But despite these differences, they were finally defeated in a manner typical of the way white Americans subdued all the Indians.

The defeat of the Sioux and the other Native Americans of the plains was just one chapter in the history of continental expansion. White Americans had begun moving across the Mississippi in the 1830s. In the decades after the Civil War, this movement increased both in speed and recklessness. By the time of Wounded Knee, white dominance in the Great Plains and the Rocky Mountains was complete.

THE LAST WEST

Until the 1840s, it was possible at each census for a mapmaker to draw a zigzag line from north to south showing how far white "settlement" had advanced in each decade. In truth, both the line and the notion of an advancing frontier were illusions. There never really had been a definite frontier line. And "settlement" was nothing more than a favored white term, meant to suggest that the Native Americans' homelands were "unsettled."

But after the Mexican War of 1846–1848, the line could not be drawn at all. The drift of pioneers into Oregon, the settlement of Texas and Utah, and the discovery of gold in California created pockets of white settlement thousands of miles beyond the old frontier line near the Mississippi. By the early 1850s, it was evident that the Pacific Coast would be "settled" fairly quickly, organized into territories, and carved into states. California had already been admitted to statehood in 1850. Oregon entered the Union nine years later.

Between the Pacific and the areas in eastern Kansas and Nebraska into which whites had pushed by the time of the Civil War, lay a vast stretch of plains and mountains. It formed an area larger than the whole territory over which George Washington had presided. This region was the last frontier, the last region to be occupied by white Americans.

The Great Plains begin in the first tier of states west of the Mississippi River and extend west to the Rockies. In 1836 the Senate Committee for Indian Affairs had declared that the Great Plains were an "uninhabitable" region. The Native American tribes there were thought to be "on the outside of us, and in a place which will forever remain on the outside." In fact, the offical government name for the plains was "The Great American Desert." The weather was dry. There was no water in many of the rivers during part of the year. The land was covered not with trees but with stubborn grass. Only the Native Americans and the buffalo seemed able to thrive.

The Rocky Mountain region also seemed to offer little to encourage settlement. For many years its great peaks and almost inaccessible high valleys were the home only of small Indian bands and a few white fur traders and renegades. And in the Southwest there were real deserts, enormous stretches of land that received less than ten inches of rain a year and were covered—if at all—by nothing more than scrub.

There were many reasons this myth that the West could never be "settled" was dispelled. Three of the most important were gold, railroads, and cattle. As miners, railroad men, and ranchers moved into the region, they systematically seized Indian lands. Then came the final pioneers of the last West, the farmers. In 1890 the Census Bureau announced that the frontier no longer existed.

THE MINING FRONTIER

The western mining frontier had begun in 1848 with the discovery of gold in California. In the next year, tens of thousands of people, most of them men, had rushed to the area around San Francisco. They quickly became known as the "Forty-Niners" and were celebrated in popular songs and stories. But the mythic version of this first American gold rush is a far cry from the reality. In most of the mining camps, somewhere between one-fourth and one-half of the men were foreign-born. Experienced and skillful miners from Mexico came by the thousands, working in hills and valleys that had belonged to their nation just a few years before. Other skilled, Spanish-speaking miners came up the Pacific coast all the way from Peru. News of the gold strike rippled around the Pacific Rim, and within three years there were 25,000 Chinese in California. (The new state government of California was quick to respond to these "foreign threats." In the first year of statehood, 1850, the California legislature passed a law requiring "foreign miners" to apply for special licenses and to pay a fee of twenty dollars a month for the privilege of looking for gold.)

Some of the Forty-Niners did strike it rich, although the people who made the most money were probably not the miners and prospectors but those who set up businesses to sell them food, clothing, tools, or whiskey. Most of the men who rushed to California were disappointed. Many of them began to drift east, through the Sierra Nevada, looking for new bonanzas. In 1858, prospectors found gold near Pike's Peak in Colorado. Soon people were pouring into new, ramshackle towns like Denver, Pueblo, and Boulder. Their covered wagons proclaimed "Pike's Peak or Bust!"—though for many, it would be Pike's Peak *and* bust. A year after the first strike, about 100,000 people—mostly men without their families—had moved into the area. Like most other western gold and silver strikes, the Pike's Peak boom did not last. The earliest prospectors soon raked off the surface gold. The remaining precious metal was buried deep in the mountains, where it could be mined only with expensive machinery that individual miners could not afford. Within three months in 1859, the population of the Colorado goldfields dwindled to about 50,000. But enough people stayed to create a pocket of white occupation in the mountains.

A similar process was under way farther west, in what is now Nevada. Miners from California found gold near the western border of the region in the late 1850s. In 1859 they discovered the famous Comstock Lode. One of the richest single mines in America, it produced over $200 million worth of gold and silver in the thirty years following its discovery. Thousands of men rushed over the mountains from Sacramento to build nearby Virginia City. Soon the town had five newspapers, a miniature stock exchange, and a horde of prospectors, saloonkeepers, prostitutes, and gamblers. A few men became enormously wealthy. Most of the prospectors, however, went away disappointed.

CALIFORNIA MINERS. These miners were photographed in 1852, three years after the California gold rush began. The three European-American men are holding the tools of their gold-mining trade, including the large pan for finding loose gold that has been washed down the sluice mixed with dirt from the digging. They seem quite pleased with themselves. The Chinese Americans at right— two of them hardly more than boys—do not seem so cheerful, partly because, as soon as the photographer left, they would take picks and shovels and go back to their backbreaking digging, and partly because none of the gold that showed up in the sluice would be theirs.

Some miners who stayed found small pockets of loose gold that could be mined with a pan or a sluice, a simple trough that runs water downhill over dirt and loose rocks, washing out the heavy gold dust. This kind of mining, called placer mining, soon washed off the free metal near the surface. This meant that the miner's frontier quickly became a corporate frontier, exploited by mining companies owned by eastern investors. Within a few years, any successful field soon became an industrial development, and the prospectors scattered again in search of a new discovery and easy pickings elsewhere.

The California gold rush that had excited so many thousands of Americans in 1849 was repeated over and over again throughout the West. In the late 1850s a small strike was made in eastern Washington, but it soon petered out. Restless

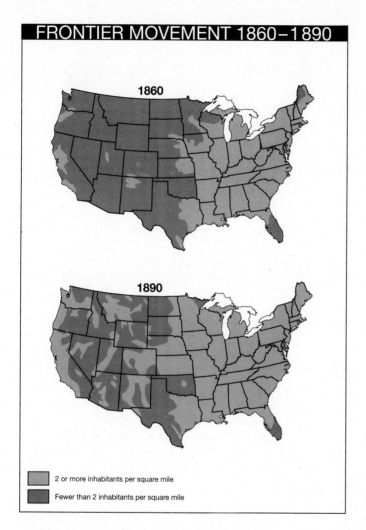

FRONTIER MOVEMENT 1860–1890

1860

1890

2 or more inhabitants per square mile

Fewer than 2 inhabitants per square mile

miners headed farther east, up the Snake and Salmon rivers into Idaho. There they built Boise, Silver City, and other new mining towns. By 1861, the start of the Civil War, there were probably 30,000 European Americans in Idaho.

While their countrymen were battling at Bull Run and Chickamauga, white miners moved from Idaho into Montana. There they struck gold and silver at Last Chance Gulch (which later became the city of Helena) and Alder Gulch (Virginia City). By 1863 Idaho had enough citizens to organize as a territory, and Montana followed a year later.

The last western gold rush occurred in 1874. In the Black Hills of South Dakota, in the heart of the Great Sioux Reservation, an army expedition commanded by Colonel Custer found traces of gold. According to a treaty between the United States and the Indians, the hills belonged to the Sioux "forever." For a short time the federal government did make some efforts to prevent whites from entering the Black Hills. But the pressure to find gold was too great. Within two years about 7,000 whites had built Deadwood and Custer City. The Sioux lands had been decisively invaded.

TRANSPORTATION WEST

The influx of of whites into the mountains, together with the growth of population of Oregon and California, led to demands for quick, safe, and economical land transportation between the East and the Far West. Every new mining town wanted to be linked to the rest of the country. People who lived on the West Coast wanted an overland route as an alternative to the long sea voyage around South America.

TRAIL, STAGE, AND PONY

The Oregon Trail, Santa Fe Trail, and other routes followed by pioneers in the 1840s and early 1850s were more or less protected by army posts along the way. But they were far from being real roads. Something else seemed necessary.

In 1858 the first stage road was finally cut through the countryside for the Butterfield Overland Express. Its route ran 2,000 miles, from St. Louis south through present-day Oklahoma, then across Texas, New Mexico, and Arizona. The ride was rough and usually very hot, and it took twenty-four days. Still, the overland trip was faster than the sea voyage. Soon other stage and freighting companies were opening additional roads across Colorado and Utah to California.

In 1860, businessmen set up a mail service known as the pony express. Small, lightweight boys rode big horses (not ponies) in relays between St. Joseph, Missouri, and Sacramento, California. The young riders were able to carry a message across the country in ten days. The pony express prospered for only about a year, however. In 1861 the first telegraph line was put through to the West Coast. The time for sending transcontinental messages was then cut to a split second.

A TRANSCONTINENTAL RAILROAD

All these ways of getting people, goods, and information across the country were only preludes to the most dramatic and successful method of all, the railroad. A transcontinental railroad had been a dream since the 1840s—to move people and goods through the West to California. The North and the South, however, had not been able to agree on the western part of the route. The North wanted a line to run from Chicago to San Francisco. The South insisted on a route through Texas to southern California.

The Civil War ended this competition. By seceding, the South lost its right to participate in the decision making. In 1862 Congress settled on a route between Council Bluffs, Iowa, and San Francisco. The same law provided for enormous financial support from the federal government. There would be two companies. The Central Pacific would build east from San Francisco. The Union Pacific (a patriotic name suited to wartime) would go west across Nebraska and Colorado. They were to meet somewhere in the middle. Each railroad would be given a right-of-way 400 feet wide. In addition, the government would lend the railroads up to $48,000 for each mile of track laid—less for flat country, more for mountain track. Most important, the railroads would be given 6,400 acres of land for every mile of track completed. In 1864 this land allowance was doubled.

The Central Pacific started building toward the east, but the work went slowly for two reasons. First, the company did not have enough capital. Second, labor was scarce in California. The first problem was eased when the Lincoln administration allowed the Central Pacific to claim flat-country miles as mountain miles, which entitled the company to the largest possible federal loans. The labor problem was solved by the brutal "importation" of thousands of Chinese laborers. Many of them were unwilling immigrants, and all of them were exploited as gang labor. They lived in extremely crude conditions, with poor food and almost no housing. And when the tracks were laid and their work was finished, they would be cast loose to try to earn meager livings in the cities and towns of California, in a society whose European-American majority was at least as bigoted toward them as to-

DEADWOOD, 1876.   The Plains Indians might clash with the United States Army, but the real menace to their society was not the cavalry but the whites' railroads, farms, and cities. This 1876 photograph shows the bustle of growth in Deadwood, South Dakota, with its liquor stores, dentists' offices, and banks. Against towns like Deadwood, the Native Americans' tepee villages had little or no hope of survival.

ward Native Americans or African Americans. But the Chinese workers endured, and their endurance was translated into rail mileage. In the first year of construction, 1864, the Central Pacific had completed only twenty miles of track. But by 1867 the pace was up to twenty miles per month, largely as a result of Chinese-American labor.

At the other end of the proposed route the Union Pacific also built slowly at first. But it picked up speed by bringing in thousands of Irish immigrants to lay rails. In 1868 alone the Union Pacific laid 425 miles of track, well over a mile a day.

In May 1869, after only five years of construction, the two work gangs met at Promontory Point, Utah, just east of the Great Salt Lake. The last crosstie put down was coated with silver; the last spike was gold. A telegraph operator cabled east and west: "Hats off—prayer is being offered." Then there was a wait of almost fifteen minutes. Again the telegraph clicked. "We have got done praying. The spike is about to be presented." Railroad officials took turns with the hammer; the first blow was a bad miss, but the work was eventually done. Two locomotives eased forward until they touched. The nation celebrated almost as wildly as it had at the end of the Civil War. Chicago's parade was seven miles long. The nation was joined, east to west, across a "desert" that an earlier generation had believed would never be settled.

During the next fifteen years three more routes were opened across the Rockies. Iowa,

Missouri, Kansas, and Nebraska were criss-crossed by rails. In the process, the government gave the railroad companies almost 180 million acres of public land, and it lent them over $100 million. Because of complicated regulations that allowed railroads to delay choosing the land they wanted to keep along their rights-of-way, they were able to keep great stretches of land for years, waiting for its price to rise.

At one point the railroads controlled—at least on paper—almost all of Iowa and Wisconsin. The Northern Pacific, whose route crossed the northern tier of states between Lake Superior and the Pacific, controlled a strip of land larger in area than many European nations. The same kind of situation developed in Arizona and New Mexico. By 1885 the railroads held land totaling almost one-sixth of the entire country.

Many of the congressmen and senators who voted these huge grants to the railroads did so in the belief that most of the land in the Great American Desert was of little value. The motive behind the first transcontinental lines was not to build a transportation network for the Great Plains and the Rockies but to build a link to the Pacific Coast. It took a generation's experience to make clear that the intervening territory was valuable, that it would be occupied and farmed. As things turned out, the railroads may have been a very efficient mechanism for disposing of the public lands, at least in some areas. The government's own land policy was confused and often corrupt, and the public interest may, on balance, have been served about as well by the railroad grants as by the government's direct land grant practices. But the "public" whose interest was at stake was, of course, solely a white public. For Native Americans, the railroads were just one more step toward disaster.

⊷━◉═⊶

FROM BUFFALO TO CATTLE

The first important effects of the railroads on the Great Plains had less to do with land ownership and cultivation than with animals. The railroads created a new industry on the plains: ranching. Building the railroads not only hastened the destruction of the buffalo herds, it made possible the systematic exploitation of another set of resources: grass and cows.

Early in the sixteenth century the Spanish had begun importing European cattle into America. Over the years the cattle had multiplied. Some had escaped and become wild, especially in southern Texas around the Nueces River. These were the famous Texas longhorns—lanky, tough, and too dangerous to be captured or herded on foot. They roamed at will over the open range, a huge expanse of grass that was part of the public domain. By 1860 there were probably 5 million longhorns in Texas.

The Civil War sent beef prices soaring in both the North and the South. The beef herd in the northern states was smaller at the end of the war than it had been at the beginning. At the same time, the population had grown by more than 20 percent. Thus the demand and price for beef had increased. A longhorn steer could be bought in Texas for as little as three dollars. The same steer in Chicago would fetch ten times as much. The problem was to get it there.

THE LONG DRIVE

By 1866 the Missouri Pacific Railroad had pushed its line west to Sedalia, Missouri, just east of Kansas City. That same year the first large group of Texans drove enormous herds north across Indian Territory (now Oklahoma) to reach the rail line. The men ran into many difficulties. Part of the route passed through dense forests. The longhorns, unaccustomed to woods, panicked and refused to be driven through the trees. Flooding rivers had to be crossed. The Native Americans (whose treaties gave them control of all white travel across their land) harassed the cowboys. This early attempt showed, however, that it was possible to herd cattle safely over hundreds of miles to the railroad, which could then carry them on to lucrative eastern markets.

EAST MEETS WEST. In the years after the Civil War, American railroad companies imported thousands of Chinese workers to help finish the rail network in the mountains and deserts of the West. Here, Chinese workers use hand labor to complete a graceful and impressive trestle on the Central Pacific Railroad in the Sierra Nevada of California.

Thus began the twenty-year era of the long drive. As the years passed, the railroads extended farther west. New cattle towns replaced Sedalia. Among them were Abilene (probably the most successful), Wichita, and Dodge City. Between 1866 and 1888, Texans drove as many as 6 million head of cattle over the grasslands to Kansas.

For those who succeeded, the profits of the long drive were enormous. Cattlemen claimed that as much as 40 percent profit per year was not unusual. Like the miner's frontier, the cattleman's bonanza soon attracted thousands of eager easterners. Each usually had a few hundred dollars and a dream of running a vast ranch. Like the prospectors, most of the would-be ranchers were disappointed. Many of them either returned home or switched to another line of work such as running a store or saloon.

The long drive, despite the romantic myth of the cowboy it fostered, was a business. It required capital if it was to succeed on a big scale. In the end, only a lucky few became cattle "barons." It was eastern and European investors, with enough capital to buy and move large herds, who eventually controlled most of the cattle industry.

The men (and occasional women) who rounded up the herds and drove them to the cowtowns along the railroads have become the most romanticized figures in American culture. In truth, they were only workers in an industry that drove them as hard as they drove cattle. On the drives, they put in brutal, dangerous, four-teen-hour days. Although they had to learn highly specialized skills, and managed herds that were worth hundreds of thousands of dollars, they typically earned less than ten cents an hour. And when they finally reached Sedalia or Dodge City, what they found was not a roaring, adventurous scene where gunfighters might face off at any moment in a saloon or on a dirt street. In reality, the homicide and crime rates in the cattle towns were probably no higher than in eastern towns and cities. Cattle ranching was an industry that, like most industries of the day, made many owners rich. But the workers in the cattle industry earned little, labored hard, and lived quiet and usually dull lives.

A considerable number of the cowboys were African Americans. But the trail and ranch foremen were always white. One black cowboy, who had been born into slavery, claimed to be the original Deadwood Dick—although the popular hero of pulp fiction was transformed into a white man. Another black ranch hand, well known for his steady nerves and great skill, said bitterly that he would have been a boss if it had not been for "my damned old black face."

An even larger number of cowboys, probably a third or more, were of Mexican ancestry. In fact, the Mexican counterparts of the American cowboys, the vaqueros (from the Spanish word *vaca*, "cow"), had mastered their trade long before Anglo-Americans reached Texas or the plains. If an American cowboy called his pony a "pinto," it was because that Spanish word meant "painted." Or if his horse was a "palomino," it was because that meant "dove-colored" in Spanish. If he roped with a "lariat," it was because the Spanish term for such a rope was *la reata*. If he preferred to say "lasso," he was using the Spanish word for a snare, *lazo*. If he called another man "hombre," if he said "vamoose" instead of "leave," or "savvy" instead of "know," it was because the Spanish *hombre* meant "man," *vamos* meant "let's go," and because he was mispronouncing the Spanish *sabe*, which meant "you know."

NAT LOVE. This African-American cowboy was born a slave in Tennessee during the 1850s. He eventually made his way west to Deadwood, South Dakota, where he claimed to have won a contest in 1876 to determine who could become known as Deadwood Dick. The mythic American cowboy was less a western reality than the creation of eastern journalists and dime-novel writers, whose audiences were mainly city people.

THE END OF THE OPEN RANGE

The long drive had a brief existence. Gradually, people north of Texas realized that as the railroads came closer, it made sense to breed and feed cattle nearby instead of driving them up from Texas. During the 1880s the long drive from Texas was replaced by an even wilder cattle bonanza in other plains territories to the north. In 1860 there were no cattle at all in the northwestern plains, and there were only a few in Kansas and Nebraska. By 1880, Montana, the Dakota Territory, Wyoming, and Colorado had great herds, totaling almost 4 million head.

THE LAST FRONTIER c.1860–1890

(Map showing the western United States with labels including:) CANADA, Tacoma, Portland, Columbia R., Last Chance Gulch (Helena), Bozeman, NORTHERN PACIFIC R.R., Yellowstone R., Duluth, Alder Gulch (Virginia City), Boise, Bighorn Mts., Deadwood, Silver City, Snake R., BLACK HILLS, Custer City, Missouri R., Chicago, ROCKY, Promontory Point, CENTRAL PACIFIC R.R., Great Salt Lake, UNION PACIFIC R.R., FIRST TELEGRAPH LINE, Omaha, Council Bluffs, PONY EXPRESS, Sacramento R., Salt Lake City, Platte R., St. Joseph, San Francisco, Sutter's Fort (Sacramento), Virginia City, Comstock Lode, Boulder, Denver, Abilene, Kansas City, Sedalia, St. Louis, Colorado R., PIKES PEAK, Pueblo, Arkansas R., Wichita, BUTTERFIELD, Dodge City, Los Angeles, Santa Fe, Rio Grande, Pecos R., GOODNIGHT-LOVING TRAIL, WESTERN TRAIL, CHISHOLM TRAIL, Mississippi River, OVERLAND, EXPRESS, Tucson, Ft. Worth, SEDALIA TRAIL, New Orleans, El Paso, SOUTHERN PACIFIC R.R., San Antonio, Rio Grande, MEXICO, GULF OF MEXICO, PACIFIC OCEAN

Legend:
- Railroads
- Cattle trails
- Mining sites
- Cattle raising areas after 1880

0   100   200   300 MILES

But the days of the open range, when cattle wandered on public land from one spring to the next, could not last long. The cattle industry soon found itself in a situation that typically afflicts large-scale agriculture: overproduction. Rapid expansion led to an overstocked range. The grass could not support so many cattle. The increased supply also caused prices to fall. Between 1885 and 1886 the Chicago price of a steer dropped from thirty dollars to ten. The following winter on the plains was the bitterest in memory. Thousands of cattle starved and froze to death. The cattle bonanza was over.

THE DEFEAT OF THE NATIVE AMERICANS

The miners, railroaders, and cattlemen brought about the final chapter in the conflict between whites and Native Americans. It was a conflict older than European "settlement," and as tragic as any aspect of American history. The whites cloaked their actions with high-sounding, abstract expressions like "civilization against savagery" or "Manifest Destiny." But the facts were simple, and not at all abstract: the whites came and took the Indians' lands.

White people in the New World had always regarded the Native Americans as a "problem." Most whites—whether they were French, Spanish, or English—saw the Indians either as a people to be exploited through trade or slavery or as a barrier to westward expansion. A few whites sympathized with the Indians and did what they could to protect them from the worst aspects of white civilization. But even to those who were sympathetic, helping meant teaching the Indians to "adjust to civilization."

The Native Americans might be a "problem" for the whites, but for the Indians the whites meant disaster. At stake for the whites was only the delay of continental expansion for a generation or so. The stakes for the Native Americans were much higher. They were in danger of losing their culture, their freedom, their identity as human beings, and, in many cases, their lives. This was true from the time the Spanish invaded Mexico to the final conquest of the tribes of the American West.

ADVANTAGES OF THE WHITES

White people's ways were overpowering. In the first place, the whites' methods of dealing with the environment were unlike those of the Native Americans. Some Indians farmed. But the whites were able to cultivate vast stretches of land, first with teams of mules or oxen, then with machinery. Some Indians, like the Navajos, made ornaments out of silver or gold. But the whites came for gold and silver in droves. Big new towns and frightening machines and explosives changed the face of the mountains and valleys of the Rockies. The Indians hunted wild animals, which seemed numerous enough to last forever. But the whites killed off the wild animals,

fenced in the range, and raised great herds of cattle instead.

These were the main weapons of the whites: farming, mining, and ranching. Along with these the whites brought strange powers and "medicine" that made the Native Americans' situation hopeless indeed: the railroad, machine guns and cannons, and the telegraph.

Another weapon of the whites against the Indians was something they only rarely used on purpose—indeed, the whites feared it themselves. This was disease. Smallpox, measles, and other sicknesses may have wiped out as many as half the western Indians before any significant number of whites even arrived in their territory. The germs traveled with traders and so preceded white migrations by decades. The Indians had no inherited resistance or immunity to many diseases of the whites, because the germs had been imported from Europe. Indians died by the band and even by the tribe from sicknesses that only made most whites uncomfortable.

Finally, the whites had an advantage that probably counted more than anything else: numbers. They poured west by the thousands. In one change of seasons, between one Sun Dance and another, the whites seemed able to throw up towns like San Francisco, Denver, or Deadwood—towns that soon had populations larger than the whole Sioux nation.

One by one, the tribes of the Great Plains, the California-Intermountain area, and the northwest coast were made to realize that the whites were a force they could neither understand nor control. Some groups, like the Sioux, the Kiowas, and the Apaches, fought back. They were sustained by their myths, their magic, and their hatred of the cavalry that invaded their villages, shooting men, women, and children. But in the end, all the tribes were defeated. Only something as unusual as Wovoka's Ghost Dance could convince Native Americans—and only a few at that—that there was any way to combat the enveloping white civilization.

DEALING WITH THE TRIBES

From the beginning, United States policy toward the Native Americans had been contradictory. On the one hand, the government treated tribes as independent nations with whom it could make treaties. On the other hand, Indians were not citizens but wards of the government, subject to federal control. In addition, the American nation was growing with incredible speed. Again and again, government aims that seemed practical in one decade were obsolete ten years later.

In California and Oregon, and in the frontier regions of the Rockies, relations between whites and Indians were poorly controlled by the government. Groups of whites simply drove the Indians out, murdering many of them in the process. The Indians of California suffered especially. They had settled around Spanish missions and learned farming and various crafts. After the Spanish missions were closed down in the 1830s, the Indians were defenseless against the greedy whites. In the ten years after the gold rush of 1849, some 70,000 of these "mission Indians" died from starvation, disease, and outright murder.

On the Great Plains, whites might band together to attack Indians. But the government and its army played a much larger role in keeping the peace there than it did farther west. After 1850 the history of Indian-white relations settled down to a fairly steady rhythm of treaties, "uprisings," war, and new treaties. The Native Americans were always the losers. Even when they won the battles, they lost in the making of the treaties.

This process began in 1851 at Fort Laramie on the Oregon Trail. To protect the trail, the government called hundreds of Indian leaders together and persuaded them to agree not to bother the wagon trains crossing their territory. Each tribe accepted boundaries to its hunting grounds. In return, the government promised to leave them in peace.

These agreements left the Indians in possession of almost all of the Great Plains. But accepting boundaries laid out by Washington opened the door to a new government tactic: getting each tribe, by a separate treaty, to give up part of its lands. By 1865 the tribes had given up all of Kansas, most of Nebraska, the central half of Utah, and almost all of Texas.

THE SAND CREEK MASSACRE

Much Native American land was surrendered peacefully, in return for promises of peace and annual shipments of government supplies, called annuities. But in 1861 in Colorado, a government attempt to move Cheyennes and Arapahoes onto a small reservation at Sand Creek resulted in the Indians' waging a three-year guerrilla war. In 1864 the leader of the warring Indians, Black Kettle, tried to make peace with the whites. The army and the territorial government refused. The unyielding commander of the Colorado militia, Colonel John Chivington, told Black Kettle: "My rule for fighting white men or Indians is to fight them until they lay down their arms and surrender."

Black Kettle led his people to a camp at Sand Creek, where he hoped to be left in peace. But the Indians woke on November 29, 1864, to find 1,000 of Chivington's militia surrounding them. The militia rushed the camp, shooting at everything that moved. When the "fight" was over, 450 Indians were dead. Only about 50 had escaped the massacre. The next year the Cheyennes and Arapahoes had to sign a new treaty with the United States. The treaty forced them to leave their Colorado plains for a barren corner of Indian Territory.

NEGOTIATIONS WITH THE SIOUX

The Sioux fared better, at least for a time. Their agreement at Fort Laramie in 1851 gave them one of the largest hunting areas in the West: most of the Dakota Territory and the region around Powder River in eastern Wyoming and southern

Montana. But by 1865, miners had crowded into Montana at Bozeman, Virginia City, and Helena. These towns soon demanded a road connecting them with the Oregon Trail. This road would cross the Yellowstone River, skirt the Sioux hunting areas around the Big Horn Mountains, and cross directly over the valley of Powder River.

In the summer of 1865 the cavalry moved into the area to construct forts and begin work on the road. A Sioux chief, Red Cloud, led his people in a two-year attack on the road and the forts. And in 1868 the government made a new treaty that seemed to give the victory to Red Cloud. The road was abandoned. But the Sioux, in return, had to agree to a reservation that included only the Dakotas west of the Missouri—the so-called Great Sioux Reservation. According to the treaty, they could still hunt in the Powder River country. For the first time, however, they had accepted a reservation to replace the large domain that their 1851 treaty had recognized.

The commission that made the 1868 agreement with the Sioux dealt with other Plains tribes in the same way. Reservations were created in Indian Territory for the southern groups: the Kiowa, Comanche, Arapaho, Cheyenne, Osage, and Pawnee tribes. Between 1868 and 1874 the northern tribes—Crows and Blackfeet, Shoshonis and others—also accepted new, restricted reservations. By 1876 the Plains Indians had given up over three-fourths of the land they had held under the Fort Laramie Treaty just twenty-five years before.

THE BATTLE OF LITTLE BIGHORN

The policy of concentrating Indians on reservations was applied once again in the Black Hills area of South Dakota. The treaty of 1868 guaranteed the Teton Sioux complete possession of the Black Hills. But in 1874, rumors of gold led to a reconnaissance of the area by a military column of the Seventh Cavalry under Colonel George Custer. Custer's men found gold, and the resulting rush into Deadwood and other mining towns made conflict between the Sioux and the whites inevitable.

The Grant administration tried for a time to hold the prospectors back. The army even removed some of them. But finally the government gave in and allowed the prospectors to enter the Black Hills "at their own risk." The next step was as cruel and illegal as any the government ever took against the Sioux. To prevent clashes between the miners and the Indians, Washington ordered all the Sioux to report to reservation agencies. Any who remained outside would be considered automatically "hostile" and subject to attack. Many of the Sioux obeyed the order. But about 8,000 of them defied the government and gathered in the area of the Big Horn Mountains for their annual summer encampment and Sun Dance.

In June 1876 the army launched powerful forces of infantry, cavalry, and artillery against these "hostile" Sioux. One column, marching north from the Platte River, met Crazy Horse's forces at Rosebud Creek on June 17. The army was beaten back in fierce fighting. Crazy Horse returned to the Sioux camp on the Little Bighorn River, where 8,000 Teton Sioux had gathered—the most powerful single assembly of Native American warriors the army would ever face. Another army column advanced from the east. On June 25 the Seventh Cavalry, again under Custer's command, rode foolishly to the attack. The Sioux killed Custer and over 200 of his troopers.

Another cycle of treaty, war, and new treaty was about to be completed. Within a year, the Sioux were forced to give up their important Black Hills area. They were now herded onto a reservation covering only the central part of South Dakota, between the Missouri River and the Black Hills. But their troubles were not over. A railroad was pushing toward the reservation, and the remaining Sioux stood in its path. Farmers and ranchers were also beginning to look longingly at the land that the Sioux still held.

CHIEF JOSEPH AND THE NEZ PERCÉS

In 1877, the year after the Battle of the Little Bighorn, another legendary Native American leader had his final confrontation with the forces of the United States. Hinmaton-Yalaktit was his name—"thunder coming out of the water and over the land." Joseph was his white man's name. He was a chief in the Sahaptin tribe, which the whites called Nez Percé—pierced nose—because of their custom of wearing nose ornaments made of shells.

In 1863 the Nez Percés had ceded most of their lands to the United States and agreed to live on a small reservation in Idaho. A "renegade" portion of the tribe, however, refused to recognize the treaty. For ten years, the government did not try to enforce the treaty, and all the Nez Percés had to do was fend off individual white squatters. This was the situation when Joseph, at age thirty-three, became chief. In 1876 the government decided to enforce the treaty and move the "renegade" Nez Percés onto the Idaho reservation. A group of Joseph's warriors, almost certainly without his blessing, went on a rampage and killed twenty or so white settlers. Reluctantly, Joseph was drawn into a situation in which he knew final victory was impossible. He decided to strike out for Canada.

The force Joseph led into the mountains contained fewer than 200 fighting men, who had to protect about 600 women and children. But Joseph was able to lead them on a superb retreat that covered hundreds of miles of difficult wilderness. He ran when he could and fought when he had to. In August 1877 he defeated the cavalry in a desperate struggle on the Big Hole River in Montana. Finally, Joseph got his people into the Bear Paw Mountains, only thirty miles from Canada.

Joseph thought he had won, and stopped to allow his dozens of wounded and helpless followers to rest. But at the beginning of October, he was overtaken by a force of cavalry, and had to decide, quickly, whether to run, surrender, or fight. He chose to fight, and kept the cavalry at bay for five days. Finally, he surrendered his beaten force: 87 men, almost half of them wounded, and about 350 women and children. To this broken remnant of the Nez Percés, Joseph made a classic Native-American speech:

I am tired of fighting. The old men are all dead. My brother who led the young men is dead. It is cold, and we have no blankets. The little children are freezing to death. My people, some of them, have run away to the hills. No one knows where they are. I want to have some time to look for my children and see how many I can find. Maybe I shall find them among the dead.

Hear me, my chiefs. From where the sun now stands, I will fight no more forever.

Joseph and his people were taken first to Kansas and then to Indian Territory, where many of them died of disease. A few were eventually returned to Idaho. But Joseph never went home. He was moved to a reservation in Washington State. Separated from his people, Joseph died in 1904. The official cause of death was entered as "broken heart."

A CHANGING POLICY

The idea of private property is so deeply rooted in white society that it is sometimes difficult to grasp the Native Americans' concept of land ownership. Most western tribes looked on the land in more or less the same way that fishermen look on the sea—as a place to hunt. No Indian thought of himself as *owning* a piece of the land. He might own his horses or his weapons, but the land itself was the "property" of the whole tribe, to be used communally and protected from other tribes.

When the various tribes of the plains agreed to give up their land, they did so as tribal units, not as individuals. When they accepted the reservations, too, they accepted them as tribes, not as individual property owners.

Reformers, most of whom lived in the East, believed that private property was an essential feature of "civilization." To break the Native Americans' ancient, communal concept of land, the reformers proposed that the reservations be divided into lots and given to individual families in "severalty"—that the Indians be treated as "several," or separate, individuals. Westerners, anxious to exploit the Indians, agreed with this proposal. Their enthusiasm was a result of some simple arithmetic. If every Native American family was given an individual farm, a lot of reservation land would be left over. There simply were not enough Indians, in most tribes, to "use" all the reservation land. The remaining acres could become available to whites.

This new policy became law in 1887 in the Dawes Severalty Act. The next year, after much argument, some trickery, and probably some bribery, whites persuaded the Sioux to accept the new plan. The one big Sioux reservation could then be broken down into five smaller ones that were, all together, less than half as large in area as the original. The same policy was applied to the other Plains Indians. One after another, the tribes settled for 160 acres per family. One after another, they realized this meant giving up about half their tribal lands. The resulting demoralization provided fertile ground for the new Ghost Dance religion. No matter what the intentions of the whites who wrote and supported the Dawes Severalty Act, it was just one more disaster for the Indians. In 1887, Indians had held about 130 million acres of land in the United States; by 1930, after forty-three years of the Dawes Act, the total had been reduced to less than 50 million acres.

With the new policy came even stronger efforts to convert Native Americans to white "civilization"—to make them "walk the white man's road," as Sitting Bull put it. These efforts hardened the conflict in attitudes between the "progressive" Indians, who accepted the new ways, and the "nonprogressives," who clung to the old ones. The division was dramatized when Sitting Bull was killed by "progressive" Indian police from his own tribe. Even after the reforms of the 1880s, American policy toward the Native Americans was a calamity. They were reduced to a condition in some ways worse than that of the freed slaves in the South. The stage had been set for Wounded Knee.

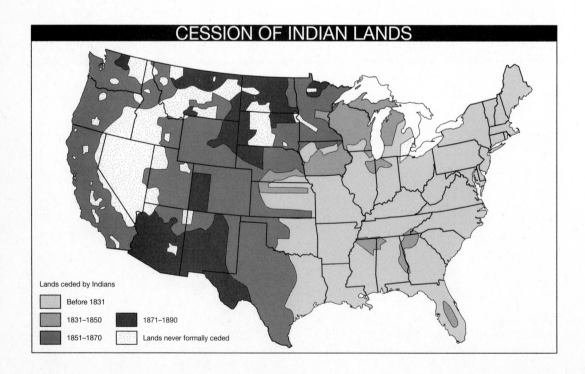

CESSION OF INDIAN LANDS

Lands ceded by Indians

- Before 1831
- 1831–1850
- 1851–1870
- 1871–1890
- Lands never formally ceded

FARMING ON THE PLAINS

Mining, railroads, and cattle ranching had created a scattered pattern of settlement on the Great Plains and in the Rockies. Miners gathered in towns that were separated by hundreds of miles. Railroads created towns, but only along their rights-of-way. And ranchers needed only a few cowhands to handle even very large herds. The actual "settlement" of the plains had to await the slower migrations of farmers away from the Mississippi and onto the dry grasslands.

THE HOMESTEAD ACT

The pace and pattern of settlement depended very much on government encouragement. In its youth, the Republican party had been the party of "free soil," which meant both agriculture without slavery and free land for any American. One of the first measures promoted by the Lincoln administration had been the Homestead Act of 1862. According to this law, any citizen (or even an immigrant who had taken the first step toward becoming a citizen) could claim 160 acres of public land, just by paying a fee of $26–$34. If he "lived upon or cultivated the land" for five years, it became his, free and forever. If the homesteader did not want to wait five years, he could pay for the land at $1.25 an acre and own it after only six months.

The Homestead Act resulted in over a half million claims, totaling 80 million acres. But if its purpose was to award most of the public lands of the West to simple farmers, it was a failure. Much more land was given to railroads and states or sold directly to speculators than was ever acquired by small farmers.

Moreover, many of the homestead claims were phony. By law it was possible to transfer ownership at any time to any other person or corporation. So, for example, a rancher could have each of his hands claim a homestead and then (for a small bribe) transfer ownership to the ranch. Any land speculator could do the same, just by paying a bribe to a stranger passing through.

OTHER LAND ACTS

Congress made the situation worse by passing several more laws that promoted corruption and what amounted to the theft of public land. First, in 1873, came the Timber Culture Act, which allowed a homesteader (or a rancher or speculator) to claim an additional 160 acres if he would plant trees on 40 of the acres. In 1877, Congress passed the Desert Land Act, which allowed an individual to claim 640 acres of land if he would begin irrigation. Under the law, ranchers took up section after section of land, especially in the Southwest, since they needed it for grazing cattle. They had their friends swear that it was "irrigated" (even if they had only poured a bucket of water on it in the presence of their "witnesses").

Even more corruption resulted from the Timber and Stone Act of 1878. This law applied to forest land that could not be farmed but that was highly profitable for timber. Under this law, any citizen or immigrant could purchase up to 160 acres of western forest for $2.50 an acre. Lumbermen used the same tricks that ranchers and other speculators used. They imported sailors, prospectors, and others to buy land and then sign it over to a company for a small fee. And since one good log sold for about $2.50, every tree after the first from any acre of land was pure profit. Under these laws, over 20 million more acres of potentially valuable public land fell into the hands of corporations and speculators.

HARDSHIPS AND SOLUTIONS

Despite the fact that many of the profits went to land speculators and big corporations, Western lands were opened to the American people. Though they might have to pay ten dollars an acre to a speculator instead of getting homestead land virtually free from the government, farmers moved out onto the plains anyway. The majority

KANSAS REST STOP. People moving west took as much with them as their covered wagons could haul. And this included as much of their old life as possible. This woman has brought along a symbol of the home she has left behind, a clean white tablecloth. Somewhere on a treeless Kansas plain, the couple has paused for a meal, which she is spreading on a makeshift table set up in the grass.

came from the states bordering the Mississippi. Most of the rest were immigrants. Almost no workers from eastern cities made the trip west. But the men and women who did settle on the plains performed a monumental task. In the thirty years after 1870 they brought more land under cultivation than had been cleared and plowed by all the generations of farmers from the settlement of Jamestown to the Civil War.

These farmers confronted problems that they had not met farther east. They found that

their old ways of plowing and planting would not work. For one thing, rainfall was scarce, rivers often ran dry, and the water table was deep. Farmers had to haul water from long distances or collect it in holes when it did rain. New well-digging machinery, invented in the 1880s and 1890s, however, enabled people to dig deeper wells to reach the water table. And steel windmills made it easier to pump the water up. Plains dwellers also developed dry farming. This technique, by which a farmer covers a plowed field with a blanket of dust, conserves the moisture in the soil.

Another problem on the plains was lack of wood. Farmers living there often made their first homes from cakes of sod. For fuel they burned old hay or dried cow dung. Fencing was also a special problem until the invention of barbed wire in the 1870s.

A farm family soon learned that, while sixty acres of land could support them back east, five times as much was needed on the plains. Nature seemed to do things on a grand scale there. In summer the wind blew hot, and twice as hard as in the East. In winter, blizzards howled down out of the mountains, burying homes and killing livestock. Tornadoes, dust storms, and plagues of locusts and grasshoppers were frequent.

Dry years drove thousands of farmers back east. Many of those who stayed barely survived. In the end, though, farmers turned the plains into the world's most efficient area for producing wheat, corn, and other grains. By 1880, American flour—like American beef and pork from the same area—was being exported in great quantities all over the world.

In all this the Native American was, of course, the great loser. The whites' successes on the plains seemed to prove what white Americans had always believed—that the Indians could not make proper "use" of their environment.

Whites were able to exploit even the tough plains environment, to draw from it enough food to feed not only most of the United States but part of the rest of the world, too. The Native Americans had developed a sustainable relationship to their environment, but one that allowed them only to feed, cloth, and shelter themselves—and this often precariously. A full century was to pass before many white Americans began to ask themselves seriously whether the Indians' "way" was not somehow at least as good as theirs. Only one thing was certain: Native Americans had lived in ways that had much less enduring impact on the land. To be sure, they used all the tools they could get—including the rifle, the horse, and the knife—to wring what they could from their world. But they were less likely to view nature as something that they could control and remake at will, as white Americans had learned to do. This, at least in part, was what the massacre at Wounded Knee was all about.

CHRONOLOGY

1849	American and Chinese miners begin California gold rush
1851	Native Americans agree to Treaty of Fort Laramie, accepting first boundaries to hunting areas
1858	Colorado gold rush;
	Butterfield Stage Road opened through Southwest to California
1859	Comstock Lode discovered in Nevada
1860	Pony express route opened between Missouri and California
1861	Civil War begins;
	Telegraph line to California established
1862	Congress establishes subsidies for transcontinental railroad construction;
	Homestead Act
1863	Idaho Territory organized
1864	Land allowance for transcontinental railroad doubled;
	Montana Territory organized;
	Sand Creek massacre in Colorado;
	Missouri Pacific railroad reaches Sedalia, Missouri; cattle era of "long drive" begins
1865	Civil War ends
1866	Sioux chief Red Cloud begins two-year war with U.S. Army
1868	Great Sioux Reservation established in the Dakotas
1869	First transcontinental rail line completed

1873	Hinmaton-Yalaktit (Chief Joseph) becomes chief of Nez Percé tribe;
	Timber Culture Act
1874	Gold discovered in the Black Hills of the Dakotas
1876	Battles of Rosebud Creek and Little Bighorn;
	Nez Percé "renegades" strike out for Canada
1877	Chief Joseph and his Nez Percé band surrender;
	Crazy Horse surrenders, enters Sioux reservation;
	Desert Land Act
1878	Timber and Stone Act
1881	Sitting Bull and his band return from Canada, surrender, and enter the Sioux reservation
1883	Senate investigating committee visits Sioux reservation
1885	Rapid collapse of Chicago price for beef
1887	Dawes Severalty Act
1889	Bitter winter severely damages cattle industry;
	Sioux learn of Wovoka's Ghost Dance religion
1890	Massacre at Wounded Knee Creek;
	Bureau of the Census officially declares that the frontier no longer exists

-›-=⊙=‹-

SUGGESTIONS FOR FURTHER READING

WOUNDED KNEE

Robert M. Utley, *The Last Days of the Sioux Nation* (1963), is a scholarly, balanced, but readable story of the gradual collapse of Sioux society under white pressure. Also important are Utley's more recent books, *Frontier Regulars: The United States Army and the Indian* (1973), and *The Indian Frontier of the American West* (1984). Stanley Vestal's biography *Sitting Bull* (1957) is important, as is C. M. Oehler, *The Great Sioux Uprising* (1959). James Mooney was an anthropologist who did extensive fieldwork among western Indians during the period. He collected his observations and many of the Ghost Dance songs in his classic *The Ghost Dance Religion and the Sioux Uprising of 1890* (republished in 1965).

THE MINING AND CATTLE FRONTIERS

A great beginning is to read Mark Twain's uproarious but informative *Roughing It* (1872). Rodman W. Paul, *The Far West and the Great Plains in Transition* (1988), is a fine survey. Patricia Limerick's *Legacy of Conquest: The Unbroken Past of the American West* (1987) is an interesting, if somewhat idiosyncratic, book. A nice discussion of the astonishing development of mining cities is Gunther Barth, *Instant Cities* (1975). The same author's *Bitter Strength* (1964) deals with the experiences of Chinese immigrants in the Far West. The unhappy social history of the Spanish-speaking natives of California is the subject of Leonard Pitt, *The Decline of the Californios* (1966). On the gold-mining areas, a somewhat dated but still usable book is G. C. Quiett, *Paydirt: A Panorama of American Gold Rushes* (1936). More modern discussions of the various mining frontiers are available in R. W. Paul, *Mining Frontiers of the Far West* (1963), and William S. Greever, *Bonanza West: Western Mining Rushes* (1963). Useful treatments of the origin and development of the cattle frontier are E. E. Dale, *The Range Cattle Industry* (1930); Lewis Atherton, *The Cattle Kings* (1961); Terry Jordan, *Trails to Texas* (1981); Robert Dykstra, *The Cattle Towns* (1968); and J. M. Shagg, *The Cattle Trading Industry* (1973). J. B. Frantz and J. E. Choate, *The American Cowboy, Myth and Reality* (1955); David Day, *Cowboy Culture* (1981); Roger McGrath, *Gunfighters, Highwaymen, and Vigilantes* (1984); and Philip Durham and E.

L. Jones, *The Negro Cowboy* (1965), are careful and realistic treatments of the highly romanticized culture that grew up around the cattle industry.

THE DEFEAT OF THE NATIVE AMERICANS

A very useful general approach to the subject is Philip Weeks, *Farewell, My Nation: The American Indian and the United States* (1990). Dee Brown, *Bury My Heart at Wounded Knee* (1955), is a sometimes moving and not always precisely accurate book. But it is still an excellent place for the student to begin reading. F. G. Roe, *The Indian and the Horse* (1955), discusses the most intimate and important relationship of the western Indians to a new animal tool. The most general and reliable scholarly discussion of the gradual ruin of Native American civilization and culture on the Great Plains is R. K. Andrist, *The Long Death: The Last Days of the Plains Indians* (1964). Also extremely useful are Francis Paul Prucha, *The Great Father: The United States Government and the American Indians* (1984), and Richard White, *The Roots of Dependency* (1983). Two general studies by Wilcomb Washburn, *The Indian in North America* (1975) and *Red Man's Land—White Man's Law* (1971), have useful information on this period. Federal policy toward the tribes is the subject of Francis Paul, *American Indian Policy in Crisis* (1976).

FARMING ON THE PLAINS

Two accounts of the way the public lands of the United States were made available for settlement and exploitation are R. M. Robbins, *Our Landed Heritage* (1942), and Paul W. Gates, *The History of Public Land Development* (1968). On farming on the plains, F. A. Shannon, *The Farmer's Last Frontier* (1945); Gilbert C. Fite, *The Farmer's Frontier* (1966); and Allen G. Bogue, *From Prairie to Corn Belt* (1963), are the basic studies. J. A. Malin, *The Grasslands Agriculture of North America* (1947), is a technical but important book. A more recent study of the water problem on the plains is Donald Worster, *Rivers of Empire: Water, Aridity, and the Growth of the American West* (1985). The impact of the railroads can be followed in G. R. Taylor and I. D. Neu, *The American Railroad Network* (1956).

The Gospel of Wealth

THE EPISODE: *On August 4, 1892, two wealthy inhabitants of the industrial city of Fall River, Mass., were brutally murdered in their home—hacked many times about the head with an ax. All the evidence pointed to a most improbable suspect— Lizzie Borden, the victims' own daughter. Lizzie was arrested and put on trial. Throughout the United States the case was headline news. Most Americans found it difficult to believe that Lizzie Borden was guilty. But the prosecution mounted a provocative case, arguing that beneath the calm, respectable surface of the Borden household lay a deep well of conflict and anger. As the trial developed, both the jury and the public followed in fascination as the prosecution and the defense presented two profoundly contrasting pictures of life in the Borden family.*

THE HISTORICAL SETTING: *Whether or not Lizzie Borden was guilty, the two competing pictures of life in the Borden household reflected two different sides of life in late nineteenth-century American cities and towns. For the well-to-do and the middle classes, life was good—on the surface. Benefiting from the great increase in national prosperity over the decades following the Civil War, these people proudly (even frantically) displayed their new wealth by building bigger houses, wearing fancier clothing, and behaving with ever more elaborate rituals of "good manners." Through their family life they found the greatest opportunity to display the signs of their public status.*

But their families were also designed to provide refuge and comfort from the tensions of life in the outside world of business and moneymaking. Women, above all, had to play both roles at once. They had to display—with their clothing, their manners, and their leisure—all evidence of family prosperity. But they also had to act as selfless sources of kindness and emotional support for their husbands, children, and parents. Playing both these roles demanded that women remain at home, away from the sordid business world where money was actually made.

Women in poorer families, however, lacked the choice of remaining at home. For these women (many of them recent immigrants or African Americans), it was necessary to earn money to supplement the meager incomes of their husbands or fathers. Usually, that meant taking menial, dead-end jobs for very low wages. So for many Americans, rich and poor alike, the family was unable to become the deep source of inner satisfaction and peace it was expected to be. The burden of this failure fell especially hard on women. Few responded the way Lizzie Borden may have done, but the tensions hidden within the Borden household were commonplaces of late nineteenth-century American life.

THE LIZZIE BORDEN MURDERS

Thursday, August 4, 1892. The summer morning was hot and sultry in Fall River, Massachusetts. It was uncomfortable everywhere—out in the city's streets and inside its textile mills, its tenements, and even its mansions.

In the house at 92 Second Street, Bridget Sullivan, the live-in Irish servant, was at work, washing the downstairs windows. At exactly 10:40 A.M. her employer, Andrew J. Borden, arrived home from his daily business rounds downtown and started to open the front door. There were two separate locks on the door, and even after Mr. Borden opened both of them, he was still faced with a metal bolt, which could be opened only from the inside. Bridget Sullivan knew what was happening, so she stopped her work and walked over to the entrance in order to help Mr. Borden. For a moment, Bridget had trouble releasing the bolt. As she fumbled with it she muttered in frustration—a sound she later reported to be "Pshaw." Her expletive was overheard by the only other person known to be in the house, Lizzie Borden, Mr. Borden's thirty-two-year-old daughter. Lizzie, standing on the top of the stairs leading up from the front hall, laughed.

Andrew Borden walked into the house without speaking to Bridget, and the maid resumed her window washing. Lizzie joined Mr. Borden, and father and daughter spoke briefly with each other. From the next room, Bridget was sure she heard Lizzie tell Mr. Borden that his wife "had a note and had gone out."

After a few minutes, Andrew Borden got up, took the key to his room from its accustomed spot on the dining room mantelpiece, and went upstairs. A few minutes later, he came down again to take a nap. Still dressed in his tie and jacket, he lay down on the couch in the sitting room, his feet resting on the carpet.

As Mr. Borden lay down, Bridget moved discreetly into the dining room, to wash the windows there. After a few moments, she was joined by Lizzie, who was carrying an ironing board and who now began to iron a stack of handkerchiefs. Quietly, Lizzie began a conversation with the servant:

"Maggie, are you going out today?" Lizzie asked. (Maggie had been the name of a previous Borden family servant, and Lizzie Borden always addressed Bridget by that name.)

"I don't know," Bridget answered. "I might and I might not. I don't feel very well." (Bridget had been vomiting earlier in the morning.)

"If you go out, be sure and lock the door, for Mrs. Borden has gone out on a sick call [to visit a sick person], and I might go out, too."

"Miss Lizzie, who is sick?"

"I don't know. She had a note this morning. It must be in town."

Soon, Bridget finished washing the dining room windows and returned to the kitchen to clean up. She was feeling ill, and she needed to rest. She climbed upstairs to her room in the attic, and without undressing, lay down on her bed. Soon Bridget heard the clock at city hall, two blocks away, strike eleven. It was too hot to sleep. Andrew Borden had now been home for twenty minutes. Bridget Sullivan continued to lie on her bed for ten minutes more. All this time, she heard nothing at all from downstairs, no doors opening or closing, no voices talking or arguing, no sound.

Until 11:10. That was when Lizzie Borden hollered up to her: "Maggie, come down!" Bridget could tell something was wrong. "What is the matter?" she called down.

"Come down quick!" Lizzie yelled back. "Father's dead! Somebody came in and killed him!"

Bridget ran downstairs and headed toward the sitting room—but Lizzie stopped her. "Oh, Maggie, don't go in," she warned. Then she said, "I have got to have a doctor, quick. Go over. I have got to have the doctor." The doctor was Seabury Bowen, who lived diagonally across the street. But Dr. Bowen was out on his rounds, so Bridget blurted the news of the murder to the doctor's wife, then quickly returned to the Borden house.

Once again, Lizzie asked Bridget to go out—this time to find her some companionship. "Go and get Miss Russell. I can't be alone in the house." (Alice Russell was Lizzie's best friend; Lizzie had visited her just the previous evening.) As Bridget went out to fetch Miss Russell, she was observed by a next-door neighbor, who noticed that Bridget was walking fast and looking pale. The neighbor, a woman named Adelaide Churchill, knew that something must be wrong. She looked out through her kitchen window and peered into the Borden house, where she spotted Lizzie Borden standing by the side door. Opening the window, Mrs. Churchill yelled across: "Lizzie, what is the matter?"

"Oh, Mrs. Churchill, do come over," Lizzie replied. "Someone has killed father!"

Mrs. Churchill rushed over and found Lizzie sitting on the inside stairs. Placing her hand on Lizzie's arm to comfort her, she asked, "Oh, Lizzie, where is your father?"

"In the sitting room."

Then Mrs. Churchill asked Lizzie a key question: "Where were you when it happened?"

Lizzie's response was the basis of the story she would continue to tell, with variations, over the next year: "I went out to the barn to get a piece of iron. I heard a distressing noise and came back and found the screen door open."

But Mrs. Churchill was more worried about the rest of the Borden family than suspicious of Lizzie's story. She realized that Lizzie's stepmother, Abby, might be in danger. Where was Abby? she asked.

"I don't know," Lizzie replied. "She had got a note to go see someone who is sick." And she added: "But I don't know but she is killed, too, for I thought I heard her come in."

Now Lizzie changed the subject, and spoke once again of her dead father: "Father must have an enemy, for we have all been sick, and we think the milk has been poisoned. I must have a doctor."

As it turned out, Dr. Bowen had just returned home, learned of the horrifying event, and headed to the Borden house. He went straight to the sitting room to examine the body, which was lying face up on the sofa. He later reported what he had seen.

His face was very badly cut, apparently with a sharp instrument. His face was covered with blood. I felt of his pulse and satisfied myself he was dead. I glanced about the room and saw there was nothing disturbed—neither the furniture nor anything at all. . . . His face was hardly to be recognized by one who knew him.

His brief examination complete, Dr. Bowen moved into the dining room. He kept repeating: "He is murdered, he is murdered." Then Dr. Bowen returned to question Lizzie Borden. Had she seen an intruder? he asked. She repeated her story that she had been out in the barn looking for a piece of iron. And she mentioned the fear she had expressed a few minutes earlier about some "enemy." But now she offered an explanation of that fear: "She said she was afraid her father had had trouble with tenants, and she had overheard loud conversations several times recently."

Meanwhile, Bridget Sullivan had found Lizzie's friend Alice Russell, and the two women returned to the house. Bridget, too, had begun to be concerned about her mistress, Abby Borden. Bridget knew there was only one person who would have been likely to ask Abby Borden to come visiting when she was sick: that was Abby's younger sister, Mrs. Sarah Whitehead. So Bridget offered a suggestion:

"Oh, Lizzie, if I knew where Mrs. Whitehead was, I would go and see if Mrs. Borden was there, and tell her that Mr. Borden was very sick."

But now Lizzie repeated her hint that Mrs. Borden might not be out after all, but might be somewhere in the house that very minute. And if she was, then why had she not come downstairs to see what was the matter? "Maggie," said Lizzie Borden, "I am almost positive I heard her coming in. Won't you go upstairs to see?"

Bridget knew very well what it was she might see, so she refused to do what her mistress asked. She said simply: "I am not going upstairs alone."

The next-door neighbor, Mrs. Churchill, said she was willing to accompany Bridget to the second floor, and the two women started upstairs together. Bridget led the way, so she was the first to spot the second body. It was in the guest room, lying face down, resting on its knees where it had fallen. The two women did not stay very long—they knew who it was and that she was dead. They headed right back to the first floor. Now Lizzie was lying down, as if expecting the dread news. But it was her friend Alice Russell who spoke first, her words tactful, almost delicate: "Is there another?" Mrs. Churchill answered: "Yes, she is up there."

The police made efforts to find a crazed intruder—but they never found a serious suspect. In fact, the possibility of such an intruder almost had to be excluded: too many people had been abroad on Second Street that morning, or watching the street from their windows. If there had been an intruder, he had somehow escaped everyone's notice. So they also pursued another avenue of investigation, trying to discover whether anyone had sufficient reason to want to kill Andrew Borden. And they could come up with no such hypothetical person, either. Andrew Borden may have had trouble with his tenants, as Lizzie had said, but extensive investigation revealed no "enemy" with any real reason to slaughter him and his wife. Finally, robbery could be excluded as a motive: nothing at all had been taken from the house, and there were not even signs of a search.

THE MURDER SCENE. This photograph of Andrew J. Borden's body was taken by the Fall River Police Department within a few hours of his murder. Examine the furnishings—comfortable, but shabby and out of fashion.

What was troubling was the extreme brutality of the murders. Each victim had been hacked in the skull some twenty times—well after the killer must have known they were already dead. Whoever killed them was crazy—or else filled with consuming rage.

Most unsettling of all, perhaps, was the fact that the two victims had been killed at least ninety minutes apart—Mrs. Borden around 9:30, and her husband shortly after 11:00. This had to mean one of two things: Either the murderer had killed Mrs. Borden and then hidden himself without detection somewhere in the house from 9:30 until after 11:00, waiting first for Andrew Borden to return home (whenever that might be) and then waiting for him to fall asleep so that he would not put up a struggle or raise an outcry, or else the murderer had sneaked into the house, not once but twice, totally unseen by neighbors or passersby. But the house had been locked and bolted all morning. And there were no signs of a forced entry.

Every one of these problems and improbabilities simply disappeared with a single alternative hypothesis: that the murderer was not an outsider at all, but a member of the household. Inevitably, then, even as the police dutifully tried to track down all other possibilities, their attention turned toward Lizzie Borden. And they found that

the pieces fitted perfectly—almost. Lizzie's guilt could explain the time that passed between the two murders and also the absence of any sign of forced entry or of struggle
on the part of either victim. Furthermore, her own account of her actions on the
morning of the murders—which she told first to her father, and then to Bridget Sullivan, Mrs. Churchill, and a variety of police officers—simply failed to hold together.
Abby Borden had not left the house earlier in the morning and then returned. In fact,
none of her acquaintances was sick that day or had sent a note asking her to come
visit. No such note was found in the Borden house. Finally, despite extensive and repeated inquiries, nobody ever came forward (either within Mrs. Borden's circle of acquaintances or outside it) to acknowledge having written one. The conclusion became
inescapable: there was no such note. Lizzie had invented the story and told it to her
father simply in order to prevent him from looking for his wife—and discovering her
bloody corpse.

There were also contradictions in Lizzie's account of her actions between the time
her father returned home and the discovery of his murder half an hour later. She
claimed to have gone out to the barn loft soon after her father's arrival—that was the
reason she had not witnessed the murder. But she was unable to keep her story
straight. To her neighbor Mrs. Churchill, she said she had visited the barn "to get a
piece of iron." To another person, she specified that the iron was intended to repair a
broken screen on a window. But later, and under oath, Lizzie testified she had gone to
the barn because she was planning to go fishing in a few days and wanted to "find lead
for a sinker." Most damning of all, a policeman who examined the barn shortly after the
discovery of the murders reported that the loft was coated with dust so thick that his
own footprints were like tracks in the snow—yet there were no other prints to be
found in the place!

The evidence was clear: Lizzie Borden had not been in the barn at all. She had remained in the house the whole time. She must have witnessed her father's killing—or
committed it herself.

Lizzie was arrested, charged, and tried for the murder of her parents, in the most
famous American criminal case of the nineteenth century.

Although the evidence against Lizzie Borden was powerful, there were some
equally powerful problems that the prosecution faced if it was to put together a case
strong enough to gain a conviction. To begin with, the evidence against Lizzie was entirely circumstantial: She had neither confessed to the crime nor been seen by any witness to have committed it. Circumstantial evidence was perfectly valid from a legal
point of view; however, jurors would have to be persuaded not only that the evidence
was airtight but that the defendant was capable of committing murders of such brutality. So the prosecution had to deal with image as well as evidence—and that was its
most difficult challenge.

In the first place, Lizzie Borden was female. As her minister put it, "To my mind,
it is an impossibility for this girl to have committed the deed." (The minister was not
alone in referring to Lizzie as a girl rather than a woman, even though she was thirty-
two years old.) She was a woman of established character—a church member, a Sunday school teacher, and an active member of the Women's Christian Temperance
Union, or WCTU. In fact, the Fall River branch of the WCTU voted to "declare our un-
shaken faith in her, as a fellow worker and sister tenderly beloved." Even the *Woman's
Journal*, a feminist magazine, declared: "The citizens of Fall River who have known Miss

LIZZIE ANDREW BORDEN. This photograph of a fashionable Lizzie Borden was taken in 1890, when she was 29 or 30. Those people who came to believe two years later that Lizzie was guilty of double murder made their point with the following ditty, first sung in the streets of Fall River's textile mill district: "Lizzie Borden took an axe / And gave her mother forty whacks; / When she saw what she had done / She gave her father forty-one."

Lizzie Borden from childhood are unanimous in their belief of her innocence. She is a solid, substantial young woman of gentle disposition and quiet habits, much beloved by her friends."

Added to the fact that Lizzie was a woman who had lived a respectable life was a closely related point: Her family was extremely wealthy. By any standards, her father was a rich man—a member of the single wealthiest and most powerful clan in the city of Fall River. A local newspaper reporter described Andrew Jackson Borden's position in these words:

He was one of the family of Bordens whose name has always been identified with the growth and business enterprises of the city. No one knows how much money he was worth, but persons who are as well acquainted with his affairs as he would allow them to be, do not hesitate to say that his estate was worth $300,000. He was president of the Union Savings Bank, a member of its Board of Trustees and Investment, a director of the Merchants Manufacturing Company, the B.M.C. Durfee Safe Deposit and Trust Company, the Globe Yarn Mills, the Troy Cotton and Woolen Manufactory and other manufacturing concerns.

It was difficult enough to believe that any woman—even some poor, working-class, immigrant woman—was capable of committing such a hideous crime. But a Fall River jury had recently been persuaded to convict a local woman of a brutal murder. That woman, however, had not been from a respectable old family. What the jury that would soon sit in judgment of Lizzie Borden would have to decide was whether a woman whose family held such a high position could have committed a murder so foul. Lizzie Borden was not only a woman, she was a "lady."

The final difficulty in persuading a jury of Lizzie's guilt was the simplest, and perhaps the most powerful, of all. Lizzie Borden was not accused of murdering some stranger but of killing her own parents. She was not only a woman, not only even a "lady," she was also the victims' own daughter. As her defense attorney put it: "To foully murder her stepmother and then go straight away and slay her own father is a wreck of human morals. Such acts as those are morally and physically impossible for this young woman."

That was the issue, then. The evidence pointed to Lizzie Borden, and to nobody else. But the evidence was all circumstantial, and Lizzie was not the kind of person who seemed capable of committing such a crime. That fact alone might be grounds for "reasonable doubt."

There was only one strategy for the prosecution to follow. It had to convince the jury that Lizzie Borden had a clear and powerful motive to commit the crimes—a motive powerful enough to overcome the doubts inevitably raised by her sex, her background and social status, and her familial role. Lizzie's past history precluded the possibility that she was demented or prone to fits of sudden rage or violence. The second murder had been committed such a long time after the first one that the killings could not have been a sudden act of unpremeditated emotion. The crime had been planned in advance. This meant the prosecution had to convince the jury that Lizzie had some reason to want her family dead—a reason so long-standing, so deep, that it could overcome all the circumstances that made it so hard to believe she could do such a thing.

The prosecution therefore attempted to undermine with a single stroke all the favorable feeling that had built up around Lizzie Borden. It did so by insisting that she was not the tender woman or the dutiful daughter she was made out to be, and that her family was not a haven of cordial affection. Instead, the prosecution argued, the Borden household was pervaded by a venomous hostility that ran so deep the family had turned into a "murderous" unit and had settled into a kind of silent warfare that divided the two generations into armed camps, each eyeing the other with constant suspicion. As the district attorney put it, "Although they occupied the same household, there was built up between them an almost impassable wall."

It was easy to show that Lizzie had remarkably little to do with her parents. She spent much of her time outside the house, and when she was at home she usually stayed in her bedroom—with the door shut. She rarely bothered to greet her parents when she entered the house. In fact, she hardly ever joined them even at mealtime—instead, she waited until they were finished, and then she ate alone.

ABBY DURFEE GRAY BORDEN.   On the morning of the murders, Lizzie Borden claimed that her stepmother had been about to go shopping for food, clothed in a housedress. Won't you change your dress before you go out? Lizzie allegedly asked, and Abby Borden replied: No, this is good enough. This trivial exchange reveals the conflict between a fashion-conscious lady and a woman who did not need to parade her status by a display of conspicuous consumption.

But the "impassable wall" that ran through the Borden house was more than a figure of speech. Lizzie and her parents had divided the house up by an elaborate series of locks and bolts and bars. The guest room (the room where Mrs. Borden was murdered) was right next to Lizzie's bedroom, and there was even a door connecting the two rooms. But Mrs. Borden used the guest room for sewing, and Lizzie made sure that the connecting door could not be used. As she reported at the inquest, "It has been locked and bolted, and a large writing desk in my room kept up against it." When Lizzie was asked how she could get from her room to the guest room, she replied: "I have to go to the front hall." (In any case, she said, she was "not allowed in that room.") In the same way, Lizzie could not get to her bedroom by walking up the back stairs—that was her father's territory. "Father's bedroom was kept locked, and his door into my room locked and hooked, too, and I had no keys."

Such arrangements affected the whole household, and the prosecution suggested that they stemmed from the particular hostility that Lizzie felt toward Mrs. Borden. There even seemed to be a plausible explanation for the hostility. Abby Borden was not Lizzie's mother at all, but her stepmother. Lizzie's own mother had died when Lizzie was only two years old, and Andrew Borden had married Abby two years later. Abby had now been living in the Borden household for twenty-eight years. Even so, when a policeman on the scene routinely asked Lizzie "if she had any idea who could have killed her father and mother," Lizzie had said: "She is not my mother, sir; she is my stepmother. My mother died when I was a child."

Just a few months before the murders, a seamstress who made clothing for the women of the Borden household had made the mistake of referring to Abby as Lizzie's mother. Lizzie quickly shot back: "Don't say that to me, for she is a mean good-for-nothing thing." That was strong language, and the dressmaker had tried to give Lizzie a chance to take it back (or, perhaps, to say even more):

"Oh, Lizzie, you don't mean that?"

"Yes, I don't have much to do with her. I stay in my room most of the time."

"You come down for your meals, don't you?"

"Yes, but we don't eat with them if we can help it."

The pattern of hostility was clear. But what was its basis? The prosecution came up with an incident it argued was an important piece of family history.

Five years earlier, in 1887, Andrew Borden had given a piece of real estate to his wife and his wife's sister—the same Mrs. Whitehead who was supposed to have written Abby Borden the "sick note" on the morning of the murders. It was an open secret that Lizzie resented this gift. And there was another open secret about the episode: it was at this very time that Lizzie began to address Abby Borden as "Mrs. Borden." Until then, she had called her "mother."

Behind Abby—behind it all—loomed the figure of Andrew Jackson Borden. It was Andrew who had married Abby, who ran the household, and who more than any other person dominated the life and the imagination of Lizzie Borden. Andrew was a well-known man around Fall River, and something of a local character. He had earned the reputation of being tight-lipped, iron-willed—and notoriously stingy. He was known as a man who loved to make money, but who hated to spend it. And his tastes determined the shape of Lizzie's life—a life she had come to loathe.

It was not that Lizzie was short of money. Several years earlier, her father had given her and her sister Emma one of the other houses he owned, and the rent from this property had provided Lizzie with plenty of spending money—enough money to buy the nineteen dresses that hung in her closet, and more. When she went out, Lizzie could dress as she wished. But in the house to which she always had to return, she was forced to live in the dark shadow of her father.

The house itself was one of Lizzie's problems. Over the previous forty or fifty years, most of the bankers and mill owners of Fall River had sold their old houses downtown and had moved to an elegant section of the city, known as the Hill, where they could look down on the factories that had made their fortune—and also on the thousands of laborers (most of them Irish or French-Canadian immigrants, and many of them children) who worked ten hours or more each day, six days a week, in those factories, and who lived crowded in nearby tenement houses that were owned by those same wealthy capitalists. Most of Lizzie Borden's wealthy cousins lived in lavish new mansions on the Hill, and so did many people with far less money. But Andrew Borden had never chosen to move up to the Hill. He and his family continued to live downtown, just two blocks away from the bank he owned (and only a few blocks from one of the largest factories in the city). Second Street was one of the busiest streets in the city. Andrew Borden's neighbors were a mixed lot of shopkeepers and professional men, many of whom took in unmarried working-class boarders to help make ends meet. One house on the street contained as many as nine boarders. The immediate neighborhood was respectable enough (even though, just a block down the street, a brothel operated openly). But Andrew Borden was its wealthiest resident—by far.

What made the situation even odder was the appearance of the Borden house. It was a modest building even for the Second Street neighborhood. The house was relatively small, and it was more than fifty years old. (There was even a barn in the backyard.) And its two stories were constructed in a style that seemed strangely out-of-date by the year 1892. The house contained no halls or corridors. The only way to reach most rooms in the house (even the bedrooms) was by walking through another room. That was the reason for all the locked doors in the house: because of the structure of the building, there was simply no other way for Lizzie or her parents to ensure privacy.

The house was old-fashioned in other ways as well. For one thing, it lacked most of the modern amenities. Fall River had dug an underground water and sewer system during the 1880s—but Andrew Borden had never chosen to have his house connected up with it. There was no indoor plumbing at 92 Second Street. The household got water from a well in the backyard (that was where Bridget Sullivan had filled her pail to wash the windows on the morning of the murders). They urinated into "slop jars" kept in their bedrooms, and defecated in a water closet down in the cellar. A decade or two earlier these had been the standard arrangements. Even in 1892 they would not have seemed unsanitary—merely out of fashion.

The house was furnished in a style that was a generation or more out of date. Police photographs of the bodies of Mr. and Mrs. Borden show some of these furnishings (see p. 168). The glossy black horsehair of the sofa on which Andrew Borden was murdered would have been replaced long ago in more fashionable households by decoratively printed cotton or velvet plush. Mrs. Borden's body lay beside a heavy wooden bedstead with a tall, elaborately carved headboard. It should by now have been replaced by a more modern metal bedstead. And the carpets in both rooms, running wall-to-wall to cover the wide, uneven floorboards, would have been replaced by smaller throw rugs over narrow, evenly joined, polished floorboards.

The house was so embarrassingly old-fashioned that Lizzie Borden's defense attorney felt obliged to confront the issue in his concluding speech to the jury, out of fear that it might provide his client with the necessary motive for murder:

> They say she killed her stepmother and father because that was a house without any comforts in it. Well, gentlemen, I hope you all live in a better way than the Borden family lived, so far as having good furniture and conveniences. Are your houses all warmed with steam? Do you have pictures and pianos and a library, and all conveniences and luxury? Do you? Well, I congratulate you if you do. This is not a downtrodden people. There are lots of comforts in our country homes. I know something of them, but I remember back in my boyhood we did not have gas and running water in every room.

The lawyer's argument was clever. He knew that the jury members were all "old-fashioned men" from the small towns around Fall River, and he was trying to persuade these men that Andrew J. Borden was basically one of them—not a miser, but a man who had remained true to solid, old-fashioned country ways. The lawyer summed up his point simply and effectively:

> Andrew Borden was a simple man, an old-fashioned man. He did not dress himself up with jewelry. He carried a silver watch [not a gold one]. He was a plain man of the everyday sort of fifty years ago.

THE BORDEN HOUSE. Andrew Borden moved here at the age of fifty-one, in 1872, after he had become wealthy enough to retire from the undertaking business. Until then, he and his family had lived with his father in an old and seedy section of Fall River. The new house was modest, even by the standards of its own neighborhood, but it was exactly what Andrew Borden wanted. Note the barn in the background at the left.

Gradually, Lizzie Borden's guilt or innocence had become tied to her father's character. The prosecution wanted the jurors to perceive Andrew Borden as a mean-spirited miser who systematically deprived his household of the most ordinary comforts. The defense wanted the jurors to see him as a conservative man who had courageously refused to surrender to the fads of the day. The ambiguity was deep and real, and it lay at the heart of the bitter feeling that pervaded and divided the Borden family, and that finally destroyed it. To understand the problem, it is necessary to probe deeper into the inner history of the family—deeper than either side in the trial cared to go.

The Borden clan had seen Fall River grow from a tiny farming village of a few hundred people in 1800 to a dynamic city of 75,000 in 1890. In 1890 more cotton textiles were manufactured in Fall River than in any other city in the entire world. And the Bordens had played an important part in the city's industrial transformation.

At the beginning of the nineteenth century, a farmer named Borden had owned the rights to operate a sawmill and a gristmill along the powerful stream that gave Fall River its name. With the beginning of industrialization around 1820, these mills had been replaced by the first cotton factories—and farmer Borden's children owned and controlled most of them. As the community began to grow in size and wealth, the Borden brothers took the capital they earned from these factories and shrewdly used it to organize a variety of other economic activities. By 1850 the Borden brothers controlled the banks that regulated the city's credit system and the new factories that produced the dyes and patterns used in the cotton factories, as well as the complex machines that powered those factories. The Borden brothers even owned the steamboats and railroads that soon connected Fall River to the commercial centers of Boston and New York City.

Over the thirty years between 1850 and 1880, the Borden brothers consolidated the family grip on Fall River by carefully passing their power into the hands of their own children—nearly twenty of them—and by engaging in a systematic pattern of arranged marriages between those children and the members of another wealthy Fall River clan, the Durfees. *The New York Times* sarcastically described the situation:

> Fall River has been more or less controlled by Durfees and Bordens, who appear and reappear as officers in most of the corporations. Of the Fall River Bleachery, Jefferson Borden is President, Spencer Borden is Treasurer, and Jefferson Borden, Spencer Borden, Richard B. Borden, Philip D. Borden, and George B. Durfee are Directors. Of the American Print Works, Jefferson Borden is President, George B. Durfee is Clerk, Thomas J. Borden Treasurer, and Jefferson Borden, Thomas J. Borden, George B. Durfee, and W. B. Durfee are Directors. Bordens and Durfees have put their sons, brothers, uncles, sons-in-law, and cousins into office, and permitted them to do nearly as they chose. This is the way the Bordens and Durfees continually break out, like small-pox, in all the industrial enterprises of that city.

From Andrew J. Borden's point of view, one fact about this *New York Times* story would have been particularly striking: his own name did not appear in it even once. Andrew would have known exactly why not. It was because he was not one of the sons of the wealthy Borden brothers. In fact, he belonged to a different branch of the family. The family had many branches. In 1892 there were no fewer than 128 heads of households in Fall River named Borden—including four named Andrew Borden. Andrew J. Borden's grandfather, a farmer, was the brother of the man who owned the original sawmill and gristmill. Andrew's father, an unskilled worker who never cared to make anything of himself, was only a cousin of the Borden brothers who "held everything commercial and industrial in their grasp." And Andrew J. Borden himself was only a second cousin of those twenty-odd children whose names "continually break out, like small-pox."

Andrew J. Borden therefore found himself in a curious situation. In a technical sense, it was accurate to describe him (as the local newspaper writer did on the day after his murder) as "one of the family of Bordens whose name has always been identified with the business enterprises of the city." But in real terms, he was not a member of that family at all; he was a classic self-made man. He had earned his fortune on his own, without any assistance from his unambitious father on the one hand or his wealthy Borden cousins on the other. A local obituary summed up his career like this:

"When he started in life, his means were extremely limited, and he made his money by saving it."

Andrew J. Borden got his start by entering the funeral business, as a casket maker and undertaker. With a single partner and a small gift of cash from his father, Borden opened the business in 1844, as a young man of twenty-three. The population of Fall River was beginning to increase rapidly in those years of dynamic industrial growth. And a larger population in turn meant that there were more people to die. In this indirect way—and in this way only—Andrew Borden prospered on account of his cousins' banks and cotton mills.

A dozen years after he went into business, Andrew Borden began to invest some of his profits in local real estate and, later, in mill and bank stock. By the time he was fifty, in 1871, he had accumulated enough capital to leave the undertaking business and spend all his time in managing his various investments, which now included a downtown office building that bore his name, and a bank and a cotton mill of which he was president, along with other real estate in and around Fall River. By the time of his violent death at the age of seventy-one, the local newspaper was able to claim that Andrew J. Borden was "regarded as one of the wealthiest men in town."

Borden did all this on his own. To be sure, his luck was good—he lived at a time of opportunity. But he worked long and hard to take every possible advantage of that opportunity. Long before his death, he had a reputation for good judgment and impeccable honesty. His creditors acknowledged that he was "safe and reliable," a "good, honest" businessman who stuck to his word and undertook no risky enterprises. His customers and tenants knew him as a man who always drove a hard bargain, but who

ANDREW JACKSON BORDEN. A few months before he was murdered, Andrew J. Borden discussed his future and that of his neighborhood. "Second Street will eventually become an overflow business highway, but it won't be in my time," he told an acquaintance. I don't like to move off the street in my lifetime.

was "scrupulously upright in all his dealings, and expected the same fairness in others." In his later years, he invariably chose to pay for investments in hard cash, and shortly before his death he told an acquaintance that "the man who didn't borrow lived the most contented life." He believed that it was his character that had made his fortune. He also stressed the contrast between himself and his wealthy Borden cousins, who had inherited their positions with no effort of their own. He had received no help from them, and he steered clear of them. He remained a loner to the end.

It is not hard to see why. Despite all the money he made, Andrew Borden remained an outsider to the Fall River industrial aristocracy. The fact that this aristocracy was dominated by his own cousins and namesakes made his own alienation even more acute. His cousins were the children and grandchildren of wealthy men. They had been raised with all the advantages (disadvantages, Andrew Borden might have said) of inherited wealth. They had been sent to prestigious colleges like Harvard, Yale, and Brown, and early in their lives they had developed fashionable and expensive tastes. One of Borden's cousins was an accomplished yachtsman. Another bred prize thoroughbred horses. A third was a collector of paintings and rare books. Almost all of them traveled widely, and several owned lavish vacation homes in places like Newport, Rhode Island. They took fully as much pleasure in spending their money as in making it.

In contrast to these industrial aristocrats, Andrew Borden never went to school at all, and to the end of his life he never developed any hobbies or outside interests. As his local obituary tactfully put it, he was "domestic in his tastes, and, although he had considerable leisure time, was rarely to be found where men are accustomed to congregate"—at their clubs or in fancy restaurants. According to the same newspaper, Borden had only a single interest in life: "money getting." To the end of his life, he remained a poor man who had made a lot of money. No wonder that when his cousins chose to build expensive mansions on Fall River's fashionable Hill, Andrew Borden never cared to follow them. No wonder that he chose to live out his days in an old-fashioned downtown house without hallways or indoor plumbing.

Lizzie Borden's aspirations were different because her youth was different. Lizzie was Andrew's daughter—but she inhabited a different world. Unlike her father, Lizzie never grew up poor. By the time Lizzie was born in 1860, her father's business was thriving, and when she entered her teens he was already a rich man. By then, Fall River was an industrial city, and people who had money were living on the Hill. It would have been hard for Lizzie Borden to avoid feeling that that was where she belonged, too. She rarely talked about it (being able to keep her mouth shut was one trait she did pick up from her father), but it seems apparent that she deeply craved to live in the kind of style her father could afford. The nineteen dresses that hung in her closet on the day of the murders provided a vivid display of the deep gulf that divided daughter and father.

The money for Lizzie's dresses came from her father. He did give her gifts of cash and a steady source of income of her own. By his own lights, he was extremely generous toward her and tried to indulge her in satisfying needs he could hardly understand. In the summer of 1890 he even treated Lizzie to a long vacation in Europe. She had a splendid time abroad, but ironically, this taste of elegance and freedom only intensified her revulsion for the household to which she had to return. As the ocean liner approached New York Harbor in November 1890, Lizzie confessed to her cabinmate that "she regretted the necessity of returning home after she had had such a happy summer, because the home she was about to return to was such an unhappy home." Leaving the house on Second Street altogether was the only thing that would have relieved Lizzie Borden's dread. But her father had no intention of ever doing that.

The silent anger that filled the air at the Borden house reflected something more complex than a gulf between generations. It was also a conflict between social classes.

What could Lizzie do? How could she escape from the prison of her parents' house? The simplest avenue of escape was simply to move out. But Lizzie did not have the money to purchase a house on the Hill. And in any event, moving into a place of her own was utterly unthinkable as long as her parents were alive and she was unmarried. By taking such an unrespectable step, Lizzie would have lost all chance of ever being accepted into the homes and parties of the Fall River upper class.

There was only one way for Lizzie to enter that world—by marrying a man who lived in it already. Only such a marriage would be able to provide her, in a single stroke, with a better house in a better neighborhood, and with the companionship of a person who shared her own values. In short, only marriage could bring her real membership in the class she aspired to join, and real independence from her family.

But now, still single at the age of thirty-two, Lizzie Borden was forced to confront the ever increasing likelihood that she would never get married. And, with it, she had to confront the likelihood that she would remain in the grubby house on Second Street until her father's death. (Lizzie knew that the Borden males were usually long-lived. Andrew's own father, her paternal grandfather, had died only six years earlier, in 1886, at the ripe age of eighty-eight. Andrew Borden himself was in fine health at seventy-one; who knew how long he might survive?) By then, Lizzie would be past her prime—it would be too late to marry, too late to enjoy the life that was left to her.

It was not that Lizzie had lacked the opportunity to get married. She was not unattractive, and in any case her father was the richest man in her neighborhood. But that was part of the problem: the young men who lived on Second Street were shop clerks and laborers, hardly in a position to give Lizzie the kind of life she craved. On the other hand, it would have been difficult for her (maybe even impossible) to find more desirable suitors. Even if she did make the acquaintance of a proper young gentleman, how could she invite him to visit her Second Street home and be entertained by her family? What would her suitor think about a stepmother who might not even bother to change out of her housedress for the occasion? About a neighborhood filled with boardinghouses and immigrants? About an out-of-date house that lacked even a toilet and running water? Lizzie Borden was in a bind, and whichever way she looked at it, her parents were the cause. And now, in the summer of 1892, the hopelessness of her situation, and of her future, was becoming impossible to deny. Lizzie was reaching a point of quiet but total desperation.

✦⇒◉⇐✦

On Wednesday, August 3, 1892—the evening before the murders—Lizzie Borden left her house to visit her old friend Alice Russell, an unmarried woman in her forties. For many years Alice Russell had been a neighbor of the Bordens on Second Street, but she had recently moved a few blocks away. She was probably Lizzie's closest friend, and Lizzie was visiting her to confide her confused and desperate feelings.

Much later, at Lizzie's trial, Alice Russell testified for the prosecution about some of the ominous and revealing things Lizzie had said to her. It was a confusing story that Lizzie had told, but also an extraordinary one—the closest she ever came to disclosing her state of mind on the day just before the death of her parents.

> I feel depressed. I feel as if something was hanging over me that I cannot throw off, and it comes over me at times, no matter where I am.

Lizzie did not (or could not) explain the cause of her depression, but she was vaguely aware that her feelings were affecting her behavior. A few weeks earlier, for example, she had turned down an appealing invitation to join a group of her friends who were planning to spend a few weeks on vacation at a seaside cottage in the resort town of Marion, Massachusetts. This was just the kind of opportunity Lizzie would ordinarily have welcomed, since it would allow her to escape from the oppressive midsummer urban heat as well as from the equally oppressive atmosphere of her family. But Lizzie had refused to join the vacationing party, offering her friends the feeble excuse that she "ought to stay home to see that everything went all right." Circumstances seemed to be getting more and more out of control, and she was not sure what was going on. Certain things were happening within the household, she confided to Alice—things that upset her profoundly, in ways she could not explain.

Lizzie reported these things to Alice Russell in rambling, half-coherent fashion. It was unclear to Alice (and perhaps also to Lizzie herself) just which statements described real events and which were simply expressions of Lizzie's fears or fantasies.

Lizzie talked about an occurrence that seemed simple enough, however unpleasant: "Mr. and Mrs. Borden were awfully sick last night," she said. "They were awfully sick, and I wasn't sick. I didn't vomit, but I heard them vomiting, and stepped to the door, and asked if I could do anything, and they said, 'No.'" Was it something Mr. and Mrs. Borden had eaten? Alice asked. Lizzie acknowledged that it might have been the household bread or milk. Then Lizzie offered a bizarre explanation of her parents' illness: "Sometimes," she said, "sometimes I think our milk might be poisoned."

Alice Russell was startled, and she tried without success to convince Lizzie that the Borden family milk could not possibly have been poisoned. But Lizzie would not hear her out. She went on to make an even more bizarre suggestion: The "poisoning," she hinted darkly, was only the latest in a series of scary events in the household. For example, she now revealed, "the barn has been broken into twice." Alice Russell, trying hard to calm her friend, reassured Lizzie that the break-in must have been nothing more than petty vandalism—nothing to worry about. "Well," Lizzie went on, "they have broken into the house in broad daylight, with Emma and Maggie and me there." And one night not long before, Lizzie had even seen a strange man "run around the house."

Lizzie was almost certain that these were not random events at all, that they were part of a pattern of conscious hostility on the part of some person who was determined to do nothing less than destroy the entire household: "I feel as if I wanted to sleep with my eyes half open—with one eye open half the time—for fear they will burn down the house over us."

Lizzie seemed unaware that the hostility she was describing was actually her own. But at this point, she unconsciously made a revealing shift in her emphasis. Up to now, she had been speaking of her parents as if they were the innocent victims of some incomprehensible malevolence. But now she began to suggest that the trouble might not be incomprehensible after all—that her father had actually provoked it by his behavior and manner.

"I feel afraid sometimes that father has an enemy," Lizzie began, and told a story (which she would repeat several times the next day, after the murders) of how her father had lost his temper at a prospective tenant who spoke to him in a sneering voice about his reputation for money grubbing.

Lizzie was unable to face her own hostility. She simply could not grasp a fact that might conceivably have saved the lives of Andrew and Abby Borden: her father's "enemy" was Lizzie herself. "I think sometimes—I am afraid sometimes that somebody will do something to him. He is so discourteous to people." For a few moments, Lizzie came close to acknowledging that her father made her feel embarrassed, threatened, and enraged.

As if to explain something about her feelings, Lizzie began to go into detail about what had happened earlier that very day, after Andrew and Abby had gotten sick and vomited. Mrs. Borden had felt concerned, and she told her husband she wanted to send for a physician—Dr. Bowen, who lived across the street (and who would examine her dead body the next day). Andrew Borden did not see the need for professional help, and he scolded his wife for her wastefulness. He told Mrs. Borden, as Lizzie recalled, "Well, my money shan't pay for it." But Abby had called Dr. Bowen anyway, and when he came over to examine her, Andrew had treated the physician with characteristic rudeness. When she told the story to Alice Russell, Lizzie did not report her father's exact words—but, for once, she directly expressed something of her own feelings toward her father. What Lizzie told Alice Russell was this: "I am so ashamed, the way father treated Dr. Bowen. I was so mortified." It was as close as Lizzie would ever come to identifying herself as her father's "enemy."

Never again would Lizzie Borden expose so much of her feelings. Barely twelve hours after her conversation with Alice Russell, Andrew Borden and his wife were lying dead, and their deaths seemed somehow to restore Lizzie's characteristic poise—and her silence. In the hours after the murders were discovered, and in the days and months of public exposure that followed, the people who observed Lizzie Borden were struck by her extraordinary emotional control. Newspaper reporters often used words like "cold" to describe her manner. She rarely broke down and cried (although at one point during her trial, she fainted—when her father's skull was displayed to the jurors).

Some people even suggested that Lizzie's composure was "unfeminine" and was evidence that she was capable after all of having committed the crimes of which she stood accused. But Lizzie's composure was her characteristic style, developed in years of hiding her feelings behind a facade of cold civility. Throughout the trial, the defense tried—and failed—to offer evidence that the Bordens had been affectionate with each other (the word they used was "cordial"). Similarly, the prosecution could not show that life in the household had been tempestuous. Even Bridget Sullivan, the servant who had lived in the house for almost two years, said that she had never seen or heard "any trouble with the family, no quarreling or anything of that kind." This kind of testimony was damaging to the prosecution's case. But the fact was that Lizzie and her parents had learned to avoid expressing their feelings—just as they had learned to avoid each other in the flesh. There were not only physical locks and bolts that kept the family from invading each other's space, there was also an elaborate, unspoken series of emotional locks and bolts that prevented Lizzie and her parents from expressing either love or hatred, and possibly from even feeling the hatred that was always there. Perhaps if these emotional locks had been opened, and if explosions of anger had been tolerated in the Borden household, Lizzie might have been able to express her hidden rage in some fashion less deadly than the form it took on the morning of August 4, 1892. The cold composure that Lizzie displayed to the world at her trial was the hard veneer of lethal civility that pervaded her life. It was almost as if she had found it easier to confront her parents with an ax than with sharp words.

When Lizzie Borden came to trial in June 1893, she never took the stand in her own defense. The only time she ever testified for the record was ten months earlier, at the private inquest hearing. Her defense lawyers realized that if she were to testify at her trial, she would probably make a poor impression on the jury—and she would be forced to acknowledge the contradictory testimony that she had given at the inquest. Fortunately for the defense, the judges refused to admit Lizzie's inquest testimony into evidence at the trial. (They decided that she should have been offered the opportunity to have a lawyer present during the inquest, so that anything she said on that occasion was therefore legally inadmissible.) The exclusion of Lizzie's inquest testimony dashed any hopes for a conviction that the prosecution might have entertained. So did the presiding judge's final charge to the jury, which was so biased in Lizzie's behalf that one newspaper called it "A PLEA FOR THE INNOCENT."

The jury was out little more than an hour. When it returned, the verdict was "Not guilty." A newspaper described the scene that followed:

> A cheer broke the stillness of the courtroom. Everybody sprang to their feet, and the greatest excitement prevailed, but the woman on whom all eyes were turned sank to the rail, with her face buried in her hands. Lizzie Borden wept as she had not for many months.

> Then, in a calm and kindly tone, Judge Mason announced that Lizzie Borden was a free woman at last. The jury came forward to shake hands with Miss Borden.

A few minutes later, Lizzie held a brief press conference in the judge's chamber. She refused to say a word about the verdict, but she did talk about her immediate plans. Her words were so conventional that they must have sounded startling, and they would be proven false soon enough. Lizzie Borden said: "I want to go home: take me straight home tonight. I want to see the old place and settle down at once."

Money, Class, and Women

The reporters who interviewed Lizzie Borden a few moments after she was found innocent must have been astonished to hear her say that all she wanted was to go home, "to see the old place," and settle down. In fact, she did not settle down in the "old place." Two years later, after the excitement had subsided and she received her share of her father's estate, she bought a mansion on the Hill and named it, grandly, Maplecroft. Then she changed her name from Lizzie—which was no nickname but her legal given name—to the fancier Lizbeth. She began to buy nice things. Maplecroft got a set of fine china, elegant furniture, the oil paintings that had been so absent from the old house on Second Street. She also bought five diamond rings and a lot of other expensive jewelry.

Still, her father's investments in real estate and industrial stock continued to grow. Lizbeth Borden died quietly in 1927, at the age of sixty-seven, a rich woman. (She left only one small bequest, to the Fall River Animal Rescue League. "I have been fond of animals," her will explained, "and their need is great and there are so few who care for them.")

Lizbeth Borden got some of the things Lizzie Borden must have wanted. But there were other things she did not get. She never married. She lived a more or less isolated life, with few friends and no invitations to balls or parties, no memberships in fancy women's clubs. She had

won her way into the physical world of the Hill, but the murder trial had cost her whatever chance she might have had for access to the Hill's society. She even lost contact with her sister. Her little bequest to the Animal Rescue League was a pathetic testament to her isolation from the social world of human beings.

What Lizbeth Borden did escape was tackiness. She got out of a shabby house, with its slop jars and its basement privy. She acquired flush toilets and running water. She got away from the embarrassing, old-fashioned horsehair sofa, the barn, and the well on Second Street. Had Andrew Jackson Borden shamed her by carrying a silver watch and not a gold one? She would have diamonds and gold aplenty.

The question of Lizzie Borden's guilt or innocence was settled legally by the jury. Most historians have decided the question the other way. She may well have killed her parents. But, on a deeper level, her legal guilt or innocence is irrelevant. What matters most is that her behavior before and after the murders says a great deal about American society at the end of the nineteenth century, particularly about the lives of middle- and upper-class Americans.

Murder, especially one like the brutal ax murder of the elderly Bordens, is a bizarre event that may have little historical significance. But the preoccupations with social class and social status that set the scene for the murder and the trial can tell us a lot about the kinds of ambitions and stresses that "normal," nonmurderous American families labored under. That is what one man suggested in a letter to a Fall River newspaper:

> A striking feature of this case is the picture it gives of life in the Borden household, and presumably in other households in Fall River—and elsewhere. I dare say that this life is so familiar to many people that they are unable to appreciate the meanness and sordidness of it.

Whether Lizzie Borden killed her father and mother might interest a jury or a novelist looking for a plot. Why Lizzie Borden might have wanted to kill her parents is a question that takes the case out of the realm of the bizarre and into the realm of history.

THE GILDED AGE

The steel baron Andrew Carnegie, one of the richest men in the world, once visited an American Indian village on the Great Plains. He noticed that the tepee of the chief looked very much like the tepees of all the other men, and he drew what he believed was the compelling lesson. In the modern world of industrial capitalism, Carnegie said, the home of the millionaire was drastically different from the home of the farmer or factory worker. The glaring extremes of wealth and poverty might seem to signal a much more severe exploitation of the poor by the rich than in a "primitive society" like that of the Indians. But the opulent life of the modern millionaire was really a sign of social progress. He lived a fantastically rich life. But his riches were the result of production. And that same production had made the average citizen wealthy, too. An ordinary family under industrial capitalism lived in a style that Carnegie believed would have made any tribal chief, or even any ancient king or emperor, envious.

Carnegie's meditation, which he made famous in a popular essay of 1888 entitled "The Gospel of Wealth," was typical of the attitudes of both wealthy and middle-class Americans in the 1880s and 1890s. One of the most obvious features of their world was wealth. And their awareness of wealth only increased their consciousness of poverty. They were not heartless people. They could pity the poor, especially the "deserving" poor and the children of poverty. They might even try to relieve suffering through philanthropy. But they seldom doubted what they believed were the inevitable twin consequences of industrial capitalism: the creation of fortunes for a small fraction but of a much better life for everyone else.

THE MONIED CLASS

In 1877, when Lizzie Borden was a teenager, Cornelius Vanderbilt died. His will, when it became public, astonished a society that was not yet accustomed to fabulous fortunes. He left an estate worth a staggering $100 million. But by the time Lizzie Borden went to trial, fifteen years later, Americans had become used to seeing newspaper stories about single donations made by men of fortune that almost equaled Vanderbilt's entire estate. By the 1890s the wealth of men like Carnegie, Rockefeller, and a dozen or so other multimillionaires had become public and legendary. Even more important, there were a hundred millionaires for every well-known multimillionaire. By the 1890s the United States had, by conservative guesses, well over 3,000 men whose holdings were worth over a million dollars. And there were even more with "moderate" fortunes of several hundred thousand dollars.

Every American city of middling size had its tight cluster of wealthy families. Around these rich people, in every town and city, were grouped a growing number of others who would have described themselves as "well-to-do" or "respectable." Like the truly wealthy, this class of Americans was increasingly a fact of ur-

NEWPORT MANSIONS. Every American city in the late nineteenth century had its fashionable neighborhoods, like the Hill in Fall River, Massachusetts, where Lizzie Borden moved after her trial. But no single place in America was as fancy or as pretentious as Newport, Rhode Island, where many wealthy Americans built summer homes—vast Victorian cottages like these along Cliff Walk. At the same time, yachting became a popular sport—and means of display—among the rich. And so began a continuing contest for the American shoreline between the wealthy and the rest of the population.

ban life. In 1880 the total value of all rural and urban real estate in the United States was still about equal. Just ten years later, the value of urban real estate had increased twice as much as rural. Even more striking was the fact that city dwellers owned almost three times as much of other kinds of property—furniture, jewels, stocks, bonds, and bank accounts—as rural people did. The average farm family owned about $3,000 worth of such property in 1890, but the average city family owned about $9,000 worth. Since a lot of city people had no money, the average wealth of those who had any at all was far above $9,000.[1]

THE PREOCCUPATION WITH WEALTH, DISPLAY, AND STATUS

This new money was not quiet, discreet, and invisible. The style of the wealthy, from the 1870s through the end of the century, was one of display. For the very rich and the moderately well-to-do, the purpose of life seemed to be to mount exhibitions of opulence. For the multimillionaire, this meant building "cottages" like Marble House at Newport; or houses with palatial dining rooms like that of the Astors in New York; or imposing mansions fronting on Central Park, like the home of Henry Clay Frick, Carnegie's partner in steel.

---

[1] *These figures can be translated into today's dollars by multiplying them by at at least seven, perhaps even ten.*

But even for people of moderate income, in smaller cities and towns, the new style permitted dramatically larger and more pretentious houses. The typical middle-class house of the period was a vast affair, with eight, ten, or even twelve rooms. Cheaper lumber and labor made its vastness possible. New methods of power milling and carving wood gave it opulent woodwork and elaborately decorated mantels and staircases. It had eleven-foot ceilings, central steam heat, running water, and gaslights. Soon it would have electricity and a telephone. But the Victorian house of the period, with its turrets and its wrought-iron fences, had one obvious purpose: to be imposing. It was to declare to the world that the family who lived within had achieved the sweet dream of success. This was exactly what the Borden house on Second Street did not declare.

The determination to display opulence and grandeur controlled the design and size not just of houses but of all the places the new middle and upper classes might frequent or pass through. Their hotels and restaurants were legendary for their elaborate gilding and marble, their ornate mirrors and high ceilings. Railroad stations, like the new Pennsylvania Station in New York, were designed to dwarf many a European palace—and many an American government building from the early days of the Republic. The Pullman "Palace" cars, in which rich and near-rich Americans traveled, were fantastic studies in conspicuous display.

For the first time, the rich became celebrities—not because of some achievement in war or politics, but simply because of their wealth. To give a dinner at the fabled Delmonico's restaurant in New York, with seventy-two guests and a total tab of $10,000, was enough to make a rich man into a famous one, with pictures and headlines not only in New York newspapers but others around the country. Simply to have and to display money seemed enough to attract attention—and, of course, envy. To return from a ride in Central Park, on beautiful horses, to a mansion facing the park was enough to draw an admiring crowd. The clatter of hooves, the men in fancy dress, including perhaps a polished top hat, the women in elegant riding costume, with brilliantly colored silk scarves trailing almost to the street—this was the stuff of which the sweet dream of success was now made. And the public attention was as important as actually having the horses, the clothes, and the mansion in the first place.

Wealthy Americans not only flaunted their money, they tried hard to consolidate their position as an upper class—and to make it clear to those who wanted to join them that there were certain definite steps and initiations that had to be passed through. Especially for young men, college now became an important rite of passage. Before the middle of the century, poor boys studying for the ministry had constituted the primary student body of many American colleges. But by the time the century drew to a close, three things had happened. First, there was a great expansion in the number and size of colleges and universities—from about 60,000 students in the 1870s to almost 200,000 twenty years later. Second, beginning in the 1870s, a number of private colleges for women were established, and many state universities began to admit women. Third, the students were now from a more homogeneous social class, almost all sons and daughters of middle- and upper-class families. Within the colleges and universities, the students heightened class consciousness even further through an array of secret societies, Greek-letter fraternities and sororities, and dining clubs—organizations that had not been a part of college life a generation earlier.

The students' parents were doing the same sorts of things. A number of institutions took root in every American town, institutions whose main purpose was to segregate people along class lines. The country club became a regular feature of the lives of the urban middle and upper class. Indeed, most cities of any size would have two or three country clubs, each precisely distinguished from the others along fine but definite lines of status. The same was true of the yacht clubs that seemed to dot every usable harbor on the coasts and lakes. Men joined downtown clubs and women formed an astonishing variety of social clubs of their own. The lodge movement, with its Masons, Moose, Odd Fellows, and the like, served many of the same functions for middle-class men. There had always been clubs, of course. The Masons was an organization much older than the American Republic. The difference now was that the clubs and lodges were not only much bigger, and consisted of many more members, they were more subtly and elaborately graded signs of class membership.

THE PREOCCUPATION WITH MANNERS

The preoccupation with wealth, display, and status gave a peculiar intensity, even desperation, to Americans' concern with "manners." A flood of manuals of etiquette poured from the presses during the decades after the Civil War. These were reinforced by regular columns in the high-circulation magazines of the day, many of which were aimed especially at women: *Ladies' Home Journal, Cosmopolitan,* and *Harper's Bazaar.* Major newspapers (whose circulation was now leaping into the millions each day), also employed women to write daily columns of advice on good form and "personal" problems.

This tremendous volume of avidly read material was all based on two assumptions. The first was clear and explicit: There was a correct way of doing everything—eating, dressing, talking, dancing, courting—and that correct way was very likely to be something complicated, unnatural, and slightly European in tone. The manuals were littered with French expressions, as though to convey ideas that were a little too subtle or too elegant to be expressed in English. Some things were *trés distingué,* which lent them an air of mystery not conveyed by the English "distinguished." Readers were warned of *faux pas,* as though a simple misstep were a dark and disgraceful thing indeed. People who were plan-

ning dinner parties might be pleased to learn that host and hostess were no longer expected to carve and serve at the table, that food should be brought to the table by servants. But that information was given an even greater air of elegance when the reader learned that this practice had originated with the Russian aristocracy and was called *service à la Russe.*

The second, somewhat hidden, assumption behind all the books and columns was that a failure to know the right fork or the proper way to invite a lady to waltz was a failure of class. The individual whose manners were not in good style—or *bon ton*—had to worry not just about a revealed weakness of personality, or even a lapse of morals, but about being betrayed in class terms, about being pegged as part of what was now called "the other half."

The world that Lizzie Borden inhabited was a world preoccupied, even obsessed, with wealth and with displays of elegance and manners. Her father was certainly rich enough to afford *service à la Russe.* But he insisted on just keeping plain Bridget. Lizzie, and thousands of other young men and women, pored over newspaper stories of the doings of the wealthy, and over books that laid out impossibly fancy designs of behavior for the proper. In one person, the response might be heightened ambition to have the money and the grand house that lay at the center of the dream of success. In another person, the response might be shame or disgust with the extent to which his or her manners and lifestyle fell short of what was considered correct. In many, the response was a simple fear of exposure of their rudeness or vulgarity, their lack of "respectability."

One book of manners gave its readers the following example of an elegant conversation. A gentleman has just offered his arm to a lady, to lead her in to table at a fine dinner party.

> The gentleman may say, "We must be careful not to step on that elaborate train," referring to the costume of a lady preceding the pair.

"Yes, indeed, that would be a mishap. But trains are graceful in spite of their inconvenience."

Her companion must answer: "Oh! I admire them, of course. Only I have such a dread of stepping on them and bringing down the wrath of the fair wearer on my devoted head."

The proposed conversation may appear comic. But it would have seemed a little bitter to Lizzie Borden, who lived in a house where a dinner party was simply an impossibility. It also suggests something of the discomfort that even the "lady" and "gentleman" had to labor under. She acknowledges that the train is an inconvenience that has to be endured because it is "graceful." He in turn reveals his dread of the wrath that will come down on him if he causes a mishap. If even the men and women in manner-book examples felt this way, their readers can only have been even more anxious.

Much of the fiction of the period explored this anxiety. William Dean Howells's 1885 novel *The Rise of Silas Lapham,* for example, dramatized a family situation that mirrored that of Lizzie Borden in some striking ways. Like Andrew Borden, the title character was a wealthy self-made man. Like Borden, too, he was an unpolished boor who did not much worry about whether his neighborhood was fashionable or his conversation elegant, and who did not easily recognize that his behavior provoked the disdain of those more refined than he. (One of these men explained the situation with supreme elegance when he asked whether the Laphams "had knowledge enough to be ashamed of their ignorance.") Silas Lapham's behavior also embarrassed his socially ambitious daughters, eager to marry into polite society. Once, when Lapham boasted openly of his wealth—a taboo subject in society—one of his daughters squirmed, muttering: "Oh, I wish Papa wouldn't brag so!" She later confided, "I thought I should die." Many young Americans, Lizzie Borden among them, would surely have understood.

In the novel, things came out all right, because Silas Lapham had a wife who was quick to grasp all the "right" things to do, and who could be counted on to coax her husband into doing them—and even to show him how. The lesson was clear: A young woman needed a mother who could and would bridge the awkward gap between an economically ambitious father and his socially ambitious children—the gap between two classes as well as two generations. It was exactly here, of course, that the parallel between the fictional Laphams and the real-life Bordens broke down. Lizzie Borden was painfully aware that her stepmother cared just as little as her father did about helping her enter polite society. If Lizzie Borden ever read *The Rise of Silas Lapham,* she would have found it a profoundly depressing book.

UTOPIAN VISION OF THE FAMILY

Americans usually remember the last decades of the nineteenth century as the age of "rugged individualism," when men (almost exclusively men) competed in a no-holds-barred contest for individual success. But the sweet dream of success was not really an individual dream. Men experienced life as members of families, and success meant the success of the family—clothes and social standing for the wife, education for the children, fine careers for the sons (and increasingly the daughters). The specter of failure was a horror the entire family had to face, a fear not so much of poverty as of losing the vague but urgent sense of being "respectable."

In fact, the American dream of success was in many ways a family dream. It was a dream that money might buy enough ease and comfort, enough space and privacy within the home, to make the family a place of harmonious refuge from a world of striving, competition, and ambition. If people could get enough money, the dream promised, then their personal problems within the home might be solved. Strife between husbands and wives, anger and resentment be-

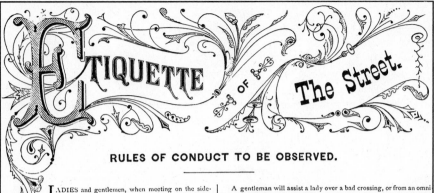

ETIQUETTE of The Street.

RULES OF CONDUCT TO BE OBSERVED.

LADIES and gentlemen, when meeting on the sidewalk, should always pass to the right. Should the walk be narrow or dangerous, gentlemen will always see that ladies are protected from injury.

Ladies should avoid walking rapidly upon the street, as it is ungraceful and unbecoming.

Running across the street in front of carriages is dangerous, and shows want of dignity.

The gentleman should insist upon carrying any package which the lady may have, when walking with her.

Before recognizing a lady on the street, the gentleman should be certain that his recognition will meet with favor.

No gentleman should stand on the street-corners, steps of hotels, or other public places, and make remarks about ladies passing by.

A gentleman may take two ladies upon his arms, but under no circumstances should the lady take the arms of two gentlemen.

Upon the narrow walk, for her protection, the gentleman should generally give the lady the inside of the walk (Fig. 21), passing behind her when changing at corners.

Allowing a dress to trail on the street is in exceedingly bad taste. Such a street costume simply calls forth criticism and contempt from the more sensible people.

A gentleman walking with a lady should accommodate his step and pace to hers. For the gentleman to be some distance ahead, presents a bad appearance.

Should protection on the street be necessary, it is customary for the gentleman to give his right arm to the lady; but if more convenient, he may give the left.

It is courtesy to give silent, respectful attention as a funeral procession passes. It shows want of respect to pass between the carriages while the procession is moving.

Staring at people, spitting, looking back after they pass, saluting people across the street, calling out loudly or laughing at people as they go by, are all evidences of ill-breeding.

The gentleman accompanying a lady should hold the door open for the lady to enter first. Should he be near the door when a lady, unattended, is about to enter, he will do the same for her.

In the evening, or whenever safety may require, a gentleman should give a lady his arm. It is not customary in other cases to do so on the street, unless with an elderly lady, or the couple be husband and wife.

Fi. 21. The street-promenade. The gentleman gives the lady the inside of the walk. ✱

A gentleman will assist a lady over a bad crossing, or from an omnibus or carriage, without waiting for the formality of an introduction. When the service is performed, he will raise his hat, bow, and pass on.

In a street car or an omnibus, the passengers who are seated should strive to give seats to those who are standing, rendering such accommodation as they would themselves desire under similar circumstances.

When crossing the pavement, the lady should raise her dress with the right hand, a little above the ankle. To raise the dress with both hands is vulgar, and can be excused only when the mud is very deep.

No gentleman will smoke when walking with, or standing in the presence of, a lady on the street. He should remove the cigar from her presence entirely, even though permission be granted to continue the smoking.

A gentleman should give his seat to any lady who may be standing in a public conveyance. For this favor she should thank him, which courtesy he should acknowledge by a slight bow. In an omnibus he will pass up the ladies' fares.

A true lady will go quietly and unobtrusively about her business when on the street, never seeking to attract the attention of the opposite sex, at the same time recognizing acquaintances with a courteous bow, and friends with pleasant words of greeting.

Swinging the arms when walking, eating upon the street, sucking the parasol handle, pushing violently through a crowd, very loud and boisterous talking and laughing on the streets, and whispering in public conveyances are all evidences of ill-breeding in ladies.

A lady should have the escort of a gentleman in the evening. A gentleman at the house where she may call may return with her if she goes unattended; gossip and scandal are best avoided, however, if she have some one from her home call for her at an appointed hour.

On the narrow street-crossing the gentleman will allow the lady to precede him, that he may see that no injury befalls her.

Should a lady stop in the street, when meeting a gentleman, it is courtesy for him to stop also. Should his business be urgent, he will apologize for not continuing the conversation, and ask to be excused. Should it be desirable to lengthen the interview, and the lady resume her walk in the midst of her conversation, it is courtesy for him to turn and accompany her. Should she desire to end the conversation, a slight bow from her will indicate the fact, when he should bid her "good day" and take his leave.

THE LADY AND THE GENTLEMAN. This page from an etiquette book—clearly meant for those people who needed elementary instruction—laid down some quite fastidious rules. It advised the ladies, for example, to lift the hem of the skirt when crossing a street, but only with one hand, for "To raise the dress with both hands is vulgar." The manual is uncertain on one point, however. It recommends in general that gentlemen give ladies the inside of the sidewalk when they promenade together. On the other hand, it admits some authorities recommend that the lady walk on the gentleman's right, so as to leave her right hand free to carry a parasol. If the lady in the picture had adopted that rule, she would have spared the gentleman from being jabbed in the chest by her parasol. But such were the valiant sufferings demanded of the gentlemen of the day.

A PROSPEROUS AFRICAN-AMERICAN FAMILY.   Eleven family members (four men, seven women) posed for this formal portrait, taken sometime between 1880 and 1900. Everything in the photograph points to the family's worldly success: the rich tapestry and the artwork adorning the wall, the ornamental rug on the floor, and the expensive organ that sits in the very center of the group. This was the kind of conspicuous consumption that Lizzie Borden could only envy from a distance— until 1893.

tween generations—all might disappear once there were goods enough, rooms enough, servants enough. For wealthy and well-to-do Americans, the ideal family had gradually become a truly utopian vision of sanctuary from a lonely, dangerous, and corrupt world.

This utopian vision of family life lay behind the astonishing support Lizzie Borden got from middle-class and wealthy Americans during her trial. In Fall River, "respectable" people immediately assumed that she was innocent, that she could not have committed such a deed, since she was a lady—not just a woman. As Lizzie Borden became a celebrity in newspapers and magazines around the country, this kind of support broadened and became even more insistent. The reasons had little to do with the facts of the case. They had to do with the profound commitment that "respectable" Americans had made to the re-

lationship between wealth and family happiness. They had assumed that money, honestly earned, could lead only to the good life, to family circles that were quiet and loving. In a very real sense, this was the American dream. For the men and women who read about the Borden murders, Lizzie had to be innocent. To admit otherwise was to admit that the dream was false, that even Andrew Jackson Borden's wealth could not buy the kind of family they wanted.

The jury that acquitted Lizzie Borden did so not only because its members had trouble believing that a woman was capable of such a crime (a Fall River jury had already convicted a woman of a sensational murder before). The jury's real problem was that its members found it threatening to believe that a woman like Lizzie Borden— who was, after all, "a Borden"—could have done such a thing. To believe this would have undercut the jury's cherished hope that wealth and prominence could produce families that would be havens of security from the troubles of the world. Convicting Lizzie Borden would have been an admission that wealth offered no sanctuary from social disaster and family nightmare.

THE MIDDLE-CLASS WOMAN'S BURDEN

The utopian vision of family put a great deal of emotional pressure on all those Americans who entered the struggle for "respectability." But it probably bore most heavily on middle-class women. Some of them were interested in political causes like getting the right to vote. A small but increasing number were looking for professional careers, attending one of the new women's colleges or one of the state universities that had become coeducational. Various kinds of jobs were becoming "respectable" options for young middle-class women: nursing, teaching, being a librarian or a stenographer or even a clerk in a fancy city store. But for a large majority of women in the white middle class, "respectability" meant staying at home, being a mother, and perhaps—at most—getting involved in church work, women's clubs, or a reform movement like temperance.

These were the women who carried the difficult burden of translating money into comfort, decorum, and elegance at home. And their task was defined in ways that made it extremely trying. For one thing, they were expected to present themselves to the world as models of purity and innocence. Even their clothing seemed designed to shut them off from contact with the world. In the 1870s the heavily corseted "wasp" waist, which enclosed women in an armor of bone or spring steel, became fashionable among the middle class. Then, about a decade later, came the bustle, heaping layer upon layer of heavy cloth between women and the world. In fact, the most marked characteristic of women's dress was becoming its heavy, complicated, encasing nature. A standard "walking costume" of the 1880s required a strip of cloth two feet wide and forty-five feet long—a total of ninety square feet. Lizzie Borden, before her parents were murdered, had many elaborate dresses hanging in her closet—as though clothes were the one way she could break through her father's determination to be old-fashioned. And she had sometimes quarreled with her stepmother because the older woman seemed as indifferent to clothing as Mr. Borden was to his house.

But even when they were properly dressed, women had to worry even more than men did about doing all sorts of things the "right" way. For men, in their working lives, there was a simple test of what was right: Did it help get and keep a job? Did it increase profit in the long run? But women were more at sea in a world where social standing seemed to depend on elegance and etiquette, where every detail of life was prescribed, and where a single misstep might lead to disgrace. One manual of manners for the period even tried to dictate the precise replies a woman ought to make to every kind of letter or note. In a "Letter Refusing a Donation to an Old Ladies' Home," one should write "I am compelled to contribute only to such objects as have my warmest sympathy." Then there was a "Letter Congratulating a Friend upon Finding a Lost Child": "God Bless Essie." Social care and caution seemed to know no limits, with every conceivable situation demanding a rule. There was even a proper "Answer to a Letter of Condolence on the Loss of a Limb": "Hoping to see you soon, maimed as I am." The book was published in 1888. One can only speculate what its author might have suggested a few years later as the proper way to answer a "Letter of Condolence upon the Ax Murder of One's Aged Parents."

Of course, for most women, most of the time, such detailed prescriptions were unnecessary. But there was no way to escape the sense that there were rules governing what was proper in "good society" for every kind of occasion, and that failure to know those rules doomed a woman and her family to being cast down into "the other half."

Even more important was the fact that the doings of the very rich were relentlessly written

LADIES' WEAR. During the period between the Civil War and World War I, wealthy women—and many who were not so wealthy—dressed themselves in more and more ornate costumes. Here two women promenade at an elegant summer garden party in fashionable Newport, Rhode Island. The woman on the left is wearing an outfit that probably weighed some twenty pounds or more. But the sight of the photographer has apparently cheered her up a bit.

up in newspapers and magazines, and paraded as models of "taste." There had always been prominent ladies, members of one kind of aristocracy or another. But now they had become public celebrities. With what mixture of awe, envy, and confusion could a young woman of Lizzie Borden's social class read the *New York Times* description of the costume Mrs. William Kissam Vanderbilt wore to a very famous ball she held in 1883?

> Mrs. Vanderbilt's irreproachable taste was seen to perfection in her costume as a Venetian princess. The underskirt was of white and yellow brocade. The figures of flowers and leaves were outlined in gold and lined with Roman red. Almost the entire length of the train was caught up at one side forming a large puff. The waist was of blue satin covered with gold em-

broidery; the dress was cut square in the neck, and the flowing sleeves were of transparent gold tissue. She wore a Venetian cap, covered with magnificent jewels, the most noticeable of these being a superb peacock in many colored gems.

It is difficult to measure the emotions of even a single individual, much less of an entire social class or group. But the levels of tension and anxiety among middle-class women in the 1880s and 1890s must have been extremely high. One of the most popular woman writers of the day asked, in 1880, "What is this curious product of today, the American girl or woman?" Her answer was tentative, but a little frightened: "She does not yet understand herself. The face of today is stamped with restlessness, wandering purpose, and self-consciousness." Isabel A. Mallon, who wrote a phenomenally successful advice column in the *Ladies' Home Journal,* put the problem this way ten years later, in 1890: "The great fault of the girl of today is discontent. She calls it by the more magnificent sounding name of ambition, but in reality she is absolutely restless and dissatisfied with whatever may be her position in life."

Two serious writers of the period wrote brilliant and chilling stories of the plight of middle-class, middle-aged women. The first was *The Awakening,* published in 1899 by Kate Chopin. The second was "The Yellow Wallpaper," by Charlotte Perkins Gilman, which was first printed in 1892.

Kate Chopin's heroine is Edna Pontellier, a woman of intelligence and acute sensitivity, married to a wealthy Creole businessman in Louisiana. The social and physical setting in which she moves is lush, picturesque, and even interesting. But she has a vague, powerful sense that her life is incomplete. She considers leaving her husband for another man but discovers that her lover thinks of her as "his" just as much as her husband does. She ponders the possibility of simply having an affair with some experienced, gentlemanly rogue. But that prospect galls. She talks to friends and to a doctor, but no one has any sort of workable advice. Edna Pontellier becomes increasingly despondent. Even the children she wants to love come to seem a trap and a burden to her. Finally, in a curiously indecisive way, she swims naked, out too far to survive, and dies with pink memories of innocent girlhood floating through her mind.

The nameless heroine of "The Yellow Wallpaper" shares Edna Pontellier's vague and powerful sense that she is trapped in an unsatisfying life. She too is married, and to a man of obvious "breeding" and success, a doctor. But she is being gnawed at by depression and anxiety. Gilman paints a classic picture of the way insanity creeps into the life of a woman who feels imprisoned by her marriage, her family, her social position. She begins to imagine that a strange woman is trapped in the vines that decorate the yellow wallpaper in her room. She starts refusing to leave the room, and as the story ends, she is con-

vinced that she is the woman in the wallpaper, where she can now hide forever, creeping invisibly around and around the room.

Both of these stories are about women who, superficially, have nothing to complain of. Both seem to have satisfied every conventional ambition for success. Both are married to men who are far from cruel, and who are rich or near-rich. Both women have "help" aplenty and well-behaved children. But both are cut off from any serious use of their intelligence or their talent. They are suffocating in a world that reduces them to social ornaments, a world ruled by a stifling decorum. And for both heroines, life becomes intolerable. One chooses suicide, the other is pictured as actively choosing insanity. Lizzie Borden would have understood.

THE OTHER HALF

The heroines of *The Awakening* and "The Yellow Wallpaper" were women for whom the domestic ideal had become a stifling, suffocating nightmare. And it is probably true that some middle-class and wealthy women experienced marriage and motherhood as a frustrating round of tedium and despair. But the domestic ideal was kept vital by one simple, inescapable fact: for most women, there was no acceptable alternative.

WOMEN'S WORK

There was one possible alternative, of course: paid work. Lizzie Borden and other women like her could have escaped the confinements of home and marriage by getting jobs. But the alternative was simply not socially acceptable. The jobs to which women had access in the nineteenth century were even more degrading and poorly paid than the jobs most men could find. For most women, a job was an unpleasant and temporary alternative to domestic life. For some others, it was an inescapable necessity, not a freely chosen way to avoid marriage, home, and children.

Women had always worked in ways for which they were not paid. Before the Civil War, about 2 million African-American women had worked as slaves, harder than most men. Women worked in their homes, whether they were wives, widowed aunts, or daughters. They cooked, they cleaned and sewed, they planted and harvested. But neither slave women nor "homemakers" were counted as part of the workforce, because they were not paid. On the record, at the time of the Civil War, only about 10 percent of American women held paid jobs, and they constituted only about 10 percent of the workforce.

After the war, the unpaid work done by women increased in at least three ways. First, many ex-slave women began not only to keep house for themselves and their families, but also to "take in" washing, sewing, and other work. They also entered into informal arrangements with white families, coming in to take care of children or to cook. These arrangements were usually not recorded, so such women did not show up on official records of who "worked" and who did not. Second, the practice of "boarding" increased, especially in American cities. By the end of the century, one out of every five Americans was a lodger in someone else's home. This meant that the women who kept all these houses had additional work to do, work that did not count as a paid job, even though it earned family income. Third, as cities grew, so did prostitution. Tens of thousands of women earned livings in this trade, most of them working now and then for brief periods. But their work did not count as part of the public record of women's employment.

The amount of unpaid work that many women had to do kept them from seeking paid jobs. Still, more and more women did find the opportunity—or, more often, the need—to work outside the home for money. In 1870, women constituted about 15 percent of the total paid workforce, an increase of about 50 percent from the proportion in 1860. And the figures climbed steadily. By 1910, despite the vast immigration of male workers from Europe and Asia, women made up 20 percent of the paid labor force. And fully 25 percent of all women worked for money.

For a few of these working women, a job was an attractive and hard-won escape from the pressures of marriage and motherhood. But for most of them—as for most men—work was a grinding necessity. The plain fact was that most men, whether they were native-born, immigrants, or blacks, could not support a family on the wages from their jobs. Because almost all Americans lived in families, the difference had to be made up somehow, and when it could not, people had to go hungry. The difference was made up, more often than not, by women. (In immigrant families, particularly, child labor also supplemented family income.)

WHICH WOMEN WORKED?

The fact that women who worked did so not because the jobs were more attractive than home, or because they wanted "careers," created a female working population with a peculiar profile. The women who worked were not typical. They were women for whom the domestic ideal was unreached or unreachable. They were black women. They were daughters of immigrants living in urban ghettos. They were native-born women who were still unmarried and who would quit work as soon as they could.

Black women were probably the women who were most often forced to work for wages, even after they married. In 1900 only about 3 percent of the white married women in America earned wages (and this percentage included many women who lived in poor, immigrant families). But among married black women (most of whom lived in stable, two-parent households), more than 25 percent held paying jobs. And the jobs were unfailingly poor. African-American women worked in about equal numbers as agricultural laborers in the South and as domestic servants in northern and southern cities. Their ability to find work as servants caused black women to migrate to northern cities much more often than black men. A careful and probably accurate census in New York in 1890 found ten black women living in the city for every eight black men.

In most of the families of the new immigrants living in the cities, cultural pressures against wives and mothers working were very powerful. In these families, some of the slack in family income was taken up by children. By 1900 fully a quarter of Americans under the age of fourteen worked for wages. But an even more typical solution to the problem was to send older unmarried daughters into the labor market. In New York in 1880, the women who held jobs were, typically, young, unmarried, native-born daughters of recent immigrants from Europe. In fact, fully 90 percent of the city's working women over the age of fourteen were single. Seventy-five percent were not yet twenty-five years old. And 90 percent were the daughters of an immigrant father or mother.

WOMEN'S JOBS

What did they do, these women who "chose" jobs? How did they earn the incomes that would almost invariably put them below the poverty line if they had been trying to support themselves, let alone a family?

A few women did manage to have careers as scientists, social scientists, doctors, lawyers, or writers. And for such women, a career was an authentic alternative to being a wife and mother.

NURSES.   At the turn of the century, there was a concerted effort to transform nursing from a branch of domestic service into a profession. One clue to the transformation was the development of a uniform. But the uniform shown here, in a photograph taken just after the turn of the century, bore the indelible marks of nursing's past. The apron and the striped dresses could have been worn by any Victorian servant whose work kept her distinct from the family who employed her. And the woman holding the batch of keys could have been any head housekeeper.

When the census takers in 1920 asked professional women—most of whom had begun their careers in the nineteenth century—whether they were married, nine out of ten answered no. But such women were only a minuscule part of the total female population of the United States. The lives of an overwhelming majority were far removed from any recognized or prestigious profession.

During the nineteenth century, two occupations had opened up to women, nursing and teaching. But nursing was still classified as "domestic service" in most areas. And as women moved into teaching, the status of the occupation fell. Salaries had dropped, and very few middle-class men were willing to take teaching jobs. As a result, most women who taught did so in exactly the same way that most white women worked at other jobs; temporarily, until they married. But teaching was not, in reality, a job that could attract middle-class women for even the short term. As late as 1911, the average woman teacher came from a family, usually headed by a skilled worker or a farmer, that earned only about $800 a year. Teachers and nurses may have yearned for gentility, but in economic terms they were no better off than most other Americans who worked for a living.

An increasing number of women went to work in manufacturing. They were an important part of the workforce in a few selected industries, like cigar making, clothing, shoes, and bookbinding. But even at the end of the century, only a small number of the industrial workers of the United States were women. And here, too, women tended to work for a few years, until marriage, at only the worst, most unskilled, and most poorly paid jobs. Industrial work did not provide a reasonable, permanent choice for middle-class women. And even working-class women left the factories as quickly as they could and returned only under the most severe economic pressure.

More women earned their wages as domestic servants than at any other job. In the last decades of the century, about a million women were working as maids, cooks, or laundresses.

(So there were about half as many female "domestics" in 1900 as there had been female slaves in 1860.) They lived at home with parents when they could. But more often they had to accept miserably paid "live-in" jobs. A few of them may have developed affectionate relationships with the families in whose homes they worked. But only a few. The rest were like the Borden household's Bridget: a little resentful, and dreaming of the day they could put away their uniforms and aprons.

The statistical records tell a clear story. The domestics were almost all single (unless they were black). They were young. About half of them were either immigrant women or the daughters of immigrant parents. Another quarter of them were black. And they did not like their work. Around the turn of the century, social scientists—mostly women—began to survey domestic servants, asking them about their working conditions and their attitudes toward their jobs. The answers were plain. Mostly, the servants testified, they missed "respect" and "freedom." As one young woman put it in an interview in the 1890s, "freedom was as dear to women as to men, although we don't get so much of it."

Lizzie Borden knew all these things. She knew that working for a living was not an acceptable alternative to marriage—especially at her advancing age. Marriage was ruled out, at least to a suitable partner, for the simple reason that a well-mannered courtship was impossible. She had no place to go, no home of her own to look forward to, and no other kind of career. Lizzie Borden probably committed murder for reasons that were partly personal and private. But she was also pushed to violence by inescapable facts about the kinds of things a respectable woman could and could not do outside the home.

American women, like American men, lived in a country where faith that hard work would lead to the good life was widespread. For women, this faith was merged with another dream—that economic success would lead to an idealized home and family. But for most workers, men and women, neither the faith in the gospel of wealth nor the vision of a gentle and refined family would alter grim reality. And middle-class women probably clung to the ethic of domestic refinement not so much because they wanted to as because they could not reach for that other ethic of work and career. Most of the men who dreamed of becoming "self-made" successes failed. But most women did not even have the chance to fail.

CHRONOLOGY

1818	First cotton textile mill constructed in Fall River		**1872**	Andrew Borden moves his family to Second Street
1821	Birth of Andrew Jackson Borden		**1877**	Cornelius Vanderbilt dies
1844	Andrew Borden goes into business as an undertaker		**1880**	Indoor plumbing comes to Fall River
			1885	William Dean Howells writes *The Rise of Silas Lapham*
1850	Fall River capitalists begin to move to "The Hill";		**1887**	Andrew Borden gives his wife a piece of real estate
	Borden brothers consolidate control of Fall River		**1890**	Lizzie Borden vacations in Europe
1860	Birth of Lizzie Andrew Borden		**1892**	Andrew and Abby Borden murdered;
1862	Lizzie's mother dies			Lizzie Borden arrested;
1864	Andrew Borden marries Abby Durfee Gray			Charlotte Perkins Gilman writes "The Yellow Wallpaper"
1870s	Heavily corseted "wasp waists" come into fashion;		**1893**	Lizzie Borden tried and acquitted
			1895	Lizzie changes her name to Lizbeth Borden, moves to "The Hill":
	Several private colleges for women are established			Sears and Roebuck begins operation
1871	Andrew Borden retires from the under-taking business		**1899**	Kate Chopin writes *The Awakening*
			1927	Death of Lizzie Borden

SUGGESTIONS FOR FURTHER READING

LIZZIE BORDEN

Edmund Pearson, *The Trial of Lizzie Borden* (1937), is an abridged version of the transcript of the inquest and trial. Books about the Borden case continue to appear, generally focused narrowly on the question of her innocence or guilt: among the most recent are Arnold Brown, *Lizzie Borden: The Legend, the Truth, the Final Chapter* (1991), and David Kent, *Forty Whacks: New Evidence in the Life and Legend of Lizzie Borden* (1992). Victoria Lincoln, *A Private Disgrace* (1967), is a strange but intriguing book written by a Fall River native who believes that Lizzie committed the murders in an epileptic seizure. Edward Radin, *Lizzie Borden: The Untold Story* (1961), argues that Lizzie was innocent—the murderer was Bridget Sullivan, the family maid. Ann Jones, *Women Who Kill* (1979), shows how murders committed by women—Lizzie Borden's among them—were treated by contemporaries as products of feminine passion.

WEALTH AND DISPLAY

Irvin G. Wyllie, *The Self-Made Man in America* (1954), examines the myth of rapid upward social mobility. Stephen Thernstrom, *Poverty and Progress* (1967), tests the reality of upward mobility in one Massachusetts community during the nineteenth century. Harold C. Livesay, *Andrew Carnegie and the Rise of Big Business* (1975), is a biography of one of the most famous self-made men in U.S. history. Frederic C. Jaher, *The Urban Establishment* (1982), is about the upper classes in five major American cities. William Dean Howells, *The Rise of Silas Lapham* (1885), is a novel of the period about social mobility and a family that somewhat resembled the Bordens. Thornstein Veblen, *The Theory of the Leisure Class* (1899), is a classic critique of "conspicuous consumption" by a man who probably shared many of Andrew Borden's values. Arthur M. Schlesinger, *Learning How to Behave* (1946), traces the development of etiquette through American history. Ann Douglas, *The Feminization of American Culture* (1976), is an analysis and criticism of consumer culture in the nineteenth century.

WOMEN AND THE FAMILY

Sheila M. Rothman, *Woman's Proper Place* (1978), traces changing ideas and practices from 1870 to the present. Alice Kessler-Harris, *Out to Work* (1982), is a first-rate history of wage-earning women. A more specialized study of maids like Bridget Sullivan is David M. Katzman, *Seven Days a Week: Women and Domestic Service in Industrializing America* (1978). Ellen Dubois, *Feminism and Suffrage* (1978), is a good account of feminism in the same period. Richard Sennett, *Families Against the City* (1970), deals with the family as a utopia, and the tensions between private and public lives in the late nineteenth century. Arthur M. Schlesinger, *The Rise of the City, 1878–1898* (1933), provides a panoramic overview of middle-class life, with a very good chapter on the domestic world of urban women. Ellen Rothman, *Hands and Hearts* (1985), is a history of American courtship practices.

The Politics of Reform

THE EPISODE: *The end of the nineteenth century saw a dramatic change in the nature of American social life and politics. Discontented with the narrow possibilities of lives as wives, mothers, and helpmates, women challenged the boundaries of convention. Strong-willed, talented, and ready to mount the podium of public life, women such as Jane Addams built new institutions through which to enter the public arena. They transformed the nature of charity and redefined social work; they broadened and deepened reform. They often did so, however, without totally casting off the ideology that ascribed a higher morality to women and a special purpose to motherhood. As Jane Addams would learn, this assumption could legitimate the movements of social betterment that she led. It was a persuasive argument in favor of votes for women. But it was also confining. When Addams turned her attention to the meaning of warfare, challenging masculine assumptions about command, heroism, and battle, she provoked a barrage of unkind and damaging criticism.*

THE HISTORICAL SETTING: *The Progressive period, from the 1890s through World War I, was noteworthy for the number of remarkable women and men who affected American political life. No doubt many of them were inspired by a sense of impending crisis. The end of the century was ushered in with vivid scenes of violence and exploitation, strikes and industrial warfare in the new manufacturing centers of the Midwest and East. In 1893, a chilling economic depression stilled factories and businesses throughout the nation. Great businessmen, happy with their enormous profits and protected by political influence, often generous with gifts for civic enterprises, conducted their lives in extraordinary splendor. They constructed urban castles, suburban mansions, and country estates that shamelessly borrowed ideas from the homes of European nobility. At the same time, vast numbers of immigrants pressed into squalid tenements, where they continued to speak foreign languages, read newspapers in their native language, and attend Catholic churches or synagogues. It appeared as if America might become permanently divided by social class, by ethnic origin, by religion, by occupation.*

This ominous situation also presented opportunities. Reform movements sprang up across the nation, powered by people deeply concerned about the evolution of American society; intrigued by new ideas about the function of government, administration, and bureaucracy; empowered by the status of new institutions devoted to social science; and inspired by a rejuvenated social Christianity. Their movement greatly changed America, founding the institutions of government and the ideas of social welfare that are, recognizably, part of our modern world.

THE MOST DANGEROUS WOMAN IN AMERICA

A stout, proper-looking middle-aged woman, escorted by a delegation wearing caps and gowns and carrying signs, "Votes for Women," strode confidently into the entranceway of the Chicago Coliseum. As she did, she stepped beneath the huge stuffed trophy-head of a bull moose. She had traveled only a slight distance across Chicago. Hull House, the South Side settlement house where she had resided since 1889, was only a short ride away. But entering the giant hall, festooned with flags and draped with patriotic bunting, Jane Addams had walked across a threshold of enormous significance. Chosen as a delegate to the Progressive party presidential nominating convention, she was about to do what no American woman before her had done: She would read a speech seconding the nomination of a leading candidate for the presidency of the United States—Theodore Roosevelt of New York. During the remainder of the summer of 1912, she delivered speeches and interviews supporting Roosevelt. After the election in November, despite Roosevelt's defeat and the somewhat bleak prospects for the new Progressive party, she remained politically active. For the next several years she spoke, wrote, and agitated for two great causes: woman suffrage and world peace. With votes for women achieved finally in 1920, and a bloody, precarious peace signed after the end of World War I in 1919, she concentrated her remarkable energy on disarmament until her death in 1935.

The Progressive convention, which Jane Addams addressed and whose delegates cheered her as she led a parade around the hall behind banners urging female suffrage, holds a fascinating place in American politics. The party existed from about 1911 to 1916, but it only lived for one real moment between the summer and fall of 1912. Like other American political parties it was an unstable alliance of idealists and political opportunists. But unlike other major parties, it existed only to elect one man. Its soul belonged to the bitter, angry, and canny ex-president of the United States, Teddy Roosevelt. Without him, it was a name without a face and a movement with no leader.

Roosevelt accepted the mantle of presidential nominee for the Progressive party partly out of pique. Having served one full term and most of another as president (1901–1909), he had hand-picked his successor, William Howard Taft. As president, Taft proved anything but a compliant and loyal friend and fellow reformer, so Roosevelt stormed back into politics to unseat him. He first tried to seize the 1912 Republican party nomination from Taft. Failing that, and complaining of a "stolen" nomination, he let it be known he would run as the nominee of the new Progressive party. Just

JANE ADDAMS. The difficulty for the photographer and for Jane Addams herself was to find an appropriate mode of portrayal. An active writer, administrator, and public figure, she is pictured here as a Victorian lady, poised to compose a letter, not an article or report.

six weeks after the Republican debacle, the Progressives came together on August 5 in Chicago to nominate Roosevelt.

While Jane Addams was only one of about twenty women delegates to the Progressive convention, she was certainly the most famous. Indeed she and Roosevelt were arguably the most important reformers of the early twentieth century. Their political alliance was remarkable not just because it brought into the political limelight a woman, who like most other women in the United States was denied the right to vote or hold office, but also because it temporarily united two very different versions of reform, two opposed sentiments that later burst apart.

For Addams and a great many of the Progressive delegates, the convention represented the culmination of years of work. The Progressive party platform was obviously built on the 1912 report on social work of the National Conference of Charities and Corrections, an organization headed by Addams in 1912. Its far-reaching suggestions for reform proposed extensive labor and social changes, including a minimum wage, regulation of hours worked, health and safety standards in industry, workmen's compensation for injury, and insurance. It promised to end politics as usual and institute the administration of virtue.

After Addams met with the platform committee, she remarked that it seemed more like a session of the National Conference of Charities and Corrections or a convention of the American Sociological Society than a political meeting. To Addams and many other delegates, the convention represented "a curious moment of release from inhibitions." What she meant by the phrase was even more curious: "that reticent men and women should speak aloud of their religious and social beliefs, confident that they would be understood." She was surely right. Religious fervor rose up to the rafters and echoed through the corridors of the Coliseum during the three-day convention in August. Political speeches were delivered and received with solemn passion. Often the delegates spontaneously broke into hymns: "The Battle Hymn of the Republic," or "Onward Christian Soldiers." Roosevelt titled his long speech to the convention a "Confession of Faith." Even before he could mount the podium, the crowd sang a special song:

> *Thou wilt not cover in the dust,*
> *Roosevelt, O Roosevelt:*
> *Thy gleaming sword shall never rust,*
> *Roosevelt, O Roosevelt*

When the convention ended, the delegates stood and sang the "doxology," as if to close a religious service and commence a dramatic crusade to gather in souls (and votes).

To Addams, the convention and the nomination continued a struggle to which she had devoted her life. At last, she told the delegates, a great political party

> has pledged itself to the protection of children, to the care of the aged, to the relief of overworked girls, to the safeguarding of burdened men. Committed to these humane undertakings, it is inevitable that such a party should appeal to women, should seek to draw upon the great reservoir of their moral energy, so long undesired and unutilized in practical politics—one is the corollary of the other, a programme of human welfare, the necessity of women's participation.

1912 CONVENTION. At the 1912 nominating convention of the Progressive party, men still very much dominated politics, both inside and outside the meeting place.

Addams believed the Progressive party represented a political opening for the special moral qualities and human experiences of women to enter the mainstream of American political life. Roosevelt no doubt agreed with her about the special talents and sensibilities of women. Justifying her prominent participation in the campaign, he told a crowd, "I think the highest life, the ideal life, is the married life. But there are both unmarried men and unmarried women who perform service of the utmost consequence to the whole people." He also strongly supported votes for women. But he put these ideas in terms dear to him, and in words that must have troubled Addams: "A vote is like a rifle," he wrote in 1913 in his autobiography, "its usefulness depends upon the character of the user."

Roosevelt's invocation of military language—of rifles and shooting and the ultra-masculine symbol of the trophy of the bull moose as a mascot for the Progressive party—underscored the personality trait that almost every observer noticed about him. He was a man's man, devoted to the strenuous life and military virtues. A devotee of big-game hunting (hence the moose head) and African safaris, a cattle rancher and United States cavalry commander, he believed in character, principle, and individual courage and responsibility. When president, he and several military cronies and cabinet officers engaged in I-dare-you "straight-line walks"—through Washington, D.C. Picking a spot around the city on the map, the group would hike straight toward it and back, swimming across creeks, climbing fences along the way. The symbolism of this could not be clearer—the good man, "the right sort" as Roosevelt put it, climbed over the obstacles of life to remain on a straight and narrow course.

In a profound way, Jane Addams was taking a calculated risk by allying herself with Roosevelt. The ex-president was volatile and headstrong. He certainly agreed with the social welfare platform of the Progressive party designed by Addams and others. He supported woman suffrage. He campaigned vigorously for these principles. But he had forced Addams to compromise on several counts and there was nothing to guarantee that he might not carry the party in further directions she could not follow. Indeed, he did this in 1916 when he led the party back into the Republican fold. But in 1912, Addams was ready to overlook two commitments that felt ominously militaristic to her. The first committed the party to building two battleships a year for the American navy. "I confess," she wrote, "that I found it difficult to swallow those two battleships." Even worse was the pledge to fortify (and thus place under absolute American control) the new Panama Canal. She was also distressed when black delegates lost the right to represent the states of Mississippi and Florida at the convention.

Yet Addams repressed her doubts and joined enthusiastically in the campaign. Up and down the land, she noted, progressivism had become the accepted language of reform, even "in the remotest farmhouse to which the rural free delivery brought the weekly newspaper; certain economic principles become current talk and new phrases entered permanently into popular speech." Women's participation in politics as voters or officeholders would eventually bring "less emphasis upon the military order and more upon the industrial order of society."

For Addams, the Progressive party represented a transitional point between two sorts of social orders: an archaic military order based on an outdated masculine tradition, and a new industrial order, or industrial democracy, that drew on the special insights and virtues of women. Jane Addams developed this theory of sociological maternalism out of years of experience with the problems of the new industrial world of Chicago. Living adjacent to the crowded slums and immigrant ghettoes of the South Side, she tested her maternal philosophy in action. In her own way, she was as practical and experienced a politician as Theodore Roosevelt.

Jane Addams ascended to this high point in her career in 1912 through a long struggle to express her acute moral commitment to improve the social conditions of the poor and exploited immigrants of Chicago. To do so she had to break the conventions that defined her as a middle-class Victorian lady. When she and a friend, Ellen Gates Starr, founded their settlement at Hull House in 1889 in Chicago, she secured a stable base to pursue her goals. Hull House quickly became America's best-known social settlement and Jane Addams the nation's most prominent woman. Unlike Lizzy Borden, who was her contemporary, she helped blaze a path along which modern women would travel.

Jane Addams was born in 1860 into a prominent family of Illinois pioneers. Her father, John Hay Addams, built a saw mill and a grist mill in Cedarville in the northwest part of the state. As he succeeded in milling and then banking, he also helped found many of the small town's early institutions: its schools, churches, and libraries. Elected to the Illinois senate in 1854, he became a friend of Abraham Lincoln and later, during the Civil War, raised a company in an Illinois regiment for service in the Union Army. A strong, dominant, morally upright man, he had amassed a fortune of a quarter million dollars by the time of his death in 1881.[1]

Jane Addams's natural mother was scarcely familiar to her, for she died in 1863 leaving Jane as an infant. When her father remarried three years later, her stepmother, Ann Haldeman, brought a new sensibility to the family, acquiring elegant furniture, china, and silver. Widely read in literature and an accomplished musician, the new Mrs. Addams introduced luxury and culture into a household that had been simple and frugal.

There is nothing really unusual in this history. Nineteenth-century families were often changed by death and remarriage. Nor was it unusual that Jane suffered from chronic illnesses that sometimes incapacitated her for extended periods. Bad health was also common in this age of unsophisticated medicine. Yet she became an avid reader, a good student, and a serious young woman. Attracted to the moral seriousness and high-mindedness of her father and yet tempted by the cultural sophistication of her stepmother, she was, by her late teenage years, an attractive, highly educated, and self-motivated young woman. She was also about to become one of the first generation of college-educated girls in American history.

Although John Addams encouraged his daughter's educational ambitions, he discouraged her from attending Smith, the new women's college that had opened in Northampton, Massachusetts, in 1872. Instead she enrolled at nearby Rockford Female

---

[1]*This sum is probably untranslatable into today's dollars, but one measure might suggest something of its value. At that time, the average schoolteacher earned about $330 per year; the average minister, $730, and a postal employee, $925.*

Seminary. Although the college did not yet award a B.A. and remained small, Jane made several close friends, including Ellen Gates Starr. The two joined the other girls in what became a lively intellectual atmosphere. Some of the students dropped out to marry, but those who remained continued to deepen and sharpen their education. They also brought themselves to a dilemma faced by almost every woman of their special generation: what to do in life with an education. For what did the reading, learning, science, and debate prepare a young woman? Would this education simply make her a more brilliant and polished jewel in the diadem of marriage? Or was there something else? A career?

In 1881 when she graduated, Jane Addams faced this question and spent the next eight years trying to resolve it. She had gained self-confidence; she had been nurtured by a special company of young women her own age. She had become a feminist in the sense of thinking first of the particular virtues and talents of women, of preferring the company of other women, of wanting to pursue what she thought of as the particular calling of women—to be of larger service to society. None of this suggested marriage, and besides, her thoughts and ambitions were already larger than most nineteenth-century marriages could encompass. Instead, Addams wanted to free women (and herself) to make their own choices, even to have a public presence.

Her first thought was medicine, and she applied to the Women's Medical College of Philadelphia in early 1881. Before she could leave Illinois, however, her father died suddenly, and her life immediately seemed rudderless. John Addams had long been the moral center of the family, the bright star in their constellation. For Jane, there was a genuine dimming of possibilities. She had, as a young girl, lived in her father's shadow, unable to believe herself worthy or equal to his affection although craving to be. In part, this doubt took a physical manifestation. In her autobiography, Jane Addams referred to herself as an "ugly duckling." Thinking herself physically plain and unworthy was akin to judging herself morally unfit. In the midst of recounting several moments of childhood anguish and embarrassment, she exclaimed (decades after the fact): "It is hard to account for the manifestations of a child's adoring affection, so emotional, so irrational, so tangled with the affairs of the imagination. I simply could not endure the thought that 'strange people' should know that my handsome father owned this homely little girl."

So, looking back over her life, even through years of achievement and fame, Addams revealed in such poignant moments, an excruciatingly sensitive feeling of self-judgment, a self-measurement against the impossible standards associated with her father.

Deprived of his guidance and inspiration, Addams determined to set out for medical school in the fall anyway. But by the second semester, she suffered what can only be described as a physical and nervous breakdown. She placed herself in the care of Dr. S. Weir Mitchell of Philadelphia, a physician specializing in the treatment of neurotic problems of women. In the fall of the next year, she underwent an operation for a spinal disorder that had periodically incapacitated her since infancy. Then she returned home to Cedarville to live with her stepmother. Thoughts of further formal education had, by that time, been dropped. Jane Addams could look forward only with indecision. She had few prospects for marriage and no apparent career.

For the next years, she continued her search for a life's commitment. To an outsider, it might appear that her major activities during the next six years were aimless and self-indulgent. During this time she took two long trips to Europe, from 1883 to

1885 with her stepmother, family, and friends, and then again in 1887 to 1888 with Ellen Gates Starr and another friend. She spent considerable energy trying to find a proper role in her own family. But beneath the surface, this was a time of gathering energy and quickening commitment, for at the end of the period, Jane Addams suddenly emerged as one of the great reformers of modern American history.

By her own account, Addams finally triumphed over the "snare of preparation"—by which she meant overeducation for any conceivably appropriate role for a Victorian lady. She did so by gradually recognizing that the rich and brilliant culture to which she had been exposed and that compelled her attention—the great literature, music, and art of Europe and America—had become, like herself, distant from the real life struggles of most individuals. Literature, particularly the deeply moralistic writings of the late nineteenth century, engaged life, but only at secondhand. How to apply its lessons, how to make education relevant to the world of life, death, and struggle, was mirrored exactly in Addams's own self-doubts. How could she too participate in life? She could not remain forever a tourist, a reader, an audience, an observer, a consumer of culture. So her two trips to Europe sharpened her belief that education and culture must be instrumental, must be put to work in the service of some cause. Finding that cause would both solve an intellectual problem and end her feeling of uselessness and abstraction.

Addams's description of the sudden choice to open a settlement house is conveyed in her autobiography with something of the urgency and drama of a religious conversion. The seeds of her decision were planted during the first European sojourn, in England, a few months after landing. Making up a portion of a party of tourists escorted by a Christian missionary on a Saturday night to London's East End, Addams witnessed a mad scramble for food auctioned off to the poor. Rotting vegetables, ill-clad men, women, and children, and an air of desperation and hopelessness painted this scene in indelible colors in her mind. Such trips to see the "submerged tenth" as it was called, were certainly not uncommon among the Victorian middle class, for whom slumming in the city, visiting immigrant districts, passing through gambling, drug, and prostitution areas was a special adventure for the hardy tourist. But the incursion made a deep impression on the young American woman. Recoiling from the horror of the experience, Addams felt a sense of shame and personal responsibility. In some manner, she felt, it was her fault. As she recounted it later, for weeks she went about London, edgy with the fear that such an encounter would intrude itself again. "In time," she complained, "all huge London came to seem unreal save the poverty in its East End. During the following years on the continent . . . I was irresistibly drawn to the poorer quarters of each city. . . ." Clearly, Addams had begun to construct the mental image of a world divided between the real and unreal, the real world of struggle and suffering on the one hand and the sphere of culture, comfort, and middle-class detachment for which her education had prepared her, on the other. To enter reality, to participate in its struggles, would mean finding her true nature and essential womanliness. But for that she had to discover how and where to make that commitment.

With a dramatic flourish, Addams recounted the moment of her decision. It came following a bloody bullfight in Madrid that she attended in 1888 at the end of her second trip to Europe. Other members of her party left the stadium in disgust, but Addams lasted through the dispatch of five bulls and a number of gored horses. It was a frightful spectacle, but she found herself numbed to the butchery and intrigued by thoughts of the pageant of historic culture being enacted before her. This ritualized encounter with death, with its lone male matador, brought a rush of historic figures and situations to her mind, recalling the ancient virtues of heroism and chivalry. When she at last joined her disapproving friends, she recognized the lesson. She was lulling her conscience with "a dreamer's scheme." All of her learning she once believed was to prepare for some great task in life. But she had been wrong. It had distracted her from the reality of suffering and violence. Culture was deceptive; history was a phantom; the world of heroes and men of military courage was destructive and violent. The reality of modern life lay elsewhere. And so as she recounts it, she and Ellen Starr determined to carry out a plan they had been discussing. She would return to England to visit the settlement house called Toynbee Hall. Then the two women would meet in Chicago to begin their own social settlement. She had forever turned from the path of acquiring culture for its own sake. Her tours of Europe had ended. She now had a career.

The foundation of Hull House settlement in Chicago in September 1889 began one of the city's—and the nation's—most important reform institutions. Despite her own account of a hasty decision and the precipitous establishment of the settlement, Jane Addams had been considering some sort of social or religious service work for several years. She had read widely in the didactic literature of the nineteenth century, which intensified her sense of social obligation. She, Ellen Starr, and others held long conversations about the possibility of opening some sort of settlement. Her religious commitment also quickened during this period, and in 1888 she joined the Presbyterian Church. What made the opening of Hull House practical, however, was the portion of inheritance she received from her father: enough money to purchase a large house and

HULL HOUSE. The imposing mansion pictured here, belonging to the Hull family, became Chicago's leading settlement house. Besides offering services to the neighborhood, it was a residence for scores of women and men who wished to learn about and assist Chicago's poor communities.

maintain much of the early work of the institution. After several trips through immigrant areas of Chicago, Addams decided to rent a large mansion belonging to the Hull family on the South Side of the city adjacent to an Italian section. The settlement quickly took the name Hull House.

Although an institution devoted to bettering the condition of the poor and exploited, Hull House was a settlement, a residence for Jane Addams, Ellen Starr, other women of her generation, and women (and some men) who had acquired an education and who wanted to do social service, but who lacked the outlet for it. Hull House released a generation from the "snare of preparation," and plunged them into what quickly became the beginning of the modern profession of social work. As guiding genius of Hull House, Addams not only shaped its activities and defined its aspirations, she also used it as a political base to push for social reform on a national and then an international scale. This was an ambitious, even daunting endeavor, and it occupied a lifetime.

The Chicago Jane Addams proposed to reform in 1889 was America's fastest growing large city. It had reached almost a million in population by 1890, making it the second city of the nation and one of the largest urban areas in the world. Certainly it was one of the most dynamic spots on earth. Thousands of immigrants poured into its railway stations daily, from southern, eastern and northern Europe and the small Midwest towns surrounding it. It contained hundreds of thousands of Germans, Irish, Swedes and Norwegians, Italians and Poles, as well as ambitious young men and women from nearby farms and villages. Streets unrolled, buildings grew up, population increased, and factories mushroomed as if erected by a perpetual-motion building machine. In the most conservative of America's older cities, these forces gave the impression of disorder and a breakdown of institutions. In Chicago, there was no doubt about it. Within a six-block radius of Hull House lived 70,000 people representing twenty-six nationalities. The only citywide institutions of note were political parties, and they were often seen as part of the problem of disorder and corruption, not the solution.

The first and perhaps most lasting impression that the city made upon Addams and her coworkers was one of disarray and the breakdown of tradition. What bonded people together, affirmed their identities, offered them help? To some extent, the Catholic Church did and so did immigrant institutions and clubs. Neighborhoods maintained a semblance of stability—sometimes—but movement in and out was constant. In fact, it seemed as if the whole city of Chicago was in motion. Impoverished immigrants poured into the center of the city and then dispersed into newer, less crowded neighborhoods as they found jobs and acquired English. Sociologists examined this complex process and called it assimilation, or, more popularly, Americanization. Captured in the aggregate figures of the census or the social scientists's calculus, this appeared a relentless process. To those who looked at it up close, it involved pain and disorientation.

Observing the world around them, Addams and her companions saw disorder, but they also saw opportunity to learn and share their learning. This took confidence and sensibility, a translation of the earnest education that Addams herself had received, into a form that could aid and not threaten her new neighbors. Over the course of several years, Hull House became the focal point of new neighborhood institutions. Quite early on, it provided a meeting place for the new University of Chicago educational extension service for after-work-hours education. It housed a branch of the Chicago Public Library. It sponsored club meetings, cultural discussion clubs, and political organizations. It began and ran a kindergarten for neighborhood children. It constructed a gymnasium for young men and women to exercise. It founded the Jane Club, a residence apartment complex for neighborhood working girls who found living in crowded boardinghouses precarious because of strikes or other troubles at work. It organized cooperative groups for the cheap purchase and distribution of coal used for heating—a serious problem in the bleak Chicago winters. It opened an art studio and gallery. As the institutions associated with Hull House grew in number and importance, it became clear that one of the primary functions of the settlement house was to initiate neighborhood organizations and then agitate for their acceptance in the city and nationwide. Its purpose was to provide the texture of institutions and culture that Addams and her coworkers defined as essential to any meaningful urban life.

Sometimes these endeavors led Jane Addams to confront the old-boy world of ward heelers and machine politicians. One of the most visible and annoying problems of the neighborhood was the immense amount of garbage and dead animal carcasses that accumulated on the streets. Chicago had a decentralized system of garbage inspection and pickup that invited corruption and inefficiency. Her response was typical of her tactics and highly effective. After an investigation of the city garbage collection system and its possible links to the high death rates in certain city wards, Addams, with the backing of two prominent businessmen, placed a bid before the city for the contract to collect garbage in the ward. Her bid was disqualified on a technicality, but the mayor of the city appointed her garbage inspector of the ward—for $1000 a year. Addams had to fight the companies that did the sloppy inadequate work as well as landlords who refused to collect and store garbage properly. Disposal of dead animals and tin cans proved to be another serious problem. But the worst was a filthy narrow street in a heavily Italian area. After Addams had eight inches of garbage removed, she finally convinced the mayor to have the street resurfaced. Neighborhood children delighted following her "garbage phaeton" (carriage) around the ward in search of such problems.

Aside from churches, which were frequently suspicious of social reformers, or saloons, which provided an uninviting environment, there were few meeting places in the ward. Hull House more than filled this need. As in other areas, the residents sought to use the settlement house to combine the interests and needs of the local population with their own middle-class education and enlightenment. Aside from educational meetings, Hull House sponsored labor union reunions. On more than one occasion Jane Addams was chosen to help mediate between strikers and owners. Famous and notorious visitors streamed to the settlement. Philosopher John Dewey and prominent social reformers Richard T. Ely and Henry Demarest Lloyd were frequent visitors. So were important members of the sociology department of the University of Chicago, who looked upon Hull House as something of a laboratory for reform institutions. Some, like the Russian anarchist Prince Kropotkin, proved more controversial. But by the end of the first decade of its operation, Hull House had become a leading model of social, cultural, and political interchange, copied and admired in the United States and Europe.

A further and especially revealing activity of Hull House was its sponsorship of middle-class cultural activities. Fearful that her cultural education had trapped her in irrelevance, as a consumer, not a user of literature and the arts, Addams hoped to build culture into the practice of the settlement house movement. The problem, she concluded during her trips to Europe, had been separation and aloofness. Hull House could overcome this distance between culture and reality, between middle-class and immigrant life. For this reason an early and abiding activity of the residents was a kind of cultural ministry to the slums. When the settlement house first opened, Addams invited her Italian neighbors in for a reading—in Italian—of a novel by the female Victorian moralist George Eliot and to view slides of Renaissance art from Florence, Italy. Her purpose was to introduce neighbors to uplifting literature as well as reveal to them their own artistic past.

This ambition pushed Addams toward some interesting insights and activities. In her own experience the separation of culture from the turbulent reality of life brought her to live at the edge of the slum. But for her immigrant neighbors, deprivation and emptiness had different causes and consequences. Condemned to toil long hours, impoverished, cut off from traditional institutions and culture, the men, women, and children of the ward suffered from futile efforts to adjust peasant European institutions to the modern industrial city. The community was separated from its origins and divided against itself. Generation bickered and fought with generation. Older people who could not make a rapid transition to the new environment and who clung to old languages, customs, and foods, suffered in particular. Traditional social and gender roles were shattered by the new demands of urban life. Children, in particular, became uprooted—heartless in their rejection of older ways and eager to absorb the flashy new popular culture arising around them. To Addams the situation was filled with dangerous potential: alcoholism and excessive drinking, family violence, prostitution, juvenile delinquency, and a general aura of discouragement and defeat among the older generation.

A fascinating response to the generational misunderstanding was the Labor Museum founded at Hull House. As Addams suspected, the distance between parents and sons and daughters extended from their different experiences in two different worlds of work and culture, between past and present. Something was required to explain generations to each other. From her numerous trips to Europe, Addams had observed handicraft and culture in their geographic and historical settings. While many men and women immigrants to the United States were skilled in these crafts and steeped in the history of their towns or villages, the new society demanded different work of them and their children. Children, especially, in their eagerness to Americanize, wanted to discard these old traditions. The past was only a reminder of the difficulties in assimilation.

The Labor Museum provided a context to bring generations back together around memories and symbols of the old country. In it, older immigrants could illustrate their skills in craft, especially in spinning and weaving. This, in turn, could be a lesson for all persons engaged in industry, for the history of cloth making contained all the elements of the history of industrialization. As Addams wrote, "Human progress is slow and perhaps never more cruel than in the advance of industry, but is not the worker comforted by knowing that other historical periods have existed similar to the one in which he finds himself . . . and is he not entitled to the solace which an artistic portrayal of the situation might give him."

The Labor Museum aimed to revive and restore tradition, half-extinguished by the rush of acculturating to the city, by exhibiting the skills and products of traditional work. Addams expected that children would view their parents in a new light and find them worthwhile, skilled and dignified. As she noted, "An overmastering desire to reveal the humble immigrant parents to their children lay at the base of what has come to be called the Hull-House Museum."

Addams brought this same thinking to her description of wayward youth. Nothing so distressed reformers as the apparent aimless and empty lives of young immigrant men and women. Without the steadiness of traditional culture and living beyond the reach of American small-town mores, immigrant youth became increasingly susceptible to juvenile delinquency. Although this term had many contemporary meanings, when applied to boys it generally referred to some form of criminal behavior against property by an under-aged youth (under eighteen). For girls it implied prostitution or an easy attitude toward premarital sex.

To Addams delinquency was a very serious matter and she wrote a popular and sympathetic book explaining it in 1909, entitled *The Spirit of Youth and the City Streets.* Once again she pointed to an absence of tradition and culture, exposing young sons and daughters of immigrants to the temptations and cheap amusements of the urban environment. Empowered with freedom, with jingling pockets of loose change, these children flocked to dance halls, cheap theaters, eateries, and amusement parks. Beyond adult supervision and untouched by claims of the past, they wandered through adolescence and misspent their youth consuming popular culture. Following fashions and fads, unprotected, they were spoiled by the temptations of the city. The most dreaded prospect wrote Addams, occurred to girls. "We see thousands of girls," she wrote, "walking up and down the streets of a pleasant evening with no chance to catch a sight of pleasure, even through a lighted window save as these lurid places provide it."

It was the responsibility of Hull House to offer alternatives, to convey proper culture to young men and women, and draw them off the street and into a healthy environment. This was so much the harder because the majority of young people worked in factories. They were exhausted and footloose, with few intellectual and moral resources to combat the popular culture of the city. So Hull House founded a boys' club and a girls' club, which taught a variety of industrial and craft skills. It offered classes in literature. It sponsored plays and held literary discussions. To compete with Saturday-night dances, it held athletic contests in the gymnasium. In each of these efforts, the goal was similar: to bring the best thought and culture to bear upon the lives of young immigrants; to help them to find their place in the confusing new world they were helping to shape. What Addams said of the Hull House Shakespeare classes could justify any of these activities: "To feed the mind of the worker, to lift it above the monotony of his task and to connect it with the larger world, outside of his immediate surroundings. . . ."

Probably the most singular story Addams recounted in her autobiography showed her uncanny insight into the problems of older immigrant women, who were most victimized by a disruption of culture. During 1912, a rumor swept the local community that a "Devil Baby" had been abandoned at Hull House. Scores of women and several men called at the settlement house to catch a glimpse of this (nonexistent) child. Addams might have dismissed the event as a remnant of peasant lore, inspired by the gossip of old ladies. Instead she found some striking, larger meanings in the experience.

The story, basically an Italian tale, centered around a curse. An atheist husband, standing in his bedroom, pointed to a holy picture on the wall and exclaimed to his cowering wife: "I'd rather have the devil in this bedroom than that picture." A Jewish version of the tale featured a father with six daughters. Before the birth of a seventh child, he exclaimed, "I'd rather have the Devil than another girl." In both cases the Devil obliges and appears in the guise of a newborn child wreaking havoc and evil upon the family.

Why this story gained such currency puzzled Addams until she began to interview the women who visited Hull House seeking a view of the monstrosity. One motivation, she concluded, was that knowledge and expertise in such matters traditionally belonged to elderly women. Confirmation of the existence of the Devil Baby would have brought these women immense prestige in their families. Addams also concluded that the story revealed the quiet desperation of immigrant women. Here was an explanation of a marriage gone bad, of brutish husbands, of strayed children. As she wrote, "The story of the Devil Baby may have made its appeal through its frank presentation of this very demonic quality, to those who live under the iron tyranny of that poverty which may any dark night bring them or their children to extinction; to those who have seen both virtue and vice go unrewarded and who have long since ceased to complain."

The sociological insight in these discussions provided a powerful argument for social reform and, even more, the necessity of a female perspective on the world of industrial problems. In her books and through her activities at Hull House, this was exactly the vision that Addams promoted, and it deeply affected the beginnings of academic sociology in the United States.

Addams's relationship to professional sociology was complex and conflicted. Although some fortunate women had degrees in higher education from eastern women's colleges or the more enlightened universities of the West and Midwest, almost none could enter the academic professions which were almost everywhere the closed clubs of men. Sociology was no exception. Although Jane Addams participated in defining sociological study, knew the great sociologists at the University of Chicago—one of the centers of the new social sciences—and wrote for professional journals, she never held a university lectureship. Her writings deeply influenced the developing profession. She was a leading American sociologist pushed by discrimination and custom into applied social work. No doubt this was also her bent, to serve as well as study the community around her. But it meant that her influence remained greatest among social workers and the professional women who became its practitioners, not among university scholars. She became best known for founding practical institutions—the Federal Children's Bureau, the Women's Bureau, and the Immigrant Bureau, not schools of thought.

This gender separation between professions, between what men and women could aspire to accomplish in their careers, only underscored a division in Jane Addams's mind between feminine and masculine culture. To her, women existed in a special relationship to society. They better understood the institutions of family and community. Their experience and instincts for nurturing children and caring generally for the weak and deprived fitted them with a special moral sense. This fortunate sensitivity made them vital to the purposes of social reform and crucial to restoring honest politics. Their moral superiority could transform the city, the nation, and the world. It was on these grounds that Jane Addams joined the campaign of 1912 and worked actively for political reform of Chicago. It was the assumption that guided her most important ideas about society. If this viewpoint extended an earlier Victorian notion about the "cult of true womanhood"[2] into the twentieth century, it also empow-

---

[2]*The notion that women were guardians of culture and morality, but too weak intellectually and physically to pursue a life in public.*

ered her to understand the modern world. At the same time it placed her in a profound dilemma.

To Addams and many other early-twentieth-century reformers, the most terrible symbol of social disorganization and exploitation was prostitution. During 1912, she wrote several essays for *McClure's Magazine* that she published the next year in a book, *A New Conscience and an Ancient Evil*. Basing her analysis on sociological studies of Chicago's juvenile delinquents and working girls and their behavior in popular public places such as amusement parks, dance halls, and theaters, Addams portrayed a sinister profession of "white slavery." Countering this was an advancing host of publicists and moralists denouncing prostitution in a growing popular literature "approaching 'Uncle Tom's Cabin'" in significance. She implied that her own book might provide the energy to end the enslavement of women, just as Harriet Beecher Stowe's great abolitionist novel had energized the antislavery movement.

Addams's choice of "white slavery" was no idle metaphor. She viewed young women as particularly susceptible to exploitation and deception. Girls became prostitutes for economic reasons, out of weakness and deception, through betrayal, or because of alcohol. In particular, the new mass culture set the stage for the seduction of impoverished working women: finery and fads demanded money. "It is perhaps in the department store more than anywhere else," she wrote, "that every possible weakness in a girl is detected and traded upon." In a city with over 320 public dance halls, 190 connected to saloons, it was impossible to regulate behavior. "The girls attending the cheap theaters and vaudeville shows are most commonly approached through their vanity," she concluded. To this temptation, the addition of alcohol was fatal. The result was wrecked lives and the spread of (incurable) venereal diseases.

If women were seduced, betrayed, or forced from desperation into prostitution, what responsibility did men have for this great social evil? To Addams, the cause was the breakdown of tradition and social control. As a result, a man's sexual nature was liberated and empowered. "The great primitive instinct," she concluded, had been freed from restraint. Modern society convinced men they stood above social control and beyond the watchful eye of the community. The only solution was establishment of a "single standard" of virtue: that sex for men and women would be limited to marriage. Only empowering women with the vote and the right to sit on juries could abolish their enslavement. "One cannot imagine that the existence of the social evil would remain unchallenged in its semi-legal protection," she concluded.

Addams's gender analysis of prostitution resembled her understanding of warfare. To this subject too, she applied a maternalist sociology, but here she encountered angry denunciations for the first time. If she was correct that a female perspective was pacifist, then during a war, women might be seen as enemies of the state. This argument could compromise the crusade for women's suffrage and cast doubt on reforms identified with women's moral housekeeping.

Her views on warfare had long been known. The male military culture, she believed, that sustained the false heroism of the past was being engulfed in "a rising tide of moral feeling." During the first decade of the twentieth century she developed a notion of a "moral substitute" for war. As with her analysis of the great primitive sexual instinct, she argued that young men needed a directed culture to divert them from warfare, something to control the instinct for belligerence. While Addams was certainly not alone among Americans in hoping for universal peace and world order at this time, neither she—nor anyone, perhaps—was prepared for the ferocity of bellicose opinion unleashed by the beginning of World War I in 1914.

When the European powers began their decimating conflict in 1914, the United States remained aloof until 1917. As the leading peace advocate in the United States, Addams could hardly remain silent. In early 1915, she became chair of the new Women's Peace Party, and in the spring she traveled to the Netherlands to attend an international gathering of women devoted to halting the war. There she was elected a delegate to visit warring heads of state to petition for peace. When she returned from Europe, she eventually gained an audience with President Woodrow Wilson of the United States.

It was a speech she delivered on July 9, 1915, at Carnegie Hall in New York City that suddenly changed her reputation and exposed the perils of her analysis of war. From that time forward Jane Addams was a deeply controversial public figure. Most painfully, the alliance she had struck with Theodore Roosevelt in 1912 was shattered. The two leading advocates of progressivism divided over the issue of gender and its relationship to understanding of and sympathy for warfare.

Addams's controversial statement was an almost offhanded, superficial point illustrating her main argument against the war. The European conflict was incited and directed by old men, she said, who had been raised in an archaic militaristic culture. The young men called upon to fight and die, however, "were not the men who wanted the war, and were not the men who believed in the war." In fact, she said, she heard rumors that commanding generals on both sides distributed alcohol to ground troops before a bayonet charge to drug them into fighting. The point was clear: young men could not possibly be in favor of war or their own suicide. They could only be forced into belligerence by the plots of sinister old men. The parallel to her argument against prostitution was clear enough, but that did not enrage critics. She had dared to cast suspicion on the ideals of patriotism, sacrifice, and heroism. She had devalued masculine pride in

MRS. P. LAURENCE, JANE ADDAMS, AND MRS. LEWIS F. POST on Henry Ford's Peace Ship. Jane Addams's efforts for peace during World War I provoked angry and damaging commentary.

warfare. She had insulted the military ethic, and men like Theodore Roosevelt would never forgive her.

The attacks on Addams that followed were bitter, personal, and instinctively focused on the argument that women had a special moral mission. But just the reverse was true, they claimed. "Jane Addams," wrote one paper, "is a silly, vain, impertinent old maid, who may have done good charity work at Hull House, Chicago, but is now meddling with matters far beyond her capacity." Some writers used the occasion to denounce woman suffrage, arguing that if women were inherently different and naturally pacifist, they should never be given the vote. Theodore Roosevelt unkindly said that Addams was "one of the shrieking sisterhood," calling her "poor bleeding Jane," and a "Bull Mouse."

For the next several years, Jane Addams persisted in opposing the war, and suffered the slights of former friends and new enemies. She had tried to make conscience the heart of a new female-centered sociology and a practical politics of reform. In the process she had also become to some, "the most dangerous woman in America."

TRADITIONAL FEMALE ROLES. This photograph, taken toward the end of Jane Addams's life, again emphasizes traditional female roles, this time with children.

In Search of the Public Interest

The Progressive movement, which made Jane Addams a national leader and achieved singular success in the presidencies of Theodore Roosevelt and Woodrow Wilson, gained much of its energy and inspiration from secularized religion. Divided and contradictory as it was, this was a movement that also revolutionized attitudes and practices of government in American society. This diverse coalition of men and women emerged primarily from the ranks of the new urban middle class. Drawing on traditional ideas of democracy and republicanism, they worried deeply about the incongruities of their society. They puzzled over the contradictions between self-interest and social interest, between progress and poverty. Steeped in nineteenth-century concepts of self-help, stewardship, and the work ethic, they were surprised and troubled by the unexpected byproducts of industrial growth. The obvious success of the capitalist economic system—its productivity, invention, and urbanization—had a threatening dark side: poverty, exploitation, and violence. Industrial development degraded work and initiated cycles of economic boom and bust, violent strikes, and political instability. Inexplicably, the Victorian economic ethic, based on saving, investing, and individualism, had spawned a generation of business leaders whose greed made a mockery of the precepts traditionally invoked to justify wealth and success.

In a justly renowned article published in 1889 (see Chapter 16), Andrew Carnegie, self-made millionaire and steel and iron entrepreneur, reflected on his society, which had grown rich and poorer at the same time. Competition, he wrote in his essay "The Gospel of Wealth," made a few men like himself very rich, but many other people poor. Because competition also stimulated the marvels of productivity, he would certainly not oppose it. But its social effects demanded attention. As he put it, finding the proper administration of wealth would bind together the rich and poor in harmonious relationship. But could it be done? Carnegie had raised the questions that most worried progressives: Could industrial progress and economic individualism continue without degenerating into violence and class warfare? Was a social gospel possible?

The depression of 1893 helped precipitate the forces that created progressivism as a national movement. This deep economic downturn shook millions of workers from their jobs. Unemployment rose from around 3 percent in 1892 to over 18 percent two years later. The gross national product (the estimated sum of goods and services produced by the economy) fell by 12 percent in 1894 and did not recover until 1897.

A measure of the depression's seriousness was the social unrest to which it gave rise. In the spring of 1894, this burst into an angry disturbance in Washington, DC. Led by Jacob S. Coxey, an Ohio businessman, a small army of supporters, dubbed the Commonweal of Christ, marched to the capital to ask for a public works bill to end unemployment. Although it posed no threat, the group was attacked by police and Coxey was jailed.

A far more threatening labor incident began in May 1894 with a strike at the Pullman Palace Car Company in Chicago. Sparked by falling wages and management opposition to unions, the strike took on national significance in June (see Chapter 16). In trying to understand these events that she saw first hand, Jane Addams invoked Shakespeare's tragic hero King Lear, who harmed those who loved him and trusted those who betrayed him. As she wrote, "Her attention was caught by the similarity of ingratitude suffered by an indulgent employer and an indulgent parent. King Lear often came to her mind." To her, the industrial world had turned values on their heads.

Why were these new industrial relations frightening to so many observers in the 1890s? There are, essentially, two answers. The industrial system encouraged the organization of powerful private institutions: corporations and labor unions that seemed pitted against each other in a ruthless struggle for power. Surely, it was assumed, society itself would be the loser in such strife. Second, the private, unregulated industrial system had created untold hardships for millions of Americans through unemployment and injury. In this uneven struggle, where did the nation stand?

CORPORATIONS VERSUS UNIONS

CORPORATIONS ORGANIZE

The most powerful economic institutions of the early twentieth century were corporations. Many of them were assembled in the waning days of the 1893 depression and in the first few years of the twentieth century. Their objective was to control markets, raw materials, and labor. By 1900 about two-fifths of total American manufacturing capital and two-thirds of railroad trackage were concentrated in the hands of large combines and corporations. Ten of the largest holding companies (that is, corporations that owned other operating companies) had assets of more than $100 million; the greatest of these, U.S. Steel, controlled over $1 billion. Such concentrations of power touched off controversy from almost the moment they appeared. In 1890, Congress passed the Sherman Antitrust Act, intended to prevent monopolies from restraining trade and competition. But business circumvented the act and, aided by the courts, turned the Sherman Act against labor unions instead.

Some capitalists ignored the adverse publicity. But others believed they had to act to deflect criticism of their private power and fortunes. Some, like Andrew Carnegie, also recognized a larger social responsibility. The successful businessman, Carnegie suggested, should administer his wealth for the good of society. Carnegie acted on his own advice and endowed over 2,000 free public lending libraries during his lifetime.

Carnegie's charitable gifts exemplified the development of professional philanthropy. But this money was not intended for the unemployed or the poor. Instead, most was given to encourage culture or to fund scientific or social research or educational projects. As Carnegie put it, his gifts provided "ladders upon which the aspiring can rise." During the first half of the twentieth century, universities also acquired large endowments from such wealthy donors. Several important institutions, such as Stanford, started by railroad magnate Leland Stanford in 1885, were founded by men with large fortunes. A number of America's great universities were created in this manner. Universities also hired professional fund raisers and used fund drives to expand their educational offerings.

In many cases, philanthropists wished to control the use of their gifts even after their own death. In others, philanthropy became a device to deflect criticism from questionable business practices. John D. Rockefeller, whose reputation for ruthless competition was national, used charitable giving to improve his public image. In 1889 he began a series of large donations to the new University of Chicago. In 1891 he hired Frederick T. Gates, a Baptist clergyman, to oversee his donations. But such philanthropy did not prevent criticism; instead, it made the very act of giving suspect. Journalists and politicians denounced Rockefeller's motives, calling him a "robber baron" and "spoiler of the state," and his charitable gifts "tainted money." Obviously, philanthropy itself was not enough.

In response to the 1893 depression and mounting public sympathy for labor unions, corporations formed two important new organizations: the National Association of Manufacturers (NAM) in 1895 and the National Civic Federation (NCF) in 1900. The NAM, especially after 1903, pushed the "open shop" movement, a movement devoted to preventing unions from forming. Particularly directed against the American Federation of Labor (AFL), this drive gathered strength in the West, where affiliated organizations sprang up to defeat union drives or prolabor legislation.

The NCF adopted a much less confrontational approach to industrial strife. Reformer and journalist Ralph Easley, its driving force, had been deeply affected by the Pullman strike of 1894. He believed that business had to negotiate with unions to prevent class warfare. Persuading Samuel Gompers of the AFL and John Mitchell of the United Mine Workers to join Ohio Republican political boss Mark Hanna and a group of financiers, businessmen, and academics, Easley created an organization devoted to moderate labor legislation.

UNIONS ORGANIZE

Unions were obviously the weaker force in the struggles of the 1890s. The problems they sought to overcome were legion: poverty, indus-

trial accidents, strikes and lockouts, exploitation. For almost all factory workers, wages were low and industrial accidents frequent. Average wages for nonfarm employees hovered around $500 a year in this period. Jobs not only paid poorly, they were dangerous, particularly in the key railroad sector. Because of lax safety standards and poor maintenance, 610 passengers, 4,534 railroad employees, and 6,695 workers in railroad shops lost their lives in the deadly year of 1907.

Before they sought to unionize an industry, labor organizers knew they would confront tough employer opposition. Employers possessed an arsenal of legal tactics to discourage unions. They could demand a "yellow-dog contract," allowing dismissal of any worker who joined a union. They assembled blacklists of workers who sympathized with unions, and they hired scabs to cross picket lines. Often they could persuade a friendly court to declare a strike illegal. As a last resort, employers could hire small armies of detectives, spies, and bodyguards to break up union gatherings.

Other obstacles to unionization arose from the nature of the American working class. Increasingly, industrial workers were immigrants from eastern and southern Europe. Divisions by language and national origin made organization difficult—a circumstance that employers often exploited.

Despite these factors, significant unions emerged toward the end of the nineteenth century. The most important and lasting of these was the American Federation of Labor (AFL), founded in 1886 by Samuel Gompers of the Cigar Makers Union. Consisting primarily of skilled craft unions, the AFL grew rapidly in the 1890s. Gompers, an English immigrant and one-time Marxist, guided his union through thirty-five years of strife and conflict. Although he gave up his belief in class struggle, he remained deeply suspicious of politicians and legislation. Everything in his experience worried him about the effects of government intervention. Gradually he developed a philosophy of voluntarism, or union independence from political parties and government intervention. Anxious to avoid the socialist unionism sweeping Europe, he devoted the political energies of the AFL to rewarding its friends and punishing its enemies. By 1900 the union had increased its membership to 400,000.

The dangers and exploitation in industrial work also bred radical organizations. The most important of these, the Socialist Party of America, was formed in 1901. Eugene Debs, of Terre Haute, Indiana, leader of the American Railway Union, epitomized the movement. Enormously popular, Debs addressed audiences across the country in speeches laced with discussions of class struggle and promises of the coming Christian brotherhood, under which the people, not the capitalists, would own the means of production.

The Socialist party, along with the revolutionary Industrial Workers of the World (IWW), also known as the Wobblies, which it helped to found, grew rapidly during the progressive era up to World War I. In 1912, when it presented a serious challenge to Wilson, the party had 118,000 dues-paying members, 1,200 public officials, and 300 socialist periodicals. With strength in old Populist strongholds of the Southwest, socialists created a movement dedicated to an "international socialist commonwealth—God's Kingdom." Although it eventually broke with the Socialist party, the IWW also grew rapidly. It achieved important, though transient, successes during widely noted strikes such as the textile strike in Paterson, New Jersey, in 1913.

MIDDLE-CLASS REFORMERS

Facing substantial industrial turmoil and large new power blocs in the economy, middle-class reformers tried to develop a program and philosophy of national public interest. They believed

government could solve the problems raised by unregulated competition and industrial struggle. As reformers, they were critical of both sides, owners and unions. They intensely disliked the selfish moneyed interests and feared the organized power of monopolies. Perhaps even more, they distrusted the industrial labor force of newly arrived immigrants. Many worried that labor unions or socialist organizations would challenge the basic tenets of American capitalism. Like Jane Addams, they proposed to create a reformed society, guided by moral principles, in which all of the contending interests would share the benefits.

The forerunners of the progressives, the mugwumps (see Chapter 15), appeared first in the sedate halls of Harvard University and the gentlemen's clubs of Boston. These genteel reformers bolted the Republican party in 1884 to vote for Grover Cleveland, the Democratic candidate. They put principle above party and supported changing the electoral system and, above all, honesty in government enforced by civil service reform. On issues of labor rights, they remained conservative; to them, reform began and ended with good government. However, they did will to the next generation of reformers a commitment to national change and an invitation to the respectable classes to enter politics.

CHURCHES AND COLLEGES

The mugwumps also bequeathed a tone of moralism and high-mindedness that progressives like Jane Addams shared. The Protestant churches in particular paid special attention to the developing evils of the industrial system. Led by Baptist minister Walter Rauschenbusch and Congregationalist Washington Gladden, ministers and churchmen advocated a new social Christianity. This "Social Gospel" proclaimed that Jesus had taught a social ethic, not individualism as conservative theologians preached. Proposing social salvation

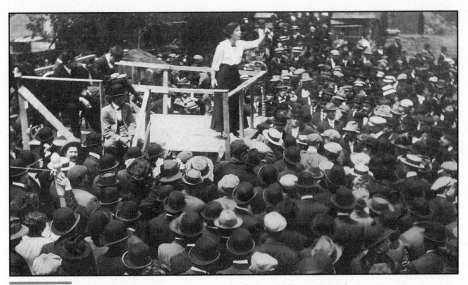

FIERY SPEAKER ELIZABETH GURLEY FLYNN addresses a crowd of workers during the I.W.W. strike at Paterson, New Jersey, in 1913. Note that she is the only person in the picture not wearing a hat, as if to emphasize the singularity of a woman exhorting an assembly of unionists.

through good works, these men sought greater and greater social cooperation. Many of them entered local good-government campaigns and crusades to regulate industry.

The intellectual climate in American universities and colleges also lent itself to new ways of thinking about society and government. Much as Princeton had done under the presidency of Woodrow Wilson, other prestigious American universities like Johns Hopkins, the University of Chicago, Harvard, and the Universities of Wisconsin and Michigan hosted new intellectual movements that swept away the cobwebs of nineteenth-century conservative individualism. The development of the new professions of sociology and social work, which underscored the importance of social engineering as the legitimate function of the state, was one such movement.

SCIENCE AND SOCIETY

Perhaps the most profound thinker of the era was Thorstein Veblen. A difficult writer and an eccentric personality, Veblen wrote several remarkable sociological works. The best known was *The Theory of the Leisure Class* (1899), in which he satirized the "conspicuous consumption" of the American middle and upper classes. In its stead, he called for the cultivation of the "instinct of workmanship," which he deemed a more natural and creative human impulse.

Veblen's attack on compulsive wastefulness and class consciousness was seconded in the philosophical and educational writings of John Dewey. Dewey belonged to a group of important American philosophers, called pragmatists, who stressed the effectiveness and efficiency of ideas rather than their religious or traditional origins.

Steeped in modern theories of science, these philosophers were impressed with the possibility of engineering new answers to old human problems. Dewey constructed a philosophical system that emphasized the possibilities for growth, change, and increasing control of the environment. In education, he emphasized the importance of work and experience. To him, education meant placing the child in an environment where he or she could understand the process of change and social evolution in a scientific way. Hence the school, in Dewey's educational plans, became the center of society and a force to rejuvenate the community. It would, he hoped, help narrow distances between social classes and strengthen American democracy.

Socially applied science also inspired the management reformer Frederick Winslow Taylor. Taylor's famous book, *The Principles of Scientific Management* (1915), made him both a hero and a villain to the public. His works were cited by some as a bible for industrial reorganization. To others, his writings constituted evidence of a management conspiracy to speed up production and reduce wages. Taylor developed a system to increase efficiency by measuring the time and motion involved in completing a task. Quite literally this meant observing and timing (with a stopwatch) the actions of a worker and then devising ways to improve his or her productivity. In many cases this meant a quicker pace and sometimes more efficient tools. In addition, Taylor urged new shop arrangements and incentive wages as well as new management techniques. Taken together, this system of organization was supposed to increase efficiency, productivity, and wages. But before Taylor died in 1915, he had been vilified for treating workers as if they were no more than robots: his efficiency revolution did not occur.

THE GOOD-GOVERNMENT MOVEMENT

Civic reformers also provided an important practical ingredient of progressivism. These city dwellers were often appalled by the powerful coalitions of urban politicos and immigrant voters, and they organized to wrest cities like New York, St. Louis, and Minneapolis from the control of the bosses. The good-government movement received national attention with the founding of the National Municipal League in 1894.

The achievements of this movement were exemplified by Tom Johnson of Cleveland, Ohio. Johnson had earned a fortune as an inventor, steel mill owner, and operator of streetcar railways. Elected mayor of Cleveland in 1901, he pushed through several impressive municipal reforms: a new garbage disposal system for the city, a low-cost municipally owned electric company, meat and milk inspection, and the construction of broad streets and parks to provide open spaces and uncongested throughways for all the city's residents. He also attacked organized gambling. Johnson quickly earned a national reputation. In the words of journalist Lincoln Steffens, Cleveland was the "best governed city in the United States," and Johnson's was "the greatest movement in the world today."

Other urban reformers focused on overcrowded living conditions, poor diet, and the ravages of poverty. Tuberculosis, typhoid fever, influenza, and other contagious diseases were sweeping American cities, fueled by overcrowding, poor sanitation and hygiene, and contaminated food.

A key instrument in conveying this terrible reality was the photograph. Although photography had been possible even before the Civil War, its potential for persuasion and propaganda was scarcely realized until the 1890s. Jacob Riis in *How the Other Half Lives* (1890) recorded a grim vision of the urban immigrant world. But it was Lewis Hine who probably most evoked pity and outrage through his photographs of working children in the first two decades of the new century. Newsboys, girl mill workers, oyster shuckers, cranberry pickers, and a legion of other working children were the subjects of his camera. Published in national journals and displayed by reform organizations, these poignant, brave children's faces made the reality of exploitation and child labor inescapable. Camera in hand, Hine helped transform poverty from private suffering into a public cause.

⤙⬗⬖⤚

WOMEN AND PROGRESSIVISM

Women contributed to progressivism in a variety of ways. Roused by a fear of disease and shoddy products, and desiring to protect their families, middle-class women organized consumer groups in the 1890s. The General Federation of Women's Clubs (1890), the National Congress of Mothers (1896), and the Consumers League (1899) hoped to safeguard American homes by improving conditions in the factories where products were made.

THE SETTLEMENT-HOUSE MOVEMENT

Women were also heavily represented in the settlement-house movement, which began in 1886 with the establishment of the Neighborhood Guild (later the University Settlement) on New York's Lower East Side. Certainly the most famous settlement was Jane Addams's Hull House, opened in Chicago in 1889. Addams articulated many of the ideals of the late Victorian reformers who peopled the Progressive movement. Well educated, with a sensitive social conscience, she rejected the roles open to her: marriage, teaching, or nursing. Unable to find an academic career in the male university world, she helped create something new: the profession of social work. Hull House, a mansion near the slums of Chicago, became a sort of resident university for women who, like herself, sought a useful profession. Addams and her fellow workers plunged into daily life in the slums, agitating for local garbage disposal, public education, and child labor laws. (The 1910 census reported that hundreds of thousands of children between the ages of ten and fifteen were employed, many of them in factories and mines.) By the turn of the century, the settlement included a gymnasium, boys' club, auditorium, and library, and offered extensive courses and club meetings making it an institution almost as large and important to the city's cultural life as the University of Chicago.

SUFFRAGE

A large segment of women reformers felt that their own rights were as much at stake in the early twentieth century as the welfare of immigrants and child laborers. Although women organized many of the important reform movements that constituted the larger progressive mood, they were still unable, by law, to vote in elections, except in some statewide contests. The women's movement in America had a long and varied history. Beginning in the mid-nineteenth century, the movement pushed a variety of aims, from the abolition of slavery to the prohibition of alcoholic drinks. But in the early twentieth century, it concentrated on obtaining women's right to vote.

Many reformers—such as Jane Addams—believed that extension of the vote was essential to a responsible public spirit. By adding the moral weight of women to the electorate, they assumed it would be easier to legislate national reforms. Some suffragists, like Mrs. George Bass when she appeared before the Senate in 1915, declared that women's duty to family should be expanded to become a sort of social motherhood: women wanted the vote because they required it to continue "the business of being a woman."

For those women opposed to the vote, a sort of reverse logic could apply, a reading of women's roles that inverted Jane Addams's interpretation. Mrs. A. J. George of the National Association Opposed to Woman Suffrage told Congress that suffrage would destroy women's special character. She explained: "The Woman-suffrage movement is an imitation-of-man movement, and, as such, merits the condemnation of every normal man and woman." The vote, she concluded, would condemn women to jury duty, and quite possibly, military service. It would, in

SETTLEMENT HOUSE WORKERS. Julia Lathrop, Jane Addams, and Mary McDowell (left to right) were three important settlement house workers in Chicago. Besides ministering to the needs of slum residents, they worked to secure national reforms such as women's suffrage.

other words, eliminate the distinctions, privileges, and responsibilities of the different genders.

Like other reformers of the progressive era, the suffragists turned to the national government for remedies. They sought an amendment to the Constitution. Finally, toward the end of the progressive period, they persuaded Congress and the president to support their initiative. The Nineteenth Amendment was passed by Congress and three-quarters of the states during World War I. It was declared in effect in 1920.

PROGRESSIVISM AS A MOVEMENT

Like Jane Addams's social workers, urban reformers and Social Gospel ministers shared a feeling of identity with the victims of society. Whatever their emphasis, the various constituencies of progressivism shared one common assumption: the public must be informed and government must assume the role of peacemaker in society.

THE HOLBROOK CARRIES THE SUFFRAGE TORCH. The campaign for women's suffrage took many forms designed to attract public attention and support. Civil disobedience and hunger strikes were eventually added to more traditional spectacles and parades.

Progressivism became a movement by establishing a national audience for reform ideas and programs that stressed social and political solutions to individual misfortune. In other words, it pushed onto a national reform agenda social problems and solutions defined by local and state reformers. It clearly relinquished the older notion of effective charity as individual stewardship in favor of the idea that society itself, as represented by government, must actively protect and promote the welfare of its most vulnerable citizens. Men like Woodrow Wilson and Theodore Roosevelt became expert in gathering public support for their reforms. But much of the attention to reform came from a new sort of journalism called *muckraking*. The technological revolution in printing that occurred in the 1890s enabled large-circulation magazines to lower prices to a dime an issue and begin printing photographic features. Newspaper chains owned by William Randolph Hearst adopted an aggressive investigative journalism. Vying for public attention, journals such as *Cos-mopolitan, Munsey's Magazine,* and especially *McClure's* began to expose corruption and corporate ruthlessness. For example, *McClure's* in late 1902 published the first installment of Lincoln Steffens's attack on urban corruption, *The Shame of the Cities.* At the same time, it included the first of several articles by Ida Tarbell on the history of Standard Oil. Almost overnight, that company became a symbol of corporate greed and monopoly.

Other journalists, taking their cue from these successful articles, began investigations of other sordid elements of modern life: poverty, corruption, and exploitation. In 1906 reporter David Graham Phillips even attacked the Senate for accepting bribes and secret contributions from corporations and lobbyists in his series "Treason of the Senate." Phillips's accusations aroused the ire of Theodore Roosevelt, who believed the journalist had gone too far. In an April speech, Roosevelt denounced journalists who raked the muck and never lifted their eyes from it. The name "muckraker" stuck.

By the early twentieth century, progressivism had begun to emerge as an important although divided political force stressing industrial regulation and a new social ethic. The problems of industrialism, immigration, poverty, social violence, and corruption were widely recognized. And middle-class reformers had begun to advocate a larger role for government to balance the contending interests of capital and labor. They had begun to articulate a vision of society controlled by men and women of good faith who had an acute sense of the public interest. At every level, in countless organizations, they clamored for an about-face in social ethics, stressing the need for social intervention to correct ills that individuals and families, by themselves, could not resolve. In the process they helped transform local and national priorities—and themselves. But the shape of public interest would depend partly on organized private citizens who pushed for social and political reform and partly on two important presidents who responded to these movements: Theodore Roosevelt and his great rival Woodrow Wilson.

⟶⟩⫯⟨⟵

THEODORE ROOSEVELT

Everything in Theodore Roosevelt's background seemed to have prepared him for his aggressive and expansive years in the presidency, which he sometimes called the "bully pulpit." Roosevelt brought a keen mind, unexcelled vigor, a talent for publicity and writing, and a love of politics to the office. He also displayed a Victorian sense of social duty, manliness, and culture.

He was born October 27, 1858, into a wealthy and established New York family. His father, whom he admired immensely, was a gentleman banker with broad interests in social reform and charities. Suffering from delicate health, asthma, and poor vision, young Theodore evoked his parents' concern. They planned long trips to the country and European vacations, and hired tutors to educate their son at home. But it was a strenuous body-building regimen begun after the age of twelve that enabled Teddy to overcome his physical weaknesses. This success dramatically affected his personality. In a sense, it made him a "self-made man," despite his wealth. It added energy to his efforts and confidence to his ambitions. At the same time, however, it tinged him with excess. Too much self-confidence sometimes became arrogance. And failure could be devastating.

Roosevelt resembled other men of his class who entered politics during the progressive era. Educated at a private preparatory school and then at Harvard, he believed firmly in laissez-faire economics, charity for the poor, and ethical government. Like Woodrow Wilson, he tested other careers before he entered politics. Like the mugwumps, he had an upper-class background, but unlike them, he made the transition to progressivism, developing and changing with the clash of events.

THE PATH TO THE WHITE HOUSE

Roosevelt rose through the ranks of the Republican party by loyally supporting party candidates and pursuing modest reforms. He earned a reputation as a civil service commissioner and later as police commissioner of New York City. In 1896, when William McKinley won the presidency, the Republicans rewarded Roosevelt with the position of assistant secretary of the navy, an appointment he relished.

Roosevelt pushed enthusiastically for a larger navy. When war broke out in April 1898 between the United States and Spain, he quit his position and rushed to organize a cavalry regiment. Telegraphing western governors for men, he assembled and outfitted a band that became known as the Rough Riders. His major enemy was time. Spain was so weak it might crumble before he could reach the battlefield. The Spanish obliged, however, and held on long enough for Roosevelt to lead a frantic charge up Kettle Hill near San Juan Ridge in Cuba on July 1, 1898. As he wrote in his *Memoirs*, "I waved my hat and we went up the hill with a rush."

Roosevelt's exploits delighted the newspapers and helped win him the nomination for governor of New York. The hero of San Juan Hill squeaked through to victory by about 18,000 votes. In his first term as governor, he pushed through civil service reform and a tax bill on corporations. And he promoted an investigation of a state insurance scandal. When the Republicans renominated McKinley in 1900, Roosevelt stood in line for the vice presidency. Republican bosses who disliked him helped steer him into this position. They reasoned that Roosevelt could do no damage in this powerless and dead-end job. Stumping the country for his ticket, Roosevelt helped deliver a huge majority for the Republicans: 292 electoral votes to 155 for William Jennings Bryan, the Democrat.

The bosses were right. At first, Roosevelt had little to do. But on September 6, 1901, while visiting the Pan-American Exposition in Buffalo, New York, McKinley was struck down by two shots fired by anarchist Leon Czolgosz, and he finally succumbed on September 14. Roosevelt was president. At age forty-two, he was the youngest man yet to assume the presidency. With a command of American and European history, widely read in American fiction, and with a speaking knowledge of French and German, he was one of the best educated men ever to occupy the office.

Roosevelt immediately announced that he would continue McKinley's policies. But in fact, he moved first to ensure his own position in the party. He also initiated a series of steps to consolidate power in his office, dramatically increasing its influence and importance. Thus, as progressivism moved into the White House, Roosevelt began a transformation of the executive branch. During his presidency, Roosevelt actively campaigned and lobbied for legislation he favored and increasingly acted as a broker among the organized national interest groups that were clamoring for or resisting reform, attempting to create

what he called a "Square Deal for the American public."

BUSINESS POLICY

Roosevelt's first administration established new guidelines for the behavior of American corporations. In 1903 Congress passed the Elkins Anti-Rebate Act, which prevented railroads from charging special low rates to favored customers. Congress also established a Bureau of Corporations under the new cabinet-level Department of Commerce and Labor. This agency perfectly fitted Roosevelt's philosophy of business regulation. The bureau could control business behavior through its power to investigate and publicize its findings about corporate concentration and monopoly.

The president took other unusual steps to intervene in the economy in the public interest. The first occasion came in 1902 during the long anthracite coal strike. In this bitter clash between mine workers and coal operators, Roosevelt leaned toward the miners. The nation demanded action as winter came. The president pushed for arbitration, against the stubborn opposition of the operators. Labeling them unreasonable, he fought to save them "from the dreadful punishment which their own folly would have brought on them if I had not acted."

Roosevelt finally persuaded the owners to accept arbitration. Workers returned to their jobs, and in early 1903 a commission granted some but not all of their demands. The judgment raised wages by 10 percent and established a conciliation board. But the miners did not win union recognition. In fact, the biggest winner was Roosevelt. He had helped end the strike and had moved labor relations to the level of federal responsibility.

Roosevelt earned the reformer's mantle in another well-publicized action. In 1902 his attorney general, Philander C. Knox, instituted a lawsuit under the Sherman Act to dissolve the Northern Securities Corporation. The company

PRESIDENT THEODORE ROOSEVELT in Asheville, NC, 1902. Part of Roosevelt's skill as a politician was his ability to sway crowds of voters. A masterly campaigner, he, as well as other progressives, took their reform message to the people.

typified what Roosevelt considered a bad corporation. Certainly he did not oppose bigness or consolidation, but a corporation that existed only to secure a monopoly was another matter. The Northern Securities Corporation resulted from a compromise between two giant railway systems (the Union Pacific–Northern Pacific and the Great Northern) fighting to control rail access to Chicago from the west. The courts decided that the consolidated company must be dissolved, and in 1904 the Supreme Court upheld this decision. Roosevelt was elated by this and other successful trust-busting suits. Thus Roosevelt could be considered either a conservative who staved off more fundamental change or a liberal who forced through a radical reorientation of government policy. Whatever the point of view, however, Roosevelt would occupy center stage of American politics for almost eight years.

With a reputation for activism and good marks earned for his intervention in the coal strike, Roosevelt won the Republican nomination in 1904. He soundly defeated Democrat Alton B. Parker in November and then began a more aggressive legislative program. The railroads continued to be a special concern. They were the nation's biggest business and the favorite target of muckrakers.

Roosevelt actively supported a new regulatory law, the Hepburn Act, named for its sponsor, Congressman Peter Hepburn of Iowa. Passed into law in 1906 after a difficult fight, the act expanded the federal Interstate Commerce Commission and added to its authority. Congress granted the commission power to regulate express companies, sleeping-car companies, bridges, ferries, terminals, and oil pipelines. Most important, the agency was granted the power to lower shipping rates that it considered excessive.

Roosevelt also responded to calls to regulate consumer products. Two pioneering measures were passed by Congress in 1906. Spurred by a broad campaign against adulteration of drugs and cosmetics and shocked by the grue-some details of the meat-packing industry re-vealed in Upton Sinclair's novel *The Jungle*, Con-gress agreed to the Pure Food and Drug Act in June, which established the Food and Drug Ad-ministration, and the Meat Inspection Act in July. The second of these acts, championed by pro-gressive Senator Albert J. Beveridge of Indiana, provided federal inspection for meat sold in in-terstate commerce. Together, the acts set up the structure to regulate a wide variety of consumer products. In many cases, the affected industries supported this legislation, which, in effect, meant a government stamp of approval for their prod-ucts. The result was reform that satisfied many activists, consumers, and businessmen. It was a model of Roosevelt's commitment to executive intervention, compromise, and reform in the na-tional public interest in a manner that would not hurt business interests.

OTHER ACHIEVEMENTS

The president's other substantial accomplish-ments came in the withdrawal of public lands from unregulated exploitation. No preservationist or sentimentalist about wildlife, Roosevelt be-lieved in conserving land for a variety of uses: parks, hunting, timbering, and mining. Working with Gifford Pinchot of the U.S. Forest Service (a part of the Agriculture Department), Roosevelt set aside about 150 million acres of public land for restricted use. And he supported reclamation legislation that created dams and irrigation pro-jects. (But when Congress canceled executive power to set aside land in 1907, Roosevelt quickly withdrew a final 16 million acres.) He called this policy of preserving resources the "principle of stewardship."

From 1906 through 1908 in particular, Roosevelt supported other important progressive reforms: establishment of the eight-hour day for railway workers, termination of child labor in the District of Columbia, and a minimum wage. Al-though Roosevelt was not able to persuade Con-gress to act on these measures, they reveal his deepening commitment to federally sponsored social reform and his greater adherence to pro-gressive goals.

Yet in other areas that deeply affected mil-lions of Americans, Roosevelt was inactive. The progressive era saw racial tension, sweeping at-tacks on the voting rights of black Americans, and rigid segregation in the South. Even some black leaders, most notably educationist Booker T. Washington, publicly embraced a strategy of racial separation. Sympathetic to Washington's theories of gradual black self-improvement, Roo-sevelt appointed several black politicians to pa-tronage jobs early in his presidency. He person-ally opposed lynchings and disfranchisement, and he even invited Washington to dine at the White House in 1901. But he did little to im-prove race relations generally. As he told students at Tuskegee vocational school in Alabama in 1905: "The race cannot expect to get everything at once. It must learn to wait and bide its time."

-∘-▸═◉═◂-∘-

WILLIAM HOWARD TAFT

In 1908 Roosevelt initiated a course of action that ended with his bitter split from the Repub-lican party in 1912: he kept his promise not to run again for president in 1908 and selected William Howard Taft as his successor. Only superficially was Taft a good choice to follow Roosevelt. A staunch party man with few po-litical debts to pay—except to Roosevelt—Taft would have preferred an appointment to the Supreme Court (which he eventually got in 1921, serving as chief justice until his death in 1930). He was an able administrator but an unimaginative leader. Taft was also unsure about his legislative goals and unsympathetic to the growing band of progressive congressmen in his own party. He lacked their commitment to us-ing government as an arbitrator between con-tending economic interests. During his four years in office, he relied more and more on con-servative Republicans, with whom he shared a natural affinity.

Taft's victory in 1908 came partly because of Roosevelt's aggressive campaign for him. But the presidency became his own. Roosevelt, in a gesture of self-advertisement, sailed off after the inauguration on an African safari to stalk "dangerous game." The new president had to find his own way in the political jungle of Washington.

Taft's cabinet appointments disappointed progressive senators but pleased House Speaker Joseph Cannon, a stalwart Republican conservative. With Senate leader Nelson Aldrich, Cannon and Taft agreed to seek a lower tariff. The president called Congress into special session in March 1909. The House managed to pass a somewhat lower tariff bill, but the Senate actually proposed increases. In a conference committee meeting the two houses compromised. When Taft signed the law in August, there were 654 decreases in rates and 220 increases. The legislation also raised a tax of 1 percent on corporate profits above $5,000. Although Taft proclaimed the legislation a victory—the best revision ever passed by Republicans—progressive congressmen complained that the president had caved in to special manufacturing interests.

Progressives supported other presidential initiatives, however. For example, Congress passed the Mann-Elkins Act in 1910, placing telephone, telegraph, and wireless companies under the jurisdiction of the Interstate Commerce Commission. Congress also established a postal savings bank system. In addition, Taft's administration initiated ninety antitrust suits against large corporations. One of these secured the breakup of Standard Oil. Another, however, against U.S. Steel, seemed an indirect attack on Roosevelt, who had given tacit approval to a giant merger of U.S. Steel and the Tennessee Coal and Iron Company during the deep recession of 1907. Taft's action implied that Roosevelt had done wrong to promote monopoly in the American economy. Other presidential initiatives helped establish administrative reform: a new Children's Bureau and a separate Department of Labor. Taft also supported the Sixteenth Amendment to the Constitution, legalizing the income tax, and the Seventeenth Amendment, establishing the direct election of senators.

This was an impressive legislative record but no proof of leadership among Republicans. In fact, Taft's hold on the party gradually weakened. Opposition came from two sources: congressional progressives and Roosevelt. By the mid-term election of 1910, the Republicans were badly split. Taft encouraged conservatives to challenge progressives. But the effort backfired. Democrats won the House, and together with Republican progressives, they also controlled the Senate. Early in January 1911, progressives meeting at Wisconsin senator Robert La Follette's Washington residence formed the National Republican Progressive League with the assumption that La Follette would be their candidate in 1912.

La Follette's chances dimmed, however, when Roosevelt bounded back on stage. Never

PRESIDENTIAL EQUESTRIAN POSE. President William Howard Taft sits astride a horse in front of the Executive Office Building in Washington, DC.

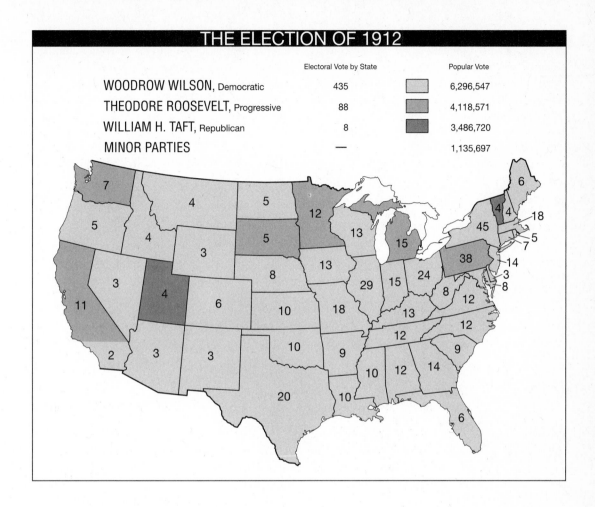

THE ELECTION OF 1912

	Electoral Vote by State		Popular Vote
WOODROW WILSON, Democratic	435		6,296,547
THEODORE ROOSEVELT, Progressive	88		4,118,571
WILLIAM H. TAFT, Republican	8		3,486,720
MINOR PARTIES	—		1,135,697

content to sit on the sidelines, the ex-president was furious at Taft's "betrayal." Taft, he said, had taken a narrow view of the presidency: "Most able lawyers who are past middle age take this view," he added disparagingly. Worse, Taft had forced Gifford Pinchot, Roosevelt's ally, out of office in 1910 in a fight over conservation policy. Taft's secretary of the interior, Richard A. Ballinger, had approved the transfer of several federal sites to private development. Pinchot, still in the Forest Service, had opposed the transfer and taken his case to the public. Forced to choose between the two men, Taft had fired Pinchot.

THE ELECTION OF 1912

The 1912 election brought progressivism to center stage in American politics and reoriented both principal parties. The groundswell of progressivism split the Republican party. The Democrats shifted away from their western Populist leader, William Jennings Bryan, to choose the urban progressivism of Woodrow Wilson. On the left, Eugene Debs challenged conservatives and progressives with his socialist proposals.

In some respects the election tested two competing philosophies of progressivism developed by two extraordinary contemporary thinkers, Louis Brandeis and Herbert Croly. Brandeis, a lawyer who both influenced and advised Wilson and whom Wilson later appointed to the Supreme Court, believed deeply in an economy based on small competing units. The power of government, he argued, should guarantee such a fair contest. But perhaps even more important, in a series of legal briefs Brandeis developed powerful arguments for the constitutionality of social reform legislation. In *Muller* v. *Oregon*, in 1908, he told the Supreme Court that the state of Oregon had the right to limit the workday for women to ten hours. The law, he asserted, had to take account of the conditions of real life. And the facts, he persuaded the justices, made the law compelling.

Herbert Croly, author of *The Promise of American Life* (1909) and editor of the influential journal *The New Republic*, approached the large questions of government from a different direction. Convinced of the importance of expert guidance of the Republic, he accepted what repelled Brandeis: bigness in industry. Croly admired the growth of huge industries, although he rejected the antisocial, selfish, and ruthless exploitation characteristic of some companies. The solution, he believed, was government regulation, not competition. A revived national spirit meant giving up the old and inappropriate Jeffersonian dream of a nation of small, competing farms and accepting the modern condition of large-scale enterprise. It meant, too, accepting the rights of unions to organize and bargain. These ideas appealed to Roosevelt, who saw them as a justification for many of his actions as president and as a plan for the future.

By February 1912, Roosevelt had stormed into the presidential race. Entering Republican primaries where he could, he piled up significant convention votes, but not enough to control the party machinery. Taft's forces engineered a narrow, but hollow, victory. Roosevelt's delegates withdrew and called for a new party. Meeting in Chicago in August, the new Progressive party nominated Roosevelt at a meeting that joined shrewd politics and revivalism. The delegates, with banners flying, broke into hymns.

Roosevelt's platform promised direct primaries, legislative initiative and referendum, the recall of judges, woman suffrage, an end to child labor, the eight-hour day, and a federal trade commission. The candidate's "New Nationalism" was designed to centralize control of the economy in the executive branch. In what was to prove an unstable alliance, Roosevelt welcomed the support of two dissimilar, prominent figures associated with progressivism. One was Jane Addams. The other was the wealthy capitalist and financier George Perkins, a power in the National Civic Federation.

Taft, the incumbent president, was odd man out. He defended his administration but did little active campaigning. The significant race pitted Roosevelt against Wilson. But Roosevelt could not overcome the effects of the Republican split. Wilson won more than 6 million votes, Roosevelt more than 4 million, Taft about 3 million, and Debs almost 1 million.

WILSON'S PROGRESSIVISM

Woodrow Wilson brought a special kind of leadership and experience to the White House. He had as deep an understanding of history as Roosevelt. But unlike the former president he had learned the lessons of command and compromise on a university campus. His sense of purpose and commitment was unyielding. He believed that his cause was also the nation's. Sympathetic to the plight of the "masses of men," and distressed by the arrogance of wealth, Wilson supported many of the progressive causes. But the new president's vision also had its bounds. His progressivism spoke nominally for the underprivileged. His vision of government—reflecting his inspired reorganization of Princeton University—consisted in the exercise of leadership by meritorious gentlemen.

Having proclaimed a "New Freedom" in the election, Wilson set about to institute it. Congress, both houses now firmly Democratic, prepared to help him. Wilson aimed first at eliminating corporate monopoly and other obstacles to free market competition. He strongly believed that the restoration of competition would liberate business talent and prevent the excesses of the greedy few. But proposing competition was easier than establishing it. Quickly, Wilson accepted reform projects more in tune with Roosevelt's New Nationalism. By the end of 1916 he had begun to advocate centralized executive power and federal economic regulation. And he put these ideals into practice after 1917. When America entered World War I, Wilson began a limited experiment in national economic and social planning.

Wilson appointed a cabinet to represent the various geographic and ideological wings of the Democratic party: Bryan as secretary of state; William B. Wilson, former official of the United Mine Workers, as secretary of labor; and William G. McAdoo, from Georgia, as secretary of the treasury. Like Taft, Wilson began with the tariff and a special session of Congress. But Wilson worked skillfully for lower tariff rates. When lobbyists and conservatives tried to stop him, he took his case to the public. Wilson relished the fight; as so many times in the past, he was convinced that it pitted principle against special narrow interests. He won the struggle. The new law, the Underwood Tariff, lowered rates by about 15 percent and attached a small income tax to make up for lost revenues.

Banking also demanded reform. Ever since the financial panic of 1907, Congress had debated the issue. Two solutions emerged. The first, proposed by Arsene Pujo, representative from Louisiana, attacked private banks. The second called for a national banking system controlled by private banks. Wilson steered toward the second position. The resulting Glass-Owen Act of December 1913 established a new federal banking system consisting of twelve regional banks controlled by a Federal Reserve Board appointed by the president. Local banks that joined the system could borrow from the Reserve banks. And the Federal Reserve system could expand or contract credit by lowering or raising the discount rate it charged member banks for loans. This new banking tool of the federal government supplied the power to create a national monetary policy. By expanding or contracting interest rates and the money supply, it could theoretically shrink or in-

crease economic activity. Although this was not a precise tool—and it was only as effective as the wisdom of its board of governors—the Federal Reserve system represented a major step in creating an institution that could potentially guide and protect the economy from the repeated shocks of recession, inflation, and overexpansion.

Trusts, monopolies, and corporations were also a primary concern of the new president. Wilson's New Freedom had promised decisive action to unclog competition. But the problem was not simple. Wilson recognized this and gradually moved away from trust busting to a regulatory approach. Passed in September 1914, the Federal Trade Commission Act, which he supported, incorporated features of Roosevelt's Bureau of Corporations. The commission of five members, appointed by the president, could investigate business combinations and issue "cease and desist" orders where combinations acted illegally. Another law, the Clayton Antitrust Act, passed a month later, defined antitrust policy more sharply and assured organized labor that it would not be prosecuted under the Sherman Act.

The second half of Wilson's first term saw reforms aimed at curbing the excesses of labor exploitation. Adoption of these progressive reforms marked a significant (and often controversial) expansion of federal power. Wilson was under considerable pressure from progressives, and he acted. In 1916 he supported the Keating-Owen child labor bill, which banned child labor under the age of fourteen in interstate commerce. (But in 1918 the Supreme Court declared the law unconstitutional.) Wilson also supported the Adamson Act, which set an eight-hour day for railway workers and established, by example, a standard for other industries to follow. He supported a workmen's compensation bill for federal employees. He also signed the Federal Farm Loan Act of 1916, which provided loans for farmers using their land and improvements as security, thus enacting legislation similar to proposals long supported by the Populists.

One of Wilson's most controversial acts endeared him to progressives but drew the ire of conservatives. He nominated Jewish lawyer and

LOUIS D. BRANDEIS. Brandeis's appointment to the Supreme Court in 1916 was noteworthy for several reasons. He was Jewish—the first person of his faith to attain this high office—and he was widely known for his successful advocacy of progressive social reform legislation.

activist Louis Brandeis to the Supreme Court in 1916. The American Bar Association and influential political and social leaders were outraged partly because of his ethnic heritage and partly because of his social views. Nonetheless, working with congressional progressives, Wilson secured the appointment. Acts such as these demonstrated the power of Wilson's leadership.

Although Wilson broke important ground by making the first appointment of a Jewish American to the Supreme Court, he followed the inclinations of his southern heritage when it came to black Americans. Wilson did nothing to defuse the explosive racial situation in the South. By this time, racism in the South, where most African Americans lived, had reached an extraordinary crescendo. In the late 1890s the South was

ravaged by hundreds of lynchings, mostly of black men accused of rape or alleged insults to white women. Mob rule executed as many as 156 in 1892 alone. Although the number fell by Wilson's first administration, conditions for blacks did not improve. Indeed, the reorganization of the Ku Klux Klan in 1915 was an ominous sign. The popularity of a 1915 film, *The Birth of a Nation*, shown at the White House and seen throughout the nation, pictured the Klansmen as heroes who saved the South from ruthless exploitation by former slaves during Reconstruction. The public acceptance of this brilliant but morally flawed film proved that blacks could count on little understanding in the North for their plight. Even the organization of the National Association for the Advancement of Colored People (NAACP) in 1910 was only a first, small step in a battle against enormous odds.

Wilson did nothing to prevent the disfranchisement of southern blacks by means of poll taxes or literacy tests. Indeed, his record was worse than the benign neglect of the Republicans. A firm believer in segregation, he allowed his cabinet to segregate federal jobs and downgrade or fire black employees. Wilson's defense of his actions suggests the serious limitations of his progressivism. Writing in 1913, he said:

> It is true that the segregation of the colored employees in the several departments was begun upon the initiative and at the suggestion of the heads of departments, but as much as in the interest of the negroes as for any other reason, with the approval of some of the most influential negroes I know, and with the idea that the friction, or rather the discontent and uneasiness, which had prevailed in many departments would thereby be removed. It is as far as possible from being a movement *against* the negroes. I sincerely believe it to be in their interest.

By 1916 Wilson had achieved party unity around his program of regulation and reform. The Republicans, still smarting from the split of 1912, nominated Charles Evans Hughes for president. Roosevelt supported him. Despite numerous advantages, Wilson won only a close victory.

Progressives and peace advocates had probably provided the margin of victory.

Ironically, although the issue of peace had helped carry the election of 1916, it was the issue of war that preoccupied Wilson's second term. Europe exploded in 1914, as the major powers rushed into battle. When the United States was drawn into the conflict in 1917, Wilson turned to progressive ideas of regulation, creating an unprecedented system of planning and control of the economy. The demands of war accelerated the tendency of the executive branch to oversee the American economy. Wilson gained considerable power to effect such changes through such legislation as the Overman Act of 1918, which allowed the president to reorganize executive agencies.

During the war, Wilson also extended his commitment to progressivism by advocating, as he had previously refused to do, votes for women. In September 1918, he urged the Senate to approve a constitutional amendment to grant suffrage to all Americans regardless of sex. He cited the unusual circumstances of a world war.

Yet by supporting restrictions on free speech and empowering a vast public relations campaign to sell the war to Americans, Wilson extended government into controversial areas. In doing so, he kindled doubts about his leadership. Did he not see that others might have a valid, if different, sense of the public's interest? Was it sufficient to be confident in a righteous cause? This single-mindedness had long been a potential problem. Now it provoked a major crisis.

Quite possibly political writer Walter Lippmann was right about Wilson—and progressivism—when he said:

> The inner contradiction of Woodrow Wilson is that he knows that there is a new world demanding new methods, but he dreams of an older world. He is torn between the two. It is a very deep conflict in him between what he knows and what he feels.

This too was the dilemma of Jane Addams. She also dreamed of a world based on an enlightened moral vision applied to politics. Yet her vision was too safely harbored in an older notion of the special moral virtues of women. It drew from the ideas of a world that was fast disappearing.

-→=◉=←-

CHRONOLOGY

1856	Thomas Woodrow Wilson born in Virginia
1858	Theodore Roosevelt born in New York
1860	Jane Addams born in Illinois
1883–1885 1887–1888	Jane Addams's trips to Europe
1889	Jane Addams opens Hull House in Chicago; Andrew Carnegie publishes *The Gospel of Wealth*
1890	Jacob Riis publishes *How the Other Half Lives*
1893	United States falls into severe depression
1894	Coxey's "Army" marches on Washington; Pullman workers out on strike
1895	Booker T. Washington delivers his "Atlanta Compromise" speech; National Association of Manufacturers formed
1896	Theodore Roosevelt becomes assistant secretary of the navy
1898	Theodore Roosevelt forms the Rough Riders
1899	Thorstein Veblen publishes *Theory of the Leisure Class*
1900	McKinley-Roosevelt slate wins presidential election
1901	Theodore Roosevelt becomes president; Robert LaFollette elected governor of Wisconsin

1902	*McClure's* magazine begins muckraker articles; Wilson becomes president of Princeton
1903–1906	Roosevelt's progressive measures enacted by Congress
1904	Roosevelt reelected president
1908	William Howard Taft elected president
1909	Jane Addams publishes *Spirit of Youth and the City Streets*
1912	Woodrow Wilson elected president over Roosevelt, Taft, and Debs
1913	Glass-Owen Act passed; Wilson appoints Louis Brandeis to the Supreme Court; Sixteenth Amendment ratified confirming right of Congress to collect income taxes; Seventeenth Amendment ratified providing direct election of senators
1914	Federal Trade Commission established; Clayton Anti-Trust Act passed
1915	Jane Addams's controversial speech for peace
1916	Keating-Owen Act passed; Wilson reelected over Charles E. Hughes of New York
1918	Eighteenth Amendment ratified imposing Prohibition
1935	Jane Addams dies

-→=◉=←-

SUGGESTIONS FOR FURTHER READING

JANE ADDAMS

The best place to begin is with Jane Addams's works. She wrote and published widely. A good sampling of this is Jane Addams, *A Centennial Reader* (1973). Her best work is her wonderful autobiography: *Twenty Years at Hull House, with Autobiographical Notes* (1911). Two interesting biographical works that take quite different positions are May Jo Deagan, *Jane Addams and the Men of the Chicago School* (1988), and Alan Davis, *The Life and Legend of Jane Addams* (1973). An excellent

work that puts Addams's career and the settlement-house movement in a larger perspective is Robyn Muncy, *Creating a Female Dominion in American Reform, 1890–1935* (1991).

PROGRESSIVISM

The literature on progressivism is both extensive and fascinating. One fine and very readable general account is Robert Wiebe, *The Search for Order, 1877–1920* (1967). A very different view of progressivism that stresses corporate interest in reforming the most flagrant and dangerous social injustices is James Weinstein, *The Corporate Ideal in the Liberal State, 1900–1918* (1968). Geoffrey Blodgett examines the politics and ideology of the forerunners of the progressives in *The Gentle Reformers: Massachusetts Democrats in the Cleveland Era* (1966). Progressivism on a state level is skillfully reconstructed by David Thelen in *Robert M. La Follette and the Insurgent Spirit* (1985). As a national movement, progressivism developed because of publicity and journalistic exposés. Louis Filler, *The Muckrakers* (1976), is a revised edition of the classic work on reform publicists.

MOVEMENTS

In some respects, progressivism was the sum of contemporary social movements. One of the most important of these was Prohibition. Jack S. Blocker, Jr., *Alcohol, Reform, and Society: The Liquor in Social Context* (1979), discusses this very significant movement in relation to other reform programs. Women played a key role in Prohibition, but, increasingly during the era, they also concentrated on securing the vote. Aileen Kraditor, in *The Ideas of the Woman Suffrage Movement* (1981), recounts the arguments for and against woman suffrage. An essential element in this turbulent era of reform was widespread interest in socialism. James Green's fine work, *Grass-Roots Socialism* (1978), documents the extensive socialist movement that grew up in the American Southwest during the progressive era. Reform inside the factory was, in many respects, as extensive as social reform at large. Daniel Nelson in *Frederick W. Taylor and the Rise of Scientific Management* (1980) examines Taylor's management ideas and their relationship to progressivism. Intellectuals as well as workers, managers, and politicians were deeply affected by the swift changes of the opening century. Christopher Lasch, *The New Radicalism in America, 1889–1963* (1965), contains an outstanding discussion of new attitudes toward the self and society. For another view of the culture of progressivism, see Robert M. Crunden, *Ministers of Reform* (1982). Nick Salvatore, *Eugene V. Debs* (1982), is a crucial biography of this popular socialist and union leader. Two recent books give very different views of the era: Morton Keller, *Regulating a New Society: Public Policy and Social Change in America, 1900–1953* (1994), and Alan Dawly, *Struggles for Justice: Social Responsibility and the Liberal State* (1991).

PRESIDENTS

The two commanding political figures of the progressive era were Theodore Roosevelt and Woodrow Wilson. George E. Mowry, *Theodore Roosevelt and the Progressive Movement* (1946), is a fine older work and a good starting place for the study of the Roosevelt presidency. A fast-paced, very readable biography of Roosevelt's early years is David G. McCulloch, *Mornings on Horseback* (1981). On Roosevelt and Wilson see John Milton Cooper, *The Warrior and the Priest* (1983). Of all the political leaders of the era, Wilson has received the closest scrutiny. Arthur S. Link set the standard for this scholarship in his excellent *Woodrow Wilson and the Progressive Era, 1910–1917* (1954). John M. Mulder, *Woodrow Wilson: Years of Preparation* (1976), is a careful and fascinating study of Wilson's early years. An ingenious medical and psychological study of Wilson is Edwin Weinstein's, *Woodrow Wilson: A Medical and Psychological Biography* (1981).

CHAPTER

20

Imperial America

Episode: The Conquests of the Philippines

PROGRESSIVE FOREIGN POLICY, FROM EMPIRE TO WORLD WAR

The Myth of America's Destiny

The Reality Behind the Myth

A New Foreign Policy

The Spanish-American War

Foreign Policy, 1901–1916

World War I

THE EPISODE: *In 1901, thousands of miles away from home, American soldiers were locked in a bloody war against an entrenched and popular guerrilla army in the former Spanish colony of the Philippines. Frustrated by a hostile population, deceived by local politicians playing on both sides, and impeded by terrible weather, jungle, and mountains, the American army vented its anger on the local population. The events on the island of Samar were among the worst aspects of this attempt to make the Philippines an American possession. The political presence of the United States, led by William Howard Taft, pursued hegemony in other ways: by improving social services and fiscal stability in government and by financing improvements such as schools and medical clinics. These two policies of force and persuasion reflected a divided and uncertain command. The result was disastrous.*

THE HISTORICAL SETTING: *By 1900 the United States had for some time been an important nation in world politics and, increasingly, a power in international economics. With a revolutionary tradition that faced inward and a policy that tried to avoid European wars and colonial expansion, the United States was, nonetheless, an active, expansive nation on the North American continent and in Latin America. By the end of the century, this isolation from Europe's politics was ending, partly to preserve the role of the United States as the*

dominant power in the Western Hemisphere. But a strong sense of moral superiority also convinced leaders like Woodrow Wilson that the United States could transform the old, tired European balance of power and lead others into a new world order based on the American experience of democracy.

The Philippine war was an important step in the development of American internationalism. In the late 1890s the United States surveyed a world increasingly divided by cutthroat competition for trade and influence. European nations pursued expansionist policies that led to a scramble to conquer the remaining area of the world lying outside established colonial empires. After the United States went to war with Spain in 1898, American leaders found themselves with important choices to make about the spoils of victory. Should they keep the Spanish islands of the Caribbean to maintain an exclusive trade and defensive zone or should they release these territories to their own devices? Should the army seize the Philippines as an American colony or grant them independence? Suddenly, the United States found itself with a colonial empire and the possibility to acquire even more. Yet by the time of World War I, the nation's leaders were determined not to become another imperialist power along the lines of European nations. Thus, the United States kept itself aloof even as it plunged into one of the most brutal European wars.

THE CONQUESTS OF THE PHILIPPINES

The month of October, in the year of 1901,
Eventful in its history for the bloodshed it had run;
Soldiers and marines received orders to proceed without delay,
And avenge a nation's honor in the blood that passed away.

The memory of those comrades, who in China side by side
Did share our tribulation with courage and with pride,
And it was in the town of Balangiga, where those martyrs at their post
Were soon despatched by bolos, for there they gave up the ghost.

PRIVATE PATRICK CATHSEM, C Company of
9th Infantry, United States Marine Corps

The eighty-eight American troops of Company C, 9th Infantry, gathered in the scorching early-morning sun of September 27, 1901, to eat breakfast. Some were eagerly reading or rereading mail that had arrived just the day before, after a long delay. Because it was Sunday, they skipped their usual duty of mustering out the larger group of Filipino workers who had been rounded up to clear the town of Balangiga, on the island of Samar, of garbage and jungle undergrowth that might conceal revolutionary troops. But it was not just any Sunday for the Marines. In fact, the American soldiers, who had just learned the terrible news of the assassination of President William McKinley, were expected to form at 8 A.M. for a eulogy and memorial Mass at the local Catholic church.

This break in the routine was not the only extraordinary event planned for that morning. The night before, the local priest had suddenly disappeared; Captain Thomas W. Connell, in charge of Company C, could not locate him to make arrangements for the eulogy service. Indeed, none of the clergy, normally found at the church, could be located.

About midnight the previous evening, a group of women had slipped into the area bearing small wooden caskets. To a suspicious American sentry, the women had explained that they were mourners, carrying the pitiful corpses of children struck down by a cholera epidemic in the countryside. The sentry ordered one casket opened, but a quick glance confirmed that a child lay inside, so he ordered the box resealed and carried into the church. Had he looked further, he would have discovered, beneath the child, a bed of bolos (deadly machetes used by Filipino revolutionaries in close combat). He also might have realized that many of the mourners were actually men in disguise.

AMERICAN SOLDIERS relax at a typical thatch-roofed mess hall in the Philippines.

So Sunday morning began with the Americans preparing to commemorate a fallen leader and the whole Filipino community anticipating an attack. It began by pre-arranged signal. The local chief of police, strolling by, stopped to chat with an American sentry. Suddenly, he seized the sentry's rifle, turned it around, and shot the American. At the same moment, armed revolutionaries poured out of the church, racing for the U.S. officers' headquarters, the mess, and the arsenal that held the company weapons. Filipinos working in the cleanup project joined in with the attackers. Captain Connell leaped out of his room, but the charging bolomen cut him down in the street. Most of the American soldiers fought with whatever weapon they could improvise: baseball bats, shovels, tent poles, and the few rifles snatched out of the arsenal before it was overrun. There were enough rifles and ammunition for one withering stand against charging bolomen. But the Americans had to retreat.

With all the other officers dead, Sergeant Frank Berton led the remaining thirty-eight men toward three dugout canoes. Leaping in, the men rowed along the island's coast until they reached the nearby town of Basey, where Company C was headquartered. All along the route they were harassed by gunfire from Filipinos shooting newly captured American rifles. When they reached their destination, only six men remained unscathed. Of the total force of eighty-eight, fifty-nine men had died and twenty-three were wounded.

Immediately, the commander at Basey assembled a troop to return to Balangiga on a revenge mission. Over fifty volunteers quickly stepped forward, including the six uninjured soldiers from Company C. Rushing back in the gunship *Pittsburgh*, the

THE PHILIPPINE ARCHIPELAGO

troops turned their cannon and Gatling guns on any movement in the jungle. When the *Pittsburgh* stopped at the shoreline, its angry American troops rushed into the town with bayonets drawn. The few Filipinos discovered were shot on the spot, although the town seemed eerie and empty. But the horrifying evidence of the attack was everywhere: weapons stolen, food stores opened and carried off, and the bodies of fallen American troops mutilated.

As the soldiers pushed on to the edge of town, they came upon an enormous freshly dug common grave waiting to receive the bodies of the Filipinos killed in the attack. Captain Bookmiller, the new American commander, halted the funeral in progress. Some of his sentries had discovered about twenty Filipino men, probably gravediggers, hiding nearby and marched them to the grave site. The commander then ordered them to pull the bodies of the Filipinos out, and bury the dead Americans in their place. This finished, the American troops held a short service. The dead Filipinos were piled together, soaked with kerosene, and burned in a huge pyre. The commander then ordered the gravediggers to face a firing squad made up of the six survivors of Company C. As the men of Company C moved back to their ship, they burned what remained of Balangiga.

When news of the attack reached the United States, the press, an active though divided player in the dramatic debate over what to do with the Philippine Islands, burst into accusations, blaming political and military leaders for coddling the Filipinos, for failing to realize that the islands had not been pacified, and for ignoring the ability of the Filipino independence movement to deliver such swift, punishing, and brutal action.

In the Philippines, General Adna Chaffee, commander of the American forces there, blamed Governor William Howard Taft and his civilian Philippine Commission for indecisiveness and for impeding a swift, decisive military victory. Taft, for his part, feared that Balangiga represented the inevitable consequences of an iron-fisted military

THESE RESIDENTS OF SAMAR, obviously dressed in their best, pose for a visiting cameraman. Much of what Americans knew about the Philippines came from such photographs.

policy. Although originally opposed to keeping the island colony as the spoils of war with Spain in 1898, he became convinced that once dominating them the United States should win over the hearts and minds of the Filipino people. To this end, he advised a program of firmly guided democracy and a reform policy of "benevolent assimilation," which was President McKinley's phrase. But two years of bloody warfare had proved that many Filipinos preferred their own self-government, whatever its character, to American democracy installed at the end of a rifle.

While the press and Congress clamored for an explanation of the surprise attack at Balangiga, the American occupation army planned to recapture the arms lost in the battle, to suppress the Filipino rebel army still controlling the island of Samar, and to avenge their fallen comrades. General Chaffee sanctioned new orders governing the behavior of American troops. Filipino attacks on Americans were redefined as murder, in which case a prisoner of war could face execution. Populations living outside the main towns in Batangas, an unpacified province south of Manila on the island of Luzon, were ordered into relocation centers, then towns, villages, and crops were burned and livestock dispersed. As news of this policy reached the United States, opponents and supporters of the war focused their attention on Balangiga and other examples of brutality in Senate hearings on the war chaired by Senator Henry Cabot Lodge.

In the Philippines, the army command concentrated on a strategy to crush the remaining rebellion in Samar. Samar was sparsely populated and lay halfway down the archipelago of the Philippines. With a spine of rugged, jungle-covered mountains, it had few towns other than Balangiga and Basey. Most of its usable land was devoted to raising hemp. The population was intensely loyal to the Philippine independence movement; the local leader, General Vincente Lukban, was the mastermind of the surprise attack on Balangiga. He and his men had become doubly dangerous because they now possessed an important store of captured American weapons and ammunition.

To suppress this pocket of insurrection, General Chaffee called on General Jacob Smith, a leader of the pacification of Batangas province and an experienced Indian fighter and veteran of Wounded Knee. Known to his men as "Hell Roaring Jake," Smith inspired fear and respect despite his diminutive stature. He organized a special force of 300 Marines, led by Major Littleton Waller, an officer with considerable experience in China and Egypt. Smith gave Waller clear and deadly orders: "I want no prisoners. I wish you to kill and burn; the more you kill and burn the better it will please me. I want all persons killed who are capable of bearing arms in actual hostilities against the United States." When Waller asked for clarification, Smith said that these orders applied to any male over "ten years of age."

Waller planned three operations for the fall of 1901: local search-and-destroy missions, a surprise attack on General Lukban's headquarters, and a forced march across the island to split the remaining rebel strongholds. Private John H. Clifford recalled the first operation in his diary:

> I never will forget this experience. I had just been taken off the sick report on Sunday, a bright November morning. A detachment went on a hike, with Second Lieutenant in charge. The first thing we got was wet feet in the rice fields; then a big hill to climb and through the woods we discovered a lonely shack built near a lot of trees. An investigation was made by the picket [an advance detachment], and the result was he found a knapsack, blanket, clothing, and the company chest. They all belonged to Company C. The boys di-

vided the goods amongst themselves. We killed pigs, hens and cattle and destroyed the plantation, and then proceeded on our way as though nothing had happened. About a mile from this place we burned six fishing boats, a large pile of hemp, and we helped ourselves to the coconuts. It was getting late, so we returned on another trail. We discovered a shack of nipanipa [made of palm fronds] between some coconut trees and a man jumped out of the window. Several shots were fired, but we never knew whether we hit him or not. In the house there was a crippled old man and a young girl, probably his daughter. She was sitting on the floor. The house was surrounded by guards; I was one of them. We found a soldier's blue shirt, trousers, shoes, and a photo of a young man in civilian dress. There were also bloodstained bolos. Evidently they had been implicated in the massacre of Company C. When the boys saw these things, it made them mad, so they put the people to death and destroyed the place.

Returning to their base camp, the Americans made their way through the jungle in the dark, walking single file to avoid the deep pits dug by Filipino revolutionaries and filled with pointed stakes. When they finally returned home, the troops were exhausted: "We were hungry, wet and tired, and several of the men had chills and fever, while many were under the doctor's care with swelling of the feet caused by long hikes, and sore eyes."

The second campaign, against General Lukban, required guile and surprise. Waller located the general's headquarters on the Sohoton Cliffs overlooking the Caducan River in the interior of Samar. On November 15, 1901, he prepared a two-pronged attack. Placing a heavy gun on a raft, he assigned a first group to move up the river. Meanwhile, he ordered a second squad to set out overland to approach the rebel headquarters from the rear. The raft was unable to penetrate close enough along the river to bring his guns into play, and Waller's naval maneuver could do little to dislodge Lukban. But his other troops reached high terrain above the camp, from which they laid down a withering machine-gun barrage that forced the terrified Filipinos to flee through a hail of bullets.

Lukban was routed and his headquarters destroyed, but his organization on Samar still remained powerful. Waller now moved into his third operation. To dislodge the organization's remnants, the commander decided to split the interior of the island. Thus he began sketching plans for his fateful march from the American base at Lanang to the town of Basey, about forty miles across the southern part of the island.

In some respects, Waller's decision is deeply puzzling. Perhaps he was reacting to a note from his commanding officer General Smith, urging him to turn the interior of Samar into a "howling Wilderness." But there was undoubtedly more to his rash decision than this cryptic biblical reference. Waller may well have believed that the march would be easy and that he could demonstrate to the Filipinos the mobility and power of his troops. Whatever his reasons, it was a mistake.

Waller and his men set out in December 1901 with only four days' supply of field rations but a full store of unwarranted optimism. The American troops and their Filipino bearers soon confronted torrential rains, swirling streams, and steep terrain. After three days, Waller realized that many of his troops were too weakened to continue, so he split his forces. He placed Captain David Porter in charge of the weaker men and in-

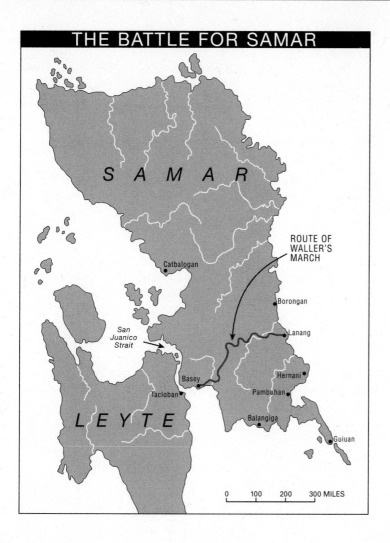

structed them to build rafts to float downstream, back to Lanang. Waller proposed to continue forward with his remaining group overland to Basey.

As instructed, Porter ordered his Filipino bearers to cut trees and fashion them into rafts. But these makeshift boats sank into the torrent. Desperate, fatigued, and low on supplies, Porter unwisely set out by foot, trying to retrace his steps to Lanang. He dispatched two messengers to catch up to Waller and inform him of his decision.

When Waller learned of Porter's move, he was shocked at the dangerous turn of events. Nonetheless, he continued forward toward Basey, hoping that common sense would force Porter either to stop or turn around again. When he finally reached Basey, Waller was sick with jungle fever and growing increasingly suspicious that his Filipino bearers were plotting against him. But he gathered fresh troops and plunged back into the jungle to rescue Porter and his men.

Unfortunately, Porter had neither stopped nor turned around. Instead, he pushed on toward Lanang, abandoning first one group of thirty-three men and eighteen bearers and then four more Marines who could not keep up. Finally, on January 11, 1902, with three other Marines he staggered into Lanang and collapsed. A relief column was immediately dispatched to rescue the two groups of men remaining in the jungle. As one survivor recalled:

> Our company got lost; we were without food, and in a terrible condition. Every man had sore feet, fever and was weak from lack of food and blind from leeches. We could not carry our belts or rifles, but just barely drag ourselves under a tree.

Facing these dire physical conditions, the thirty-three Marines who remained behind, commanded by a Lieutenant Williams, discovered another danger: a possible insurrection by their bearers. Increasingly nervous about the stock of bolos used by the Filipinos to cut through the jungle, Williams demanded that the weapons be kept under American guard at night. But several disappeared. Suddenly one evening when Williams ordered the bearers to gather some firewood, the missing bolos reappeared in Filipino hands. Several of the bearers attacked Williams, but failing to kill him, fled into the jungle. Furious, the lieutenant decided that next morning all the bearers should be shot. At this point, the relief column from Lanang appeared and escorted the exhausted men back to the American base. Ten of the bearers straggled into Lanang shortly thereafter.

Waller, now desperately ill and delirious from fever, returned to Basey, only to receive messages of the disaster that had befallen Porter and Williams. Worse, he heard rumors of a plot by Filipinos in Basey to repeat the massacre of Balangiga. The accused ringleaders, a merchant and the local mayor, were shot by a military firing squad. Waller then ordered two more conspirators to be executed and their bodies placed in a public square as a visible lesson to others.

At this point, a ship from Lanang arrived, carrying the ten Filipino bearers in chains. When he heard of the attack on Williams in the jungle, Waller became enraged and ordered the men shot. Survivors of the march crawled out of their sickbeds to volunteer for the firing squad. Without trial or a moment's hesitation, the Filipinos were dispatched, with their bodies left in the square of Basey to impress other would-be opponents of the Americans. As standard procedure Waller informed his commander, General Smith, who in turn relayed the information to the army commander of the Philippines, General Chaffee.

When Waller's outfit was finally relieved on February 26, 1902, he and his men sailed back to the main U.S. naval base at Cavite in Manila Bay, heroes to the American soldiers who had heard of his dangerous trek and his vengeance against the Filipinos. Few questioned the reasoning behind his strategically inept traipses back and forth through the jungles of Samar. And certainly few sympathized with the surprise greeting that awaited Waller in Cavite: a summons to appear at a court-martial trial.

The shocked Marine commander appeared before his fellow officers on March 17, 1902. After some initial sparring over procedure, the court began its deliberations, with the astute Waller overseeing his own defense. At first, he claimed justification for all his decisions in the guidelines set out in the Army General Orders 100, a handbook outline of field practices. But when the prosecution convinced his commander, General

PHILIPPINE PRISONERS OF WAR, held in a makeshift camp. The apparent relaxed attitude of prisoners and their guards, posed for the photographer, misrepresents the ferocity of the war.

Smith, to testify against him, Waller switched his defense. He produced written orders and confirmations of the verbal instructions he had received from Smith to burn, kill, and destroy. The court had little choice but to acquit him. Now the deflected guilt fell on Smith, who was ordered before the court.

In May, Smith began his testimony, defending himself and his orders also on the basis of the General Orders 100. Unrepentant to the end, he refused to acknowledge that he might have spoken metaphorically: he meant literally what he had told Waller. The only way to win the war was to shoot and burn out the "treacherous savages," he declared. Almost without choice, the court convicted the general of "conduct to the prejudice of good order and military discipline." This admonition was his only sentence.

The ordeal of Samar did not end with the conviction and mild reproof to Smith. For a time it threatened to engulf General Chaffee, Secretary of War Elihu Root, and Theodore Roosevelt, the new president of the United States and an enthusiastic and early proponent of seizing the Philippines as an American colony. Democratic party newspapers, as well as groups and journals associated with the anti-imperialist movement (opposed to keeping the Philippines), proclaimed that Samar and other American examples of brutality and torture proved their case against colonialism. America, in setting out on a course of empire, ran the risk of betraying its national principles.

Imperialism incurred more costs than any of its eager supporters had anticipated. The war against Spain that had brought the United States sovereignty over the Philippines had inflicted only a few hundred battle casualties (many more were lost to disease); it ended in 1898 almost as soon as it was declared. But the war to control the once-Spanish colony of the Philippines lasted three bitter years. Over 4,000 American lives were lost, with 20,000 Filipino combatants killed and an estimated 250,000 Filipino civilians dead from starvation, disease, and combat. A deeply divided American nation, with a curious set of crossed purposes and conflicting aims, had stumbled into a policy that had enormous consequences.

The situation was also filled with ironies. At almost the same time that Samar and other holdout areas of the Philippines were crumbling under the military offensive, the U.S. Congress, on July 2, 1902, passed the first organic act of the Philippines. This comprehensive bill, designed to codify the relationship between the United States and its new colony, defined that relationship in terms of American law, culture, and political power. It signaled benevolent intentions. For example, all Filipino citizens would be protected by a bill of rights to guard against arbitrary government. Following a census, the United States would establish an elected assembly that could pass laws (subject to the approval of the U.S. Congress). But the islands would not be independent.

The United States arrived at this position after several years of military intervention and a protracted argument over policy. The ordeal on Samar was a final, bitter incident in the unexpected guerrilla war that the United States had fought for three years. But this had never been the American intention. The United States had acquired title to the Philippines as a result of the short war and treaty with Spain in 1898. However, the actual dispute and the war between Spain and the United States had nothing to do with the Philippines.

The Spanish-American War began and ended auspiciously; in fact, it lasted barely three months. After a naval victory in Santiago, Cuba, and two widely reported and publicized army victories in the hills around that city, including Theodore Roosevelt's celebrated charge up San Juan Hill, there were few important engagements except in the Philippines. There, on May 1, 1898, the United States fleet cornered and destroyed the Spanish fleet in Manila Bay. The war for the independence of Cuba ended. Now the war for the conquest of the Philippines was about to begin, although at this point it was not clear who the enemy would be: the remaining Spanish colonial troops or the Filipinos themselves.

By the end of the first week in May 1898, President McKinley acknowledged the confusing situation in the Philippines, although he had not developed a clear policy. From Admiral Dewey he learned that about 10,000 Spanish troops still held Manila and other Philippine cities. He also discovered that Filipino revolutionaries opposed to the Spanish had massed as many as 30,000 troops around Manila. McKinley quickly ordered Major General Wesley Merritt to gather an American expeditionary force in San Francisco. The first troops arrived in the Philippines on June 30, 1898, 7,000 miles from home and without a clear purpose other than to eliminate the Spanish army.

Awaiting American troops, Admiral Dewey, operating out of the naval base at Cavite across the bay from Manila, decided to employ the Filipino revolutionaries against the remaining Spanish army forces. He had invited their leader, Emilio Aguinaldo, in exile in Hong Kong, China, to join him as soon as possible. Aguinaldo and his aides arrived at Cavite on May 19 and immediately set out to reinvigorate the Filipino rebellion against the Spanish. Very quickly, local Filipino militias and revolutionary groups joined Aguinaldo, so that by mid-June, even before the American troops arrived, Spanish power on the central island of Luzon and in other parts of the nation

EMILIO AGUINALDO dons a Western-style uniform. Although this dress gives the impression of a European leader (and that was, no doubt, its purpose), Aguinaldo was forced, by circumstances, to lead a guerrilla army.

was crumbling. Town after town surrendered to the Filipino revolutionaries, many without even a struggle.

Perhaps to an uninformed outsider, Aguinaldo's quick success in organizing military and civil support would have seemed nothing short of miraculous. But then, few outsiders knew that the revolution against the Spanish was persistent and deep among Filipinos or that Aguinaldo was one of its tested leaders. Born into a mixed Chinese-Filipino family of moderate wealth, Aguinaldo was an important nationalist leader in a tradition that extended well back into the nineteenth century.

There were various threads of independence movements in the Philippines by the 1890s, but the most important one was the Katipunan, a secret society combining both intense revolutionary and religious sentiments. When the Spanish discovered the society, members were forced to declare independence prematurely, then turned to armed struggle on several of the largest islands. Aguinaldo was a latecomer to the Katipunan, but he quickly rose to leadership because of his military and administrative skills. He also wrote a Philippine framework for government based on the American Constitution.

Despite some early successes in 1896 against the Spanish, Aguinaldo's forces were defeated, so he retreated to a mountainous region near Manila to pursue a guerrilla war. Finally, a peace treaty of sorts was signed. In exchange for Aguinaldo going into exile, the Spanish promised reforms and the payment of damages. But by 1898, peace had broken down again as both sides reneged on their promises. In March 1898 the insurrection burst forth again and Aguinaldo prepared to return to the Philippines. When escorted to Luzon by the Americans, the Filipino leader was returning to an established, ongoing revolutionary struggle, with a long history and a developing sense of nationhood and a personal history of participation.

As Spanish power declined, Aguinaldo stepped in to build a revolutionary government in its place. On May 24, 1898, he proclaimed himself dictator and promised to institute a civilian government as soon as the islands were completely liberated. In late June he issued proclamations calling for local and municipal elections. Effective control of the islands, in all but a few areas, principally Manila, now lay in the hands of the revolutionaries. While they waited for troops, the Americans in the Philippines recognized two major forces to contend with: the remnants of the Spanish army holed up in Manila, and Aguinaldo's revolutionary Filipino government.

Understandably, relations between Aguinaldo and the American commander worsened. Aguinaldo presumed that the Americans supported Philippine independence; after all, they had summoned him to organize his revolutionary army and allowed him to increase his hold on the areas outside Manila. At the same time, however, American military men treated Aguinaldo with growing hostility. In part, they were guided by instructions from Washington. On May 26 the secretary of the navy cabled Dewey, warning him against any permanent arrangements with Filipino forces that might limit future U.S. actions. By mid-June, messages from Washington instructed Dewey to avoid any agreement with Aguinaldo that might appear to legitimize the power of the revolutionaries. Finally, the American expeditionary force began to arrive.

When they took up their positions, the American soldiers found that Filipino revolutionaries had the Spanish pinned down in Manila. Aguinaldo reluctantly allowed American forces to station themselves around the city, in effect replacing some of his own troops. Then on August 1 General Merritt arrived to take command. With a total contingent of 10,000 men, the Americans considered that an assault on Manila was now possible.

American preparations for an assault dramatically increased tension with Aguinaldo's forces. Two armies, in effect, planned to attack Manila. Each of these "allies" regarded the other as an intruder. But because of his superior firepower, Merritt insisted on the sole right to attack and occupy Manila. When the strike finally came on August 13, American forces advancing into the city met almost no resistance. Spanish power in most of its colony had already faded. Now in control of the capital, Merritt insisted that Aguinaldo and his forces retreat to the outskirts of the city; joint occupation was not possible. In one day, with the miserable remnant of Spanish power crushed, the two uneasy allies became enemies. The American and Filipino armies now turned their guns on each other.

Four days later the U.S. commander received a message from Washington suggesting that the assault on Manila had probably been unnecessary. Spanish and American representatives had signed a protocol on August 12 ending the war. Among other things, Spain granted the United States the right to occupy Manila until a formal treaty would settle all the unresolved issues between the two nations. The message also ordered Merritt to insist that the Filipino insurgents recognize the legitimacy of American occupation. Furthermore, Merritt was commanded to enforce this order with "whatever means in your judgment are necessary to this end."

Thus the fate of the former Spanish colony now lay with Washington, although the administration ducked taking a clear stand. Over the summer, pressure on President McKinley grew as senators, the press, and other groups urged him to keep the Philippines. Of many justifications, that of Britain's counsel was particularly persuasive. Fearing the rise of German and Japanese naval power and imperial adventurism, Britain urged America to keep the entire nation, not just Manila or even a naval base.

In late August, General Elwell S. Otis replaced Merritt as commander of the Philippines, while Merritt embarked for Paris, where peace negotiators from Spain and the United States were gathering. He assured all parties that Aguinaldo's rebellion was limited; there would be no violence if the Americans took over administration of the islands.

While he was making these unfounded claims, sporadic fighting had already broken out between American troops and Filipinos. Some incidents resulted from drunkenness or insults to natives by American soldiers. But more serious clashes occurred as Filipino and American armies jockeyed for position around Manila. After a tense standoff in early September, Aguinaldo drew his troops back away from American lines. But in October, General Otis demanded that Aguinaldo pull back even farther. The Filipino general agreed because at the moment he was concentrating on extending his power over the rest of the islands. By fall he had largely succeeded. The Americans controlled the seas and the cities of Cavite and Manila. Aguinaldo's government assumed power elsewhere.

Although President McKinley generally understood the military situation in the Philippines, neither he, General Otis, nor his advisers fully realized the consequences of annexing the island nation. Furthermore, the president had to make his decision within an increasingly furious fight in Washington about imperialism. A real calculation of the costs in lives and money was rarely visible as the press and congressmen debated their fantasies about the potential role of the Philippines.

The "imperialist" side of the debate was led by such stalwarts as Senator Henry Cabot Lodge of Massachusetts and prodded by enthusiasts such as Theodore Roosevelt, supported by a skilled chorus of journalists, whose ability to invent reasons to embark on overseas ventures was as brilliant as their knowledge of conditions in the islands was vague.

Four main arguments in support of keeping the islands emerged. Economically, the Philippines would protect and enhance a trade route to China. Strategic reasons centered on keeping the islands as a buttress against Japanese and German expansionism. A third rationale was promoted by Protestant missionary groups, who saw the islands as fertile ground for conversion (a great many Filipinos were already Roman Catholics). The fourth reason was vague but still compelling: it was America's destiny to conquer and hold the Philippines, to dominate the Pacific, and push the march of its civilization westward.

And yet Americans were not united at all. A powerful group of public figures led by William Jennings Bryan of Nebraska joined a group of distinguished writers, journalists, and intellectuals in opposing imperialism. Their arguments against imperialism warned of violence to American tradition in ruling over a subjected people. What would happen, these anti-imperialists asked, to sacred proclamations like the Declaration of Independence and the Monroe Doctrine? Would anything remain of the unique American civilization if the nation joined the unseemly European scramble for empire? Would acquiring territory compromise the American Republic? Might Americans be dragged down into the whirlpool of imperialist struggles with the aging empires of Europe? And what fate did Americans intend for the brown-skinned Filipinos, who would never be accepted as equals in a segregated American society?

Senator Beveridge had a chilling answer to all these objections. There was no compromise of tradition if one thought about the treatment of Native Americans as a precedent. Furthermore, there was even an important lesson to be learned in the comparison:

> Our Indian wars would have been shortened, the lives of soldiers and settlers saved and the Indians themselves benefited, had we made continuous and decisive war; and any other kind of war is criminal because ineffective. We acted toward the Indians as though we feared them, loved them, hated them—all at the same time—with a mingling of foolish sentiment, inaccurate thought, and paralytic purpose.

The senator's desired clarity and decisiveness were the very qualities missing from Philippine policy making. Even those who opposed acquisition of the Philippines failed to agree on reasons for their opposition, nor did they ever unite into a single-purpose political group. They raised questions about acquiring colonies that may now seem remarkably farsighted, but they lost the argument at the time. Debate, dispute, vagueness of purpose, contradictory reasoning, and outlandish claims determined the outcome. This confusion defined the context in which President McKinley had to formulate his policy toward the Philippines.

The president was a cautious man. In moving toward war with Spain and then asking for colonies as a part of the peace treaty, he had appeared passive and vague. The United States in 1898 had been reluctantly belligerent against Spain. During peace negotiations in September, the president wrote (somewhat disingenuously) to his negotiating team in Paris that the United States had no intention of seizing the Philippines. Nevertheless, he reasoned:

> We cannot be unmindful that without any desire or design on our part the war has brought us new duties and responsibilities which we must meet and discharge as becomes

a great nation in whose growth and career from the beginning the Ruler of Nations has plainly written the high command and pledge of civilization.

Still somewhat reluctant, but leaning more and more toward acquisition, McKinley turned to prayer, as he explained, "for light and guidance from the 'Ruler of Nations.'" The inspiration he received strengthened his growing inclination. It was, he decided, America's duty to take the islands, to "educate the Filipinos, and uplift and Christianize them." On October 23, 1898, the president wired his commissioners in Paris. The United States, he declared, now demanded not just a naval base in Manila Bay; not even the central island of Luzon would be sufficient; the United States insisted on acquiring the whole archipelago. In return, he tendered the Spanish $20 million. Having little choice or desire to resist, Madrid agreed on December 10, 1898.

McKinley still faced two important obstacles. The first was the U.S. Senate, which had to consent to the treaty. Several strong and vocal members promised a bruising battle. Thus the struggle became a fight for American public opinion. The second impediment was Aguinaldo and his Filipino army, which already controlled most of the Philippine Islands except Manila and the nearby naval base at Cavite. Would he and his army exchange independence and self-rule to become an American colony?

Before the bar of American opinion, McKinley won his case easily. In elections in early November, Republican candidates, touting victory over Spain and promising the annexation of the Philippines, defeated the Democrats in key congressional races. They also gained the governorship of New York, where Theodore Roosevelt, charging into electoral politics, won an important victory by whipping up patriotism. "If you choose to vote for America," he declared bluntly, "if you choose to vote for the flag for which we fought this summer, then vote Republican." The Democrats, fearing the challenge, did not oppose annexation strongly, but the issue hurt them anyway.

Weeks of political maneuvering in the Senate followed the election, with promises, pork-barrel agreements, and strident speeches. Finally, a vote was scheduled for February 6, 1899. Immense pressure focused on a few wavering anti-imperialist senators from the South and West. In the final tally, the treaty passed by a margin of two. Why the Senate finally approved this agreement is a complex question of party loyalty, opportunism, and response to public opinion. Perhaps more than anything, the issue had become one of patriotism and national unity. Having acquired the Philippines almost by default, it seemed easier in terms of domestic politics to keep them than to establish an informal protectorate to block German or Japanese encroachment or allow Aguinaldo's revolutionaries to take over.

Yet few Americans realized that keeping the Philippines committed the United States to conquering them first. There had been some warning, but it came too late. On February 5, 1899, just before the crucial Senate vote, war broke out. General Otis, continuing his pressure on Aguinaldo to retreat from Manila, insisted that the Filipino army abandon more of its positions close to the city. When the Filipinos refused, he alerted his men to fire on any military personnel approaching disputed territory. On February 4, U.S. troops opened fire on a group of revolutionary soldiers. The next day, Otis launched a general attack, backed up by heavy guns from Admiral Dewey's warships, anchored within easy range of the Filipino lines.

Charging through the Filipino lines, shouting the "Montana Yell," American troops decimated the ill-equipped and startled revolutionaries. Trapped by charging cavalry, as many as 3,000 Filipino soldiers died. There were only about 60 American casualties. The pattern of war was set. Otis marched out to engage and destroy Aguinaldo's army, then returned to the safety of the Manila area. This first phase of the war to conquer the Philippines resembled traditional warfare. Although the Filipino forces had few weapons or trustworthy artillery, they sought, at first, to engage the American force in pitched battles.

Despite efforts to negotiate a truce, Aguinaldo refused to give in; consequently, American troops extended their control over major cities on Luzon and some of the other islands. At the same time, McKinley initiated plans for a civilian government, sending the first Philippine Commission to the islands. On April 4, 1899, the commission (including Dewey and Otis as members) proclaimed eleven "regulative principles" establishing the outlines of colonial government. In matters of sovereignty, the United States would be supreme. The regulations guaranteed civil rights and liberties and promised maximum local self-government, improved education and economy, and speedy and fair justice. But there would be no Philippine independence.

Enforced by unrelenting military pressure, this policy was designed to win the allegiance of the Filipinos, particularly the elite groups who dominated the social, cultural, and economic life of the islands. Thus pacification proceeded along two lines: military and civilian. But time and again, just when the Americans believed they had won the allegiance or cooperation of local officials, their trust proved premature as Filipinos cast their lot with Aguinaldo.

As a result, General Otis concluded that he must destroy Aguinaldo's army and capture the revolutionary general. During the summer of 1899 Otis succeeded in the first of these aims. At the same time, the commission's pacification policies proceeded. The Army distributed $100,000 worth of texts on arithmetic, geography, U.S. history, and English, and school supplies, including American flags. Roads were repaired and other public works undertaken. A vaccination program against smallpox began. Proud of these efforts, Otis assured Washington that he had won the war for the Philippines.

But while clashes between Aguinaldo's forces and the U.S. Army diminished over the summer of 1899, this did not mean the country had been pacified. The Filipino general had the loyalty of a great many of his people even if he could not field an army. Nonetheless, the United States government proceeded as if pacification was complete. In March 1900 the second Philippine Commission landed at Manila. Its purpose was to assume power in civilian matters from the army. Secretary of War Elihu Root instructed the commission to collect taxes, appropriate public funds, and establish courts. The commission was to act as the legislative power of the colony. Root also replaced General Otis on May 1 with General Arthur MacArthur, who promised that the islands would be "submerged immediately under a tidal wave of education."

William Howard Taft led the second commission. A man of immense girth and considerable talent, who had a close and valuable friendship with Theodore Roosevelt, Taft had once opposed taking the Philippines because, according to his wife, they "would only add to our problems and responsibilities without increasing in any way the effectiveness and usefulness of our government." But he now believed that America

THE GENTLEMEN OF THE FIRST PHILIPPINE COMMISSION in 1899 included Jacob G. Schurman, Admiral George Dewey, Charles Denby, and Dean C. Worcester.

could offer the islands efficient and businesslike reforms. Taft, unlike many military men—especially enlisted men—viewed the Filipino situation with optimism. It was widely believed in the islands that he had coined the phrase "our little brown brothers" to betoken his warm feelings for the Filipinos. But soldiers recited a bit of broken verse that recorded more hostile feelings:

> I'm only a common soldier-man in the blasted Philippines.
> They say I've got Brown Brothers here, but I dunno what it means.
> I like the word Fraternity, but still I draw the line;
> He may be a brother of William H. Taft, but he ain't no friend of mine.

A month after arriving in Manila, Taft confided his impressions of the Filipino people in a letter to Root: "The population of the Islands is made up of a vast mass of ignorant, superstitious people, well-intentioned, light-hearted, temperate, somewhat cruel, domestic and fond of their families, and deeply wedded to the Catholic church." Although this statement shows a paternalistic view of the Filipinos, it also suggests that the commissioner suffered from what might be called "culture shock" or an extreme misunderstanding of the customs of another society. Mrs. Taft was obviously amused by her husband's sensitivity to Filipino characteristics. As she noted in her diary: "The first conclusion he [Taft] reached in Manila was that the people knew nothing about the value of time, and it must have been a strain on his temperate-zone nervous system to watch a squad of men at work in his garden."

While Taft designed a policy of benevolence, General MacArthur increased military pressure. Not surprisingly, divergent U.S. civilian and military interests hard-

YOUNG FILIPINOS dress up and carry flags to celebrate America's independence (not their own). By their looks, these children seem more interested in another American importation: the camera.

ened into a dispute over how to pacify the Philippines. The behavior of American civilians and soldiers underscored the differences. Military men frequently referred to Filipinos as "gugus" or "niggers." The soldiers' bad handling of debts, drunkenness, and rude behavior increased tensions between them and Filipino citizens, despite the polite reception that Taft and his wife gave to the elite Philippine families of the capital city.

This contradictory policy reflected the profound division in the United States over the Philippines that continued throughout 1900. The debate became an issue in the election of 1900, which pitted the Republican President McKinley and his new vice presidential candidate, Theodore Roosevelt, against the Democrat William Jennings Bryan. Imperialism was a highly visible issue that divided the parties. Although this issue may not have decided the election, newspapers returned again and again to the debate. Republicans publicly doubted the patriotism of Democrats who opposed the war; Democrats accused imperialists of undermining the Constitution. Yet Bryan proved to be a poor crusader for anti-imperialism. Considered unreliable on the issue, he lost the support of some of the most vocal opponents of the war.

The overheated rhetoric of the campaign did nothing to clarify Philippine policy or justify continued U.S. occupation of the islands. But it did convince Aguinaldo and his forces that a Bryan victory might lead to American evacuation and Philippine independence. Partly to influence the election, Aguinaldo's army increasingly shifted to active guerrilla tactics over the summer of 1900. In a certain sense, they had no choice; superiority in men, arms, and mobility meant the Americans could win any direct, pitched battle. Against lightning strikes, ambushes, and surprise attacks carried out by citizen soldiers who then melted back into the population, the American army of occupation had far less success.

Partly out of frustration, the Americans responded with antiguerrilla tactics that carried warfare to the population harboring the revolutionaries. MacArthur's men burned barrios near the scenes of attacks, destroyed crops, and killed work animals. Because secrecy and surprise were the weapons of guerrilla warfare, the American troops commonly relied on torture to extract information from prisoners. The approved method was the "water cure." Water was forced into the mouth of a suspect held on the ground, until he talked. The sensation was like drowning, and, if not stopped in time, could lead to death.

While conditions in the Philippines deteriorated and relations between Mac-Arthur and Taft grew more hostile, the decisive electoral victory of McKinley and Roosevelt in November squelched the last hopes of the Filipino revolutionaries. MacArthur immediately toughened his policy after the election. He increased censorship of the news, and announced that captured revolutionaries would henceforth be treated as criminals, not soldiers, making them susceptible to the death penalty. He initiated a policy of population concentration, gathering peasants into monitored areas where they could not support the guerrillas. In certain respects this policy resembled the treatment of Native Americans in the final struggle for control of the West after the Civil War.

Although this tough policy seemed to bear fruit—more weapons and taxes were collected—MacArthur was replaced in February 1901 by Brigadier General Adna R. Chaffee. Secretary of War Root declared that civilian authorities, led by William Howard Taft, would now exercise increased power. In part, this victory of Taft over MacArthur indicated that the United States government believed the war was coming to a close.

Further evidence of victory came in March 1901 with the capture of General Aguinaldo in northern Luzon. Aguinaldo had sent secret correspondence to his brother asking for more troops, but the U.S. Army intercepted the message. General Frederick Funston devised a ruse to enter Aguinaldo's headquarters. Filipino troops loyal to the United States disguised themselves in revolutionary uniforms while Funston and four other American officers posed as their prisoners. Welcomed into rebel headquarters during the celebration of Aguinaldo's birthday, the troop of conspirators opened fire. Most of Aguinaldo's men panicked. The Americans seized the leader and rushed to the coast to a waiting ship.

A month later, in captivity and persuaded of the futility of continued resistance, Aguinaldo issued a proclamation from prison urging the Filipino people to lay down their arms and accept American rule. But the movement headed by the Filipino general lived on without him. The guerrilla war continued, particularly in the southern area of Luzon and on the island of Samar. Important pieces of the revolutionary government remained intact, although the ordinary people and even elected officials hid their loyalties to the rebels.

In most respects, Chaffee continued MacArthur's tough policy of carrying the antiguerrilla war to the civilian population. Under his command, final plans were drawn up to subdue Samar. He ordered American troops to occupy Balangiga, where the September 1901 attack on Company C took place.

The ordeal of Samar had far-ranging effects. A Senate investigation of the Philippine pacification revealed bungling, torture, atrocities. The population concentration policy resulted in cruelties. General MacArthur defended the suspicious casualty ratio among Filipinos. Explaining why there were fifteen dead to only one wounded (when in the U.S. Civil War there had been about one dead to five wounded), he denied that the Army had killed prisoners and wounded men. The general simply said that "inferior races" died more easily than Anglo-Saxons.

Although such harsh statements did not force practices to change immediately, they may well have contributed to the growing sentiment that the occupation was a mistake and that the United States should grant independence to the Philippines as soon as self-rule became possible. A number of Americans remained uneasy about the intervention. *The Sultan of Sula*, a successful theatrical spoof of imperialism that played in Chicago and other cities in 1902, expressed some serious second thoughts about the whole endeavor. In the play, a chorus of American soldiers sings ironically about "benevolent assimilation."

> *We want to assimilate if we can*
>   *Our brother who is brown*
> *We love our dusky fellow-man*
>   *And we hate to hunt him down.*
> *So when we perforate his frame,*
>   *We want him to be good.*
> *We shout at him to make him tame,*
>   *If he but understood.*

Promises of changes in policy came rather quickly. The Jones Act of 1917 officially guaranteed independence as soon as the nation achieved "a stable government." Even superimperialist Theodore Roosevelt soon concluded that the islands were our "Achilles' heel."

In the Philippines, MacArthur and Chaffee's tough tactics finally convinced most of the populace that struggle was futile. Taft successfully negotiated an arrangement with the Catholic Church to pay for large tracts of land confiscated from it. The Filipino elite recognized that they had nothing more to gain and much to lose by supporting the revolutionaries.

As the fighting diminished, Taft and the commissioners could pay more attention to new government institutions and health and social reforms. Whether these improved the lives of the Filipino people significantly has been widely debated. Furthermore, traditional Philippine institutions proved more resilient (and resistant) than anyone anticipated. For example, despite an influx of missionaries, Protestantism made little headway in the largely Catholic population. Only about 3 percent of Filipinos in 1980 could trace their religious beliefs back to the efforts of these proselytizers. Political corruption, wide class differences, inefficiency, and slow economic growth continued. The islands benefited only marginally from special tariffs that allowed their products to enter the United States at lower rates than foreign goods.

Ultimately, confusion of purpose, indecision at home, and squabbling between American military and civilian authorities probably worsened the conflict with Filipino revolutionaries. Left without clearly formulated policies or instructions, local commanders fell back on their own experiences, improvising their response to the bitter guerrilla warfare. Because a great many of the officers had recent experience in fighting Na-

PAGEANT AT MANILA. Shortly before they left the Philippines in 1904, the Taft family, pictured here with two aides (left and right standing), held a costume ball. There could scarcely have been a more incongruous celebration, to imagine Manila as Venice and Taft as the cultured doge who helped inspire the Renaissance.

tive Americans in the American West, almost inevitably their actions and their attitudes recalled that bitter conflict. That is what Senator Joseph R. Burton of Kansas had in mind when he compared the antiguerrilla warfare tactics to the extermination of Indians at Wounded Knee. Both were, he noted, "entirely within the regulations of civilized warfare." After all, he told his fellow senators, "you cannot fight a barbarous foe in the same way you can a civilized enemy."

Progressive Foreign Policy, from Empire to World War

Nationalism, benevolence, dreams of manifest destiny, economic self-interest, and a missionary zeal to spread Protestantism and Western civilization—these different notions lay behind U.S. involvement in the Philippines after the Spanish-American War. If it is true that foreign policy reflects domestic circumstances, it should be no surprise to find that during a period of striking transition in American society between an agrarian past and an industrial future, such deep contradictions and uncertainties of purpose also appeared in foreign affairs.

Led by dynamic leaders who held strong opinions, with nationalism burgeoning, the United States confidently, but cautiously, stepped into a competitive and dangerous world. Problems at home seemed difficult but surmountable. A reform movement that preached efficiency, organization, and professionalism promised to solve domestic economic and social problems by applying the right combination of compassion and expertise. This also became the policy of America toward a world in the last throes of colonialism and bracing for its first wave of modern revolutions. The United States would offer progressive reform to the world.

In some respects, the war in the Philippines tested this offer. Its frustrating results anticipated much that happened in the next two decades of foreign policy. The same pattern seemed to repeat itself: the best intentions of policy makers

brought unpleasant and often dangerous involvement with other nations. Facing this predicament, Americans were assailed by doubts about the aptness of trying to export institutions. The conflicting purposes that underlay policy reemerged. As a result, the nation turned toward isolationism again in the 1920s, skeptical that American ideas could be exported, suspicious of the motives of reformers, and with renewed worries about entangling alliances and colonial wars. There appeared to be a lesson in this: in a turbulent world, events had a way of flying out of control, whatever the objectives of policy makers. But there was also a profound question: Could America really stand for principle in a world where everyone else seemed motivated by cutthroat economic and political competition?

THE MYTH OF AMERICA'S DESTINY

After about 1896 the United States increasingly looked outward, toward the acquisition of an empire and then, warily, toward active participation in the conflicts between European nations. Every step of the way was accompanied by questions and debate over two issues: How should Americans treat the peoples of the undeveloped countries they encountered? Should the United States become permanently involved in alliances and covenants with European nations? If America was to remain the unique civilization that so many thinkers had proclaimed it to be, then these problems demanded a resolute answer.

The architects of a more engaged and activist foreign policy often found justification in their unusual interpretations of history. A great many Americans at this time were influenced by the idea of American "exceptionalism," the theory that America had a special destiny in the world born out of a combination of its European, principally Anglo-Saxon, racial and cultural heritage and its experience as a frontier civilization. Their ideas about the mission of the United States were similarly born out of the feeling of belonging to a uniquely successful society. It is these ideas that convinced Americans they were duty-bound to try to set the world right.

The words of journalist William Allen White capture the intense spirit of this idea: "It is the Anglo-Saxon's manifest destiny to go forth as a world conqueror. He will take possession of the islands of the seas. That is what fate holds for the chosen people. It is so written. It is to be." Ambrose Bierce, another journalist, whose biting realism vividly rendered the terrible battlefields of the Civil War, was a late convert to imperialism. Speaking of the gift of Western civilization to be granted to the Filipinos, he wrote:

> Of all it may safely be said that their only hope lies in subjugation by a master race. Such advancement as they may be capable of is not to be effected by suggestion or advice. Like all backward peoples, they fight against the light and will accept it, if at all, only when it is flashed upon them by the sword.

Indiana Senator Albert J. Beveridge, much given to hyperbole and handsome turns of phrase, justified taking the Philippines on all these grounds—and then some. Having visited the islands himself, he described the natives as a "barbarous race." America had a destiny to transform the world: "Of all our races He [God] has marked the American people as His chosen Na-

tion finally to lead in the regeneration of the world." Climbing down from religious to patriotic metaphors, he called the flag the emblem of this movement: "That flag has never paused in its onward march." Beveridge's use of the term *race*, which he meant as something akin to "cultures" or "civilizations," had a certain urgent appeal to it. It could satisfy Americans who were increasingly puzzled by a dangerous and competitive world where history appeared to have chosen the nation to play a grand role.

Still the United States had picked up the burden of empire after some reluctance. The nation was a late entrant in the expansion race. It quickly acquired a string of colonies and protectorates, but then withdrew from the contest. However, it did not retire from the scene; its overseas ambitions merely assumed a different form. In the Western Hemisphere, Americans began a series of interventions in the affairs of Latin American countries that continued, sporadically, for several decades. By 1917 the United States would weigh in to tip the balance of power in one of the gravest conflicts in human history.

These events inspired a new national self-consciousness. They gave rise to new ideas about national power, to a belief that because of its history and culture the United States was uniquely fitted to guide the destinies of other nations. Yet these events simultaneously aroused doubts. Would America's new activist role in the world forever compromise the special qualities of affluence, social mobility, and democracy in the New World?

Such questions found their way into serious political discourse. Indeed, a great many Americans were talking about the nation's destiny in terms of world leadership. Of course, words like *leadership, destiny,* and *mission* had always been part of the American political vocabulary. In the mid-nineteenth century, writers and politicians often spoke of the nation's manifest destiny to populate a continent bounded by two vast oceans, on the east and the west, and by two different cultures, to the north and the south. But with that geographic destiny fulfilled in the 1890s, with most of the fertile land already occupied and millions of new immigrants pouring into the cities of the East and Midwest, the idea of manifest destiny acquired a new meaning. American institutions of political democracy and economic mobility still seemed superior to the class-conscious societies of Europe, but many Americans wondered how this superiority could survive.

Frederick Jackson Turner, a historian at the University of Wisconsin, in a celebrated and influential essay about the American spirit, summed up the effects of the frontier on American society and offered a vision of continued expansion. Turner asserted that American democratic institutions came from the frontier experience. As settlements pressed across the continent, civilization and wilderness repeatedly intermingled. Savagery refreshed society, while civilization tamed the wilderness. Thus had Americans progressed in a westward trek for almost 300 years.

When he described his frontier thesis at the World's Columbian Exposition in 1893 in Chicago (to commemorate Columbus's voyage 400 years earlier), Turner used the language of popularized evolutionary theory. Struggle and competition on the frontier, he declared, created a survival ethic of individualism and democratic cooperation. But the historian issued a warning. The frontier, he said solemnly, "has gone and with its going has closed the first period of American history."

Would there be a second, equally rich period of American history? Movement, restlessness, and a desire for opportunity still remained the essence of the American spirit. The lure of the West had not died. It drew thousands of young men and women onto what remained of the frontier. Many failed to make their fortune, but the dream of fleeing the workaday cities of the East remained irresistible. Perhaps some Americans could find escape in the fictional heroism and new frontier worlds of popular fiction: westerns, science fiction, and adventure tales. But could the nation survive the loss of the energy and creativity that had once come from opening up new frontiers?

Turner did not think so. Nor did he believe that the nation could prosper unless it continued to grow economically. So he advised continued expansion in world trade. In effect, the world was to become America's economic frontier. Many of his contemporaries agreed with Turner that the 1890s represented a watershed in American history. With the frontier officially closed and westward expansion blocked by natural and cultural boundaries, the only feasible economic expansion lay overseas in trade or empire. But there were dangers. Could America avoid falling into the traps that ensnared Spain, Britain, and France in costly colonial ventures? Would America's new activism in the world economy mean entangling alliances with European powers?

Those American policy makers who advised a new activism—a new foreign policy—believed American society would flourish because of its cultural superiority. They believed America was a nation of Englishmen purified by the encounter with the frontier. Long implicit in American thinking, this theory of Anglo-Saxon supremacy emerged full-blown in the early twentieth century. Many Americans believed that an English background bestowed a special racial heritage. America would survive world competition because of its superior racial stock, culture, and high principles. Nor was this thinking confined to a few diplomats or politicians. It was a myth that found a huge audience among all classes of Americans.

American cultural supremacy was the argument Theodore Roosevelt used to justify America's policy of Indian removal in his book *The Winning of the West*. "It was wholly impossible," he wrote, "to avoid conflicts with the weaker race unless we were willing to see the American continent fall into the hands of some other strong power." Progressive senator Albert Beveridge, speaking of America's destiny, called the nation "the purest race of history." "Fellow Americans," he proclaimed in 1898, "we are God's chosen people." Even William Jennings Bryan, who opposed acquiring colonies, solemnly spoke of the nation's mission "to liberate those who are in bondage."

THE REALITY BEHIND THE MYTH

The men who developed America's new foreign policy at the turn of the century subscribed to this notion that the nation had a special destiny. Most believed in the superiority of the Anglo-Saxon "race." Some based their position on social Darwinism, a popular translation of evolutionary theory into a proclamation of the right of the "fittest" individuals and the strongest nations to rule over others. Many were influenced by the ideas that Turner had enunciated in his "frontier thesis." But they were also hardheaded realists who recognized the political and economic benefits of an activist foreign policy. They realized that the United States had to begin to exercise more power in the world because its economic position among nations had become preeminent.

The profoundest changes in America's world position were economic. In 1877 the United States struck a favorable balance of trade (more exports than imports). Forty years later, during World War I, the nation became a world creditor, owing less to other nations than it had lent out. This evolution toward financial independence reflected a dynamic economic growth. Rapid development in the 1880s and 1890s greatly increased the percentage of manufactured

goods in American exports. This, in turn, focused the interest of American industrialists on maintaining and increasing overseas markets.

Much of the increased American economic activity abroad came in the form of investments, especially in underdeveloped nations. In Mexico, for example, by 1910 about 1,100 American firms held about $500 million worth of assets. In effect, American capital controlled most of Mexico's railroads and a large share of its ranching, lumber and paper industries, and banking. United States companies also dominated Mexican mining and oil extraction.

During the progressive era, exports constituted only between 6 and 7.5 percent of total American production, but this was a vital part of the nation's commerce. From 1890 to 1914 the share of trade with Latin American and Asian countries increased dramatically. Something of the nature of this trade can be illustrated by one highly successful firm, the Singer Sewing Machine Co. Founded in Boston by Isaac Merritt Singer un 1850, it became, by the first decade of the twentieth century, an extraordinarily successful American enterprise. In 1913 it had almost 6,000 branches in the United States and abroad, with over 60,000 salesmen. Besides its special marketing program, it operated branch factories in Canada, Scotland, Germany, and Russia. Other nations manufactured sewing machines, but

AMERICAN EXPORTS BY VALUE AND DESTINATION, 1896–1924

Year	Total*	Canada	Cuba	Mexico	UK	France	Germany	China
1896	$ 883	$ 60	$ 8	$ 19	$ 406	$ 47	$ 98	$ 7
1900	1,394	95	26	35	534	83	187	15
1904	1,461	131	27	46	537	84	215	13
1908	1,861	167	47	56	581	116	277	22
1912	2,204	329	62	53	564	135	307	24
1916	5,483	605	165	54	1,887	861	2	32
1920	8,228	972	515	208	1,825	676	311	146
1924	4,591	624	200	135	983	282	440	109

*Millions of dollars.
Source: U.S. Department of Commerce, Bureau of the Census, Historical Statistics of the United States: Colonial Times to the Present, *bicentennial ed. (Washington, D.C.: Government Printing Office, 1975), Vol. II, p. 903.*

American companies, with Singer taking the largest share, dominated the world market.

A slogan picturing the sewing machine as "the great civilizer" reiterated the company belief, and the larger American assumption, that the export of Yankee know-how would transform the world. There were, however, other views of this American dominance of world markets. For example, during the Spanish-American War of 1898, newspapers in Madrid called for a boycott of Singer products. One journal accused Singer of being an "immense octopus whose tentacles encircle Spain and crush it, snatching from it the savings of its workers in order to aggrandize the miserable, iniquitous, cowardly, disgusting North American nation."

The potential for even larger sales for other companies was alluring. Yet success bred worries. Power shifts in Europe and instability in Asia, South America, and Africa increased the aggressiveness of leading European powers. The rapid industrialization and armament of Germany and Japan threatened the dominance of Great Britain. After a scramble for colonies in Africa during the 1880s and 1890s, the major powers looked covetously on the weak Spanish empire in Asia. China appeared to be tottering. Even the unruly Latin American republics seemed in danger of intervention by European powers.

After many years of relative isolation, the United States suddenly had to rethink its foreign relations. Thus the new American foreign policy at the turn of the century was defined in the context of serious challenges as well as opportunities. If industrial nations divided the world into competing, closed empires protected by high tariff walls, United States trade and influence would collapse, with American products excluded from markets. If the European nations and Japan insisted on expanding their empires, the United States might be shut out from the world economic frontier. To make matters more urgent, many American business and political leaders concluded during the severe depression of the 1890s that agricultural and industrial overproduction were permanent American problems. They could be solved only by exporting more.

A NEW FOREIGN POLICY

The men who formulated the new American foreign policy of the progressive era were in fundamental agreement: They insisted that the United States pursue a more active role in the world. They were deeply influenced by ideas and worries about America's destiny. They realized the opportunities and problems created by rapid industrial development. But they disagreed sharply about how far the United States should go toward acquiring a formal empire of naval bases and colonies. This practical question dominated debate over foreign policy at the turn of the century.

The major shift toward a new, activist foreign policy began during the second presidency of Grover Cleveland, in the depths of a depression. Three unsettling events pushed the president toward new policy initiatives. The first was a revolt in the Hawaiian Islands in January 1893. Dominated by American planters, the islands became increasingly important because of the fine port at Pearl Harbor and the islands' strategic position along trade routes to the Far East. Immigration of Chinese and Japanese settlers in the 1880s, plus the growing economic importance of Americans, led native Queen Liliuokalani to assert her powers. But the white settlers in Honolulu, led by sugar planters like Sanford Dole and supported by the U.S. minister to the island, John L. Stevens, overthrew the queen and asked for American annexation.

When Cleveland entered office in 1893, he faced a decision to accept or reject annexation. He refused, angrily saying that the revolt was dependent for its success on "the agency of the United States." Cleveland desired trade and influence in Hawaii, but he was reluctant to annex the islands as a colony of the United States.

A second crisis developed in South America in a dispute between Great Britain and Venezuela that challenged the Monroe Doctrine of 1823, which had provided the principle for American hemispheric foreign policy: no further encroachment by Europeans in the Americas. The British

SINGER IN SOUTH AFRICA. The caption to this advertising card from Singer reads, "This is a fertile, well-watered country of South Africa, on the Indian Ocean, and forms a part of the region known as Kafraria. The native Zulus are a fine warlike people of the Bantu stock, speaking the Bantu language. The language extends over more than half of Africa and is one of great beauty and flexibility. The Zulu bids fair to be as forward in civilization as he has been in war. Our group represents the Zulus after less than a century of civilization. Worth wins everywhere. Our agent at Cape Town supplies both the European and native inhabitants of Zululand, The Transvaal, and Orange Free State with thousands of Singer Machines."

navy had generally supplied the shield for this policy. Now, suddenly, the British themselves threatened a Latin American republic.

The dispute was a long-standing one about the boundary between Venezuela and the British colony of Guiana. At stake was the Orinoco, a large navigable river whose upper reaches tapped trade and gold prospecting areas of Venezuela. Cleveland supported Venezuela's claims and pressed Britain to submit the dispute to international arbitration. On July 20, 1895, Secretary of State Richard Olney demanded that the British negotiate. In his message he reminded Britain of America's power: "Today the United States is practically sovereign on this continent."

When the British response came, it was curt and inflammatory. No arbitration and no recognition of the Monroe Doctrine. Cleveland's next move edged the United States toward war.

He sent a message to Congress on December 17, 1895, calling upon the nation to resist the "willful aggression" upon Venezuelan rights. Talk of war flared but then subsided quickly. Already overextended elsewhere, the British agreed to arbitration.

THE SPANISH-AMERICAN WAR

No sooner had the Venezuelan crisis ended than a rebellion flared in Cuba that quickly became the center of American attention. One of the last outposts of the crumbling Spanish empire, Cuba had gravitated into the U.S. economic orbit. American exports to the island reached $24 million in 1893, larger than to any other Western Hemisphere nation save Canada, and larger than all of America's Asian trade. In February 1895,

QUEEN LILIUOKALANI OF HAWAII. Queen Liliuokalani ascended the throne of the Hawaiian Islands in 1891. Her attempts to assume wider powers persuaded American residents on the islands to demand annexation by the United States in 1893.

Cuban rebels demanded independence. Too weak to enforce order, Spain nonetheless insisted that the rebels surrender. As fighting spread, American-owned sugar plantations and mills suffered from arson and looting. The whole structure of American investments on the island—$50 million worth—hung in the balance.

At first, Cleveland sympathized with the Spanish, and he never wavered from his desire to see the rebellion end. But continued violence eroded his patience. Moreover, Cuban rebels gathered significant support in the United States. Many Americans became openly sympathetic to their cause after Spanish general Valeriano Weyler introduced martial law and his "reconcentration policy." Begun in October 1896, this policy pushed thousands of peasants into the cities to depopulate the countryside and end guerrilla warfare. But Weyler miscalculated, and thousands of Cubans died of starvation and disease in crowded city quarters. Newspaper publishers William Randolph Hearst and Joseph Pulitzer, who knew how to provoke sympathy (and circulation), played up the brutality of this policy by chanting: cruel Spain, corrupt Spain, heroic Cubans. Like their Progressive counterparts, the muckrakers, these "yellow journalists" discovered the importance and malleability of public opinion. When war finally began, Hearst ran a headline in his *New York Journal:* "How Do You Like the *Journal's* War?"

Under the circumstances, Cleveland could only increase pressure on Spain to end the rebellion. He was not prepared to go to war over Cuba, yet he defined peace in the rebellious colony as key to American interests. Thus when he left office in 1897, he passed on to William McKinley, the new president, the task of protecting America's interests in this explosive situation.

McKinley's inauguration brought a new group of foreign-policy makers and advisers to power. They were more willing to push ahead in places where Cleveland had been reluctant. The most prominent of these new men was Theodore Roosevelt, the new assistant secretary of the navy, although other members of the group were also important: Senator Henry Cabot Lodge of Massachusetts, diplomat John Hay, historian Brooks Adams, and Admiral Alfred Thayer Mahan.

Although their views differed somewhat, most of the new men agreed with the strategic proposals outlined by Mahan in his book *The Influence of Sea Power upon History* (1890). Mahan proposed an export and investment network based on naval power. His tactics centered on building a Panama canal, acquiring protective bases around it, and then colonial stepping-stones across the Pacific to Asia. This would ensure American trade and influence in Latin America and the Orient. These goals, Mahan proclaimed, were far greater than mere national self-interest. "Every expansion of a great civilized power," he wrote, "means a victory for law, order, and righteousness." Overseas empire was America's destiny.

Spain was the major obstacle in America's route to empire when McKinley entered office in 1897. Senator Henry Cabot Lodge expressed

ANTI-AMERICAN PROPAGANDA. A Spanish journalistic view of America during the war of 1898. The American pig courts the Lady of Spain with flowers and a handy money bag.

ANTI-SPANISH PROPAGANDA. Portrayals of Spanish authorities as brutal murderers in journals and newspapers in the United States helped incite American public opinion in favor of war against Spain in 1898.

what many in the administration, as well as many other Americans, believed about Spain, writing that the Spanish were a people who "stood for bigotry and tyranny as hideous in their action as any which have ever cursed humanity." Spain also held the strategic islands of Puerto Rico, Guam, and the Philippines.

The new president hoped to avoid direct intervention in Cuba. But unlike Cleveland, he committed himself to a more expansionist foreign policy, including acquisition of the Virgin Islands in the Caribbean, and Hawaii, and eventually removal of all vestiges of European colonialism from the Western Hemisphere. His first priority was to end the divisive pressure on domestic politics and the economy caused by the Cuban rebellion. So he stepped up pressure on the Spanish. In June 1897 he called on Spain to end its "uncivilized and inhumane conduct." Again in the fall, he warned the Spanish not to seek allies among the European powers.

As Spain moved from one inept policy to another, the United States pressed its case harder.

By the end of 1897 the two nations were on a collision course. The Spanish minister to Washington, Enrique De Lome, in a letter to a friend in Cuba referred to McKinley as "weak and a bidder for the admiration of the crowd." The letter was intercepted and published February 9 in the *New York Journal*. Sensationalists needed no more evidence of Spanish duplicity.

A far more serious event on February 15 almost ignited war. The U.S. battleship *Maine*, anchored in Havana harbor in Cuba, exploded mysteriously. Of the 350 officers and seamen aboard, 260 perished. Although the perpetrators of the act (if indeed there were any) were never captured, many Americans blamed the Spanish authorities. Once again, the sensationalist press resounded with cries for war.

As pressure on Cuba increased, the United States flanked the Spanish empire in the Pacific. Assistant Navy Secretary Roosevelt ordered Admiral George Dewey to anchor his fleet at Hong Kong. In the event of war, he was to destroy the Spanish navy in the Philippines. In late March, McKinley again demanded an end to hostilities in Cuba, proposing an immediate six-month armistice and American mediation. Spain accepted part of the proposal and hedged on the rest. Both nations prepared for war.

McKinley decided to ask Congress for a declaration of war on April 11, 1898. He gave a number of reasons, but they all revolved around one assumption: peace in Cuba was necessary to the domestic tranquility of the United States. As he said, there was an "intimate connection of the

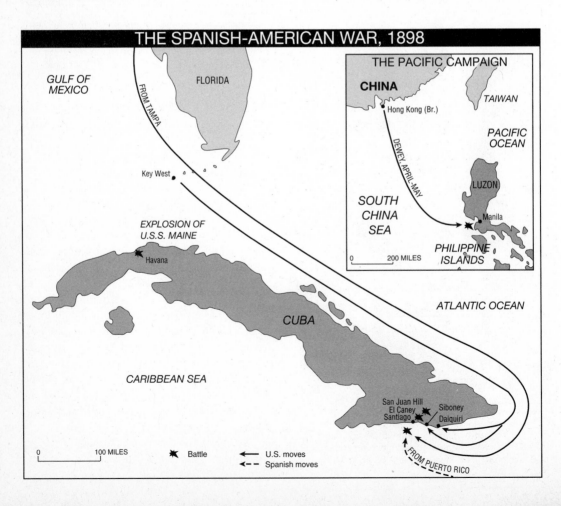

THE SPANISH-AMERICAN WAR, 1898

GULF OF MEXICO

FLORIDA

FROM TAMPA

Key West

EXPLOSION OF U.S.S. MAINE

Havana

CUBA

CARIBBEAN SEA

ATLANTIC OCEAN

San Juan Hill
El Caney
Santiago
Siboney
Daiquiri

FROM PUERTO RICO

0   100 MILES

★ Battle   ← U.S. moves   ←-- Spanish moves

THE PACIFIC CAMPAIGN

CHINA

TAIWAN

Hong Kong (Br.)

PACIFIC OCEAN

DEWEY APRIL-MAY

LUZON

SOUTH CHINA SEA

Manila

PHILIPPINE ISLANDS

0   200 MILES

Cuban question with the state of our own Union." In what became a rehearsal for policy in the Philippines, the president refused to side with the rebels; his intent was to end the rebellion. "Final military victory for either side seems impracticable," he concluded. America's purpose, in other words, was to preserve order in an area where U.S. interests were involved. On April 19, Congress declared war; one day later it proclaimed the Teller amendment renouncing any intention to annex Cuba.

Enthusiasm for the war ran high. After voting, congressmen burst into song, harmonizing to "Dixie" and the "Battle Hymn of the Republic." Much of the popular poetry of the day underscored this feeling of enthusiasm and unity. The opposing sides of the Civil War were reunited in a splendid struggle against decadent Spain. As a *Baltimore News* poet rhymed in 1898:

> *Those who wore the blue and gray,*
> *And they'll fight for common country,*
> *And they'll charge to victory*
> *'Neath the folds of one brave banner*
> *Starry banner of the free!*

For many Americans this was a romantic war, a chance for a man to prove his heroism and courage. But the conflict was over in less than four months. American casualties were slight— only 385, although deaths from disease, accidents, and other hazards pushed the total to 2,446.

In Asia the war began as a naval operation. Dewey, as ordered, steamed to the Philippines in late April and discovered the Spanish fleet huddled under shore batteries in Manila Bay. Dewey ordered an attack on May 1. Passing before the harbor and pouring fire into the motionless ships, Dewey's forces devastated the Spanish fleet. The Americans sustained no casualties at all. The city of Manila surrendered on August 13. Elsewhere in the Pacific, U.S. forces took the island of Guam on May 10, and Congress annexed Hawaii in early July.

By the time Spain sued for peace in August, the outlines of an American empire existed: a protectorate over Cuba, with claims to Puerto Rico, Guam, and the Philippines. Hawaii with its port of Pearl Harbor now belonged to the United States. The question that remained was, should the United States annex the Philippines? The islands lay thousands of miles east of America. Here was a problem that required rethinking the whole history of American foreign relations. To take the islands meant embarking on colonialism. McKinley weighed these factors carefully. He agreed that a naval station at Manila was highly desirable. But he doubted it could be defended without holding the island of Luzon and perhaps all of the Philippines. If the United States moved out, on the other hand, European powers such as Germany seemed prepared to move in. McKinley made his decision. The president forwarded his demands for the peace negotiations; Spain had no choice but to cede the islands to the United States in the Treaty of Paris, signed in December 1898. The treaty was sharply contested and barely passed the Senate, largely because of its provisions on the Philippines. America had, reluctantly, picked up the "white man's burden."

RESULTS OF THE WAR

America plunged deep into colonialism when it took the Philippines, and this decision touched off a furious debate about the meaning of the new foreign policy. Two major groups emerged: the imperialists and the anti-imperialists. But these designations are somewhat misleading. Both sides agreed that America should intervene in areas of American interest. Both wanted a dynamic international trade. But there were real differences.

The imperialists generally favored acquiring colonies. They believed that these new territories could be administered by the United States without any serious compromise of tradition or the Constitution. The anti-imperialists, led by Grover Cleveland, William Jennings Bryan, Andrew Carnegie, and civil service reformer Carl Schurz, together with a host of reformers, argued against keeping the Philippines. They drew a dividing line through American history. In the first period—up to 1899—they praised legitimate continental and territorial expansion. But taking the Philippines meant European-style colonialism. How, asked Schurz, could the United States absorb populations "incapable of becoming assimilated to the Anglo-Saxon"? For Bryan, principle overshadowed questions of race. America's mission was to liberate, "not place shackles upon those who are struggling to be free."

Most of the anti-imperialists believed that trade could be increased without colonies. They wanted a limited number of bases—a strategic empire—but not the Philippines. As many as 30,000 Americans joined the Anti-imperialist League and almost prevented passage of the peace treaty with Spain. And by 1913, they had reversed the initial victory of the imperialists regarding the formal possession of colonies. The new president, Woodrow Wilson, agreed that the Philippines should eventually be granted independence.

The Spanish-American War had other serious effects. It moved the United States closer to the sort of entangling alliances it had traditionally avoided. In the late nineteenth century, Great Britain faced a loss of its world predominance and looked around for new friends. The swift rise of Germany in Europe had upset the balance of power. Britain moved to court the Americans. After the near-collision in Venezuela, Britain strongly affirmed U.S. claims against the Spanish. In return, the United States expressed sympathy for England in its bitter colonial war in South Africa with the German-backed Boers.

The new informal alliance of Anglo-Saxon nations paid off handsomely. Britain also supported American efforts to retard Japanese, German, and Russian efforts to carve protectorates out of the Chinese empire. Secretary of State John Hay's brash "Open Door" notes of September 1899 and July 1900 demanded that European powers stop partitioning China and that they treat all nations equally in their spheres of interest. This, he hoped, would prevent the collapse of China and the exclusion of American commerce. The British agreed in principle. Other nations were far less compliant, but China did manage to avoid being partitioned by the contending European nations.

Probably more significant, Britain agreed in 1901 to the Hay-Pauncefote Treaty, which canceled prior agreements for joint U.S.-British construction of a canal across the Isthmus of Panama. The treaty freed the United States to dig the canal alone. As Hay wrote of it, the developing American-British friendship was "a sanction like that of religion which binds up to a sort of partnership in the beneficent work of the world."

—∗=◎=∗—

U.S. FOREIGN POLICY, 1901–1916

ROOSEVELT AND THE PANAMA CANAL

When an assassin's bullet brought Roosevelt into the White House in 1901, it elevated to power America's leading advocate of an activist foreign policy. But Roosevelt's actions disclosed that even he believed foreign policy had important limitations. By 1901 most of the pieces of an American empire had already fallen into place; only the Panama Canal remained to be built—"by far the most important action I took in foreign affairs," wrote Roosevelt.

By securing the independence of Panama and an American monopoly for a canal, Roosevelt reached into someone else's yard and plucked the ripest fruit. Panama had been the northernmost—and most troublesome—province of Colombia. Its greatest natural asset was favorable terrain for a shipping canal. Roosevelt encouraged Panamanian rebel leaders, who declared their independence in late 1903. Roosevelt ordered U.S. naval vessels to protect the fledgling government, and almost immediately afterward the United States signed a treaty with Panama. The new nation granted the Canal Zone to the United States plus exclusive rights to construct a canal. In exchange, the United States paid $10 million to the new republic.

Ownership of the Canal Zone and a network of bases and possessions focused American attention on the perennial instability of Central America. In December 1904, Roosevelt issued his corollary to the Monroe Doctrine. The situation of economic chaos and potential foreign intervention he described in Central America was acute. Speaking of the need to preserve "civilized society," the president declared that he would intervene in any country to restore order and decent government. If a nation "keeps order and pays its obligations," it need not fear the United States, he said. But if chaos invited foreign interference, America would intervene. Roosevelt backed up his statement with action in 1905, when he sent troops to the Dominican Republic to force it to pay its international debts.

On a very different front, Roosevelt played the role of arbitrator in the Russo-Japanese War of 1904–1905. This bitter conflict between two rising powers in Asia brought huge casualties, civil unrest in Russia, and the shocking defeat of a European nation by Japan. Roosevelt skillfully negotiated a peace treaty that called for Russian evacuation of portions of Manchuria and their withdrawal from Korea. It divided Sakhalin Island between Russia and Japan. To careful observers, this struggle portended an emerging new world in which Japan would become a leading participant and in which older European empires would be challenged. The war also confirmed the importance of naval power. For his efforts, Roosevelt won the Nobel Peace Prize. But perhaps most significant from the American perspective, he negotiated a settlement that prevented either

A GROUP OF DIGNITARIES in top hats, led by William Howard Taft, on an inspection trip of Panama Canal construction.

Japan or Russia from becoming the dominant power in East Asia.

TAFT AND "DOLLAR DIPLOMACY"

As president from 1909 to 1913, William Howard Taft continued most of Roosevelt's policies but under a new name: Dollar Diplomacy. He did not mean this term to sound crass; he merely wanted to play down the use of force. But like so much else in his administration, good intentions tripped over a bad choice of words. Taft left much of his policy making to Philander C. Knox, the new secretary of state. Knox reorganized the State Department into more efficient regional and topical divisions. Overt interventions in Latin America continued—in the Dominican Republic again, and in Honduras and Nicaragua. The purpose was to enforce order and security in areas around the Canal Zone. Taft's other purpose was to increase American economic dominance in the area. As he told Congress in 1912, he intended to support "every legitimate and beneficial enterprise abroad." He also worked hard to open European development consortiums in China to American investors.

Taft pursued this policy because he was convinced that foreign capital remained the only practical way to engineer progress in the undeveloped world and because he wished to aid American investors. Based on his experience in the Philippines and also in dealing with Cuba and Panama, he concluded that American institutions and investments would help bring enlightenment to the nonindustrialized areas of the world. Taft's legacy was, therefore, continued activism and intervention in support of American economic, political, and strategic interests without Roosevelt's rhetoric and daring.

WILSON AND MISSION DIPLOMACY

Taft's administration bridged the empire-building years of McKinley and Roosevelt with the mission diplomacy of Woodrow Wilson, which began in 1913. Wilson's assumption of the presidency brought leading anti-imperialists to power. With William Jennings Bryan as secretary of state, Wilson invoked a high moral tone in foreign relations. But much had changed since the debate over the Philippines. The United States had acquired an empire and the Panama Canal. It had established an informal alliance with the British. Involvement in the affairs of Latin American republics had increased. Wilson did not intend to undo any of these developments, but he did commit his administration to what he believed was a more responsible exercise of power.

When Wilson assumed office, ideas about America's world destiny were still very much in the air. Anglo-Saxon cultural consciousness, based on pseudoscientific theories of racial superiority, combined with traditional notions of moral mission to create a special American sense of purpose. At the same time, Americans were beginning to develop a view of the world as filled with social rebellion, insurrection, and imperial struggle.

Under Woodrow Wilson, the United States pursued a diplomacy that the president believed would confront these dangers and set new standards for international behavior. The next eight years proved the possibilities and limitations of this hope. When Wilson became president, the problems that had launched America's new foreign policy had grown more complex. The balance of power in Europe had continued to swing away from Britain; there were new rebellions in the nonindustrialized world; and American economic and political interests abroad had increased significantly. By 1917 these problems had helped draw the United States into World War I.

At first, Wilson hoped to wean American foreign policy away from the interventionism of his two predecessors. But he did not give up the idea that it was America's responsibility to act to suppress chaos. Nor did he wish to retard the growth of American trade and investment. This placed him in something of a dilemma. For example, he sympathized with the goals of the social revolutionaries in Mexico, but he intervened

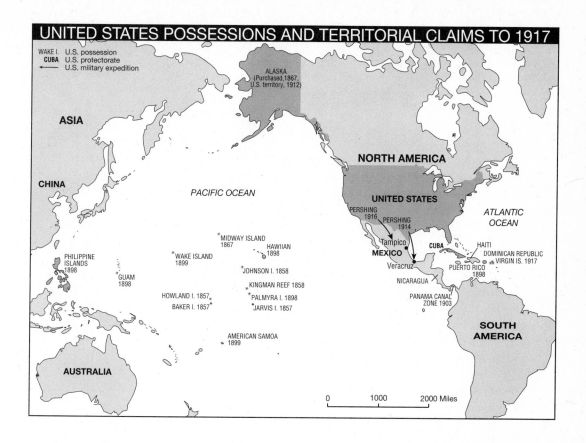

in that nation when he thought events were headed in the wrong direction. Although he found Dollar Diplomacy distasteful, he nonetheless worked to protect American trade and investments abroad. He desired to prove America's right to moral leadership, but he convinced some critics that such aims were delusive or, worse, hypocritical.

In October 1913 Wilson proclaimed a new Latin American policy: "Human rights, national integrity, and opportunity," he declared, "as against material interests—that, ladies and gentlemen, is the issue which we now have to face." In China, he terminated Taft's attempts to bring Americans into investment consortiums with European powers. And he supported Secretary of State Bryan's efforts to win international treaties of arbitration to prevent war. As a gesture, Bryan had several old swords belonging to the War Department melted down and fashioned into miniature plowshares, which he presented to the president and his cabinet.

The symbolism was clear, but the policy proved much more difficult to shape, particularly in the Western Hemisphere. From the first days of his administration, Wilson faced increasing problems with Mexico. Under the friendly regime of Porfirio Díaz up to 1910, American capital streamed into Mexico. This had two important effects: It gave control of much of the Mexican economy to Americans. And economic development increased the social strains, which in turn precipitated the Mexican Revolution. When it broke out in 1910, therefore, the revolution had serious implications for U.S. policy.

Although Wilson wanted the revolution to pursue democratic goals, he could not guide or control it. At first he tried nonrecognition as a means of convincing Mexican revolutionaries to moderate their policies. When this failed, Wilson

THE U.S. CAMPAIGN AGAINST PANCHO VILLA, 1916. In order to retaliate against Mexican revolutionary leader Pancho Villa for his raids across the American border, General John J. Pershing led an expeditionary force 300 miles into Mexico. Pershing never did capture Villa, but the American presence in Mexico greatly complicated U.S. relations with that country.

intervened militarily. Responding to what he interpreted as an insult to the nation, Wilson ordered the seizure of the Mexican port of Vera Cruz in April 1914. Eventually, General John Pershing led an American expeditionary force into Mexico during the spring and summer of 1916 to capture a Mexican troop led by Pancho Villa that had attacked across the U.S. border. At this point, however, Wilson backed off and withdrew American soldiers. But for dire events in Europe, Wilson might have intervened further. Nevertheless, considerable damage had been done. American-Mexican relations suffered for many years. Anti-Americanism became a strong element in Mexican politics. With the best of intentions, Wilson had made a bad situation worse.

WORLD WAR I

The increasingly desperate war in Europe curtailed Wilson's Mexican adventure. World War I began in late July 1914. Like the gears of a giant machine, the alliances of Europe engaged the British, French, Italians, and Russians (the Allies) against the Germans, the Austro-Hungarian empire, and Turkey (the Central Powers). Other nations joined the struggle, but the key battlefields developed in northern France and western Russia.

The outbreak of hostilities occurred in the Balkans, the most politically volatile area of Europe; it infected two tottering empires, Russia and Austria-Hungary; and it quickly spread to the most advanced industrial nations. Since the 1870s and the swift industrialization of Germany, Europe had embarked on an arms race, with each side fearing isolation and encirclement. Germany formed the Triple Alliance with Austria-Hungary and Italy. France signed an agreement with Russia and then an *entente cordiale* ("friendly understanding") with Great Britain. Competition between these two groups of nations had worldwide ramifications. Germany sought to overcome Britain's predominance in international trade and to acquire the colonies and naval bases befitting a modern imperial nation. Rivalry between these two powers inevitably came to involve other industrial nations, including the United States.

The war broke out along the explosive boundaries of Austria-Hungary and Russia. Austria-Hungary sought to repress Slavic nationals, who were supported by Russia in areas bordering the Ottoman empire (present-day Turkey), Greece, and Romania. On June 28, 1914, a member of Black Hand, a Serbian nationalist group, assassinated Archduke Francis Ferdinand, heir to the Austro-Hungarian crown. Austria declared war, the Russians (supported by France) mobilized, and Germany declared war on Russia August 1 and on France August 3. Britain entered the war against Germany August 4.

Even before its official declaration of war, Germany had initiated what it planned to be a rapid, fatal blow to France. On August 1, German troops, in accordance with the Schlieffen Plan (named after the former chief of staff), attacked. Disregarding treaties, Germany poured troops through neutral Belgium and toward northern France, hoping to trap the bulk of the French army up against heavy German defenses that lay along the northeastern borders of France. Then, with France knocked out of the war, the German armies could shift rapidly by railroad to battle the Russians.

To the dismay of the French and the British, the Schlieffen Plan worked well. Belgium reeled and collapsed under the hammer blows of the advancing German armies. British troops rushed to northern France. By early September, German armies had occupied important areas of northern France. The Allies chose this moment to counterattack along the Marne River. The battle raged from September 5 to 12, resulting in 500,000 casualties. Despite its indecisive result and lack of a clear winner, the German advance now stalled; France was spared. German plans had not anticipated the resilience of the French and British armies nor the logistical difficulties of supplying and commanding an extensive force over long lines of communication. Now the war settled down to a stalemate, disrupted by intermittent bloody thrusts to secure limited territory. Both sides constructed elaborate networks of trenches and defensive positions ringed with barbed wire and separated from each other by a "no-man's-land."

The relative immobility of the forces in France was dictated by the technology available to each side at the time. The principal weapons, artillery and the machine gun, exacted a terrible price in manpower but could not, in themselves, turn the tide of battle. Mounted cavalry, which had always been important in earlier wars, proved ineffectual. New weapons like tanks and airplanes were too few to be decisive yet. Understandably, each side sought tactics or new weapons that might tip the balance. The Germans developed and employed poison gas, which they first used in 1915. To overcome their inferior naval position, the Germans deployed submarines, which effectively attacked British shipping.

On the eastern front, the Germans were more effective because they excelled in equipment, training, and command. Joined by the Ottoman empire and Bulgaria, Germany and Austria inflicted huge losses on the Russians. Despair, disorganization, starvation, and revolution stalked Russia. The czar was deposed in March 1917, and the Bolsheviks, led by V. I. Lenin, took power in November. In mid-December, Russia signed an armistice with Germany, whose troops were now freed for a final push on the western front.

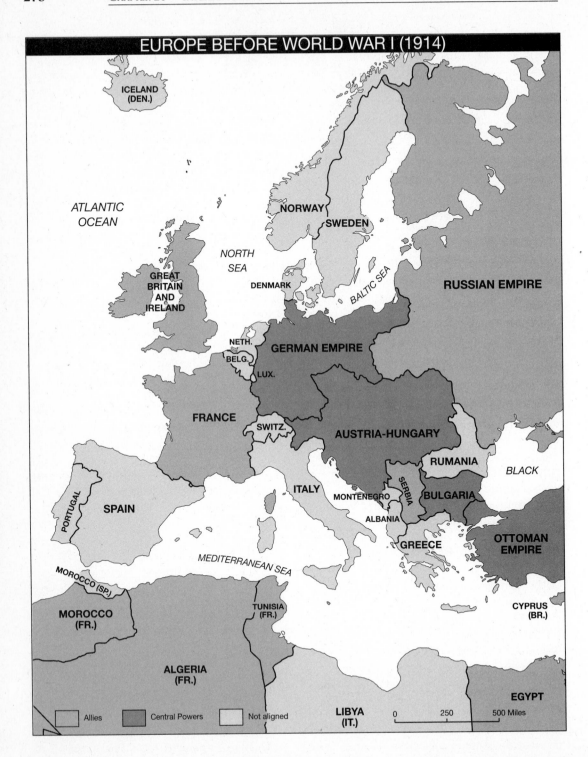

EUROPE BEFORE WORLD WAR I (1914)

ICELAND
(DEN.)

*ATLANTIC
OCEAN*

NORWAY

SWEDEN

*NORTH
SEA*

GREAT
BRITAIN
AND
IRELAND

BALTIC SEA

DENMARK

RUSSIAN EMPIRE

NETH.

GERMAN EMPIRE

BELG.

LUX.

FRANCE

SWITZ.

AUSTRIA-HUNGARY

RUMANIA

BLACK

ITALY

MONTENEGRO

SERBIA

BULGARIA

PORTUGAL

SPAIN

ALBANIA

GREECE

OTTOMAN
EMPIRE

MEDITERRANEAN SEA

CYPRUS
(BR.)

MOROCCO (SP.)

MOROCCO
(FR.)

TUNISIA
(FR.)

ALGERIA
(FR.)

EGYPT

LIBYA
(IT.)

| | Allies | | Central Powers | | Not aligned |

0   250   500 Miles

Despite this victory, Germany was still badly overextended. Its allies, the Turks and the Austro-Hungarians, suffered discouraging defeats. More serious was the tight economic blockade around Germany enforced by the British navy. Consequently, the German general staff decided in the winter of 1917 to try one last, decisive assault. In the spring of 1918 the Germans initiated a massive ground offensive, hoping to win the war before the entrance of the United States into the conflict could turn the tide.

THE UNITED STATES: FROM NEUTRALITY TO WAR

From the very beginning of the war, American economic power and trade became a major prize in the contest between the Allies and Germany. Both sides hoped to use American economic resources to their own advantage. In such a world it was extremely difficult for Wilson to maintain American neutrality, but he tried despite his Anglophilia. On August 19, 1914, the president appealed to Americans to remain "impartial in thought as well as in action." He promised that the United States would not be drawn into the conflict. Inevitably, his stance enraged war enthusiasts Theodore Roosevelt and Henry Cabot Lodge.

Try as he might, Wilson could not control events, nor did most Americans remain neutral. Many believed that Germany had ruthlessly crushed neutral Belgium. They despised German militarism and feared their new weapons such as submarines and poison gas. On the other hand, the British had angered the United States with their attempts to control American policy. Much of the large Irish-American community rooted for the defeat of England.

Wilson's greatest problem became protection of American trade and commerce, an economic traffic that became more and more oriented to the Allies. In late August 1914 the British navy (which for all practical purposes controlled surface traffic on the seas around Europe) initiated an economic blockade of the Central Powers and announced it would search ships

for contraband. Most of the goods that the Germans wished to import and the Americans hoped to export were on the banned list. Strict enforcement of the blockade caused periodic breaches between Britain and the Wilson government, particularly in the fall of 1915 and the summer of 1916.

The British tried to appease American objections while they vigorously pressed their economic strangulation of Germany. Skillful diplomacy and a large increase in British purchases of American goods made the policy work. For example, when the British placed cotton on the contraband list in 1915, they simultaneously bought American cotton to make up for the lost trade. In 1914 the value of American trade with Britain was about $600 million annually. By 1917 it had increased to over $2 billion. Smaller to begin with, German trade fell to almost nothing in 1917.

In effect, Wilson accepted the British blockade. The Germans, therefore, had to choose. They could let British-American trade flourish, or they could block it and risk sinking American ships. Germany tried at first to impose a blockade against the British Isles. Its only effective weapon was a fleet of submarines. Although no match for naval vessels on the surface, these U-boats (from *unterseeboot*, meaning "submarine") wreaked havoc on undefended merchant ships.

For two years the Germans pursued an intermittent policy of sinking merchant ships. But they dared not use their full powers for fear of forcing the United States into war. This possibility loomed in May 1915 when, without warning, a German U-boat sank the British passenger ship *Lusitania*. Although carrying some war materiel, the ship had 2,000 passengers aboard. Struck by a torpedo, the ship sank; 1,200 people, including 128 Americans, perished.

Rejecting any excuses or explanations, Wilson demanded that the Germans immediately end their attacks on merchant ships. William Jennings Bryan, rather than send this ultimatum (which he believed betrayed American neutral-

THE FACE OF MODERN WARFARE.   Hidden in trenches, looking across no-man's-land, a German soldier prepares to throw a grenade into Allied lines.

ity), resigned as secretary of state. His successor, Robert Lansing, was far more antagonistic to the Germans. But the crisis died down by summer, when the German government promised to refrain from attacking passenger ships.

The next serious confrontation occurred in the spring of 1916, when a U-boat sank the *Sussex*, an unarmed Channel steamer. This time Lansing sent an ultimatum to Germany. Either stop attacking "passenger and freight carrying vessels" he warned, or the United States would break diplomatic relations. Germany retreated again. In the meantime, America and the Allies moved closer, as Wilson allowed the British and French to borrow large sums of money from American bankers.

WAR AND PEACE

Wilson had always made it clear that in or out of the war, the United States desired a hand in settling the peace. This was the essence of his mission diplomacy. On January 22, 1917, he informed the Senate of his goals: peace without victory, the spread and support of self-government in Europe, freedom of the seas, and world disarmament. He also outlined an organization that would later become the League of Nations. The unspoken assumption was that to gain such goals, America would probably have to enter the war. Thus when Germany attacked and sank several U.S. ships early in the spring of 1917, war was inevitable, and Wilson had already anticipated how the final peace treaty might be drawn.

By the winter of 1916–1917, the Germans had decided they must win the war quickly by attacking all shipping to the Allies. In effect, they had opted for war with America. An exacerbating factor was an intercepted note from Alfred Zimmermann, the German foreign secretary, that spoke of an alliance with Mexico—with recovery of Texas, New Mexico, and Arizona as part of the agreement—which helped persuade Wilson of the necessity for war. Then on February 1, 1917, Germany declared unrestricted submarine warfare against shipping. Three days later the United States severed diplomatic relations.

The declaration of war was passed by an overwhelming majority of Congress: 82 to 6 in the Senate and 373 to 50 in the House. American troops did not reach the front until the latter part of 1917, but the navy and merchant marine rushed to protect trade routes to England and France. In 1918, before American soldiers could make a difference, the Germans tried for a quick, decisive victory. They struck five times between March and July. Successful in some respects, these moves ultimately exhausted and disheartened the German troops. Over the summer and fall, the Allies struck back. By this time, fresh American troops had entered the contest. After a final offensive in September, the Allies advanced sharply and the Germans retreated. By November, Germany had been routed. On November 11, 1918, the two sides signed an armistice, and maneuvering for a peace settlement began. Germany, Austria-Hungary, and the Ottoman empire watched helplessly as the Allied powers redrew the maps of Europe and the Middle East. Europe, meanwhile, lay devastated, with transportation, industry, and agriculture in shambles, governments in turmoil, and over 14 million dead. These were Wilson's most glorious and tragic moments.

Early in January 1918 Wilson had publicized his peace proposals, the Fourteen Points. Some of these, such as the return to France of Alsace-Lorraine and independence for the peoples of the Austro-Hungarian and Turkish empires, coincided with Allied aims. But others did not. For example, freedom of the seas and removal of trade barriers could be construed as an attack on the British empire. Among all the points, the proposed League of Nations to guarantee world peace was most important to Wilson, although some Allies viewed it with indifference.

The president traveled to Europe in early 1919, a hero to the huge crowds who greeted him. But in the peace negotiations he had no real power to impose his demands on the Allies. Thus he compromised: punitive territorial and economic measures to be exacted from the Germans; the German protectorate of Kiachow in China to be transferred to the Japanese. He did, however, win on the League of Nations. On June 28 the Germans, under duress, signed the treaty in the splendid Hall of Mirrors at the palace of Versailles outside Paris. Although something of a personal victory for Wilson, the negotiations had taken a heavy toll. One observer remarked: "I found him looking utterly worn out, exhausted, often one side of his face twitching with nervousness." In fact, he was very ill.

Wilson brought the treaty back to a deeply divided and war-weary America. The Democratic party had lost control of Congress in 1918, and Henry Cabot Lodge, an opponent of the treaty and the League of Nations, now headed the Senate Foreign Relations Committee. To such opponents, the treaty, and especially the League of Nations, seemed destined to entangle the United States forever in the machinations of European politics. To some, this appeared not to be a fitting culmination of a war to end wars and make the world permanently safe for democracy; it seemed, instead, to risk recurring wars by tying America's fortunes to the political struggles of the Europeans. Moreover, the war had caused enormous strains in American society.

WAR AT HOME

Organizing for war was a test of Wilson's progressivism. Because of long-standing hesitations, the president only acceded to a cautious and tempo-

DEFENSE EXPENDITURES BY SERVICE, 1895–1920

Year	Army	Navy
1895	$51,805,000	$28,798,000
1899	229,841,000	63,942,000
1903	118,630,000	82,618,000
1907	149,775,000	97,128,000
1911	197,199,000	119,938,000
1915	202,060,000	141,836,000
1919	9,009,076,000	2,002,311,000

Source: U.S. Department of Commerce, Bureau of the Census, Historical Statistics of the United States: Colonial Times to the Present, bicentennial ed. (Washington, D.C.: Government Printing Office, 1975), Vol. II, p. 1114.

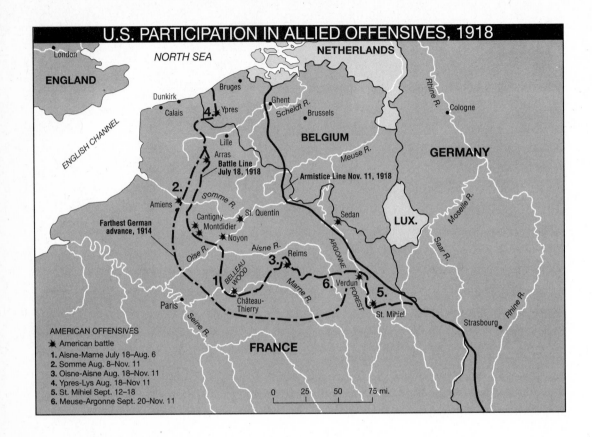

U.S. PARTICIPATION IN ALLIED OFFENSIVES, 1918

AMERICAN OFFENSIVES
✳ American battle
1. Aisne-Marne July 18–Aug. 6
2. Somme Aug. 8–Nov. 11
3. Oisne-Aisne Aug. 18–Nov. 11
4. Ypres-Lys Aug. 18–Nov 11
5. St. Mihiel Sept. 12–18
6. Meuse-Argonne Sept. 20–Nov. 11

rary experiment in executive-branch centralization. Financing the war was accomplished largely through the sale of government bonds, dubbed "Liberty" loans, rather than increased taxes. Besides training and deploying troops, the federal government's greatest tasks included coordination, supervision, and stimulating production of war goods and food. This it conducted largely through the activities of the War Industries Board, the Railroad Administration, and the Food Administration created in the spring of 1917.

Given the immense problems and the minimal coercive powers granted to these agencies, much was accomplished that had lasting effects. One notable example was the standardization by size, weight, and shape of American industrial commodities, which helped create a national market of interchangeable parts and products. In many industries, employment and wages went up, while increased demand raised farm profits. There were also huge profits to be made by companies engaged in war production.

War profiteering was only one risk of the new intimacy between government and business. The close relationship that began during the war remained afterward to undercut the broad premise of the progressive hopes for a pluralistic public interest. Moreover, Wilson's reluctance to use the power of government to regulate and guide the economy during the war opened the way for—perhaps even required—ideological coercion. This was inspired by an enthusiastic and occasionally excessive nationalism that was sometimes misdirected against unions and immigrants.

VIVE WILSON! This electric sign in Paris (which translates as Long live Wilson!) was part of the hero's welcome accorded to President Woodrow Wilson when he traveled to Europe in 1919 to negotiate a peace treaty. Despite his personal popularity, Wilson won only a compromise from America's European allies when he asked for a less harsh and punitive treaty against Germany.

Wilson's strategy of persuasion was to encourage support for the war and compliance with his economic programs through advertising and public agitation. Consequently, in 1917 he appointed progressive reformer George Creel to head the Committee on Public Information. Creel took to his job energetically, overseeing a nationwide speaking campaign of 75,000 "Four-Minute Men" (so named to recall Revolutionary War Minutemen). The committee also published 75 million pieces of prowar literature. But its strident, all-or-nothing tone led to a rigid definition of patriotism. Clearly, some of these strains must be blamed on Wilson. He had allowed the overzealous Creel to wage a vociferous propaganda campaign in favor of the war. Unfortunately, the committee had oversold its case.

Attacks on civil liberties also soured Wilson's efforts. The Espionage Act of June 1917 and the Sedition Act of May 1918 effectively outlawed criticism of the American government, its leaders, and its national symbols. Intolerance was also aimed at German-Americans by Americans with other backgrounds. In areas of large German immigrant populations in the Midwest, local authorities tried to suppress the German language and German culture. In their fiction popular writers depicted Germans as degenerate beasts. Suddenly, ethnic identity and nationalism became a dividing line. Racial intolerance also flared in this charged atmosphere, in part because African Americans moved north to fill war production jobs. One of the worst incidents was a violent race riot in 1917 in East St. Louis,

EUROPE AFTER WORLD WAR I (1925)

ICELAND
(DEN.)

*ATLANTIC
OCEAN*

NORWAY

SWEDEN

FINLAND

ESTONIA

BALTIC SEA

LATVIA

LITHUANIA

U.S.S.R.

*NORTH
SEA*

DEN.

IRISH
FREE
STATE

GREAT
BRITAIN
AND
N. IRELAND

NETH.

BELG.

LUX.

GERMANY

EAST
PRUSSIA
(GER.)

DANZIG

POLAND

FRANCE

SWITZ.

AUSTRIA

CZECHOSLOVAKIA

HUNGARY

RUMANIA

BLACK SEA

PORTUGAL

SPAIN

ITALY

YUGOSLAVIA

BULGARIA

ALBANIA

GREECE

TURKEY

CYPRUS
(BR.)

MOROCCO
(FR.)

ALGERIA
(FR.)

TUNISIA
(FR.)

MEDITERRANEAN SEA

EGYPT

LIBYA
(IT.)

Countries created after World War I

0   250   500 Miles

Illinois, in which thirty-nine blacks and nine whites died.

Attacks on radical political groups were also intense. This "red scare" drew energy from fears of the Russian Revolution of 1917, whose new government signed a separate peace with the Germans. The organization of revolutionary communist organizations in the United States, which changed the face of American radicalism, and a series of widespread strikes aroused fears that revolution might spread to America. Socialist leaders like Eugene Debs who spoke against the war were imprisoned. The federal government attacked the Industrial Workers of the World, seized their records, and deported many of their members. In this atmosphere of fear and suspicion, it was easy to conclude that America's active participation in the war—its pursuit of the new foreign policy—had resulted in contaminating the nation with the class struggle and the disorders of Europe. It seemed to threaten to compromise American uniqueness.

For a nation worried about such questions, the Versailles treaty was both too full of idealism and too riddled with compromises. Worse, it tied the United States to a permanent world organization. Wilson demanded its acceptance. Trying to arouse public support, to work around strong and articulate opposition in the Senate, he embarked on a futile speaking tour in the late summer of 1919. On September 25, 1919, in Pueblo, Colorado, he renewed his vision of America's destiny: "We have accepted the truth of America's moral vision and we are going to be led by it, and it is going to lead us, and through us the world,

out into pastures of quietness and peace such as the world never dreamed of before."

These were the words of a man who saw not just a dream of world peace but perhaps also his own final peace. The next day he suffered a stroke, collapsed, and never fully regained his old vigor. The Versailles treaty languished in Congress; Wilson refused to compromise on the League, and the Senate refused to accept the treaty as written. The dream of putting the world in order receded.

During his last year in office, Wilson rarely appeared in public. Most decisions issued in his name were made by advisers or his second wife Edith, although for a confusing period in 1920, he talked about running for a third term. By the approach of the election, issues had degenerated into considerations of personalities, and the winner of the race, Republican Warren G. Harding, took no clear stand on the problems that most divided the nation. Thus Wilson's final days trailed off into helpless frustration. He even spoke plaintively in the last year of his life of accepting a college presidency again.

The political leader who had possibly best understood the revolutionary new world that the Spanish-American War and the struggle for the Philippines brought had failed to persuade his compatriots to follow his vision of a new, democratic world order. He had personally failed, moreover, to understand the costs and pitfalls for the nation in pursuing this elusive vision. The costs of the new moral order contained in the fourteen Points were, from the perspective of the end of the war and the hindsight of many Americans, simply too high.

CHRONOLOGY

1890   United States census marks end of frontier;

Alfred T. Mahan publishes *The Influence of Sea Power upon History*;

Frederick J. Turner presents his "frontier thesis;

Grover Cleveland rejects annexation of Hawaii

1894   Cuban rebellion begins

1898 (Feb.) Battleship *Maine* explodes in Havana harbor

(Apr.) Congress declares war on Spain;

American fleet sinks Spanish fleet in Manila Bay

(Aug.) American army seizes Manila;

Spain sues for peace

1899   Philippine insurrection begins

1900   William H. Taft heads Philippine Commission;

Secretary of State John Hay announces "Open Door" policy

1901   Hay-Pauncefote Treaty signed by Britain and the United States

(Mar.) Filipino revolutionary Emilio Aguinaldo captured

(Fall) Pacification efforts begin in Batangas province

(Sept.) Massacre of American soldiers at Balangiga, Philippines

1901-1902

(Dec.–Jan.) The ordeal of Samar;

Court-martial of General Smith

(July) First Organic Act creating colonial government in the Philippines;

Pacification of the Philippines ends

1903   Panama rebels against Colombia

1909–1913 William H. Taft serves as president

1913   Woodrow Wilson announces new Latin American policy

1914 (July) World War I begins in Europe

(Sept.) Battle of the Marne, France

1915 (May) *Lusitania* sinks

1916   General John Pershing leads American troops into Mexico

1917 (Feb.) Germany announces unrestricted submarine warfare

(Apr. 2) Congress declares war on the Central Powers

(Nov.) Bolshevik revolution in Russia

1918   Wilson publishes his Fourteen Points

(Nov. 11) World War I armistice

1919(June) Treaty of Versailles completed

1920   United States debates Treaty of Versailles and rejects membership in League of Nations

SUGGESTIONS FOR FURTHER READING

DIPLOMATIC HISTORY

The field of American foreign relations at the turn of the century has recently undergone a rich and fruitful debate. The best early works in the field established the outlines of American diplomatic history. Samuel Flagg Bemis, *The Latin American Policy of the United States* (1943), is a classic study of the intricacies of diplomacy. Dexter Perkins, *A History of the Monroe Doctrine, 1867–1907* (1955), traces the development of American attitudes toward other Western Hemisphere nations. Charles S. Campbell, *The Transformation of American Foreign Relations, 1865–1900* (1976), provides an excellent, balanced, and updated account of American foreign policy in this period.

Much of the dispute over the meaning of America's foreign relations was initiated after the publication of William Appleman Williams, *Tragedy of American Diplomacy*, rev. ed. (1962). This work began a critical reevaluation of the motivations and accomplishments of foreign policy. Another principal work in this vein is Walter LaFeber, *The New Empire: An Interpretation of*

American Foreign Expansion, 1860–1898 (1963), which explores the economic and ideological impulses that triggered the American quest for empire. An excellent study in this tradition that focuses on the Orient is Thomas J. McCormick, *The China Market: America's Quest for Informal Empire, 1893–1901* (1967). Robert H. Ferrell, *Woodrow Wilson and World War I* (1985), writes convincingly of the president's successes and failures. For a good discussion of domestic policy during the war, see David M. Kennedy, *Over Here* (1980). Edward Coffman, *The War to End All Wars* (1968, 1983), provides an excellent account of the American military experience in World War I.

IMPERIALISM

A key problem to emerge in the debate over foreign relations was the meaning of imperialism and the degree to which American policy makers shared imperialist ambitions. Thomas G. Paterson, ed., *American Imperialism and Anti-Imperialism* (1973), presents the writings of imperialists and anti-imperialists as they debated such questions as acquisition of the Philippines. The best examination of the leading participants in the debate is in Robert L. Beisner, *Twelve Against Empire: The Anti-Imperialists, 1898–1900* (1968). In connection with this issue, a fascinating and influential document is Alfred Mahan, *The Influence of Sea Power upon History* (1957). Ernest R. May, in his thoughtful *American Imperialism: A Speculative Essay* (1968), offers

a different view of the origins and nature of the imperialism debate at the turn of the century. Kenton J. Clymer, *Protestant Missionaries in the Philippines, 1898–1916* (1986), explores the role and impact of the evangelicals. See also Stuart Creighton Miller's excellent *Benevolent Assimilation: The American Conquest of the Philippines 1899–1903* (1982).

LATIN AMERICAN POLICY

American foreign relations in the progressive era related largely to Latin America. Theodore Roosevelt helped establish a new foreign policy toward America's southern neighbors. A good place to begin study of Roosevelt is John Morton Blum, *The Republican Roosevelt*, 2d ed. (1977). A lively and interesting account of the Spanish-American War is Frank Freidel, *The Splendid Little War* (1958). Freidel also has an excellent book on World War I: *Over There: The Story of America's First Great Overseas Crusade*, rev. ed. (1990). P. Edward Haley, *Revolution and Intervention: The Diplomacy of Taft and Wilson with Mexico, 1910–1917* (1970), untangles the complicated and very important relations of the United States with Mexico prior to World War I. See also Arthur Link, ed., *Woodrow Wilson and a Revolutionary World, 1913–1921* (1982). Joseph Smith in *The Spanish-American War: Conflict in the Caribbean and the Pacific, 1895–1902* (1995), has the latest word on this era of expansionism.

Mass Culture and the Jazz Age

THE EPISODE: *In 1926, a New York hotel manager offered a prize of $25,000 to the first person to fly an airplane nonstop from New York to Paris. During the next two years, four planes crashed making the attempt. And in those four crashes, six aviators died and several others were badly hurt.*

But there were still men and planes ready to dare for the celebrity and the money that would come to the first who succeeded. By May 1927, no fewer than three aircraft were poised at the edge of the dirt runway of Roosevelt Field on Long Island, New York, ready to make the attempt. Two of them were large, multi-engined craft, with crews of several men. The third, called the Spirit of St. Louis, was a small, single-engine plane that could carry only one man. His name was Charles A. Lindbergh, and he and his airplane were about to become the most adored objects of a decade that was hungry for celebrities and symbols. When the other crews were waiting for the weather to improve, Lindbergh decided to chance a difficult takeoff from a rainy and muddy field. He would make it to Paris. More importantly, he would make it into the minds and hearts of the first generation of Americans who had the means to confer instant media fame on the people they chose as their heroes.

THE HISTORICAL SETTING: *Lindbergh's feat was in many ways only a stunt and of no practical importance. For the historian, the significance of the flight does not lie in what it reveals about him or about the history of aviation. Instead, the significance of Lindbergh's flight lies in the terms in which it was celebrated, the ways the American public—the white, middle-class public, at least—transformed a stunt into a feat and transformed Lindbergh himself into a symbol of what they wanted to believe America was all about: youth and innocence combined with daring and technological mastery.*

Much of what makes up the romantic images of the 1920s—the notion of the "Roaring Twenties" or the "Jazz Age," or the idea of the "Lost Generation"—began to take shape in the progressive period. And the echoes of the 1920s lasted far beyond 1930. Nevertheless, the 1920s were the decade in which all the pieces necessary for the formation of a relatively homogenous middle-class media "public" fell into place—the press, radio, motion pictures, and urban affluence.

The 1920s had another side, of course. Intellectuals produced an impressive body of writing and art that was extremely critical of the so-called "New Era." For the first time, a truly remarkable community of African-American artists and writers assembled in Harlem and generated what became known as the Harlem Renaissance. And white writers, musicians, and artists in centers like Chicago, New York, and Paris produced an equally imposing body of novels, poetry, music, and painting that explored the dark side of the decade.

LINDBERGH'S FLIGHT

The captain was a little man, dapper and very French. But he sought a big prize: $25,000 for the first person to fly an airplane from New York to Paris. His name might sound somewhat strange—even funny—to American ears: René Fonck. But his reputation was formidable. He had been the youngest French air ace in the Great War (as World War I was called until World War II). Without being seriously injured himself, he had shot down at least seventy-five German planes. In a war that had turned the new aviators into overnight heroes, Fonck's reputation for skill, courage, and dash was probably greater than that of any other pilot. Now, in the summer of 1926, he was preparing for a flight that could make him an even greater hero, both in France and in the United States.

Compared with any of the planes Fonck had flown during the war, his new silver-colored craft was very large. It had three engines and two pairs of wings—a "biplane," it was called. Its large cabin was equipped for a crew of four: a pilot, a copilot, a mechanic, and a radio operator. The main problem that Fonck faced was simply getting the big plane off the ground with enough fuel to fly the 3,600 miles to Paris. All summer he carefully tested the plane in New York, gradually increasing the gasoline load for each test.

At daybreak on September 21, Fonck's plane was pulled onto the east-west runway at Roosevelt Field, a small airport on Long Island. The wind was blowing from the west. So Fonck would take off from east to west. To get the plane off the ground, he and his crew would have to attain a speed of eighty miles an hour. One by one, the three engines were turned up to their maximum power. The blocks were pulled away from the wheels, and the plane began to move. It lurched slightly, under the weight of 2,000 gallons of gasoline, and chased its own awkward shadow down the dirt runway.

When the plane passed the halfway point on the runway, it did not have the speed needed for takeoff. The small crowd of onlookers waited for Fonck to cut power and abort the takeoff. But something had gone wrong, either with the pilot or with his controls. The plane simply roared on. The runway ended. The plane took a sharp, short drop into a gully, then exploded and burst into flames. Somehow Fonck got out, and so did his navigator. But the copilot and the radio operator burned to death.

Despite the crash, the man who had offered the $25,000 prize—Raymond Orteig, a Frenchman who managed two hotels in New York—announced that his offer still stood. For a while Fonck's crash made headlines and kept alive the idea of a New York–Paris flight. Late in February 1927 others began to announce that they would make the flight. It was soon obvious that a real contest was developing. It would not be merely a battle between one airplane and the Atlantic Ocean but a race among several aviators and their planes. The stage was set for what the public began to sense would be the greatest "thrill" of the decade.

By the end of March 1927 there were four serious contenders. One was the *America*, a plane piloted by Admiral Richard E. Byrd, who had already gained fame as the first man to fly to the North Pole. Byrd was backed with over $100,000 from a wealthy New York merchant. His three-engine plane, with a wingspan of over seventy feet, was enormous by the standards of the day. It seemed to have the best chance.

A second entry was another three-engine craft, the *American Legion*, named after and supported by the veterans' organization. It too was backed with $100,000. Unlike Fonck's plane and Byrd's *America*, the *American Legion* carried only two men. A third entry was a plane known as the *Columbia*, a single-wing, single-engine craft. The *Columbia* would soon set the world endurance record by flying nonstop for over fifty hours. Finally, there was a French entry, a single-engine biplane called the *White Bird*. Its pilot and copilot, a pair of French flying "aces" from the Great War, planned to make the flight in reverse—from Paris to New York. The *White Bird* was said to have the most powerful gasoline engine ever put into an airplane.

By mid-April the weather had warmed up enough to make flight over the North Atlantic possible. On April 16 Admiral Byrd took his *America* up from a New Jersey airport for its first test flight. Byrd and three crewmen flew the plane for a few hours and then brought it down for its first landing. The heavy landing gear touched ground smoothly, but almost at once there was a sound of splintering wood and wrenched metal. The *America* flipped over and skidded to a halt on its back. All four men managed to escape. Byrd had a broken wrist, and two of the other crewmen were badly hurt. They would not be able to fly again for weeks.

Ten days later the *American Legion* was at Langley Field, in Virginia, undergoing its last test flight. The plane had flown well in earlier attempts, but both its designers and its pilot knew it was too heavy. To find out whether the plane could make the Paris flight, the pilot and copilot decided to fly it from Virginia to New York with a full load of gasoline. The takeoff was slower than usual. For a moment it seemed the plane would not clear a line of trees at the end of the runway. To avoid them, the pilot banked to the right a few degrees. But even this slight turn was too much, upsetting the delicate balance of the plane. The *American Legion* rolled over and went down into a wet marsh, on its back. The pilot and copilot were trapped inside, hanging upside down in the cabin, which filled first with gasoline fumes and then with water. By the time rescuers came wading through the marsh, the two men were dead.

Four men had been killed and three others hurt, and the race over the Atlantic had not yet begun. On both sides of the ocean, in America and in France, newspapers stirred public excitement to a high pitch. Surely one of the planes would make it, sooner or later. But no one knew what might happen next or who might be injured or killed. The race to Paris had the competitive excitement of a baseball World Series or a heavyweight championship fight. And it had the danger and drama of war. In the United States the race gained as much importance in the press as had the war of 1898, the sinking of the *Lusitania,* or even the declaration of war in 1917. In France the excitement was heightened by the memory of Fonck's crash. The excitement was fastened on the two young "air aces," Charles Nungesser and Francis Coli, who would fly the *White Bird*. Both had been wounded in air combat during the war—a total of twenty-six times. Between them they had won almost every medal that the French government could award.

At dawn on May 8, Nungesser and Coli took off for New York from Le Bourget airport near Paris. A great crowd gathered to watch. Nungesser got the wheels off the ground, but too soon. The White Bird dropped back down onto the runway with a thud. Finally, it gathered speed and left the ground, almost two-thirds of a mile down the long strip.

The next morning, American newspapers reported that the plane had been sighted over Newfoundland. Paris celebrated with an excitement that almost matched that of the day of the armistice. Nungesser and Coli had dropped their landing gear over the ocean, to save weight and lessen wind resistance. New Yorkers watched the harbor, where the Frenchmen hoped to land on the water and keep afloat until they could be reached by waiting boats. But the *White Bird* was never seen again. In France the premature celebrations quickly came to a shocked end.

The death toll in the New York–Paris race had reached six in less than a year. The world's most experienced pilots—backed by large sums of money, flying the best airplanes that modern technology could provide, with the most powerful motors ever developed—had all failed.

The man who was finally going to win the race to Paris had been reading every newspaper report he could find on all the airplane tests, takeoffs, and crashes. When Fonck's plane burned, Charles Lindbergh was flying airmail between Chicago and St. Louis. When Byrd and the others announced they would enter the competition, Lindbergh was in San Diego supervising the construction of a new plane for himself. When Nungesser and Coli took off from Paris, he was waiting in San Diego for the weather to clear over the Rocky Mountains and the Great Plains, so he could fly east to St. Louis. From there he would go on to New York to make his attempt.

Lindbergh had only $2,000 of his own money, carefully kept for him by his mother in Detroit. He was only twenty-five years old—too young to have flown in the Great War. He looked even younger, so that almost everyone called him a "boy." Worst of all, he decided on what struck everyone as a suicidal idea: to make the flight in a single-engine plane with only himself in the cockpit. He had been able to persuade some St. Louis businessmen to back him with $15,000. But this was a small sum compared to the support that Byrd's group and the American Legion had. Still, late in the summer of 1926, just before Fonck's crash, Lindbergh had come to an almost religious conviction that he could make the Paris flight.

At first Lindbergh had tried to negotiate with several large aircraft companies for a plane. He was turned down. No one wanted to risk a company's reputation on an insane stunt like flying from New York to Paris alone. Then Lindbergh sent a plain but daring telegram to Ryan Airlines, a small, little-known factory in California:

FEB. 3, 1927

RYAN AIRLINES, INC.
SAN DIEGO, CALIFORNIA

CAN YOU CONSTRUCT WHIRLWIND ENGINE PLANE CAPABLE OF FLYING NONSTOP BETWEEN NEW YORK AND PARIS? IF SO PLEASE STATE COST AND DELIVERY DATE.

The answer came surprisingly quickly. The small company could build the plane, and it could do so for the amount of money Lindbergh had at his disposal. But it would take three months, the telegram said. Lindbergh answered:

FEB. 5, 1927

RYAN AIRLINES, INC.
SAN DIEGO, CALIFORNIA

COMPETITION MAKES TIME ESSENTIAL. CAN YOU CONSTRUCT PLANE IN LESS THAN THREE MONTHS? PLEASE WIRE GENERAL SPECIFICATIONS.

Again the company answered quickly, making as much of a guess as a calculation. It could build a plane capable of carrying 380 gallons of gasoline at a cruising speed of 100 miles per hour, with an engine rated at only 200 horsepower. (This was less than half the power of the big engine that had taken the *White Bird* out over the Atlantic. It was also much less than the power supplied by the three engines of Byrd's great *America*.) Most important, the company promised to have the plane ready in time.

By the last week in February, Lindbergh was in San Diego working out the details on his plane. Neither Lindbergh nor the engineer who designed the plane even knew exactly the distance between New York and Paris. They drove to the San Diego public library to measure it off on a globe with a piece of string. Lindbergh remembered it this way:

"It's 3,600 miles." The bit of white grocery string under my fingers stretches taut along the coast of North America, bends down over a faded blue ocean, and strikes the land mass of Europe. It isn't a very scientific way of finding the exact distance between two points on the earth's surface, but the answer is accurate enough for our first calculations. The designer was making quick calculations in pencil on the back of an envelope. "Maybe we'd better put in 400 gallons of gasoline instead of 380," he concludes.[1]

Lindbergh's project was simple, almost amateurish: hastily drafted telegrams, bits of string stretched across a globe, figures on the back of an envelope, and "maybe" calculations. But with no more detailed or expert plans, he decided to go ahead.

The mechanics and carpenters at Ryan started work at once on the plane that Lindbergh would call the *Spirit of St. Louis*. They built it almost literally around the pilot. The narrow, simple cockpit was just large enough to hold Lindbergh's tall, skinny body (and then only if the wooden overhead ribs were scooped out a little to make room for his head). In the end, the plane would be only about three feet taller than Lindbergh himself. It would have a much smaller engine than any of the other planes in the race. But this was the secret of Lindbergh's plane: simplicity. He would build the smallest, simplest plane possible, a machine designed with only one purpose: to carry enough gasoline for the trip. Everything else—comfort, safety, navigating equipment—would be sacrificed to save weight, which could be devoted to more gallons of gasoline.

---

[1]*Quotations from* The Spirit of St. Louis *by Charles A. Lindbergh are reprinted with permission of Charles Scribner's Sons, an imprint of Macmillan Publishing Company. Copyright 1953 Charles Scribner's Sons; copyright renewed 1981 Anne Morrow Lindbergh.*

BEFORE THE FLIGHT. This publicity photograph of Lindbergh and the *Spirit of St. Louis* was taken some time before the flight. Lindbergh may have been shy, but he fully understood the need to publicize his daring effort. And he knew how to emphasize the solitary nature of his flight by posing himself and his plane as though they were partners.

On April 26, the day the two pilots of the *American Legion* were killed in Virginia, the *Spirit of St. Louis* was finished. Two days later Lindbergh was ready for his first test flight. He squeezed himself into his seat in the cockpit. He could touch both sides of the tiny cabin with his elbows. To the front, the cockpit was blind. Shiny metal sloped all the way up from the engine to the top of the wing. There were only two side windows and a glassed-in skylight overhead. For takeoffs and landings he had to lean out of one of the side windows. But the plane was designed for only one important takeoff and landing. The rest of the time, over the Atlantic, there would be nothing to see but ocean, clouds, sun, and stars.

Directly in front of Lindbergh's face was a small cluster of instruments: an airspeed indicator, a turn-and-bank indicator, a fuel-flow meter, a compass, and one or two others. The plane carried a pitifully small survival kit containing a rubber raft, a flashlight, a canteen of water, some matches, and string. Surrounding the cockpit were nothing but gasoline tanks. One tank rested in the nose between the pilot and the engine. Another lay behind the cockpit in the fuselage. And there were more tanks in the wings overhead. There was no radio, no heater to provide warmth at freezing altitudes, no sextant for navigational sightings, not even a parachute. The *Spirit of St. Louis* was built to carry only its pilot and the all-important gasoline—over a ton of it, as it turned out, weighing more than the plane and the pilot put together.

But to Lindbergh, as he walked onto the sunny runway in San Diego, the *Spirit of St. Louis* was a thing of beauty and awe:

> What a beautiful machine it is, resting there on the field in front of the hangar, trim and slender, gleaming in its silver coat! All our ideas, all our calculations, all our hopes, lie there before me, waiting to undergo the acid test of flight. For me, it seems to contain the whole future of aviation.
>
> "Off! Throttle closed."
>
> I'm in the cockpit. The chief mechanic turns the propeller over several times.
>
> "Contact!"
>
> He swings his body away from the blade as he pulls it through. The engine catches, every cylinder hitting. This is different from any other cockpit I've been in before. The big fuel tank in front of me seems doubly large, now that I'm actually to fly behind it.
>
> I signal the chocks [blocks] in front of the wheels of the plane away. The *Spirit of St. Louis* rolls lightly over the baked-mud surface of the field.

The *Spirit of St. Louis* moved very quickly. Its tanks were almost empty for this first test flight.

> The tires are off the ground before they roll a hundred yards. The plane climbs quickly, even though I hold its nose down. There's a huge reserve of power. I spiral cautiously upward. I straighten out and check my instruments. I circle over the factory, watching little figures run outdoors to see the machine they had built actually flying overhead. I rock my wings and head across the bay.

During the next week Lindbergh tested the *Spirit of St. Louis* for speed, control, and, most important, takeoff under load. More and more gasoline was filtered by hand into the tanks for each run. With a load of slightly over 300 gallons, the plane took off easily. But continued landings with large loads were dangerous. Lindbergh decided to stop the tests.

The *Spirit of St. Louis* had needed a little more than 1,000 feet of runway to take off with 300 gallons of fuel. From this and other data, the Ryan designers made a rough calculation: fully loaded with 400 gallons the plane would need 2,500 feet of firm runway to get into the air safely. Rather than tempt fate by testing this calculation—as the crew of the *American Legion* had done—Lindbergh decided to trust the plane and the designers' arithmetic. He was ready. And he knew Byrd's *America* had been repaired and was undergoing final tests. The *Columbia*, too, was ready. Both planes were poised on Long Island. Time counted more than tests.

But time seemed to work against Lindbergh. A big storm blanketed the western United States and was creeping eastward. Lindbergh had to wait several days until the rain and clouds cleared. On the evening of May 10 he began the first leg of his trip, from San Diego to St. Louis. He flew the 1,500 miles in record time. It was the longest nonstop solo flight ever made. After just one night's sleep, he headed for New York.

Lindbergh arrived on Long Island May 12. He had set another record, for the fastest transcontinental flight in history. The crews of Byrd's *America* and the *Columbia* came over to shake his hand and wish him luck. A crowd gathered. Newspaper

INSIDE THE *SPIRIT OF ST. LOUIS*.
The cockpit of Lindbergh's plane was a model of stripped-down efficiency. The wicker seat may have been uncomfortable, but it was lightweight, and weight was Lindbergh's main concern. The plane had only side windows, so the pilot could not see much—for most of the flight, though, there was nothing to see. In any case, the most important thing Lindbergh had to watch for was ice on the wings.

photographers and reporters pushed and shoved their way to Lindbergh, shouting for pictures and answers to their questions. A horde of people climbed to the roof of a small building next to the hangar where Lindbergh parked the plane. Their weight caused a wall to collapse. Something new and strange was happening to Lindbergh. The newspapers and the public were making him into a hero, almost an instant American myth.

Even without Lindbergh, the New York–Paris contest had all the elements of an exciting publicity event: death, drama, and competition. But Lindbergh's entry into the race added new elements. He was going alone, thus he could become an object of hero worship in ways that the crews of the other planes could not. He was tall, thin, blue-eyed, and handsome in a boyish way. And along with his youthful good looks went other personality traits that soon endeared him to the newspapers. Above all, he was modest, shy, and simple.

All these traits combined to present a picture of an innocent young man ready to dare the impossible, alone. Lindbergh was the honest, plainspoken, cowboy-like young man from the West. He was an attractive underdog, a modern David challenging the

Eastern Goliaths, with their money, their experience, their financial backers—and their head start. The *Spirit of St. Louis*, too, was simple and seemingly innocent compared with the other, more sophisticated aircraft in the race. It quickly became a sentimental favorite in the newspapers.

Lindbergh could not leave his hotel room without being mobbed by people anxious to touch him, "just for luck." And the newspapers played his story for all it was worth. They nicknamed him "Lucky," "The Flyin' Fool," or just "Lindy." (He had always been "Slim" to his friends.) All the hero worship that the Americans of the 1920s usually reserved for baseball players like Babe Ruth or movie stars like Rudolph Valentino was now showered on the twenty-five-year-old airmail pilot. The worship was made more serious by the fact that "The Flyin' Fool" was doing something real and dangerous, not merely hitting baseballs or posing for motion picture cameras.

In most ways this public personality created for the new "celebrity" had little to do with reality. Lindbergh may not have had Byrd's $100,000, but he had finally obtained solid backing from St. Louis businessmen. And even if the *Spirit of St. Louis* was smaller than the other planes, it was still a sophisticated piece of machinery, created by advanced technology. It was a little silly for newspapers to write of Lindbergh and his plane as though they were a cowboy hero and his beloved horse.

Nor was Lindbergh's background as "simple" as the newspapers tried to make it appear. He came from a well-to-do, educated family. His father had been a congressman. Lindbergh had been to college for a time and held a commission as captain in the Army Air Service Reserve and the Missouri National Guard. He had been chief pilot for an airmail company in St. Louis. He was, despite his youth, an experienced professional pilot, flying a state-of-the-art machine.

But there was just enough truth to the mythical picture to make it stick. It probably infected Lindbergh somewhat, too. He had always been a bit "wild," even though he *was* shy. Cars, motorcycles, ice boats—anything that involved speed—had always fascinated him. When he was just twenty he dropped out of college to learn to fly. He bought his first craft, a war-surplus plane, even before he had made a solo flight, and he almost crashed it on his first takeoff.

Lindbergh had "barnstormed" all over the West, crashing regularly and surviving only with luck. He had walked on airplane wings while in flight and done dangerous parachute jumps for one "aerial circus" after another. Four times he had been forced to parachute for his life from planes that had collided, run out of gas, or gotten lost at night.

All this, combined with Lindbergh's seeming boyishness and his determined faith in himself and his plane, did smack of something faintly supernatural and mythical. So the hero worship that began almost as soon as he reached Long Island was probably inevitable. At times the publicity and the public attention irritated Lindbergh. Reporters went so far as to burst into his hotel room without knocking to discover what kind of pajamas, if any, he wore to bed. But the irritation could not overcome the excitement. Lindbergh was becoming, even before takeoff, a national hero.

The *Columbia* was scheduled to take off May 13, the day after Lindbergh reached Long Island. But the weather was closed in over New York and the North Atlantic. The same storm that had delayed Lindbergh in San Diego was making its slow progress north and east. So the *Columbia* had to wait. Lindbergh was able to test and tune his engine, to check and recheck every instrument. A noisy crowd that sometimes numbered over a thousand gathered around the hangar to watch him. By May 16 he was ready. As far as he could tell, Byrd was ready too. In the *Columbia* organization there was a legal quarrel over who would be the pilot. One of the men who had trained for the flight had secured a court order preventing the plane from taking off without him. But the court order could be lifted at any minute. So there seemed to be a real chance that two or possibly even three planes would take off from Roosevelt Field on the same morning.

The spring rains persisted for three more days. Then, on the evening of May 19, the forecast called for clearing skies. Though it was not clearing rapidly, Lindbergh made his decision. He would fly, even if it meant taking off into a rainy sky from a muddy field—not the firm runway the Ryan designers had assumed in their calculations of how much gasoline their plane could lift. He bought five sandwiches "to go." A few hours later the *Spirit of St. Louis* was towed to the west end of the Roosevelt Field runway. Lindbergh had decided to take off before dawn. Not far behind his plane was the scorched area where René Fonck's plane had burned. The spot was still marked by a bent propeller stuck into the ground as a tribute.

Slowly, carefully, mechanics strained 5-gallon cans of gasoline into Lindbergh's plane. The oversize tanks had a capacity of 450 gallons instead of the 400 that the designers had planned earlier. Lindbergh decided to fill them to the brim, even though it meant a dangerous overload for a takeoff in the mud. In the hangars of the *America* and the *Columbia*, there was only darkness and silence. No one else was going to risk flying on this wet morning.

As he looked over the situation, Lindbergh also wondered whether he should make the attempt. He was overloaded with gasoline. The wheels of the *Spirit of St. Louis* sank into the wet earth, as though warning him that flight was out of the question. The wet weather affected the engine, which turned about thirty revolutions per minute slower than it should have at full power. Worst of all, the process of getting ready took so long that Lindbergh lost the dawn wind. By the time he was ready, the breeze had shifted to his back, creating a dangerous tailwind of five or six miles per hour. This meant he would need even more speed on takeoff.

Lindbergh's only guidelines were the San Diego calculations. They had shown, roughly, that with 400 gallons of gas he should be able to take off in 2,500 feet on a dry field, with no wind, and with full engine power. But he had 450 gallons of gas, a soggy field, a laboring engine, and a wind at his back. At the end of the Roosevelt Field runway were a ditch, a parked tractor, some telephone wires, and then a hill with a line of trees. He had to clear them all. He considered towing the *Spirit of St. Louis* through the misty rain and mud to the other end of the runway to get the help of the wind. He thought about postponing the flight altogether. But he decided instead to go.

Lindbergh looked around at the crowd that had gathered to watch. Nearby were mechanics, some engineers, and several policemen, all looking into the dark cockpit at his pale face.

> Their eyes are intently on mine. They've seen planes crash before. I lean against the side of the cockpit and look ahead, through the idling blades of the propeller, over the runway's glistening surface. I study the telephone wires and the shallow pools of water through which my wheels must pass. A curtain of mist shuts off all trace of the horizon. Sitting in the cock-

pit, in seconds, minutes long, the conviction surges through me that the wheels will leave the ground, that the wings will rise above the wires, that it is time to start the flight.

I buckle my safety belt, pull goggles down over my eyes, turn to the men at the blocks, and nod. Frozen fingers leap to action. I brace myself against the left side of the cockpit and ease the throttle wide open.

The *Spirit of St. Louis* feels more like an overloaded truck than an airplane. The tires rut through mud as though they really were on truck wheels. Even the breath of wind is pressing me down. The engine's snarl sounds inadequate and weak.

A hundred yards of runway passes. How long can the landing gear stand such strain? I keep my eyes fixed on the runway's edge. I must hold the plane straight. Pace quickens— the tail skid lifts off ground—I feel the load shifting from wheels to wings. The halfway mark is just ahead, and I have nothing like flying speed.

The halfway mark streaks past. Seconds now to decide. I pull the stick back firmly, and— the wheels leave the ground! The wheels touch again. I ease the stick forward. Almost flying speed and nearly 2,000 feet ahead. The entire plane trembles. Off again—right wing low—pull it up—ease back onto the runway. Another pool, water drumming on the fabric covering the fuselage. The next hop's longer. I could probably stay in the air, but I let the wheels touch once more.

The *Spirit of St. Louis* takes herself off next time. Full flying speed. The controls taut, alive, straining—and still a thousand feet to the telephone wires. If the engine can hold out one more minute. Five feet, twenty, forty. Wires flash by underneath. Twenty feet to spare!

Green grass below—a golf links. People looking up. A low, tree-covered hill ahead. The *Spirit of St. Louis* seems balanced on a pinpoint, as though the slightest movement of controls would cause it to topple over and fall. Five thousand pounds suspended from those little wings. Five thousand pounds on a blast of air.

Now I'm high enough to steal glances at the instrument board. The earth inductor compass needle leans steeply to the right. I bank cautiously northward until it rises to the center line—65 degrees—the compass heading for the first 100-mile segment of my great-circle route to France and Paris. It's 7:54 a.m. Eastern daylight time.

Back in San Diego, when Lindbergh and the designer of the *Spirit of St. Louis* had measured the distance of the flight across a library globe, the string had made a straight line between New York and Paris. But on a flat map, where the lines of longitude are straightened out into parallels, the route had to bend into an arc known as a "great circle." The route Lindbergh would take curved north and east from New York, up the coast over Cape Cod, then out over the ocean to Nova Scotia. Lindbergh planned to change his compass course every hundred miles (about one hour's flying time). He would head a few degrees farther south and east across the southern coast of Newfoundland and then out over the North Atlantic.

As Lindbergh flew up the coast on this route, people waited on streets and housetops to watch him pass. Despite the fact that his navigating equipment was primitive, he managed to reach the Nova Scotia coast only a few miles off course. Every hour, excited messages were telephoned to New York giving details of his progress. In the twelfth hour of his flight, Lindbergh passed over St. John's, Newfoundland, then out over the ocean:

> I come upon it suddenly—the little city of St. John's—after skimming over the top of a granite summit. Farther ahead, the entrance to the harbor is a narrow gap with sides running up to the crest of a low coastal range. Twilight deepens as I plunge down into the valley. It takes only a moment, stick forward, engine throttled, to dive down over the wharves (men stop their after-supper chores to look upward) and out through the gap. North America and its islands are behind. Ireland is 2,000 miles ahead.

Throughout the flight, Lindbergh faced the ever-present hazards of engine failure, storms, and the possibility of a structural weakness in the plane itself. But between Newfoundland and Ireland there were two additional dangers. The first was sleep. Lindbergh had not slept at all the night before his takeoff. During the next night and the day after, as he flew over the ocean, he fought back the terrible temptation to close his eyes for just a few seconds of rest. The *Spirit of St. Louis* was not a very stable plane. Lindbergh knew that if he relaxed his hold on it for more than a moment, he might crash. He had to hold his eyes open with his hands. Once he even had to hit himself full force in the face to keep awake.

The second peril was ice. This danger came upon Lindbergh suddenly after he had climbed over 10,000 feet, trying to clear a bank of clouds about 200 miles east of Newfoundland. He was suddenly aware of being cold himself. (He had left the glass out of the side windows of the plane, hoping that the fresh air and engine noise would keep him alert.) Cold? He jerked himself wide awake. If he was cold, what about his plane?

> Good Lord! There are things to be considered outside the cockpit! How could I forget! I jerk off a leather mitten and thrust my arm out the window. My palm is covered with stinging pinpricks. I pull the flashlight from my pocket and throw its beam on a strut. The entering edge is irregular and shiny! Ice!

> I've got to turn around, get back to clear air—quickly!

But Lindbergh fought the urge to make a sudden turn. He knew that if he did, the ice on the wings might cause the plane to go out of control. Instead, he eased the *Spirit of St. Louis* around in a long, slow curve back toward Newfoundland.

> I throw my flashlight beam onto the wing strut. Ice is thicker! Steady the plane. Everything depends on the turn indicator working till I get outside the cloud. Just two or three more minutes.

> My eyes sense a change in the blackness of my cockpit. I look out through the window. How bright! What safety have I reached! I was in the thunderhead for ten minutes at most, but it's one of those incidents that can't be measured by minutes. Such periods stand out like islands in a sea of time.

After this brief but dangerous encounter with the night sky, Lindbergh picked his way cautiously toward Ireland and dawn. (Since he was flying west to east, into the sunrise, he was experiencing the shortest night any person ever had.) He sipped cautiously at his quart canteen of water. The rest of the time, he just flew his plane, waiting for moonrise, then sunrise. Then came the twenty-eighth hour of his flight.

> I keep scanning the horizon through breaks between squalls. Is that a cloud on the northeastern horizon, or a strip of low fog—or—can it possibly be land? It looks like land, but I

don't intend to be tricked by another mirage. I'm only sixteen hours out of Newfoundland. I allowed eighteen and one-half hours to strike the Irish coast.

But my mind is clear. I'm no longer half asleep. The temptation is too great. I can't hold my course any longer. The *Spirit of St. Louis* banks over toward the nearest point of land.

I stare at it intently, not daring to believe my eyes, watching the shades and contours unfold into a coastline. Now I'm flying above the foam-lined coast, searching for prominent features to fit the chart on my knee. I've climbed to 2,000 feet so I can see the contours of the country better. Yes, there's a place on the chart where it all fits—Valentia and Dingle Bay, on the southwestern coast of Ireland! I can hardly believe it's true. I'm almost exactly on my route, closer than I hoped to come in my wildest dreams back in San Diego. What happened to all those detours of the night around the thunderheads? Where has the swinging compass error gone?

Intuition must have been more accurate than reasoned navigation.

The southern tip of Ireland! On course, over two hours ahead of schedule; the sun still well up in the sky, the weather clearing!

Now it was easy. So easy that Lindbergh himself fell into the temptation of making a myth out of his own achievement:

I'm angling slowly back onto my great-circle route. I must have been within three miles of it when I sighted Ireland. An error of fifty miles would have been good dead reckoning under the most perfect conditions. Three miles was—well, what was it? Before I made this flight, I would have said carelessly that it was luck. Now, luck seems far too trivial a word, a term to be used only by those who've never seen the curtain drawn or looked on life from far away.

After Ireland the landmarks appeared rapidly—a lighthouse, the coast of England and then the coast of France, "like an outstretched hand to meet me." For the first time, Lindbergh felt hungry. He ate one of the sandwiches he had bought in New York, stale and dry now. He picked up a series of beacons marking the route between London and Paris. Then the city rose before him. He circled the brightly lit Eiffel Tower and then turned northeast to look for Le Bourget. "You can't miss it," he had been told, as though he were some sort of tourist.

It was almost ten o'clock at night in Paris. Lindbergh was confused by an incredible number of lights around the dark spot where the airport ought to be. A factory? he wondered. He did not know that he had suddenly become the most famous man in the world. Thousands of Parisians had rushed out to the airport to greet the American flyer. The roads leading to Le Bourget were jammed with cars with headlights blazing.

Finally, Lindbergh was able to pick out floodlights showing the edge of a runway. He dragged the field once, flying low over it to check for obstructions—a tractor or maybe some sheep let out to crop the grass, he thought. Then he brought the plane in as carefully as possible, as though he were teaching a student to fly. The plane felt sluggish. By his guess he still carried a lot of gasoline. His own reflexes seemed slow. Lind-

THE HERO'S WELCOME HOME. Lindbergh probably became a more famous celebrity, more quickly, than any American ever had. Here, in a parade in New York City, he is welcomed home among the crowds, the fanfare, and the flags that followed him everywhere.

bergh had never landed the *Spirit of St. Louis* at night. He glided in at an angle so he could peer out of his side window.

> It's only a hundred yards to the hangars now. I'm too high, too fast. Drop wing. Left rudder. Careful. Still too high. I push the stick over. Below the hangar roofs now. Straighten out. A short burst of the engine. Over the lighted areas. Sod coming up to meet me. Careful. Easy to bounce when you're tired. Still too fast. Tail too high. Hold off. Hold off. But the lights are far behind. Ahead, there's nothing but night. Give her the gun and climb for another try?
>
> The wheels touch gently. Off again. No, I'll keep contact. Ease the stick forward. Back on the ground. Off. Back, the tail skid too. Not a bad landing, but I'm beyond the light. Can't see anything ahead. The field must be clear. Uncomfortable, though, jolting into blackness. Wish I had a wing light, but too heavy on the takeoff. Slower now, slow enough to ground-loop safely. Left rudder. Reverse it. The *Spirit of St. Louis* swings around and stops rolling, resting on the solidness of earth, in the center of Le Bourget.
>
> I start to taxi back to the floodlights and hangars. But the entire field ahead is covered with running figures!

Society and Culture in the 1920s

When Lindbergh completed his ground loop at Le Bourget, about 100,000 French men and women broke through police lines to rush onto the field, almost hysterical over this new hero. All day, the transatlantic cables, the newspapers, and radio had been full of news of the flight. And for hours before Lindbergh landed, Parisians had been fighting heavy traffic to drive out to Le Bourget to greet this "Flyin' Fool."

As soon as the *Spirit of St. Louis* touched down, the crowd rushed the plane. Lindbergh was afraid (as he was to be for months, whenever he made announced landings anywhere in the world) that the overexcited people would run into his spinning propeller. When he tried to climb out of his cramped cockpit, the crowd grabbed him. For a long time, he could not even set foot on French soil, but was passed over the crowd, from shoulder to shoulder. In the din, he shouted for a mechanic, someone to protect the plane; but no one could hear or understand him.

In the log he kept of the flight, Lindbergh made this brief, slightly bitter entry: "May 20, Roosevelt Field, Long Island, New York, to Le Bourget Aerodrome, Paris, France. 33 hours. 20 min. Fuselage fabric badly torn by souvenir hunters." The first part of the entry, the flight, was what was significant to Lindbergh. But the second part, the half-crazed hero worship of the crowd, is just as important to understanding the full significance of what Lindbergh had done and become. In Paris, but even more in New York and dozens of other American cities, Lindbergh was adored. From the time he landed at Le Bourget, his life was not his own. People crowded around wherever he went. They stole his hats in restaurants. He could not keep shirts, or even underwear, because laundry employees swiped them for souvenirs.

More than any other person of his generation, Lindbergh captured the imagination of his contemporaries. Newspapers printed more stories about him and his flight than they had about the death of President Wilson. More people—4 million, the police said—turned out to see him in a New York parade than had ever come out to look at any president. Something about Lindbergh and his feat touched a responsive chord in the America of the 1920s.

On the face of it, there was no overwhelming reason for Lindbergh's fantastic fame. As a matter of cold fact, his flight had proved nothing—except that a superb pilot, blessed by some luck, could fly a specially built airplane 3,600 miles. The *Spirit of St. Louis* could carry no passengers and no cargo. In fact, Lindbergh had refused to carry even one pound of mail, though he was offered $1,000 to do so. Lindbergh was not even the first man to fly across the Atlantic. Eight years earlier, in 1919, a British dirigible had done it twice. That year, too, an American seaplane had crossed from New York to England, landing several times on the ocean. And in the same year, two pilots had made it nonstop from Newfoundland to Ireland, to win a prize of $50,000—double Lindbergh's prize. For a variety of reasons, when Lindbergh made his flight in 1927 almost no one seemed to remember these earlier feats, and "Lucky Lindy" quickly became a household word.

The causes of Lindbergh's incredible celebrity have to be found outside his actual accomplishment. They lie in deep changes that had occurred in American society. Americans were excited about Lindbergh for reasons that had more to do with them than with him. They projected more significance into the event than it really had. When masses of people experience such excitement, they tend to see historical actors as demons or heroes. They oversimplify the world and thus make some new kind of sense out of their own lives. This process often has very little to do with reality. Lindbergh became a symbol. His contemporaries saw in him what they wanted to see, making him into a sort of mirror for the technological and social changes that had transformed American society in the twentieth century.

-→=◎=◄-

REACHING A MASS AUDIENCE

One of the reasons for Lindbergh's rapid rise to fame was the intense publicity he received from the press and the radio. Since the 1890s the newspapers of the United States had been increasing in number and circulation. They competed fiercely for the attention of the public. This expansion of newspapers was only part of an important revolution in communications that began in the nineteenth century—and still continues.

One by one, new inventions brought people's lives closer together. These included the telegraph, the telephone, the phonograph, the camera, the radio, and the motion picture. They created a world in which whole nations and continents could share almost simultaneously in distant events. Lindbergh's flight was covered intensely by the press, which transmitted its stories over telegraph and telephone lines. Lindbergh was also photographed mercilessly. His activities were recorded both in newspaper photographs and in the newsreels that accompanied the early silent motion pictures. Hour-by-hour reports of his flight were transmitted on the radio—an invention that had come into widespread use only a few years before. As soon as Lindbergh landed in Paris, the news was flashed back to the United States by transatlantic telegraph cable.

In many ways, Lindbergh the hero was the creation of the mass communications "media." He was the first national celebrity to have the full advantage of every modern form of mass communication (except television, which did not come into wide use until after World War II).

THE COMMUNICATIONS REVOLUTION

The revolution in communications began with the telegraph, which linked California and New York more than half a century before Lindbergh's flight. During the same period, newspapers began to attract a mass audience. The telephone, too, contributed to the rapid and widespread circulation of information. In the first part of the twentieth century the number of telephones in use skyrocketed, from just over 1 million in 1900 to more than 10 million in 1915. By the time Lindbergh took off for Paris, practically every middle-class urban American home had its own telephone.

But the communications revolution did not gather full speed until the invention of the radio. The principle of wireless transmission of sound was almost as old as the telephone. In 1887 a

German scientist had proved the existence of electrical waves in space. He speculated that they might be turned into signals. An Italian inventor, Guglielmo Marconi, applied the theory to wireless transmission of telegraph signals in 1896. From then on it was only a matter of assembling the appropriate tubes, transmitters, and receivers.

In 1920, Americans heard their first commercial radio broadcast. The station was KDKA in Pittsburgh, and the program was a news report on the 1920 presidential election. Soon after that, the winner of the election, Warren G. Harding, installed a radio set in the White House. Gradually, Marconi's invention was transformed from a toy into a commercial reality. By the time Lindbergh made his flight to Paris, an estimated 10 million radio sets were in use in the United States.

Two other inventions, the phonograph and the camera, furthered the revolution in mass communication. Thomas A. Edison found a way of capturing and re-creating sound that was to make music available to millions at an instant. George Eastman's perfection of the camera made it possible for newspapers to publish photographs on their pages.

All these changes allowed millions of people to participate indirectly in events they were not able to witness in person. In other words, these developing communications facilities had created a potential public that could witness any happening, frown at any villain, worship any hero.

A MIDDLE-CLASS PUBLIC

The new public that celebrated Lindbergh's flight with such enthusiasm should not be confused with the whole nation. Lindbergh's fame was primarily a middle-class phenomenon. He was, in some ways, a media creation, and the media that made him catered primarily to white, well-to-do

THE POWER OF COMMUNICATION. This Hood River County, Oregon, farm family instantly became closer to the rest of the nation through their new radio. What once might have taken weeks to reach them—or be dismissed as rumor—was now immediately available "information."

citizens. Even newspapers were aimed primarily at a middle-class audience. Radios and telephones were still the property of the middle class almost exclusively. In 1927 the phonograph and the camera were alien novelties to many millions of poor Americans. Whole great subpopulations—blacks, many poor white farmers, millions of immigrants in the cities—were practically excluded from the new "public" that the mass media helped create.

Eventually, of course, the new inventions (and the television sets that completed the communications revolution) would become the common property of almost every American, rich or poor. But in the 1920s, and for some time after, they were still middle-class conveniences. If Lindbergh was a symbol of popular "values," they were not necessarily values that belonged to all of America. They were the beliefs and hopes of white, middle-class citizens. At the time, it was easy and tempting for the members of this restricted public to believe that they *were* America. Most of them would have agreed quickly with the American ambassador to France, who said that Lindbergh represented "the spirit of our people." Similarly, the *New Republic*, a magazine with a small, highly educated audience, could say confidently that "Lindbergh is US personified." But the ambassador and the *New Republic* spoke carelessly. The "people" and the "US" they referred to were in fact only the public defined by the media.

As for the others, the majority—the poor, the blacks, the immigrants—there is no way to know what (if anything) they thought about Lindbergh. In all likelihood, if they noticed Lindbergh at all, it was only for a moment and with no special sense of identification with him or his feat. Like most of the cultural content of the so-called "Roaring Twenties," the Lindbergh phenomenon occurred mainly within the very class from which he had come. In fact, he may have served the need of this class to believe that it really *did* possess the spirit of the whole nation.

THE MACHINE AND THE MAVERICK IN A TECHNOLOGICAL SOCIETY

Americans were fond of calling the period after World War I the "New Era." Much of what they meant by the phrase was summed up symbolically in Lindbergh's airplane. The New Era was above all a machine age, a triumph of advanced technology. Compared with a modern jet aircraft or a moon rocket, the *Spirit of St. Louis* was a very primitive machine. But to millions of Americans of the 1920s it was the final and glistening outcome of the industrial and technological revolution that had begun in the preceding century. It symbolized what they believed was happening in the United States: the creation of a new kind of civilization, a miracle of "progress" in which every barrier to human comfort and achievement would be broken by industry and invention.

The United States of the mid-1920s was even more thoroughly industrialized than it had been at the turn of the century. Total steel production, for example, quadrupled during the period between the death of William McKinley and Lindbergh's flight to Paris. The total value of all manufactured goods increased about eight times in the same brief period. The number of people engaged in agriculture declined to about one-fourth of the total population. American cities grew at an astounding pace. By 1930, three years after Lindbergh's flight, 40 percent of the total population of the United States lived in twenty-five large metropolitan centers. In short, Lindbergh appealed to a society that was industrial and urban, and fundamentally dependent on machines and factories.

ELECTRIC POWER AND ASSEMBLY LINES

In some ways the New Era was an extension of the revolution in industry that had occurred after the Civil War. The factory system had continued to expand. New and more complex forms of machinery had been developed to produce more and more goods. But if the basic trends were the same, there were some new elements too. The New Era, to a far greater extent than the old, was powered by electricity and organized around assembly lines.

In 1870, when the industrial revolution was still in its first phase, steam and water-power were used equally to drive industry. Steam continued to be the main form of motor energy in industry until about 1917. But steam engines had many drawbacks. It was the introduction of electricity and electric motors that made possible the extraordinary advances in industry that took place in the 1920s.

Again, the basic inventions belonged to the nineteenth century. Within the ten-year period from 1877 to 1887, the dynamo for generating electricity and the electric motor for converting it into motion were both perfected. This was largely the work of Thomas Edison. During these same years, Edison's incandescent light was introduced into homes and streets. In 1882 the first commercial electric power station, the Edison Illuminating Company, was built in New York.

While electric lighting brightened life in offices, houses, and streets, the electric motor helped transform industrial production. In 1900, electric motors provided only one-twentieth of the power used in American industrial plants. By World War I this figure had increased to about one-third. When Lindbergh flew to France, just ten years later, electricity provided almost two-thirds of the total industrial power in American factories and mills. Between 1870 and 1920 the amount of raw energy used by American industry, measured in horsepower, increased by well over 1,000 percent.

The development of the moving-belt assembly line also had far-reaching effects on industrial production. Assembly lines were first introduced on a large scale by Henry Ford at his automobile plant in Michigan in 1913. The principle was a simple one. Workers were placed in a row in the order of sequence of their jobs. As the product (in this case the automobile) moved past, each worker performed an assigned task. The idea might be simple, but the savings in time and motion were dramatic. Each worker, using a specialized tool to perform a small task, could now produce much more in a given day. Ford's assembly line was copied by dozens of other industries. By the middle of the 1920s it was a standard technique.

EFFECTS OF MECHANIZATION

The changes brought about by the electric motor and the assembly line made the lives of most Americans in 1927 very different from a generation or two earlier. More and more, the ways in which people lived and worked were determined by machines and technological innovations. More and more, mechanical devices replaced human energy and skill.

This process of mechanization had two deep effects on American society. First, it made modern Americans more conscious of the efficient use of time and effort than any other people in the history of the world. Second, it threatened to standardize life by reducing the area of imagination and individuality in people's daily working environment. The celebration of Lindbergh was connected to both these consequences.

In planning his flight, Lindbergh was almost ruthlessly efficient. The *Spirit of St. Louis* was a nearly perfect machine. It was designed to perform one simple task in the most effective way, with a minimum of wasted energy. Like a machine in a modern factory, the plane represented the harnessing of energy to a carefully designed instrument for the performance of a rigidly defined task. Much of what Americans admired in Lindbergh was precisely what they admired in their own society: technological achievement and mechanical efficiency.

But there was another side to Lindbergh. He was perceived as a "maverick." Some of the pet names the newspapers gave him, like "The Flyin' Fool" and "Lucky," made his daring seem more important than his technical skills. Lindbergh seemed to go against the trend toward the mechanical standardization of life in the New Era. He represented individual imagination, as well as engineering and piloting knowledge. A large part of Lindbergh's fame probably rested on this seeming opposition between machinery and personality. His flight could be pictured as *both* a triumph of technology and a victory for individual daring.

WHEELS AND WINGS: THE MOTOR AGE

The development of electricity had a powerful effect not only on industry but also on American homelife. New inventions like the electric washing machine and refrigerator (which utilized small, inexpensive motors) changed the working and eating habits of American families. And a dozen other smaller electric appliances, from toasters to thermostats for home furnaces, helped usher in the American consumer's vision of a New Era.

PERFECTING THE AUTOMOBILE

The largest change in American social life was brought about by the gasoline engine. The basic principle of the internal combustion engine was understood by the middle of the nineteenth century. The first was built and operated in the 1860s in France. Instead of burning fuel externally to convert water into steam, the internal combustion engine burned fuel in an explosive way inside a chamber. The force of the explosion was then used to drive a piston or a rotor. Power for the new engine was available in the form of gasoline—which had once been a waste product

in the making of kerosene, the basic fuel oil of the nineteenth century.

It was only a matter of time, then, until someone perfected the engine, mounted it on a "horseless" carriage, and so created the automobile. No one, however, could have begun to guess at the end of the nineteenth century just how rapid the development of the automobile would be. Nor could anyone foresee the range of consequences it would have on the ways Americans lived.

The first man in the United States to build a workable automobile powered by a gasoline engine was probably Ransom E. Olds. (His rickety machine was the forerunner of the present-day Oldsmobile.) Five years later, in 1895, Henry Ford began to put together his first car. The new machine was noisy, unreliable, and expensive. Still, a few Americans were willing to pay the price and stop their ears against the noise. By 1900 there were about 8,000 of the curious new machines operating in the country.

But Ford was not so much an inventor of the automobile as an inventor of a style and a method of production. In the early years of the century Ford began simplifying the automobile. He cut away every fancy decoration and convenience that had been adapted from the luxurious horse-drawn carriages of the day. He also reduced costs by turning out standardized, mass-produced machines. The results were astonishing. In 1907 the average price of an automobile was over $2,000. The next year, Ford introduced a model selling at only $850. By 1914 he was able to cut the price to a little over $500. By the mid-1920s Ford was selling his assembly-line Model T for less than $300. The car was similar in many ways to the *Spirit of St. Louis*. It was the simplest machine possible, designed to do a plain task in the most efficient way.

Other automobile makers began to imitate and compete with Ford. The result was an exploding new industry. By the 1920s the manufacture of automobiles was by far the largest consumer-products industry in the United States. It employed tens of thousands of workers at large and growing factories centered around Detroit. The automobile had a remarkable impact on other industries, especially steel and rubber, which provided the raw products for the assembly lines. The oil industry also underwent a major expansion. The automobile turned gasoline into the main stock-in-trade of the petroleum companies.

LIFE IN THE MOTOR AGE

The most obvious impact of the automobile was not on industry but on American social life. By 1927 Ford had made 15 million cars. About 20 million American families owned an automobile. The immediate result was that horses and other draft animals almost disappeared from the streets of cities and towns.

But the automobile had other, less obvious and predictable effects. First, it encouraged those Americans who could afford a car to move farther and farther out of their cities, into suburbs. Second, cars and buses transformed American education, especially in small towns and farm areas. The school bus made it possible to consolidate school districts into larger units. Gradually, the common one-room schoolhouse, with one or two teachers for all the grades and pupils who all walked to school, practically disappeared.

Finally, the automobile, the truck, and the bus began a process that would take another thirty years to complete: the near-destruction of the railroads—the principal technological innovation of the nineteenth century. At first, in the 1920s and 1930s, the car and the bus cut mainly into the railroads' local traffic. But as roads and engines improved, the competition became more and more severe. As for freight, the trucking industry began to compete for what had been almost a railroad monopoly. The train, with its mighty steam engine, had been the great symbol of the industrial revolution up to the 1920s. By the middle of the twentieth century, much of the railroad industry was ailing and unprofitable, no longer able to survive as a private enterprise.

In the long run, the automobile proved to have unwanted as well as unpredicted consequences. Among these, the modern decay of central cities was the most serious. Gradually, large sections of cities like New York, Boston, and Chicago became the slums of the poor, who could not afford either cars or suburban homes. Also, although no one in Lindbergh's day could have predicted it, the automobile caused a major problem of air pollution. Smog resulted from the exhausts of millions of cars and trucks burning hundreds of millions of gallons of gasoline every year.

To most Americans, though, the automobile was an unquestioned miracle. To those who could afford it, it meant freedom to move at will through the city or the countryside. It also provided status, as manufacturers introduced more elaborate models, some costing ten times as much as Ford's Model T. And the automobile meant adventure. Middle-class Americans could get behind the wheel of a powerful, complicated piece of machinery—just as Lindbergh had climbed into the cockpit of the *Spirit of St. Louis*—and be off on an exciting journey of motion and speed every day. Like Lindbergh, too, Americans went beyond a concern with efficiency and practicality to a romantic affection for their machines. They polished them, paraded them, and gave them pet names like "the old bus," the "flivver," the "tin Lizzie," and the "merry Oldsmobile." Americans—those with the money to pay for one, at least—loved the car, despite its effects on their air, their cities, and their social traditions.

AIR TRANSPORTATION

For the first quarter of the twentieth century, the automobile had the greatest impact on American transportation. The development of the aircraft industry and airline passenger service did not become truly important until years after Lindbergh's flight. Like the automobile, the airplane depended on the small, powerful, and efficient gasoline engine. But the airplane was in many ways more thrilling than the automobile. (This was why Lindbergh and other pilots could make a living in the 1920s barnstorming across America in their "aerial circuses.")

The first men to fly a real airplane were Orville and Wilbur Wright. In 1903 they brought a primitive biplane to Kitty Hawk, North Carolina (a location they chose because it had strong and steady coastal winds, plus a great expanse of beach). The plane had a tiny gasoline engine, which turned two push-type propellers. The first successful test flight came in December, after a series of dangerous and frustrating failures. This first flight lasted a little less than a minute, and covered only about 800 feet. But the Wright brothers were soon experimenting with larger planes and engines. In 1909, after six years of work, they sold the first plane to the United States Army.

World War I brought about a dramatic spurt in design sophistication, not only in the United States but in Europe. The new planes had larger and better engines and a much more rigid construction than the Wrights' original. The war also romanticized flight and created a new type of military hero, the "aviator." Lindbergh, then, was able to capitalize not only on advances in technology but on a new image of the heroic and daring "ace."

The first important civilian use of the airplane was to carry mail. The government began service in 1918. Later, private companies (like the one Lindbergh had worked for in St. Louis) took over the service. The operation was dangerous, and many pilots were killed in crashes during the early years. But by the mid-1920s there was regular, all-weather airmail service between most major cities in America.

Lindbergh's flight, combined with the introduction of larger airplanes like Byrd's *America*, did more than any other single event to encourage the growth of air transportation. Lindbergh had faith in the future of aviation. Soon after his return to America in 1927, he began a flying tour of the country to promote airmail and air transportation. By 1930, just three years after his solo transatlantic flight, there were forty-three domestic airline companies, operating over 30,000 miles of flying routes.

NEW MANNERS AND MORALS

All these changes—the development of mass communication, the expansion of industry, the introduction of a new technology—brought about another revolution. This revolution marked a dramatic difference in the manners and morals of many Americans. Americans of the 1920s knew they were living in a time when the world was undergoing rapid change. They coined new phrases, like "the Roaring Twenties," the "Lost Generation," and "Flaming Youth," to describe what was happening to them. Many young Americans—especially those who were urban and middle-class—were adopting habits and moral standards that their parents found shocking and offensive.

A REVOLUTION FOR WOMEN

At the center of the revolution in manners were young, middle-class white women. The revolution that would change women's lives did not begin in the 1920s. During the first two decades of the twentieth century, many middle- and upper-class women had adopted new patterns of behavior (including divorce) that broke the traditions of nineteenth-century Victorian America. But because of the impact of World War I and the influence of books, radio, and advertising, the trend that had started at the turn of the century began

SMOLDERING YOUTH.   Many Americans of the 1920s were intensely conscious of the changing ways men and women behaved toward each other socially and sexually. At the center of the supposed changes was the "flapper," the young woman scantily dressed, hatless, with bobbed hair, at home with alcohol, frankly provocative, and carefully posing in ways designed to seem altogether natural. In truth, the consciousness of change probably ran considerably ahead of the changes themselves. This cartoon of 1927 wildly exaggerates the degree of public nakedness most women were willing to risk—or most men to accept.

new experience of education and work increased the number of women who were likely to remain single, or, if they did marry, to get divorced. The divorce rate in 1930 was twice what it had been before World War I. This did not mean that marriages were more unhappy, but that women were less likely to put up with a bad marital situation. They would demand their freedom instead.

There was an even more obvious revolution in the way women dressed. The ideal that gradually emerged in the decade of Lindbergh's flight

SIMPERING YOUTH.   Dancing was one of the main preoccupations of the popular culture of the 1920s. White people appropriated, and drastically modified, black dances—just as they did black music. (They managed to do this, usually, with no apparent change in their racial attitudes.) Here a young couple are shown doing the Charleston. The effect they are striving for in this staged photograph is one that combines open sexuality with youthful innocence; their own highly patterned intimacy is mixed with an awareness that they are not so much dancing as they are performing for a public.

to affect ever-widening circles of women. By the 1920s a sexual revolution was in full swing.

Politically, women actually were new creatures. After decades of agitation, they finally won the right to vote with passage of the Nineteenth Amendment in 1920. But this new political role was only a small part of the emancipation of women. The new middle-class woman of the 1920s wanted to do "everything," and everything included many more social and economic choices than her mother or grandmother had had.

The "new woman" was much more likely than her mother to attend college. She might very well go to work, too. By 1930, 10 million women were employed in the American labor force. This was that of the "flapper." She wore her dress short—above the knees rather than at the ankle. And the dress was not only shorter, it was made of thin material, designed to move with her body as she walked or danced—designed, too, to give an occasional glimpse of thigh above the hemline. The flapper discarded the corsets that her mother had worn, and dispensed with the bustle, too. She put on much more makeup and perfume, and jangled with much more jewelry at her neck and wrists. In advertisements and in movies—and in real life, too—she was likely to pose with a cocktail in one hand and a cigarette in a long holder in the other—the essence of a new "sophistication."

Like Lindbergh, though, the flapper and the liberation she symbolized were primarily a middle-class phenomenon. College, careers, divorce, and emancipated dress still touched only a minority of American women. Even though the right to vote now belonged to every woman, in practice that right was exercised primarily by middle-class women. For the rest, life continued to be quite confining. And when women did leave the home to take jobs, they still suffered from a systematic discrimination in wages and opportunities. In the final analysis, the flapper, like Lindbergh, had a significance that was more symbolic than real.

THE JAZZ AGE

The new woman was part of a changing culture. A freedom of action and belief unheard of before seemed to go hand in hand with the triumph of industrial technology, with its prosperity and sense of unlimited possibilities for life. Both men and women listened to new music—jazz—and danced new steps. Instead of formal waltzes and other Victorian dances, they moved to the fast

BESSIE SMITH. One of the effects of the communications revolution was to turn previously obscure musicians into public celebrities, and art forms that had been folk music into commercial properties. This was particularly true for black artists and their music. Bessie Smith, shown here dressed in the ideal movie-queen costume of the period, made the blues into a form that managed to combine superb talent with commercial success. As a phenomenon, the celebrity was nothing new. But there were more of them than ever before, their variety was more striking, and their fame more instantaneous and widespread.

Charleston and the Black Bottom. They also danced close together in the slow "fox-trot." Many older Americans were shocked by these changes. But these dances became part of the new culture, sweeping their way through high school gymnasiums and college campuses, and dance halls across the country.

The sexual mores of Americans were changing, too. The ideas of the Austrian psychologist Sigmund Freud about sex began to be discussed at the dinner table and in the polite magazines of the middle class. Words like "bitch" appeared in novels published by respectable publishers and read by respectable people. "Petting" and "necking" became part of the everyday vocabulary of magazine readers and even ministers. In the movies, sex became a major box-office attraction. Stars like Theda Bara and Clara Bow appeared on the screen in wispy clothing, locked in long, passionate embraces with their leading men. When Clara Bow was advertised as "the It girl," hardly anyone needed to ask what "It" meant.

Middle-class Americans drank more alcohol, too. Although it was illegal, liquor was easy to obtain. So millions of Americans became technically criminals every time they bought from their regular "bootlegger," or went to one of the many illegal drinking establishments known as "speakeasies." Terms like "bathtub gin" became part of the national language. Especially in colleges, drinking became a regular pastime of the "flaming youth" of the decade.

A BLACK RENAISSANCE

The Jazz Age was a distinctly urban phenomenon. It was also an outcome of the greatest large-scale influence black music, dance, and style had ever had on white, middle-class Americans. And these two facts reflected two important changes in the African-American experience.

The first of these changes was one of the most massive and significant migrations in American history. In 1910, nine out of ten African Americans still lived in the South, almost all of them in rural areas where they worked for meager incomes as sharecroppers or day laborers. But blacks were beginning to leave the farms for the cities in great numbers. In the 1920s, 1.5 million African Americans moved into urban areas, most of them in the North.

The second great change in black experience was vocational. Those blacks who had managed to get an education during the decades after the end of Reconstruction had almost all been confined to careers as ministers or teachers in small towns, or managed to get work as clerks in a special environment like Washington, DC. In 1910 there was exactly one black judge and two state legislators in the entire United States. But things were beginning to change. Black colleges were turning out hundreds of graduates every year, and a few blacks were able to graduate from old-line white colleges and universities. (The first black football players to be singled out as "All-Americans," in 1916 and 1917, played for elite, private white colleges, Brown and Rutgers, and each was the first black ever to play varsity sports for the school.) The migration to northern cities made it possible for ambitious young blacks to pursue careers—as lawyers, actors, singers, writers, journalists that would have been nearly impossible in the rural South.

The place where these two changes came together to produce remarkable results was the part of Manhattan known by the old Dutch name of Harlem. The district, which ran north from 125th Street, had already become a black neighborhood by 1920. It was a neighborhood with real style, the place where every young black with ambition to be a doctor or a poet, a playwright or a lawyer, took his or her dream.

W. E. B. Du Bois had brought his magazine, *The Crisis*, to Harlem at the beginning of World War I. After the war the National Association for the Advancement of Colored People (NAACP) moved its headquarters to Harlem (and at the same time replaced a predominantly white board of officers with a group of blacks headed by poet and lawyer James Weldon Johnson). Du Bois and Johnson were typical of the kinds of people who were going to lead black movements in the 1920s in one important respect: They were not just political men interested in social justice. They were also intellectuals, writers, and poets with an intense interest in art and culture. Soon they were joined in Harlem by a remarkable generation of black intellectuals and artists, many of them immigrants from the West Indies. Together they produced what they themselves referred to with justifiable pride as the Negro Renaissance, or the Harlem Renaissance.

The literature of the Renaissance was varied in tone and manner. Langston Hughes's poetry

THE CRISIS. In this twentieth-anniversary cover for *The Crisis*, artist Aaron Douglas brought together several themes and artistic techniques. The highly stylized female head is partly an assertion of pride in African origins, partly an allusion to the long-necked female figures of the great Italian painter Amadeo Modigliani (who had died nine years before), and partly an exercise in the newer vogue of abstract expressionism. The sun that is rising among the skyscrapers of New York is crowned with the letters NAACP.

moved easily from bitterness to gentleness, as did the poems of the Jamaican Claude McKay. Some writers explored the contemporary world. Some discovered the African past and its dense culture. Jean Toomer wrote a stunning collection of stories about black life in the 1880s in rural Georgia, *Cane.* But for all the differences in tone or subject matter, the writers of the Harlem Renaissance produced a body of work that had a recognizable unity.

This unity derived from the fact that the Renaissance was not just an intellectual flowering, it was an act of faith. The faith centered on a willingness to embrace black culture, history, and personality as something "beautiful." The poet and essayist Langston Hughes put it simply: "Creative blacks intend to express our individual dark-skinned bodies without fear or shame." He would be glad, he went on, if whites were pleased with this kind of "expression," but if they were not, it would not matter. "We know we are beautiful."

Embracing an idea like this meant that black artists and intellectuals were doing more than producing art. They were making a political statement as well. In the 1920s the work of leading white writers and artists often ended in a repudiation of their culture and politics, questioning its vitality and authenticity. The Harlem Renaissance was attempting to do the opposite, to discover in the African-American experience sources of something that could be both authentic and vital, a basis for the emergence of what came to be called the "New Negro." And for black intellectuals, this required not a separation of art and politics (as it did for an increasing number of white writers), but a fusion between the two. Deciding where you stood as an artist required you to decide where you stood as a black man or woman, both in relation to other blacks and in relation to white society.

The act of faith, the decision that to be black was a thing of beauty, did not translate into a single obvious political position. Out of the 1920s came a spectrum of proposed agendas. Perhaps the most conservative—though terms

LANGSTON HUGHES. The artist Winold Reiss made this portrait of Langston Hughes about 1925. The portrait emphasizes Hughes's vocation as a New York writer, framed in ways that associate him with an emphatically avant-garde artistic modernism. The background is done in the style known as Cubism, abstractly joining Hughes's bed and slippers, some random stairs to nowhere and jazz notes, with continuous clouds and curtains and the buildings of Harlem.

like "conservative" are of limited use in this matter—was the position of the NAACP. Under James Weldon Johnson's leadership, the NAACP continued to struggle for legal equality and integration through the enforcement of the Fourteenth and Fifteenth amendments to the Constitution.

W. E. B. Du Bois and his followers, on the other hand, continued to believe that black pride and black culture, not integration through legal means, was the solution. In this view, the work of

what Du Bois called the "talented tenth" among blacks—the teachers, poets, and other intellectuals—was critical.

An alternative vision was put forward by A. Philip Randolph, who vigorously edited the newspaper *The Messenger*. Randolph believed more in labor militancy than the NAACP leadership did. And he believed more in the crucial role of the black working class than Du Bois did. His solution centered on getting blacks to join unions, like the Brotherhood of Pullman Porters he organized.

A very different kind of program was put forward by the West Indian Marcus Garvey. Garvey was a black nationalist, whose vision involved promoting a "return to Africa" and the creation of a new black nation. In the meantime, he also urged the development of black capitalism in the United States as a way of making African Americans as free as possible from any necessary economic contact with whites.

Garvey's ideas had little appeal to the men and women who made the Harlem Renaissance. They were interested in finding ways to embrace their own racial culture, but they were also interested in being intellectuals. They wanted to reach into their own past—into slavery, into Africa, into rural poverty in the South—but they also wanted to reach out to the high culture of European and American whites. They traveled to England and to France. They attended parties in Harlem where they met their white counterparts. Many of them cultivated a new and fragile connection with white artists and writers who lived and worked downtown in Greenwich Village.

The connection did generate at least the beginnings of biracial culture in New York. The noted avant-garde playwright Eugene O'Neill wrote two plays with leading roles for a black man, *The Emperor Jones* (1920) and *All God's Chillun Got Wings* (1924). They were performed at the now-legendary Provincetown Theater in the Village, and *The Emperor Jones* had a brief run on Broadway. They even got some favorable notice in establishment papers like *The New York Times* and the *World.*

The Provincetown Theater was also the scene of a moment of great symbolic importance for the Harlem Renaissance. In 1925 a young and gifted singer, Paul Robeson, performed a concert of spirituals, or sorrow songs. The moment was important partly because these songs were rooted in slavery and in the sufferings of poor blacks since emancipation. The small black middle class had usually preferred to forget about such music. It belonged to the past they were trying to leave behind. But for the Renaissance, it was important to see the black experience as something to be embraced, not left behind. And a brilliant singer like Robeson (with the help of some ingenious musical arrangements) could make the songs do what Langston Hughes had called for, make them "express our individual dark-skinned bodies without fear and without shame." Du Bois wrote the next day, "It was very beautiful."

But the moment was equally important because the audience was composed mostly of whites—artists, writers, musicians, journalists, and other intellectuals—most of them in formal evening dress. And when they rose in thunderous applause after each song, it was clear they had found a form of black expression that they could embrace without hesitation. They could see the spirituals as the gentle, innocent expression of a gentle and innocent people. In a different setting, the songs had a different meaning. When Robeson made some recordings later in 1925, Hughes happened to be in Georgia. He wrote Robeson, "The great truth and beauty of your art struck me as never before one night this summer down in Georgia when a little group of us played your records for hours there in the very atmosphere from which your songs came." There, in Georgia, it was probably not gentleness or innocence that the spirituals evoked, but deprivation, suffering, and resentment.

PAUL ROBESON. In 1943, during the first season of Robeson's great Broadway performance in the role of Shakespeare's *Othello,* Betsy Graves Reyneau painted this portrait, capturing all the majesty and force that Robeson brought to the part, one of the most demanding in all of Shakespeare. Robeson had acted the part in London in 1930, but had to wait more than a decade before he was allowed to be the first African-American Othello on Broadway.

The problem was, from the point of view of the men and women who made the Harlem Renaissance, that most blacks in Georgia and elsewhere were more likely to buy "race" records of splendid and innovative jazz and blues artists like Louis Armstrong or Bessie Smith than they were to buy the carefully arranged spirituals of Robeson. The intellectuals of the Renaissance were learning what white artists and writers had learned: that fine painting or music or writing often failed to reach large audiences. Jean Toomer's *Cane* was a powerfully written book. But the first edition sold only 500 copies. And the opposite side of the coin was that black artists could please white audiences most when they fell into stereotypes. An all-black "revue" was a tremendous success on Broadway in the early 1920s—a hundred times more successful than O'Neill's *Emperor Jones,* even with Paul Robeson in the title role. But the revue was a musical comedy whose content was in keeping with its title, *Shuffle Along.*

A SEARCH FOR INNOCENCE

The white middle-class public, in the end, gave little notice to the Harlem Renaissance. They had other things on their mind. As their own lives became more and more confused and complicated, white Americans began to celebrate innocence. In their movies and sports they created simple, naive heroes who were guided by straightforward codes of justice and virtue. The most popular type of movie hero of the decade was the cowboy, a symbol of pure, preindustrial man. And the most popular movie star of the period, Rudolph Valentino, played roles that put him on horseback in a country far removed from Fords and factories and modernity. It was no accident, too, that the greatest sports hero of the decade, George Herman Ruth, was nicknamed "Babe."

Lindbergh stirred the deep urge of people to believe in innocence. His youth, honesty, and simple determination made him seem much purer than the public that worshiped him. Lindbergh did not smoke or drink. He displayed no interest in women, at least at the time of his flight. And his boyish face looked out at the world through clear blue eyes. They seemed to say that everything was still the same, that the world had not lost its innocence after all.

RUDOLPH VALENTINO. Valentino, shown here dressed for his role in *The Sheik* (1921), was the most popular male movie idol of the 1920s. Valentino and his directors emphasized the curious intensity of his apparent passions, using stares like the one he has adopted for this publicity photograph. But they also armed him to the teeth, with knives, swords, and bullets, whenever his roles allowed for it. The resulting effect of violence and lust was made acceptable partly by the fact that he often played some sort of "foreigner" from a culture distant in time and place. In such realms, any fantasy could seem appropriate, even to the most conservative middle-class moviegoer.

ILLUSIONS OF DISILLUSIONMENT

In the midst of all this change and confusion, intellectuals offered very little guidance to their middle-class public. Before World War I, a generation of scholars and intellectuals had produced a remarkable body of writing on the workings of society, economics, and politics. In the 1920s a new generation of intellectuals began to turn out a profusion of superb novels, plays, and essays—as rich a cultural flowering as the country had ever produced. But their work embodied a marked shift away from a concern with social and political problems. With a few exceptions, the new writers either ignored society altogether or viewed it as the enemy, to be mocked or damned.

All in all, the viewpoint of the writers of the 1920s fitted the writer Malcolm Cowley's description quite well: "Society was something quite alien—a sort of parlor car in which we rode, over smooth tracks, toward a destination we should never have chosen for ourselves." This self-conscious sense of alienation from social structures and purposes governed the literary culture of the decade. It was what prompted the idea that the writers of the period belonged to a "lost generation." The result was a rush of great art that pointed in no particular social direction whatever.

The dominant theme of the writers of the 1920s was disillusionment. Their heroes and heroines usually entered their novels, plays, and stories caught up in some sort of innocent faith— in religion, civilization, progress, freedom, or the like. But, typically, this faith was broken by experience, and the outcome was a ripping away of old illusions. In the typical novel of the decade, the illusions were not replaced by any working new beliefs, but instead by a brooding sense of mistrust and disappointment, and a curious kind of boredom with the world.

The first great subject for disillusionment was the war and the mistaken peace that followed. Several of the best young writers cut their teeth on the war experience—William Faulkner, Ernest Hemingway, John Dos Passos, and others—and for most of them, the conclusion was simple: the war had proved the bankruptcy of what people called civilization. Hemingway summed up the experience in a story called "Soldier's Home," about the shattered illusions of a veteran named Krebs: "Krebs acquired the nausea in regard to experience that is the result of untruth or exaggeration." The same logic governed Maxwell Anderson's popular play *What Price Glory,* E. E. Cummings's *The Enormous Room*—a hilarious but bitter book on his arrest and imprisonment in France—and the two war novels of Dos Passos, *One Man's Initiation* and *Three Soldiers*. The only way to escape the "nausea" brought on by the war was to make what Hemingway called a "separate peace."

Actually, when looked at carefully, the American war novels were not so much about the war at all as about what the writers thought lay behind the war: technology, bureaucracy, and propaganda. For people like Faulkner and Dos Passos, the war was not so much a subject as a dramatic metaphor. In many of Hemingway's books and stories of the 1920s—*A Farewell to Arms* (1925) and *The Sun Also Rises* (1926) among them—the war was only the most violent phase of modern civilization. It had only brought into more vivid focus the cruelty and inhumanity that were an inherent feature of contemporary social life.

When the writers looked at peacetime subjects, the result was much the same. Sinclair Lewis's riotous parody of the consciousness of a Midwestern businessman in his novel *Babbitt* (1922) was just as "disillusioned" as any of the war novels. In *Winesburg, Ohio* (1919), Sherwood Anderson looked behind the drawn blinds of a small town with exactly the same sense of alienation and distaste. Dos Passos's voluminous novel *1919* made little or no distinction between war and peace. All in all, the writers of the decade agreed with the judgment of the poet Ezra Pound that Western civilization was "an old bitch gone in the teeth." Another poet, T. S. Eliot, summed up the attitude in the title of his most popular work of the period, *The Waste Land* (1922).

For many intellectuals, the only solution seemed to be expatriation. In *The Sun Also Rises,* Hemingway portrayed the aimless confusion of American and British intellectuals in Paris. And for those who did not actually leave the country, there were other forms of withdrawal. William Faulkner—probably the best writer of the period, technically—stayed stubbornly in his small Mississippi town. From that vantage point, he wrote social novels, but they were novels about a rural society whose problems were hardly those of an industrial and urban society. In novels like *The Sound and the Fury* (1929), Faulkner resorted to disarmingly traditional and innocent solutions to human problems—honesty, decency, and even simple modesty. At times, he even seemed to propose religious faith as the only authentic alternative to meaninglessness in modern life.

The writer who best caught the spirit of the Jazz Age—as he called it—was F. Scott Fitzgerald. *This Side of Paradise* (1920) rocketed him to a precocious fame. But his reputation was quickly confirmed by *The Great Gatsby* (1925). Fitzgerald's characters inhabited a world of money and sophistication. They were literate and articulate, young and dashing. They drank and smoked and danced their way toward disaster. They were a curious mixture of innocence and disillusionment.

Jay Gatsby, easily Fitzgerald's most memorable hero, was in some ways a cynical man. He was a criminal who had become extraordinarily wealthy and had invented a false and cultured identity for himself, complete with a great vulgar mansion on Long Island. But there was another side to Gatsby, very like Lindbergh. He was a boy from the Midwest who had read Benjamin Franklin, worked hard for success, and dreamed an innocent dream—that he might find and marry the girl he had loved as a youth. It was this dream, this "romantic readiness," that made Gatsby great. And if the naive dream led only to corruption and murder, that seemed to Fitzgerald to capture the inner meaning of his generation's experience.

In a sense, Gatsby and Lindbergh were opposite manifestations of the same heroic figure. Both were simple in the midst of complexity, daring in a world that had become increasingly routine and bureaucratic. Both were driven by a private conviction that had little or no social significance. The difference was that Fitzgerald's hero ended in defeat and death; Lindbergh won success and fame and married the daughter of a wealthy financier.

CHRONOLOGY

1890	Ransom Olds builds his first workable gasoline-powered automobile
1899	W. E. B. Du Bois publishes *The Philadelphia Negro*
1903	Orville and Wilbur Wright make first powered heavier-than-air flight at Kitty Hawk, North Carolina;
	Du Bois publishes *The Souls of Black Folk*
1905	Du Bois and other black leaders found Niagara Movement
1907	Henry Ford introduces the Model T automobile.
1910	National Association for the Advancement of Colored People founded
1913	Ford introduces assembly-line production in automobile plant
1914	World War I begins in Europe
1916	First African American named as "All-American" football player
1917	United States enters World War I;
	Beginnings of Harlem Renaissance;
	James Weldon Johnson publishes *Fifty Years and Other Poems*
1918	World War I ends;
	Pan African Congress founded;
	Airmail service inaugurated
1919	Sherwood Anderson publishes *Winesburg, Ohio*
1920	Eugene O'Neill's *Emperor Jones* performed in New York, with African American in title role;
	First commercial radio station, KDKA, opens in Pittsburgh, Pennsylvania;
	F. Scott Fitzgerald publishes *This Side of Paradise*
1921	John Dos Passos publishes *1919*
1922	Sinclair Lewis publishes *Babbitt;*
	T. S. Eliot publishes *The Waste Land;*
	Claude McKay publishes *White Shadows*
1923	NAACP moves headquarters to Harlem;
	Urban League begins to publish *Opportunity*
1925	Paul Robeson introduces spirituals at New York's Provincetown Theater;
	Ernest Hemingway publishes *A Farewell to Arms;*
	Fitzgerald publishes *The Great Gatsby*
1926	Hemingway publishes *The Sun Also Rises*
1927	Charles Lindbergh completes first New York-Paris flight
1929	William Faulkner publishes *The Sound and the Fury*

SUGGESTIONS FOR FURTHER READING

LINDBERGH'S FLIGHT

The most engaging way to begin reading about Lindbergh's feat is to start with his own story, which is a twice-told tale. Immediately after the flight, he wrote *We* (1928). A quarter of a century later, he took a longer, somewhat romanticized second look, in *The Spirit of St. Louis* (1953). There are three intelligent modern biographies: Kenneth S. Davis, *The Hero: Charles A. Lindbergh* (1959); Walter S. Ross, *The Last Hero: Charles A. Lindbergh* (1968); and Leonard Mosley, *Lindbergh* (1976).

THE COMMUNICATIONS REVOLUTION

The following books are helpful discussions of the new media: David M. White and Richard Averson, *Sight, Sound, and Society* (1968); Ronald Gellatt, *The Fabulous Phonograph* (1965); Beaumont Newhall, *The History of Photography* (1964); Erik Bernouw, *A Tower in Babel: A History of Broadcasting in the United States to 1933* (1966); Susan J. Douglas, *Inventing American Broadcasting, 1899–1922* (1989); and Frank Luther Mott, *American Journalism* (1962). On advertising, see Daniel Pope, *The Making of Modern Advertising* (1983).

TECHNOLOGY

A workable introduction to the new technology of mass production is Sigfried Giedion, *Mechanization Takes Command* (1948). Changes in business practice are treated exhaustively in Sanford M. Jacoby, *Employing Bureaucracy* (1985). Ford's career may be tracked in the exhaustive and sympathetic study by Allan Nevins and Frank E. Hill, *Ford* (three volumes, 1954–1962). But the more interesting approach is through the writings of some of the molders of technological change, such as Henry Ford, *My Life and Work* (1922), and Wilbur and Orville Wright, *Papers* (1953).

POPULAR CULTURE

Two classics from the period, the first charming, the second influential, are Frederick Lewis Allen, *Only Yesterday* (1931), and R. S. and H. N. Lynd, *Middletown* (1929). Stanley Coben's *Rebellion Against Victorianism* (1991) is a good general introduction to the decade. An interesting study of the definition of a generation is Paula Fass, *The Damned and the Beautiful: American Youth in the 1920s* (1977). William Henry Chafe, *The American Woman* (1974), is a plausible place to start reading on women in the 1920s. There is also much valuable material in Nancy F. Cott, *The Grounding of Modern Feminism* (1987); Linda Gordon, *Woman's Body, Woman's Right: A Social History of Birth Control in America* (1976); J. Stanley Lemons, *The Woman Citizen: Social Feminism in the 1920s* (1973), and Susan Strasser, *Never Done: A History of American Housework* (1982). Interesting and usable books on mass entertainment are Harold Seymour, *Baseball* (two volumes, 1960–

1971); Edward Wagenknecht, *Movies in the Age of Innocence* (1962); and Robert Sklar, *Movie Made America* (1975). The social impact of the automobile is discussed in James Flink's fine *Car Culture* (1975). The development of the suburbs is the subject of Kenneth Jackson, *Crabgrass Frontier* (1985). Gilbert Osofsky, *Harlem: The Making of a Ghetto* (1965), is essential reading. Useful treatments of the Harlem Renaissance are Nathan Huggins, *Harlem Renaissance* (1971); David Levering Lewis, *When Harlem Was in Vogue* (1981); Mary Campbell, *Harlem Renaissance: The Art of Black America* (1987); and *Color, Sex, and Poetry: Three Women Writers of the Harlem Renaissance* (1987); Manning Marable, *W. E. B. Du Bois: Black Radical Democrat* (1986), is thorough and sympathetic. Two useful books on Marcus Garvey are Judith Stein, *The World of Marcus Garvey* (1986), and Theodore Vincent, *Black Power and the Garvey Movement* (1971). The black experience in the cities is the subject of Ira Katznelson's fine *Black Men, White Cities: Race, Politics, and Migration in the United States, 1900–1930, and Britain, 1948–1968* (1976). A superb study of a great black artist and activist is Martin Duberman, *Paul Robeson* (1989).

INTELLECTUALS

Two classics of criticism from the period are Malcolm Cowley, *Exile's Return* (1934), and Edmund Wilson, *Axel's Castle* (1931). The two best general books on the literary history of the period—though both must be used very cautiously—are still Alfred Kazin, *On Native Grounds* (1942) and Frederick Hoffmann, *The Twenties* (1955).

Capitalism in Transition

Episode: Defeat of the Bonus Marchers

THE EPISODE: *In 1932, thousands of veterans of World War I began to gather in Washington, D.C., to demand immediate payment of a $1,000 "bonus" that Congress had scheduled to be paid to them in 1945. So they organized themselves into a "Bonus Army" and set up camps near the Capitol and at Anacostia Flats on the southeastern fringe of the city.*

During the spring and early summer, Congress debated the bonus. Finally, in June, the House passed a bonus bill, but the Senate rejected it—as thousands of angry bonus marchers waited on the Capitol steps. Even after this failure, the Bonus Army did not leave the city. Some veterans were leaving, but others were coming to the capital every day to take their places in camps, rallies, and parades. Gradually, the government grew more tense. The president finally decided the Bonus Army was led by "radicals" and was a threat to the stability of the government itself. He ordered the army to clear the veterans from the District of Columbia, and soon the veterans faced bayonets and tanks of the same army in which they once had served.

THE HISTORICAL SETTING: *The Bonus March of 1932 occurred at the moment of deepest crisis the United States had experienced since the Civil War. After a decade of apparent prosperity in the 1920s, stock prices suddenly collapsed on Wall Street, and the economy entered the most severe depression in American history. Within months, millions of people lost their jobs. Millions of others lost homes or farms or family businesses. So the desperation that drove the Bonus Army veterans to Washington was just one symptom of a much more widespread despondency.*

The administration that ordered troops to move against the Bonus Army was led by Herbert Hoover, the third in a succession of Republican presidents. But he was about to be replaced by Franklin Delano Roosevelt, who was promising a "New Deal." The marchers did not get their bonus, but the nation was about to get a seven-year tide of legislation that would permanently transform traditional assumptions about the relationship between the federal government and the American people.

The Great Depression, as people came to call it, was a world phenomenon that crippled the economies of all the industrial nations. All around the world, authoritarian leaders were gaining power over distressed and frustrated populations. The question posed by the Bonus March—and by the New Deal—was: Could industrial capitalism in the United States be saved within the framework of constitutional government, or was Hoover's use of the United States Army against freely assembled citizens the first step toward a major distortion of the American political system?

DEFEAT OF THE BONUS MARCHERS

The witness shifted nervously in his chair, but was clearly determined to hold his ground. Having waited a long time to testify, he was not going to be put off. He did not address the committee formally, or even begin with a polite "Good afternoon, Gentlemen." He simply began with the story of how he had walked all the way from New Jersey to Washington:

> My comrade and I hiked here from nine o'clock Sunday morning, when we left Camden. I done it all by my feet—shoe leather. I come to show you people that we need our bonus. We wouldn't want it if we didn't need it.

The witness was Joseph T. Angelo, veteran of World War I. He was addressing a committee of the House of Representatives of the United States Congress. The year was 1931, and the committee was hearing testimony about a controversial matter: the immediate payment of a "bonus" to all the veterans of World War I.

The country was in the second year of the most severe economic depression in its history. The bonus would pay about $1,000 each to over 3 million men and their families. Congress had set up the bonus (a combination of life insurance and a pension) in 1924. It was not due to be paid until 1945, except to the heirs of veterans who died earlier. The amount of money involved was enormous. (A thousand dollars in 1932 was comparable to at least fifteen thousand of the dollars of the 1990s.) If the bonus was paid now, it would be the greatest program of direct relief for the poor ever undertaken by the federal government.

For six days officials of the Republican administration testified. President Herbert Hoover was opposed to the bonus. The testimony of government officials reflected this opposition. A few congressmen and one or two officers of veterans' organizations spoke out for the bonus, but they were outnumbered by a long string of firmly Republican bank vice presidents, insurance executives, and other businessmen. The testimony was dull and full of statistics, designed to prove that the bonus would bankrupt the federal treasury and bring about a dangerous inflation.

But now for the first time, an ordinary veteran, with no job, a hungry family, and a plain man's English, was testifying. Before Joe Angelo had finished, the committee and the audience were stirred to a mixture of laughter, admiration, and stunned confusion.

> I have got a little home back there in Camden, New Jersey, that I built with my own hands after I came home from France. Now, I expect to lose that little place. Last week I went to our town committee and they gave me $4 for rations. That is to keep my wife and child and myself and clothe us; and also I cannot put no coal in my cellar.

Here, in the poor grammar and tired face of the witness, was the whole meaning of the depression that had begun in 1929. Angelo said he spoke for hundreds like himself in New Jersey. But he spoke, too, for millions all over the country who had not worked for a long time, who stood in bread lines, and who built the shacks in the shabby little neighborhoods they wryly called Hoovervilles.

But Angelo was also a veteran. So he spoke from his experience of the two most important events in his time: the war that people still called the Great War and the depression they were beginning to call the Great Depression. There was no economic theory or political philosophy in his testimony. He was just a hungry man who had fought in France.

> All I ask of you, brothers, is to help us. We helped you, now you help us. My partner here has a wife and five children, and he is just the same as I am. He hiked down here at the same time with me, and our feet are blistered. That is all I have to say. And I hope you folks can help us and that we can go through with the bonus. We don't want charity; we don't need it. All we ask for is what belongs to us, and that is all we want.

Some of the congressmen were confused. Others were curious. Following the custom of congressional committees, they began to question the witness:

MR. FREAR: What is your business?

MR. ANGELO: Nothing. I am nothing but a bum.

MR. FREAR: You say you have not worked for two years?

MR. ANGELO: I have not worked for a year and a half. But there is no work in my home town.

MR. RAINEY: You are wearing some medal. What is it?

MR. ANGELO: I carry the highest medal in America for enlisted men, the Distinguished Service Cross.

MR. RAINEY: You have a Distinguished Service Cross? What is that for?

MR. ANGELO: That is for saving Colonel Patton.

George S. Patton was already a well-known Army officer. (In World War II he would become one of the most famous and controversial of America's generals.) Congressman Rainey continued the questioning and pressed Angelo for details. Angelo responded with a startling tale. He had been part of a 305-man unit attacked by German machine guns in the Argonne Forest in 1918. When the battle was over, he said, most of the men were dead. Colonel Patton was wounded, and only Angelo was left standing. Then Angelo showed the committee a tiepin made from a bullet he said was taken from Patton's leg in France. Neither the tiepin nor the medal had ever gone to "Uncle" (Angelo's nickname for the pawnshops that had swallowed up most of his other possessions).

The afternoon was wearing on, but Angelo had roused the attention of the committee members and the audience as none of the other witnesses had. So the congressmen began to ask about his life. As Angelo answered, the audience sometimes laughed, sometimes applauded. He told them of working in a Du Pont plant, making munitions for the British before the United States entered the war. When Congress declared war in 1917, he enlisted at once. But he was almost rejected because he weighed a mere

107 pounds. Only after ten doctors had examined him and a general had watched him do a handspring and jump a table was he accepted.

Then, obviously agitated, Angelo wound up with another statement:

> I can make money. I can make lots of money. Now, I could go bootlegging. It is just the same way I could have went to France and I could have run out on my outfit. Which is the best, to be a live coward or a dead hero?

> When this was put on me, brothers, I wasn't worried when I went through. I don't have nothing to worry about. I wasn't married, and I got a wonderful sendoff when I went to France. My father throwed me out. [Laughter] And when I came back, I went home to my father. I saw a big, fat woman sitting in the seat. I knowed her from next door. I said, "She is the last woman you want on earth. Pop, what is she doing here?" He says, "That is my wife." I says, "Oh, My God!" She says, "Get out of here," and that was my welcome home, and I got out. [Laughter]

> So, folks, I tell you all I will say to you is, help us through with the bonus. That is the best answer for you folks to give to the fellow at home. Don't forget me for a job. [Applause]

Joe Angelo was three things: a veteran, a bum, and a victim of the most serious economic depression in American history. In each of these roles he was not just an individual grappling with purely personal problems; he represented over 4.5 million soldiers (about half of whom had actually been sent to Europe) suddenly discharged into civilian life in 1918 and 1919. These veterans organized, like other veterans in America's previous wars. More than a million joined the new American Legion and the Veterans of Foreign Wars. They thought of themselves as a special type of citizen, with a special claim on their country's gratitude.

As a bum, Angelo also spoke for countless people, many of them veterans, who had worked unsuccessfully at one job or another but mostly drifted through the 1920s. Naturally, the depression added millions of new bums. Angelo, who had not been able to find work for a year and a half, was only one of a great, restless mass of unemployed people. When he appeared before the congressional committee, at least 5 million men and women were officially classed as unemployed. Probably another 5 million were able to find only part-time work. Almost half the workers in America had their wages cut after the stock market crash of 1929. Few people could doubt in 1931 that unemployment was one of the most serious problems the United States had ever faced.

Joe Angelo's instinct was to turn to Washington for help. On his walk from Camden, he had met other small groups of veterans with the same idea. The unemployed, the veterans, and the bums (often one man, like Angelo, was all three) were looking more and more to the federal government for relief. They had one fairly good chance of getting help from a reluctant Congress and a stubborn president: payment of the bonus. This, in Angelo's words, was "the best answer for you folks to give."

Angelo wanted $1,000 immediately, instead of waiting until 1945 to collect a larger amount. This was the heart of an issue that was about to create the most dramatic crisis of the depression—the massing in Washington of a Bonus Army. Behind the crisis lay the old task of writing a final chapter to the war and the new, complicated task of dealing with the depression. But for the marchers in the Bonus Army, the problem was quite simple: when and how would they be able to collect their bonus in full?

Veterans could already borrow a little money against the promised bonus. Over 2 million had taken out loans that averaged $100 each—just enough to pay a back grocery bill, buy some coal for winter, or meet a medical emergency. But veterans everywhere were beginning to ask for ten times more, the payment of the entire bonus. And they found some sympathetic ears in Congress. Representative Wright Patman of Texas introduced a bill to authorize printing almost $2.5 billion in new paper money to pay the bonus. As time passed there was more and more talk of the bonus, not only in Washington but wherever knots of hungry veterans gathered.

For two years the president had been telling the nation that the depression was not so serious and would soon end. Administration officials played down unemployment statistics, portraying the crisis as a "temporary" economic slump that would soon "cure itself." Meanwhile, Hoover kept to his principle that the federal government should not provide direct relief to poor individuals. The veterans who were hitchhiking and jumping freight trains headed toward Washington were not so sure of their principles. Certainly they lacked the president's political experience and skills. But they knew that they needed the bonus.

In November 1931 a group of veterans left Seattle to ride freight trains to the capital. All over the country others were doing likewise. A movement had begun that would shake the Hoover administration. In May 1932, 300 men from Portland, Oregon, left for Washington in a group. They called themselves the Bonus Expeditionary Force—a play on the name of the American army in France, the American Expeditionary Force. They elected a leader, Walter F. Waters, once an army sergeant, then foreman in a fruit cannery, now unemployed. They rode freight cars east and by late May reached East St. Louis, Illinois. There they tried to hop new trains going farther east. When railroad police told them to leave, they began to break up trains by uncoupling cars. They also soaped the rails in some places, making it impossible for engines to move.

The state called for its National Guard to drive the veterans away. A scuffle occurred, but no one was hurt badly. The marchers were soon on their way again—in National Guard trucks that Illinois had provided in return for their promise to leave the state peacefully. But, most important, for the first time, the Bonus Army had won the attention of the newspapers and the public. Other veterans soon followed suit.

The scene was repeated everywhere. Merchants and mayors, railroad officials and governors, found it easier to supply trucks or boxcars than to stop the veterans. Thus a steady stream of bonus marchers was pouring into Washington. Each group had a leader or two, and their purpose was the same. They were in Washington to demand their bonus, even if they had to wait there until 1945 to get it.

One man deeply interested in the veterans' cause was Pelham D. Glassford, a West Point graduate and the youngest American in the war to become a brigadier general. In 1931 Hoover appointed Glassford superintendent of Washington's police force. He would have to deal with the Bonus Expeditionary Force in the capital.

Glassford hoped that the Bonus Army either would not come or would go home quickly. But when the marchers arrived, he became sympathetic and helpful. He called them his "boys." He even assigned them "quarters" in abandoned buildings on Pennsylvania Avenue, at the heart of official Washington, between the White House and the Capitol.

At Glassford's suggestion, also, the marchers made a "muster," or list of their groups, to make it easier to track down criminals and keep out "reds" and "radicals." Gradually, the veterans formed themselves into "companies" and then "regiments." They elected Walter Waters, leader of the Portland group, as their commander. He appointed junior officers and divided the men into companies named after states. Soon the Bonus Army had a structure of command like the regular army.

Glassford's original decision to let the marchers camp along Pennsylvania Avenue was based on his hope that few would come. Soon it was obvious that the Bonus Army was much too large and dangerous (and embarrassing to the administration) to be at the center of things. Glassford sent most of the marchers to a new campsite a few miles southeast of Capitol Hill, at Anacostia Flats, a muddy landfill near the fork of the Potomac and Anacostia rivers. There about 6,000 veterans built a shabby but orderly camp, with shacks and tents arranged in winding rows.

At Anacostia Flats the veterans tried to re-create their old army life. They woke to bugles, conducted roll calls, and had inspections. A company of men was assigned every day to KP. Waters exercised strict discipline.

Other aspects of camp life were more relaxed. Some men had brought their wives and children. The Salvation Army set up a post office, a library, and a recreation room.

IN CAMP AGAIN. At their Washington campsites, the bonus marchers tried to maintain military order. Among other things, this meant setting up kitchens to cook and to serve large groups of men. Here, one ex-soldier ladles out a dish of food for another. The stove is a trench, covered by a steel beam, with a rude chimney at the cook's left.

Glassford managed to borrow some field kitchens and other equipment. He supervised the distribution of food donated by Washington citizens, American Legion posts, and others. At one point Glassford gave several hundred dollars of his own money to buy food. There was even a camp newspaper to keep the veterans informed about the progress of bonus legislation in Congress.

By June 6, 1932, the veterans were ready for their first direct action. About 7,000 left their separate camps around the city and lined up neatly in six "regiments" to parade through Washington. The men felt fairly hopeful as they moved along. The Patman bill, which was in the House, seemed likely to pass soon. The rumors that they were controlled by "communists," spread by some politicians to smear the Bonus Army, were not being given much credit. Best of all, their parade had drawn a crowd of about 100,000, made up mostly of Washington clerical workers. Every time another company with its American flag passed, the crowd applauded.

Shortly after dark the long line of marchers reached a circle near the Capitol. (They were forbidden to pass the White House or go to the Capitol itself.) Orders were given to fall out, and the marchers broke ranks to walk quietly back to Anacostia. They had heard that in less than a week the House would vote on the bonus bill. If it passed both the House and Senate and was signed by Hoover, most of the veterans could collect the $1,000 needed to get their hungry families through another depression year.

The parade was simply a beginning. Veterans kept coming to Washington—the police estimated 100 every hour. On June 15, when the House passed the bonus bill, there were probably 15,000 veterans, plus some wives and children, scattered around Washington. Anacostia Flats was crowded, but new shacks kept going up. By now the ex-soldiers had stripped half the city of every stray board and door, every spare piece of tin and canvas. One man moved a burial vault onto the flats and took up residence in it. The camp was about level with the river, and had to be protected by a levee. When it rained, mud was a foot deep. But the Bonus Army kept building.

Obviously, some kind of crisis might soon develop. Health officials predicted a typhoid epidemic. Waters predicted victory if 100,000 more veterans arrived. Hoover's advisers predicted that "communists" would take over the Bonus Army.

The Bonus Army and the administration were both waiting for the Senate to vote on the Patman bill. Hoover was sure he would win. The House elected in 1930 was Democratic. Since it was the first body of politicians to graduate from the depression, it was full of representatives who had recently promised their constituents direct action. But only one third of the Senate had been elected in 1930. The majority were still firmly Republican and loyal to the president. Both houses were striving for a July adjournment. (It was an election year, and everyone wanted to get home to campaign.) The administration hoped that the Bonus Army would simply disappear after the Senate voted and Congress adjourned.

On June 17 the Senate would debate and vote on the bonus. Waters commanded his marchers to go to the Capitol and fill the galleries, steps, and grounds. By noon there were 10,000 veterans in and around the Capitol.

VETERANS ON PARADE.   In July 1932 the Bonus Army held this shirtsleeve parade from the Washington Monument, shown in the background, to the Capitol. The marchers maintain their ranks and files in good order and are absolutely in step, in spite of the lack of a band. They are obviously trying to emphasize both their military skills and their patriotism.

Inside, the Senate debated. Men would leave the gallery every few minutes to report to the marchers out on the steps. Opponents of the bill argued Hoover's position on what should be done about the depression: the government ought to cut spending, not spend more. Direct relief to individuals was not a federal responsibility. Recovery would come as large banks, businesses, and railroads regained their health. Then jobs would become available, and the economy would escape from radical tinkering.

Many senators supporting the bill argued that since the veterans were hungry and would be able to collect the bonus in thirteen years anyway, they should have it now. But one or two senators gave a more complicated justification for the bonus. In a depression, they insisted, the government should spend money, not save it. If the government printed 2.5 billion new dollars for the bonus, the money would swiftly circulate. The veterans would be only the first to gain. The stores where they spent their payments would get the money. These stores, in turn, would order more goods from wholesalers and manufacturers. So every bonus dollar would become a dollar in motion, moving through the economy and stimulating all business. Naturally, when the depression was cured, the government could stop "deficit spending"—that is, spending more than it raised in taxes. The economy would return to "normal."

Though the debate went on, it soon became clear that only a political miracle could save the bonus. The Senate was much too conservative to experiment with such legislation. Even some of the senators who usually opposed Hoover questioned the bill. What was needed, they said, was a general bill for relief of *all* the unemployed. Veterans should receive no special favors.

Finally, after 8 P.M., someone came from the Senate gallery and whispered to Waters. The bill had lost decisively, by a vote of sixty-two to eighteen. Waters climbed the steps and turned to face the largest body that had ever gathered in Washington to demonstrate for a cause. The marchers had been waiting for hours, and for a moment it seemed they might riot. Marines were stationed nearby, just in case. Members of the administration had wanted to set up machine guns, but Glassford persuaded them not to. Waters shouted:

> Comrades! [a term from the war, and not necessarily a communist greeting] I have bad news. Let us show them we can take it on the chin. Let us show them we are patriotic Americans.

There was a muttering from the crowd. Then a gigantic roar came from 10,000 throats. Waters pleaded for calm:

> We are not telling you to go home. Go back to your camps. We are going to stay in Washington until we get the bonus, no matter how long it takes. And we are one hundred times as good Americans as those men in there who voted against it. But there is nothing more to be done tonight.

The situation was tenser than any in the capital since the Civil War. Ten thousand disappointed people, who had kept good discipline for weeks, were ready to break and mob the Senate. Waters played a final card to keep order: "I call on you to sing 'America,'" he shouted. After a few false starts, the men obeyed. Gradually, the song gathered strength.

The emergency was over, at least for the moment. The singing died out, and bugles sounded assembly. The men milled about, looking for their outfits for the march back to camp. It was dark now, and the nervous political men waiting inside the White House and the Capitol could take a deep breath. The bonus was dead, at least until Congress reconvened in December, after the presidential election of 1932.

But the Bonus Army did not disappear. The Hoover administration issued statements that the men were leaving. But the police revealed that new recruits were arriving about as fast as old ones left. Estimates of the size of the group issued by the government, the police, and the newspapers varied wildly. At its largest, the Bonus Army probably numbered about 20,000. Membership shifted constantly; perhaps as many as 50,000 veterans came to Washington at one time or another during June and July of 1932.

The Hoover administration decided to try a bribe, and offered to "lend" the veterans train fare or gas money to leave town, plus seventy-five cents a day for other "expenses." Many veterans simply took the money and stayed in town. Others used it to

ON THE CAPITOL STEPS. The high point of the bonus march was probably this scene on the steps of the Capitol. Inside, while the veterans waited, the Senate was debating the Patman bill, which would have given them early payment of the bonus they had come to ask for. The bill's defeat nearly triggered an angry confrontation between the veterans and U.S. Marines, who had been called out to keep order.

recruit new members. Thus a month after the Senate had defeated the Patman bill, there were about as many marchers as ever. The police estimated 15,000, two-thirds of them crowded into Anacostia Flats.

By late July, with no hope of a bonus from Congress, the veterans' mood soured. Their newspaper published more militant calls for action. Waters began to allow the small group of about 150 communists to eat occasionally at the Anacostia mess. (He had always thrown them out before.) He even began to talk about a permanent organization of veterans in politics, which he would call the Khaki Shirts, in imitation of the Brown Shirts that Adolf Hitler had recently organized in Germany.

In the White House, too, opinions were getting stronger. After the Senate defeated the bonus, President Hoover decided the marchers had no business "squatting" on government land. He also decided they were not truly "patriotic" veterans asking for relief. Instead, he believed they had been

> organized and promoted by the communists, and included a large number of hoodlums and ex-convicts determined to raise a public disturbance. They were frequently addressed by Democratic congressmen, seeking to inflame them against me.

The differences grew sharper, the summer hotter, and tempers shorter. On July 16 the most serious incident so far broke out at the Capitol. Congress was about to adjourn. Waters ordered his men to make one last symbolic demonstration. By midday, nearly 7,000 bonus marchers were at the Capitol. Their mood was much uglier than a month before, at the time of the Senate vote on the Patman bonus bill. Senators and congressmen crowded near every window to watch. Even Glassford lost his nerve.

Glassford ordered Waters taken into custody and moved to the basement of the Capitol. When the veterans saw what was happening, they stopped cheering Glassford and began to boo and jeer. "Waters! Waters!" they chanted. Glassford was forced to bring the Bonus Army's commander back out of the Capitol building, onto the platform. After a short, harsh exchange with Glassford, Waters tried to calm his people. Then he ordered them to move to the middle of the great stairway that leads up to the Capitol's main floor:

> Use the center steps. But I want you to keep a lane open for the white-collared birds, so they won't rub into us lousy rats. We're going to stay here until I see Hoover!"

The demonstration had turned dangerous. Several congressmen came out of the Capitol to speak to the demonstrators, trying to cool them down. Finally, the Speaker of the House, John Nance Garner, agreed to meet with Waters and a committee of his aides inside the building. Garner handled the situation well. He made a few empty promises of help and was photographed with Waters. When the conference was over, Waters went back outside and ordered his followers back to their camps. For a second time, an extremely touchy and potentially violent situation had been controlled.

In the White House, however, tempers were also growing shorter. Hoover had just been renominated by the Republicans to run for a second term. The Democrats would meet soon to nominate Franklin D. Roosevelt, the governor of New York, as their candidate. Hoover knew the campaign would be rough. But he believed he could win if he could overcome the widespread idea that he was somehow personally responsible for the depression.

A favorite tactic of Hoover's closest associates was to picture him as the firm opponent of all kinds of "radicalism." Hoover had always opposed the bonus. Now he and his advisers decided to move firmly against the veterans. Some even hoped for an incident. Then it would appear that the government had to defend its very life against a radical "insurrection."

A few days after Congress adjourned, the administration decided to move. The tensest point in Washington was two blocks on the south side of Pennsylvania Avenue, just a block from the Capitol and a mile from the White House, an area known as the Triangle. The buildings were vacant structures that had been condemned to make way for a government building program. All over the Triangle, veterans had camped in and around empty and half-demolished buildings, creating political eyesores that embarrassed the administration. On July 21, on instructions from the Treasury Department, the commissioners who governed the District of Columbia ordered the veterans to evacuate the two blocks. For various reasons the order was not carried out at once. But Waters told his people to be ready to leave. Glassford was locating another site farther away, where they could take their few possessions and settle again.

VETERANS AND THE POLICE.   A group of bonus marchers try to defend their tents against the advancing police. The Bonus Army was one of the few organizations in America that was more or less integrated racially, and the group shown here includes at least a couple of determined African Americans. The most intense struggle seems to concern whether the marchers or the police have a better right to the flag.

Finally, at about 10 A.M. on July 28, Treasury officials accompanied by Glassford and his police entered the area. The veterans began to evacuate the buildings and their makeshift shanties, leaving behind everything they could not carry or push along in small carts or baby carriages. Everything went peacefully, though a few veterans had to be taken out under arrest. Before noon the first building was empty. In the meantime, a large crowd of Washington citizens had gathered to watch. Their sympathies were divided between the police and the veterans.

Then, a little past noon, veterans from the other camps filtered into the area, mixing with the crowd. One group came to stage a formal demonstration. Paul Anderson, a journalist, described what happened next:

> At noon, three bonus men, one carrying a large American flag, started across the block, followed by several hundred. When the leaders encountered a policeman, he grabbed the flag. There was a scuffle, and one of the marchers was hit on the head with a night stick. He wrested it from the officer and struck the cop, and there was a shower of bricks from the buddies in the rear. It looked like an ugly mess, but the cops kept their heads, and no shots were fired.

> Glassford dashed into the heart of the melee, smiled when a brickbat hit him on the chest, and stopped the fighting. Within two minutes, the veterans were cheering Glassford.

For another half hour the police continued their work. The veterans were leaving the buildings, but they stood around outside, many on big piles of bricks. No one is certain what happened next. Some witnesses said a policeman tried to clear veterans out of a building that had not even been ordered vacated. They resisted. Another observer said that a policeman started climbing some makeshift stairs, lost his balance, and fell. In a panic he pulled his revolver and began to fire wildly into a crowd near him. Glassford gave what may be the most accurate account:

> I was about twenty yards away from the building when I heard a commotion. I went to the second floor. One officer had started up the steps, and near the rear, I heard some say, "Let's get him!"
>
> As he started up the steps, bricks started falling on him [Glassford was not certain whether the bricks were being thrown or were just falling], and as I leaned over the railing above, I saw him fall and draw his gun, firing two shots.

Other policemen also started shooting. Then veterans began to throw bricks at every policeman in sight. Again Glassford acted quickly to prevent a vicious riot. He ran outside, shouting, "Stop that shooting!" The firing ended, and the bricks stopped flying. Ambulances rushed in to take away the injured. One policeman was hurt seriously by a brick. One bonus marcher was dead; another died later of gunshot wounds.

The battle of the Bonus Army might have ended here. Glassford had the situation in hand. The veterans were moving out of the buildings as they had been ordered. On the whole they were reluctant but still willing to cooperate. Waters had supported Glassford every step of the way. Within another hour or two, evacuation of the two blocks would have been complete. But the administration also had decided to act. Hoover had ordered the chief of staff of the army, General Douglas MacArthur, to bring troops into the city to "restore civil peace."

The troops—about 500 at first, then later over 1,000—formed up behind the White House. They came armed with bayoneted rifles and heavy blue canisters of tear gas. There were cavalry with sabers, a machine-gun squadron, several infantry companies, and even a half-dozen tanks. MacArthur put the troops under the command of General Perry L. Miles. But, as he later wrote, "In accordance with the President's request, I accompanied General Miles." With MacArthur was his aide, Major Dwight David Eisenhower. And with the cavalry was George S. Patton (who had no way of knowing that Joe Angelo had come back to Washington and was out in the troubled city with about 12,000 of his buddies, waiting).

At about four o'clock the cavalry led the way, the iron shoes of their horses clattering on the asphalt of Pennsylvania Avenue. Then came tanks, more cavalry, the infantry, and the mounted machine gunners. They rode, walked, and rumbled up to the Triangle, pushing the crowds back and surrounding the buildings. Without any conference or hesitation, the troops (who wore gas masks and carried fixed bayonets) began to throw tear-gas canisters into the buildings. They were going to clear the entire area.

The veterans did not resist. A few hung back and had to be jabbed at with bayonets. Mostly they stumbled out of the area and toward Anacostia. MacArthur, who also

MACARTHUR AND EISENHOWER. The command of the military force that finally chased the Bonus Army out of Washington was in the hands of General Douglas MacArthur, shown here on the left, with his aide, Dwight David Eisenhower. MacArthur insisted that the bonus marchers were a fundamental threat to the government.

had tears streaming down his face from the gas, ordered most of his men to herd the veterans south. Another detachment moved west, to attack the buildings where the few dozen actual communists who were part of the Bonus Army had been forced by Waters to set up a separate encampment.

Suddenly, it became clear that General MacArthur intended to clear the entire District of Columbia. In the Triangle, smoke began to rise: The troops had set fire to the shacks, tents, and scattered belongings of the Bonus Army.

MacArthur's forces kept pushing the straggling veterans before them with bayonets and sabers. The sun was going down behind the troops. Ahead lay the drawbridge to Anacostia. The Bonus Army's rearguard hurried across the bridge at about sunset. Waters had already given the order to evacuate Anacostia and had sent word to MacArthur asking for time to move at least the women and children out of the camp. On the flats about 7,000 men were scurrying around, trying to keep order in a forced retreat.

From the time the troops first appeared, the bonus marchers gave no resistance. They booed, they swore—but they moved. MacArthur left his tanks north of the river and paused before Anacostia Flats for an hour before sending in the infantry. But when they went onto the flats, the soldiers threw gas everywhere. Stragglers were treated very roughly. The soldiers then set fire to the camp. (Many of the veterans had already put matches to their borrowed army tents.) Next the infantry moved beyond the camp up a nearby slope where many of the veterans still stood, watching their shacks burn. As the troops rushed up the hill (which was not federal property) they continued to throw tear gas. One woman, whose baby had actually been born at Anacostia Flats, told this story:

> The troops came up the hill, driving the people ahead of them. As they passed by the house [the shack where the woman was living], one of them threw a tear-gas bomb over the fence into the front yard. The house was filled with gas, and we all began to cry. We got wet towels and put them over the faces of the children. About a half an hour later, my baby began to vomit. I took her outside in the air and she vomited again. Next day, she began to turn black and blue.

A few days later the baby died—the third and last fatality of the battle of the Bonus Army.

The day after the action was a time for summing up. The White House and other administration officials issued statements. MacArthur gave his version in a press conference:

> That mob was a bad-looking mob. It was animated by the essence of revolution. They had come to the conclusion, beyond the shadow of a doubt, that they were about to take over either the direct control of the government, or else to control it by indirect methods. It is my belief that had the President not acted today, he would have been faced with a grave situation. Had he let it go on another week, I believe that the institutions of our government would have been severely threatened.

To this version of the ominous threat posed by the Bonus Army, MacArthur added a claim that it was the veterans who had burned their own shacks in the Triangle.

Another kind of summing up came from Joe Angelo, who told a newspaper reporter his story. He was at Anacostia Flats, watching a group of infantrymen in gas masks overrun the shack he had been living in. They were urged on by a tough, confident officer. Angelo blinked the burning tear gas out of his eyes and recognized George S. Patton. Then, like the rest of the Bonus Army, he ran. Soon he was back home in Camden, where he had started his long hike to Washington a year and a half before. No one knows whether he pawned his medal or the tiepin made from his souvenir bullet.

Crash, Depression, and a New Deal

Most of the veterans who went to Washington in 1932 to ask for their bonus were as politically innocent as Joe Angelo. Some of their leaders had a little political sophistication; but only the tiny fraction who were communists thought they understood the basic problems of American society and sought a revolutionary solution. The rank-and-file marchers were simply caught in a web of circumstances they neither understood nor desired.

The bonus marchers' experience was defined by the two great events they had participated in, the Great War and the Great Depression. Between lay the decade of the 1920s, the "Jazz Age." But most of the veterans had experienced very little "jazz." Like most Americans, they had passed through a curiously contradictory decade. On the one hand, American society of the 1920s really was characterized by tremendous innovations—some technological, others social. But alongside all the newness and experimentation, the 1920s had been a decade of profound, sometimes violent, conservatism. Both in formal politics, centered in Washington, and in the informal politics of organized movements, the keynote had been not innovation but restoration.

Conservatism in politics received a kind of endorsement from the economy. The 1920s was a period of apparent prosperity. In some sectors, the economy underwent a sustained boom. And this burst of prosperity had made it appear to many Americans that the country had returned from the "distortions" of progressive reform and war to what President Warren G. Harding called "normalcy." It took the depression to show that normalcy was an illusion, and that the 1920s had contained profound distortions of its own.

A TIDE OF REACTION

For millions of Americans, the uncertainties of modernity, the wave of progressive reforms, and the moral crusade of the war were all extremely unsettling. Even before the war was over, millions of people had already decided that change had gone too far, that the Republic was in desperate danger of losing its stability and virtue. For some, the threat was simple: The country was being overrun by "foreigners," and by "alien" political ideas. For others, the problem was alcohol, and the loose life associated with it. Still others viewed blacks as the principal threat. For many, the danger lay in the growing number and power of Jews and Catholics. Some complained about the inroads new scientific ideas were making on traditional values and beliefs.

Not every American participated, by any means, but a large and very active segment of society—especially in the South and the Midwest—joined in a series of movements and organizations to "save" their country from what they saw as the perils of change. Sometimes the results were merely quaint, as when the sale of alcohol was forbidden by an amendment to the Constitution. Or when schoolteachers were prosecuted for explaining Charles Darwin's theory of evolution in their classrooms. At other times, however, the results were more serious, even tragic, as when dozens of African Americans were lynched by mobs, or hundreds of immigrant "radicals" were hounded in court and even sentenced to die for their supposed crimes. This was part of the character of "normalcy," the darker face of the Jazz Age.

THE RED SCARE

The conservative reaction focused sharply on "radicalism." The Russian Revolution of 1917, which had brought the communist government of the Bolsheviks to power, was followed by communist uprisings in Germany and Hungary. These developments created an atmosphere of fear in the United States. Many people, including a number of powerful leaders in federal and state governments, believed that a communist "conspiracy" was at work to "overthrow" the American government.

In 1919 a series of spectacular labor strikes and an outbreak of political sabotage fed the fear. In the spring of that year, two small groups of anarchists attempted to bomb the homes and offices of a number of government officials and businessmen. The bombs, most of which were sent through the mail, were probably the work of mentally unstable persons. Certainly they had nothing to do with the tiny organized Socialist and Communist parties of the country.

In fact, the bombers were incompetent. Many of the bombs were never delivered because they did not have enough postage. One bomb only damaged the house of its intended victim, but it blew the bomber himself, an Italian anarchist, to bits. Another, addressed to a Georgia politician, was opened by his maid (a black worker, not a "capitalist"). She lost her hands as a result. But the bombings did convince many people that revolution was at hand.

One of the people who was most convinced was Woodrow Wilson's attorney general, A. Mitchell Palmer. Like Wilson, Palmer was both a liberal and a strong antiradical. He also happened to have his eye on the Democratic nomination of 1920. So he used the "red" scare to make his department the center of the action. He obtained a special appropriation for hunting down radicals. With the money, he formed a new antisubversive division of the Justice Department, headed by J. Edgar Hoover.

Beginning in November 1919, the Justice Department conducted a series of raids against radical groups, seeking out suspected communists at union meetings, at Communist party headquarters, and in their homes. The most spectacular of the raids, which came on New Year's Day 1920, resulted in the arrest of 6,000 people. In the end these "Palmer raids" led to the conviction of only a handful of citizens, most of them for minor crimes. Immigrant aliens, who were Palmer's main target, suffered more; about 600 were eventually deported, mostly to the Soviet Union.

Palmer's campaign created an atmosphere of near-hysteria among many Americans. It led to one episode that did more than any other single event of the 1920s to divide Americans of different political beliefs. In 1920 two Italian anarchists, Nicola Sacco and Bartolomeo Vanzetti, were arrested in Boston on a charge of robbing a shoe company and murdering two of its employees. Their trial soon became a political event, a test of the established authority against political "radicalism."

The trial was unfair. But in the political climate of the red scare, Sacco and Vanzetti were convicted and sentenced to death. The appeals process was long and unsuccessful. Finally, in 1927, the year of Lindbergh's flight, both men were executed in the electric chair. To many American liberals and radicals of the 1920s, Sacco and Vanzetti were the century's greatest martyrs, contemporary counterparts of the victims of the Salem witchcraft trials of the 1690s and the Haymarket affair of the 1880s. But to

SACCO AND VANZETTI. Here, in 1927, Nicola Sacco and Bartolomeo Vanzetti enter the courtroom to make their last plea for justice. Some recent evidence seems to show that at least one of them may have been guilty of the crime he was charged with. But no amount of new evidence can set aside the fact that they were unfairly tried and unfairly convicted.

most Americans, they were just dangerous "aliens," Italian radicals who had been properly punished.

The bonus marchers of 1932 had to contend with the lingering effects of the red scare. They were accused of being communists and serving as tools in a foreign conspiracy. When Douglas MacArthur marched on their camp at Anacostia, he did so in the belief that he was protecting the country from a powerful revolutionary movement. The irony was, however, that the marchers themselves accepted much of the ideology of "Americanism" that fueled the red scare. Their response to the charge that they were communists was to insist on their own patriotism, and to point proudly to their record of military service. Most of the marchers were probably just as devoutly anticommunist, just as insistent on their own "100 percent Americanism" as their critics.

The red scare also made it possible for those Americans who feared immigrants and their ethnic and religious differences to restrict immigration. In February 1921 (over the veto of President Wilson), Congress passed a law that limited immigration, especially from countries in southern and eastern Europe. According to the law, the number of immigrants from a country in any given year could not exceed 3 percent of the number of people of that nationality who were already in the United States in 1910. In 1924 the law was made even more restrictive. Quotas would now be based on resident population in 1890, immigration limited to 150,000 per year after 1927, and Asians totally excluded. The effect of the laws was to end, almost at once, the flow of immigration.

PROHIBITION AND REACTION

Like the red scare and the movement for immigration restriction, the prohibition of alcohol in the 1920s had its roots in the progressive period. In 1919 the necessary number of states had approved the Eighteenth Amendment, which empowered Congress to prohibit the sale of alcoholic beverages. The amendment marked the victory of a long campaign for "temperance." It provided another rallying point for conservative, small-town Americans. They divided society into the "drys" and the "wets" and opposed any politician who did not favor Prohibition.

The Prohibition movement failed to stop Americans from drinking. In most cities, people continued to drink whiskey in illegal bars that became known as "speakeasies." The sale of "bootleg" whiskey was controlled largely by organized gangs of criminals, like the one led by Al Capone in Chicago, which bribed public officials and policemen to cover up their operations. But for most conservative Americans, Prohibition was above all a moral crusade. It was an issue they could use to split their country into two camps: one composed of "decent" people, the other of "riffraff."

Another conservative campaign of the 1920s was the attempt of many Protestant Americans—again, especially in the South and the Midwest—to prevent schools from teaching "dangerous" or "un-American" ideas. In several southern states this crusade was aimed mainly at the idea of evolution. The notion of biological evolution was an old one. It became scientifically respected in the nineteenth century through the work of Charles Darwin, who published his landmark book, *The Origin of Species*, in 1859. By the 1920s practically every scientist in the world believed that animals, including human beings, had evolved over a long period of time. But this idea seemed to many people to be a serious challenge to the fundamentals of their religion. They saw it as a challenge to the Genesis account of creation.

Several state legislatures forbade schools to teach the theory of evolution. In 1925 John Scopes, a schoolteacher in Dayton, Tennessee, decided to challenge the law. He was arrested, and his trial became almost as much a spectacle as the trial of Sacco and Vanzetti. Reporters from every major American newspaper—and several European papers—covered it closely.

Scopes was defended by the most famous criminal lawyer in the United States, Clarence Darrow of Chicago. The prosecution was led by William Jennings Bryan, who had been the Democratic presidential candidate three times, and had served as secretary of state in the administration of Woodrow Wilson. Bryan, now an aging but still powerful leader of millions of Protestant fundamentalists, stood ready to smite the forces of "modernism."

Bryan was forced by Darrow to take the witness stand, and he was publicly humiliated by Darrow. But Scopes lost the case and was fined $100. The Tennessee law stayed on the books. After the Scopes trial, however, the direction of education in the South and elsewhere shifted away from Bryan's intellectual conservatism toward the acceptance of modern science. Bryan's crusade, like many other conservative movements of the 1920s, was only a temporary victory over twentieth-century ideas and social habits.

THE KU KLUX KLAN

The most bizarre conservative movement of the 1920s was the Ku Klux Klan. The Klan, which had all but disappeared after Reconstruction, was reorganized in 1915 in Georgia. Its membership grew slowly until the war was over. Then, taking many of its cues from the red scare, the Klan began to gain support. Much of its strength still lay in the rural South and Southwest. But there was a new element in this second growth: now, millions in the northern states, many of them city dwellers, joined the organization. At one time or another, about 5 million Americans took up membership and donned the white sheets that were the uniform of the Klan. The strongest Klan state was not in the South at all but Indiana, where the organization appeared for a time to control even the state government.

The Ku Klux Klan was a fringe organization, attracting only the most conservative citizens. The white robes and hoods, the secrecy and the rituals, the burning of crosses in the night, all demanded considerable dedication from its members. They had to be able to

THE KKK ON THE MARCH. The Ku Klux Klan is shown here, in 1926, in one of its favorite kinds of moments. The robed Klansmen are marching publicly and openly, declaring to all the world their patriotic purposes and determination to save the country from a host of "perils." And yet, even in this aggressively public setting, the marchers preserve the air of secrecy, mystery, and ritual that is so important to many of its members. ("Ku Klux" was an adaptation of the Greek *kuklos*, meaning "circle" or "band." "Klan," of course, was an adaptation of "clan.")

stomach a good deal of violence and torture. And they had to be able to tolerate a large element of the ridiculous, as in the titles of Klan officers, like "dragon," "kleagal," and "kludd." Nevertheless, the Klan gained considerable political power. The "grand dragon" of Indiana claimed that he had controlled the election of one of the state's governors, and the Klan had an important influence on the Democratic presidential nomination in 1924.

In the long run, the Klan—like the Prohibition movement and the fundamentalist attempt to prevent the teaching of evolution—was destined to lose. Blacks would not be lynched in great numbers forever, the freedom to drink alcohol would return, new scientific theories would get taught, eventually. But in the political atmosphere of the 1920s, it was possible for millions of Klansmen, and millions of other conservatives

who did not join the organization, to convince themselves that their victory was close at hand, that the country would be saved, after all.

THE POLITICS OF CONSERVATISM

The political instrument of salvation, restoration, and "normalcy" was to be the Republican party. As the war ended, the Republicans could see as plainly as anyone else that there was a change in the political atmosphere. The policies of reform and military crusade, on which Woodrow Wilson and the Democrats had built their success in national politics, were clearly falling into disrepute. The Republicans met at Chicago in their national convention of 1920 full of hope. They were still the majority party, they knew. And no Democrat on the horizon represented a real threat to the election of a Republican president. Wilson's illness, the failure of the League of Nations, the doings of A. Mitchell Palmer—all had helped to disorganize the Democrats.

The only question seemed to be whether the Republicans could unite on a candidate. The convention deadlocked for six ballots. Then a few party leaders huddled in one of the most famous "smoke-filled rooms" in American history and chose a surprise candidate: Warren Gamaliel Harding, senator from Ohio.

WARREN G. HARDING

Harding was a small-town newspaper publisher and politician, reminiscent of the Republican style of the late nineteenth century. He had risen carefully through the party system in Ohio to become a senator. His political virtues were, primarily, loyalty to the organization and a discreet silence on most issues. A handsome but simple man, he was puzzled by complicated issues like taxation, the tariff, and foreign affairs. He was "one of the boys," who enjoyed a night of whiskey and poker with his cronies. He had never proposed an important law or policy, nor made an important speech, in his whole career. But he had a face that voters wanted to trust. And the people who ran the party knew they could trust him, too. He was a party "regular." He would not have any strange ideas about regulating business or supporting labor unions, nor would he propose any odd reforms. He was, in a word, conservative.

For vice president, the Republicans nominated Calvin Coolidge, another small-town politician, who had first won a national reputation as a tough antilabor man during the strikes of 1919. Coolidge was governor of Massachusetts when Boston's police organized as an AFL local and went out on strike. Without attempting to settle the strike peacefully, Coolidge sent armed troops into the streets of Boston. The protest of Samuel Gompers, the AFL president, was met with one of Coolidge's most famous terse retorts: "There is no right to strike against the public safety, anywhere, anytime."

Coolidge was less a party regular than Harding, but he was even more conservative in matters of policy. Except for his odd flair for succinct statements, he was a lackluster man with a crabbed countenance, a striking contrast to Harding's handsome geniality. In any case, no one at the Republican convention thought that they were choosing anything but a vice president.

The Democrats nominated a lackluster candidate of their own, James M. Cox. However, they tried to spice up the ticket with a dashing young New Yorker, Franklin D. Roosevelt. Roosevelt had served as assistant secretary of the navy under Wilson. The convention hoped the Roosevelt name would attract voters who remembered his cousin Theodore. But probably no Democratic ticket could have won in 1920. The voters wanted a change. Sixty percent of them voted for Harding. They also sent large Republican majorities to both the House and the Senate, making it one of the most complete victories in the history of American national politics. Harding carried every state outside the Democrats' Solid South and cracked even that by winning Tennessee. The repudiation of Wilson's New Freedom seemed complete.

RETURN TO NORMALCY

Harding took office with a slogan that coined a new word. He said the country needed a return to "normalcy." No dictionary contained this word, but it was easy enough to guess what the new president meant. Harding believed that there had been too much "experimentation," too many attempts to regulate the economy and the working lives of Americans, too much speculation about new diplomatic arrangements such as the League of Nations. "Normalcy" meant letting things take their "natural" course—not interfering in the decisions of businessmen or in the complex affairs of other nations. "Normalcy" meant, in short, an attempt to return to supposedly simpler times and uncomplicated politics.

Harding's relaxed conservatism was not a well-defined policy. Rather, it was a wish for fewer policies and less activity by the government. For his cabinet, the president chose people sympathetic to the practices of industrial and business leaders. His most important appointment, in fact, was Secretary of the Treasury Andrew Mellon, a Pennsylvania industrialist who owned the only important company then making aluminum in the United States.

Mellon helped shape the small amount of legislation that the Harding administration presented to Congress. His pet bill was one cutting the maximum income tax on the wealthy from 65 percent to 25 percent. (Congress at first reduced the limit to only 50 percent, but Mellon later got most of what he wanted.) He also proposed, and got from Congress, much higher tariffs on imports, a policy that benefited American business and industry by limiting foreign competition.

THE OHIO GANG

Specific legislation was less important in Harding's conservative administration than its general relaxation of federal controls over business. Harding did not try to tear down the established regulatory agencies, like the Interstate Commerce Commission or the Federal Reserve Board. Instead, he merely appointed people to these agencies who were so friendly toward corporations that they administered the law gently or not at all. And Harding named as his secretary of commerce Herbert Hoover, who had made a fortune as a mining engineer and investor.

Hoover was clearly the most distinguished of Harding's appointments. He had made an enormous reputation during the war as head of the federal Food Administration. Unlike most of his colleagues in the Harding administration, Hoover was a thoughtful man, with a fairly clear-cut ideological position. He was a promoter of what he called "individualism." His central faith was that private enterprise, left to its own devices, could end poverty and usher in a new era of prosperity and progress.

To Hoover, the modern corporation was, ultimately, an instrument of social justice. Capitalism had, he believed, emerged from its nineteenth-century youth into a "mature" period of development. In their new maturity, corporations would be less concerned with sheer competition for profits and more determined to produce goods efficiently. In the process, the corporations would also contribute a great deal of what Hoover called "service" to society—technological innovation, education, the redistribution of income, and so on—until ignorance, poverty, and disease were banished.

The role of government, Hoover believed, should be to help this process along by providing information and assistance to businesses, not to hinder them through wasteful and inefficient regulation. This was the logic that Hoover applied as secretary of commerce. And this was the logic he would later bring to the White House.

Harding brought to Washington a group of friends who soon became known as the Ohio Gang. Some held seemingly harmless positions, like "Old Doc" Sawyer, a doctor in less than good standing with the medical profession. Old Doc became the White House physician, with the rank of army brigadier general. Other gang members were given more important positions, such as attorney general and secretary of the interior.

After two years in office, Harding, who was personally honest about money, began to realize that his appointees were stealing and peddling influence. In the spring and summer of 1923, two administration officials committed suicide while being investigated. In June, Harding began a long vacation in the West. As he left, he complained to a journalist, "My God, this is a hell of a job. I have

no trouble with my enemies. But my friends! They're the ones that keep me walking the floor nights!"

Two months later, in California after a trip to Alaska, Harding suffered what Old Doc Sawyer called food poisoning. Harding now had to pay personally for this political appointment, for Sawyer was wrong. The president had suffered a heart attack; on August 2 he died. In a way, Harding was lucky. He was mourned by his country almost as much as Lincoln had been. He was spared the knowledge of a new scandal that would later become almost synonymous with his name.

Albert Fall, Harding's secretary of the interior, had finagled Interior Department control of oil reserves on public land, set aside for the use of the navy. There were two large reserves, at Elk Hill in California and at Teapot Dome in Wyoming. Private oil interests were willing to pay almost any price to drill on the land. And they did.

Two oil company executives, Edward L. Doheny and Harry F. Sinclair, gave and lent Fall almost a half-million dollars in return for secret leases allowing them to drill on the reserves. The secret leaked out faster than the oil. The government managed to cancel the leases, but Fall went

to prison for a year. He was the first cabinet officer in American history to be put behind bars.

COOLIDGE AND BUSINESS

When Harding died, Vice President Calvin Coolidge became president. Though privately a talkative man, Silent Cal, as Coolidge was called, spoke very little in public. He kept most of Harding's appointees and basically followed his predecessor's policies for the rest of the term. As the 1924 election approached, there was little doubt about what the Republicans would do. Their convention enthusiastically nominated Coolidge.

The Democrats experienced a struggle between two wings of their party. One represented the rural South and West, the old Bryan supporters. The other wing, newer and based in the northern cities, was made up mostly of opponents of Prohibition and depended heavily on the support of immigrants (many of them Catholics or Jews). Neither wing of the party had enough delegates to control the convention. After 103 ballots the convention finally settled on a compromise candidate, John W. Davis.

Davis was as conservative as Coolidge. The Democratic candidate was associated with the financial firm of J. P. Morgan, almost a perfect symbol of corporate capitalism. The time seemed right to revive the third-party idea that had worked so well in 1912. This time, the Progressive candidate was Robert La Follette, now nearly seventy but still a fiery opponent of business interests. He did well. Although Coolidge won the election easily, with 15 million votes, La Follette managed to get almost 5 million votes, and to carry Wisconsin. Davis and his badly split party could muster only 8.5 million votes, less than a third of the total, and the party's worst showing since the Civil War.

Coolidge's second term in office was a continuation of the conservative policies of the earlier years, but without the scandals of 1921–1923. Mellon and Hoover still exercised great influence. The new administration went on supporting high tariffs, low taxes on corporations and the wealthy, and a hands-off policy on trusts and monopolies. It had an essentially do-nothing approach to farm problems and a negative attitude toward labor as well. The entire conservative politics of the 1920s was summed up in Coolidge's most famous statement: "The business of America is business."

Still, the president was popular, and doubtless he could have been nominated for a second full term and won. But his second most famous statement was: "I do not choose to run." Coolidge may have meant to put the heavy emphasis on "choose," meaning simply that he *would* accept a draft by the Republican convention. But, for once, "Silent Cal" had spoken too soon and said too much. The Republicans took him literally and turned to Herbert Hoover, the most prestigious official in the administration.

THE DEMOCRATIC CHALLENGE OF 1928

The Democrats partially healed their old split, hoping to rebuild the party after the disasters of 1920 and 1924. Governor Alfred E. Smith of New York won the nomination easily. Smith and Hoover were almost perfect contrasts. Hoover was conservative, even gloomy. He dressed in neat blue suits and was the perfect representative of stability and efficiency. Above all, he opposed any extension of federal power over private enterprise (unless, as with tariffs, federal power could be used to help business).

Smith, on the other hand, was an amiable, talkative, cigar-chomping Irish-American politician. He wore a brown derby and checked suits and talked with a New York twang. During the campaign, Hoover accused Smith of "socialism" because the New Yorker favored federal ownership of electric power-generating facilities.

However different their personalities and political backgrounds may have been, Smith and Hoover actually ran on similar platforms. To head his campaign, Smith chose a Republican executive from General Motors, a man who admitted he had actually voted for Coolidge in 1924. And in a variety of other ways, the Democrats strained to capture the political center by hewing to a very cautious policy line. On the surface, at least, the election was a contest between personal styles and religious convictions.

Smith's Catholicism got most of the publicity. Some of the charges were merely nasty, as when the Methodist bishop of Virginia referred to Smith as "this wet Roman Catholic chamberlain of the Pope of Rome." But even literate, liberal Protestant newspapers and magazines were concerned. The *Christian Century*, one of the most popular Protestant journals, said that Smith's victory would be the victory "of an alien culture, of a mediaeval Latin mentality, of an undemocratic hierarchy and of a foreign potentate."

Smith's stand on Prohibition also alarmed many voters. Hoover called Prohibition a "noble experiment," and it may have been this stand, not Smith's religion, that won Hoover powerful support in the South and Southwest. Smith, on the other hand, was a publicly announced "wet," who believed that Prohibition was not only a failure but an act that unfairly deprived urban workers of their modest "pleasures."

In the end, Hoover won what appeared to be a landslide. With 58 percent of the popular vote, he almost equaled Harding's record. In fact, because the turnout was unusually heavy, Hoover amassed 21 million votes—more than the combined votes of Coolidge and La Follette in 1924. In the process, Hoover cut deeply into the traditionally Democratic South, where he carried Virginia, Tennessee, North Carolina, Florida, and Texas.

But there was another side to the election, an aspect that was almost lost in the apparent landslide. Smith had made some gains, too. Although he had won fewer electoral votes than any Democrat since Reconstruction, Smith had succeeded in taking two eastern states, Massachusetts and Rhode Island. This was an indication of a powerful new source of support that the Democrats might be able to capitalize on later— support from immigrants and the children of immigrants in eastern cities. In 1924 Coolidge had swept all twelve of the largest cities in the nation, and by a large margin. In 1928 Smith won more urban votes than Hoover.

Despite this straw in the wind, however, the Republican ascendancy was still in full swing. Hoover could look toward the inauguration and the future with confidence. The powerful and profitable industrial system, watched over at a discreet distance by a sympathetic government, did seem to be ushering in an era of unprecedented prosperity for millions. So it looked in the winter of 1928–29.

BOOM AND BUST

On the surface, at least, the 1920s was a decade of great prosperity. Progress seemed undeniable as more and more cars, radios, washing machines, and other goods poured off assembly lines. More workers were producing more goods than ever before. The United States seemed to have created an economic miracle.

American buyers and investors were confident. The New York Stock Exchange, where the economy's pulse seemed most vital, enjoyed an amazing boom period after 1923. Sales on the exchange quadrupled between 1923 and 1930. As sales increased, so did the prices of stocks. Americans were on a speculative binge. The total amount of money kept in stocks and bonds increased faster than any other economic factor during the period (much faster, for example, than the actual production or sale of goods).

Much of the speculation was made on credit. According to the rules of the New York Stock Exchange, investors could buy stock by putting some money down and owing the rest to their brokers. These "brokers' loans" showed how little of the investment rush was real money and how much was pure speculation. By 1927 almost $4 billion was still owed on such loans. The whole structure of the stock market was rickety.

Such investment was really a form of gambling. If a stock cost ten dollars a share and an investor expected it to go up, he or she could buy a share for a dollar. When the price went up, say to twelve dollars, the investor could sell the stock, pay the nine-dollar broker's loan, and pocket the two-dollar profit—a magical profit of 200 percent. A few such deals, done on a much larger scale, could make a speculator rich in short order. There would be a serious problem, though, if the price of the stock went down. Then, when the broker's loan was due, the investor might have to sell not only the shares of stock but other assets as well. If the stock price fell too far and too fast, the investor could quickly be ruined.

Year after year, the gambles paid off. More and more ordinary people, with only small amounts of money to invest, began to play the market. The prospering economy appeared to justify their confidence.

A WARPED ECONOMY

But prosperity was very unevenly distributed through the population. There were large pockets of people who did not share in it at all. Blacks in both the South and the North did not benefit much. Nor did most farmers, whose lives had long been difficult.

The problems of farmers were especially pressing. In the second half of the nineteenth century, an agricultural revolution had provided the foundation for industrial expansion. Then, during the war, farmers had prospered because of high demand and government supports. The end of the war brought a sharp drop in the demand for exports, and an end to federal aid. At the same time, something odd happened in the domestic market. Improvements in diet slightly increased the demand for vegetables and fruit, but the demand for cereal grains dropped, partly because men released from heavy labor by machines needed fewer calories. In addition, the prevailing Victorian ideal of a sturdy, almost obese figure for men and women had given way to a new, much more slender image of the ideal American.

Meanwhile, farmers were trapped by the high-volume, technologically sophisticated agriculture that had made many of them successful during the preceding two generations. In wartime, especially, they invested heavily in expensive machines, and they continued to do so even after the demand for their crops had fallen off. In the 1920s, in fact, the number of working tractors on American farms quadrupled.

The effect of these changes was to cause farm prices to drop and production to increase. In 1920 the income of farmers represented about 15 percent of the total national income. By 1929 this proportion had fallen to only about 9 percent. Several million farmers and agricultural laborers were driven off the land. They drifted to the cities, where many of them remained permanently unemployed. Those who stayed in farming very often lost ownership of their land and had to become either tenant farmers or hired hands.

One solution to the problem was government intervention. Grain farmers, especially, supported a scheme that would guarantee farmers a fair price for their crop. The scheme involved two things. First, a tariff on imported foodstuffs was needed to prevent foreign producers from taking advantage of an artificially high price on the American market. Second, the domestic price of grain needed to be set at a level that was the average for the ten years preceding 1914. The result would be "parity," or a kind of rough equality of agricultural prices and other prices. Under the sponsorship of a senator from Oregon, Charles McNary, and a congressman from Iowa, Gilbert Haugen, a bill providing for parity for grain crops was introduced in the 1924 Congress, but it was defeated in the House.

Two years later, in a bid for southern support, the McNary-Haugen bill was broadened to include cotton, tobacco, and rice. In 1927 it passed both houses of Congress but was turned back by a Coolidge veto that could not be overridden. The next year, 1928, Congress again passed the act, but President Coolidge once more exercised his veto power. The principle of parity would have to wait.

For industrial workers, the situation was a little better. Real wages—the actual purchasing power of earned dollars—rose during the decade by over 20 percent. And some corporations began to behave a little like Herbert Hoover's model, with programs of "enlightened capitalism." Sanitary and safety conditions were improved in some of the more modern factories. Some companies started pension funds that gave workers a tiny share in the stock of the corporations that employed them. But the major purpose behind these progressive practices was to undercut the growth of industrial unionism. The AFL, meanwhile, pursued a cautious policy throughout the decade. The failure of strikes in 1919 and several succeeding years made many workers hesitate to join even a conservative union like the AFL. The outcome was a decline of about 15 percent in union membership, despite an increase in the total number of factory workers.

Those at the outer edges of the industrial system—blacks, most women, the many underemployed recent immigrants in the cities—simply did not participate in the prosperity of the decade. Such soft spots in the economy led to a very serious distortion. Technological innovation increased productivity rapidly. The question was, simply, how would the increased production be absorbed? Who would buy the washing machines, the cars, the clothes, all the products of a sophisticated industrial system? The total quantity of goods for sale was increasing much faster than the population. Either wages would have to rise dramatically, so that workers would have more money to spend on all the things being made, or prices would have to fall, so that everyone could afford more. Otherwise, the gap between production and sales would grow until inventories were clogged with unsalable "surpluses" of consumer goods.

But business owners generally raised wages less than they should have. They also kept prices higher than they should have. In the short run, of course, their practices could bring in higher profits—and higher profits for corporations meant that the price of their stock rose. They could either invest the profits in still larger factories and produce still more goods, or they could invest them in stock and heat up the stock market even more. Many corporations did both.

The result was a warped economy. The amount of goods being produced ran far ahead of the people's power to purchase them. Sooner or later an adjustment had to be made. Otherwise, factories would have to close until the cars, clothes, tools, and other items could be sold. For a time the problem could be avoided in two ways. The "surplus" products could be sold, on credit, to people who could not really afford them. A family could pay for a car, for example, over two or three years. Or goods could be exported to foreign countries. But both credit and exporting could help a distorted economic system only briefly.

THE STOCK MARKET CRASH

These facts were difficult to see. On the surface, the economy had never looked better, and Americans continued to bet on the future by speculating in stocks. In 1928 the average price of indus-

trial stocks increased by about 25 percent. Then, after a few rumblings and warnings, the bubble burst. In 1929, reality finally caught up with Wall Street.

In September the most popular index of stock prices stood at 452. Two months later it was 234. What this meant, in plain terms, was that the market value of stocks on the exchange had been halved. Most of the people who owed the $4 billion in outstanding brokers' loans were ruined. So were many of the brokers, when they could not collect. On what came to be known as "Black Thursday," October 24, investors lost $3 billion. Brokers piously announced that the worst was over. But five days later came the worst day of all, an even blacker Tuesday. On that day, stockholders lost a staggering total of $10 billion. The great glamour stock of the 1920s, RCA—the Radio Corporation of America—which had recently peaked at a giddy $450 a share, fell to $32. And coming days were almost as bleak and ruinous. Stock prices continued to slide. They reached bottom in 1933. Then, most stocks were worth little more than one tenth of their cost in September 1929. The Great Depression had begun.

It was difficult then, and still is, to understand why the wild panic on Wall Street should have had any effect on the real economy. The factories were still there, ready to roll out goods. The farms were still there, ready to produce food. All the hands and minds that were willing and able to work before the crash were still there, still willing and able to work.

But month by month, the entire economic machine ground down. The stock market crash was the crucial link in the chain of events leading to this breakdown. It caused people to make the grim decision not to buy or invest. So storekeepers sold less. And factories produced less or closed down altogether. Many foreclosed on loans made to others because they needed money to pay off their own loans.

Farmers behind on their payments lost their farms as banks desperately tried to collect hard cash. The banks needed cash because millions of people with savings accounts, frightened now, lined up at tellers' windows to withdraw their money. The banks often could not produce the cash because they had invested or lent it. So even the banks began to fail, leaving depositors penniless.

Builders of houses and offices stopped construction because they could not borrow money to continue. Down at the bottom of this tangle were workers who, by the millions, received notices that they need not come to work anymore. Their jobs disappeared. Since they could not work, they could not buy; since they could not buy, others could not sell or make goods.

The new "jobless" were not just the old-line poor. Many had been solid, middle-class citizens, such as bank tellers and factory foremen. Others were farmers, who had barely managed to survive a rough decade. Now they had lost their farms forever. They moved to the cities, looking for food and work, or they began to drift, looking for migrant workers' jobs. People combed garbage heaps for food for their families. They made soup from dandelions. Mostly, however, they waited in a cold, gloomy fog of despair for something to happen.

HOOVER'S OPTIMISM

The question posed by the depression and symbolized by the Bonus Army was simple. Could the federal government be used as a tool for dealing with economic disaster? In the past the answer had been no. Other depressions had been allowed to run their course without any federal attempt to bring early recovery or relieve human suffering. But the Great Depression was by far the worst ever. Now the industrial economy was so large and complicated that its collapse affected far more people. Countless millions were unemployed; banks were failing by the hundreds; hundreds of thousands were threatened with starvation.

At first, the Hoover administration was optimistic. The stock market crash was called a "needed adjustment." The economy, Hoover announced, was "fundamentally sound." Recovery would be natural and would come soon. Meanwhile, no federal action of any kind was needed.

Surprisingly, most Democrats agreed. In the congressional elections of 1930, the Democrats made Prohibition as big an issue as the depression. Nor did the voters heavily punish the administration for its failure to bring about recovery. The Democrats did win the House, but the Senate stayed Republican. Hoover was still predicting that a return to prosperity was just around the corner.

But things kept getting worse. In 1929 over 600 banks shut down; in 1930, over 1,000; in 1931, 2,000. For farmers, there seemed to be no bottom. Wheat sold for 36 cents a bushel in 1931, compared to $1.03 in 1929. No one even knew how many people were unemployed by 1932, but guesses ran as high as 15 million. For those who still had jobs, pay envelopes grew smaller. By 1932, wages in industry were less than half what they had been in 1928.

As he faced all these facts—or, sometimes, tried not to face them—the president grew gloomy and confused. He tried to stay optimistic in public, believing business "confidence" was crucial to recovery. In private, however, he was trapped between two different beliefs. A humane man, he did not like to see people suffer. But he still thought government should not interfere in the economy. Free enterprise would bring the nation back to its feet.

Most important, Hoover believed that the federal government must never give direct relief to the poor, unemployed, and hungry. Direct federal welfare, he thought, would destroy people's "moral character," making them "dependent" instead of healthy, strong personalities. This set of attitudes, which he referred to as "individualism," made Hoover seem insensitive and cruel. He became the target of bitter jokes. Homeless people named their makeshift shantytowns "Hoovervilles" and called an empty pocket, turned inside out, a "Hoover flag." Reluctantly, Hoover decided that the government must act.

NEW FEDERAL POWERS

Early in 1932 Hoover signed a law creating a new federal agency, the Reconstruction Finance Corporation (RFC). It could lend up to $2 billion to banks, insurance companies, and railroads. These loans, the administration believed, would be used, especially by the banks, to make other loans to businesses. Businesses would in turn use the money for new construction or to reopen factories. This would create new jobs and save old ones. Thus RFC loans would eventually end up in the pockets of workers, who would then spend the money and create new demand, resulting in more new production, and so on, in a circle of recovery.

The president also went against his own beliefs by signing another law empowering the RFC to lend relief money to state governments. But the amount of the loans was too small to help much. Pennsylvania, for example, could borrow only enough to provide three cents a day to its unemployed workers. Also, the RFC loans to business were far too small to aid the economy effectively. Compared to previous government activity, Hoover's actions were bold experiments in the use of federal power. But measured against what was actually needed, they were too little too late, as the bonus marchers recognized.

THE NEW DEAL

THE ELECTION OF 1932

Herbert Hoover was not a cruel man. His reluctance to meet the crisis of the depression was not a result of hard-heartedness but of confidence. He devoutly believed that the nation's economy was healthy and that it needed only adjustment.

But the Democratic party was about to nominate a man who was altogether willing to define the depression as a crisis. Franklin Roosevelt had been working diligently for the nomination for months. By the time the party held its convention in Chicago during the summer of 1932, he had lined up the necessary support.

The contrast between Hoover and Roosevelt was striking. Hoover was methodical, brooding, and cool. Roosevelt was cheerful, brash, and smiling. He had been stricken by polio in 1921 but had made a ten-year effort, with braces and canes, to look healthy and powerful. One of his main political tools was a wide, exaggerated grin. And he was ready to present himself as a leader who would not be bound by tradition. He broke precedent by going to Chicago to accept the nomination in person—and doing so in an airplane, not by train.

He quickly made it clear to the cheering delegates that his strategy would be simple and relentless: to define the depression as a real crisis and to flay the Republicans for their failure to meet it:

> Republican leaders not only have failed in material things, they have failed in national vision, because in disaster, they have held out no hope. I pledge you, I pledge myself to a new deal for the American people.

Roosevelt's campaign speeches never made clear just what his "new deal" would be. He made vague promises that he would relieve suffering, create jobs, and make the economy work again. And this, plus the fact that voters had come to blame Hoover for causing the depression, was enough to give Roosevelt a smashing victory. He received about 23 million votes, against about 15 million for Hoover. Just as important, the Democrats won large majorities in the House and Senate for the first time in modern history.

On March 4, 1933, Roosevelt took his oath of office with a ringing pronouncement that he would have both the courage to admit that a disaster had befallen the nation and the courage to deal with it. And he seems to have believed that courage was the key to the problem. "Let me assert my firm belief," he said in a bluff, confident voice, "that the only thing we have to fear is fear itself. This nation asks for action, and action now."

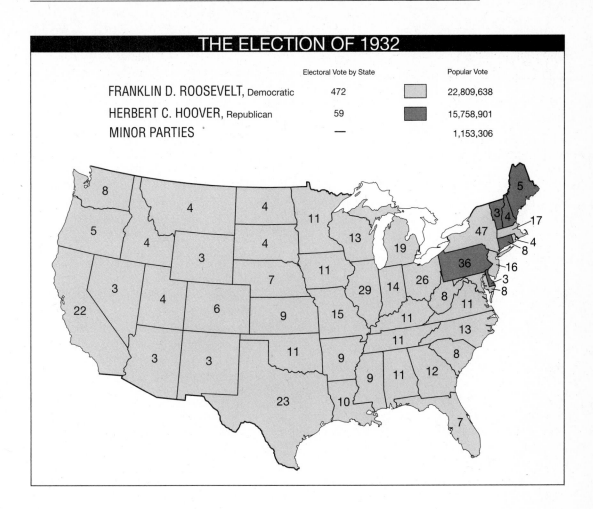

THE ELECTION OF 1932

	Electoral Vote by State		Popular Vote
FRANKLIN D. ROOSEVELT, Democratic	472		22,809,638
HERBERT C. HOOVER, Republican	59		15,758,901
MINOR PARTIES	—		1,153,306

LAUNCHING THE NEW DEAL

Roosevelt's inaugural proclamation was a little il-logical—and even echoed Hoover's preoccupation with restoring "confidence." For men and women out of work, with hungry children, there was in fact plenty to fear besides "fear itself." But what counted was not the accuracy of Roosevelt's statements but their bravery. And the statements had to be brave because there was a growing sense of despair and even panic in the nation. Millions of men were roaming the country looking for work. Radios played popular songs like "Brother, Can You Spare a Dime?" Every city had its "Hoovervilles" and its lengthening "bread lines." Middle-class Americans, who might still

have their jobs and their houses, were frightened by the plague of bank failures, which seemed to be a sign that the economy had simply, perhaps finally, collapsed.

The banks were the most immediate problem Roosevelt chose to face. If they did not work, nothing else would. On his last night in the White House, Hoover declared: "We are at the end of our rope." After his inauguration, Roosevelt made it clear that he intended to pull the rope, at once. He boldly declared a "bank holiday," shutting down all banks, sound and unsound, until further notice. At least a closed bank could not fail, and the money that was supposed to be in people's accounts would still be there.

Then, five days after he became president, Roosevelt sent to Congress an Emergency Banking Relief Act, which empowered the federal government to buy stock in failing banks, providing the cash to pay off its depositors if they demanded their money. Astonishingly, the act passed through Congress in eight hours. The New Deal—whatever it was to be—had begun.

THE DEBATE OVER MEANING

Ever since the 1930s, Americans have debated, sometimes in anger, the meaning of the New Deal.

For some, including both partisans and critics of Roosevelt, the New Deal was a kind of "revolution." According to this view, Roosevelt's programs broke the normal patterns of politics and economics and brought radically new federal control and regulation of economic and social life.

For others, the New Deal did not represent much of a departure from the patterns of history. This argument claims that Roosevelt was, in essence, a conservative. His basic motive was to leave the Constitution and the capitalist economy intact. In fact, this picture of Roosevelt's administration is one of a program whose deepest wish was to preserve the American system from the kinds of convulsions and revolutions that had been occurring in Europe since World War I, including the Russian Revolution of 1917 and the explosive rise of fascism in Italy and Germany.

Both these pictures of the New Deal have a good deal of truth to them, depending on what kinds of comparisons are being made. Compared to other peacetime presidents, Roosevelt does seem something of a revolutionary. But when compared to the wartime presidencies of Abraham Lincoln and Woodrow Wilson, Roosevelt's administration seems much more normal. Regarded as part of a progressive tradition reaching back to Populism, to Theodore Roosevelt's Square Deal, and to Wilson's New Freedom, the New Deal looks moderate, even tame. Finally,

measured against the dramatic changes the Russian Revolution had brought, or the kinds of changes that Benito Mussolini and Adolf Hitler were bringing to Italy and Germany, the New Deal can fairly be described as a program of preservation rather than of change.

The difficulty is that the arguments and the comparisons often assume the New Deal was a coherent, unified program based on a clear political and social theory. In fact, it was a loose bundle of laws and executive orders that were designed by many men and women. Most of the new policies were established as practical steps to solve immediate problems. There was only one crude idea behind it all: that the federal government's power should be used to meet any national crisis.

What held the New Deal together, in fact, was not a program but Roosevelt himself. And he was a curious, contradictory, and sometimes confused man.

FDR

Franklin Delano Roosevelt was forty-seven years old when the stock market failed, and he was fifty-one when he won the presidency—young by the standards of the day. But he was old enough that his ideas about the world had already been formed, and there is little evidence that the depression changed any of those ideas very much.

He was, in many ways, a very traditional man. He came from a wealthy family of Hudson River aristocrats. He went to exclusive private schools and then to Harvard. He owned a great country estate, where he liked to play at being a gentleman farmer. In private life, he was a practicing, though not especially devout, Episcopalian. He was also a practicing, though not especially devout, capitalist. And he was a Democrat because his branch of the family were Democrats. Unlike some other great presidents—Jefferson, Lincoln, or Wilson—he was neither a scholar nor a gifted writer. All in all, he was a suave, smiling,

FRANKLIN D. ROOSEVELT AT A CCC CAMP. The Roosevelt administration tried to help unemployed young men by creating the Civilian Conservation Corps, a quasi-military group that was supposed to plant trees, improve public land, and otherwise "conserve" the landscape. Here the president, third from right, takes lunch out of a mess plate with a group of uniformed members of the corps. Second from the left is Roosevelt's trusted adviser from the 1920s, Louis Howe. To the president's left is Henry Wallace, who would run for president in a controversial third-party bid in 1948. To Wallace's left is Rexford Tugwell, a member of the Brains Trust.

public man; fond of dogs, children, and women; a man whose most striking characteristic was not his lameness but the intensity of his desire to be president.

On the other hand, Roosevelt's sense of personal confidence—combined perhaps with his determined victory over polio—made him open to experiment in a way Hoover could never have been. Roosevelt was ready to try a variety of things and, if they did not work, to try others. He was also ready to appoint a large number of advisers with ideas of their own. The inner circle, composed heavily of academic economists and social scientists, became known as the Brains Trust. Some of its members did have theories of government and the economy. And some were

much more radical than Roosevelt and worked to make the administration reflect their wishes.

But the president remained secretive, and even a bit coy, about what he had in mind. As it turned out, Roosevelt seemed to think always in very specific and concrete terms. He was willing to send to Congress a bewildering set of proposals for new agencies and programs, many of which became known by their initials. This gave rise to a popular joke that the New Deal was an "alphabet soup." But the master chef—who was also popularly called by his initials, FDR—had no master recipe. This became obvious during the first whirlwind weeks of his administration, which became known as the Hundred Days— after the Hundred Days of campaigning that followed Napoleon's escape from Elba and ended at the Battle of Waterloo in 1815. It was during these weeks that Roosevelt became a leader of heroic proportions in the minds of many Americans. And to them, Roosevelt would always be more important than the sum of all the programs and agencies and laws that would make up the New Deal. Debates about the New Deal's successes and failures can never erase the fact that no modern president has been so loved and trusted by so many Americans for so long a time.

RELIEF AND STABILIZATION

The New Deal functioned on two very different levels. First, it involved direct efforts to feed people and to calm the economic panic, to achieve what people were calling "relief" and "stabilization." Second, it included measures aimed at long-term reform. During the Hundred Days, and for some time afterward, relief and stabilization were the primary goals and concerns.

The simplest approach to relief was to distribute direct aid. The Federal Emergency Relief Act of 1933 distributed billions of dollars to the states, which in turn doled out the money to needy people.

But the most characteristic New Deal solution to hunger and poverty was not a dole but jobs. Roosevelt and his advisers were willing to make the federal government the employer of millions of men and women. The Public Works Administration (PWA), created in 1933, eventually spent over $4 billion, employing people to construct roads, public buildings, and other such projects. In 1935 the PWA was joined by a new agency, which scrambled the initials a bit. The Works Progress Administration (WPA) employed Americans in every kind of project, from construction to producing plays, concerts, paintings, and sculpture, to library work and scholarship.

The PWA and the WPA were designed to give people a steady income. But the New Deal was just as preoccupied with the other side of middle-class economic life: property. Some of its most important measures were designed to protect farmers from losing their land and homeowners from losing their houses because of unpaid debts or mortgages. In 1933 a Farm Credit Administration was created, with power to lend mortgage money to harassed farmers. In the same year, a Home Owners' Refinancing Act created a federal corporation to give government-financed mortgages to hard-pressed families threatened with foreclosure of their privately financed mortgages.

Direct relief meant much to the men and women who got jobs in the PWA or WPA, and to farmers who were able to save their land. But Roosevelt's administration was perhaps even more interested in getting the economy stabilized. Calling a bank holiday might help in the short run, but something more was needed to prevent bank failures in the future. Since banks failed because their depositors got frightened and suddenly withdrew all their money, the New Deal solution was simplicity itself. The Glass-Steagall Act of 1933 established a Federal Deposit Insurance Corporation (FDIC). This agency simply stood behind the banks, guaranteeing to pay every depositor his or her money—up to $10,000 for each account—if the bank failed. Presumably, neither banks nor their customers would have to worry any more about sudden and disastrous runs of withdrawals that left the banks' vaults empty.

The same sort of logic lay behind the two programs that were most central to the New Deal—both of which suffered heavily from attacks in the courts. The National Industrial Recovery Act and the Agricultural Adjustment Act, both passed in 1933, were aimed at regulating private industry and farming, respectively, without changing the basically private and capitalistic nature of either.

The National Industrial Recovery Act was, at its heart, simply a repeal of parts of the Sherman Antitrust Act. That law, which represented nineteenth-century confidence in the idea—if not the reality—of competition, forbade businesses to get together to set prices. It did not work, at least not very well. The new law recognized this fact and tried to build on it. It set up a National Recovery Administration (NRA), with the mission of encouraging corporations and businesses to work together to set and hold prices and production quotas.

For workers, the new law provided that the companies should agree on uniform wages and hours. And when some businesses were slow to cooperate, the NRA itself established wages and hours for industries. The companies that did cooperate won the right to fly a flag with the NRA's symbol, a blue eagle, as evidence of their civic conscience.

The Agricultural Adjustment Act attempted to deal with the farmers' peculiar problem: When prices fell, they were driven to produce even more food for the market. This simply sent prices further down, creating a spiral of oversupply and falling incomes. The act created the Agricultural Adjustment Administration, with the power to give farmers money *not* to plant crops. The AAA could also buy up excess amounts of crops like cotton and wheat and store them. The goal was to control production and marketing, to drive farm prices back up to the prosperity levels of 1909–1914, a level of parity.

In the short run, at least, the AAA seemed to work, though some of its measures seemed misguided to the men and women rummaging in garbage heaps for scraps of food. The AAA plowed under millions of acres of potatoes and other crops. It also killed and dumped about 5 million pigs. But the result was apparently successful. In 1933, farm prices stood at about 55 percent of parity; in 1939, the ratio was 90 percent.

REFORMS OF THE NEW DEAL

Programs aimed at direct relief and at economic stability made up the bulk of the New Deal, at least as measured in new laws. But Roosevelt and his advisers made efforts to introduce other, more fundamental and lasting changes in American life. These reform measures seem mild and timid in comparison to later exercises of federal power. But to many men and women of the 1930s, they seemed innovative, even radical or revolutionary.

One of the most visible of Roosevelt's measures was the Civilian Conservation Corps. The CCC set up camps for unemployed young men, put them into uniforms that looked military, and set them to cleaning up parks and planting countless trees all across the country, not only on federal property but on public lands of all kinds. Here was an astonishing, though short-lived, fact: a uniformed federal corps, not an army, working along hundreds of highways and lake-fronts, doing things that were far removed from traditional notions of federal responsibility.

A more daring and enduring effort was the Tennessee Valley Authority. The TVA was established to build dams and generate electrical power in the backward, flood-ravaged valleys of the Tennessee and Cumberland rivers. But the responsibilities of the TVA went further: to reforest, to reclaim marginal land, to improve health and recreation for the people of the valleys. Opponents charged that the plan was patterned on "Soviet" dreams. But others saw the matter differently. For its supporters, the TVA was a magnificent effort to salvage some of the most economically and socially depressed areas of five states.

The National Labor Relations Act of 1935—popularly known as the Wagner Act, after a New York congressman—was another effort at social reform. The Roosevelt administration used the act to enable the federal government to intervene in relations between labor and capital in a more forceful way than in the past. The Wagner Act made it illegal for an employer to refuse to bargain with a union chosen by the employees. The act also outlawed a list of "unfair labor practices" by employers, a list that could be extended indefinitely. It was a major victory for unions, and gave the federal government a much greater role in protecting organized labor than it had ever had before.

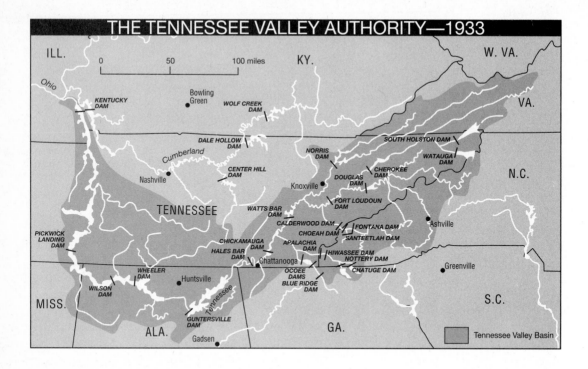

THE TENNESSEE VALLEY AUTHORITY—1933

Partly as a result of the Wagner Act, union membership tripled between 1933 and 1939—from about 3 million to over 9 million. And the character of the unions changed too. The American Federation of Labor had organized workers by craft and trade. An employer could then negotiate—if willing to negotiate at all—with a series of separate organizations, each representing a fraction of the company's workers. Now a more radical vision of unionism gained force: industrial unionism, based on the idea that all the workers in a particular industry—steel, say, or automobiles—ought to be organized into one union rather than into a number of small craft unions. The most striking development of the 1930s in labor history was the emergence of the Congress of Industrial Organizations (CIO).

The organizing leadership of the CIO contained a number of labor radicals and even some communists. But its rank-and-file members were committed to the simple idea that collaboration was as necessary to workers as to corporations, that the only way to achieve fair bargains between

workers and industrial giants was through wholesale solidarity among all the workers in an industry. Employers resisted, of course. Bitter battles were fought. A massive sit-down strike at General Motors in 1936–1937, in which the workers did not leave the plants but "sat down" at their places, ended in partial victory for the CIO. In 1937 the steel industry (notoriously anti-union for decades) was forced to submit to bargaining with the CIO.

In the perception of the New Deal, old people needed federal assistance even more than industrial workers. The Social Security Act of 1935 was an attempt to create an insurance and retirement system for American workers. It provided for small contributions from workers and their employers to be paid into a common fund. This fund could then pay a pension to men and women who retired, or benefits if they became disabled, or support for their children if workers died prematurely. The payments were small at first. But the Social Security Act was still a long first step in the direction of what critics of the New Deal referred to as a "welfare state."

There were a number of reform possibilities that the Roosevelt administration shied away from. There was no civil rights legislation. There was no attempt to massively redistribute income through taxation. In fact, there was no attempt to tamper with existing relationships between social classes, between races, or between men and women. His enemies might charge him with "Sovietism," but Roosevelt's own perception of the possibilities of federal action were far from drastic. Some of the young men and women who supported and worked in the administration might hope for more. But that more lay well over the historical horizon—beyond further years of depression and then years of total war.

TWO-THIRDS OF A NATION

In one of Roosevelt's most memorable speeches, he said that one-third of the nation was "ill-housed, ill-fed, and ill-clad." His fraction may have been too high or too low, depending on what he meant by "ill." But there is one fraction about which there can be no serious dispute. Two-thirds of the nation was unequally treated. This majority of Americans was deprived of fair access to work, education, medical care, recreation—to what many Americans liked to call their "way of life"—for the simple reason that they happened to have been born women or members of a particular racial or ethnic group. For such people, both the depression and the New Deal had special and sometimes contradictory meanings.

WOMEN

At the outset of the depression, in 1930, over 10 million women held paying jobs. Most of these working women—about three out of four—were single. Some of them worked alongside men in fields and orchards as migrant farm labor and were not included in official statistics. Many others were part of an informal economy of domestic

labor and thus were also left off the official rolls. In business, industry, and government work—where records *were* kept—women workers tended to be segregated into jobs that were considered appropriate as "women's work." In 1930, 98 percent of all nurses were women. So were 95 percent of all telephone operators, and 81 percent of all schoolteachers. Jobs classified as clerical were about equally divided between men and women, though women usually held the jobs at the bottom of the ladder.

When the depression hit, it caused less unemployment among women workers than among men because it struck hardest at manufacturing—steel and automobiles, for example. Nurses and teachers were less likely to be fired than male steel or auto workers. In fact, the number of women with paying jobs actually increased during the 1930s, from about 10 million to about 13 million. Women made up about 30 percent of the paid work force in 1930, but 35 percent in 1940.

As a result, there was a lot of uninformed talk about women taking jobs that ought to be held by male "breadwinners." Some states even passed laws against married women working in civil service jobs or as teachers. And the Roosevelt administration for five years of the depression refused to allow the federal government to employ more than one person from a family. If a husband and wife each held a government job, the woman usually was the one to quit, since she earned less money. But the truth was that women and men competed for very few jobs, and that most working women were single and needed to work to live.

For women who did not work, the depression was a tough experience. But because of sexual stereotyping, they may not have suffered as much as their husbands and brothers. In reality, women who did not have paying jobs were probably more intensely employed than they had been before 1929. They still had their jobs—cooking, mending, washing, and the rest of the daily round of domestic tasks. And the economic crisis actually increased the importance of this kind of unpaid work, as stretching family resources by skillfully making clothes and food last longer and go further became essential. But the depression did prove one thing: Most people, male and female, continued to believe firmly that men were the proper "head" of the family, even if they were unemployed and even if their wives had assumed a larger role than ever in enabling families to survive.

At least that is what most Americans *said* they still believed, when opinion polls asked them the question. But in thousands of families, men found it increasingly difficult to look their wives and children in the eye. The contradiction between belief and fact was hard to bear in a world where men were expected to be providers and family heads. Not being able to be the first made it very difficult to continue to be the second. It is true that the divorce rate actually declined during the depression, but the birthrate went down even more sharply. The reasons for these trends are difficult for historians to know, since they involve forms of human intimacy that are often not understood even by people who experience them. But the declining divorce rate may only have been a reflection of an increase in the rate of desertion, in families where the legal idea of divorce had lost its practical meaning. Unemployed men do not normally pay alimony or child support. Also, poor people often did not take the trouble to get a divorce until they decided to marry someone else, and the depression made this decision less likely. The declining birthrate may have been the result of rational calculations about how many children a family could afford. But it may also have been the result of a more subtle and cruel process, a form of private, psychological depression that brought the ugly reality of the public, economic depression home. For people whose lives had become melancholy and pathetic, the idea of sex and new children may have been an increasingly unlikely assertion of hope.

One unemployed woman from Minnesota described her hours in an unemployment office this way: "So we sit in this room like cattle unable to work, unable to get food and lodging, un-able to bear children. Here we must sit in this shame looking at the floor, worse than beasts at a slaughter." She was convinced that the inability to find work had made her unable to have children, as though she had been made sterile and fit only for a slaughter. There was an obvious rage in people who felt these things. But the rage was muted, translated into a sense of helplessness and shame. And this sense of things, which she shared with millions of other women and men, would have made the idea of divorce seem irrelevant, and the idea of sex and childbearing distant and forbidding.

AFRICAN AMERICANS

The depression and the New Deal had mixed effects on African Americans. Most black people were much worse off to start with than whites. In 1930, infant mortality was twice as high among blacks as among whites. Black life expectancy was ten years below that of whites. And the depression made things worse. Unemployed whites were now willing to take jobs that had usually been filled by blacks, such as janitor or garbage collector. And governments and businesses were all too willing to replace black workers with whites. This pushed black unemployment up to rates as high as 50 percent in many industrial cities (compared to about 30 percent for whites).

Even some well-intended New Deal programs had negative effects on African Americans. One of the main agricultural programs was to encourage farmers not to produce "surplus" commodities like cotton. This was designed to help farmers by reducing supply and so raising prices. But the program helped only those farmers who owned their land. In the South, where more than half of black families lived in rural areas, most of them did not own land but worked it as sharecroppers. White landowners, paid by the government not to plant crops, simply ordered sharecroppers (black and white) off the land. Between 1930 and 1940 the number of sharecropper families in the South fell by one-third.

ROOM IN NEW YORK, 1932. No American artist was more gifted than Edward Hopper at capturing the kinds of personal depression that brought the Great Depression into people's daily lives. Here, he shows a childless couple framed in the window of an apartment that most people would have called "middle class." But the room is small, the furniture plain and almost shabby. The man is hunched over his newspaper, and the woman turns away, not to play the cheap piano but to toy with one key. They have lost touch with each other and with the world on the other side of their window.

Overall, the New Deal's modest efforts to redistribute wealth touched black families—and poor families in general—very little. Between 1929 and 1941 the share of the wealth owned by the richest 20 percent was cut a little, from about 54 percent to about 49 percent. But most of the loose money and property found its way into middle-class pockets. The middle 40 percent of Americans soaked up about four-fifths of this redistributed wealth. Not all poor people were black, but almost all blacks were poor people, so they benefited very little from the modest efforts of the Roosevelt administration to promote economic equality. Most blacks worked in jobs that

were not covered by Social Security and not protected by any of the new labor legislation.

But there were fragile signs of promise and change. Some of the signs were merely symbolic. In 1939 the black opera singer Marian Anderson sought to give a concert in Washington. The Daughters of the American Revolution, which owned the Constitution Hall theater, refused to allow her to use its building. Eleanor Roosevelt, in a dramatic gesture, promoted a much larger concert by Anderson on the steps of the Lincoln Memorial. (But there were limits to even Eleanor Roosevelt's willingness to make such gestures. A year later, a similar problem was provoked by

No crop, no share. These sharecroppers have been evicted from their homes in Missouri. They told the reporter who took this photograph that they were sent away by their white landlords because the Agricultural Adjustment Administration government was paying landowners *not* to grow crops. The picture was taken in January, 1939, and the stove will be badly needed when night comes.

plans for a Washington benefit concert starring the great black singer Paul Robeson. The First Lady at first joined a committee to support the controversial concert, but she withdrew her name when she learned that the sponsors included an organization that was thought to be connected with the Communist party.)

The commitment of the president's wife, and of a few other prominent Democrats, to public support for blacks was very effective in political terms. Most black voters seem to have become deeply convinced that however meager, or even damaging, the specific economic impact of the New Deal was on their lives, the Democratic party was their only political hope. In 1932, after three years of the depression, 80 percent of black voters were still loyal to the Republicans, the

party of Lincoln and emancipation. In the next four years, an astonishing shift occurred. By 1936, 75 percent of the African Americans who voted chose Roosevelt. With the large number of ethnic voters who had shifted to the Democrats, blacks became part of a new Democratic coalition that was to play an important role in national politics for half a century.

Another fragile sign of promise and change for blacks grew out of an incident that at first seemed to offer only more proof of the power of racism. In the spring of 1931 a freight train pulled into the yards just outside the town of Scottsboro, Alabama. Riding the train were about twenty hoboes, black and white, male and female, part of the hungry and shifting debris of the depression. Armed sheriff's deputies were waiting

THE SCOTTSBORO BOYS. Authorities in Alabama allowed a photographer to take this carefully staged photograph of Attorney Samuel Leibowitz and his clients. The picture was designed to assure the public that "justice" was being done, that the defendants were indeed represented by a lawyer and had access to him. But it was also designed to assure racially fearful whites that this "conference" was watched over by troopers, who only partially cover their pistols with their hands.

for the train and arrested nine young blacks, accusing them of assaulting some white men on the train. Then two white women named Ruby Bates and Victoria Price stepped forward. They were probably just as scared and just as hungry as anyone else on the slow freight. After all, women like them were routinely arrested for prostitution, and raped in jail to satisfy their jailers' commitments to "public decency" and "order." The two women also understood that poor white women had one defense against their powerlessness: they could accuse some black man of rape. Whatever their motives, the two women did claim that they had been sexually assaulted by the nine young blacks.

White justice was swift in Alabama. Before two weeks had passed, eight of the black youths

had been convicted and sentenced to death. The ninth, who was twelve years old, was not found innocent by the twelve white male jurors; the jury was unable to agree on a verdict in his case.

But at least the boys and young men had not been lynched without trial. So there was a tiny crack in the system, the possibility of an appeal to the federal judiciary. In 1932 the United States Supreme Court ruled that the defense lawyers—court-appointed white men—had not presented a competent case for their black clients. The convictions were struck down, and Alabama had to choose whether to drop the charges or begin new trials. The prosecution chose new trials. But this time, the "Scottsboro Boys," as they had become known in the press, were defended by a skilled lawyer, Samuel Leibowitz. He had been hired by the International Labor Defense League, a Communist party affiliate. The local prosecutor sneered at Leibowitz in open court, and boasted that "Alabama justice cannot be bought and sold with Jew money from New York."

In the second trials, Leibowitz introduced medical evidence that clearly proved that Bates and Price had not been raped on the train. But the white jury still brought in a verdict of guilty against the first defendant. This time, the Alabama judge, James Horton, somehow found the courage to overrule the verdict. But the authorities found a new judge and held new trials. Again, the first defendant to be tried was found guilty. This time, the Supreme Court threw out the conviction on the ground that Alabama law excluded blacks from juries.

In 1936 a fourth round of trials took place. Only five of the nine original defendants were tried, but the five were convicted and sentenced, one to seventy-five years and the others to life. Only after fourteen more years were all five men free, four on parole and one by escape. For the thousands of African Americans who were carrying on the struggle for civil rights and social equality, there was not much to celebrate. But at least the Supreme Court had saved eight people from hanging, and set four of them free. The Court had also ruled, not for the first time, that state courts could not systematically exclude blacks from juries. The stage was being set for new efforts to use the Constitution and the courts to protect the basic rights of black citizens—a struggle that would reach a climax after World War II, in the 1950s and 1960s.

For those who would not wait, there was one final consolation to be wrung from the New Deal. It came in 1941, when it was becoming increasingly clear that depression and the New Deal were about to give way to war. A. Philip Randolph, the brilliant and militant leader of the black union movement, decided that the time had come for blacks to demand justice from their government. He proposed a grand, all-black march on Washington. The Roosevelt administration was anxious to prevent "disorder" in the capital. And some officials were afraid that "communists" would infiltrate the movement. Roosevelt decided to negotiate. He told black leaders that if they would call off the march, he would establish a Fair Employment Practices Commission, with at least some power to try to enforce equal treatment for black and white workers in the few industries where working conditions could be federally regulated. Randolph and his colleagues accepted the deal, and the commission was established in the summer of 1941, just a few months before the United States entered World War II. As one black newspaper put it, most African Americans thought they had little choice but to support Roosevelt and the Democrats, "until the real thing comes along."

MEXICAN AMERICANS

A large migration of Mexican laborers into California and the Southwest, where most of them became migrant farm workers, had taken place in the 1920s. But the irresistible forces of the depression turned on them severely. Hundreds of thousands of white farm families of the South and Southwest were losing their land or their sharecropping arrangements and heading west to California. The result was a dramatic reversal of the tides of migration. At the beginning of the crisis, only a small minority of the migrant workforce on California farms had been North Americans. By the end of the decade, the North Americans— the "Okies" and the "Arkies" and the rest—made up nine-tenths of that labor force, doing the toilsome and low-paying jobs that had once been left to Mexicano "braceros."

The result was a huge outmigration of Mexicans and Mexican Americans. In the first five years of the depression, about half a million left. The U.S. census—woefully inaccurate when it came to minority groups—counted only half as many Mexican-born people in 1940 as it had in

MEXICANOS ON STRIKE. The striking "braceros" on this truck were unarmed. But they were threatening to arm themselves unless the landowners they usually worked for put down their own weapons and stopped hiring private armies of thugs to harass striking workers.

1930. This drop was just about equal to the number of landless North Americans who had wandered into California looking for work. But the Mexicanos were not only discouraged by the economic crisis, they also were encouraged to go by governments like California's, which offered one-way tickets to Mexico, free of charge, to anyone willing to leave. And to offers like this, local police and bureaucrats often added harassment and ugly treatment. A government official in California said that Mexicans are "trash." "We herd them like pigs." (His command of English was weak. He was obviously trying to say that he thought Mexicans were like pigs, to be herded. But his sentence could also mean "We herd them as though *we* were pigs.")

Some of the Mexicanos did resist, did refuse the free tickets home, and did try to do something about their difficult jobs and miserable earnings. In the 1930s, Mexicano workers began to organize, to resist exploitation at the hands of *norteamericano* landowners—and exploitation, too, at the hands of fellow Mexicanos who organized work gangs and wrote contracts with the farmers. They organized a union, the Confederación de Uniones de Campesinos y Obreros Mexicanos (Confederation of Unions of Mexican Campesinos and Workers. There is no easy translation of *campesino*. Literally, it means only "people of the fields." It is sometimes translated as "peasants." But its meaning in Mexico and Central America covered a variety of forms of agricultural experience that included most of the rural poor, even those who owned small farms.) The Confederación supported a number of bitter and sometimes bloody strikes during harvest seasons in the 1930s. In the largest strike, which took place in 1933, 18,000 Mexicano pickers refused to harvest the cotton crop in the rich San Joaquin Valley of California. But two strikers were murdered, and the violence eventually broke the strike. Still, during the next seven years, the Confederación promoted twenty-five major strikes.

By the end of the decade most landowners had shown that they preferred to hire North American workers, if they would work for the same low wages. The North Americans proved to be more docile than those Mexicanos who had stayed in the United States. As for the federal government, it tried to assist migrant farm workers by setting up camps run by the Farm Security Administration, camps that could provide decent temporary housing for laboring people. But the camps were established only in 1937, and the men who ran them, like the landowners, showed a definite preference for assisting North American migrant families. (John Steinbeck's famous novel about the sufferings of migrant workers in California, *The Grapes of Wrath,* was a moving and sympathetic book. But it did not have a single Mexican or Mexican-American character. His depiction of a Farm Security Administration camp is of an institution with no Mexicanos—or blacks, either.) Since agricultural workers were not covered by major New Deal programs like Social Security or the Wagner Act, and since only proven citizens were eligible for federal relief, the Mexicanos got little or no benefit from the New Deal.

NATIVE AMERICANS

For Native Americans, economic depression was nothing new. For half a century Native Americans on reservations had lived in increasingly miserable conditions. Their main resource was land. But land ownership was governed by the rules of the Dawes Severalty Act of 1887 (see pp. 155–156). Under the terms of this law, land that tribes had once owned in common became the property of individual families. But with each passing generation, a fixed amount of land had to be divided among several children. The only alternative was for new generations to leave the reservations altogether, and try to cope with hardship and discrimination in towns and cities.

So the inevitable long-term effect of the Dawes Act was to promote poverty and want.

The situation was perhaps worst in Oklahoma, which had once been the Indian Territory. During the nineteenth century the federal government had crowded about thirty different tribes onto a skimpy expanse of land that was not very fertile in the first place. Increasing populations were unable to feed themselves adequately. Disease, especially tuberculosis, was epidemic. To Native Americans, the news that there was something called a "panic" on a street named Wall would have had a significance that was mainly ironic or bitter. And it appeared that help was not going to come to them any sooner than it was coming to the Mexican Americans. In 1929 the Hoover administration ruled that Native Americans living on reservations were not eligible for even the meager relief funds being provided by the federal government.

Then, in 1933, Roosevelt appointed a new commissioner of Indian affairs, John Collier, a former social worker. Collier made a number of decisions that were of real benefit to Native Americans who lived on reservations. Some of the decisions were of genuine symbolic importance. He ordered the bureaucrats who administered federal programs to respect Native American customs, language, and dress. He told them to stop doing what they had been doing for half a century, trying to force Indians to dress and talk and act like white people—or somebody's idea of the way white people ought to dress and talk and act. Other decisions were of more immediate and practical importance. Early in the New Deal, Collier persuaded Congress to fund the Indian Emergency Conservation program. It worked like the Civilian Conservation Corps, giving young men jobs building dams, planting trees, and improving roads. By the end of the 1930s about 90,000 Native Americans had worked in the program—nearly one third of the total Indian population. Paradoxically, life on the reservations during the Great Depression was probably better than it had been during the "prosperity" of the 1920s.

But it was clear to most Native Americans that something more than emergency relief measures was needed. Federal policy had to be changed. Tribal leaders worked with Collier to produce one of the decade's most significant pieces of legislation, the Indian Reorganization Act of 1934, which reversed many of the practices of the preceding fifty years. It recognized the basic concept of tribal ownership of land in common. It provided money—though never enough—for tribes to buy new land. The act also provided that tribes could write their own constitutions, which would be recognized as law by the federal government. And the act formally ended all restrictions on Native American ceremonies, dress, and language.

The Indian Reorganization Act did not touch the lives of those Native Americans who did not live on reservations, but some indirect assistance came to them through the Johnson-O'Malley Act of 1934. This law gave federal money to schools, hospitals, and other social agencies to encourage them to extend their services to Native Americans. Despite these measures, Native Americans probably remained the most impoverished of America's visible minorities—though the possessors of one of its richest cultures. As with blacks and Mexican Americans, it would take one more generation for their pride in that culture to become a public fact of indisputable significance.

END OF THE NEW DEAL

Franklin Roosevelt did everything he could to make the election of 1936 a test vote of the people's confidence in his efforts. And he won resoundingly. His Republican opponent, Governor Alfred Landon of Kansas, took only Maine and Vermont. No American president had ever received such a ringing endorsement for such a controversial program of action.

But victory did not bring more of the New Deal. If anything, it brought less. For the New Deal now had to face a set of distressing realities.

The first problem, though minor, was noisy and irritating. A third-party candidate, Congressman William Lemke, had polled almost a million votes in 1936. The vote itself did not matter, but it did seem to be the tip of an ominous political iceberg. Lemke had put together the votes of a number of critics of the New Deal who were demanding more radical action on a number of fronts. Senator Huey Long of Louisiana, an eccentric and fiery figure, was promoting a simple "Share Our Wealth" plan that held out the promise "Every man a king." A much quieter man, Dr. Francis Townsend of California, had created a movement for more adequate pensions for the elderly, a movement organized into thousands of Townsend Clubs. And an anti-Semitic Catholic priest, Father Charles Coughlin, had used the radio to generate a passionate belief in millions of people that "the Jews" were responsible for the depression and that they controlled the Roosevelt administration. Hindsight makes it obvious that Lemke, Long, Townsend, and Coughlin had little in common and no chance of success. But their movements raised serious doubts about the workability of the New Deal.

A much more trying problem for Roosevelt, however, was the failure of his efforts to end the depression. The gross national product would not budge. Federal deficits remained high, despite Roosevelt's personal commitment to a balanced budget. Unemployment refused to drop significantly. And no sooner was Roosevelt inaugurated the second time than a new wave of economic panic struck. The depression of 1937—a sort of depression-within-a-depression—shook the confidence not only of many voters but of many New Dealers themselves. The congressional elections of 1938 brought a coalition of Republicans and conservative Democrats to power, a coalition that made it virtually impossible to achieve any new legislative victories.

Finally, Roosevelt had to deal with an increasingly troublesome federal judiciary. In 1935 and 1936, parts of the Agricultural Adjustment Act and the National Industrial Recovery Act were ruled unconstitutional by the Supreme

-–‡–◉–‡–

CHRONOLOGY

1917	Russian Revolution
1919	Red scare begins;
	Eighteenth Amendment introduces prohibition
1920	Warren G. Harding (Republican) defeats James M. Cox (Democrat) in presidential election;
	Nicola Sacco and Bartolomeo Vanzetti convicted of murder in Massachusetts
1921	Immigration restricted by federal law
1923	Harding dies; Calvin Coolidge becomes president;
	Teapot Dome scandal;
	Stock market enters six-year boom
1924	Congress establishes bonus for World War I veterans, to be paid in 1945;
	Immigration further restricted, with Asians totally excluded;
	Ku Klux Klan plays important role in Democratic party national convention;
	Coolidge defeats John W. Davis (Democrat) in presidential election
1925	Scopes trial in Dayton, Tennessee
1927	Sacco and Vanzetti electrocuted
1928	Herbert Hoover (Republican) defeats Alfred E. Smith (Democrat) in presidential election
1929	Stock market crash begins the Great Depression
1930	Democrats gain majority in House of Representatives
1931	Congressional hearings on early payment of veterans' bonus;
	Scottsboro trials begin

1932	Veterans form Bonus Army;
	Hoover administration creates Reconstruction Finance Corporation;
	Senate defeats plan for early payment of veterans' bonus;
	Bonus marchers routed from District of Columbia by federal troops;
	Franklin Delano Roosevelt (Democrat) defeats Hoover in presidential election
1933	New Deal begins with "bank holiday";
	Works Progress Administration;
	National Labor Relations Act;
	Social Security Act
1935–1936	Agricultural Adjustment Act overturned by Supreme Court;
	National Industrial Recovery Act overturned by Supreme Court
1936	Roosevelt re-elected, defeating Alfred A. Landon (Republican);
	Sit-down strike at General Motors
1937	Roosevelt proposes to "pack" Supreme Court with additional justices;
	Congress of Industrial Organizations (CIO) gains members rapidly
1939	World War II begins;
	Eleanor Roosevelt sponsors Marian Anderson concert at Lincoln Memorial
1940	Roosevelt re-elected, defeating Wendell Wilkie (Republican)
1941	Fair Employment Practices Commission established in response to pressure from African Americans;
	United States enters World War II

Court. Roosevelt became convinced that unless the Court could somehow be changed, the Wagner Act, the TVA, and the Social Security Act would not be safe.

He made a daring move. He proposed a scheme to "pack" the Supreme Court, suggesting that Congress empower the president to increase the size of the Court by one for every justice over seventy years of age who did not retire.

What followed was a political fight lasting for months into Roosevelt's second term. In the end, he both won and lost. He won because some justices did decide to retire and others shifted their votes. This change gave rise to one of the cleverest newspaper headlines of American history, "A switch in time saves nine." But Roosevelt also lost, for public opinion seemed to turn markedly against him. Voters apparently disliked the idea of "tampering" with the Constitution (though the Constitution is in fact silent on the number of justices who sit on the Supreme Court). The Court fight virtually ended the New Deal. From that point onward, the attention of Roosevelt, and increasingly of everyone else, turned across the Atlantic and the Pacific, to fields of revolution and battle that would soon involve the nation in another world war, even more terrible than the Great War of 1914–1918.

SUGGESTIONS FOR FURTHER READING

THE BONUS ARMY

The two full-scale histories of the Bonus Army are Donald Lisio, *The President and Protest: Hoover, Conspiracy and the Bonus March* (1974), and Roger Daniels, *The Bonus March* (1971). The first is more concerned with what went on inside the Hoover administration; the second pays more attention to the marchers themselves. The *Reminiscences* of Douglas MacArthur (1964) are an interesting route into the peculiar mind of one important participant.

CONSERVATIVE REACTION

Robert K. Murray, *The Red Scare: A Study in National Hysteria, 1919–1920* (1955), is colorful and readable. The best place to begin reading about Sacco and Vanzetti is still Justice Felix Frankfurter's *The Case of Sacco and Vanzetti* (1962). It should be supplemented with William Young and David E. Kaiser, *Postmortem: New Evidence in the Case of Sacco and Vanzetti* (1985). The best account of Prohibition is Andrew Sinclair, *Prohibition: Era of Excess* (1962). The only book-length story of the Scopes trial is Ray Ginger, *Six Days or Forever? Tennessee* v. *John Thomas Scopes* (1958). Norman Furniss, *The Fundamentalist Controversy* (1954), is still a useful general treatment. The persistence of Christian conservatism can be followed in Leo Ribuffo, *The Old Christian Right* (1983). On nativism and the Klan, see John Higham, *Strangers in the Land* (1955); Kenneth Jackson, *The Ku Klux Klan in the City* (1965); and David M. Chalmers, *Hooded Americanism* (1965).

THE POLITICS OF CONSERVATISM

A fine general history of the Republican administrations of the 1920s—though an aging one—is John D. Hicks, *Republican Ascendancy* (1960). On the Democratic side, see David Burner, *The Politics of Provincialism* (1967), and Paula Elder, *Governor Alfred E. Smith* (1983). Two unusually sympathetic discussions of the most conservative presidents of the period are Robert K. Murray, *The Harding Era* (1969), and Donald R. McCoy, *Calvin Coolidge* (1967). An intriguing biography is *The Shadow of Blooming Grove: Warren G. Harding* (1968), by Francis Russell. Burl Noggle, *Teapot Dome* (1962), is excellent. Allan J. Lichtman's *Prejudice and the Old Politics* (1979) is a fine quantitative study of ethnic voting patterns. A valuable discussion of farm problems and policies is David E. Hamilton, *From New Day to New Deal: American Farm Policy from Hoover to Roosevelt, 1928–1933* (1991).

BOOM AND BUST

The crash and what brought it can be approached best through John Kenneth Galbraith's fine little book, *The Great Crash, 1929* (3d ed., 1972). A good treatment of the economic history of the 1920s and 1930s is Jim Potter, *The American Economy Between the Wars* (1974). Robert S. McElvaine, *The Great Depression* (1984), is an excellent general study. Useful discussions of Hoover's reaction to the onset of the depression are available in Joan Hoff Wilson, *Herbert Hoover, Forgotten Progressive* (1975); Martin Fausold, *The Presidency of Herbert Hoover* (1985); and William J. Barber, *Herbert Hoover, the Economists, and American Economic Policy, 1920–1933* (1985). Good firsthand accounts of the way the depression affected people are available in Richard Lowitt and Maurine Beasley, eds., *One Third of a Nation* (1981), and Robert McElvaine, ed., *Down & Out in the Great Depression* (1983). The victims of the crash speak eloquently in Caroline Bird, *The Invisible Scar* (1966); Studs Terkel, *Hard Times: An Oral History of the Great Depression* (1970), and the Federal Writers Project, *These Are Our Lives* (1939).

THE NEW DEAL

The literature on Roosevelt and the New Deal is vast. For a sampling of some of the ways the New Deal has been judged, see Harvard Sitkoff, ed., *Fifty Years Later: The New Deal Evaluated* (1985). The most readable, though thoroughly biased, general account is the three volumes of Arthur M. Schlesinger, Jr., *The Age of Roosevelt: The Crisis of the Old Order, The Coming of the New Deal, The Politics of Upheaval* (1957–1960). A useful and briefer account is Albert Romasco, *The Politics of Recovery* (1983). The Roosevelt administration's welfare policies are discussed in the early chapters of James Patterson, *America's Struggle Against Poverty* (1981). For an unsympathetic treatment of Roosevelt and his policies, see Gary Dean Best, *Pride, Prejudice, and Politics: Roosevelt Versus Recovery* (1990). Three excellent special studies of crucially important aspects of the New Deal are James Patterson, *The New Deal and the States* (1969); Ellis Hawley, *The New Deal and the Problem of Monopoly* (1966); and Barry Dean Karl, *Executive Reorganization and Reform in the New Deal* (1963). A fine, general, and brief book is William Leuchtenburg, *Franklin Roosevelt and the New Deal* (1963). The most ambitious study of Roosevelt is Frank Friedel, *Franklin D. Roosevelt* (4 vols., 1952–1973). For a briefer treatment, see the same author's *Franklin D. Roosevelt: A Rendezvous with Destiny* (1990). Good studies of workers and unions are John Barnard, *Walter Reuther and the Rise of the Auto Worker* (1983); Ronald W. Schatz, *The Electrical Workers: A History of Labor at General Electric and Westinghouse* (1983); and Lizabeth Cohen, *Making a New Deal: Industrial Workers in Chicago, 1919–1939* (1991). A fascinating look at radical opposition to the New Deal is Alan Brinkley, *Voices of Protest: Huey Long, Father Coughlin, and the Great Depression* (1982). Equally useful is William Ivy Hair, *The Kingfish and His Realm: The Life and Times of Huey Long* (1992).

WOMEN AND MINORITIES

The best study of women in the 1930s is Susan Ware, *Holding Their Own* (1982). Also useful are Alice Kessler-Harris, *Out to Work* (1982), and Winifred Wandersee, *Women's Work and Family Values* (1981). For the way the depression accelerated the transformation of Harlem into an African-American ghetto, see Gilbert Osofsky, *Harlem: The Making of a Ghetto* (1966). Gunnar Myrdal's classic study, *An American Dilemma* (1944), is still extremely useful. The relationship of the New Deal to black people is well treated in Nancy Weiss, *Farewell to the Party of Lincoln* (1983), and Harvard Sitkoff, *A New Deal for Blacks* (1978). The standard account of the Scottsboro trials is Dan T. Carter's very readable *Scottsboro* (1969). For the experiences of Mexican Americans and Mexicans in America, see Rodolfo Acuna, *Occupied America* (1981); Mark Reisler, *By the Sweat of Their Brow* (1976); Abraham Hoffman, *Unwanted Mexican Americans in the Depression* (1975); and Wayne Cornelius, *Building the Cactus Curtain* (1980). Kenneth Philip, *John J. Collier and the Crusade for Indian Reform, 1920–1954* (1977); Lawrence C. Kelly, *The Assault on Assimilation* (1977), and Christine Bolt, *American Indian Policy and American Reform* (1987), all contain careful and thorough discussions of federal policies affecting Native Americans. Donald Parman, *Navajoes and the New Deal* (1976), is a specialized book, but it contains a fine summary of changes in federal policy toward Native Americans.

A Global Nation

THE EPISODE: *There are few more dramatic events of the twentieth century than the explosion of atomic bombs over Hiroshima and Nagasaki, Japan. These terrible instruments of war convinced the already defeated Japanese to surrender. Exclusive possession of these weapons by the United States gave the nation an arms lead over the Soviet Union that remained decisive for only a few years after 1945. The atomic bomb also became a symbol for the cold war, the threat of a nuclear engagement that menaced the existence of humanity. Yet the atomic bomb and, particularly, the decision to build it in secrecy had a profound impact inside the United States also, affecting relations between scientists and government, between research and funding and deployment of weapons. Atomic research helped to shape not just relations with the Soviet Union and the rest of the world, but the way the American government related to science in the postwar world.*

THE HISTORICAL SETTING: *The explosion of the atomic bomb seemed to signal the beginning of a new age. Indeed, there were dramatic changes in American foreign policy after 1945, as the nation emerged from the war at the head of a coalition determined to prevent the expansion of Soviet influence and the spread of communism. Among the exhausted participants of the war only the United States had the energy and capacity to undertake this crusade.*

Atomic weaponry was, necessarily, a major element in any such strategy. But development of the bomb occurred in the peculiar context of an alliance of enemies against the Germans and the Japanese during World War II.

After almost a decade of appeasement, isolation, and fruitless negotiations, Britain, the United States, and the Soviet Union found themselves fighting a desperate war against Germany, Italy, and Japan. Their tenuous alliance, upon which the shape of the postwar world depended, fell apart rapidly after the war ended because of irreconcilable differences that were only temporarily submerged. Determined to enhance the influence of the USSR, Joseph Stalin gradually exerted control over vast areas of eastern Europe occupied by the Red Army. The United States organized its European allies into a military and economic coalition and undertook to rebuild Germany and Japan. As the sides hardened there were a number of dangerous flash points: jointly occupied Berlin, eastern Europe, and, in Asia—on the periphery of China—Taiwan, Korea, and, ultimately, Vietnam.

Yet, remarkably, the atomic bomb was not used again. Each side eventually manufactured hundreds of atomic bombs and warheads for delivery by bombers or missiles. Each side spent billions, finally, on a weapon that by anyone's account had changed the rules of modern warfare forever but had made those rules obsolete.

HIROSHIMA

On a cold day in early spring 1955, a U.S. Air Force plane circled over Mitchell Field on Long Island, New York. Plunging into the turbulence, the aircraft landed and released its cargo: twenty-five young Japanese girls, "the Hiroshima maidens." Disfigured, some crippled, they huddled together, waiting to be taken to Mount Sinai Hospital for surgery to release their limbs, twisted by radiation and burns, and to smooth their swollen and distorted features. They were a fortunate few among the victims of the atomic bomb, brought to the United States by a group of religious workers and concerned citizens. It was a small, private gesture of reparation by Americans for the terrible destruction of Hiroshima.

Ten years earlier, shortly after eight o'clock on a warm August morning, a U.S. Army Air Force B-29 droned high over the center of Hiroshima, Japan. Most of the residents were only vaguely aware of its presence, reminded briefly, perhaps, of an earlier air-raid alert, which had then been followed by the all-clear signal. Most of the twenty-five girls were in the basement of their public school preparing erasers and chalk for classes. Most adults were on their way to work. Other schoolchildren were getting ready to resume their labor of clearing fire lanes in the city. This safety precaution, of pulling down crowded wooden houses and buildings in wide swaths across the city, had become necessary to prevent the firestorms from American incendiary raids that had obliterated whole square miles of Tokyo and other cities. Thus far, Hiroshima had been spared. Built on the flat delta of the Ota River, Hiroshima had become an important manufacturing center for the Japanese war effort. Most of its population lived along inlets connected by bridges, and most of the city was built of wood or other flimsy materials.

On the morning of August 6 the weather was clear. No antiaircraft fire or fighter planes met the American bomber, the *Enola Gay*, as it cruised smoothly toward its mission. Suddenly over target, the ship released its five-ton bomb and dived sharply to the right. The weapon drifted down slowly on a parachute, giving the plane forty-three precious seconds to escape. Then, shortly before it reached the ground, the bomb's altitude detectors triggered the device.

The burst flashed far brighter than the sun at midday. Waves of concussion pulverized everything at its center, and in an instant the enormous heat ignited the splintered debris. Inrushing winds thrust smoke and dust 40,000 feet into the atmosphere within two minutes. Still close by, but safe, the *Enola Gay* was buffeted by shock waves. One crew member looked back and remarked that it was "like boiling dust." The B-29 continued on its long trip back to base at Tinian Island. Built on a coral ridge, its six 2-mile runways, constructed especially for heavy bombers, made it the world's largest airport. It had launched the *Enola Gay* and, with it, a new era in world history.

In Hiroshima, the devastation was instantaneous. About 80,000 people were killed or seriously wounded, most by burns, pressure from the blast, or falling buildings. Fires leaped out over the precautionary fire lanes. There was no way to fight them. The explosion had destroyed most firehouses, roadways were blocked, and scores of firemen were dead. Of the city's 200 doctors, 180 were killed or injured; of 1,780 nurses, 1,654 had died or were disabled. Some residents who survived, like Mrs. Futaba Kitayama, working about 2,000 yards from the blast, were terribly burned. Fearing that the bomb contained incendiary powders, she recalled, "I rubbed my nose and mouth hard with a *tenugui* [towel] I had at my waist. To my horror, I found that the skin on my face had come off in the towel." Farther out, people fell sick from radiation poisoning; many more died painfully within weeks. The Hiroshima maidens scrambled out of their collapsed school, some badly burned by fire or radiation. Nothing remained of their classrooms or schoolmates.

Of all the feelings experienced by Hiroshima survivors, perhaps the most universal was shock followed by a protective numbness. The single bomb, the single plane, surprise, and then enormous destruction—the combination wiped out all sense of proportion and disrupted the logic of cause and effect. It left only shock. As a Japanese poet wrote later:

> *There is nothing for us to sing*
> *Whose eyes are closed,*
> *When we, in tears, gaze through*
> *The clear sky's depths.*
> *We find that all is lost and scattered;*
> *Suppose our brains have turned to ashes,*
> *Soaked in the River Ota, flowing in its blue;*

> *You people,*
> *Believe us;*
> *We find that all is washed away.*
> *What song is there for us to sing whose eyes are closed?*
> *But a song of tears?*

Three days later, the United States dropped a second atomic bomb, this time over the city of Nagasaki. Although different in composition from the first, the device had an equivalent destructive force. But because of the hilly terrain and the greater prevalence of concrete buildings, the city sustained somewhat fewer casualties. Still, the general effect was similar: a bewildered population, the breakdown of social services, and a landscape littered with splintered trees, twisted girders and towers, and the debris of what once had been a place of human habitation.

In August the Japanese had been on the verge of surrender: their cities shattered, their navy sunk, and their air force limited to defensive operations and suicidal

HIROSHIMA.   This picture of devastated Hiroshima captures the bewildering destructiveness of the atomic-bomb raids on Japan.

kamikaze attacks against U.S. ships. Two days after Hiroshima, the Soviet Union declared war on Japan and marched rapidly into Japanese-held Manchuria. Against overwhelming odds on land, and facing extinction from the air, the Japanese sued for peace after Nagasaki. With their surrender, World War II ended on August 14.

✦⟶══◉══⟵✦

The decision to drop the atomic bomb on two Japanese cities had been one of three key decisions relating to atomic energy that American policy makers had confronted during the war. The first decision was to build the bomb; the second, to use it; and the third, to try to maintain its secrets as an American monopoly during and after the war. None of these decisions was made lightly, for as the president, his scientific advisers and administrators, and the few other officials brought into the process knew well, the shape of the postwar world depended on the wisdom of their deliberations.

The decision to develop an atomic bomb was, initially, made out of fear that the Germans would create this awesome weapon first. And there was no doubt that they would use it if they acquired it. Germany's blitzkrieg (lightning war) invasion of Poland in September 1939 had demonstrated the importance of technological superiority in winning battles. World War II was, as British prime minister Winston Churchill aptly called it, "a wizard war." By this he meant that inventions were decisive. The opposing

NAGASAKI BEFORE ATOMIC ATTACK. Nagasaki, a port city and shipbuilding center, was the target of the second atomic bomb dropped on Japan at the close of World War II. Built on a series of hills, the city was devastated by the single blast on August 9, 1945.

nations spurred their scientists to develop weapons that would turn the tide of this desperate struggle. As Albert Speer, the German Reich's minister for armaments and munitions, said in 1946, even to the last moment the German population believed that some new "miraculous weapon" would save them from defeat.

The Americans and the British feared the potential of Germany's pure science and its sophisticated industrial plant. German military tactics, demonstrated in Poland and then in Belgium and France in the spring of 1940, underscored the advantages of a military strategy harnessed to science and industry. During the war, German science fielded several new weapons, including self-guided rockets and a new jet fighter plane.

Had the jet been developed more quickly, it might have reversed Allied air supremacy in the last days of the war.

American and British science was also active in the development of weapons technology. A new radar system invented by the British helped deflect Hitler's effort to achieve air supremacy over England. Sonic systems to detect submarines, proximity fuses for mines, and a host of other engineering triumphs helped turn the tide of battle in favor of the Allies. None of these accomplishments, however, matched atomic power. Whoever tamed this energy first could command the gods of war.

The American scientific community, led by a distinguished group of European physicists who had fled German and Italian fascism, had good reason to fear German atomic science. In 1938, German scientists had demonstrated the possibility of nuclear fission, the basis for a chain reaction in radioactive material. The practical question was, could a chain reaction be harnessed and detonated as a bomb? In March 1939, physicists Leo Szilard (from Hungary) and Enrico Fermi (from Italy) directed successful fission experiments. Deeply worried that the Germans had made similar advances, Szilard went to the world-renowned scientist Albert Einstein. Einstein agreed to sign a letter to President Roosevelt warning him that Germany might be on the verge of developing atomic weapons: "It is conceivable," the letter concluded, "that extremely powerful bombs of a new type may be constructed."

Roosevelt undoubtedly knew little about the scientific basis of this prediction, but he was impressed enough by this warning to appoint a uranium committee inside the National Bureau of Standards. By early 1940 he had agreed to spend significant sums of money on atomic research, even though the United States officially remained at peace with Germany and Japan. Moreover, he determined that these activities should be pursued in secrecy; only a few scientists and only his closest political associates knew of the project.

In early summer 1941 Roosevelt appointed a larger committee to muster science in the cause of defense. Headed by Vannevar Bush, president of the Carnegie Institute and a noted engineer, this new National Defense Research Committee took over the work of the Uranium Committee. Bush reorganized the uranium group, adding more scientists and removing some of the military representatives. Then word reached Washington that the British had begun their own atomic program, dubbed MAUD in secret code. The British warned that a bomb was practical and could probably be built in two years.

Spurred to move faster by the British report, Roosevelt pushed through another reorganization during the fall of 1941, this time creating an advisory group called Section 1 and making it part of the recently formed Office of Scientific Research and Development. Section 1 consisted of Bush; James B. Conant, president of Harvard University; Secretary of War Henry L. Stimson; Army Chief of Staff George C. Marshall; and Vice President Henry Wallace. In March 1942 Roosevelt turned the actual building of the bomb over to the War Department, which put Brigadier General Leslie R. Groves of the Army Corps of Engineers in charge of the project. By then, it had acquired a new name, the Manhattan Project, and a large, secret budget, hidden even from Congress.

Bureaucratic shuffling, agency reorganization, and new liaison committees were clues to the growing importance of atomic research. Roosevelt, by his actions, was also

ENRICO FERMI. One consequence of fascism in Italy and Germany was the flood of scientists and intellectuals who sought refuge in the United States during the 1930s. Some of these scientists, like Fermi, conducted crucial experiments that enabled America to construct the first atomic weapons.

tightening federal control over the research, giving the military a dominant role in guiding it. By the time the project ended, it had spent about $2 billion. Over 100,000 people had worked on various aspects of the endeavor at thirty-seven military, scientific, and industrial installations—all to create a device that would cause about thirteen pounds of plutonium to release its energy. Yet this work had been accomplished with a degree of secrecy unknown in American history. Even many of the scientists did not know the precise objective of their research.

The project began in earnest in late 1942. General Groves appointed J. Robert Oppenheimer, a physicist from the California Institute of Technology, to direct the nuclear facility at Los Alamos, New Mexico, where much of the work was completed. In December, Enrico Fermi, working in an abandoned squash court at the University of Chicago, created the first self-sustaining chain reaction. Thus by early 1943, American scientists had acquired the basic knowledge and the facilities to develop a bomb. Ironically, at almost precisely the same time, German scientists concluded that an atomic weapon was not feasible. Yet no one knew of the Germans' decision for sure. In fact, Arthur Compton, a Manhattan Project participant, reported that the United States worried so much about German atomic progress that "when the Allies landed on Normandy France beaches on 6 June, 1944, certain of the American officers were equipped with Geiger counters," to detect traces of atomic weapons.

Secrecy, compartmentalization, and hierarchy characterized Groves's administration of the project. By dividing up the research and keeping any one scientist in the project from having access to more information than was required to answer a specific question, Groves prevented leaks of information. He possibly also slowed the progress of the project. More important, however, he stopped scientists from discussing the larger implications of their work: whether or not a weapon should be used and under what conditions. Furthermore, he angered a number of scientists with his security-conscious rules and bureaucracy, for this contradicted the fundamental tenets of scientific research.

Groves, however, was not the only policy maker who wanted to hide the project. Bush and Conant hoped to exclude the British, to prevent their gaining atomic weapons. At first, Roosevelt seemed to agree, but in the summer of 1943 he reversed himself. At an August conference with Churchill in Quebec, Canada, the president agreed to a full exchange of information. This left only the Soviet Union, America's other principal ally, out in the cold. In fact, the decision not to tell the Soviets while keeping the British informed became one of the most momentous of the war, for it came to symbolize the lack of trust and cooperation between the opponents of Germany. Apparently, Roosevelt never seriously considered informing the Soviets about the project or keeping them abreast of scientific developments. As Groves later declared, "There was never, from about two weeks from the time I took charge of this Project any illusion on my part but that Russia was our enemy."

Although atomic research always aimed at production of a usable bomb, its actual deployment remained uncertain and controversial. Depending on its completion date, a bomb could be dropped on Germany or Japan or both. If one or the other of the Axis powers was knocked out of the war—and by early 1945, Germany was rapidly crumbling—it would have to be used exclusively on the sole enemy survivor.

In 1944, as the bomb moved from the drawing board to construction, several scientists began to discuss the wider implications of atomic power. The resolve to use the bomb was implicit in its creation and in the momentum the Manhattan Project gained in 1944 and 1945. But the decision could have been reversed, and a few of the scientists working on the project or familiar with atomic energy desperately pressed for a reconsideration. They recognized that the bomb was more than just a new, powerful weapon. Its development and its use, they contended, would have vast implications in shaping the postwar world. This was a difficult position to take, for the bureaucratic structure governing the Manhattan Project was designed to prevent broad discussions of any sort—especially those that challenged the use of the bomb. Any halt to plans for deploying the bomb would have to come from the very top, from the few civilian leaders like Churchill and Roosevelt who knew the details of the weapon's development.

As the weapon became more of a likelihood in 1944, several scientists became uneasy about the choice of a target. Increasingly, it appeared that Germany would not be the victim. That country was rapidly falling apart under the massive attacks from west and east by Allied armies. That left Japan, a nation that could not develop a bomb of its own but that still clung tenaciously to its extended empire of Pacific conquests. Allied commanders estimated that to knock the Japanese out of the war would require a two-stage invasion of Japan—the first in November 1945 with a landing on the island of Kyushu, and a second, full-scale attack in the spring of 1946. Estimated Allied casualties in the two assaults were placed at somewhere around a million men. If this were the case, the atomic bomb might prove decisive. But it was also possible that the Japanese would give up before such a costly assault became necessary.

Other questions worried scientists as early as 1943. Niels Bohr, a Danish refugee and key theorist in the field of atomic science, firmly believed that atomic information should be shared among all the Allies, including the Soviets. If not, he warned, an atomic arms race might develop after the war. In several memoranda to Roosevelt, he urged international control of atomic energy. He urged the president to inform the Soviet Union of the Manhattan Project. Scientists could help in promoting an

> understanding of how much would be at stake should the great prospects of atomic physics materialize, and in preparing an adequate realization of the great benefit which would ensue from a whole-hearted co-operation on effective control measures.

Roosevelt postponed taking any such initiatives, so Bohr tried to persuade Winston Churchill. The scientist traveled to England in the spring of 1944 with letters of recommendation and waited impatiently for a meeting with the prime minister. When it finally occurred, Churchill showed himself hostile to sharing atomic secrets with the Soviet Union. Bohr left the meeting knowing he had failed: "We did not even speak the same language," he later remarked. Other scientists active in the project, such as Bush, eventually came to share Bohr's fears that attempting to maintain a monopoly on atomic secrets would stimulate an arms race between the United States and the Soviet Union. But by the end of 1944, Roosevelt clearly agreed with Churchill: the two allies would not share atomic knowledge with the Soviet Union.

By the spring of 1945 the Soviet issue had even complicated the question of using the atomic bomb. Decision making became more difficult still in April. President Roosevelt died suddenly on April 12, leaving to the new President, Harry Truman, the decision about dropping the first atomic weapon in history. War was racing to a climax in Europe. The new president had to face the hard task of designing a peace in an atmosphere of growing competition with the Soviets. Truman had limited experience in foreign affairs; he had little sympathy for the Soviets; and he was not aware of the plans or promises Roosevelt had made. Most important, he did not even know about the atomic bomb.

At a White House meeting on April 25, Stimson and Groves informed the new president of the weapon about to be placed under his command. Secretly ushered into the president's office, Groves made several points: The United States would soon test an atomic device; the United States and Britain held a monopoly on the world's fissionable materials; the Soviets were probably spying on the Manhattan Project. Stimson took a very different tack, warning the new president of the dangers atomic bombs presented to international diplomacy:

> In the light of our present position with reference to this weapon, the question of sharing it with other nations and if so shared, upon what terms, becomes a primary question of our foreign relations.

Truman's sole initiative at this meeting was to appoint an interim committee to choose targets in Japan.

Once the Germans had collapsed, in early May, Truman turned his attention to formulating a European peace and to ending the war in Asia. Increasingly, these two efforts became intertwined. The president was deeply distressed by news reaching Washington: the Soviets, occupying Europe as far west as central Germany, were consolidating their hold on eastern European countries, including Bulgaria, Poland, Hungary, and Czechoslovakia. The Japanese, he believed, were preparing to defend their island empire to the last inch. In both situations, the atomic bomb might be important. In Europe, exclusive American possession of a successful bomb might convince the Soviet Union to cooperate with the United States on its plans for the shape of postwar Europe and Asia. In Asia, its use might save hundreds of thousands of American and Japanese lives.

Truman had both possibilities in mind when he scheduled a meeting at Potsdam, Germany, with Stalin and Churchill in July. The timing coincided with the first testing of the atomic bomb, the news of which Truman expected to reach him during the conference. As expected, on July 18 word flashed from Alamogordo Air Base, near Albuquerque, New Mexico: a successful explosion with "the brightness of several suns at midday." The president then proceeded to use the information. On July 25 he wrote in his diary:

> We met at 11 a.m. today, that is, Stalin, Churchill and the U.S. President. But I had a most important session with Lord Louis Mountbatten and General George Marshall before that. We have discovered the most terrible bomb in the history of the world. It may be the fire destruction prophesied in the Euphrates Valley Era, after Noah and his fabulous Ark.

The president then recorded his thoughts about using the bomb:

> This weapon is to be used against the Japanese between now and August 10th. I have told the Secretary of War, Mr. Stimson, to use it so that military objectives and soldiers and sailors are the target and not women and children. Even if the Japs are savages, ruthless, merciless and fanatic, we as the leader of the world for the common welfare cannot drop this terrible bomb on the old capital Kyoto or the new Tokyo.

Truman believed that the bomb would save lives and that its use was inevitable, since the Japanese, even after warnings, would not surrender: "It is certainly a good thing for the world," he concluded, "that Hitler's crowd or Stalin's did not discover this atomic bomb. It seems to be the most terrible thing ever discovered, but it can be made most useful."

Truman's private musings contained at least three dubious assumptions or misapprehensions. The first was that the bomb incontestably had to be used. There were strong rumors at the time that the Japanese were on the verge of collapse. With Germany out of the war, Japan was isolated. On July 18 Stalin informed Churchill of a message from the Japanese emperor suing for peace. With the imminent prospect of a Soviet declaration of war on Japan, surrender—without the use of the bomb—was at least possible. Second, Truman had assured himself that the targets selected were primarily military. This was only partly the case, for both Hiroshima and Nagasaki were cities with large civilian populations. Finally, Truman believed the weapon could be useful. Perhaps he meant useful to end the war. But possibly he also meant that it would intimidate the Soviets.

If making the Soviet Union more cooperative was one purpose of the bomb, it did not entirely work. When Truman hinted to Stalin at Potsdam about the new weapon, the Soviet leader replied calmly that he hoped it would be used against the Japanese. The conference resumed and eventually reached certain limited agreements about the shape of the postwar world. But as Truman later wrote:

> What a show that was! But a large number of agreements were reached in spite of the set up only to be broken as soon as the unconscionable Russian Dictator returned to Moscow! And I liked the little son of a bitch.

By August, Truman had determined not to share any secrets with the Soviets, and he was committed to dropping two bombs. Last-minute appeals of atomic scientists to reverse his decision failed to convince him. A committee of Chicago scientists had warned in early June that a surprise attack against the Japanese would initiate an arms race with the Soviet Union. However, Truman's own Scientific Advisory Committee, made up of several eminent scientists, recommended using the weapon:

> We can propose no technical demonstration likely to bring an end to the war; we see no acceptable alternative to direct military use.

One last serious attempt to stop the bomb came from Chicago scientists on July 17. Leo Szilard authored a petition and gathered the signatures of sixty-eight other atomic scientists. The document urged President Truman not to drop the bomb:

> The development of atomic power will provide nations with new means of destruction. The atomic bombs at our disposal represent only the first step in this direction, and there is almost no limit to the destructive power which will become available in the course of their future development.

No nation, Szilard concluded, would ever be safe from destruction.

This petition, as well as other serious reservations expressed by other scientists, failed to reach the president. Project director Groves refused to pass them on because "no useful purpose would be served in transmitting either the petition or the attached documents to the White House." And besides, by the time the petition reached Groves, Truman was already in Potsdam. Having built this terrible weapon, and seeing its apparent multiple advantages—in ending the war immediately and in impressing the Soviets—Truman, Stimson, and other policy makers were determined to use it.

On July 26 the United States, Britain, and China issued a new warning to Japan and a final demand for unconditional surrender. The proclamation vaguely threatened the "utter devastation of the Japanese homeland," but it did not mention the bomb. The Japanese rejected the call, still holding out for preservation of the power and status of the emperor. The decision to use the bomb had now become irreversible.

On August 6 President Truman in a dramatic report to the nation announced the explosion of the atomic bomb over Hiroshima. "Sixteen hours ago an American airplane dropped one bomb on Hiroshima, an important Japanese army base," he said. Then he described the size and power of the weapon. It was, he proclaimed, "the great-

THE CREW OF THE GREAT ARTISTE.   In this posed reenactment, Major Chuck Sweeney, commander of the B-29 that dropped the atomic bomb over Nagasaki, illustrates how he briefed his crew before taking off on the mission.

est achievement of organized science in history." It had been built in secret, and it would be continued in secrecy:

> It has never been the habit of the scientists of this country or the policy of this Government to withhold from the world scientific knowledge.

> But under present circumstances it is not intended to divulge the technical processes of production or all the military applications pending further examination of possible methods of protecting us and the rest of the world from the danger of sudden destruction.

Truman's decision to maintain secrecy about atomic research and development was, like the decision to drop the bomb, very much the product of past decisions. Having already excluded the Soviet Union, and believing that sole possession of the weapon by the United States would make them more amenable to American wishes for postwar Europe, Truman and his advisers were dubious about sharing America's scientific advantages. But any decision can be reversed, and there were some compelling reasons to do so in this case. In the first place, many scientists argued that there were no secrets. In the words of Albert Einstein, "There is no secret and there is no defense." Second, the administration recognized that Russian espionage was likely to penetrate American security anyway. This possibility was confirmed in September 1945, when the Canadian prime minister revealed details of an atomic spy ring operating in the United States and Canada. Furthermore, to hold scientists captive to the secrets they discovered in their research betrayed the very essence of free scientific inquiry. Finally, there was the possibility of an arms race. As a scientist at the University of Chicago put it in 1946:

> If we seek to achieve our own security through supremacy in atomic warfare, we will find that in ten years the whole world is as adequately armed as we, and that the threat of imminent destruction will bring about a "preventive war."

These were grave risks: dependence on secrets that might not be safe, excessive government direction and interference in scientific research, and an arms race.

Nevertheless, to Truman they were risks worth running. By late 1945 he had become convinced that a monopoly on the atomic bomb would allow the United States great flexibility in foreign policy without the cost of a large standing army. On October 27 he declared that American possession of the bomb was a "sacred trust" for humanity. Nonetheless, Truman made at least one serious effort in early 1946 to demilitarize nuclear energy. But the spring of that year was a tense time to formulate a treaty based on mutual trust. In February 1946, news of the Soviet spy ring operating from Canada had been made public. In consequence, American and Soviet foreign policies both stiffened. Still, a committee in the State Department devised a plan for international control of atomic energy. The group was headed by David Lilienthal, former head of the Tennessee Valley Authority and future head of the Atomic Energy Commission. After serious debate, the committee suggested a scheme in March that would give the United Nations control over the mining, refining, and utilization of atomic raw materials. Each nation, under this plan, could retain control over the peaceful uses of nuclear energy. In many respects this was an extraordinary proposal because it implicitly challenged American national sovereignty. It meant giving up a right and a power to an international body that, in some matters, would be superior to the United States. It implied a serious venture into world government.

Truman endorsed the plan and appointed the elderly financier Bernard Baruch to present it to the UN Atomic Energy Commission. Baruch agreed to serve but insisted on the right to make changes. His modifications almost guaranteed a Soviet refusal. He proposed total disarmament, not just control of nuclear weapons. His plan included dire punishments for nations who violated the agreement and private, not international, control of mining and manufacture. Finally, he proposed abolishing the Security Council veto in atomic energy matters. The Soviet Union rejected the plan in the summer of 1946. Almost immediately, the United States resumed atmospheric nuclear bomb testing, and the Soviet Union continued their drive to develop a bomb.

Public opinion, which might have contributed significantly to the extended debate about the bomb, atomic secrecy, and the role of science, was splintered, confused, and often anxious. A Gallup poll taken August 16, 1946, disclosed that about 85 per-

THE FAR EAST, 1945

U.S.S.R.
*(declared war on Japan
August 8, 1945)*

MONGOLIA

MANCHURIA
*(controlled by
Japan, 1932-1945)*

JAPAN
(surrendered August 14, 1945)

Peking (Beijing)

SEA OF
JAPAN

KOREA
*(controlled by
Japan, 1910-1945)*

Tokyo

Osaka

Hiroshima *(first U.S. atomic bomb
dropped August 6, 1945)*

Nagasaki
*(second U.S.
atomic bomb
dropped
August 9, 1945)*

CHINA
*(at war with
and partially occupied
by Japan)*

Shanghai

EAST
CHINA
SEA

PACIFIC
OCEAN

SOUTH
CHINA
SEA

INDOCHINA
*(occupied
by Japan)*

THE PHILIPPINES
*(occupied
by Japan)*

0   500   1000 Miles

cent of Americans approved the bombings, 10 percent disapproved, and 5 percent had
no opinion. In the context of the war's end, this result is hardly surprising. Mixed into
the approval were certain strong American beliefs: admiration for science and technology, a long-standing faith in air power as a kind of ultimate weapon, and a faith in
progress. Shortly after the war, David Dietz captured this spirit in his book *Atomic Energy in the Coming Era*. Dietz predicted a plane that traveled more than 1,000 miles an
hour and a moon rocket ship powered by atomic chain reactions. He also promised an
automobile engine fired by "tiny explosions of Uranium 235." These, he proclaimed,
were only a few of the "miracles just ahead for mankind in the coming Era of Atomic
Energy whose dawn was heralded Sunday, August 5,[1] when the first bomb of atomic
energy exploded over the Japanese city of Hiroshima."

Nonetheless, many Americans worried about the bomb, especially after the initial
euphoria of the war's end died down. They did not believe General Groves, who told a

---

[1] *Because Japan is on the other side of the International Date Line, the blast occurred there on August 6.*

Senate hearing that radiation poison was "a very pleasant way to die." Church leaders in particular condemned the bomb. Roman Catholic spokesmen denounced the weapon because, contrary to expressed intentions, the explosion did not spare civilians. Thirty-four leading Protestant clergymen sent President Truman a petition calling the bomb an atrocity. In 1946 the Federal Council of Churches of Christ wrote of its anguish at the attack:

> As American Christians, we are deeply penitent for the irresponsible use already made of the atomic bomb. We are agreed that, whatever be one's judgment of the ethics of war in principle, the surprise bombings of Hiroshima and Nagasaki are morally indefensible.

It was not the moral outrage of churches that touched the American public so much as the book *Hiroshima*, written by novelist John Hersey. Hersey traveled to Japan in October and November 1945 and brought back material for an extended article for the *New Yorker* magazine. Ordinarily a witty and fashionable periodical known for its sardonic cartoons, the magazine suspended its humor for a single issue in August 1946. It printed no satire, cartoons, or verse, and even excised some of the more inappropriate advertising. The issue sold out four hours after it hit the newsstands. Hersey's article was subsequently reprinted in fifty newspapers and then became a best-selling book.

Hersey wrote about the bomb in a way that most Americans could understand: through the eyes of six survivors. He clothed bare statistics with the details of the life and death of ordinary people. He captured the essential experience of surprise, nakedness, and numbness before a force that was incomprehensible. This approach cut through the depersonalized, abstract—often bigoted—way America had judged its enemy.

The effectiveness of Hersey's story aroused a response from the bomb's defenders. Hollywood produced a quick propaganda film in 1947, *The Beginning or the End?* showing the president troubled by the fateful decision to employ the weapon but the scientists in favor of its use. Some of those who had helped guide the construction of the bomb, like Henry Stimson, wrote articles in popular magazines to defend its use. In the end, most Americans remained convinced that the bomb had been necessary. Neither guilt nor fear of atomic warfare translated into significant opposition to relying on a nuclear monopoly in foreign policy. On the contrary, the public increasingly worried about keeping nuclear weapons a secret.

In July 1945, just before the end of the war, Vannevar Bush had submitted a report titled *Science—The Endless Frontier* to the president, outlining his suggestions for a new relationship between science and the government. The war had created this new relationship and Bush wished to institutionalize it. The government should coordinate and support broad research programs, he wrote,

> but we must proceed with caution in carrying over the methods which work in wartime to the very different conditions of peace. We must remove the rigid controls which we have had to impose, and recover freedom of inquiry and that healthy competitive spirit so necessary for expansion of the frontier of scientific knowledge.

Bush's worries about government interference and rigidity were well founded, for three major groups were contending for the control of science and atomic research after the war. These included the scientists themselves, the civilian branch of the federal government, and the military. In the end, something of a compromise was worked out, and basic scientific research in the United States evolved into a partnership between scientists and the civilian and military branches of government. But to some researchers, this compromise severely limited their freedom to speak and publish and, above all, to determine the uses of their work. For them research in peacetime remained too much like secret research under conditions of war.

In the next several years, three federal institutions were developed to direct and finance scientific research in the United States. The precedent of the Manhattan Project, the commitment to secrecy, and the desire to advance science in competition with the Soviet Union played a significant role in their foundation. The first was the Atomic Energy Commission (AEC), established August 1, 1946, which guided and controlled the development and application of nuclear energy in a variety of military and nonmilitary areas. The National Science Foundation, set up in 1950, became the major institution to fund and direct basic scientific research (some of it relevant to weapons development and much of it not). The third institution was the military administration and funding of large weapons projects by the Defense Department.

The AEC had many of the characteristics of the Manhattan Project. Its by-laws prevented international cooperation on atomic energy development, and its employees had to pass an FBI investigation. But tightly run as it was, the AEC represented a significant compromise. Scientists who had balked at tight security and army interference on the Manhattan Project demanded freedom to do research. Some of them organized the Federation of Atomic Scientists in 1945 to oppose any efforts to impose direct military control of research. It successfully blocked legislation that would have placed military representatives in a dominant position on the commission.

The question of federal funding for basic scientific research ended in much the same sort of compromise. In his report on science, Vannevar Bush proposed a new agency to underwrite basic research. Run by civilians and scientists, it would direct research in a wide variety of fields, not just those related to military weapons. Although this proposal appealed to scientists, President Truman rejected the plan because it appeared to be independent from federal control. Thus in 1947, when a bill to create an independent National Science Foundation passed through Congress, Truman vetoed it. Lacking close executive branch supervision, Truman argued, the proposed foundation would be divorced from control by the people "to an extent that implies a distinct lack of faith in democratic processes." What he meant was that government would not have sufficient power to direct and focus the agency's activities.

Unable to agree on the shape of a new science foundation, the federal government still forged ahead with funding basic scientific and weapons research. Military planners pushed hard for weapons research. In particular, the Office of Naval Research, created in August 1946, funded large military research contracts. Many universities and corporations were initially skeptical about secret peacetime research, but by 1949 the office had spent more than $20 million on 1,200 projects at some 200 institutions. And most of this work was undertaken without public knowledge.

Militarily funded research met the immediate needs of a growing defense establishment, but it did not fill the place of a broader, federally funded science research program. This came, finally, in 1950 with the establishment of the National Science Foundation. The new agency would report directly to the president—a victory for Truman. Its purpose was to fund basic research in the sciences—a victory for scientists. Weapons development would remain primarily under the control of the military.

Thus by 1950, cooperation between scientists, the federal government, and the military had been established. Federal funds were lavished on research in ways hitherto unheard of in peacetime. A mode of operating in secret, yet with some latitude, had been established. Science had become the willing servant of federal policy. But there was a price.

In August 1949 the dream of scientific superiority over the Soviet Union turned into an anxious nightmare, when American scientists detected traces of a Soviet atomic blast experiment. The monopoly had been broken. The public and Congress demanded to know how the secrets had been lost. Scientists had often warned that there were, essentially, no secrets, but few had been willing to listen. In fact, the successful explosion of a bomb revealed its greatest secret: that it could be done. This was even truer in 1949. In this atmosphere of recrimination and spy stories, President Truman pushed ahead to try for a monopoly on a new super weapon. In January 1950 he accelerated research into a hydrogen bomb. Two and one-half years later the United States tested its first fusion device. (Fission and fusion are, in some respects, opposite reactions. In the first, heavy nuclei are split; in the second, two lighter nuclei are combined.) By 1954 the Soviets had also tested a fusion bomb. American superiority had evaporated quickly again in an arms race in which equality was probably the best that could be hoped for.

Rather than stimulating debate over fundamental issues, the growing stalemate in nuclear terror pushed concern about secrecy and security to a frenzied pitch. In a reversal of fortunes, the most important scientist of the Manhattan Project, J. Robert Oppenheimer, fell victim to this mood. From the very beginning, Oppenheimer, the physicist who had led the Los Alamos scientists to their triumph, had been viewed suspiciously by military and security experts. Some of his associates in the 1930s had been political radicals, including his wife and his younger brother. But during the years of the Manhattan Project, Oppenheimer always received security clearance. Moreover, Oppenheimer had supported using the bomb. Now, after the war, his independence of mind began to carry him away from established policy, and he started to question some of the assumptions of the arms race.

In 1948, shortly before the Soviets exploded their first atomic bomb, Oppenheimer proposed making small tactical weapons. He wanted to develop atomic explosives suitable for use against military targets. He opposed building huge bombs to hold civilian populations hostage. Working for the AEC General Advisory Committee in 1949, he spoke against committing massive resources to developing the hydrogen bomb. Losing this debate, he also earned the suspicion and opposition of scientists who were advocating the larger bomb, such as Edward Teller. Teller's opposition was well

THE ATOMIC ARMY.   During the 1950s, the United States and the Soviet Union carried on extensive open-air nuclear weapons testing. Frequently, as pictured here, American soldiers were stationed close to the test blast area for training purposes. The risks of such exposure to radiation were, at the time, rarely acknowledged.

founded, for Oppenheimer had changed many of his views about atomic energy. Shortly after the decision to build a hydrogen bomb, Oppenheimer told a radio audience:

> The decision to seek or not to seek international control of atomic energy, the decision to try to make or not to make the hydrogen bomb, these are complex technical things, but they touch the very base of our morality. It is a grave danger for us that these decisions are taken on the basis of facts held in secret.

As Oppenheimer astutely saw, the decision to build the hydrogen bomb compressed almost every question surrounding atomic energy research into one momentous problem. Secrecy, international control—practically all the elements of the nuclear debate were involved. He decided he could not support such a decision.

By raising these doubts, Oppenheimer challenged developing policy and, thereby, raised suspicions about his politics. By 1953 he was rarely being called in for advice. Nonetheless, during that year the doors of secrecy were unceremoniously closed on him, shutting him out of any further research in the atomic field. Outraged

SCHOOL CHILDREN IN 1951 DUCK FOR COVER DURING A PRACTICE ATOMIC BOMB RAID. Such experiences made the nightmare of World War III seem a plausible part of the waking world.

by Oppenheimer's apparent change of heart on nuclear weapons, a former staff member of the congressional Committee on Atomic Energy had sent a long denunciation of the scientist to the FBI in mid-1952. The writer said that Oppenheimer "more probably than not . . . was a sufficiently hardened Communist [and] that he either volunteered espionage information to the Soviets or complied with a request for such information." Agency director J. Edgar Hoover reassembled Oppenheimer's clearance file, reworked it, and forwarded the letter and the dossier to the newly inaugurated President Eisenhower. The president acted quickly, barring Oppenheimer from access to all atomic secrets and government research facilities. The scientist was officially notified on December 24, 1953.

Oppenheimer decided to fight the decision, and the AEC set up a special panel to hear his plea. Meeting in April and May of 1954, the three-member board heard thirty witnesses, among them most of the principal atomic scientists of the nation. In late May, the board reported. Oppenheimer was cleared of all charges of disloyalty and espionage, but the panel voted anyway to remove his security clearance. The policy became official in late June: the father of the atomic bomb was now permanently barred from further work on atomic energy.

In a sense, Oppenheimer was a scapegoat for an unworkable policy of secrecy. Although he was accused and then cleared of divulging secrets to the Soviet Union, his real crime had been to challenge the policies he had helped create during the Manhattan Project. He now discarded the role of government servant and used his reputation as an independent scientist to argue in public against the building of the hydrogen bomb. In doing so, he rejected the fundamental premises that had guided the Manhattan Project, the release of bombs over Hiroshima and Nagasaki, and postwar arms research. In 1946 he had argued that weapons development would make the "problem of preventing war not more hopeless, but more hopeful." Now he had changed his mind. But it was too late. America could not undo the damage of the bombs that had been dropped. It could only treat a few of its victims, like the Hiroshima maidens who came to the United States in 1954. Secrecy was now too entrenched in weapons research and deployment to be reversed. Both the United States and the Soviet Union held the power to eliminate civilization in a flash having the "brightness of several suns at midday." Only the equality of mutual terror—the fear of a thousand Hiroshimas—could now prevent the further use of atomic weapons.

The brilliant achievements of American science had thus altered the nature of war and peace. In 1945, after the first successful test of the atomic bomb, Secretary of War Stimson had congratulated science administrator James B. Conant for his work on the project. Conant had replied: "Yes, it worked. As to congratulations, I am far from sure—that remains for history to decide."

World War and Cold War

Those three vital decisions about the atomic bomb—to build it, to use it against Japan, and then to hide its scientific secrets in tight national security—can best be understood in the context of a developing cold war between the United States and the Soviet Union. Indeed, the hostile standoff between the two great powers and their allies required a new vocabulary to describe it. The idea of a cold war perfectly suited the situation of a total conflict that threatened but never fully erupted except at the periphery. This grim falling out between allies did not occur suddenly. It grew gradually out of the conduct of World War II, a long history of U.S.-Soviet antipathy, the antagonistic war aims of West and East, and the remarkable shifts in the world balance of power that the war confirmed. In the degenerating relationship between the USSR and America, the bomb was at first only a minor irritant, a symbol of distrust. By 1945 it provided leverage that the United States hoped to use to modify the Soviet Union's postwar behavior. By 1949 it had become a doomsday weapon possessed by both sides in a contest that seemed to have no other logical outcome than the destruction of humanity.

The atomic bomb was also a scientific and technological achievement that represented a vast federal commitment of money and administration. Like winning the war itself, building the bomb required careful planning, centralized authority, and an almost unprecedented intervention of the government into the economic and political life of the nation. After the war, this interference and control persisted for several reasons. Policy makers continued to believe that the federal government had to take a more activist role in economic planning to prevent the recurrence of depression. Ongoing confrontation with the Soviets led to large peacetime military budgets that required extensive government direction and planning of the economy. Maintaining secrets related to research strongly implied that the federal government might also legitimately investigate and monitor the political beliefs of individual citizens—as it did in the case of J. Robert Oppenheimer.

THE WORLD WAR II ALLIANCES

The shape of the cold war developed from the circumstances of the alliance against the Axis powers of Germany, Italy, and Japan. In their struggle against them, the Americans and British worked closely together. They integrated their military command and supply structures and consulted frequently on strategy. Scientific cooperation was also important, although the United States admitted Britain only as a junior partner in atomic research. Relations with the Soviet Union, on the other hand, were very different. Although an ally after 1941, the USSR was never a full partner. Britain's leader, Winston Churchill, distrusted Stalin's motives. The American president, Franklin Roosevelt, worked hard to win the cooperation of the Soviet Union, but the relationship was never much more than an alliance of convenience.

When the war ended in mid-1945, it left a legacy of unresolved problems, economic and political competition, and old hostilities that quickly degenerated into a cold war between the United States and the Soviet Union. Opposition to Germany and Japan forged the alliance of the United States, Britain, China, and the Soviet Union, but it was a union of desperate partners.

The military crisis of 1939 and the beginning of World War II had their origins in the economic catastrophe of 1929 and the harsh peace imposed upon Germany after World War I. The Great Depression, symbolized by the stock market dive in New York in October, signaled the beginning of a long, unnerving, and costly decline in production in most industrial nations. Stock values fell in Germany, England, France, and the United States, while unemployment rose and agriculture stagnated. Production worldwide fell by almost 40 percent, and international trade shrank by two-thirds. In 1930, unemployment in nations that kept such records reached 30 million persons, with other millions uncounted.

The continued depression brought political instability. In the United States, it created the impetus behind the New Deal and the energy to create the modern welfare state. In Europe, the effects were grave. Following World War I, most industrial societies were seriously divided between contending ideological factions: socialists, communists, fascists, and liberal and conservative capitalists. In Italy in 1922, fascists led by Benito Mussolini forced a change of government, consolidated power, and eventually eliminated democratic rule. Mussolini instituted censorship, curtailed the vote, repressed labor unions, and founded a secret police.

The totalitarian order of fascism appealed elsewhere in western European nations, including Spain, Portugal, and France, where major fascist movements sought power. But fascism achieved its greatest triumph in Germany. Led by Adolf Hitler, the National Socialists (Nazis) seized control of the German government in 1933 and, once in power, initiated a virulent totalitarianism. Political parties (aside from Hitler's National Socialists) were abolished, unions were disbanded, and a cruel and efficient secret police force, the Gestapo, was established. Hitler then embarked on a broad rearmament program while Germany muscled its way to dominance in eastern European economic markets. Hitler's aim, as he repeatedly announced, was to establish Germany's preeminence among European nations, by whatever means.

The threat of communism, which Hitler invoked to justify his quest for power, also alarmed other European nations touched by political and economic chaos. France swayed between conservative governments and a socialist-communist alliance called the Popular Front. In the late 1930s in Spain, civil war pitted an elected Popular Front government against fascist revolutionaries. In the Far East, Japan, swept by some of the same economic and political currents and frustrated in its search for markets and power, initiated attacks against China.

In this unstable world, alliances were valuable but difficult to achieve. Italy and Germany agreed in 1936 to form a fascist Axis, with Japan added later as an ally. For Britain and France, forging military ties was more difficult. One potential ally, the United States, although worried about the advance of fascism, remained officially neutral. The second most powerful nation in Europe, the Soviet Union, represented a force that many in Britain and France detested.

THE WAR BEGINS

Hitler recognized this conflict and vacillation among potential allies, and he brilliantly exploited it. In 1936 he renounced the Versailles treaty and fortified the Rhineland. He also aided the Spanish fascists. In 1938 he annexed Austria and began to claim German ethnic areas inside Czechoslovakia. Despite treaties with France, the Czechs were forced to concede large areas of

ADOLPH HITLER IN NUREMBERG IN 1935. A pretentious little man in an ill-fitting uniform and unkempt hair, Hitler inspired hysteria and obedience from his enthusiastic followers.

territory—in effect, dooming that nation. Britain and France feared war and willingly appeased Hitler, hoping to satisfy his desire for expansion. But they miscalculated. After signing a Non-Aggression Pact with the Soviet Union in August 1939, Hitler invaded Poland on September 1 and World War II began.

Here, for the first time, Hitler met resistance. The Poles refused to relinquish areas that Germany demanded. For the time being, the German leader had neutralized any potential interference by the Soviets because the Non-Aggression Pact with them promised to respect their claims to territory lost to Poland in 1920. On September 1, German armored divisions and aircraft swept across western Poland while the Soviets moved into eastern areas of that nation. On September 3, France and England declared war on Germany. But Poland fell in less than a month.

The strategy of the Germans and their European allies in World War II was an extension of World War I plans, carefully revised to avoid the failure that resulted from fighting on two distant fronts. The Germans in studying their loss in 1918 realized the importance of mobility and logistics: the ability to deliver firepower rapidly and in massive amounts. Their strategy centered on tanks and mobile artillery with tactical air support.

The Japanese, Americans, and British during the 1930s also studied the successes and failures of World War I—in particular, the problems and potential of landing troops and materiel quickly, under fire, onto hostile shores. The Americans and Japanese also emphasized the aircraft carrier, which proved to be a superb attack weapon, superior to traditional naval vessels because of the striking force of the fighters and dive bombers it carried.

All of the major nations developed air power, but with varying success. Germany did not, at first, fully recognize the potential of long-range bombing and tended to use fighters primarily in aid of infantry. The British better understood the potential of long-range offensive air power as well as the need for an effective defense. The Americans also developed long-range weapons, culminating in the B-29 bomber, which dropped the atomic bombs on Japan.

As in World War I, Germany fought a war in two directions, but this time with far greater success. After a lull following the conquest of Poland, Hitler invaded Denmark and Norway. On May 10, 1940, German troops swept through Holland and into Belgium, conquering both nations by May 25. Hitler then sent his armored divisions into northern France. Facing a sometimes poorly equipped army and a divided Allied command, the Germans broke through. British troops pinned up against the English Channel were spared only because Hitler halted his armies to allow his air force to batter the British. The Allies were able to mount a desperate evacuation at Dunkirk while the Royal Air Force fought off the German Luftwaffe.

Hardly a victory, this evacuation saved 350,000 troops, but it left the French to fend for themselves. After only five days, German armored divisions were nearing Paris. The French military abandoned the city on June 13. On June 16 the French government—in disarray and retaining only a bleeding remnant of its army—surrendered. The Germans, to save themselves the costs of a total occupation, established a puppet government in southern France quartered at Vichy. Now Hitler aimed at Britain.

Hitler's strategy for the invasion of England hinged on establishing air superiority. Despite the new British radar system and a valiant defense, he almost succeeded. After sustaining days of strategic bombardment, the British retaliated with bombers over Berlin. Infuriated by this attack on their capital, the Germans shifted their attention to London and away from British defense installations. This decision allowed the British to concentrate their defenses, greatly raising the cost of air attacks. On September 30 the Luftwaffe made its last daylight raid. Hitler had to cancel plans to conquer England.

Throughout the spring and summer of 1941, the Germans and Italians moved against British positions in the Mediterranean and conquered Yugoslavia, Greece, and Crete. Germany's major objective, however, became the destruction of the Soviet Union. Hitler's divisions struck in June 1941, hoping to conquer Russia before winter. They almost succeeded, advancing hundreds of miles toward Moscow and Leningrad [now St. Petersburg]. To the very last, Stalin believed that Hitler would honor the Non-Aggression Pact. The Soviets suffered over 1.5 million casualties, with a similar number taken prisoner. The Germans lost about 800,000 men. Despite superior equipment, training, and command, the Germans failed to deliver a

THE BATTLE OF BRITAIN, 1940. St. Paul's Cathedral stands amid a Nazi air raid. The relentless bombing of London by the German Luftwaffe in the fall of 1940 failed to break the resistance of the population or secure Axis air superiority. The British fought back valiantly and gained the admiration and support of many Americans.

decisive blow, and the Soviets, with British and American aid, began to rebuild their armies. By December 1941 Hitler's empire was vast, but the short war he had anticipated had turned into a grueling battle of attrition.

JAPAN

In Asia as in Europe, war began gradually through incidents of escalating aggression. Japan, which had long planned the conquest of China, moved against this weaker power beginning in the early 1930s. Japanese armies captured large areas of Chinese territory but could not eliminate the nationalist forces of General Jiang Jie-shǐ [Chiang Kai-shek] or the Chinese communists, who controlled territory to the north. By 1940 the Japanese

had turned toward conquest of the colonies belonging to European nations under occupation or attack: France, Britain, and the Netherlands. These areas held rich natural resources that the Japanese required to continue their war effort. The only significant powers standing in the way were Britain (now desperately fighting for survival in Europe) and the United States.

Japanese war planners realized the impossibility of outproducing or directly defeating the United States. Their plan called for surprise destruction of the American navy, simultaneous seizure of Southeast Asia, and defeat of any counterattacks. They counted on the problem of maintaining long supply lines, and America's low level of preparedness, to discourage the United States.

THE UNITED STATES ENTERS THE WAR

Roosevelt responded to these desperate events in Europe and Asia in two ways. He pushed for American rearmament and established close working relations with the British. He approved plans to initiate research into building an atomic bomb. Although still officially neutral, the United States became the armorer for the opponents of Germany and Japan. In the summer of 1939 the United States informed Japan that it intended to terminate its trade treaties with that nation. Following the invasion of Poland, the president called Congress into session to repeal America's neutrality acts, which had made it difficult to trade arms to belligerents. After extensive debate, Congress repealed some of the more stringent elements of these acts.

Following the fall of France, Roosevelt pushed harder for rearmament and direct aid to Britain. Moving around legal obstacles and obstinate public opinion, the administration agreed, in September 1940, to exchange destroyers for British bases in the Western Hemisphere. Most reaction to this agreement was favorable, but an America First Committee was formed to oppose U.S. participation in the war. Led by such celebrities as Charles Lindbergh, the committee galvanized the remaining opposition to war.

In early spring 1941 the United States took a giant step toward more direct involvement with passage of the Lend-Lease Act, which empowered the president to sell, lend, or otherwise dispose of defense materials to any country deemed strategic to American defenses. The original sum made available for this aid was set at $1.3 billion, but it quickly ballooned. As shipments to Britain increased, so did the risk to U.S. ships that had to cross the submarine-infested waters around the British Isles. Over the summer the United States began escorting convoys of merchant ships; by fall, the navy had engaged in skirmishes with German submarines.

The Japanese decided the timing of America's actual entry into the war in dramatic fashion. Over the summer of 1941, Roosevelt announced that he would freeze the assets of the Japanese and end all trade in strategic materials if Japan proceeded to attack the French colonies in Indochina. When the Japanese imperial armies moved in this direction, the president acted. Although the Japanese continued to negotiate, they were secretly preparing a broad attack on U.S., British, and French possessions in Asia. During the summer of 1941, U.S. intelligence broke the Japanese diplomatic code. Intercepted messages pointed to an attack in early winter. On November 27, 1941, Washington warned commanders in the Pacific. Minimum defense steps were taken at the giant naval base at Pearl Harbor, Hawaii, including the fatal bunching together of fighter planes to prevent sabotage.

On December 7, again by decoding Japanese diplomatic messages, the United States learned of an impending attack. Washington sent out alerts to the Pacific, but these failed to reach the commanders in Hawaii on time. Even radar failed to detect the first wave of bombers and fighters that took off in early morning from the Japanese fleet lying secretly about 250 miles north of the Hawaiian island of Oahu.

Three waves of fighters and dive bombers plunged down out of the calm Sunday morning sky. The attack lasted about two hours. When it was over, the Japanese had devastated the navy air force, killed 2,403 Americans (about 1,000 of whom died when the battleship *Arizona* exploded), and sunk or damaged the bulk of the U.S. Pacific fleet. Other U.S. bases and possessions came under attack. Wake Island fell, and Roosevelt ordered General Douglas MacArthur to move his command from the threatened Philippines to Australia. By May the Philippines had fallen and the Japanese had taken most of the territory in their master plan. They now turned to menace Australia and India.

Despite these early successes, the Japanese had achieved a precarious victory at best. Their attacks exposed the weak defenses and inadequate planning of American forces in the Pacific but they also mobilized American public opinion. Roosevelt denounced the "sudden criminal attacks perpetrated by the Japanese in the Pacific" and asked for and got a declaration of war. On December 11, Hitler joined his Japanese ally and declared war on the United States.

Expansion of the armed services had begun before the United States entered the war. The army had reached 1.4 million men by July 1941. But after total mobilization, this number moved up rapidly. By 1945 over 8 million men were in the army. (The Women's Army Corps—WAC—reached about 100,000 at this time.) The navy experienced a similar expansion, reaching 3.4 million, with the marines constituting about 500,000 of this total. The air force (administratively part of the army) also expanded rapidly.

Military service touched all populations in America. By the end of the war about 1 million African Americans had participated in the various services, for example. The American armed forces in World War II mixed ethnic groups and social class, but in a curious way. Universal conscription threw together northerners and southerners, autoworkers and college professors. But if this necessitated a kind of melting pot culture in the barracks, it did not mean that democracy or racial harmony prevailed. For example, black soldiers were segregated into units commanded by white officers. Often they were relegated to stevedore or construction work. Japanese Americans were placed in special ethnic units such as the Nisei 442 Infantry Regiment, which fought in Italy. Thus, despite the commitment to defeat Nazism—the most virulent racism of the twentieth century—few Americans saw anything paradoxical in establishing and maintaining racial segregation throughout the military. This is even more curious because American war films often pictured foxholes as representative democracies, and such films as *Bataan* (1943) even implied that racial integration existed where it clearly did not.

Once the United States had entered the war, Roosevelt decided on a strategy of attrition to defeat the Axis powers. He planned an enormous economic effort in which superior resources, supplies, productivity, organization, and scientific breakthroughs would overwhelm the enemy. This emphasis on weapons, he believed, would minimize American casualties. With this aim in mind, he authorized the secret building of the atomic bomb. His commitment made the science laboratory and the factory assembly lines as important as the front lines of fighting men.

THE WARTIME ECONOMY

The war buildup also meant new federal economic controls. After Pearl Harbor isolationist opposition crumbled and Congress granted sweeping powers to the executive branch. On January 16, 1942, Roosevelt created the War Production Board, which had the power to channel civilian production into armaments manufacture and to contract for the construction of new defense plants. With the massive reorientation of production, the draft of millions of men, and a rise in employment, the United States suddenly faced labor shortages. War orders wiped away the huge unemployment left from the depression. The War Manpower Commission was organized to recruit new workers for the booming defense sector.

The largest pool of untapped potential employees was women, and millions of them eagerly took over jobs in aircraft, shipbuilding, and munitions plants. They went to vocational schools and learned trades and skills that transformed their lives. They were crucial in building the vast array of weapons that poured from the factories. They constructed B-29 bombers like the *Enola Gay* that carried the first atomic bomb; they built the tanks and ships that shattered the Nazi armies and the Japanese navy.

While the employment of women in factories was expected to be temporary, it had profound and lasting effects. Several million women attended vocational schools. As early as 1942, over 35 percent of the American workforce was female. By the end of the war, surveys revealed, a

World War II opened economic opportunities to millions of underemployed workers. African Americans from the South joined the many women streaming into defense plants.

majority of these working women hoped to keep their positions. But telltale signs during the war suggested that "Rosie the Riveter" would eventually be pushed aside. Differential wages for men and women, hostility in the workplace, antagonism from unions, and, most of all, failure of the Roosevelt administration to support the Equal Rights Amendment to the Constitution (part of the 1944 Democratic national platform) suggested that gains made could be undone.

Another large group of potential workers were African Americans. At first, they were generally excluded from defense employment opportu-

nities. But A. Philip Randolph of the Brotherhood of Sleeping Car Porters threatened a protest march on Washington in the summer of 1941 unless equality of employment was offered. This helped persuade Roosevelt to order integration of defense industries. By the end of the war, hundreds of thousands of black workers had found jobs in war production. Despite these gains, however, they continued to suffer discrimination in the workplace and in housing. Racial tension often erupted when they took new jobs or moved into new areas to work in defense industries. Such was the case in Detroit in June 1943, when a bloody race riot that broke out killed 34 persons and had to be quelled by troops.

Mexican-American workers also flocked to defense-industry cities. In Los Angeles, where the concentrations of this population were high, tensions between servicemen and Mexican-American teenagers exploded in 1943 during the "Zoot-Suit Riots" when soldiers and sailors attacked civilians wearing floppy zoot-suits and sporting long hair. Over a hundred persons were treated for injuries in this battle over clothing styles and ethnic symbolism.

Eventually, full employment and shortages of consumer items like automobiles fueled inflation and labor unrest. The federal government stepped in here too, setting up the War Labor Board in January 1942 to prevent strikes and runaway wage increases. After several skirmishes with labor, the board established the "Little Steel" formula, worked out first for smaller steel-producing companies. This formula, which applied to other industries as well, placed a limit on pay hikes. Labor disputes did not disappear, but in general, the War Labor Board did much to ease the pressure on wages, and it allowed unions to raise their membership extensively.

Another new agency, the Office of Price Administration, tried to limit price rises by setting maximum prices for standard items. It also oversaw the rationing of scarce items such as coffee, canned foods (to save tin), shoes, and gasoline (to save rubber tires). Although many workers earned more money than before the war, there were few goods to spend it on; even a thriving black market could not supply them.

Extensive government control over the economy was matched by increased federal attention to shaping public opinion and preventing possible subversion. An Office of War Information worked with radio and other media to advertise savings bonds and drives to collect scarce raw materials. Sometimes in this climate, civil liberties suffered. Of course the military censored news from the front. There was little serious opposition to the war, but even so, the administration overreacted as demands for

security and secrecy increased. For example, it brought a group of inconsequential American fascists and right-wing opponents of the war to trial.

JAPANESE-AMERICAN INTERNMENT

Much more serious was the treatment of Japanese Americans. In early 1942, American military commanders on the West Coast argued that Japanese residents must be removed. This fear of sabotage scarcely concealed a long-standing racial antipathy toward the Japanese in California. (There was no corresponding internment of Japanese residents of Hawaii, where race relations were better.)

Thus, on February 19, 1942, President Roosevelt issued Executive Order #9066, which permitted removal of alien Japanese, Germans, Italians, and all persons of Japanese ancestry, whether citizens or not, from any military area. These sensitive areas included California and parts of Oregon, Washington, and Arizona. In practice, exceptions were made for other groups so that only the Japanese were actually removed. Legal protests to the Supreme Court proved fruitless.

This policy may have had military considerations as its justification, but it also continued a history of exclusion and racial segregation. In 1924 Congress had denied further immigration to the Japanese, abrogating a "gentlemen's agreement" of 1907–1908 between the United States and Japan in which Japan promised to restrict immigration. Despite the burden of this history and various local laws that discriminated, the Japanese community had achieved considerable success in agriculture and small businesses. Their largest communities were centered on Los Angeles and Seattle, with much smaller contingents in San Francisco.

By June 1942 over 100,000 Japanese had been forcibly removed, their property and jobs stripped away. Most were placed in ten crude, dusty army camps and provided with tarpaper barracks, cots, common toilets, and shared bathing and laundry facilities.

THIS SIMPLE, WOODEN SIGN, posted in the desert, marked the entrance to the Manzanar relocation center for Japanese families uprooted from their homes, primarily in the Los Angeles area. Other camps housed still more Japanese Americans, rounded up and deported from the coastal areas of the western United States.

One internee recalled a camp set on a bleak plain behind Los Angeles:

> There was a lack of privacy when we first went to Manzanar. The barracks were not actually completed. There were terrible wind storms that swept through the Owens Valley which brought dust through the cracks in the door. I think there were two months running where we suffered from diarrhea. The food was not properly prepared.

Many of the internees gained their release before the end of the war, but few ever recovered their farms, businesses, or homes. In 1988, forty years after the fact, Congress passed a law apologizing to Japanese Americans and promised $20,000 in compensation for each internee.

THE WAR IN EUROPE

While the administration worked to organize production, it defined its strategy to win the war. In practical terms, the United States had disagreements with both of its major allies. Roosevelt opposed Britain's desire to hold on to its vast colonial empire. And he was reluctant to allow the Soviets to establish control over the invasion routes across eastern European nations. The president tried to circumvent potential friction

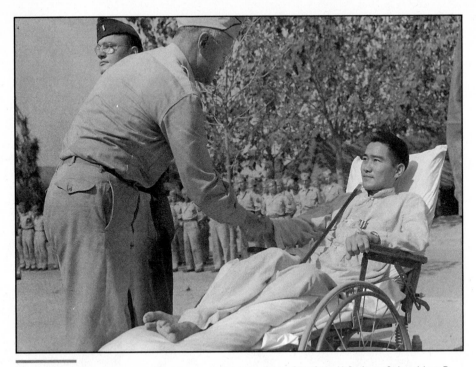

HOWARD Y. MIYAKE, a Japanese American, receives the Silver Star from U.S. Army Colonel Lee D. Cady. Some Japanese Americans were allowed to participate in units in the European theater.

through face-to-face encounters with Churchill and Stalin. Several conferences shaped the course of the war and established general principles for a peace settlement. In 1941, even before the United States entered the war, Churchill and Roosevelt met and signed the Atlantic Charter, a document that outlined international rights and responsibilities and promised self-determination, free trade, and the abandonment of force after the war. They also agreed to focus on defeating Germany first. Even after Pearl Harbor, this meant that a substantial portion of war supplies went to Britain and the Soviet Union; the Asian war took second place.

Churchill and Roosevelt made a second major decision at Casablanca, Morocco, in January 1943. There the two leaders agreed to demand unconditional surrender of the Axis powers in order to fix blame for the war on Hitler and Mussolini; no negotiated or partial peace with the fascist leaders would be tolerated.

For the Soviet Union, the immediate and paramount problem was the opening of a second front—by an Allied invasion of France—so as to divert the German armies and relieve the enormous pressure that Hitler had brought to bear on the Soviet Union. Their armies were reeling before the German onslaught, sustaining huge casualties and losses of territory. A longer-range Soviet strategy was to gain control of those areas through which the Germans had twice invaded during the twentieth century.

Roosevelt and the U.S. Army commander, Dwight Eisenhower, agreed with the proposal for a second front, but Churchill twice convinced Roosevelt to postpone a landing, arguing that preparations remained incomplete. In August 1942 Churchill explained to Stalin why the

United States and Britain had chosen to invade North Africa instead of France. Preparations for the attack advanced, and in November 1942, Allied forces landed in French North Africa. At first, French troops loyal to the Vichy government resisted, but Eisenhower negotiated a capitulation with Admiral Jean François Darlan. American and British troops pushed into Tunisia to engage German forces led by General Erwin Rommel ("the Desert Fox"). By May 1943 the battle for North Africa had ended. Rommel was defeated and a large contingent of his army captured. But the Soviet Union still stood alone with no second front in sight.

Once again, in the spring of 1943, the western Allies postponed the invasion of France. This time the United States and Britain decided to attack Sicily and knock Italy out of the war. Once again, the Soviets were angered and suspicious that Britain and the United States wanted them to continue to bear the brunt of the European struggle. Nonetheless, the Allied command went ahead; troops landed in Sicily on July 9, 1943, and took thirty-eight days to conquer the island, although the bulk of the German army escaped into Italy.

This victory led to the fall of the Italian fascist leader, Mussolini. A provisional government signed a peace treaty with the Allies on September 3, and Italy switched sides in the war. On the same day, British and American troops invaded Italy itself, and gradually they pushed a fiercely entrenched German army toward the north. The British and Americans agreed to administer liberated portions of Italy jointly, excluding the USSR from any significant participation in shaping postwar Italy. Stalin considered this a precedent for his treatment of eastern European nations liberated from the Germans by Soviet armies.

As German front lines collapsed in the east and receded in Italy, Hitler began the terror bombing of England, using V-1 and, later, V-2 rockets. This belated attempt to terrify the British public could not, however, stanch German losses.

GERMANY CAPITULATES

The western Allies finally launched the second front, in Operation Overlord, in early June 1944. When it came, it demonstrated masterly planning and execution. Although German defenders expected an attack, they misjudged its location. Allied troops established major beachheads in Normandy, designated by the Allied command as Utah and Omaha beaches. Landing massive amounts of materiel and troops, and protected by superior air cover, they fought their way inland. By late June the port of Cherbourg was liberated, then Caen in early July. A counterattack ordered by Hitler failed, and the Germans fell back rapidly. For the Nazis the war was practically over. The Soviet armies, who had turned the tide of battle in late 1942, rushed toward Poland and eastern Germany. Paris was liberated on August 25, 1944, and the Germans retreated behind the Siegfried Line along the German border. So hopeless was the war that a group of military officers attempted to assassinate Hitler on July 20 to hasten a German surrender.

In early 1945 Eisenhower ordered an offensive, moving into Germany and taking the Ruhr Valley during February and March. The Soviet army had entered Warsaw on January 17, and on April 13 they took Vienna. On April 30 Hitler committed suicide in his bunker in Berlin. At the last minute, German leaders offered to surrender to the United States, but Eisenhower refused. Germany had made war against all the Allies; Germany would have to surrender to all of them. Soviet troops took Berlin. Finally, on May 8, Germany surrendered. The Third Reich ended in flame and ruin. Allied troops finally stopped the murderous regime that in its frenzy had executed millions of Jews, Poles, gypsies, communists, homosexuals, and others.

Not only did Hitler prolong the war until every last pillbox and redoubt fell, his policy of exterminating Europe's Jews at death camps set up in eastern Europe continued methodically to

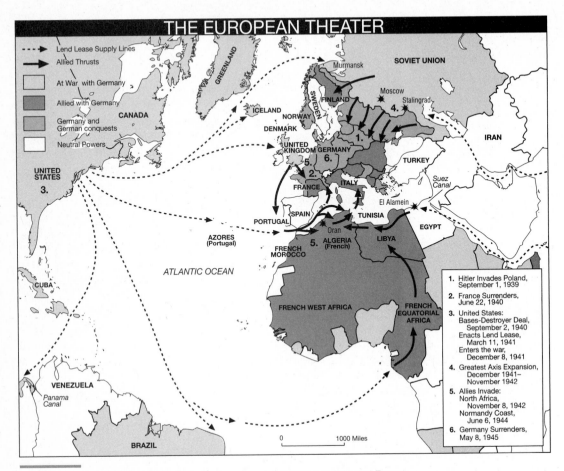

THE EUROPEAN THEATER

Lend Lease Supply Lines
Allied Thrusts
At War with Germany
Allied with Germany
Germany and
German conquests
Neutral Powers

GREENLAND

CANADA

ICELAND

UNITED
STATES
3.

CUBA

VENEZUELA
Panama
Canal

BRAZIL

ATLANTIC OCEAN

AZORES
(Portugal)

SOVIET UNION

Murmansk

SWEDEN
FINLAND
NORWAY
DENMARK
UNITED
KINGDOM GERMANY
FRANCE
SPAIN
PORTUGAL

Moscow
Stalingrad
4.
1.
6.
5.
2.
ITALY
TUNISIA
Oran
ALGERIA
(French)
FRENCH
MOROCCO

IRAN

TURKEY

Suez
Canal

El Alamein

LIBYA

EGYPT

FRENCH WEST AFRICA

FRENCH
EQUATORIAL
AFRICA

0   1000 Miles

1. Hitler Invades Poland,
   September 1, 1939
2. France Surrenders,
   June 22, 1940
3. United States:
   Bases-Destroyer Deal,
   September 2, 1940
   Enacts Lend Lease,
   March 11, 1941
   Enters the war,
   December 8, 1941
4. Greatest Axis Expansion,
   December 1941–
   November 1942
5. Allies Invade:
   North Africa,
   November 8, 1942
   Normandy Coast,
   June 6, 1944
6. Germany Surrenders,
   May 8, 1945

THE EUROPEAN THEATER. American strategy, once war was declared in Asia and Europe, necessitated a massive mobilization and military buildup. Since American productive supremacy in Asia was never in doubt, military planners emphasized the critical situation in Europe. Given their commitment to unconditional surrender, the Allies intended not only to defeat Germany and Italy but to destroy fascism. Their first object, however, was to relieve pressure at two critical points: on the Russian front and in northern Africa, where the Germans threatened to seize the Suez Canal.

the very end. When the Holocaust ceased, this grotesque corruption of science, efficiency, and bureaucracy had eliminated 6 million men, women, and children, while the rest of the world, including the United States, did little to stop it or welcome Jewish refugees.

By May 1945, Allied armies occupied practically all of Europe—from France eastward through Poland and south through Italy. As the

Allies had foreseen, this created immense political problems. Churchill, Stalin, and Roosevelt had hoped to forestall some of these problems at the Tehran Conference in 1943 and the Yalta meeting in February 1945. Roosevelt tried to restrain British hostility toward the Soviet Union. (He had opposed Churchill's suggestions for an invasion of Germany through the eastern end of the Mediterranean to head off the Soviet forces.)

THE LANDING BY ALLIED TROOPS IN NORMANDY, FRANCE, in 1944 required the huge movement of men and equipment and a mammoth effort of planning and coordination—one reason it came so late in the war.

Roosevelt hoped to enlist Stalin's peaceful cooperation with the United States after the war. He had come to sympathize with the Soviet desire to control the invasion routes of eastern Europe over which German armies had poured practically unopposed twice in the twentieth century. He encouraged Stalin to expect reparations to reconstruct his battered nation. In exchange, he wanted Stalin's help against the Japanese in Asia. But Roosevelt did little to implement these policies and postponed hard decisions about redrawing European boundaries and reconstructing governments.

By the time of the Potsdam Conference, Germany had been defeated, Roosevelt was dead, and the new president, Harry Truman, had to make the decisions that Roosevelt had put off. Truman was more suspicious of Soviet motives than Roosevelt had been, but more important, the United States now possessed a workable atomic bomb. But if the new president hoped this weapon would convince Stalin to compromise, he was mistaken. The most contentious issue was Poland. Occupying Soviet forces changed the boundaries of that nation, incorporating eastern portions into the Soviet Union and in compensation, pushing Poland's western boundaries to the Oder-Neisse line, thus giving Poland control over territory that had formerly been a part of Germany.

The issue of reparations also separated the Allies. The USSR demanded huge compensation from Germany to restore some of the vast industrial losses it had suffered. But the amount and type of reparations could not be settled. Consequently, the Soviets dismantled whole factories in their zone of occupation and sent them eastward by railroad. On the issue of the occupation of Germany, the Allies agreed, after much dispute, to four zones: a Soviet zone, including jointly controlled Berlin; a French zone, bordering on eastern France; an American zone in southern and central Germany; and a British zone to the north. But the alliance of convenience had degenerated swiftly into a contest between the United States and the Soviet Union, with each side blaming the other for blocking its legitimate aspirations, and with the atomic bomb playing an increasingly crucial role in the strategies of both sides.

THE WAR IN THE PACIFIC

The war in the Pacific did not involve the Soviet Union until the very last days of the struggle. The chief burden of fighting the Japanese fell to the United States and China, with some aid from Australia and particularly from the British in areas like Burma. Although given a lower priority, the contest was bitter and protracted. American strategy, carried out by General Douglas MacArthur and Admiral Chester W. Nimitz, focused on seizing control of the air and the seas, retaking the Philippines, then moving from island chain to island chain toward Japan. This proved to be a brilliant strategy.

By midsummer of 1942 the Japanese advance in Southeast Asia had slowed. After furious fighting on land and sea, the United States held Guadalcanal in the Solomon Islands near Australia. By early 1943 the United States prepared to take the offensive. Gradually, American forces moved northward, skipping heavily fortified islands to outflank the Japanese. After several months of battle around the Philippine Islands, MacArthur finally retook Manila on March 4, 1944.

The island-hopping American forces, now superior against the crippled Japanese navy and air force, took Iwo Jima in early 1945 and Okinawa, near southern Japan, in April 1945. These conquests provided a final, crucial link in the American strategy: bases from which to bomb the Japanese homeland. From air bases on these islands and from Tinian and Saipan in the Marianas, new long-range B-29 bombers began to pound industrial and population centers in Japan. General Curtis E. LeMay took command of the bomber operations in late August 1944 and developed tactics that showed the terrible potential of the new planes. Using incendiary devices, LeMay began systematic attacks on Japanese cities designed to start firestorms and terrorize the population. In March 1945, for example, B-29s destroyed about a quarter of the city of Tokyo. Still the Japanese refused to surrender and prepared for a desperate, even suicidal, defense of their island nation.

Air raids became more spectacular and punishing, culminating in the devastating attacks on Hiroshima and Nagasaki. Faced with obliteration from the skies and destruction of their armies by the Soviets, the Japanese sued for peace on August 10. After maneuvering to save the Japanese emperor, the government capitulated August 14. Final surrender took place September 2 in Tokyo Bay, aboard the battleship *Missouri*.

The occupation and reconstruction of Japan remained principally an American task. The Soviets were not granted a share in the occupation, although by agreement they acquired important territory in northern China and on Sakhalin Island. By agreement also, Soviet armies accepted the surrender of the Japanese north of the thirty-eighth parallel in Korea, while Americans administered the area to the south.

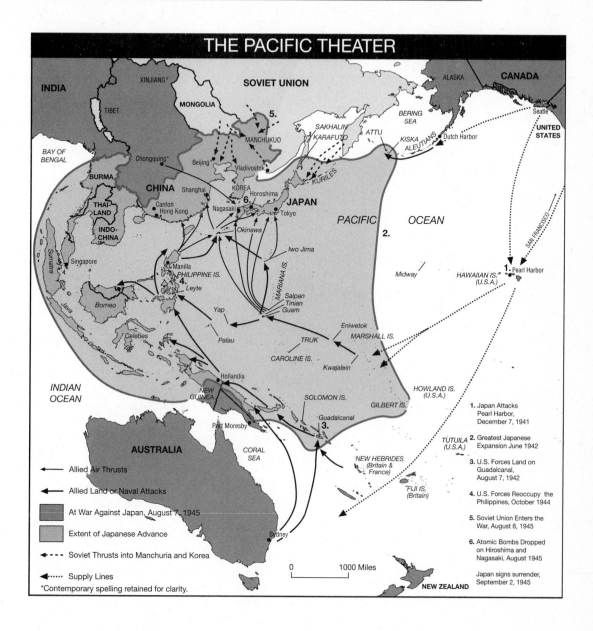

THE PACIFIC THEATER

INDIA

XINJIANG*

SOVIET UNION

ALASKA

CANADA

TIBET

MONGOLIA

BERING
SEA

Seatle

BAY OF
BENGAL

Chongqing*

MANCHUKUO

5.

SAKHALIN/
KARAFUTO

ATTU

KISKA
ALEUTIANS

Dutch Harbor

UNITED
STATES

BURMA

CHINA   Shanghai

Beijing

Vladivostok

KOREA

KURILES

THAI-
LAND

Canton
Hong Kong

Nagasaki

Horoshima

6.

JAPAN

Tokyo

PACIFIC   OCEAN

SAN FRANCISCO

INDO-
CHINA

Okinawa

2.

Sumatra

Singapore

Manilla

PHILIPPINE IS.

4.

Iwo Jima

MARIANA IS.

Midway

HAWAIIAN IS.
(U.S.A.)

1.

Pearl Harbor

Leyte

Java

Borneo

Yap

Saipan
Tinian
Guam

Celebes

Palau

TRUK

Eniwetok

MARSHALL IS.

CAROLINE IS.

Kwajalein

INDIAN
OCEAN

Hollandia

NEW
GUINEA

SOLOMON IS.

HOWLAND IS.
(U.S.A.)

GILBERT IS.

Port Moresby

Guadalcanal

3.

AUSTRALIA

CORAL
SEA

NEW HEBRIDES
(Britain &
France)

TUTUILA
(U.S.A.)

FIJI IS.
(Britain)

← Allied Air Thrusts

← Allied Land or Naval Attacks

At War Against Japan, August 7, 1945

Extent of Japanese Advance

◀--- Soviet Thrusts into Manchuria and Korea

◀····· Supply Lines

*Contemporary spelling retained for clarity.

Sydney

0   1000 Miles

NEW ZEALAND

1. Japan Attacks
   Pearl Harbor,
   December 7, 1941

2. Greatest Japanese
   Expansion June 1942

3. U.S. Forces Land on
   Guadalcanal,
   August 7, 1942

4. U.S. Forces Reoccupy the
   Philippines, October 1944

5. Soviet Union Enters the
   War, August 8, 1945

6. Atomic Bombs Dropped
   on Hiroshima and
   Nagasaki, August 1945

   Japan signs surrender,
   September 2, 1945

A more fundamental Asian problem was China. All Japanese troops in China were instructed to surrender to Chinese leader Jiang Jieshī. But in northern China, communist rebel forces led by Mao Zedong took power from the Japanese and confiscated their war supplies. Troubled by conflict between these two Chinese factions during the war, the United States tried fruitlessly in 1945 to arrange a cease-fire while continuing to aid Jiang. But in late 1949 Jiang's corrupt and inefficient government was driven out of mainland China to the offshore island of Taiwan by the communists. Nothing short of full-scale intervention by the United States could have prevented this.

DEMOBILIZATION AND POSTWAR ALLIED COOPERATION

Despite intensifying hostility between the United States and the Soviet Union in 1945, the United States proceeded rapidly to demobilize its war economy and armed forces. Even before Germany's surrender on May 8, 1945, the Truman administration began to cancel war orders and dismantle economic controls. By the end of 1945, most controls had been lifted and the economy was returning rapidly to civilian production. The American army demobilized under irresistible pressure from GIs and from their families at home. "Bring Back Daddy" clubs sprang up in the United States, and soldiers stationed abroad agitated for immediate release. Troops were hurried home and mustered out of the service as quickly as transportation could be arranged. Total personnel in the armed services fell from over 12 million in 1945 to 3 million in 1946 and 1.5 million in 1947.

But demobilization did not by any means imply that the federal government had suddenly ceased to intervene in the lives of Americans or in the economy. After a long debate, Congress agreed to the Employment Act of 1946, which pledged the government to maintaining an active role in directing the economy. Government officials also encouraged the shift of women out of the workforce. The great and successful experiment in training and employing women was undone almost as fast as it had been achieved. Finally, defense spending and direction of scientific research in such fields as atomic energy required large expenditures and tight federal controls. Continued military production required that hundreds of decisions shaping the American economy be made in Washington. Even in the late 1940s, when defense spending was relatively low, it still consumed over 25 percent of the federal budget. Scientific research increasingly fell

under the direction of federal agencies like the Atomic Energy Commission.

Other federal activities profoundly shaped the postwar world. To reward soldiers for their sacrifices, the U.S. government passed a generous bonus for returning solders in the form of the Servicemen's Readjustment Act of 1944. State governments often added their own system of financial rewards and preferential hiring. Over 2 million soldiers used this GI Bill to attend college after 1946. The result was a significant democratization and expansion of American higher education.

Many Americans hoped that postwar peace could be maintained by the United Nations, a new institution organized around the wartime alliance against Germany and Japan. The UN Charter, signed in 1945, created two chambers: a Security Council and a General Assembly. The Security Council was made up of five permanent members (Britain, France, China, the United States, and the USSR) and ten elected representatives of other nations. A permanent member could veto any Security Council undertaking. The General Assembly consisted of all member nations, each with one vote. But even in this peaceful endeavor, competition between the United States and the Soviet Union erupted. Finally, a compromise on membership was reached: The USSR received three votes in the General Assembly (Ukraine, Byelorussia, and the USSR), and the United States secured membership for Argentina (a profascist power but counted as a friend of the United States) and ensured the legality of regional alliances like the Organization of American States.

On the trial of war criminals, the Allies remained united. After arresting German leaders in the summer of 1945 (those who had not committed suicide or escaped), the Allies opened trials in Nuremberg, Germany, in November. Four judges—one each from Britain, France, the United States, and the USSR—presided over the hearings. Prosecutors accused Nazi officials of crimes against peace (for undertaking aggressive

YOUNG MAO ZEDONG, 1939. Chinese communist leader Mao Zedong found his greatest support among peasants and made them the basis for his opposition to the invading Japanese armies and the official Chinese government headed by Jiang Jie-shī

war), breaches of accepted war conduct, and crimes against humanity in the death camps. What went unexamined, however, was the failure of the Allies to act in decisive ways during the war either to inform the public of the Holocaust, accept Jewish refugees, or halt the activities of the death camps.

The first Nuremberg trial lasted 216 days; on October 1, 1946, nineteen of twenty-two defendants were found guilty; twelve were sentenced to hang, three to life imprisonment, and four to long prison terms. In addition, the judges declared four Nazi organizations to be criminal in character. In Japan much the same procedure was followed. When all the trials ended in 1949, 2,647 persons had been convicted, with 689 death sentences handed down. The purpose had been to stamp war guilt irrevocably on the German and Japanese leadership and to proclaim wars of aggression to be illegal.

COLD WAR IN EUROPE

Despite agreements between the United States and the Soviet Union, a cold war quickly developed in international relations. On Roosevelt's death in 1945, Truman came into office ill prepared in foreign policy matters, yet facing urgent unfinished business. Sentiment to return to prewar neutrality was overpowered by the sense that the United States had to enforce its own interests and goals upon a turbulent world. This meant that the United States remained on a semiwar footing. Naturally, secret weapons research and development became a high policy priority. Just as inevitably, the federal government retained much of the power over research, allocation of resources, and direction of the economy that it had acquired during the war.

The impetus for military security also generated an atmosphere of suspicion. The arms race that had once been directed against the Germans now resumed against the Soviet Union. But the growing sophistication of weaponry only increased the vulnerability that many Americans felt. Every confrontation with the Soviet Union stimulated the arms race and underscored the necessity for secrecy. More and more, these demands for control strained the assumption that a peacetime society ought to tolerate dissent and free scientific inquiry. The bitter conflict even convinced some Americans that they should try to define the purposes of their society more narrowly and perhaps exclude from it those who did not appear to agree.

Disputes between the United States and the Soviet Union at first focused on the restoration of Europe. The frightful destruction of war had created economic havoc in Germany, France, and eastern Europe. Political instability in France, Italy, and Greece brought local communists close to power. In Greece, civil war broke out in 1946 between British-backed royalist forces and communist-supported insurgents. But Great Britain was exhausted by the struggle against Germany and too feeble to play more than a minor role in Greece. Either the United States or the Soviet Union would fill the vacuum.

To exercise a decisive role in Europe, the Truman administration had to overcome several problems. One was traditional American reluctance to become involved in European politics. Truman eventually won the support of Republicans for a new activist policy in Europe. A second problem was the rapid disintegration of American military preparedness. The president could not rely on conventional military forces to oppose the huge Soviet army in Europe. As a result, the temporary monopoly on the atomic bomb (despite very small numbers in existence) and the defense potential of the American economy were crucial to foreign policy decisions.

At the war's end in Europe, the Soviet Union occupied Romania, Hungary, Czechoslovakia, and Poland, and in these nations Stalin insisted on governments friendly to the USSR. Given the traditional bitterness toward the Soviets in these areas, this often meant that only communists were willing to play such a role. And the placement of communists in power contradicted American desires for free elections and wholly independent nations in the region.

Acrimony between America and the USSR broke out in a dispute over control of Iranian oil resources in early 1946. The Soviet Union had stationed several thousand troops in northern Iran but was eventually compelled to withdraw them. Negotiations at the United Nations over internationalization of atomic energy control failed

FEDERAL RESEARCH AND DEVELOPMENT FUNDS, 1947–1970
(IN MILLIONS OF DOLLARS)

Year	Total for R & D	For Defense	For AEC*	For NSF†
1947	619.5	469.3	39.9	
1953	3,106.0	2,577.3	309.9	2.3
1959	6,693.5	5,161.6	699.8	60.4
1965	14,614.3	6,796.5‡	1,240.7	187.2
1970	15,340.3	7,360.4‡	1,346.0	289.0

*Atomic Energy Commission
†National Science Foundation
‡After 1962, large amounts of research and development funds were funneled to the National Aeronautics and Space Administration (NASA). Some of these funds, because of their application to missile development, may be considered defense expenditures.
Source: U.S. Bureau of the Census, Historical Statistics of the United States (Washington, D.C.: U.S. Government Printing Office, 1975), Part 2, p. 966

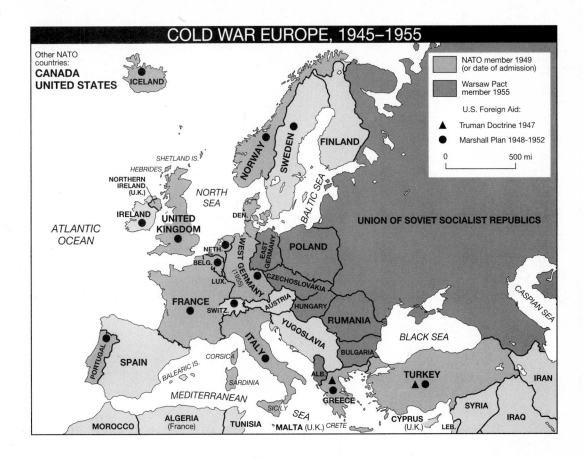

COLD WAR EUROPE, 1945–1955

Other NATO countries:
CANADA
UNITED STATES

NATO member 1949 (or date of admission)

Warsaw Pact member 1955

U.S. Foreign Aid:

▲ Truman Doctrine 1947

● Marshall Plan 1948–1952

0   500 mi

in the early summer. And the United States rejected a Soviet request for a large loan to help rebuild its shattered economy. As prospects for a comprehensive peace receded, the United States and the Soviet Union began to create separate political and economic institutions in their German occupation zones. The Truman adminstration even began to plan for universal military training for all eighteen-year-old men.

In these trying times, Americans attempted to understand how the peace of 1945 had become so fragile. In a speech on March 5, 1946, Winston Churchill provided language that seemed to describe what had happened to the world. Speaking of Soviet influence in Eastern Europe, Churchill warned that "an iron curtain has descended" across Europe. Probably more influential in defining American policy toward the Soviet

Union were ideas authored by George Kennan, counselor at the American embassy in Moscow. First in a long telegram in 1946 and then in an essay published under the pseudonym "Mister X," Kennan provided a plausible rationale for American foreign policy. He argued that the United States had to "contain" Soviet expansion and hope that this action would cause the communist nation to change internally. A number of American leaders were convinced by this notion of containment, although they often exaggerated its military aspects.

In early 1947, Kennan's principle of containment became a fundamental part of American foreign policy. This occurred in two ways. On March 12, 1947, the president announced the Truman Doctrine, which promised aid to Greece in its struggle against insurgents. Truman argued that the world was divided between two types of societies: Western democratic capitalist nations and Eastern communist nations. The outcome of the struggle between the two sides in Europe, he proclaimed, was "of grave importance in a much wider situation." Truman asked for military assistance for Greece and Turkey, and Congress obliged by voting funds on May 15.

Truman put forward the second stage of his policy in early summer. George Marshall—formerly a general, now secretary of state—proposed a plan of economic assistance for Western Europe. The Marshall Plan, as it became known, promised to revive the economy of Europe and eliminate conditions that communist politicians could exploit. The program offered economic assistance to war-torn countries of Western Europe and even to the Soviet Union and its allies, but they refused. Communist parties in countries like France demonstrated against the plan. Nonetheless, sixteen European nations eventually agreed to a joint plan for economic recovery, signed in September 1947. Congress funded the project in March 1948.

The Soviets responded to the growing integration of the western European nations by increasing their control of occupied territories such as Poland, Czechoslovakia, and Hungary. In 1948, with the United States and western European nations contemplating a military alliance, with the Soviet's former ally Yugoslavia pursuing an independent course, and with the integration of the separate western zones of Germany to form one single political and economic entity, Stalin acted. After the United States introduced a single West German currency into West Berlin in late June, the Soviets clamped a blockade on all ground and water entrances into the city. Truman had to make the next move: either abandon Berlin or force a reopening of supply routes.

The American president chose a third way. He initiated a massive airlift to supply the city. Finally, in the spring of 1949 the Soviets lifted their ineffective blockade. Not only had Stalin's tactics failed, they had helped pressure Western nations into forming the North Atlantic Treaty Organiza-

tion (NATO) in mid-1949. Britain, France, Belgium, the Netherlands, Luxembourg, Portugal, Denmark, Norway, Italy, Iceland, Canada, and the United States joined. West Germany was admitted in 1954. This formal military alliance designed to contain communism became the mainstay of America's European policy and effectively prevented further deterioration of U.S. influence in Europe.

In September 1949, Truman announced that the Soviet Union had exploded an atomic bomb. The short-lived American monopoly had been broken. The president ordered American scientists to begin serious development of hydrogen weapons to regain U.S. supremacy. In four short years, the peace of 1945 had degenerated into a new arms race and new entangling alliances.

THE KOREAN WAR

The defeat of Jiang Jie-shī 1949 touched off recriminations in the United States over who had "lost" China to the communists. In Asia, the victory of Mao Zedong created a major new revolutionary force. In this context, the Truman administration faced a serious crisis in June 1950. For two years the divided sections of Korea had glowered at each other with increasing hostility. Separated only by the thirty-eighth parallel as part of the postwar settlement, two nations had sprung up: North Korea, supported by the Soviets, and South Korea, dependent on the United States. On June 25, 1950, North Korean troops, with Stalin's approval, plunged into the south. Truman had to decide quickly: stand and fight, risking a large-scale Asian war, or abandon an ally. Because of withering criticism of his foreign policy by Republicans and public doubts about the loyalty of some members of his government, Truman probably had no real choice.

The Korean conflict employed many of the weapons and tactics developed during the total war experience of World War II, but on a limited terrain and for limited goals. It was to prove a model for a series of later military encounters.

A KOREAN WAR SCENE. A familiar sight during war on the Asian mainland in World War II and then the Korean conflict: Soldiers advanced to the front lines while civilians fled in the opposite direction, carrying what possessions they could.

This contradiction between potential means and narrow goals meant, for example, that the United States rejected use of the atomic bomb against North Korea and communist China. It meant, also, that each side operated from privileged sanctuaries: the United States from naval and air bases in Japan, and the Chinese from behind their border at the Yalu River on the northern edge of North Korea. The battlefield in Korea, however, witnessed a war that was as bitter and bloody as World War II.

On June 27 President Truman called on Douglas MacArthur, commander of U.S. armed forces in the Far East, to defend South Korea. The United Nations (with the Soviet Union absent because of a boycott) voted to demand North Korean evacuation and offered supporting troops. Eventually, small contributions came from France, Britain, Turkey, Greece, New Zealand, the Netherlands, Belgium, Ethiopia, and others. Most of the troops, however, were supplied by the United States and South Korea.

Hemmed in by the rapidly expanding communist offensive, American and South Korean troops retreated to the area in the extreme south around Pusan. But on September 15, 1950, the American army took the offensive. At the same time, a surprise amphibious landing near Seoul at Inchon, behind communist lines, broke North Korea's offensive and shattered its army. United Nations troops drove rapidly to the north and crossed the thirty-eighth parallel into North Korea, capturing the capital, Pyongyang, on October 20.

General MacArthur, after conferring with President Truman, drove farther north on two fronts toward the border of China. His purpose was to destroy the North Korean army. Disregarding warnings from the Chinese communists, he approached the Yalu River border. On November 25, Chinese troops, ferried across the

GENERAL DOUGLAS MACARTHUR.
General Douglas MacArthur was chief
of Southwest Pacific operations in
World War II, administrator of
postwar Japan, and commander of
United Nations forces in Korea.
Because he disagreed with the
limited American objectives in the
Korean conflict—and said so
publicly—President Truman removed
him from command.

river, attacked in force, compelling the UN troops to retreat to the thirty-eighth parallel. MacArthur's brilliant maneuver at Inchon was thus undercut by his grave miscalculation.

Offensive and counteroffensive followed. MacArthur's outspoken advocacy of a wider war made his dismissal by Truman in April 1951 inevitable, if very unpopular. Costly battles pushed the front back and forth over the thirty-eighth parallel until July 1953, when a permanent armistice line was established somewhat north of the original line. For this eventual small exchange of territory there were perhaps 1.5 million casualties on the communist side and perhaps 450,000 on the UN side (including 33,710 Americans killed in action and several thousand more who died as prisoners of war). In terms of tactics and materiel, the United States Navy had com-

pletely dominated sea lanes and harassed North Korean coastal installations at will. The United States had also controlled the air over North Korea, although U.S. Sabre jet fighters met stiff resistance from Soviet MIG planes stationed at bases inside China.

By the middle of 1953 the first armed confrontation between the United States and communist troops had finally ended. War had been confined to a small portion of the globe. The United States and the Soviet Union had avoided using the doomsday weapons that they now possessed in abundance. But the arms race and the cold war became, if anything, more serious in a divided and restless world. Peace was further away than it had been in 1945 when the war ended and when American scientists had developed a weapon to end all wars.

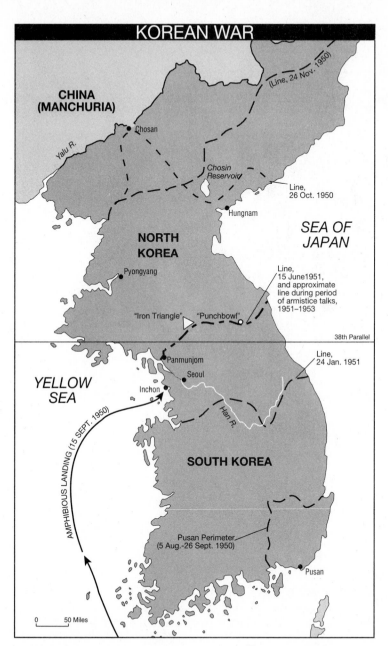

KOREAN WAR

CHINA
(MANCHURIA)

(Line, 24 Nov. 1950)

Yalu R.

Chosan

Chosin
Reservoir

Line,
26 Oct. 1950

Hungnam

NORTH
KOREA

SEA OF
JAPAN

Pyongyang

Line,
15 June1951,
and approximate
line during period
of armistice talks,
1951–1953

"Iron Triangle"   "Punchbowl"

38th Parallel

Panmunjom

Line,
24 Jan. 1951

YELLOW
SEA

Seoul

Inchon

Han R.

SOUTH KOREA

AMPHIBIOUS LANDING (15 SEPT. 1950)

Pusan Perimeter
(5 Aug.-26 Sept. 1950)

Pusan

0   50 Miles

COLD WAR AT HOME

At home, worry about military secrets and ideological purity increased. J. Robert Oppenheimer was not the only American to fall under scrutiny during this security-conscious era. In 1950 Julius and Ethel Rosenberg were arrested, charged, and convicted of passing atomic secrets to the Soviet Union. They were executed in 1953. From 1949 to the mid-1950s, suspicion of communism focused on schools, teachers, books, and government workers. Charges of communist infiltration into the government and

Senator Joseph McCarthy and *The Daily Worker*. McCarthy used communist party publications such as the *Worker* during Senate hearings to cast suspicion on his opponents. Favorable mention in such a publication would often bring charges of disloyalty from the Wisconsin senator.

into the Democratic party became an effective campaign slogan, especially for opportunistic Senator Joseph McCarthy of Wisconsin. But McCarthyism became a corrosive element in politics because it also fed on the insecurities of Americans who were uneasy about rapid social change. Groups reluctant to accept the admission of labor unions or African-Americans into the political consensus sometimes saw the hand of communist conspirators behind these movements. It was no accident that segregationists charged that integration was a communist plot or that some Americans feared that the United Nations was communist-dominated.

In this charged atmosphere President Truman saw his task principally as defending the Democratic party against accusations of being "soft" on communism. This helps explain his swift, early action on federal employee loyalty. In 1946 he appointed a Temporary Commission on Em-

ployee Loyalty to design a security program. Following the commission's suggestions, he asked the attorney general to draw up a list of subversive organizations. He also established federal departmental loyalty boards that checked each employee. Five years later, about 20,000 federal workers had been screened: a little over half had been cleared, 3,000 cases were still pending, 2,500 employees had left service voluntarily, and 400 had been dismissed.

Despite Truman's extensive and overzealous scrutiny of federal workers, Congress, the Republican party, and a substantial part of public opinion remained skeptical. Between 1945 and 1952 over eighty congressional investigations of communism were held. Many of them explored federal agencies. The most important of these inquiries were held by the House Un-American Activities Committee (HUAC). Very little legislation emerged from this committee, but it did provide a forum to attack Truman. It was a favorite strat-

CHRONOLOGY

1931	Japan invades Manchuria
1939	Hitler conquers Czechoslovakia;
(Aug.)	German-Soviet Non-Aggression Pact;
(Sept. 1)	Hitler invades Poland;World War II begins;
(Sept. 3)	France and Britain declare war on Germany
1940	United States begins serious atomic weapons research;
(May)	Germans conquer Holland and Belgium;
(Sept.)	Destroyers-for-bases deal between FDR and England;
(fall)	Battle of Britain;
(Nov.)	FDR elected to third presidential term
1941	Britain begins atomic development program called MAUD;
(Mar.)	Lend-Lease program enacted;
(June)	Germany invades Soviet Union;
	Atlantic Charter meeting between FDR and Churchill;
(Dec. 7)	Japanese attack Pearl Harbor
1943	Casablanca and Tehran Conferences held;
	Allies recapture North Africa;
	Detroit race riot;
	zoot-suit riots in Los Angeles
(Sept.)	Italy changes sides in the war;
	Mussolini executed
1944	
(June 6)	Invasion of Normandy
1945	
(May 8)	Germany surrenders;
(Aug. 6)	Atomic bomb dropped on Hiroshima;

1945 (cont'd)	
(Aug. 14)	Japan surrenders
1945–1946	Nuremberg war trials held
1945–1947	American armed forces demobilized
1946	George Kennan outlines "containment" policy;
	Atomic Energy Commission established;
(Mar.)	Winston Churchill sounds alarm about "iron curtain";
(Aug.)	John Hersey publishes *Hiroshima*
1947	
(Mar.)	Truman Doctrine announced
1947–1948	Marshall Plan for Western Europe enacted
1948–1949	Berlin blockade
1949	Nationalist Chinese flee mainland for Taiwan;
	North Atlantic Treaty Organization formed;
	Soviets test atomic bomb
1950	National Science Foundation established;
	Julius and Ethel Rosenberg convicted of espionage;
	Alger Hiss convicted of perjury;
(Feb.)	Senator Joseph McCarthy begins anti-communist crusade;
(June)	Korean conflict begins
1950–1953	United States participates in Korean conflict
1953 (July)	Korean cease-fire signed;
	The Rosenbergs executed
1955	"Hiroshima maidens" come to the United States

egy of some conservative southerners on HUAC to use the committee as a platform to charge that integration was un-American.

The principal anticommunist, antisubversive legislation of the era came in 1950 with the pas-sage of the Internal Security Act. The bill required the Justice Department to register the names, fi-nances, and membership of all communist or front groups. All literature from these groups passing through the mail was to be stamped "Communist."

Known party members could not obtain passports. Most controversial was a provision to set aside internment camps for suspected disloyal Americans in time of emergency. Truman angrily vetoed the act, saying that it subverted elementary ideas of a free society. Congress thought otherwise and overrode his veto.

The Internal Security Act symbolized Congress's growing initiative on the anticommunist front. In 1948 Alger Hiss, an important New Deal adviser and well-connected lawyer, had been charged with passing secrets to the Soviets in the late 1930s. His accuser was Whittaker Chambers, a self-confessed spy, a man of many aliases, a writer and later an editor for *Time* magazine. Chambers accused Hiss before HUAC and then in public, on NBC's *Meet the Press*. Hiss sued for libel, but in 1950 he was charged with and con-

victed of perjury. HUAC investigators, led by Congressman Richard Nixon, established a strong circumstantial case to fit Chambers's eyewitness accounts. Truman, Secretary of State Dean Acheson, and many liberals refused to believe in Hiss's guilt. But their attitude only increased the desire of some congressmen like McCarthy to expose communists in government. By 1952, issues of defense, secrecy, and spying threatened to overwhelm American political discussion. Under the circumstances, the commitment to building more bombs and maintaining secrets was hardly questioned. Only a few short years after the end of the war, fear and suspicion had invaded American policy at home and abroad. Even the scientists who had won the "wizard war" were subjected to loyalty oaths, extensive investigations, and suspicion.

SUGGESTIONS FOR FURTHER READING

HIROSHIMA AND THE ATOMIC BOMB

The effect on American society of building and deploying nuclear weapons is difficult to overestimate. Martin J. Sherwin, *A World Destroyed: The Atomic Bomb and the Grand Alliance* (1975), is an insightful account of the creation of the first atomic weapons. Gregg Herken, *The Winning Weapon: The Atomic Bomb in the Cold War, 1945–1950* (1980), details the role of nuclear weapons in policy making. Of the many accounts describing the effects of the bomb, John Hersey, *Hiroshima* (1946), is the most personal and poignant.

WORLD WAR II AND ITS EFFECTS

For an accessible and comprehensive discussion of battles and strategies during the war, Richard Ernest and Trevor N. Dupuy, *Encyclopedia of Military History* (rev. ed., 1977), is indispensable. Alan S. Milward, *War, Economy, and Society, 1939–1945* (1977), and Richard Polenberg, *America at War: The Home Front, 1941–1945* (1968), are two excellent discussions of the effects of war on American society. Otis L. Graham, *Toward a Planned Society: From Roosevelt to Nixon* (1976), focuses on the role of federal economic plan-

ning during and after the war. In *Another Chance: Postwar America, 1945–1968* (1985), James Gilbert examines some of the long-range effects of the war. For a discussion of the failure to save the Jews, see David S. Wyman, *The Abandonment of the Jews* (1984). A fascinating book on the memories and lives of children who grew up during the war is William M. Tuttle, *Daddy's Gone to War: The Second World War in the Lives of America's Children* (1993).

A fine, brief discussion of the long-term economic effects of the war may be found in Harold Vatter, *The U.S. Economy in World War II* (1985). Paul Boyer, *By the Bomb's Early Light: American Thought and Culture at the Dawn of the Atomic Age* (1985), is a chilling appraisal of the effects of this new technology. Michael S. Sherry, *The Rise of American Air Power: The Creation of Armageddon* (1987), debunks the importance of air power in World War II.

THE COLD WAR

The origins of the cold war have been extensively debated. John Lewis Gaddis, *The United States and the Origins of the Cold War, 1941–1945* (1985), carefully and comprehensively explores the issues. An excellent account with substantial coverage of Soviet policy is Adam B. Ulam, *Expansion and Coexistence* (1968). Lloyd C. Gardner, *Architects of Illusion: Men and Ideas in American Foreign Policy, 1941–1949* (1970), sheds considerable light on the complex motivations of American policy makers. The central political figures of the cold war era have left excellent memoirs. In his *Memoirs* (2 vols., 1955–1956), President Harry S Truman proves to be a marvelous storyteller and competent defender of his administration. George Frost Kennan, *Memoirs, 1925–1950* (1968), is a brilliant and intriguing account by a key policy maker and commentator. His recent book, *Sketches from a Life* (1989), adds important

material to this story. James MacGregor Burns, *Roosevelt: The Soldier of Freedom* (1970), is a masterly description of the Roosevelt presidency during the war years. James B. Conant, *My Several Lives: Memoirs of a Social Inventor* (1970), is an account by one of the leading figures in the politics of wartime and postwar science. See also Walter LaFeber, *America, Russia, and the Cold War 1945–1980* (5th ed., 1985). A very important addition to this enormous literature is Melvyn Leffler, *A Preponderance of Power: National Security, the Truman Administration and the Cold War* (1992). Another new book that takes a long harsh look at the Soviet Union is Richard Pipes, *Russia Under the Bolshevik Regime* (1993).

The American Century

THE EPISODE: *The extension of civil rights was not initiated by government act; civil rights were won through a long and bitter struggle of people determined to seize the citizenship that was their birthright. Deprived of political and business opportunities for a century, bright young black men and women turned to the black church to express their hopes, energies, and aspirations. This was particularly true in the segregated South. But during the 1950s the accumulation of change began to wear the edges of racial separation thin. When a young scholar, Martin Luther King, Jr., returned from Boston University to take up the ministry at Dexter Avenue Baptist Church in 1954 in Montgomery, Alabama, he had no hint that a nationwide civil rights movement would soon swirl around him or that his name would be linked with the great march on Washington of 1963 that would help open the floodgates of integration. What made King one of the most famous Americans of his day was the energy of a suppressed American culture, which he articulated into a momentous political and moral awakening. Its successes were his; its failures revealed his limitations and exposed the deepest barriers to equality in American life.*

THE HISTORICAL SETTING: *By reputation the 1950s (when the modern civil rights movement began) was politically conservative, perhaps even backward-looking. This representation is misleading. The 1950s was a time of consolidation in politics, when Republican president Dwight Eisenhower confirmed the welfare state and the broad tenets of guidance of the economy established during the New Deal and World War II. In fact, a variety of programs were expanded, even if the exuberant experimentalism of Roosevelt was relinquished. Beneath an apparently placid surface, American life was changing dramatically. The new consumerism of the era celebrated peace and prosperity and the virtues of family, not public, life. Centered on a dream of owning a home, raising children, and holding a good job, the new social ideal celebrated suburbs and their distance from old urban problems.*

Even in these communities ringing American cities there were rebellions of sorts. The surprising demographics of the postwar period (steep rises in marriages and births, declines in divorce rates) crested about 1957. After a brief period, women began to return to the workforce. Children increasingly explored new cultural forms emanating from the city ghettos, from working-class and from African-American culture. The restive experimentalism in culture rampant in the next decade had its origins in this time. And the civil rights movement, which energized so much of what was to come, shimmered like an ebony ribbon through the period, transforming American life and culture.

Martin Luther King, Jr.—
The Pursuit of Liberty

At about one o'clock on the afternoon of Friday, May 3, 1963, the public safety commissioner of Birmingham, Alabama, Theophilus Eugene "Bull" Connor, stood next to the city's mayor, Arthur Hanes. Connor, a fleshy, heavy-jowled man, whose glass eye gave him a peculiar stare, watched the entrance to the Sixteenth Street Baptist Church. Nearby policemen, and farther on a line of police and firemen with high-pressure hoses, backed up by a dog squad with several German shepherds, also waited and watched. They were determined to prevent black civil rights demonstrators from marching. Connor, their commander, was a national symbol of old-style violent enforcement of race separation. Although this was just one more day in a series of rolling demonstrations that had continued for almost a month, it proved to be decisive. The Reverend Martin Luther King, Jr., leader of the demonstrators inside the church, had demanded "promises and action." "We are ready to negotiate," he claimed. "But we intend to negotiate from strength." Connor just as adamantly had promised to arrest every demonstrator, even if it filled every cell in the city jails. King, he scoffed, "would run out of niggers."

Hanes nudged Connor. "Here they come," he said. Connor's men swept back a crowd of about 100 jeering white onlookers and turned on the demonstrators. Police Captain G. V. Evans ordered the emerging group to halt and disperse: "Or you're going to get wet." The first 50 blacks continued to march. Most were young and carrying signs. Suddenly, the hoses squirted on. High-pressure water splattered the crowd. Some demonstrators fled. Some fell to the ground, upended by the force of the spray. Others skidded down the pavement, like debris in a gutter.

Now a large crowd of almost 2,000 blacks who had been waiting in nearby Kelly Ingram Park grew restless. Firemen turned their hoses on this more formidable group. Instead of dispersing, however, many in the crowd responded by hurling rocks, bricks, bottles, and chunks of concrete at the police. The situation had reached a breaking point. Connor signaled and his dog squad advanced. The enraged animals snapped at demonstrators, separating them into smaller groups, as other police moved in for arrests. But hundreds of demonstrators retreated into side streets, where they continued to pelt the advancing police. Finally, James Bevel, an assistant of King's, negotiated a quick truce. If the police called off the dogs and shut down the water cannons, he would urge the demonstrators to go home. Gradually, the riot subsided, and Birmingham drew back once again from full-scale fighting. But the mask had fallen from Connor's segregation. The next day, in almost every newspaper in the country, and all over

FORCE USED AGAINST CIVIL RIGHTS DEMONSTRATORS.   In Birmingham, Alabama, police resorted to the use of attack dogs to threaten participants in a demonstration pushing for civil rights. The ferocious animals (notice the destruction one has levied on a man's pants) were not enough to keep people from demanding what was rightfully theirs.

the world, one photograph told the story of Birmingham: a snarling police dog, scarcely restrained by an officer, lunging at the chest of a black demonstrator.

The violence in Alabama broke the impasse by escalating the confrontation. In Washington, Attorney General Robert Kennedy issued a sympathetic statement: "These demonstrations are understandable expressions of resentment and hurt by people who have been the victims of abuse and deprivation of their most basic rights for many years." Then he warned King against further marches. But quite clearly, the federal government had decided to intervene. Kennedy dispatched Assistant Attorney General Burke Marshall to Birmingham to negotiate a settlement between King and the local business community. Connor and Hanes were conspicuously left out of the talks.

Kennedy chose this tactic because of the chaos in Birmingham's government. Connor and Hanes were still in office only because of stubbornness and confusion. In November 1962 the voters of Birmingham had altered the old city government structure that was dominated by Connor. When the new structure went into effect in April

1963, Connor ran for mayor but lost to a milder segregationist, Albert Boutwell. Then, switching tactics, Connor claimed that he and Hanes could not be unseated, whatever the new frame of government. They would serve out their terms of office under the old system. Thus when the new mayor was sworn in on April 15, Connor and Hanes prevented him from taking office. The matter stood, in early May, before the courts.

Connor's use of police power to enforce segregation had pushed the situation to a crisis. Extremist elements in Birmingham and from the rest of the state, including the Ku Klux Klan, rallied to support Connor. Some of them pushed for further confrontations, in hopes of a declaration of martial law. To them, anything was better than integration.

In this explosive atmosphere, Burke Marshall began his negotiations with a group of city business leaders to end the most painful and public customs of segregation. From Washington, President Kennedy stepped up pressure as cabinet members persuaded corporate friends to ask Birmingham's business elite to support a compromise. What King and his forces demanded was not easy to grant: desegregation of lunch counters, rest rooms, fitting rooms, and drinking fountains in all downtown stores; job placement for blacks as clerks and salespeople; release of prisoners arrested for demonstrating; and establishment of a permanent dialog between white and black leaders.

Marshall and his negotiating team raced against a short, sputtering fuse of racial violence, meeting in long sessions with white and black leaders. In the streets of Birmingham, the violence accelerated. King refused to call off demonstrators, even though confrontations with city police had escalated. Complicating matters, Alabama's governor, George Wallace, sent in reinforcements to aid Connor. By Tuesday evening, 575 riot-equipped state troopers were camped out around the city. On Tuesday night, however, Marshall hammered out a tentative agreement, and King and his forces canceled further demonstrations. The city waited . . . Wednesday. . . then Thursday, until the final details were worked out. Friday morning King announced the accord. Most of his demands had been met. The back of segregation was broken.

Nevertheless, segregationists tried to disrupt the agreement. Governor Wallace denounced the agreement with "lawless Negroes." He would never, he promised, compromise on segregation. On Saturday night, shortly after a joint Georgia-Alabama Klan rally in Birmingham, a car sped past the house of A. D. King, brother of Martin Luther King, Jr. Passengers tossed two dynamite bombs out of the car, blasting the house. Minutes later, four white men threw two more bombs at the Gaston Hotel, where King himself had been staying.

Although these bombings had caused no serious injuries, Birmingham's African Americans poured into the streets. Picking up anything handy, they pelted policemen, smashed car windows, and beat up white bystanders. When police reinforcements arrived with the dog squad, the crowd became still more enraged. Even state troopers could not calm the situation. Finally, black leaders persuaded the crowd to disperse. The riot ended, but not before flames had consumed several white-owned businesses in the black section of town. Still, the agreement held. The events made King's words, uttered during the campaign, all the more prophetic: "I stand alone in the middle of two opposing forces in the Negro community. One is the force of complacency. . . . The other force is one of bitterness and hatred and comes perilously close to advocating violence."

Gradually, peace returned to Birmingham. The reign of Bull Connor ended May 23, when the Alabama Supreme Court unanimously certified Mayor Boutwell's election and right to office. The businessmen's agreement was implemented. But racial hatred and white resistance continued. On September 14 white terrorists hurled a dynamite bomb through a window of the Sixteenth Street Baptist Church. It exploded in a crowded Sunday school class, killing four young girls. Twenty other children were injured. In a eulogy sermon, King tried, as he always did, to channel sorrow and shock into something positive: "Their death says to us that we must work passionately and unceasingly to make the American dream a reality."

Birmingham was a grim and inevitable rendezvous for the southern civil rights movement—a protest movement that had begun almost spontaneously in Montgomery, Alabama, in 1955. The success in Montgomery had been astounding, in no small measure because of King, who was thrust into leadership of the new movement. But Montgomery was also deceptive. It represented only one wall breached, the first battle in a war of attrition against southern strongholds of segregation. One by one they fell, some in violence, some peacefully. But some strongholds, like Birmingham, held out.

King's generalship of this movement was crucial. His strategy was honed in failure and success. He recognized, where others did not, the great energy and moral force of southern black religion. But he also understood the tenacity of segregation and the ultimate necessity of federal intervention. He realized that integration had to force its way into the American conscience, but without allowing fear to prevail in the white community. He knew that even northern liberals had to be pushed into support for action. This line between vision and threat was a precarious one.

MARTIN LUTHER KING, JR., CORETTA SCOTT KING, AND THEIR FIRST DAUGHTER, 1956. Despite his growing fame, King always depended on his wide family network for support and aid. Here he stands with his wife and first child on the steps of Montgomery's Dexter Baptist Church, his first pastoral position; the capitol building of Alabama is in the background.

King was a new resident of Montgomery in 1955. He had arrived there just one year earlier, with a new Ph.D. and his wife, Coretta, to answer a call from the Dexter Avenue Baptist Church. King had grown up in Atlanta, where his father was a prominent minister at the Ebenezer Baptist Church. His mother was the daughter of Ebenezer's previous pastor.

An outstanding student academically, King entered public school and then switched to the private laboratory school at Atlanta University. From there he attended Atlanta's only black high school, Booker T. Washington. He skipped ninth grade and graduated at the age of fifteen. Like his father before him, he went on to Morehouse College. During this period he began to think seriously about the ministry. He began preaching at the age of seventeen and shortly thereafter became assistant pastor at Ebenezer.

But at this point, King's career diverged from his father's, which had always been limited to the black community and to the black educational institutions of Atlanta. Young King wanted a deeper, wider, more committed education. Thus in 1948 he enrolled at Crozer Theological Seminary in Chester, Pennsylvania, a predominantly white school. During his three years there, he also attended philosophy courses at the University of Pennsylvania.

In his studies, King immersed himself in the social philosophy of Marx, Hegel, and other Europeans, and in the writings of the American Protestant theologian Reinhold Niebuhr. He avidly studied the Social Gospel, an earlier theological movement that stressed working for social justice. He read deeply in the writings of Mahatma Gandhi, the pacifist leader of the Indian revolution against British colonial rule. King interwove ideas from these sources into the fabric of his experience. His developing philosophy brought together his understanding of the economic exploitation of his race, his admiration for nonviolent tactics, and the traditions of southern black religion as he had experienced them. Could he, he wondered, transform the quiet, emotional, and accommodating religion of southern blacks into a force for change? Could he do this without inciting a violent backlash?

When King became a graduate student at Boston University, he did not yet know the answers although he was determined to succeed. There is also evidence he took a shortcut by plagiarizing part of his doctoral dissertation. Being a young man, he was often concerned with matters other than research and social change. While working for his doctorate in philosophy, he met a young woman, Coretta Scott, who was studying at the New England Conservatory of Music. He decided immediately that this was the woman he wanted to marry. After their first meeting, he said to her abruptly: "You have everything I have ever wanted in a wife."

For Coretta, the decision was more difficult. As her affection for King grew, she was torn. Should she give up a promising career in music and marry a Baptist minister? She finally consented, and the couple wed in June 1953. Coretta joined the Baptist church and put aside her career. In 1954 the Kings accepted the call from the church in Montgomery. Within a year, King, only twenty-six years old, had become the leader of a bus boycott that initiated the modern civil rights movement.

⋆⋈◉⊜⋈⋆

On December 1, 1955, Rosa Parks, a black woman, exhausted from her shopping and her job as a seamstress, entered a crowded bus in front of the Fair department store in Montgomery to pay the driver. She then got off the bus and walked to the "colored" entrance in the rear, where she boarded the bus again. Finding most seats at the rear occupied, she moved forward and sat down in a row immediately behind the section reserved for whites. The bus resumed its route, stopping again at the Empire Theater. Six white passengers entered the front of the bus, paid and moved back. But there were not enough seats in the white section. Seeing this, the driver called on the nearest black passengers to vacate their places. All of them did, except Rosa Parks. Too tired, or perhaps mindful of earlier incidents of rudeness by white drivers, she refused. James F. Blake, the driver, left the bus and returned with a policeman, who arrested Mrs. Parks for violating Montgomery's segregation laws.

The incident was not entirely unexpected. Others had previously defied the law, and they had been arrested. But Mrs. Parks was different. She was a well-known figure in Montgomery's black community and a member of the city's National Association for the Advancement of Colored People (NAACP). The times were also different. The Supreme Court on May 17, 1954, in *Brown* v. *Board of Education*, had ruled school segregation unconstitutional: Separate could never be equal, the Court maintained. On May 31, 1955, the Court had ordered lower federal courts and school authorities to integrate schools "with all deliberate speed."

Yet nothing much had changed in Montgomery or the rest of the South. Few black citizens could vote, although the number of black voters was growing slowly. The "deliberate speed" of school integration meant no speed at all. Still the indignities of segregation continued to pervade private custom and public commerce. From birth to death, the races were separated. Hospitals, prisons, and graveyards were divided by race. Marriages across racial lines were strictly forbidden. Swimming pools, golf courses, movie theaters, and airport and railroad waiting rooms were segregated. So were drinking fountains and bathrooms. Stores often served blacks, if at all, from a separate back or side door.

Mrs. Parks's arrest electrified the black community. Immediately after the incident, she telephoned E. D. Nixon and his wife, who went to the police station to seek her release. Nixon was head of the local NAACP and an official of the Brotherhood of Sleeping Car Porters. His wife was a member of the black Women's Political Council. In Mrs. Parks, the Political Council found a symbol they could organize around, and they quickly decided on a boycott of Montgomery's bus system. E. D. Nixon organized ministers' groups to support the boycott. Unable himself to assume leadership of the group because of his work for the union, he began to telephone local ministers searching for endorsements of the boycott. One of those whom Nixon called was Martin Luther King, Jr. On the afternoon of December 5, King accepted leadership of a new boycott group, the Montgomery Improvement Association (MIA).

The initial demands of the group were cautious. They did not ask for an end to segregation. They asked only for courtesy from drivers, equal reserved seating (equal numbers of seats for blacks and whites), and black drivers on predominantly black

ROSA PARKS, the woman who defied the segregation laws of Montgomery and thus began the bus boycott of 1955, was able to take a front seat on a city bus a year later, after the Supreme Court banned segregated public transit in Montgomery.

routes. This modest plan would have made segregation work more harmoniously, not end it. But after a fruitless meeting between the MIA, the City Commission, and the bus company, a lawyer for the company declared: "If we granted the Negroes these demands, they would go about boasting of a victory that they had won over white people, and this we will not stand for." The lines were drawn hard and fast.

By early winter both sides had stiffened their determination. But developments among the whites became ominous. The White Citizens' Council, a group devoted to preserving segregation, enlisted thousands of new members, including the mayor and the city commissioners. Abusive telephone calls frequently disturbed the King household. On the evening of January 30, 1956, a bomb blast on the front porch of the King residence split the porch and shattered windows in the house.

Faced with inflexible opposition to bus integration, the MIA decided to challenge segregation laws through the courts. On February 1, with help from the NAACP, Fred Gray, one of two black lawyers in the city, filed his case in federal court. At the same time, a group of white businessmen, the Men of Montgomery, began negotiations with the MIA. Sales in downtown stores had fallen, and the bus company was losing about $3,000 a day. Finally, in mid-February, elected officials and the MIA leadership met, but without results. The city was willing to back down, but it was too late for halfway concessions. Now Montgomery African Americans demanded equality in bus transport. Weeks of struggle had led them to make bigger demands. In a shifting and increasingly explosive situation, King and other MIA leaders pressed for a more extensive program of integration. There was no other way to retain their leadership.

The city responded with tougher tactics. In late February, King and ninety others were indicted for breaking an old antiboycott law. Their trial began on March 19 before Judge Eugene Carter. On March 22 King was convicted: his sentence was a fine of $500 or thirteen months at hard labor. His lawyers appealed the decision. Meanwhile, the boycott continued. In mid-May a federal district court declared Alabama's bus segregation laws unconstitutional. The city immediately appealed to the Supreme Court.

SEGREGATED SOCIETY IN THE SOUTH.   Throughout the South, public facilities were carefully designated white or colored. This custom persisted well into the 1960s.

As the boycotters stood firm through the spring and summer, they attracted more and more national and international attention. King spoke several times in the North, and funds raised by outside black congregations and by white liberals began to flow into the city. Finally, on November 13, word came that the Supreme Court had declared Alabama's bus segregation laws unconstitutional. The boycott remained in effect until December, when the decision was implemented.

For King, the lessons of the fight had been painfully learned. He realized the crucial role of religious leadership in the black community. He recognized, too, the tenacious hatred of the segregationists. He understood that nonviolence, to be successful, would require outside intervention. King also gained insight into the problems of leading the currently inert but potentially explosive black population. This could be a dangerous and volatile situation, given a constituency that was unpracticed in politics.

King's success in Montgomery elevated him to national leadership, but the movement remained unorganized, diffuse, and still without an articulate philosophy. He was determined to change this. King knew the old answers and their modern equivalents: the accommodationism of Booker T. Washington, the legal integrationism of W. E. B. Du Bois and the NAACP, and the black separatism of Marcus Garvey. None of these strategies had deeply touched the masses of Southern black Christians. King's strategy was to organize his constituency around the black churches. He favored a philosophy that could transform the quiet strength of Southern blacks into an aggressive force for change. The ability of black men and women to suffer, to face indignities calmly, was the foundation on which he erected his program of nonviolence. His ultimate goal was clear: integration of black Americans as equals into the full benefits of citizenship.

In early 1957, King, the Reverend Ralph Abernathy, and other ministers from the South met in New Orleans to organize the Southern Christian Leadership Conference (SCLC). The group, headquartered in Atlanta, selected King as head. One of King's first strategies was to capitalize on his national visibility to press for federal legislation. After leading a prayer vigil in Washington, he met with Vice President Richard Nixon in June. The result of this and other pressure was the Civil Rights Bill of 1957, a law that established a Civil Rights Commission to monitor voting rights violations.

King's general strategy was to force immediate change. Using nonviolence, he led masses of demonstrators into confrontation with segregationists. These nonviolent tactics had a special meaning in the American context. When Mahatma Gandhi led the nonviolent movement for Indian independence, he represented a majority of his society pitted against a small, vulnerable British colonial government. Once the Indian masses decided to be independent, probably nothing could have stopped them. But King had to use nonviolence in a society where African Americans were only a minority.

Thus nonviolence depended ultimately on some form of national action, inspired either by agreement with the goals of integration or by fear of the social disorder that might be created by confrontation. King hoped it would be the former, for this would make ultimate accommodation between the races easier. It would also channel the raw anger of the black community. But there were great risks. King recognized that nonviolence would breed disenchantment among blacks who demanded speedy change.

This was precisely the complaint of the young integrationists who later challenged King. In February 1960 white and black college students began sit-ins in Durham and Greensboro, North Carolina, demanding service at the segregated lunch counters of Woolworth dime stores. The movement spread to fifty-four other cities in two months. By mid-April the Student Nonviolent Coordinating Committee (SNCC) had formed. King maintained cordial relations with the young leaders, but he eventually lost influence over the group.

In the next few years, the desegregation movement spread rapidly, and King struggled to maintain his leadership and a national vision of the goals. From 1961 through early 1962 he supported the "freedom rides" organized by another black group, the Congress of Racial Equality. These rides on integrated buses into the South called national attention to the problem of segregation, particularly in bus stations. The first ride left Washington in May 1961; its purpose was to integrate southern transportation facilities. The trip was uneventful until the bus carrying the freedom riders was bombed and burned by whites near Anniston, Alabama, on May 14. Other groups that ventured out later were attacked in Birmingham and Montgomery. As these attacks grew, so did national concern. By the end of the month, a freedom ride that left for Jackson, Mississippi, was assigned an escort of the National Guard and army helicopters. Responding to an intolerable situation, the Interstate Commerce Commission in December prohibited segregation aboard buses and in terminals.

A freedom ride to Albany, Georgia, in December 1961 to integrate a railway station marked the beginning of a newer, broader tactic employed by King, but one that also exposed the movement to counterattack and potential defeat. Black leaders in the city called in King to help organize a movement that had been stirred up by the freedom ride. The local SCLC leader hoped to focus protest on the entire race and caste system of the city. As in other southern cities, public segregation was only symbolic of deeper divisions and exploitation in jobs, wages, social benefits, and political rights. On December 16 King and the Albany leadership organized a march to demand change in all of these areas. Over 700 demonstrators were arrested. King refused release on bond and called for more demonstrators to come to the city.

A temporary compromise was reached two days later. King left jail, and the railway station was integrated. Civil rights leaders were optimistic. But the city had not really budged. All of its parks, libraries, movie theaters, and buses remained segregated. So King and his allies decided to launch a selective boycott against white businesses and the bus company. The city struck back and reneged on an informal promise to integrate the buses.

By July 1962 King faced failure and mounting criticism of his leadership, so he turned to new tactics—civil disobedience to force Albany city leaders to grant SCLC demands. Groups of blacks fanned out across the city to integrate parks, lunch counters, bowling alleys. On July 20, however, a newly appointed federal judge granted the city an injunction against all demonstrations. Simultaneously, thousands of Ku Klux Klansmen gathered outside the city. Tension broke into angry rioting after a deputy sheriff brutally beat Mrs. Slater King in Camilla, Georgia. Mrs. King (no relation to Martin Luther) was the wife of an Albany civil rights leader. On the evening of July 24 a group gathered in Albany to protest the beating. Police moved in to break up the meeting. When they did, the long-suffering blacks of Albany reacted, just as King feared they might. Before long, thousands of demonstrators were battling police.

This outbreak of violence deeply distressed King. He had lost control of the movement; his nonviolent tactics had not worked. His first reaction was to pull back and avoid further demonstrations. The Kennedy administration in Washington was profoundly disturbed and embarrassed by events in Albany, but not enough to act. Scores of white northerners who had poured into the city to bolster the movement were preparing to leave as fall approached. The segregationists were holding firm. In September, with most white integrationists gone, they initiated selective revenge against local black leaders. Several churches were dynamited. Public facilities remained segregated or closed. The Albany movement had failed.

This setback represented a personal defeat for King. It resulted from poor planning, divided leadership, and inconclusive and uncoordinated tactics. Furthermore, he had failed to engage either national sympathy or, more important, federal support for his cause. He could either retreat or assault an even more dangerous citadel, Birmingham. It was a risk that threatened the whole movement, for by 1963, Birmingham had become a symbolic center of resistance to integration. The new Alabama governor, George Wallace, elected in 1962, had vowed undying opposition to integration. Birmingham's tough police had a leader pledged to enforce laws that rigidly separated both the public and private lives of Birmingham citizens. As King described it:

> Birmingham is probably the most thoroughly segregated city in the United States. Its ugly record of police brutality is known in every section of the country. Its unjust treatment of Negroes in the courts is a notorious reality. There have been more unsolved bombings of Negro homes and churches in Birmingham than any city in this nation. These are hard, brutal and unbelievable facts.

King decided to risk failure and violence. He and the SCLC worked closely with local leaders headed by the Reverend Fred Shuttlesworth. They decided that their movement should be clearly focused, well planned and financed, and designed to elicit maximum sympathy from northern liberals and the federal government. If the city used violence against demonstrators, this would attract outside attention and intervention.

King and the SCLC planned Project C (for confrontation) to be launched during Easter week to disrupt the season's sales. This assault on business was designed to force economic leaders in the city to negotiate with integrationists. Several hundred volunteers worked to train black Birmingham in nonviolent tactics. B-day (the first day of protest) had to be postponed until April 3 to avoid disrupting the local mayoral election. B-day began twelve hours after Albert Boutwell's victory at the polls.

At first, it appeared that Bull Connor might also play by the rules of nonviolence. During the first few days, demonstrations and sit-ins occurred without serious incident. Then on April 10 a local judge issued an injunction against all further demonstrations. King decided to break the law and suffer the consequences. In itself, this was an important turning point. Jail meant national attention. But more important, King crossed a threshold by defying a court order. Until now, he had respected such orders. His defiance represented a deeper attack on segregation and the legal structure that supported it.

On April 12, Good Friday, King and several volunteers set out on an illegal protest march. Connor and his police allowed them to proceed several blocks and then moved in for arrests. Connor arrested King and held him in solitary confinement. He was allowed no calls or visitors. In Atlanta, his wife waited anxiously for word that did not come. Anything was possible in Connor's jail. So she telephoned Wyatt Walker, one of the Birmingham leaders. Together they agreed that she should call the president.

Mrs. King's call to Kennedy forced the president's hand. While Kennedy had expressed sympathy for integration, he had done little to push it publicly. But pressure in the North was building for action. Press commentary around the world sharply criticized government inaction in the face of brutality. Mrs. King tried several times to reach the president at the White House, without success. Then she tried Vice President Johnson, but he too was absent. Finally, a sympathetic operator, sensing her desperation, suggested that she telephone the president's aide Pierre Salinger. He promised to notify Kennedy immediately. A short time later, Attorney General Robert Kennedy telephoned to promise his help. But he warned: "Of course, Birmingham is a very difficult place." Within fifteen minutes the phone rang again. It was King. He was safe.

King's eight days in the Birmingham jail were critical ones for him and for the fate of the integration movement. At first, he pondered the hope and despair of his situation. As he wrote: "You will never know the meaning of utter darkness until you have lain in such a dungeon, knowing that sunlight is streaming overhead and still seeing only darkness below."

What bothered King more, however, was the fate of the movement he headed. Had he led it also into darkness, violence, and disarray? Were his tactics of challenge, which brought out the bitterest attacks from segregationists, inevitably doomed? Did the violence of Birmingham indicate that the doors to integration might remain forever shut? Was he going too far; was he in danger of losing the vision of racial justice that appealed to whites?

This last question was posed to him by eight white Alabama clergymen on April 12. In their "Public Statement Directed to Martin Luther King, Jr.," they wrote: "We are now confronted by a series of demonstrations by some of our Negro citizens, directed and led in part by outsiders. We recognize the natural impatience of people who feel that their hopes are slow in being realized. But we are convinced that these demonstrations are unwise and untimely."

King received the statement while in solitary confinement and almost immediately began his response. At first, he penciled his thoughts in the margins of a newspaper. When this proved inadequate, he continued his reply on sheets of paper brought in by a friendly black guard. Finally, he secured a pad of legal paper from his attorney. When finished, he dated and titled it: April 16, 1963, "A Letter from Birmingham Jail."

King answered the three charges of the clergymen: that he and his organization were outsiders, that he should be patient, and that his tactics endangered the whole community. His reply was careful but passionate. King realized from the tone of their letter that the eight clergymen defined him and all blacks as being outside the community of equal citizens. Thus in his response, he tried to find the language and symbols that would locate a place for southern blacks in the community in which they had always lived but to which they had never belonged.

He bristled at the suggestion that he was an outsider. "We are," he said, "caught in an inescapable network of mutuality, tied to a single garment of destiny. Whatever affects one directly affects all indirectly. Never again can we afford to live with the narrow, provincial 'outside agitator' idea. Anyone who lives inside the United States can never be considered an outsider anywhere in this country."

As for the question of patience, King rejected the ministers' advice. "For years now," he recalled, "I have heard the word 'Wait!' It rings in the ear of every Negro with a piercing familiarity. This Wait has almost always meant 'Never.'" How long, he retorted, while African nations had emerged into political sovereignty could American blacks remain "smothering in an airtight cage of poverty in the midst of an affluent society."

King did acknowledge the risks of violence. But he argued that only "creative tension" could push the white majority into negotiation. Breaking the law—the unjust and illegal law of segregation—was a duty, he continued. "In no sense do I advocate evading or defying the law as the rabid segregationist would do. This would lead to anarchy. One who breaks an unjust law must do it openly, *lovingly*."

⊰⊱═⊙⊂═⊰⊱

If, as King believed, Birmingham represented the risk of failure and violent resistance from a closed community of bigotry, the march on Washington of August 1963 represented a chance to express, before a national audience, the vision of a new American community that King had sketchily defined in his Birmingham letter. The march, and King's dramatic speech there, represented a high point in the impulse to open America to all its citizens. It was so because he succeeded in making integration and equality for African Americans the very center of a new sort of patriotism.

King had always recognized the limitations of a southern movement and an all-black movement. He had long sought allies in the white community, among ministers, political liberals, and labor unions. His strategy was to force Americans to recognize southern segregation as a national problem. In part, this was because the federal government tolerated the special status of southern laws. The Democratic party allowed segregationists a veto over its presidential nominees as well as over civil rights laws. To break the tentacles of power that radiated out from the South, King had forced federal intervention in Montgomery and then in the bloody situation in Birmingham. But the problem also required a national vision. Change would not come without firm civil rights laws and some national manifestation of solidarity. These were the goals of the march planned for the nation's capital.

Yet this was no easy task, for government at all levels of American society was often divided between reluctant sympathy to civil rights and aggressive hostility. This divided attitude even characterized the federal government. In 1961, FBI chief J. Edgar Hoover instructed his agents to assemble a file on King that he hoped would discredit the black leader. At first, Hoover worried about some of King's radical supporters and advisers, but this concern soon faded, as Hoover began an intensive campaign to document King's extramarital affairs. King's sexual adventures threatened the movement. This second operation culminated in 1964 when the FBI sent incriminating tapes to King's home with an anonymous note urging him to commit suicide: "You had better take it [your life] before your filthy abnormal fraudulent self is bared to the nation." Thus King and his movement had to struggle at every level of society; there was no automatic refuge or sympathy anywhere.

At the center of national and international attention now (indeed, criticized for this by younger black leaders, who referred to him as "De Lawd"), King tried to turn the "creative tension" of Birmingham and its accompanying publicity into a broad national movement. President Kennedy had finally been forced to act—and not just to preserve peace in the South or to deal with a specific injustice. In early June the president spoke warmly of civil rights. New civil rights legislation in Congress was stalled by southern opposition. Birmingham and the rest of the South seemed to be a powder keg, ready to explode. Arrests of civil rights demonstrators were shooting upward, totaling almost 14,000 during the year. In his speech, Kennedy reiterated the proposition that King had enunciated so forcefully in his Birmingham letter:

> We are confronted primarily with a moral issue. It is as old as the Scriptures and is as clear
> as the American Constitution. The heart of the question is whether all Americans are to be

afforded equal rights and equal opportunities; whether we are going to treat our fellow Americans as we want to be treated.

Only passage of civil rights legislation, Kennedy concluded, could solve the crisis. This was the commitment that King had long sought. But was it enough? Could the movement relent and wait outside the legislative halls for progress? King believed it could not, and together with other leaders—the aging A. Philip Randolph of the Brotherhood of Sleeping Car Porters and representatives from most of the other civil rights organizations—he planned the march on Washington for late August. As first conceived, demonstrators were to engage in civil disobedience and sit-ins on Capitol Hill. But planners rejected this idea. The march would be a simple demonstration of solidarity for "jobs and freedom" to stir the nation's conscience.

Yet from the beginning, the march was controversial. The president refused to endorse it, although he agreed to meet with civil rights leaders afterward. His wariness only underscored the risks. If there was violence or, worse, if only a small crowd assembled, the damage might be irreparable. But other political leaders were not so hesitant as Kennedy. Mayor Robert Wagner of New York City spoke in favor of the march and proclaimed August 28 "Jobs and Freedom Day." Support from some labor unions was strong: the United Auto Workers (a major contributor to the civil rights movement) and the International Ladies Garment Workers Union (ILGWU) sent representatives. Church leaders and rabbis endorsed the march. The National Council of Churches even prepared box lunches for sale at low prices during the march.

Other leaders and groups were reluctant or even hostile. Former president Truman deplored the demonstration, although he approved its goals. Governor Wallace tried to convince the Southern Governors Conference to denounce the march. A number of newspapers across the country warned of a possible backlash. They proposed that black Americans seek redress in Congress and in the courts, not in the streets. At the fringe, Robert Welch of the right-wing John Birch Society accused King of aiming to create a "Soviet Negro Republic," headquartered in Atlanta, with himself as president.

In the face of uncertainties and attacks, planning continued. At first, response was weak. Silence from the urban black ghettos and the rural South numbed the organizers. Then suddenly, in August, the headquarters of the march was swamped with requests for information and help. Special trains and buses had to be hired. Car caravans were organized. Some set out early on foot. In Washington, predictions of attendance went up and up. More marshals had to be recruited to control the crowd. The demonstration would be enormous.

August 28 was bright and hot, the sort of Washington summer day when humidity and bright light make the stark white government buildings and monuments shimmer in the glare. Marchers began pouring into the city, into Union Station near the Capitol, and into the Fourteenth Street bus terminal. Cars and chartered buses jammed the side streets around Capitol Hill. Diesel fumes and dust stirred up by hundreds of demonstrators hung over the gathering crowd as it moved toward the staging area at the Washington Monument for the march to the Lincoln Memorial.

By one o'clock a crowd of over 200,000 had assembled around the Reflecting Pool and the grassy approaches to the memorial. Most carried banners proclaiming

"Freedom Now" or placards identifying the marcher with his or her hometown, church group, or labor union. The crowd had a look rarely seen at political gatherings in Washington: a sea of black faces set off by white shirts or made somber by the well-worn blue gabardine of Sunday-best suits. Sharecroppers, students, women with broad sun hats moved in an undulating mass. Fewer in number, but readily visible, were white faces, evidence of the racial solidarity that King had worked for.

The ceremonies began slowly. First, "The Star-Spangled Banner." Then a speech from Fred Shuttlesworth of Birmingham. Then words from Ralph Abernathy and greetings from 1,500 Americans abroad. Then a speech by A. Philip Randolph, who represented a venerable voice of continuity with old struggles and old battles. "We are," he proclaimed, "the advance guard of a massive moral revolution for jobs and freedom. This revolution reverberates throughout the land, touching every city, every town, every village where black men are segregated, oppressed, and exploited."

In the hot sun, the demonstrators shifted from foot to foot and swayed to catch the words carried out to them by loudspeakers. They had come to move and be moved, but so far the words had not done that. John Lewis, the new chairman of the Student Nonviolent Coordinating Committee, spoke angrily about the failure of government, the failure to achieve change. His remarks had been muffled by censorship: Patrick A. O'Boyle, the Catholic archbishop of Washington, had refused to appear at the march if Lewis directly attacked the Kennedy administration. But Lewis made his intent clear. Concerning the pending civil rights bill, he declared, "We support the bill with great reservations, for it is too little and too late." When he had finished, every black speaker shook his hand. Every white speaker on the platform ignored him.

As the speeches continued, some of the demonstrators began to drift back to their cars and buses. The march had been impressive, but they were tired or anxious to return home. Then the gospel singer Mahalia Jackson stood before the microphones. She began to sing an old hymn: "I Been 'Buked and I Been Scorned." As the words rolled out over the crowd, her familiar deep and resonant voice caught and stopped many of those who were departing:

> I'm gonna tell my Lord
> When I get home
> I'm gonna tell my Lord
> When I get home
> Just how long you've
> Been treating me wrong

When the echo of the song had died out, the crowd answered back, shouting, waving, screaming, moving tighter together around the memorial.

Then, finally, King rose to speak. When he mounted the rostrum, a burst of applause greeted him. He waited calmly for it to subside, showing no signs of fatigue and the late night he had spent finishing his speech.

He began by invoking the memory and language of Lincoln, and of the emancipation that had been frustrated by a century of racism and segregation: "Five score years ago a great American in whose symbolic shadow we stand today signed the Emancipation Proclamation." He continued:

THE MARCH ON WASHINGTON.   King addressed a huge crowd of civil rights supporters August 28, 1963. Standing on the steps of the Lincoln Memorial, he faced the Washington Monument, symbol of the foundation of the Republic, and the crowd roared approval as he proclaimed, "I have a dream." [Note that he is wearing religious garb.]

When the architects of our Republic wrote the magnificent words of the Constitution and the Declaration of Independence, they were signing a promissory note to which every American was to fall heir. This note was a promise that all men—yes, black men as well as white men—would be guaranteed the inalienable rights of life, liberty, and the pursuit of happiness.

King directed these words at every American, but particularly at white Americans. He mentioned the three most famous documents of American history: the Gettysburg Address, the Declaration of Independence, and the Constitution, all of which defined freedom. Yet none of them had extended freedom to all Americans. King was demanding the payment of an old debt.

He then spoke of the question of caution. Was it time to be tranquil, to quiet the voice of protest? King firmly rejected this possibility. He called for new alliances, reaching out to those white Americans who would help. But he also warned that blacks would never be satisfied while "our children are stripped of their adulthood and robbed of their dignity by signs stating 'For Whites Only.'" As a leader, he would not rest until "justice rolls down like waters and righteousness like a mighty stream." Then he urged, "Go back to Mississippi, go back to Alabama, go back to South Carolina, go back to Georgia, go back to Louisiana, go back to the slums and ghettos of our Northern cities, knowing that somehow this situation can and will be changed."

From the beginning, the crowd had listened, straining to catch each word as it swept through the loudspeaker system. Most were now standing. A few murmured their approval. He had them with him as he returned to his opening words: "I still have a dream. It is a dream deeply rooted in the American dream. I have a dream that one day this nation will rise up, live out the true meaning of its creed: 'We hold these truths to be self-evident, that all men are created equal.'"

King could have stopped then. The speech had been a great one, evoking a vision of hope and the fulfillment of American ideals. The crowd was ready to burst into applause and movement. But he struck deeper. He also had a personal dream to confess: that his own "four little children will one day live in a nation where they will not be judged by the color of their skin but by the content of their character." "I have a dream," he repeated, "that right there in Alabama little black boys and black girls will be able to join hands with little white boys and white girls as sisters and brothers." The crowd roared its approval.

"I have a dream today," he continued, moving out and beyond any specific reference to the civil rights movement or the march or his own family. "I have a dream," he continued, now quoting words of biblical prophecy from Isaiah 40:4:

> I have a dream that one day every valley shall be exalted, every hill and mountain shall be made low. The rough places will be made plain, and the crooked places will be made straight. And the glory of the Lord shall be revealed, and all flesh shall see it together.

THE FIRST LINE IN THE 1963 MARCH ON WASHINGTON. This group of men suggests the broad base of support organized by Martin Luther King, Jr.: religious, political, and union leaders; black and white Americans.

Every time he repeated the words "I have a dream," his voice rising, the crowd roared in response, moving with him as he revealed his vision. "I have a dream," he shouted again, this time quoting the words of the patriotic anthem "America" that someday "all of God's children will be able to sing with new meaning, 'My country, 'tis of thee, sweet land of liberty, of thee I sing.'"

As he finished, King wove these words into a final vision of America—an integrated America, in which the black experience would express the essence and meaning of the national experience:

> When we allow freedom to ring—when we let it ring from every city and every hamlet, from every state and every city, we will be able to speed up that day when all of God's children, black men and white men, Jews and Gentiles, Protestants and Catholics, will be able to join hands and sing in the words of the old Negro spiritual, "Free at last, Free at last, Great God a-mighty. We are free at last."

An Era of Promise

The civil rights movement that Martin Luther King, Jr., led in triumph to Washington in the summer of 1963 was, in some regards, the culmination of a very old process in American history. Previous groups, such as labor unions and ethnic groups, had demanded and achieved legitimacy in American society. Now after nearly a century of struggle, it was the turn of black Americans to win the rights that others had been granted. Although this struggle was much harder and more bitter than any that preceded it, it nevertheless succeeded. If this was not what Henry Luce, editor of *Time* magazine, meant when he predicted an "American Century" in 1941, it was, nonetheless, a stunning victory for the nation.

King's triumph was possible because of a political consensus that gradually developed during and after World War II. This agreement was based on three fundamental assumptions about the nature of American society: (1) that an expanding economy would make it possible for all groups to share in the material bounty of the nation; (2) that a fundamental political program could be defined that would satisfy the diverse interests in American society; and (3) that government should be a major instrument to achieve these goals of bounty and social harmony.

The origins of this postwar liberal vision lay in the New Deal. In the 1930s, Franklin D. Roosevelt used the federal government to protect millions of forgotten men and women from the hardships of depression. He built a remarkable political consensus to support his programs, a consensus that included farmers, Catholics, urban workers, the Solid South, and northern ethnic groups. Broad as this group was, however, it did not fully embrace American blacks.

In 1944, when Roosevelt delivered his State of the Union message—what he called his economic bill of rights—he spoke of rights for all Americans, regardless of race or creed. These included the right to food, clothing, education, and a useful job. They included the right of every family to a decent home, medical care, and support in times of misfortune or old age. But these were words with little force or meaning for African Americans. Indeed, between Roosevelt's enunciation of a new program of rights and the beginnings of the civil rights movement in the mid-1950s, traditional phrases about liberty and equality had first to acquire a new content. This was the point of Martin Luther King's speech; he created a new language of equality that really did include all citizens.

Had Congress enacted Roosevelt's economic rights with serious attention to racial, class, and ethnic equality, it would have initiated perhaps the greatest social revolution in American history. But legislators scarcely paid attention to Roosevelt's stirring suggestions. The Democratic majority in both houses had long since ceased to be a liberal majority. A coalition of Republicans and Solid South Democrats could, and did, veto any wide-ranging social legislation.

Yet Roosevelt's vision in his economic bill of rights, however seriously he intended it, was important. It promised a broad extension of the basic social programs of the 1930s. With its twin emphases on equality and inalienable social rights, it set an agenda that others, such as Martin Luther King, Jr., then only fifteen years old, would be able to seize upon and transform in the postwar period.

THE PEACETIME ECONOMY

Roosevelt's immediate plans for postwar society concentrated on rapid conversion to peacetime production. Controls enacted by Congress generally had a time limit triggered by the end of the war. In late 1944 and early 1945 the economy was set to return to civilian production. There was little momentum to continue New Deal reforms or extend social planning. Yet one piece of legislation, passed to reward soldiers for their combat service and to prevent their reentering the labor force too quickly, profoundly affected the social status of millions of Americans. This was the so-called GI Bill of Rights.

This program, enacted in the Servicemen's Readjustment Act of 1944, provided federal subsidies for college attendance and home buying. The federal government would pay tuition charges as well as a small living allowance to any serviceman with two or more years of duty. It offered low-interest mortgages for the purchase of houses and businesses. Veterans were also granted preference in federal and state employment. Together, the various federal and state programs to aid veterans amounted to a massive affirmative action plan that allowed millions of young men—men who might not otherwise have had the chance—to enter college, buy a house, or find a job in the public sector.

The GI Bill put millions of returning soldiers in school who otherwise might have joined the ranks of the unemployed. This, plus pent-up consumer demand for products that were scarce during the war, kept the economy booming. The favorable position of the United States in world trade also proved significant. Raw materials and energy supplies were cheap and easily available. Progress in aviation, television, and information systems, plus new inventions and materials, created whole new industries. These factors, along with constant federal intervention in the economy mandated by the Employment Act of 1946, guaranteed important gains in worker productivity, personal income, and gross national product.

What Roosevelt would have done to spread this bounty to the groups that did not yet share it will never be known, for he did not live to see the end of the war.

When the president announced he would seek reelection in 1944 for a fourth term, most voters fully expected him to serve four more years. In fact, he was already quite ill. Thus when he and the party leaders chose his running mate in 1944 they were, in effect, selecting the next president. Their choice, Harry S Truman, senator from Missouri, proved a controversial one. Truman's qualifications for the vice presidency rested principally on his political support. Labor, represented by the CIO's Sidney Hillman, agreed that he was acceptable. As a border-state senator, he could count on backing from southern Democrats. He also had a good reputation for his clear-headed and tough investigation of war industries. Most significant, his leading competitors, including the current vice president, Henry Wallace, all had serious liabilities.

TRUMAN'S FIRST ADMINISTRATION

Like any vice president who graduates to the presidency in a crisis, Truman's first problem in the spring of 1945 was to establish command of the office. Although he pledged to pursue Roosevelt's policies, he did not. Nor could he. He lacked Roosevelt's consummate political skill. Moreover, Roosevelt had not really defined a postwar policy except in the vaguest way. So Truman was on his own.

Much of what Truman did during the eight years of his presidency was dictated by his attempts to find and secure a political constituency. He had to hold on to the coalition that Roosevelt had assembled during the 1930s and perhaps try to extend it, particularly to strengthen it among African Americans, who had migrated to northern cities during the war in large numbers. Inevitably, he had to compromise among the conflicting interests of this coalition.

Like Roosevelt, Truman planned a rapid reconversion to peacetime production. In the last months of the war, he canceled hundreds of defense contracts. Only two days after V-J (Victory over Japan) Day, he modified controls over prices, wages, and raw materials. In November 1945 he terminated control of wage hikes exercised by the National War Labor Board. By the summer of 1946 he had reluctantly eliminated many controls over consumer prices. When the Republicans gained control of Congress in the elections of 1946, he eliminated the remaining price controls.

Deregulation of labor controls caused economic stress and brought serious political headaches to the new administration, which counted on unions for support. During the war, organized labor had rapidly increased its membership from 10 million in 1941 to 14 million in 1945. Wage increases were modest during the war, but overtime and fringe benefits pushed up earnings. After the war, labor sought large increases, and management was just as determined to prevent them. The result was an outbreak of strikes as substantial as any in the twentieth century. Walkouts at General Motors and in the oil and steel industries involved hundreds of thousands of workers. In April 1946 the United Mine Workers went out. Finally, when railroad workers threatened a strike in May, Truman seized the railroads.

This rash of strikes fueled public hostility to unions and energized the successful Republican congressional campaign of 1946. When it met in 1947, the new Republican-controlled Congress pledged to curb New Deal labor legisla-

tion. During the first four months of the session, members submitted seventy bills on this single issue. Finally, the Labor Committee chairmen in each house hammered out a compromise law. On the Senate side, conservative Robert A. Taft of Ohio provided leadership. In the House of Representatives, this was done by Fred A. Hartley, Jr., of New Jersey. The resulting Taft-Hartley Act outlawed the closed shop, in which every worker was required to join a union before employment. It required unions to file annual financial reports with the Labor Department. Right-to-work laws passed by states (that forbade requiring workers to join unions once on the job) were legalized, and the president was granted power to interrupt strikes with an eighty-day cooling-off period.

Passed by Congress on June 9, 1947, the bill went to Truman for his signature. Fully aware of the political consequences, he returned the bill with a sharply worded veto message. He denounced the legislation as contrary to the "national policy of economic freedom." It was, he continued, "a clear threat to the successful working of our democratic society." Congress thought so little of his arguments that it overrode his veto the following day. The bill became law.

In practice, the Taft-Hartley Act was not what either side claimed. It neither seriously limited the activities of organized labor nor destroyed democracy. In some ways, it represented the basis for a more permanent peace between management and labor, for while it trimmed the powers of unions, it certainly did not seriously limit them. However, the political fight surrounding the act helped overcome suspicions of Truman in the union movement.

Truman's vigorous defense of labor in his veto message was one key to his successful 1948 reelection campaign. Another was his overture to black voters. Trying to hold on to and expand Roosevelt's electoral coalition, Truman realized that he needed the support of African Americans. The steps he took to win their votes were small but significant.

Following the Republican victory in 1946, Truman issued an executive order creating a special Civil Rights Committee headed by Charles E. Wilson, president of the General Electric Company. Other members included representatives from labor organizations and the NAACP. The group was charged with writing proposals to improve the lives of American blacks. Several months later, on October 29, 1947, it submitted its suggestions. These included home rule for the largely black city of Washington, D.C., an end to racial segregation in the U.S. armed forces, protection of voting rights in state primary elections, an end to restrictive covenants in housing sales, a permanent commission on civil rights, and equal treatment in and access to facilities in interstate commerce.

Truman was certainly not prepared to push ahead on each one of these demands. Indeed, it took twenty years, the rise of new leaders like Martin Luther King, Jr., and a social convulsion of extraordinary proportions to realize most of them. But the president did include some of this agenda in his 1948 civil rights message to Congress. And by July 1948 he had started desegregation of the armed services, gradually phasing out all-black combat units. (It was not until October 1954 that the last segregated army unit was abolished.)

THE ELECTION OF 1948

Truman's initiative in civil rights earned him support from black leaders and from Democratic liberals, but it splintered his allegiances in the South. Bedrock southern conservatives revolted against his nomination in 1948. When northern liberals placed a strong civil rights plank in the party platform, a group of "Dixiecrats" bolted the party, met in Birmingham, Alabama, to found the States' Rights party, and nominated Governor Strom Thurmond of South Carolina for president.

The Republicans helped Truman hold on to what remained of his coalition by presenting a distinctly conservative alternative. Their nominee in 1948, Governor Thomas Dewey of New York, a candidate in 1944 against Roosevelt, had earned national praise for his attacks on organized crime and was known as a staunch conservative and a foe of the New Deal. As a cam-

paigner, however, he left much to be desired. Dewey lacked the visible energy, humor, and humanity of Truman. The president's campaign was also aided by a splinter party to the left of the Democratic party. A new Progressive party nominated Henry Wallace, one-time vice president and then Truman's secretary of commerce. Running on a program criticizing Truman's cold war foreign policy and with Communist party support, Wallace actually deflected criticism away from the president. Truman could accurately claim that he represented the political center of the Democratic party, and perhaps the nation.

Truman relished nothing so much as a good fight. Once Congress had adjourned from a special session called during the summer, Truman began an energetic campaign trip by train across the nation. Punching away at the overconfident Republicans, he stressed the continuities between his presidency and the New Deal. The results of the November election proved how successful this strategy had been. He won 24 million votes to Dewey's 21 million. He had held the New Deal coalition together despite some defections in the South. He had also helped lay the political groundwork for federal support for civil rights.

TRUMAN'S SECOND ADMINISTRATION

Truman began his second term in office with the promise of swift and extensive social reform. His rousing address in Congress on January 15, 1949, called for a "Fair Deal." His words and his program echoed many of Roosevelt's 1944 ideas. He began by defining the purpose of government: to use the nation's wealth "for the benefit of all." This definition implied intervention in the economy to maintain healthy production and regulation to ensure a fair distribution of goods and services. Specifically, Truman wanted a rise in taxes, repeal of the Taft-Hartley Act, a higher minimum wage, farm price supports, an increase in Social Security benefits and expansion of the system, a national prepaid health insurance system, and government construction of more low-cost public housing units.

But the president failed to translate his surprise victory in November into legislative success. Despite a Democratic majority returned to the Senate and the House, the party remained divided over reforms. Medical insurance and Truman's agricultural program fell to intensive lobbying by doctors and farm groups. Repeal of the Taft-Hartley Act could not attain a majority, and the claims of racial minorities were ignored despite the promises of the civil rights plank of the Democratic platform. Thus although civil rights had entered the legislative agenda, it had not yet become a compelling part of it. Only in the extension of Social Security coverage and in housing did the president achieve major successes. The 1950 amendments to the Social Security Act of 1935 extended coverage and raised benefits. The Housing Act of 1949 mandated construction of 810,000 low-cost units.

Spy convictions and Senator McCarthy's anticommunist crusade also helped weaken Truman in the last two years of his administration and slow the momentum for reform. Nothing went well for the president. The war in Korea touched off a constitutional crisis when the commander of the U.S. forces, General Douglas MacArthur,

PRESIDENT TRUMAN, during his "whistlestop campaign of 1948." This old-fashioned style worked one more time, but the Democratic coalition that elected him was seriously strained and the railroads were already in severe decline.

openly criticized Truman's policy of limited warfare in 1951. He wished to pursue the North Koreans to defeat rather than accept a restricted definition of American goals. In effect, MacArthur challenged the power of the president to set policy. As commander in chief of the armed forces, Truman had no choice but to remove the popular general if he wished to maintain civilian control of the military. In Congress, his Fair Deal failed to generate support. Scandals and accusations of communist influence surrounded the Democratic party. Clearly, Truman had become a serious liability.

THE EISENHOWER YEARS

THE SHIFT TO THE SUBURBS

The disintegration of Truman's support came partly from opposition to his leadership and partly from shifts in social structure and demography that began after the war. New Deal rhetoric began to lose some of its power to galvanize voters, as memories of the depression faded and the new affluence of the 1950s took hold. Much of this affluence became visible in the suburbs that sprang up around cities. Of course, American cities had long had suburbs, but traditionally these were built out along commuter rail lines. In the 1940s and 1950s, suburbs were connected to central cities by means of new highways. Because of available loans and favorable tax laws, it was often cheaper to buy a new house than to refurbish or even rent an existing urban dwelling. As the suburbs proliferated, they tended to depend less on the central city and more on their own booming economies. In effect, suburbs had begun to compete seriously with central cities for industry, jobs, population, and political power.

The suburbs won a quick victory. After the war, most cities lost jobs in manufacturing and trade while gaining modestly in service industries. Employment in all three of these categories soared in the suburbs. By 1960 the central cities had lost almost 300,000 jobs. They were also left with diminished tax bases. Responding to this

shrinking opportunity, increasing numbers of affluent or aspiring whites abandoned the central cities. Their places were taken by African Americans and Hispanics. In 1950 the black population of central cities was about 12 percent of the total. Twenty years later, the percentage had doubled. (But the much smaller proportion of blacks in the suburbs remained about the same.) Political power followed affluence to the suburbs.

If the predominant image of the early 1950s was suburban life, the focus of that image was the family. Newspapers, magazines, radio, movies, and the new medium of television extolled the virtues of family life. Behind this publicity lay a surprising change in American demographics. After World War II, divorce rates fell sharply and the marriage rate (the percentage of eligible persons who in fact marry) rapidly increased. So too did the birthrate, which shot up from 20.4 births per 1,000 population in 1945 to 25.0 per 1,000 in 1955. This increase reversed decades of decline in the number of children born to American families.

Added to the family-centered and child-centered focus in popular culture and social mores was an emphasis on leisure living and informality inspired by California. During the war, the federal government had invested huge amounts of capital in industries there. By 1945, 9 percent of all federal employees worked in the state. And this was only part of the boom. By the mid-1960s, California's population increased from 5 to 10 percent of the U.S. total. For those who did not live there, the state remained the most popular place to visit. Of all the states in the Union, California exhibited an accelerated and exaggerated version of contemporary social trends. It was the most urbanized (and suburbanized) state. It had the most extensive freeway system. It had a huge modern aircraft and defense industry. Its lifestyles were the subject of countless Hollywood films and television shows, as well as the visual backdrop for most commercials. In a sense, California was America's future and a symbol of the new postwar economy and culture.

THE ELECTION OF 1948

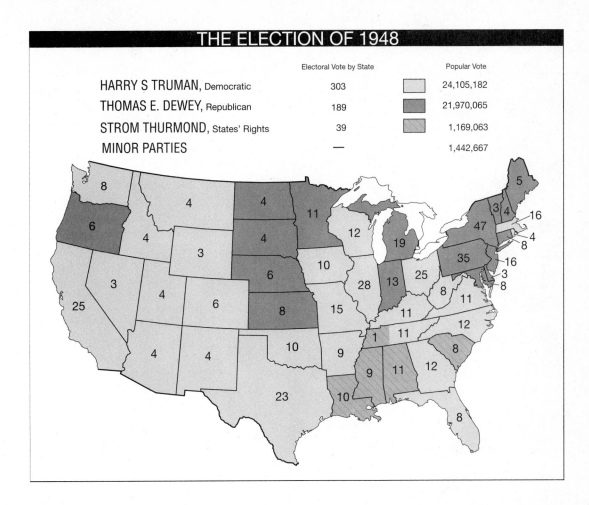

	Electoral Vote by State		Popular Vote
HARRY S TRUMAN, Democratic	303		24,105,182
THOMAS E. DEWEY, Republican	189		21,970,065
STROM THURMOND, States' Rights	39		1,169,063
MINOR PARTIES	—		1,442,667

That new economy and culture can best be understood in a single word: consumerism. While there is nothing new about an economy of abundance that depends upon widespread purchase and credit, the United States was transformed by a huge increase in the quantity and nature of this consumption. In fact, the economy of the postwar period can best be understood by paying attention to the increasing numbers of Americans who clamored to enter this marketplace and how they spent their money. This may be seen in the automobile industry during the 1950s. In order to snare an ever larger market for cars, Ford, General Motors, and Chrysler (and Packard, Hudson, Nash, and Studebaker) radically changed model designs every year, creating extraordinary-looking vehicles with garish colors, huge chrome breastworks, and fins. These automobiles, in turn, inspired a huge spin-off of other consumer goods and services: road building, drive-in restaurants and theaters, shopping malls, and service stations. To enter this marketplace as equal participants was the goal of every group: union members, recent immigrants, and African Americans.

THE ELECTION OF 1952

Some of these social and economic changes began to register first in the 1952 election. The Republicans' vice presidential candidate, Richard M.

only 2 simple controls
TURN IT ON ⊙ - ⊙ SELECT STATION - *that's all!*
BRAND-NEW and BEAUTIFUL CONSOLE gives life-size pictures at lower cost!

Motorola TELEVISION

THIS ELEGANT NEW TELEVISION SET was disguised to look like a piece of living room furniture. But the boy turning up the volume shows by his costume that television is his own window to an outside world of imaginary dramas and endless consumer delights.

Nixon, was a congressman and senator from California. The mood of the electorate tended toward conservatism, reflecting in part the new priorities of suburban life. More important, the Democratic coalition reestablished by Truman in 1948 began to show some signs of age and strain, as the weight of political power shifted away from the central cities to the suburbs, and from the old industrial East to the new industrial West.

Both sides bitterly contested the 1952 election and, consequently, issues were sometimes lost in the flurry of flimsy and preposterous charges and countercharges. Republican chances appeared very good, but so had they in 1948. However, this time the party's choice of a candidate—General Dwight David Eisenhower—proved to be enormously popular.

Born in 1890, "Ike" grew up in Abilene, Kansas. From the time he entered the U.S. Military Academy in 1911, Eisenhower's life was defined by the army. Mischievous, handsome, and athletic as a student, he rose, rank by rank, to become commander of the allied armies in Europe during World War II.

Eisenhower's lack of civilian experience cost him very little in his political career. His position in the army required the exercise of every skill needed by a politician. Furthermore, he apparently owed no political debts. In fact, he had been approached earlier by the Democrats seeking him as a candidate. Thus when he declared his willingness to run as a Republican in 1952, he quickly became the front-running candidate. To heal any breaches in the party between moderates and conservatives, Eisenhower offered the vice presidency to Richard Nixon, a man known for his hard-line anticommunist views and popular with conservatives. The party adopted a relatively moderate platform, but the rhetoric of the campaign charged treason in high places and promised to crusade against communism, corruption, and the war in Korea.

For the Democrats, the choice was not easy. Truman realized his unpopularity but still wanted to play kingmaker. Adlai Stevenson, governor of Illinois, secured Truman's favor and the nomination, but he had an almost impossible task. He had to endorse the previous twenty years of Democratic rule, yet declare his independence from Truman. He also had to hold on to the Democratic coalition that was increasingly divided on such questions as civil rights. Unfortunately for him, Stevenson's personality became an issue. Witty and elegant in his speeches, he earned loyal support from liberals. But to conservatives he appeared to be the incarnation of the suspect eastern intellectual lambasted by McCarthy.

Despite a momentary shock when it appeared that Richard Nixon might have to withdraw because of charges that he had operated an illegal slush fund of campaign donations, the Republicans stayed on course. Nixon convinced most critics that the charges were groundless. Af-

DIAPER SERVICE IN CALIFORNIA. This obviously staged photograph is a picture of a 1950s dream: a bungalow project, a crowd of mothers and children, and diaper service at every door to suggest that it was all just beginning.

ter his famous explanatory "Checkers speech" (named for the pet dog his daughter had received as a gift), Nixon deflected criticism from the issue and convinced Eisenhower he was not a liability to the ticket. When Eisenhower promised to go to Korea, implying he would end the war, the outcome was all but decided. On November 4, Eisenhower won a landslide victory: 33 million votes to 27 million for Stevenson. The voters also swept Republican majorities into the House and Senate for the first time since 1946.

EISENHOWER'S FIRST ADMINISTRATION

Eisenhower's concept of government was a conservative one. He believed in balanced federal budgets and minimal intervention in the econ-

omy. But he did not seek to undo New Deal reforms. He hoped, instead, to create a harmonious partnership between business and government that would generate prosperity and opportunity. In large measure he succeeded, except in the area of civil rights. Within American society, the forces that touched off the Montgomery boycott and brought Martin Luther King, Jr., to national prominence proved to be irresistible. Over the rest of the world, the rise of former colonies to independence and the wholesale liberation of formerly subjected peoples brought issues of racial equality to the bargaining tables of international relations. Increasingly in the contest between capitalism and communism, the United States could ill afford to persist in old ways of racial injustice, for at least in part, the

THE BABY BOOM: TOTAL BIRTHS AND RATE PER 1,000 POPULATION

	Number of Births	Births per 1,000 Population
1935	2,377,000	18.7
1940	2,559,000	19.4
1945	2,858,000	20.4
1950	3,632,000	24.1
1955	4,097,000	25.0
1960	4,258,000	23.7
1965	3,760,000	19.4
1970	3,731,000	18.4
1975	3,144,000	14.6
1980	3,612,000	15.9
1984	3,697,000	15.7

Source: U.S. Department of Commerce, Bureau of the Census, Statistical Abstract of the United States, 1986 (Washington, D.C.: Government Printing Office, 1985) p. 56.

outcome of that contest lay in winning support in the Third World of black and brown peoples. By the beginning of the Kennedy administration in 1961, such issues had reached the flash point. Would American society finally accept its black members as equal participants? Or would the civil rights movement end in confrontation and violence?

Eisenhower's first priority on assuming the presidency was to defuse the anger and hostility in American society that his election had tapped. The president had to fend off Joseph McCarthy, whose attacks had become progressively wilder. At first, Eisenhower treated McCarthy with caution, although he personally disliked the senator's extremism. Eisenhower had caved in to pressure during the campaign and shied away from defending former Secretary of State George Marshall, an old friend, who was under attack by McCarthy. Once in office, he still refused to challenge the senator, at least in

public. When McCarthy attacked "reds" in the army in the summer of 1954, Congress, not the president, finally decided he had gone too far and voted to censure him.

On the issue of Korea, the new president did act decisively. Shortly after the election, in December 1952, Eisenhower visited Korea as promised. He renewed talks with North Korea and the People's Republic of China, and by summer, he had achieved an armistice. Thorny questions of repatriating soldiers were finally resolved. After three years of bitter struggle, peace was restored in 1953, but victory had eluded both sides.

In defense policy, the president developed what he called the "New Look" strategy to replace the large and expensive conventional military buildup pushed by Truman. This policy projected small, efficient defense budgets, allowing Eisenhower to redeem a campaign pledge to keep budgets balanced. Production would concentrate on sophisticated nuclear weapons and delivery systems in a strategy that would also provide deterrence against attacks from the Soviet Union.

The New Look plan had other implications. It concentrated on rearmament and self-defense for European nations, including West Germany. It did help the president maintain relatively low federal spending, with a balanced budget in three years and minimal deficits in two other years. It also enabled Eisenhower and Secretary of State John Foster Dulles to declare a policy of "massive retaliation." By this, Dulles meant that the United States would employ its vastly superior nuclear weapons arsenal against the Soviet Union in case of aggression.

Dulles's grand strategy based on U.S. nuclear superiority, however, had two flaws. First, it proved to be part bluster. The verbal commitment to "roll back" communism talked about by Republicans in 1952 turned out to be a hollow promise; twice, the United States stood by while the Soviets crushed popular movements in Eastern Europe. Second, it was a policy that had

IKE IN KOREA. President-elect Dwight Eisenhower toured Korea in December 1952. His campaign for the presidency succeeded, in part, because of promises that he would be able to end the war quickly.

minimal effect on turbulent Third World countries. Policies aimed at securing formal alliances against the Soviet Union had little to offer millions of people struggling to cast off colonialism, military dictatorships, and corrupt oligarchies. When revolutions occurred in the Third World, the American response was often worried and hostile. Lacking a flexible view of the dynamics of social and economic change, the United States frequently intervened secretly to retard or even overthrow such movements. Thus throughout the Eisenhower years, the Central Intelligence Agency (CIA) carried on clandestine operations in such countries as Iran, Guatemala, and Vietnam.

If some Republican conservatives hoped to undo the New Deal welfare state, they were not heartened by the president's domestic program. Eisenhower did agree to legislation that lowered farm parity supports from 90 percent to 70 percent on most commodities. These price supports

were designed to guarantee a minimum living standard to farmers, but cutting them slightly did not in any way constitute a return to free-market competition. Two other programs actually increased federal spending: a Social Security Act in 1954, which extended coverage to self-employed workers, and a new public housing program. In May 1954 Eisenhower signed a bill to construct the St. Lawrence Seaway, a waterway that would join the Great Lakes to the Atlantic Ocean via the St. Lawrence River. Two years later, the president signed an act to fund a system of more than 40,000 miles of interstate highways. It was the largest public works project in American history.

Inadvertently, Eisenhower initiated activism in an area where he had hoped to avoid change. Early in his administration, the president appointed California governor Earl Warren to be chief justice of the United States. But he did not anticipate that Warren would lead the

Supreme Court into a period of social activism that would help redefine and broaden government guarantees of equality and civil rights. The Warren Court's most important decision came quickly, in the case of *Brown* v. *Board of Education* (1954). This unanimous decision revised the language of American democracy. Citing the evidence of experts, the Court rejected the prevailing and still legal school segregation on the grounds that any separation causes psychological damage. In addition, the *Brown* decision ratified the commitment of a growing number of Americans to equal rights. Like the GI Bill, it emphasized equality of education as the means to achieve equal citizenship.

For integrationists, the Supreme Court decision fixed their tactics. They could now confront local and state segregationists knowing that ultimately they could depend on the courts. Certainly this did not eliminate the risks they ran, but it did help determine the outcome of the struggle. This was the strategy that Martin Luther King, Jr., applied in the Montgomery boycott two years later and in Birmingham in 1963.

Justice Warren's decision put Eisenhower in a difficult position. The president did not wish to push desegregation, although he had agreed to integration of the armed forces. During the remainder of his years in office, he refused to speak in favor of school desegregation and never affirmed his agreement—moral or otherwise—with the *Brown* decision. This excessive caution and lack of leadership encouraged some white southerners to believe that the inevitable would never occur. But they were wrong. Even Eisenhower was finally forced to act. In 1957 he signed a weak but significant civil rights bill. More important, when Governor Orval Faubus of Arkansas tried to stop the integration of Little Rock Central High School in September 1957, the president was obliged to intervene. Faubus disobeyed a court order and installed the National Guard in front of the school to prevent black students from entering. After serious rioting, sparked by the governor's

inflammatory remarks, Eisenhower dispatched federal troops to the city and appealed for calm. It was a small step, taken reluctantly. But it had enormous implications for the future pattern of civil rights agitation, for it put the federal government publicly on the side of the integrationists.

THE ELECTION OF 1956 AND THE DAWN OF THE YOUTH CULTURE

Even though he delegated a great many tasks, Eisenhower's congenial and low-key administration focused attention and power on his own leadership. Thus his sudden heart attack on September 24, 1955, pointed up how fragile his administration was. He improved rapidly but then suffered a serious attack of ileitis in the spring of 1956, which required intestinal surgery. During neither illness was the president completely incapacitated, but attention nevertheless focused on Vice President Nixon. Viewing him with suspicion, some party regulars talked openly of a new vice presidential candidate in 1956. But speculation quickly fizzled, and the Republicans renominated Nixon along with Eisenhower.

The Democrats turned once again to Adlai Stevenson, who then allowed the convention to select the vice presidential candidate. Their choice was Estes Kefauver of Tennessee, a liberal senator with a reputation for racket and crime investigation. But he was unpopular with party bosses, whom he had offended in his investigations.

Another leading (but unsuccessful) candidate for vice president was John Fitzgerald Kennedy, senator from Massachusetts. Kennedy's rise to national attention in the late 1950s signaled the beginnings of a political and cultural transformation that came to fruition in the early 1960s. This new politics emphasized youth and activism, reflecting important changes in American lifestyles.

Beginning in the middle and late 1950s, American culture exhibited changes that began to

CENTRAL HIGH SCHOOL IN LITTLE ROCK, ARKANSAS. The airborne troops, sent to ensure integration, watch as a few African-American students are escorted through a jeering mob of white students.

disrupt the conservative, family-oriented assumptions of the immediate postwar period. The suburban culture that only a few years earlier had seemed to settle permanently on American society suddenly showed flaws. Beyond the books and articles that now criticized the smugness and conformity of the suburbs, many suburban children were defying their parents' values. These young people absorbed a new youth culture that differentiated them seriously from their elders. While it too exhibited strong elements of conformism—its customs were organized around rituals of romance, "going steady," and marriage—the new youth culture also had a more restless side, reflected in the emergence of new popular heroes such as movie stars James Dean, Marlon

Brando, and Natalie Wood. Dean, in particular, in such films as *Rebel Without a Cause* (1955), captured a mood that rejected the preselected social and sexual roles for youth. His sensitive and emotional acting challenged a stereotyped postwar image of the American male as a military figure complete with crew cut.

Also of immense importance to the burgeoning youth culture was rock 'n' roll, a new popular music that had sprung out of America's urban black ghettos. With dramatic and direct sensuality, this music expressed feelings of love, hate, and other emotions in ways that delighted teenagers and appalled their parents, teachers, and religious leaders. Although groups of white artists capitalized on the success and energy of the new sound, its creative origins in the black experience were never far from the surface. Moreover, with the appearance of Elvis Presley, the new music absorbed energy and inspiration from a long tradition of country music.

The mass media played a crucial role in developing and popularizing this distinctive new youth culture. Magazines such as *Seventeen* informed teenage girls of changing styles and customs. Recorded music became available to almost every young person because of the mass marketing of long-playing plastic records and because of a dramatic growth in radio stations aimed at the youth market. Hollywood films, once produced for the entire family, increasingly targeted specific audience segments, and often the most lucrative of these seemed to be youth. Consequently, film companies produced scores of movies in the late 1950s featuring delinquency and rock 'n' roll, seen by teenagers packed into the drive-in theaters that dotted the suburbs.

In a more subtle way, this generation of teenagers (the first suburban generation and the older brothers and sisters of the postwar baby boomers) seemed adrift and in search of belief. Many of them, although they could not vote, were attracted by John Kennedy, with his youthful political style and his glamorous wife. They were not as hesitant as their elders to face a new world of changing social and racial relations.

ACTOR JAMES DEAN had a brief but brilliant screen career before his fatal auto accident in 1955. Dean evoked a good deal of sympathy from teenagers for his roles of anguished and misunderstood youth.

But in 1956 the political stage still belonged to the moderate Republicans, and Eisenhower and Nixon won a dramatic victory, garnering 35.5 million votes to Stevenson and Kefauver's 26 million. This endorsement of Eisenhower's administration did not extend to Congress, where the Democrats held on to majorities in both houses. It seemed that the American public wanted moderation at the presidential level and continued activism in Congress.

EISENHOWER'S SECOND ADMINISTRATION

Despite his great personal victory in the election of 1956, Eisenhower faced serious problems in the remainder of his presidential years. Beginning in 1957 and extending into 1958, a serious recession gripped the economy. Unemployment rose from about 4 percent to 7 percent, and the gross national product fell back by about 1 percent. Eisenhower refused to apply federal stimuli, and he rejected calls for a tax cut or public works projects. He insisted that the best policy was to allow the economy to correct itself. This stance, added to an influence-peddling scandal that forced the White House Chief of Staff, Sherman Adams, to quit, hurt Republicans in the 1958 congressional elections. After November, the Democrats controlled the House by 283 seats to 153 and the Senate by 64 to 34. Then, on November 26, the president suffered a mild stroke. He recovered quickly but was left with a slight speech impediment.

Facing a revived Democratic party that claimed to have uncovered a "bomber gap" in 1956 and a public that was shocked when the Soviet Union launched *Sputnik*, the first successful space satellite, in October 1957, Eisenhower had to struggle to maintain his modest defense budget strategy. Pressure to increase defense spending and invest in huge civil defense programs came from all sides. But Eisenhower gave little ground. He knew that the Soviet missile and defense program was limited, but he could not say so in public without revealing secret spy sources. He did, however, step up funding for space programs and created the National Aeronautics and Space Administration (NASA) in 1958. In September 1958 he signed the National Defense Education Act, which provided about $1 billion in loans and scholarships for the study of mathematics, the sciences, and foreign languages.

In the last two years of his administration, Eisenhower revived attempts to negotiate with the Soviets. After the new Soviet premier, Nikita Khrushchev, took office in March 1958, he announced a suspension of open-air nuclear testing. The United States followed suit in late summer. Eisenhower's most astute move was an invitation to the Russian leader to visit the United States in the fall of 1959. Khrushchev and his party toured the country, visiting farms, cities, and Disneyland in California. Final negotiations at Camp David, Maryland, set a spring summit meeting for Paris in 1960. The Soviet premier's trip had been controversial, touching off scattered demonstrations, but he impressed many Americans with his energy and self-confidence.

Despite its possibilities, the opportunity for rapprochement with the USSR was lost. Shortly before the Paris conference in the spring of 1960, the Soviets announced the downing of an American U-2 aerial reconnaissance plane deep inside their territory. Eisenhower's secret source of information had been revealed. On May 9, one week before the summit meeting, Eisenhower accepted responsibility for the overflight. When the conference began, Khrushchev seemed determined to disrupt it, demanding a personal apology from the president. When Eisenhower refused, the Soviet premier left Paris, and negotiations ended.

Perhaps all of these troubles sobered Eisenhower's thinking. As he left office in 1961, he delivered an address to the nation that was more warning than farewell. He underscored the basic themes of his administration. He had tried to keep defense spending down. He had wanted to avoid acrimonious and divisive issues such as civil rights. He had hoped that a stable economy would satisfy those who preferred quick social change. But now he feared a push for larger budgets, more social legislation, and an adventurous foreign policy. He warned the nation of a military-industrial complex and a technological power elite that might destroy American democracy:

> In the councils of government, we must guard against the acquisition of unwarranted influence, whether sought or unsought, by the military-industrial complex. The potential for the disastrous rise of misplaced power exists and will persist. We must never let the weight of this combination endanger our liberties or democratic processes.

This final cautionary statement about a defense establishment growing out of control had little effect on the exuberant young politicians about to take office. It seemed misplaced and excessively conservative. The day belonged to a new generation of leaders, to the Kennedys and the Kings. They were determined to face with new strategies some of the social and economic questions that had been gathering attention during the last eight years.

THE KENNEDY YEARS

THE RENEWED PROMISE

In November 1960, American voters chose a president who exemplified change and action. But John F. Kennedy defeated Richard Nixon by only a slim margin. At first, the action he proposed aimed at ending the slump in economic growth of the late 1950s and the impasse in foreign relations that Eisenhower had reached. But the new administration quickly became the focus for social forces that were transforming American society. Young, photogenic, with a richly accented voice, Kennedy radiated self-assurance. As a Catholic of Irish origins, he personified an era of rising expectations and growing confidence among groups formerly defined as being outside the mainstream of American politics. Together with more and more Americans, he believed that government could bring the nation a fuller and more satisfying life. Government could help correct the injustices of the past and fulfill the aspirations of the present.

Kennedy was simultaneously a tough-minded practical politician and a man of legend. The myths that surrounded him came in part from his wealth and his highly publicized accomplishments. In part they were inspired by his heroism in the Navy during World War II. The second son of Joseph Kennedy, an Irish Catholic millionaire who was a major contributor to the Democratic party, John grew up to live out the ambitions of his father. Able to move easily and gracefully in the public eye, he won the acclaim and political power that had eluded his father.

Kennedy's nomination and election in 1960 represented a departure in American poli-

tics, and it symbolized the growing political importance of groups once held at arm's length in presidential politics. He was the first Roman Catholic to be elected president—resolving an issue heavily debated in some sections of the country. Some Protestants, like the leadership of the 9-million-member Southern Baptist Convention, opposed him because of his faith. But his extraordinary proportion of Catholic votes (81 percent) neutralized most of this opposition.

The Catholic issue was just the first of many obstacles to Kennedy's nomination and victory. He also had to satisfy the various constituents of the Democratic party: liberals like Eleanor Roosevelt, labor leaders like Walter Reuther of the United Auto Workers, politicos like Harry Truman, and southern conservatives. At best this road was tortuous, but Kennedy managed to neutralize his most serious opponents. His record as senator from Massachusetts had not been particularly distinguished, but he made up for this weakness with political attractiveness and energy. Labor was reluctant to support him at first because of his tenacity in investigating the Teamsters Union for corruption. Liberals wondered aloud why he had never opposed Joseph McCarthy, a friend of his father, Joseph Kennedy. Yet the political organization he built and the support he gathered helped swing the party to him and create an electoral majority.

During the campaign, Kennedy had pledged to get the American economy moving again. This meant, primarily, attacking the current recession, with its high unemployment and low productivity. Like Eisenhower, Kennedy could have waited for natural market forces to pull the economy out of its lethargy. But he had promised action. Moreover, a major element among his advisers subscribed to the general theories of the British economist John Maynard Keynes. They believed that the federal government should, as required, intervene in the economy to expand or contract expenditures. These fiscal measures, based on enlarging or shrinking the federal budget in relation to tax revenues, might temporarily increase budget deficits, but

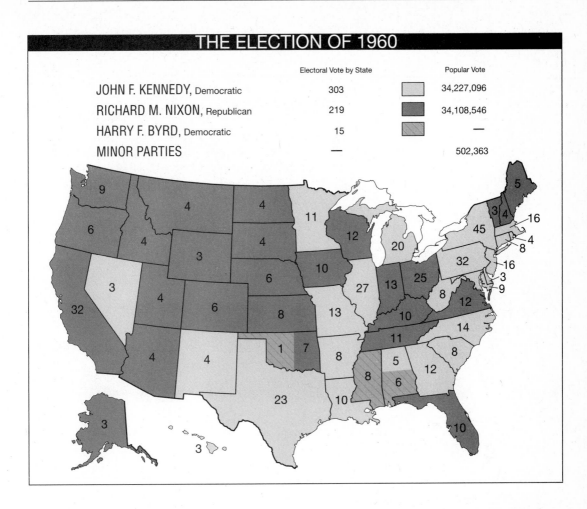

THE ELECTION OF 1960

	Electoral Vote by State		Popular Vote
JOHN F. KENNEDY, Democratic	303		34,227,096
RICHARD M. NIXON, Republican	219		34,108,546
HARRY F. BYRD, Democratic	15		—
MINOR PARTIES	—		502,363

they promised to touch off strong growth that would fill federal coffers later.

Kennedy's advisers were also convinced that the free-market system inevitably left serious problems unresolved. Despite the successes of the Eisenhower years, 39 million Americans, or about 22 percent of the population, lived below the minimum poverty level set by government economists. Moreover, rapid changes in the economy had left residues of serious unemployment in rural areas of West Virginia, New England, and the South. In the cities, large numbers of working men and women had been left behind by technological unemployment (joblessness due to lack of the skills demanded by new industries). Underlying all these economic problems was a broad shift in the American economy away from farm and blue-collar employment into jobs in government and in the service, retail, and communications industries. The private economy, these advisers argued, excluded too many Americans. Only a large new spurt of growth stimulated by the federal government could sweep these eddies of poverty back into the mainstream.

The president was initially very cautious about adopting these ideas, but he eventually accepted the principles behind his advisers' suggestions. His first economic proposals in early 1961 focused on securing supplements to unemployment benefits, increased Social Security benefits, a higher minimum wage, and aid for seriously distressed areas. All these measures

POVERTY IN THE MISSISSIPPI DELTA.   Poverty was not restricted to African Americans in the 1950s and 1960s across the South. Nonetheless, some of the poorest Americans were African Americans with small farms in the cotton belt.

passed through Congress by September. But his proposals for withholding taxes on stock dividends and interest earnings and his attempt to narrow expense-account deductions met stiff resistance. He did succeed, however, in winning larger tax deductions for business investment in new equipment.

Nonetheless, business leaders were distressed by the Democratic administration. They distrusted Kennedy and the growing consensus among his inner circle of advisers that the federal government should intervene more decisively in economic and social matters. Kennedy was keenly aware of his unpopularity with business, and he tried to mend his fences. In early 1963 he

delivered several speeches designed to win business over to a new program of moderate tax reform. His major proposal, however, was a large individual income tax cut that would save taxpayers over $13 billion. Something of a gamble, it passed finally in 1964 and paid off handsomely by helping stimulate a burst of growth that actually increased tax revenues and narrowed the federal budget deficit.

KENNEDY AND CIVIL RIGHTS

Kennedy's strategy for solving social problems rested on two tactics. He attempted to stimulate economic growth as a way of bringing underpriv-

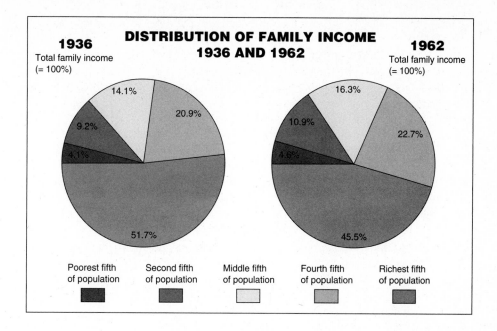

DISTRIBUTION OF FAMILY INCOME 1936 AND 1962

1936
Total family income
(= 100%)

14.1%
9.2%
4.1%
20.9%
51.7%

1962
Total family income
(= 100%)

16.3%
10.9%
4.6%
22.7%
45.5%

| Poorest fifth of population | Second fifth of population | Middle fifth of population | Fourth fifth of population | Richest fifth of population |

ileged elements of the population into the mainstream. He worked to maintain the political support of the diverse coalition that had elected him. But he remained reluctant to employ the power of the federal government to end segregation because of the political controversy it would stir.

During the campaign, Kennedy had called for Americans to dedicate themselves to high principles. This suggested his support for civil rights. But campaign hints proved difficult to translate into action. Initially, the president did little to reverse segregation. In fact, he appointed several men to federal judgeships who were hostile to civil rights. On the other hand, he chose several African Americans for ambassadorships. His brother Robert, responding finally to the Freedom Rides in 1961 and other demonstrations, worked in the Justice Department to desegregate interstate transportation facilities in the South.

Still, pressure mounted to fulfill one specific campaign pledge: his promise to eliminate "with the stroke of a pen" the segregation maintained in federally financed housing projects. The president waited until June 1962 to act, partly because he hoped to create a new Department of Housing and Urban Development and appoint an African American, Robert Weaver, as head. Too much pressure, he reasoned, would raise the opposition of southern congressmen and jeopardize his whole program.

Yet the idealism of which Kennedy spoke so often in public increased expectations that his administration would do something about the spreading confrontation between integrationists and segregationists. The president had to act in the fall of 1962 to protect James Meredith, the first African-American student to enter the University of Mississippi, from mob violence. When Governor Ross Barnett blocked a court order allowing Meredith to enroll, and used the threat of violence to intimidate Meredith, Kennedy federalized the Mississippi National Guard and ordered in federal troops. Before the confrontation ended, two persons were killed and almost 300 arrested. The young African-American student had to accept the protection of U.S. marshals for several months thereafter.

Kennedy had to intervene again in the spring of 1963, during the explosive Birmingham marches, to restrain police violence against demonstrators. These actions deepened resentment against the president in the white South. Gallup polls taken over the summer revealed profound national concern about integration, with a significant group of Americans worried that it was proceeding too fast.

Recognizing the growing momentum and importance of the civil rights movement, Kennedy believed that federal action on a broad scale had become necessary. In early June 1963 two African-American students tried to enroll at the University of Alabama in Tuscaloosa. George Wallace, governor of the state, stood symbolically in the doorway of the registration hall and read a proclamation denouncing federal interference in his state's business. Facing him, Deputy Attorney General Nicholas Katzenbach, sent by Kennedy, read a statement ordering the governor to end his obstruction of a court order to integrate the university. Confronted by federal power, Wallace stepped aside and the African-American students enrolled.

As Kennedy moved closer to acclaiming the goals of the civil rights movement, Martin Luther King, Jr., reached the height of his power and influence. During the massive march on Washington of August 28, 1963, King proclaimed a new meaning and content for the old promises of equality and freedom. These words, he declared, now meant for the first time equality and freedom for African-American men and women. Kennedy did not endorse or attend the march, but he invited its leaders to the White House afterward. A few weeks earlier, he had evoked his own vision of American citizenship and called for support of a new civil rights bill because, as he told a national television audience: "We face a moral crisis as a country and as a people." Kennedy's bill proposed to end segregation in public accommodations, strengthen voting rights, and speed school desegregation.

Extensive reforms to aid other slighted populations in America made up Kennedy's 1963 legislative package: medical insurance for the elderly and subsidized care for the indigent, aid to education, and a new Urban Affairs department of the federal government. Toward the end of the summer, he instructed his advisers to begin sketching out legislation for a concerted drive to end poverty. Kennedy thus proposed to move the federal government aggressively into the realm of social reform.

By the fall of 1963, the administration had embraced broad and ambitious new programs to expand the power of the federal government to guarantee the rights and well-being of minority, poor, and disadvantaged groups in America. It was a task worthy of the vision of Martin Luther King, Jr. But it was also, as King himself realized, a difficult undertaking filled with great personal danger.

KENNEDY'S FOREIGN POLICY

As in domestic affairs, Kennedy promised activism in foreign policy. Unwilling to rely solely on nuclear weapons to preserve a stalemate between the United States and the Soviet Union, the new president believed that his country should intervene in Third World revolutions. Kennedy hoped that the United States could woo these nations into the Western camp. Or, failing this, he was willing to use military means to support wars against communist insurgents. Similarly, in January 1961 the Russian leader Nikita Khrushchev proclaimed his support for "wars of liberation." Thus both the Americans and Soviets planned to increase their involvement in the unstable politics of the Third World.

Kennedy's policy was based on financial, technological, and economic aid coupled with military intervention. In March 1961 the president announced the Alliance for Progress for South America. This aid program promised assistance to Latin American nations for schools, roads, and health facilities. The president intended to strengthen middle-class elements in

MRBM LAUNCH SITE 3
SAN CRISTOBAL, CUBA

LAUNCH AREA

PROB NUCLEAR WARHEAD BUNKER U/C

MID-RANGE BALLISTIC MISSILE SITE IN CUBA.   Aerial reconnaissance over Cuba on October 23, 1962, indicated that work was proceeding on Soviet-supplied missile sites in Cuba, despite the warnings of President Kennedy and the announcement, a day earlier, of a blockade around the island. On October 28 the Russians agreed to dismantle the bases in exchange for an American pledge not to invade Cuba.

Latin America who were sympathetic to reform and who would steer their societies away from military dictatorship or Soviet influence. At the same time, the president announced the Peace Corps, a project to send young American volunteers into Third World countries to aid in agricultural efforts and community development.

Both these programs appealed to young Americans, who took them as symbols of a new and idealistic foreign policy. At the same time, however, Kennedy pushed readiness for military intervention. He encouraged the armed forces to develop plans for counterinsurgency, and he pushed creation of a new, sophisticated strike force for use against guerrillas, called the Green Berets.

Kennedy's first military intervention proved a fiasco. Toward the end of the Eisenhower administration, Cuban rebels led by Fidel Castro overthrew Fulgencio Batista, the ruthless dictator of the island. Castro was determined to secure agricultural reform, nationalization of foreign companies, and industrialization. His program brought harsh criticism from American business and the Eisenhower administration. During 1960 the CIA began planning Castro's overthrow, but Eisenhower decided to let his successor carry out the plans. Despite some hesitations, Kennedy approved a landing of American-trained and supplied Cubans who opposed Castro. When the landing party moved ashore at the Bay of Pigs, Castro's forces were ready. Most counter-revolutionaries

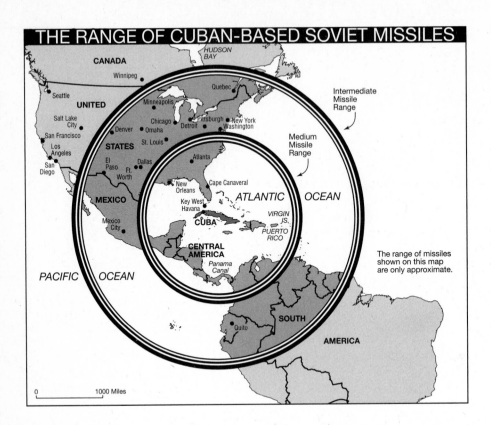

THE RANGE OF CUBAN-BASED SOVIET MISSILES

The range of missiles shown on this map are only approximate.

0   1000 Miles

were captured. Leaks to the press and circumstantial evidence linked the Kennedy administration with the invaders. Subsequently, Kennedy admitted U.S. involvement.

In October 1962, Cuba was once again the site of international conflict, but this time the incident involved a direct confrontation between the United States and the Soviet Union, now Castro's ally. On October 14, U.S. Air Force spy planes photographed missile sites being constructed in Cuba by Soviet technicians. Both the Soviets and the Cubans were fearful that Kennedy still planned an invasion of the island. The Soviet leader also wished to counter American missiles stationed close to his territory in Turkey. Khrushchev ordered the installation of rockets capable of delivering atomic weapons to almost every corner of the United States. A number of warheads were already in Cuba and required only about five hours to arm and fire.

Kennedy, of course, was gravely concerned. He could not allow deployment of these missiles, if only because of the intolerable political risks at home. But to destroy them would risk nuclear war with the Soviets. He chose, instead, a public confrontation, declaring a blockade of Cuba to prevent further Soviet supply of the missiles, and private negotiations. On October 28 the USSR agreed to dismantle their bases in exchange for an American pledge not to invade Cuba. Within a few months the phase-out of Jupiter rockets in Turkey began. This tangled web of misunderstandings, incomplete reconnaissance, and inaccurate readings of motivations on both sides brought the world closer to nuclear war than at any other time. The preservation of this armed detente, however, plunged Cuba deeply into the Soviet economic and strategic system, transforming the island's political and economic system into a state-run, Communist-style government.

CHRONOLOGY

1944	FDR enunciates his economic bill of rights;	**1956**	Eisenhower reelected president over Stevenson;
	GI Bill passed by Congress		Interstate highway system funded
1946	Employment Act passed;	**1957**	Southern Christian Leadership Conference formed;
	Postwar rash of strikes in American industry;		Eisenhower signs civil rights bill;
	Republicans capture control of Congress;		Soviet Union launches *Sputnik* satellite;
	Truman creates Civil Rights Committee	(Sept.)	Eisenhower sends troops to Little Rock, Arkansas
1947	Report of the Civil Rights Committee;	**1957**	United States enters recession
	Taft-Hartley Act passed over Truman veto	**1958**	NASA established
1948	Truman begins desegregation of armed forces;	**1959**	Khrushchev visits the United States
		1960	U-2 incident ruins Paris summit meeting;
	Truman reelected president		John F. Kennedy elected president over Richard Nixon
1949	Truman announces Fair Deal;	**1961**	Kennedy announces Alliance for Progress;
	Housing Act		
1952	Nixon delivers Checkers speech;		Bay of Pigs invasion of Cuba fails;
	Eisenhower elected president;		Cuban missile crisis;
	Republicans regain control of Congress;		SNCC founded
(Dec.)	Eisenhower visits Korea	**1961–1962**	Freedom rides in the South
1953	Korean cease-fire signed	**1962**	Kennedy appoints Robert Weaver secretary of HUD;
1954	Congress censures Senator Joseph McCarthy;		James Meredith enters University of Mississippi
	Construction of St. Lawrence Seaway begins;	**1963**(Apr.)	King jailed in Birmingham, Alabama;
	Supreme Court decides *Brown* v. *Board of Education*;	(May)	Birmingham riots;
1955	*Rebel Without a Cause* opens;	(June)	Governor George Wallace tries to stop African Americans entering University of Alabama;
	Eisenhower suffers heart attack;		
	Martin Luther King, Jr., accepts Montgomery ministry;	(Aug.)	King leads civil rights march on Washington;
(Dec.)	Rosa Parks arrested in Montgomery;	(Nov. 22)	Kennedy assassinated in Dallas
	Montgomery bus boycott		

Despite the risks incurred by intervention in Cuba, Kennedy approved stepped-up intervention in the more intricate affairs of Vietnam. At first, the president feared that communists would gain control of neighboring Laos, but his attention quickly focused on Vietnam. To Kennedy, Vietnam became a testing ground for his theories of nation building and counterinsurgency. The president recognized the complexity of the political and military situation in Vietnam. He understood that the division of the former French colony into two entities, one communist and the other supported by the United States, created instability. The communist-led insurgency that had driven out the French was now directed at expelling the Western-supported government in the south. But Kennedy believed that with United States support, the government of South Vietnam, headed by Ngo Dinh Diem, could survive.

Nonetheless, American intervention did not work as intended. The Diem government became more unstable than ever. Counterinsurgency could not stem government loss of control over the countryside. Diem spoke of reform, but he isolated himself from the political and religious majorities of the south. The military situation continued to deteriorate because the South Vietnamese army, despite its sophisticated equipment and training, proved unreliable in battle. Opposing revolutionaries, now called the Viet Cong, drew increasing support from the embattled rural population. The whole nation was becoming an armed camp.

By 1962, American advisers had approved more drastic policies: defoliants to destroy jungle cover, napalm, and a "strategic hamlet" program to isolate revolutionaries by moving the peasantry into armed camps. Still, the internal political situation was shaky. Diem clung obstinately to unpopular dictatorial policies.

In the spring of 1963 Kennedy signaled his ambassador in Saigon that the United States would accept a replacement for Diem. However, when Diem was overthrown in November, the violence of the coup shocked the administration. Instead of a new order, corruption and brutality continued to rule South Vietnam. Insurgents operated freely and successfully despite 20,000 American troops and advisers. Kennedy himself was growing suspicious of optimistic military and intelligence reports from American military officials. The struggle had come to a crossroads. The president either had to increase American participation or slow it down and face Republican criticism. As in domestic policy, Kennedy was faced with serious choices. What he would have done will never be known, for he was assassinated on November 22, 1963, in Dallas, Texas.

SUGGESTIONS FOR FURTHER READING

MARTIN LUTHER KING, JR., AND CIVIL RIGHTS

Richard Kluger, *Simple Justice: The History of Brown v. Board of Education and America's Struggle for Equality* (1976), details the complex forces and events that converged on the Supreme Court when it delivered its landmark desegregation ruling. Richard Polenberg, *One Nation Divisible: Class, Race, and Ethnicity in the United States Since 1938* (1980), provides an interesting perspective for understanding some of the larger issues in American racial and ethnic attitudes. Coretta Scott King, *My Life with Martin Luther King, Jr.* (1969), is stirring and poignant. David Lewis, *King: A Biography* (1978), is far more critical, but ultimately it is a sympathetic portrait. Two superb additions to King scholarship are David Garrow, *Bearing the Cross: Martin Luther King, Jr., and the Southern Christian Leadership Conference* (1987), and Taylor Branch, *Parting the Waters: America in the King Years, 1954–63* (1988). No picture is complete without some acquaintance with the entanglement of the FBI and J. Edgar Hoover in King's life and works. For this see Michael Friedly, *Martin Luther King, Jr.: The FBI Files* (1993). Another view of King may be explored in the play, *The Meeting*, by Jeff Stetson, which describes a fictitious encounter between King and Malcolm X.

THE COLD WAR AT HOME

The issue of domestic anticommunism and the subsequent prominence of Senator Joseph McCarthy began during the presidency of Harry Truman. A good assessment of Truman is Alonzo L. Hamby, *Beyond the New Deal: Harry S Truman and American Liberalism* (1973). A controversial look at the effects of McCarthyism is David Caute, *The Great Fear: The Anti-Communist Purge Under Truman and Eisenhower* (1978). Richard H. Rovere, *Senator Joseph McCarthy* (1959), is a very readable account of the rise and fall of the senator from Wisconsin. A newer look at anticommunism demonstrates the great absurdities to which this fear extended. See Steven J. Whitfield, *The Culture of the Cold War* (1991).

For a discussion of the Korean War, see Burton Kaufman, *The Korean War: Challenges in Crisis, Credibility, and Command* (1986). The Cuban missile crisis is well-documented in James Blight's *Cuba on the Brink: Castro, the Missile Crisis, and the Soviet Collapse* (1993).

THE 1950s

An excellent economic history of the 1950s is Harold G. Vatter, *The United States Economy in the 1950s* (1963). The effects of prosperity during this decade were controversial. One book that set the tone for much of the subsequent criticism of 1950s lifestyles was David Riesman, *The Lonely Crowd* (1950). *The Affluent Society* (1956), written by the noted American economist John Kenneth Galbraith, details some of the problems of prosperity. On the other hand, David M.

Potter, *People of Plenty* (1954), argues that abundance has had a generally positive effect on society. On suburban life, see Kenneth T. Jackson, *Crabgrass Frontier: The Suburbanization of the United States* (1985). An important corrective to the picture of a totally quiescent women's movement in the 1950s is Leila J. Rupp and Verta Taylor, *Survival in the Doldrums: The American Women's Rights Movement, 1945 to the 1960s* (1987).

THE EISENHOWER ADMINISTRATION

One good place to begin study of the Eisenhower presidency is Herbert S. Parmet, *Eisenhower and the American Crusades* (1972). More recently published material in *The Eisenhower Diaries* (1981), Richard H. Ferrell (ed.), reveals the president to be a very complex and thoughtful leader. Robert L. Branyan and Laurence H. Larson (eds.) have collected important public documents from the era in *The Eisenhower Administration, 1953–1961: A Documentary History* (2 vols., 1971).

Liberalism in Decline

THE EPISODE: *Political convention sites in 1968 were chosen as much for security as to anchor a campaign in a particular section of the country. For the Democrats, Chicago seemed a safe place. Mayor Richard J. Daley controlled a political machine that delivered votes with perennial regularity. The Democrats had to be wary of demonstrations against the war in Vietnam. Practically driven from the presidency by rising discontent with the war, President Lyndon Johnson nonetheless maintained a tight grip on the Democratic party. Opponents of the war were pushed to the periphery; leaders such as Senator Robert Kennedy and Martin Luther King, Jr., were both dead. Under the circumstances, political dissenters had to make either what seemed like unreasonable compromises or take to the streets. The choice for many was easy because opponents of the war already felt at home in the arena of public protest. Elements of the new left, the civil rights movement, and the counterculture had transformed pickets, marches, and street theater into a new language of politics perfectly suited to the age of television. Mayor Daley, on the other hand, commanded an old-fashioned force of tough and angry policemen with no sympathy for the protesters or interest in their right to demonstrate. The stage was set for an extraordinary confrontation.*

THE HISTORICAL SETTING: *The pitched battle between antiwar demonstrators and Chicago's police was the culminating moment of the presidency of Lyndon Johnson, a major turning point in America's determination to continue the war in Vietnam, and a crucial step in the decline of the Democratic party. It marked a shift of the new left and the counterculture in a more ideological, and ultimately self-destructive, direction. The year 1968 also marked the victory of a new sort of political movement, as yet vaguely conceived and clumsily organized, but important nonetheless. This was a new conservatism based on growing hostility to demonstrations, civil rights marches, protests, urban riots, and crime, and on hostility to the liberal legislative agenda.*

Of course, one event—even a year—cannot account for such shifts. Changes happen over time and flow from a wide variety of causes. Nonetheless, the political riots of Chicago, 1968, and the election of Richard Nixon (which in no small way depended on this political debacle) confirmed a serious reorientation in American life. Significant developments in lifestyles, popular culture, and social relations continued. Demographic changes in the labor force and in family life continued to alter the shape of institutions. The sexual revolution did not falter, and integration, while it did not achieve all its goals, gradually eliminated the most overt and distasteful elements of racism in American life. Nonetheless, the riots of 1968 tested the limits of political liberalism.

Chicago, 1968

Giants lived here once. It was that kind of town, thirty years gone, that made big men out of little ones. It was grand for great deeds then, as it is grand for small deeds now.

—*Nelson Algren*

Dear Students for a Democratic Society:

I'm twelve years old, and I wish to join the society. Because of the conditions at school your hair must not be two inches above the eyebrow. You must wear white socks. If you wore any other color you'd be punished and this is the reason I want to join the society.

—Letter to the Editor,
New Left Notes, 1968

SURREALISM IN CHICAGO

Dallas Morning News

Jerry Rubin mounted the stage at the Grant Park bandshell in Chicago shortly after 4 P.M. on August 28, 1968. His arms circling a large, squirming pig, he shouted out to the delighted crowd of 10,000 students and other demonstrators: "Today is a historic day for America—we are proud to announce the declaration of candidacy for the presidency of the United States by a pig." The crowd roared its approval of Pigasus.

Rubin, with his shaggy hair and unkempt beard, was well known to police guarding the edges of the park. So friends had smuggled the pig through the crowd in a burlap bag from a nearby car. (Earlier in the week, Rubin had tried the same stunt at Chicago's Civic Center, but police had arrested him before he could start his speech.)

Milling around in anticipation, the crowd had already listened to several speakers. Whiffs of tear gas rose from the grass or drifted across from the nearby flagpole area. Only a short time before, police had charged into a group of demonstrators trying to haul down the American flag. Tear gas exploded and police waded through the group, flailing nightsticks. Volunteer medics dragged the injured to safety.

David Dellinger, longtime peace advocate and leader of the National Mobilization Committee to End the War in Vietnam, a group that helped organize the demonstration, now rose to address the crowd. He announced a march out of the park, across Chicago's Loop (the business district), to the Amphitheater, where the 1968 Democratic convention was in session. There was no permit for the demonstration, but Dellinger insisted the march was a question of free speech. "This is a peaceful march," he cried. "All those who want to participate in a peaceful march, join our line. All those who are not peaceful, please go away and don't join our line."

A few small groups, some wearing helmets, their eyes smeared with Vaseline to protect against the chemical Mace and tear gas, broke off. But most of the demonstrators followed Dellinger up Columbus Drive at the edge of the park until they ran up against a solid line of Chicago policemen. The demonstrators stopped and sat down. Dellinger went off to negotiate with the police. But the officials refused to budge: no march would be permitted. Hearing this, the crowd began to clump into thick knots, which then moved around the police line and toward the bridges that led from the park, hoping to make their way over the railroad tracks and into the heart of the city. National Guardsmen standing on the bridges prevented this by firing tear gas. But the demonstrators quickly discovered one unprotected bridge toward the north and raced across it. They poured down Michigan Avenue to the Conrad Hilton Hotel, headquarters for several candidates and a symbol of the Democratic convention. The stage was set for a violent battle between police and demonstrators, a battle that shocked the nation and shook the Democratic party to its foundations.

YOUTHS FRUSTRATED, BITTER

Boston Evening Globe

The origins of the confrontation in Chicago lay in opposition to the war in Vietnam. The brutal course of this war had battered the presidency of Lyndon Johnson. Early in 1968 a Viet Cong insurgent attack against South Vietnamese and American troops (the Tet offensive) had brought the war into the streets of every city in South Vietnam. Although the Viet Cong fell back with terrible losses, the campaign was a debacle for American homefront support for the war. Optimistic predictions by government officials and body counts of enemy killed melted before the reality of the conflict. Many Americans concluded, as they watched the nightly accounts on television news, that the war was neither winnable nor worth the rising casualties.

The Tet offensive was just one element of a growing political crisis that forced President Johnson out of the race five months before the convention. Johnson had staked his reputation and fate on winning the civil war in Asia. But after three years of heavy escalation and commitment of American resources to the war, casualties were still mounting with no end in sight. Opposition, particularly within the Democratic party, was growing rapidly. At first, it gathered around Senator Eugene McCarthy of Minnesota, who came close to defeating Johnson in the March 12 New Hampshire

ROBERT F. KENNEDY. In 1964 Bobby Kennedy ran a successful campaign for election as a U.S. senator from New York: here he is overwhelmed by upstate admirers. During the presidential primaries of 1968, Kennedy attracted equally enthusiastic crowds and growing support. Acceptable to some Democratic party bosses as well as to much of the antiwar movement, he was, perhaps, the only candidate who might have held the party together. But he was assassinated in June 1968.

presidential primary. Predictions for the upcoming primary in Wisconsin were even bleaker for the president. So Johnson, in a surprise national television broadcast on March 31, announced his withdrawal from the race.

Nonetheless, Johnson had no intention of bowing out of politics. He remained determined to choose his own successor. He believed that McCarthy was only a marginal threat; the real danger to the continuation of his policies was Robert Kennedy, who could rally antiwar support and win approval from Democratic party regulars. As his own candidate, Johnson pushed Hubert Humphrey, his vice president. But he made his support contingent on Humphrey's firm commitment to pursuing the war in Vietnam to victory.

In late spring, Kennedy's chances for the nomination mounted, as support for McCarthy dwindled and Humphrey failed to attract much popular support. On June 4 Kennedy won the crucial California primary and seemed well on his way to unseating Humphrey, the party front-runner. Then in the early morning of June 5, at a victory celebration in Los Angeles at the Ambassador Hotel, shots suddenly rang out. An Arab immigrant, Sirhan Bishara Sirhan, fired at Kennedy from close range. The candidate died twenty-five hours later. This second murderous attack on the Kennedy family removed the only viable antiwar candidate from the race. Humphrey was as good as nominated.

The Republican party proved even less hospitable to antiwar sentiment, counting on polls that showed a majority of Americans still supporting the war. When Republican conventioneers gathered in Miami, Florida, they had no trouble agreeing to nominate Richard M. Nixon. Nixon opened his campaign to the center and the right, to gather up critics of Johnson and the Democrats, and to take advantage of a growing backlash against civil rights and antiwar demonstrations. He was vague and noncommittal on the issue of Vietnam. He promised to end the war but declined to say how.

For those who opposed the war—and significant numbers of Americans did—there was no place to go: no political haven, no believable candidate, and no welcome from either party. Nor was there a meaningful third-party alternative. Thus when the Democratic party shut its doors to the antiwar movement, it almost inevitably pushed that movement out onto the streets of Chicago.

CHICAGOANS AWAIT PROTESTERS WITH TEETH, FISTS CLENCHED

Los Angeles Times

Although many voters disapproved of the war in Vietnam, it was young people who took to the streets to manifest their opposition. Two groups in particular organized and led the Chicago demonstrations: the Yippies and student radicals.

The Youth International Party (YIP), founded in early 1968, dedicated itself to a world revolution led by youth. During late 1967 and early 1968, student protests against the war escalated across the United States. Student movements and crippling strikes also rocked France, West Germany, and other European nations. Many young Americans concluded that they were part of a rising generation destined to change the world. The Yippies capitalized on this sentiment and wove together diverse elements of youth culture: political protest and experimental lifestyles associated with the hippies living in San Francisco and around large university campuses like Berkeley. As Allen Ginsberg, poet and troubadour of the movement, described it, it drew together:

> younger people aware of the planetary fate that we are all sitting in the middle of, imbued with a new consciousness and desiring of a new kind of society involving prayer, music, and spiritual life together rather than competition, acquisition, and war.

The Yippies formed originally from a group of ex-college radicals living on New York's Lower East Side. They worked at shelters for runaway teenagers and held music festivals and street theater for the growing hippie community and drug culture of that area. During a large antiwar protest march October 21, 1967, on the Pentagon in Washington, two future Yippie leaders, Jerry Rubin and Abbie Hoffman, demonstrated their genius for combining politics, culture, and humor. They built the protest into a media event and urged the crowd to circle the huge building to "exorcise" the evil inside. They astutely recognized the enormous importance of such symbolic gestures. Photographs and newsreels of demonstrators planting daisies in the gun barrels of troops guarding the building brought more attention to the march than did speeches, lobbying, or slogans.

The tone of Yippie protests was mocking and anti-establishment, but it was not entirely unfamiliar. Indeed, the exploits of Rubin and Hoffman belong to the anarchic vein of American humor exemplified by the Marx brothers in their best political films, such as *Duck Soup*, shot in the 1930s. In a gesture that might have fitted such a film, Hoffman and a group of friends burst into the New York Stock Exchange in August 1967. Standing on the balcony above the bustling exchange floor, they threw dollar bills over the side. Some of the brokers below them jeered and shook their fists; others

YIPPIE POLITICAL THEATER IN CHICAGO. Yippie demonstrations against the Vietnam War were dramatic, outrageous, and effective. Marching under the symbol of death, Yippies marked the "Unbirthday" of President Johnson on August 27 during the Democratic convention.

scrambled for the bills that floated downward. Those demonstrators who escaped arrest rushed to the front entrance of the building and chanted "Free! Free!" while they shredded and burned dollar bills.

The Yippies decided to organize as a political movement in February 1968. As Hoffman related:

> There we were, all stoned, rolling around the floor. . . . Yippie! . . . . Somebody says oink and that's it, pig, it's a natural, man, we gotta win. . . . Let's try success, I mean, when we went to the Pentagon, we were going to get it to rise 300 feet in the air. . . . So we said how about doing one that will win.

The purpose of the Yippie organization was to turn the Chicago Democratic convention into theater of ridicule. The tactic was to organize a "Festival of Life," a giant counterculture rock concert to be held at the same time the Democrats nominated a candidate for president. As singer and Yippie member Phil Ochs said, "They wanted to be able to act out fantasies in the street to communicate their feelings to the public."

On March 17, at the Americana Hotel in New York, Hoffman, Rubin, Ochs, singer Arlo Guthrie, and others announced further details of their Festival of Life. It would feature a concert with Guthrie, Judy Collins, the Fugs, Country Joe and the Fish, and other popular music groups. Leaders promised to cooperate with Chicago officials, to secure proper permits for the concert and permission for the audience to sleep in the city parks. But Mayor Richard J. Daley of Chicago refused to grant permits for the festival, believing that a tough line would restrict the numbers who came to the city during the convention.

Without permits, several performers withdrew. But the obstinacy of the city suited Yippie purposes. As one flyer put it, YIP was a "National disorganization whose sole purpose would be the Theater of Disruption." Accordingly, the Yippies revised their plans. They still planned a concert, but the highlight of their mock celebration would be the nomination of Pigasus for president. This act had a special significance. *Pig* was urban ghetto slang for "policeman." By nominating a pig for president, the Yippies were proclaiming that the United States was a police state.

Through the summer the Yippies tried, without success, to persuade Chicago officials to grant a permit for their festival, although they made no effort to hide their purpose of disrupting the convention. The list of demands they released to the press was designed to shock, rather than to form the basis for any negotiations. They insisted on an end to the war in Vietnam, legalization of marijuana and other psychedelic drugs, freedom for prisoners, the disarming of police, and the abolition of money. As for events of the festival, they "predicted" activities in Chicago that would disrupt the entire city: an "unbirthday party" for President Johnson on August 27, a plan to dump LSD into the Chicago water system, a stall-in on city traffic arteries, the release of greased pigs throughout the city, and the recruitment of "230 hyper-potent hippie males into a special battalion to seduce the wives, daughters, and girlfriends of convention delegates." As the Yippies and their supporters began to converge on Chicago in late August, Hoffman proclaimed: "I use guerrilla theater as a medium for creating what I call blank space. Blank space is where you use media so that the observer, the audience, becomes a participant, becomes involved." But for Mayor Daley and the police and convention officials, the Yippies' agenda was not theater but political warfare, not humor but a threat of public disorder.

Far larger than the Yippie group was the contingent of demonstrators that came to Chicago from the more subdued and serious student antiwar movement. The largest of the political action groups, the Students for a Democratic Society (SDS), founded in 1962, refused to participate officially. Its leaders believed demonstrations to be ineffective, and they feared violence from the police. They also wanted to remain separate from any movement that might support the candidacy of Senator McCarthy. Nonetheless, two former SDS leaders, Tom Hayden and Rennie Davis, played leading roles in Chicago. Moreover, the days of protest had a profound effect on radical organizations like SDS.

The National Mobilization Committee to End the War in Vietnam (MOBE), headed by David Dellinger, was the umbrella organization that included most of the important student radical groups that came to Chicago. It was MOBE that had organized the 1967 demonstration at the Pentagon. Its leaders occasionally worked with the Yippies, but the Yippies never officially joined it. Their strategy was theater, not serious politics.

In February 1968, MOBE opened a Chicago office and chose Davis and Hayden to coordinate activities. Their first job was to secure demonstration permits from the city for a march on the convention. At a planning session held in late March, Hayden and Davis defined their aims. They wanted peaceful, legal demonstrations during the convention. But they anticipated police violence that would "dramatize to the world the large numbers of people who feel unrepresented, and in fact disgraced and used, by our government's policies on the crisis of Vietnam and racism and the mockery that democracy has become." Hayden hoped that demonstrators would converge on Chicago:

> The final funeral march on the Democratic convention, beginning as the first ballot is taken, should bring a half a million people demanding a choice on the issues of peace and justice; citizens who have come to 'make the democratic process work' by pinning the delegates in the International Amphitheater until a choice is presented to the American people.

MOBE leaders agreed that the final march to the Amphitheater would be their central aim. But Johnson's announcement in March that he would not seek reelection put these plans on hold. The violent response of Chicago police to the ghetto riots that erupted after Martin Luther King's assassination in April also gave pause. Mayor Daley had encouraged the police to take stern measures against looters and arsonists. Observers warned that he would also be very tough on demonstrators.

Nonetheless, MOBE leaders meeting in Cleveland in mid-July decided to proceed. They appropriated money for the Chicago office and organized a legal group to help out with arrest and bail problems. Medical groups, including the Committee on Human Rights and the Student Health Organization, were asked to set up first-aid support services. MOBE clearly expected trouble.

During the summer, Davis and Hayden still hoped for official permission to march. After several fruitless phone calls and letters, they finally set a meeting with city officials in early August. When the officials stalled on a permit, MOBE pressed for a court injunction. But the judge ruled on August 21 that the city was not obligated to issue a permit. The city did make one counteroffer of a location for a march at least ten miles from the Amphitheater and well away from the business heart of the city. MOBE refused this. Finally, during the convention, the city did issue one permit, for the afternoon rally at the Grant Park bandshell on August 28.

Quite clearly, the city intended to frighten protesters from coming to the convention by making marches and demonstrations illegal. In part, they succeeded. Chicago officials put MOBE leaders in an awkward position. By planning illegal demonstrations, were they not inciting to riot? On the other hand, did they not have a duty to exercise their right to assembly and free speech? The MOBE leadership chose to proceed, believing that if violence occurred, it would be initiated by the police. This in turn would discredit the Democratic party and the presidential nominee. David Dellinger promised: "We are not going to storm the convention with tanks or Mace. But we are going to storm the hearts and minds of the American people."

Other protest groups decided to come to Chicago during the convention, but they played a minor role. The Black Panthers did not officially join the demonstrations, but their representatives sometimes spoke at meetings. The Panthers, founded in Oakland, California, in 1966 by Huey Newton and Bobby Seale, were a black power group that advocated self-defense and political coalition with white radicals. Shadowed closely by police agents, Panther leader Seale spoke in Chicago, but the organization generally kept in the background. The black leader who participated most actively in the demonstrations was comedian and civil rights advocate Dick Gregory.

Chicago also attracted large numbers of young McCarthy supporters, who came to demonstrate for their candidate. Originally, they did not intend to join the Yippies or MOBE, but many of them crossed over to the radical lines after the first bloody encounters with police. Finally, Chicago drew several literary celebrities, including novelists Norman Mailer, Terry Southern, and William Burroughs, poet Allen Ginsberg, and French playwright Jean Genet.

CHICAGO: CITY OF MUSCLE, IN INDUSTRY AND POLITICS

New York Times

The Democratic party had chosen Chicago as a convention site partly because of the tough reputation of Mayor Richard J. Daley. One of the last old-time city political bosses, he ran Chicago as his own personal fiefdom. Labor unions, the police, and city employees all marched to his tune. If anyone could maintain an orderly city and keep control over local arrangements, Daley seemed the one.

With one firm hand on the convention site in Chicago, the Democratic party was ruled by another firm hand in Washington. Johnson's power in the party remained strong, and he was determined to prevent the convention from adopting either a platform or nominating a candidate that questioned American participation in the war in Vietnam. Thus Johnson prevented Humphrey from accommodating the antiwar forces in the party. He made sure that the credentials committee did not lean toward antiwar delegates in deciding disputed seats. He also insisted that the platform committee write a prowar plank. All these moves were successful, but they stripped Humphrey of power and a separate identity. In fact, Humphrey had so little influence that when he wrote to ask Daley to grant parade permits to demonstrators, his request went unanswered.

From the beginning, Mayor Daley and his police advisers prepared for a confrontation. They took Yippie "predictions" seriously. In January the city established a joint planning command with the police department, the mayor's office, the fire department, the U.S. Secret Service, and military intelligence. This committee met every two weeks until August, when it stepped up the tempo of its conferences. One function of the committee was to assess intelligence gathered by agents assigned to infiltrate

MOBE and Yippie meetings or taken from publications in the underground press. The committee paid special attention to possible participation by Chicago's African Americans. After the violent riots in April, Daley feared renewed outbreaks. Should white radicals enlist support from the black ghetto, the mayor feared he might not be able to control the city.

Daley channeled his antiriot efforts through the police task force, which in April had been the backbone of the crackdown on demonstrations and riots in the ghetto. This agency borrowed a large tear gas dispenser from the U.S. Army, which it mounted on a city sanitation truck. It organized police helicopter surveillance of routes leading to the convention center.

Squads of police were assigned to the two major city parks: Lincoln Park on the north side, which became the demonstrators' headquarters, and Grant Park, across from Michigan Avenue and the railroad tracks, facing the Conrad Hilton hotel. All leave was canceled for the period, and twelve-hour shifts were instituted. The fire department was put on special alert. Police officials also issued special riot equipment to officers: nightsticks, helmets, service revolvers, and disabling Mace spray. A number of officers, on their own, purchased plastic face shields to attach inside their helmets. Instructions issued to officers stressed the need to maintain calm, especially while making mass arrests:

> Mass arrests made by police in a helter-skelter manner will serve absolutely no purpose as far as maintaining law and order is concerned. However, arrests made in an orderly and well-planned manner indicate a trained force prepared for such emergencies and will help convey to the demonstrators and the rest of the city that they are dealing with a superior force.

Mayor Daley also asked for support from the Illinois National Guard. Following several weeks of negotiations with the guard, the governor's office, and the U.S. Fifth Army, the governor, Samuel Shapiro, announced that the guard would be activated. Approximately 5,000 guardsmen were stationed in armories around Chicago by August 23. In addition, 6,000 federal riot-control troops were brought to the city (U.S. Air Force C-141 jet cargo planes were assembled to ferry the troops). With about 11,000 reinforcements, Daley and his police force probably outnumbered the demonstrators who planned to come to Chicago.

Security around and inside the convention hall was tight. Barricades prevented any unauthorized persons from approaching the entrance. Police assigned to the inside of the Amphitheater were supplemented by Andy Frain, Inc., ushers who were generally to be seen on duty during Cubs baseball games at Wrigley Field. Entrance would be by ticket only, and delegates would receive new tickets each day. Any delegate or any newspaper or television reporter without proper identification would be removed from the floor or the galleries of the hall.

Mayor Daley also increased security around the city's water system in view of the Yippies' warning that they might dump LSD into the reservoirs. Special police were assigned to the two main pumping stations. Elements of the canine section of the task force guarded filtration plants.

Daley apparently took one further step to control the protest. An International Brotherhood of Electrical Workers strike, begun prior to the convention, remained unsettled. (It was settled immediately after the convention ended.) Daley intervened enough to ensure that live television coverage would come from the convention itself, but networks were not allowed to set up live coverage facilities around possible demonstration focal points. They could still film, but the film had to be carried to network facilities at the Amphitheater for processing. A story in *Television Digest* on August 26 explained the problem:

> Networks encountered several new labor disputes last week and were told by Chicago police they couldn't park videotape vans on streets outside major hotels. They also are prohibited from locating cameras outside hotels or in windows overlooking streets.

> New difficulties brought back into prominence earlier charges that Democrats were deliberately attempting to curb TV live coverage outside Convention Hall. CBS News President Richard Salant saw difficulties as part of "a pattern well beyond simple labor disputes, logistics, and security problems."

The news media also made special preparations for the convention, partly because of these obstacles. Besides the large contingent of reporters and camera operators assigned to the Amphitheater, the major networks, news services, and newspapers like *The New York Times* assigned about 300 reporters and photographers to follow the demonstrators. Each major news service was handed a special introduction to Chicago published by the police department. It opened: "Welcome, Newsmen! Welcome to Chicago, the City of 'The Front Page,' with an outstanding tradition of competitive journalism. Another tradition has been the excellent rapport between the Chicago police and newsmen." The news services, however, did not anticipate excellent rapport. In fact, they prepared for the worst. *The Washington Post*, for example, issued the following warning in its list of instructions:

> *Tear Gas Protection.* Reporters traveling in areas that have been heavily gassed have encountered significant problems. Each of the cars is now being equipped (in the trunk) with small containers of oxygen, and with watersoaked cloths. The cloths, enclosed in plastic bags, should be used to sponge out eyes and remove the gas from the skin. An additional small supply of oxygen containers will be kept in the radio room cabinet. This style of tear gas protection was decided upon since the Army-type of gas masks would tend to make reporters targets, and are quite uncomfortable to users who are not accustomed to their use.

IN THE HALL:
BLACK CREPE AND ANGER
IN THE STREETS:
TEAR GAS AND CLUBS

The Washington Post

Despite the overwhelming force of the city and its troop reinforcements, and with the press anticipating trouble, the Yippies and the MOBE leadership refused to retreat. The city's unwillingness to grant a march permit anywhere near the Amphitheater or to allow demonstrations, plus police refusal to allow anyone to sleep in the parks, meant that almost any action was, by definition, illegal. In the tightly surveyed and tense city, any act of political protest threatened to become a confrontation.

Neither the MOBE nor the Yippie leadership (even if they desired it) had much control over the thousands of young people who began to assemble in the city over the weekend of August 24. MOBE did train several hundred marshals to control crowds during marches, but they proved totally ineffective in the chaotic conditions of police confrontation. Communications between leaders and followers were spotty and often tardy, carried by word of mouth or by flyers pasted to walls. Moreover, the two principal wings of the protest, MOBE and the Yippies, had different aims. MOBE had a more traditional belief in the effectiveness of demonstrations and protests to attract attention to their message of opposition to the war. The Yippies also opposed the war, but their vehicle for protest was any public event that brought shock, anger, or amusement. Under such circumstances, the initiative belonged to the police. They determined the nature and extent of the pitched battles that followed.

The police had the further advantage of an informer close to Jerry Rubin. Posing as a member of the motorcycle gang the Headhunters, Robert L. Pierson, a private investigator employed by the Chicago Police Department, met with Rubin and Hoffman and secretly relayed information about demonstration plans back to police headquarters. In order to convince the Yippies of his loyalty, Pierson had to be active in the demonstrations. As one newsman reported:

> One such hell-raiser—Robert L. Pierson—has indiscreetly told the *Chicago Tribune* (as published August 31) how he gained Rubin's confidence and, to confirm his credentials, threw rocks and bottles, hurled epithets at the police and even participated actively in lowering the American flag and raising a red flag in Grant Park—an action that touched off a police assault.

Those demonstrators who were prepared to brave what they realized could be physical danger headed for Lincoln Park, about two miles north of the city's center. There, in a large area that separated Lake Michigan from Old Town (Chicago's bohemian center) the Yippies set up their headquarters. Many of the demonstrators planned to take advantage of housing offered by nearby residents, but others brought sleeping bags to spend the night in the park.

At about the same time, convention delegates began to stream into town and fill the hotels in downtown Chicago. The media set up to report on two simultaneous events: the opening of the convention and the first confrontations between police and demonstrators. The two stories became point and counterpoint in the nomination process. As Humphrey's selection moved inexorably forward, it was increasingly punctuated by events outside the Amphitheater, by the growing tension and violence between police and demonstrators.

Yippie and MOBE strategists hoped to keep media attention focused on their protests, and to build support and momentum for the large (illegal) march on the convention center Wednesday evening, the time of the nomination vote. During the weekend and first two days of the convention, television and newspapers were filled with pictures of Yippies camping in the parks, holding rock concerts and news conferences, practicing *washoi* (linked-arm marching tactics borrowed from Japanese radicals), and of Allen Ginsberg chanting Indian mantras. On Tuesday, they reported the mock "unbirthday party" for Lyndon Johnson, featuring music by the Holocaust No-Dance Band, songs by Phil Ochs, and speeches by writers opposed to the war.

Yet the high jinks of the Yippies were gradually overshadowed by the violence that occurred nightly in a battle for the parks. The city insisted on closing the parks in the evening. Each night, as police swept through Lincoln Park, spraying tear gas and exploding smoke bombs, the atmosphere became more ominous. Demonstrators increasingly fought back and, when forced out of the park, continued their harassment of police from nearby streets. More and more, the police struck and arrested first, and asked questions later. Reporters were caught in the middle and then, increasingly, on the side of the demonstrators. By Tuesday, many of the journalists and their parent news services were convinced that they were watching a police force riot out of control.

The convention floor was also a battlefield of sorts. Dissenters and antiwar delegates faced the same unfavorable odds. The convention's rules and credentials committees, which had convened a week earlier, evidenced the first sharp encounters. Antiwar delegates pledged to McCarthy challenged Humphrey's forces in an effort to demonstrate that the convention was boss-ridden. They were only partly successful. Surprisingly, Humphrey delegates joined to push through several dramatic changes in the rules relating to Democratic party conventions. They agreed to abolish the unit rule,

DAYS OF RAGE. After the failure to end politics as usual at the Democratic convention, some elements of the new left decided upon a strategy of continuing disruption. In this picture, Tom Hayden addresses a crowd of activists in Lincoln Park in October, before they marched into Chicago's loop to try to interrupt business as usual.

whereby a state could require all its votes to be cast for the same candidate. They voted to ask the convention to reexamine its manner of selecting delegates. A Reform Commission was chosen to suggest how these changes might be implemented. But of course, these reforms would not apply to the 1968 convention.

On the question of the platform Humphrey's forces were unbending. They wrote a plank praising Lyndon Johnson's conduct of the war. The minority of the platform committee that wanted to commit the party to a quick end to the war vowed to carry their fight to the convention floor.

CHICAGO NOTEBOOK: TERROR IN THE STREETS BILLY CLUBS AND BLOOD IN A NO-MAN'S LAND

Seattle Times

On Wednesday, although the convention had not yet nominated a presidential candidate, one outcome of the contest had already been decided. As predicted, Yippie tactics had brought enormous publicity. Action shots, music, wild dress, and extravagant statements were far more interesting than the droning speeches inside the convention. None of this theater of the absurd, however, blunted the point of the demonstrators: they were there to protest the continuing war and the police were determined to stop them.

As police violence mounted, the nation watched in astonishment. Reporters and television commentators increasingly sided with the students. Their photographs and video clips showed police beating protesters. Police attacks on reporters only increased their partiality. By Tuesday night, protests from major news organizations like CBS began to pour into Chicago city headquarters, demanding that Mayor Daley control the police. Even several Chicago aldermen, usually quiet on such matters, denounced police brutality. As Frank Sullivan, press officer of the Chicago police, bitterly put it: "[the demonstrators] are a pitiful handful. They have almost no support. But, by golly, they get the cooperation of the news media."

On Wednesday the spirit of confrontation even entered the Amphitheater. For a brief time, the convention itself was threatened. As the press increasingly criticized Daley, he and his aides packed the spectator section of the hall with city workers who waved American flags and signs supporting Daley. On the floor, with the Illinois delegation, Daley watched the proceedings in sullen silence. Late in the afternoon, the convention began debate on the majority (Humphrey) and minority (McCarthy) Vietnam planks. The peace delegates fervently cheered speakers who called for a speedy, negotiated end to the war. But Humphrey's forces were too numerous. When the votes were tallied, the Humphrey-Johnson position on Vietnam had won: 1,567 3/4 to 1,041 1/4. The Democratic party was now pledged to support President Johnson's position on the war. This accomplished, the convention adjourned until evening. But many of the delegates remained in their seats. New Yorkers broke into peace songs. The convention band, in reply, blared out the tune "This Will Be the Start of Something Big." Several

California delegates moved over to the New York standard and joined in the singing. The band retorted with "California Here I Come" and "Happy Days Are Here Again." Strains of music overlaid shouts of "Stop the war!" as the last stragglers filed off the floor.

At about this time, the Grant Park bandshell demonstration broke up and David Dellinger tried to lead protesters out of the park. He and other leaders, however, lost all control when the crowd discovered the unguarded northern bridge, swarmed over to Michigan Avenue and then ran down the avenue toward the Conrad Hilton. Now about 3,000 strong, the crowd approached a police line across Michigan Avenue at East Balbo Drive blocking their route. Another police line stretched west of the Hilton on Wabash Avenue. Guardsmen, reporters, and television trucks waited in front of the hotel.

When they encountered the police line on Michigan Avenue, several demonstrators began shouting and chanting slogans and insults. Blue-helmeted officers repeatedly ordered the crowd to leave the street. A few demonstrators tried to flank police lines by heading west and then south toward the Amphitheater. Most were turned back after brief, violent scuffles. They rejoined the growing crowd blocked on Michigan Avenue.

Then, at about 7:30 P.M., a small contingent of black demonstrators following a mule train (a symbol of tenant farmers) tried to make its way through the crowd south on Michigan Avenue and past the Hilton. To do so it had to pass through the demonstrators and the police lines. This group, led by the Reverend Ralph Abernathy of the Southern Christian Leadership Conference and including old people and children, had a legal permit to march. A police wedge allowed them through and they continued south on Michigan and then west away from the hotel.

By this time, the corner of Balbo and Michigan had become an undulating mass of confusion. Segments of the crowd tried to push forward, shouting "Pig!" at the police who blocked them. Others tried to sneak through police lines behind the SCLC demonstrators. The protesters were determined to continue their march toward the Amphitheater. The police were determined to stop them. Where the two groups butted against each other, violent incidents flared. In the twilight, police and television floodlights cast an eerie and ominous glow.

Police again tried to warn the crowd to leave Michigan Avenue. But in response, a large number of young people sat down in the street. Another group split off and headed west on Balbo until they ran into an advancing phalanx of officers with clubs in their hands. The protesters retreated, shouting epithets and throwing rocks and bottles. Police guarding the front of the Hilton were struck by objects hurled down from the front windows of the hotel.

At about 7:57 P.M., police advancing along Balbo neared the main body of demonstrators on Michigan Avenue. Suddenly, they charged into the crowd, trying to clear the street and grabbing at random to make arrests. Nightsticks flying, they trapped a mass of demonstrators that was so large and hemmed in, it couldn't move. Part of it pressed up against the police line on Michigan Avenue, and these officers, too, began to swing their clubs. Rocks and other thrown objects thudded onto the helmets of police as they advanced.

Reporters and news cameras focused on incident after incident of brutal beatings by the police. Even the deputy superintendent of the police department rushed into the

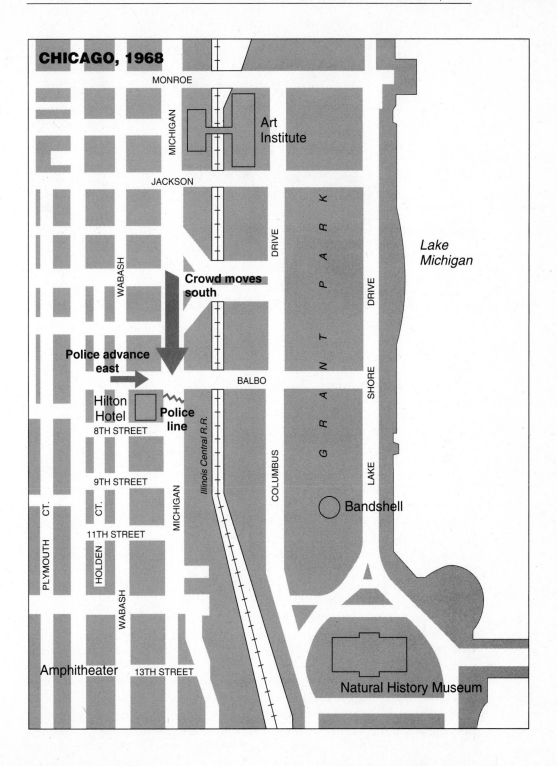

CHICAGO, 1968

MONROE

MICHIGAN

Art
Institute

JACKSON

DRIVE

WABASH

G R A N T   P A R K

Lake
Michigan

**Crowd moves
south**

SHORE

DRIVE

**Police advance
east**

BALBO

Hilton
Hotel

**Police
line**

8TH STREET

Illinois Central R.R.

9TH STREET

MICHIGAN

COLUMBUS

Bandshell

CT.

CT.

11TH STREET

PLYMOUTH

HOLDEN

LAKE

Amphitheater

WABASH

13TH STREET

Natural History Museum

THE BATTLE FOR MICHIGAN AVENUE.
During the short, violent confrontation in front of the Conrad Hilton hotel on August 28, 1968, enraged police charged into crowds of demonstrators. The major casualty, however, was Hubert Humphrey, whose nomination was associated with violence and riot.

crowd to stop his officers from their attacks. One witness testifying at later hearings on police violence reported a typical beating by police:

> When they caught him, they began to beat him with their nightsticks until he fell to the pavement. They continued to beat him briefly after he fell. Then they dragged him about 30 feet to a paddy wagon.

As the police drove demonstrators back up Michigan Avenue, away from the hotel, a group numbering about 200 pushed through police lines and raced toward the entrance of the Conrad Hilton. Officers attacked the edges of this group using Mace spray. They pushed the bulk of the group up against the hotel and the plate glass windows of its Haymarket Lounge. Suddenly, a shattering noise burst above the roar of the crowd. The large window had crashed inward under the pressure, sending several demonstrators sprawling into the lounge among the shards of glass. A squad of police lunged into the bar after them, beating fallen victims and anyone else who looked like a protester.

Outside, the riot continued. The bulk of the crowd, now massed along the side of the avenue on a small strip of park facing the Hilton, began to chant: "The whole world is watching!" Indeed it was. Spotlights poured onto the crowd, and television cameras picked out the bloodied, angry, sobbing faces.

Police reinforcements continued to pour in, and they gradually cleared the intersection, arresting anyone who dared enter it. Several units of the Illinois National Guard moved up from the south on Michigan Avenue toward the hotel. Here and there, police struck or arrested a demonstrator, but the battle had ended. Nevertheless, a crowd of about 5,000 remained facing the Hilton, while the police and National Guard occupied the streets.

THE MAYOR AND THE CANDIDATE. Mayor Richard J. Daley of Chicago (left) looks on approvingly as Hubert H. Humphrey delivers his acceptance speech to the Chicago convention, which nominated him for president on the Democratic ticket.

Back in the Amphitheater, the delegates had reconvened at 6:30 to complete the final business of the convention—nomination of the presidential candidate. The nomination speeches proceeded slowly, and as they did, the delegates gradually learned what was happening back at the Conrad Hilton. Tension inside the hall mounted rapidly. Most of the attention was riveted on Daley. As the delayed films from the riot on Michigan Avenue arrived at CBS headquarters, the director of news gave the go-ahead for a live interview with the mayor. As Daley sat whispering and nodding to the Illinois delegates around him, CBS news intercut scenes of the police beating demonstrators and dragging off reporters for arrest. Then the interview began. Dan Rather, standing next to where Daley was sitting, leaned down to talk to him. From the floor Rather wasn't seeing any of the taped material from downtown, of course.

> "Mayor? Sir? Mayor Daley, Walter Cronkite is reporting downtown the police have used tear gas and there is considerable turmoil around the Hilton hotel."

Daley remained placid. He assured Rather that the police had complete control of the situation. But television viewers at home saw dizzying pictures of soldiers in riot gear, bayonets fixed, advancing on demonstrators; of gas bombs exploding; of Chicago police rushing after protesters, beating them.

During a seconding speech for Humphrey, a Colorado delegate interrupted the proceedings and shouted: "Is there any rule under which Mayor Daley can be compelled to end the police state of terror being perpetrated?" The mayor sat scowling. Then when Abraham Ribicoff, senator from Connecticut and an old Humphrey friend, was placing Senator George McGovern's name in nomination, he abruptly departed from his text. With McGovern as president, he declared, "We would not have these Gestapo tactics in the streets of Chicago!" Mayor Daley leaped from his seat, joined by friends and supporters, cursing and shouting at Ribicoff.

With order restored, the nomination process continued, and Humphrey edged toward inevitable victory. At about 11:30 P.M. his vote total passed into a majority. Watching back at his headquarters in the Conrad Hilton, the new candidate was surrounded by well-wishers and congratulations. He rushed over to the television set and threw his arms around the screen.

If anything, however, Humphrey had embraced his worst enemy. Television was part of his undoing in the election that followed. Scenes from the riot in front of his hotel had been continuously intercut into live broadcasts from the convention. Thus the violence, which had ended about 9 P.M., seemed to punctuate the whole long process of nomination. There was no way the new candidate could undo the impression that he had been chosen in the midst of a riot and that he had silently acquiesced in the violence.

DEMOCRATS AWAKE TO A PARTY IN RUINS

Washington Post

The physical devastation of that Wednesday-evening battle for Chicago was serious: almost sixty policemen and many more demonstrators injured, and the Hilton hotel reeked of gas and stink bombs, its posh lounge closed for repairs. But the immediate political damage to Humphrey and the Democratic party was far greater. Unable or unwilling to accommodate antiwar sentiment, the convention had chosen a candidate who represented the continuation of bitterly opposed policies. Nominated in an atmosphere of violence and brutality, Humphrey could never generate enough enthusiasm to carry him to victory. Selected behind the closely guarded doors of the Amphitheater, Humphrey was defeated in Chicago's streets and in the nation's media. Much of the press and television commentary concluded that the police had rioted out of control. Despite a spirited defense of his actions and charges that "terrorists" had "set out to destroy the purpose of this national political convention," Mayor Daley was convicted in the press of inciting a riot because he would not tolerate peaceful demonstrations.

In the face of these recriminations, and Richard Nixon's close presidential victory in November, the Chicago demonstrations reverberated through the next year. In October, the House Un-American Activities Committee convened hearings to discuss possible "connections, if any, of certain leaders of the demonstration with foreign powers." They called Hoffman, Rubin, Davis, Hayden, and Dellinger as witnesses. At the first hearing, Hoffman appeared wearing an American flag for a shirt and was promptly arrested. The committee struggled to maintain a serious atmosphere, but witnesses replied to questions with attacks on the credentials of the members. After several exasperating attempts, the committee gave up.

In 1969 a federal grand jury indicted several of the MOBE and Yippie leaders under the 1967 Federal Conspiracy Act Law, which made it illegal to cross state lines to incite to riot. The trial began in late September before Judge Julius Hoffman of the U.S. District Court in Chicago. An elderly justice with a reputation for firmness, Hoffman quickly lost both his temper and control of the courtroom. In the turbulent days that followed, he delivered blistering attacks on the defense attorneys, prevented defense witnesses from appearing, and openly sided with the prosecution.

Nothing could have better suited the Yippie theatrics of Abbie Hoffman and Jerry Rubin. Once again, they won a media victory. Perhaps Judge Hoffman's worst mistake was to refuse Bobby Seale, a codefendant, the right to independent counsel. When Seale protested and disrupted the court, the judge warned that he had the power to restrain the defendant: "I don't want to do that. Under the law you may be gagged and chained to your chair." When Seale continued to object, the court bound him and refused to let him speak.

The long, ludicrous trial ended in the spring of 1970. The jury returned a guilty verdict on lesser counts than conspiracy, but the judge sentenced Rubin, Davis, Hayden, Hoffman, and Dellinger each to five years in prison. To this he added 175 contempt citations for their behavior in the courtroom. He also ordered the trial lawyers imprisoned for contempt. By piling legal outrage upon legal outrage, however, Judge Hoffman set himself up for easy reversal. When the U.S. Court of Appeals heard the case in November 1972, it reversed the convictions and sternly rebuked Judge Hoffman and the prosecution. Later, most of the contempt charges were also rescinded. This final act of the Festival of Life thus ended with a vindication of the Yippies and a reaffirmation of the rights of protesters.

In one sense, however, the victory was shallow and belated. A great many Americans despised the radical demonstrators and turned to conservative politicians to restore law and order. American participation in the war in Vietnam dragged on for a further five years. It came to a bloody and chaotic conclusion finally in 1975 when the North Vietnamese seized Saigon. The innocence of radical students had died in the Chicago confrontation. Small elements of SDS, mistaking public attention for public sympathy, slipped underground and advocated violence against symbols of power. Other student radicals turned to heavy and fruitless theoretical debates. The thrust of the movement faltered. The Yippies also found their following confused and splintered. Some turned to drugs; others dropped out of politics entirely. Some joined exotic Eastern religions.

One almost unnoticed event of the convention suddenly loomed very large in the next few years. This was reform of the party structure. In 1969 George McGovern was appointed to chair the Democratic Party Reform Commission. His working staff of researchers and writers were young political activists and veterans of the 1968 campaign. Taking the commission across the country for hearings on ways to democratize the party, the staff interviewed representatives of local black movements and women's rights organizations. It concluded that a variety of changes were necessary to eliminate control by political bosses such as Mayor Daley.

Its most radical proposal along these lines concerned quotas or proportional representation for racial and ethnic groups and for men and women. Although the proposal finally adopted was vague, its implications were not: Each state delegation to the 1972 convention must have a "proportion of women, minorities, and young people not less than the proportion of each group in the state represented." In this way, the struggle for Chicago had ended in victory for the demonstrators. They had triumphed over the old Democratic party. Many of them were now on the inside. But the party itself had been crippled and its constituencies bitterly divided against each other.

The Limits of Politics

The young protesters who clamored to enter the Democratic party convention of 1968, those who shouted their defiance at symbols of authority, were assaulting the foundations of the postwar political consensus. The target of their ire, Hubert Humphrey, the candidate nominated by the party to run against Richard Nixon, was a man of impeccable liberal credentials. His record on civil rights stretched back to the 1948 Democratic convention, when he engineered a strong plank on black rights. Throughout the 1950s and 1960s he had championed the cause of organized labor. He stood behind most of the social reforms passed by the Kennedy and Johnson administrations. Yet the Chicago protesters dismissed him with contemptuous cries of "Dump the Hump!" They demanded, instead, a very different sort of politics than that practiced by men like Humphrey.

In the brief eight years between the election of John F. Kennedy and the Chicago convention, much had happened to fragment the consensus in American society and to convince a variety of interest groups to repudiate political compromise. The result by the end of the decade was growing acrimony, confrontation, and violence. In 1968 it appeared as if the political center could no longer hold and that politics would splinter into competing ideological groups.

To some extent, the breakup of the liberal coalition of the 1960s resulted from the rising and unfulfilled expectations of social reform, and the increasing costs and unfulfillable aims of the war in Vietnam. The promise of the civil rights movement foundered on white resistance and splits in the black movement. Reformers and elected officials pledged more than they could deliver. From the middle of the Kennedy administration, through the five years of Johnson's presidency, the war in Vietnam was a constant drumbeat. At first only audible as a kind of background noise, the war eventually drowned out the voices still calling for social reform. By 1968, opposition to the war in Vietnam had all but consumed the impulse to reform, as the war frustrated the expectations aroused in the early years of the decade.

The march on Washington of 1963 represented the high point of hope that the ideals of King and the practical political sense of Kennedy could be intertwined to achieve major civil rights legislation. It was not optimism, however, but violence and tragedy that eventually persuaded Congress to pass the Civil Rights Act as well as Kennedy's other reform projects.

Late in the fall of 1963, most of the president's program was stalled in Congress. The Civil Rights Bill, toughened and amended, languished despite Kennedy's support. The centerpiece of his economic program, an extensive tax cut designed to stimulate production and jobs, remained unpassed. Work had begun in earnest to develop a program to fight large poverty pockets in rural states and urban areas, but hopes for passage of such a program were not bright.

Partly as an effort to win support for his faltering legislation, partly to shore up his presidency for the election one year away, Kennedy embarked on a speaking tour in late November. One of his stops was Dallas, Texas, a center of opposition to his programs. On November 22, Kennedy rode through the center of the city in an open car. Suddenly, rifle fire exploded and the president slumped forward. Two bullets had shattered his skull and throat. John Connally, governor of Texas, who was sitting in front of Kennedy, was also wounded. The driver of the car sped to a nearby hospital, but the president's wounds were fatal. His administration had begun in a burst of enthusiasm and media attention. Now millions of Americans watched on television the last scenes of its tragic ending: the murder of the accused assassin, Lee Harvey Oswald, and then the Kennedy funeral. Although a presidential commission presided over by Earl Warren, Chief Justice of the Supreme Court, concluded that Oswald was the only perpetrator, a great many Americans remained skeptical of these findings.

--=◎=--

JOHNSON AS PRESIDENT

It was Lyndon Baines Johnson's genius to turn this tragic moment into triumph. Assuming the presidency, Johnson stood back from the rituals of bereavement, acting to consolidate his power. In many ways this was a difficult task, for Johnson represented a different constituency of the Democratic party. He was a Texan, boisterous and crude in manner. He had mastered the clubroom politics of the U.S. Senate, which had brought him enormous legislative influence during the late 1950s. But most of the Kennedy entourage of advisers and cabinet officers considered him an outsider. Now, suddenly, he was president.

SOCIAL PROGRAMS

On the other hand, Johnson believed even more strongly than Kennedy in the power and duty of the federal government to guarantee the rights of marginal or poor citizens. Seizing the stalled leg-islative program of the Kennedy administration, Johnson vowed to win its passage as a memorial to the slain leader and, perhaps, as testimony to his own right to the presidency. But there was an irony to this. Johnson succeeded in pressing reform legislation through Congress that dwarfed Kennedy's accomplishments. Yet he could never elicit the enthusiasm that his predecessor had.

Johnson grasped the wheel of government firmly. Five days after the assassination he addressed Congress, pledging to continue the policies of Kennedy. By early 1964 his efforts bore fruit. Congress enacted bill after bill: a major tax cut to stimulate the economy; the Economic Opportunity Act, setting up the structure for a "war on poverty"; and, most significant, a major civil rights act. To push civil rights legislation through Congress meant overcoming strong southern opposition. Johnson built a majority by calling in debts owed him by other senators. Particularly important was the Republican support he gathered. Convincing the Republican leaders, Everett Dirksen of the Senate and Charles Halleck of the House, ensured victory.

Johnson also did what neither Eisenhower nor Kennedy had done: he adopted the language of the civil rights movement itself. On March 15 he appeared before Congress to speak for civil rights. The United States, he demanded, must "overcome the crippling legacy of bigotry and injustice." Delay, hesitation, and compromise were intolerable. Then he paused and repeated slowly and deliberately the most important slogan of the civil rights movement: "And . . . we . . . shall . . . overcome."

The new Civil Rights Act did not end discrimination, but it strengthened voting rights, outlawed segregation in public facilities, increased federal capacity to enter desegregation cases, and bolstered the Civil Rights Commission. When the new tax-cut legislation passed, it worked as anticipated, although part of the stimulus may have come from the escalation of the war in Vietnam. Economic growth rates increased rapidly in 1964, 1965, and 1966. Unemployment shrank, and the federal budget hovered almost in balance. This economic growth, in turn, helped

THREE DEMOCRATS. In the early 1960s, John F. Kennedy (left), Eleanor Roosevelt, and Lyndon Baines Johnson represented three versions of Democratic party liberalism and the continuity between the New Deal of the 1930s and the pragmatic liberalism of the 1960s.

improve the ratio of black to white family income from .55 in 1960 to .64 in 1970.

The Office of Economic Opportunity (OEO) was largely Johnson's project. The Economic Opportunity Act of 1964 centralized federal antipoverty activities into one comprehensive executive agency. It created a job training corps, agricultural loan programs, incentive loans to hire the hard-core unemployed, and education benefits, plus later education programs such as Head Start and Upward Bound. While some of this amounted to sleight-of-hand transfers of existing programs to a new agency, a substantial portion of the OEO represented an innovative, broad-scale attack on poverty.

THE ELECTION OF 1964

By mid-1964, Johnson had clearly established legitimate claims to the office of president. His renomination was assured. The only question was a running mate. The Democratic convention, meeting in Atlantic City, New Jersey, in August, chose liberal Senator Hubert Humphrey of Minnesota. Campaign strategy centered on defending Johnson's legislative record and turning the conservative Republican opponent, Senator Barry Goldwater of Arizona, into the issue.

Goldwater attacked the Johnson administration on domestic and foreign policy. Goldwater's grass-roots campaign in the Republican party represented a temporary triumph over political professionals. He aroused considerable enthusiasm among voters who opposed Johnson's use of the federal government to redress social and economic inequalities. Much of his support was concentrated in the rapidly growing Sunbelt, the South and Southwest, where opposition to integration and social programs was strongest.

In some ways, the Goldwater movement was premature. His campaign was troubled by public distrust of some of his right-wing supporters. And he did not completely capitalize on growing hostility to civil rights demonstrations and liberal legislation. Governor George Wallace of Alabama had illustrated the significance of this backlash vote in primary elections in Wisconsin, Maryland, and Indiana. But Goldwater could not build a movement strong enough to block the Johnson landslide.

THE WAR IN VIETNAM

One relatively unimportant campaign issue was the war in Vietnam. During his year in office, Johnson had proceeded cautiously, without calling attention to the implications of his actions,

COMPARISON OF WHITE AND BLACK FAMILY INCOME (IN CONSTANT 1975 DOLLARS)

	White Families	Black Families	Ratio
1950	$7,702	$4,178	.54
1955	9,271	5,113	.55
1960	10,604	5,871	.55
1965	12,370	6,812	.55
1970	14,188	9,032	.64
1975	14,268	9,321	.65
1980	20,502	12,380	.60

Source: U.S. Department of Commerce, Bureau of the Census, Statistical Abstract of the United States, 1981 (Washington, D.C.: Government Printing Office, 1981), p. 436.

but he moved the United States toward far greater involvement in the war. Early in 1964 he made several important decisions. He approved plans for covert harassment of North Vietnam, and he agreed to bombing missions against the north in the event of provocation. He also appointed General William Westmoreland to head military operations. These moves rested on two assumptions: first, that North Vietnam was responsible for and could control the insurgent Viet Cong in the south; second, that American intervention in the form of air strikes and ground troops could be decisive. Johnson and his advisers did not believe that American actions would increase the fighting in the south or cause an uncontrollable infiltration of troops and arms from the north.

The pretext for full-scale intervention came in late July 1964. On July 30 South Vietnamese PT (patrol torpedo) boats attacked bases in the Gulf of Tonkin inside North Vietnamese waters. Simultaneously, the Maddox, an American destroyer, steamed into the area to disrupt North Vietnamese communication facilities. On August 2, possibly seeing the two separate missions as a combined maneuver against them, the North Vietnamese sent out several PT boats to attack the destroyer. The Maddox fired, sinking one of the attackers, then radioed the news to Washington. Johnson ordered another ship into the bay. On August 3 both destroyers reported another attack, although somewhat later, the commander of the Maddox radioed that he was

THE WAR ON POVERTY: EDUCATION, EMPLOYMENT, AND TRAINING FUNDS, 1960–1980

	1960	1965	1970	1975	1980
Percentage of federal budget	1.1	1.8	4.4	4.9	5.3
Amount (in billions of dollars)	1.0	2.1	8.6	15.9	30.8

Source: U.S. Department of Commerce, Bureau of the Census, Statistical Abstract of the United States, 1981 (Washington, D.C.: Government Printing Office, 1981), p. 248.

not sure. Nonetheless, the president ordered American planes to retaliate by bombing inside North Vietnam.

Johnson then sought congressional support and justification for his action. He quickly received it. Senator William Fulbright guided a resolution through his Foreign Relations Committee and then through the Senate in less than a week. Fulbright's action was perhaps related to his fear that Barry Goldwater might use the Vietnam issue in the forthcoming election. Neither he nor anyone else in the Senate had been told all the facts about the Gulf of Tonkin skirmish, and later critics would question whether or not an attack had actually occurred.

Like the Korean War and the cold war, the origins of the war in Vietnam lay partly in unresolved questions left over from World War II. American participation in the struggle was by accumulation, some of it public and some of it secret. This made it a process and a cause that few Americans understood very well.

The fighting in Vietnam began in 1945, at the end of Japanese occupation, and terminated in 1975, when North Vietnamese and Viet Cong soldiers marched into Saigon, the South Vietnamese capital, thus putting an end to the last American-supported government. This thirty-year struggle by communist-led forces sought to eliminate first French and then American influence in Vietnam. Essentially a civil war, it was complicated by French colonialism, by international agreements, by encouragement and aid from outside nations, and by a massive effort of the United States to thwart the communists.

When the French reconquered most of their former colony of Vietnam after World War II, communist forces inspired by Ho Chi Minh began an uprising that eventually defeated the French in 1954 at the battle of Dien Bien Phu. From 1950, the United States supplied the French with war materiel but declined direct intervention. During the Eisenhower administration, the president and his advisers sympathized with the French, gave them aid, and hoped to prevent the further spread of communist influ-

ence in Asia. But Eisenhower also understood the extreme risks of direct involvement in another Asian war after the unpopular conflict in Korea.

Exhausted and defeated after Dien Bien Phu, the French agreed to a peace conference in Geneva, Switzerland, in July 1954. The Geneva Accords provided for French withdrawal and temporarily divided Vietnam into two administrative areas: the north, occupied by the communist Viet Minh, and the south, organized by pro-French Vietnamese. Reunification elections were mandated to decide the permanent fate of the nation. The United States sent observers to the

A VIETNAMESE CASUALTY.   Both sides in the Vietnam War inflicted heavy casualties on innocent civilians. Photographs such as this one, featured in American newspapers and on nightly television newscasts, convinced many Americans that the fight could never be won without a savagery and brutality that they would not support.

Geneva conference but did not sign the accords. In fact, the Central Intelligence Agency worked secretly to undermine the agreements, to disrupt the economy of the north, and to install a pro-American ruler in the south. This last goal was accomplished when Ngo Dinh Diem became prime minister of the putative Republic of Vietnam. Diem asked for and received advice and aid from the United States. He also refused to participate in reunification elections. Partly to counter this, Diem's opponents, aided by the north, turned to insurgency.

From this time onward, American financial and military support poured in as five American presidents, from Eisenhower to Ford, attempted to salvage American interests in the area. For the United States, however, intervention had no really distinct beginning. War was never officially declared, although the Gulf of Tonkin Resolution

authorized the president to protect American forces and interests in the area. American participation grew in small increments, sometimes openly and sometimes secretly. By 1965 there were 181,000 American troops in South Vietnam; by 1968 there were 536,000.

Like the Korean War, the war in Vietnam was fought within serious constraints and a desire to minimize costs. The ultimate suppliers of war materiel (the United States, the USSR, and China) were not attacked, and supply lines into Vietnam remained open on both sides for most of the war. The victory the United States sought was the permanent establishment of a Western-oriented government in South Vietnam. But the means to achieve this were, from the beginning, controversial.

The nature of warfare in Vietnam was determined by the jungle terrain and by the sympathy of many South Vietnamese for the rebels. In the absence of fronts or battle lines, the Viet Cong (South Vietnamese rebels) and North Vietnamese troops could choose the time and place of engagement. After a battle, they could slip into dense jungles or hide among supporters in the peasantry. Their weapons were sometimes crude—they used booby traps and captured arms—but they also possessed more-sophisticated Soviet and Chinese equipment. The United States, adapting to jungle warfare, relied most heavily on helicopters, which gave great flexibility to troop movements. After 1964, American tactics focused on preventing supplies from reaching rebels in the south. Intensive bombing and defoliation of jungles with herbicides disrupted supply routes, but eventually intensive bombing of North Vietnam was undertaken to cut supplies off at the source.

In his first year in office, Johnson prided himself on the consensus he had achieved in domestic and foreign affairs. In dealing with Vietnam he appeared to be a moderate. In some re-

spects he was. But he locked himself in by three assumptions that gradually convinced him to commit more men and more resources to the Indochina war. The first of these beliefs was the "domino theory," originally propounded by Eisenhower. This notion assumed that if South Vietnam fell to the communist-supported insurgents, other Southeast Asian nations would topple into the communist camp. The second assumption was that gradual escalation, covert action, and misinformation could hide the war from the American people and thus preserve consensus. (The war would be over before anyone realized its extent or cost.) Finally, Johnson wanted to save face. He believed that the United States could not afford to withdraw or back down without inviting a barrage of accusations that he had sold out to the communists. Having lived through one period of McCarthyism, he was determined to prevent another.

Believing the optimistic appraisals of his military advisers and the "hawks" in his adminis-

A HELICOPTER SWOOPS INTO BATTLE TO PICK UP A WOUNDED AMERICAN SOLDIER. The helicopter gave troops great mobility and the sound of choppers was a link to the safer world of American bases outside the confusing and gruesome battlefields in the countryside.

tration, he gradually committed American troops and prestige to the jungle war. He cut himself off from the "doves" (war opponents) in Congress. Planning strategy and defending his decisions against mounting public criticism became his preoccupations. By pursuing this policy, he convinced many Americans that the Democratic party had fallen to the control of a narrow group of professional politicians who could not understand why any reasonable person might oppose the war.

The Vietnam War was only one factor that undercut support for the liberal consensus on which Johnson depended. There were growing numbers of critics of the federal activism of the Kennedy and Johnson administrations. Opponents of integration and conservatives in general rejected the notion that government should intervene in the economic and social order to guarantee a fair distribution of opportunity and rewards. From the opposite point of view, students, the civil rights movement, the poor, and then the growing women's movement criticized the federal government for delaying social reforms.

THE NEW RIGHT

Large numbers of disaffected Americans joined the "new right." Born in the troubled 1950s from the marriage of traditional conservatism and a new, vociferous right wing, this movement captured the Republican party temporarily in 1964 and exercised a strong influence on the direction of the party thereafter. Combining a strident anticommunism with a rejection of liberal reform, this movement assailed the Democratic party with increasing effectiveness.

REACTION TO THE WARREN COURT

The new right originated in dissatisfaction with the Eisenhower administration and, in particular, with the Warren Court decisions that liberalized American society. Besides *Brown* v. *Board of Education*, the Warren Court in *Watkins* v. *United States* (1957) upheld the rights of witnesses testifying before a congressional committee. In effect, this decision made future McCarthy-like hearings less likely. Another decision, *Reynolds* v. *Sims*, (1964), ruled that state legislative districts had to be apportioned evenly according to population. This decision deprived rural (and generally conservative) areas of much of the political power they had exercised in state government. A later case, *Miranda* v. *State of Arizona* (1966), ruled that a person apprehended for a crime must be informed of his or her rights, including the right to remain silent, before any statement relating to the crime could become legal evidence.

These Court decisions, together with many others—on civil rights, definitions of obscenity, and protection of free speech—greatly strengthened minority civil rights. They opened the federal courts to a wide variety of lawsuits brought by groups claiming discrimination. The Warren Court thus took the lead in expanding the rights of citizens and the power of the federal government to intervene in the lives of every American. Because of this activism, the Court also became the target of extensive and angry criticism.

The John Birch Society was founded in 1958 by candy manufacturer Robert Welch from Massachusetts. The society (named after an anticommunist missionary who died in China) became the most strident center of criticism of the Warren Court. Welch had been deeply disappointed by Eisenhower's refusal to undo New Deal reforms. He concluded, in fact, that the Republican party had been infiltrated by communist agents. Welch discovered support for his views across America and particularly in southern California and the nation's eastern suburban areas. In 1960 the Birch society launched an "Impeach Earl Warren" campaign. By 1964, Birch members controlled a significant portion of the

Republican party, enough to ensure the nomination of Goldwater.

INTELLECTUALS AND EVANGELISTS

A growing number of right-wing intellectuals were among those who attacked government-mandated egalitarianism. One of the most important among them was William F. Buckley, whose *National Review* magazine, founded in 1955, became a center for opposition to the liberal postwar consensus.

Other conservative forces, which were at first less clearly focused or politically motivated, centered on Protestant revivalism. The early leader of this movement was the Reverend Billy Graham. Beginning in the early 1950s, Graham led successful revival crusades in cities across the nation. Although the political message of his sermons and books was sometimes muted, he preached salvation by individual redemption, not by government regulation. He appealed to elements in society who were disturbed or left behind by rapid social change. Praising "rugged individualism," he criticized social legislation and labor unions while remaining silent on questions like integration. This stand captivated a strong element of white southerners, who were most affected by the turbulence of civil rights.

SEGREGATIONISTS

In fact, the gains of civil rights caused consternation among many white Americans, and not just those of the South. Repeatedly, Gallup polls in the 1950s and 1960s demonstrated white America's divided conscience on this issue. Gradually, most white Americans, even in the South, accepted at least a limited version of the goal of integration. But most at the same time feared the means used to accomplish it, such as marches and demonstrations.

WALLACE SUPPORTERS, LANSING, MICHIGAN. Confusion in the Democratic party and the moderate line taken by Republican candidate Richard Nixon in 1968 bolstered third-party presidential hopeful George Wallace of Alabama. Wallace also ran in 1964. He gained support from disgruntled conservatives frustrated with the limited war policy in Vietnam, demonstrations, and racial integration.

Some of the opposition to integration rallied around Governor George Wallace of Alabama. Defeated in several local showdowns with federal officials over Alabama's segregation policies, Wallace became a symbol of resistance to federal erosion of local power. In 1964 he gathered significant support as a presidential candidate inside the Democratic party, although not enough to win the nomination. In 1968 he ran for president on the ticket of the American Independent party and won about 13 percent of the popular vote (some of them former Democrats), coming close to forcing the election into the House of Representatives. He campaigned on a platform calling for "law and order" (thinly veiled anti-integration code words), the suppression of urban rioting and of protest marches against the war in Vietnam.

─═◎═─

SPLINTERING OF THE LEFT

The most important element to break away from the liberal consensus was the civil rights movement. In some respects, this break was only partial. Organizations such as the NAACP and the Urban League continued to work closely with the Democratic party and the federal government. Black voters repeatedly demonstrated their allegiance to Democratic candidates. Congress and the courts still played a major role in enforcing and extending the rights of minorities. But what Martin Luther King, Jr., had feared might happen did occur after the summer of 1963 and the passage of the 1964 Civil Rights Act. Despite the progress in legal rights, the plight of many African Americans remained little changed. Integration proceeded slowly; job opportunities especially remained scarce. In order to gain support, the civil rights movement had aroused the expectations of every black American. Inevitably, these expectations were frustrated.

King was cautious (many in the movement said too cautious) about exhausting white tolerance for civil rights progress. During the summer of 1964, before the presidential election, a voter registration drive in Mississippi led by SNCC and the NAACP brought hundreds of college students to the state. After three of them were murdered in Philadelphia, Mississippi, King became so worried about such incidents of violence and the possibility that Republicans might successfully exploit them to focus hostility on civil rights that he called for a temporary moratorium on demonstrations. But groups like SNCC and CORE refused.

BLACK UNREST

Lack of visible progress toward either racial equality or improved living standards became apparent in northern cities during the mid-1960s. Fed by mass migration from the rural South during and after World War II, the black population in northeastern cities more than doubled between 1950 and 1970, while the white population actually fell in the same areas. Consequently, urban tax bases eroded, and city social services were overburdened. At the same time, discrimination in hiring, poor schools, and inadequate training kept much of the black population unemployed or underemployed. The network of federal social services could not fill every gap. Inflamed by incautious police enforcement and violent incidents, urban ghettos exploded into rioting in 1964–1967 and particularly in 1968.

Increasing violence precipitated a split in the unwieldy civil rights movement that Martin Luther King, Jr., had tried to guide. The African-American community had never been entirely unified. Enormous regional and class gulfs split the black population. Generational differences divided leadership. Gradually, a gulf widened between proponents of alliances with white liberals and the federal government and advocates of all-black organizations. The charismatic Black Muslim leader Malcolm X, for example, preached a separatism that appealed to many urban blacks. Although Malcolm X was assassinated in 1965, his position continued to attract the more radical elements of the northern ghettos. He became a legendary figure with the publication of his autobiography in the same year.

The first major urban riot occurred in the summer of 1964 in Harlem. Then violence exploded in the Watts section of Los Angeles the following summer. Other cities were struck in 1965–1968. Most of these disturbances followed the same pattern. An incident in the ghetto would bring police action. Unable to control the situation, police would call for reinforcements. Then ghetto residents would pour out of tenement buildings, attacking and looting stores and setting fires. As the conflagration spread, snipers sometimes appeared. Police and, finally, the National Guard would isolate a riot area, proclaim a curfew, and arrest thousands of residents. Frequently, the police and guard put down riots with excessive force. During 1967, a year in which seventy cities were besieged by riots, more than eighty people died—most of them African Americans—and thousands were arrested.

King still clung to nonviolence in the midst of this disorder. But groups like SNCC were less hesitant about condoning violence. In 1966 Stokely Carmichael, the leader of SNCC, advocated self-defense for blacks. He also popularized the term "black power," which implied cutting ties with white liberals and pushing for gains using exclusively black organizations.

After 1967, relations between black civil rights leaders and the administration deteriorated sharply. In the spring, Martin Luther King, Jr., broke with the president over the war in Vietnam. For the civil rights leader, this was an anguished moment. In 1965 King had briefly criticized the war, but Johnson had applied enormous pressure, and King had reversed himself. Now, however, he believed that the war could not be ignored. Its incessant funding demands had cut into poverty programs. The draft and college deferments (primarily exercised by young white men) placed a disproportionate percentage of black soldiers on the Asian front lines. Despite the company of white radicals and black power advocates that an antiwar stance placed him in, King sharply attacked the war. The United States, he declared, was "the greatest purveyor of violence in the world today." Carl T. Rowan, a black journalist, wrote: "By urging Negroes not to respond to the draft or to fight in Vietnam, he has taken a tack that many Americans of all races consider utterly irresponsible." King's decision of conscience speeded a process of alienation that took civil rights off the federal agenda. But the leader had already begun to falter and the move-

ment he headed was deeply divided over goals and strategies. The doors to the house of reform were, indeed, being shut.

The black civil rights movement endured one further, and perhaps fatal, loss in the spring of 1968. King was planning a "poor people's campaign" and demonstration in Washington to rekindle the smoldering movement. He also participated in a strike of black garbage workers in Memphis, Tennessee. The strike was a bitter one, called after two workers were accidentally killed on the job. The strikers demanded better wages and working conditions. King worked hard to prevent violence. On the evening of April 4, as he prepared to leave his Memphis motel for dinner, King stepped out on the balcony for a moment to speak to his driver below. A rifle cracked and King fell, mortally wounded.

The news of King's death blew through the ghettos of American cities like a ravaging wind. Riots erupted in over 100 cities. Buildings burned, businesses were looted. The National Guard and police once more moved in with force. Mayor Daley of Chicago, which suffered one of the worst riots, spoke of a need to "shoot to maim or cripple" looters if riots broke out again. When the soldiers and police finally withdrew, the civil rights movement, and much of the sympathy it had engendered, had been gutted.

STUDENT RADICALS

King and other black civil rights leaders had, by their example, inspired the country's white student radicals. Young white Americans had been among the most enthusiastic supporters of President John Kennedy. His New Frontier appealed to a generation that rejected the secure and smug middle-class world they associated with their parents and the suburbs where they lived. Kennedy's inaugural address in early 1961 struck a responsive chord. The new president dedicated his administration to reviving America's traditional mission in the world: the protection and extension of political freedom. To the "tempered," "disciplined," and "proud" new generation of

Americans he addressed, he promised an endeavor whose glow would be a beacon for the world. He asked of others only what he required of himself: "not what America will do for you," but "what together we can do for the freedom of man." But these were words of warning as well as promise, strident as well as imposing, for implicit in their fervent rhetoric of sacrifice lay the seeds of the confrontational policies that led to intervention in Cuba and escalation in Vietnam.

Such lofty goals as Kennedy articulated were inevitably compromised in the real and hard world of politics. Like civil rights advocates, with whom they shared much in common, young white Americans had rising expectations for their society. They desired not only civil rights for blacks but a much greater voice for themselves in the direction of society. Their goals consisted of a patchwork of radical reforms of politics, of culture, of universities and schools, and of social and sexual relationships. These aims were eventually focused in two related movements: the "new left"

and the "counterculture." At first, student radicals found themselves in alliance with the Kennedy and Johnson administrations. Pleased by some of the reform legislation and inspired by the stirring rhetoric, the new left and the counterculture nonetheless gradually moved away from the political center of American society. By 1968 they were in open confrontation with it.

The new left and the counterculture originated in the 1950s. The more politically minded students were profoundly dissatisfied with the politics of the Eisenhower era. The slow pace of integration, the tense standoff between the United States and the Soviet Union, McCarthyism, and widespread poverty and social discrimination inspired a group of university students in 1962 to found a new sort of political organization, the Students for a Democratic Society (SDS). Unlike the "old left," which they dismissed as ineffectual and conservative, these student radicals wanted to break with the prevailing liberal consensus, or at least to stretch it far beyond its cur-

THE AFTERMATH OF THE URBAN RIOTS. Riots in black ghettos in 1968 transformed the cores of American cities into war zones occupied by troops (the National Guard).

rent dimensions. With other young radicals, Tom Hayden, a student at the University of Michigan, wrote the "Port Huron Statement," a document that proposed a new political system of "participatory democracy" and called for an end to racial discrimination and the cold war.

By the early 1960s, SDS was only part of a larger political stirring on campuses across the country. Much of this movement took its inspiration from the civil rights marches and demonstrations. Northern white students joined in picketing national corporations such as Woolworth that practiced discrimination in their southern branches. Or they joined in freedom marches and voter registration drives in the South, particularly during the "Mississippi Summer" of 1964. Other students became politically active around opposition to the investigations of the House Un-American Activities Committee. By 1964 the radical movement had organized on several large university campuses: Michigan, the University of Chicago, Wisconsin, and, particularly, the University of California at Berkeley.

Berkeley became the center of national attention during the fall of 1964. The centerpiece of the prestigious California system of higher education, Berkeley enjoyed a reputation for liberal regulations and a distinguished faculty. But as an institution it was also large, impersonal, and bureaucratic. In 1964 the administration altered rules governing campus areas set aside for student political meetings and recruitment drives. Students reacted quickly and angrily. They organized a Free Speech movement and held large demonstrations and sit-ins. Eventually, they took over administration buildings. Most of these tactics were borrowed from the civil rights movement.

Frightened by the rising anger and organization on campus, and pressured by state officials, the university called in the police. Now the students declared a general strike and shut down most of the campus. Eventually, the new restrictions were lifted. But the student movement remained strong. Indeed, Berkeley set an example for students across the country, who in turn began to protest unwanted rules and restrictions on

THE BEATLES (John, Ringo, Paul, and George) early in their careers. Their conservative dress more than anything else reveals their working-class origins. The group, their music, and their styles evolved enormously during the 1960s.

THE COUNTERCULTURE. During the 1960s, two symbols represented the counterculture: a V sign, meaning peace in Vietnam, and the word LOVE. Both signified the desire of many young Americans to revise the nature of sexual, social, and political relationships.

their own campuses. At the same time, student radicalism became an issue for conservative political campaigns. Ronald Reagan's successful quest for the governorship of California in 1966 gained energy and focus from his promise to deal firmly with Berkeley.

THE COUNTERCULTURE

Whatever coherence the radical student movement attained depended in part on a growing network of counterculture. The counterculture was not necessarily political in orientation, but it was opposed to many of the practices of adult culture. It traced its origins to the 1950s and rock 'n' roll music, which at first was almost entirely a teenage phenomenon.

By the 1960s this youth culture had spread and deepened. The anti-establishment character of the youth rebellion became more and more explicit. The youth culture acquired advocates like writers Allen Ginsberg, Jack Kerouac, and Paul Goodman, whose book *Growing Up Absurd*, published in 1960, explored the anguish of the younger generation. Also by the 1960s the counterculture had absorbed more-sophisticated versions of rock 'n' roll in the music of the Beatles

and the protest songs of Bob Dylan. Equally important, many young people had begun to experiment with illegal drugs: marijuana, hashish, and LSD.

The young people who experimented with drugs and new sexual relationships were seeking a congenial and hospitable environment. Their lifestyles represented a sharp contrast to the daily grind of work shifts and overtime. So some of them "dropped out" or sought comradeship in communal living on farms or in rural areas. This emphasis on a return to nature and a rejection of modern industrial life, materialism, and artificiality eventually became a strong element not just of the counterculture but of the rest of American society as well.

By the mid-1960s many young people had begun to reject the liberal consensus of Kennedy and Johnson, largely because of the war in Vietnam. Not only did the war starve social programs that many young radicals supported, it weighed heavily on their own lives because of the draft. Many of them received deferments while in college or graduate school. But this special status, which exempted them from duty in the jungles of Asia, only increased their uneasiness with their privileged positions in society.

Increasingly, the war split America. It cut off students, the civil rights movement, and intellectuals from the established consensus. It divided those who believed the war could not be won from those who believed it must be won at all costs. Justification for the war, however, rested on the basic assumptions of post–World War II American foreign policy. Thus failure either to win the battle in Asia or to convince the American public to support it wholeheartedly frayed the fabric of faith in politics that had been unchallenged for twenty years.

AMERICAN WOMEN

One further rift in the social consensus came gradually to a head during the 1960s, as a result of the postwar experience of American women. In 1945, *House Beautiful* magazine addressed its female readers in an article on returning soldiers entitled "Home Should Be Even More Wonderful Than He Remembers It." As the author put it, "He's head man again. Your part in the remaking of this man is to fit his home to him, understanding why he wants it this way, forgetting your own preferences."

As this article suggests, the postwar years left women with an ambiguous experience that touched their identity and particularly their social image. During the war, they had been welcomed, and even encouraged, to enter the labor force to take the place of men drafted into the armed forces. Now they were encouraged, and sometimes forced, to leave. Many of them, however, did not leave; they simply could not afford to stop working. But most of these women took up jobs that were traditionally labeled women's work, such as waiting on tables or nursing. Married women who remained in the workforce found themselves shouldering a double burden: a job from nine to five and housework and cooking afterward. Statistics demonstrate that the percentage of working women shrank after 1945, but did not fall as low as prewar levels. In fact, after the initial drop, the number and percentage of working women resumed a steady increase.

These abrupt changes in women's activities gave rise to contradictory and conflicting pictures of the proper role of women in American society. During the war, the popular press, newspapers, and government publications stressed the contributions of women to the war effort. Of course, there were exceptions: In 1943, government and the press alike lamented the fate of "latch-key children," who returned from school to an empty house and unfilled hours of loneliness. Generally, however, when women enlisted to work for the duration of the war, they were well received. Indeed, during the war, both major political parties endorsed an Equal Rights Amendment guaranteeing constitutional equality to women. This change would have improved wages and job op-

---

PERCENT OF BLACK VOTING AGE POPULATION REGISTERED IN ELEVEN SOUTHERN STATES, 1960–1980

	Total	Ala.	Ark.	Fla.	Ga.	La.	Miss.	N.C.	S.C.	Tenn.	Tex.	Va.
1960	29.1% (White–61.1%)	13.7	38.0	39.4	29.3	31.1	5.2	39.1	13.7	59.1	35.5	23.1
1975	58.3% (White–60.8%)	55.8	52.2	53.1	69.5	58.8	60.7	49.2	44.0	64.2	61.9	49.8
1980	57.7% (White–79.4%)	57.5	59.9	61.4	51.9	61.3	64.1	55.3	55.8	66.7	54.8	54.1

Source: U.S. Department of Commerce, Bureau of the Census, Statistical Abstract of the United States, 1981 *(Washington, D.C.: Government Printing Office, 1981), p. 495.*

portunities for women; however, both Secretary of Labor Frances Perkins and Eleanor Roosevelt, the president's wife, declined to support it.

After the war, government, business, and labor unions pressured women to return home. Women's magazines were filled with articles urging meticulous housekeeping, giving suggestions for improving domestic skills, or showering readers with new beauty and fashion tips. Eventually this pressure, and the desire of many women to live up to ideals of femininity derived from novels and movies, affected a wide range of behavior. It also led to a family-first ideology that dominated American culture during the 1950s, giving that period a tone of orthodoxy and conservatism. According to the new domestic philosophy, women—whatever else they did—should put family above all else. As girls, their goal was marriage; as women, their duties revolved around caring for children and maintaining a home.

Statistics suggest that the revived ideology of domesticity was linked to changes in family-related behavior. From 1945 to the end of the 1950s, family stability increased. After a momentary postwar rise, the divorce rate in the United States fell until about 1960; thereafter, it increased sharply and then zoomed upward in the 1970s. After the war, the marriage rate also increased; not only were more persons of eligible age actually married, but the average age for marriage had also dropped. For women, this meant that about half married before the age of twenty. Most significant, the birthrate rose sharply after the war, reaching a peak in 1956. Simply put, more women were having more babies, thus reversing, temporarily, a twentieth-century American trend toward smaller families.

By the end of the 1950s, most of these trends began to shift. The marriage and birth rates declined, the divorce rate increased, the family appeared less stable, and the role of women was no longer clearly defined. Pressure to appear a model mother remained, but women increasingly found the role irrelevant. The suburban home, touted as the ideal environment in the 1950s, could be a barren place, where boring and empty days drove many women to various addictions (alcohol, barbiturates) in an effort to disguise their aimlessness. Perhaps more important, lifestyles were changing. Increasing access to the means for birth control (the pill and intrauterine devices and, considerably later, legal abortion) made it easier for women to control reproduction. And economic necessity, the need to pay for the affluent lifestyles that modern families sought, often required women to work.

Perhaps no greater change affected American society beginning in the 1960s than the rise of organized feminism and the general increase in the consciousness of women as to their second-class citizenship in the United States. While this was in many respects a worldwide movement, American women became leaders in raising their own awareness, in finding and restoring their own history, in recognizing and combating discrimination in every sort of public and private institution. Like other movements for liberation, the women's movement both raised consciousness and generated opposition. One of the first casualties was the radical political movement itself, where women found themselves employed as secretaries, helpers, and bedmates. As everywhere else in society, women recognized that they had to become political in their own right and for their own causes.

--->=○←---

JOHNSON'S PRESIDENCY

After his electoral triumph of 1964, now president in his own right, Johnson believed he had created a durable political consensus for further domestic reforms. He was aware of opposition from the political right and left, but he was also sure of his mastery of government. Consequently, in 1965 and 1966 he placed before a heavily Democratic Congress an astonishing program of reform legislation. Congress passed and funded Medicare insurance for the elderly and Medicaid to provide free medical services for those unable to afford them. An important Voting Rights Act of August 1965 eliminated literacy tests and other obstacles to participation in elections by minority voters. In the same month, Johnson fulfilled Kennedy's promise to establish the Department of Housing and Urban Development (HUD). Other legislation poured out of the hopper: a Clean Air Act, highway beautification, federal funding of urban transit. Each act testified to the president's legislative skill.

Nonetheless, many of these "Great Society" programs lacked coordination and adequate funding. Legislation sometimes promised much more than it could deliver. Johnson himself seemed more interested in passing laws than in administering them. Bureaucratic inertia and local opposition slowed implementation. Most ominous, however, was the war in Vietnam, which by 1965 and 1966 had begun to divert funds away from social programs into the bottomless pit of an Asian land war.

THE WAR ESCALATES

Although the Gulf of Tonkin Resolution gave Johnson a mandate to protect American lives and interests in Vietnam, its implications were not clear until early 1965. Then, on February 6, Viet Cong rebels attacked an American base at Pleiku. In response, the president ordered sustained bombing of the north. He also authorized search-and-destroy sorties by American troops and, by the end of the year, had approved the dispatch of nearly 180,000 American personnel to Vietnam. A stepped-up strategic enclave policy was also initiated. During the summer of 1965, the president added to the bombing by approving regular B-52 saturation raids on enemy strongholds in the south and increased strategic raids on the north.

By the beginning of 1966 a seemingly unchanging pattern had been established in which several interlocking factors relentlessly escalated the war. American bombing and added troop strength (which mounted to 486,000 in 1967

and 536,000 in 1968) destabilized South Vietnamese society and increased northern infiltration. Northern infiltration further destabilized the south and led to even greater U.S. intervention.

Johnson did not present the issues or the costs of the war to the American public in a forthright manner. He underestimated costs in 1966 and declined to ask for increased war taxes until early 1968. (Eventually, the war cost the United States about $100 billion, with defense spending rising 16 percent in 1966, 15 percent in 1967, and 3 percent in 1968.) He responded to his critics with scorn, sarcasm, and charges of unpatriotic behavior. Nonetheless, he tried to give the impression of flexibility. On several occasions (December 1966, February and December 1967, and March 1968) he ordered a halt to the bombing and suggested negotiations. But neither North Vietnam nor the Viet Cong would agree to his terms, which were intended to guarantee the independence of South Vietnam.

Because the war remained unresolved and promises of an early victory proved false, Johnson faced mounting opposition. The burgeoning student radical movement, intellectuals, civil rights groups, Republicans angry that the war dragged on without victory, and many others chided the president. A Gallup poll revealed profound public division and confusion about the war. American goals seemed unclear. In part because of his inability to articulate clear and believable aims, the president's popularity plummeted. His carefully constructed consensus, built around fulfilling the idealism of the Kennedy years, disintegrated.

LBJ AND CIVIL RIGHTS

Meanwhile, continuing summer outbreaks of riot in American cities took their toll on Johnson's civil rights achievements. Not only split over the war in Vietnam, the United States was quickly becoming more seriously divided than ever over racial questions. Johnson attempted to prevent this polarization and to preserve the ties of the civil rights movement with his administration. In

1967 he appointed a National Advisory Commission on Civil Disorders, headed by Governor Otto Kerner of Illinois. The report, when issued in 1968, warned of the degeneration of American society into two warring racial cultures. The commission also blamed "white racism" for the urban riots. But a Gallup poll found that only a third of Americans accepted this conclusion.

Following the disorders of 1967, Johnson also secured passage of a new civil rights act in early 1968 that barred discrimination in most American housing. But while he recognized the need for quick action to correct social injustice, Johnson opposed riot and confrontation as a means of attaining such goals. After the riots of 1967 he declared: "Violence must be stopped, quickly, finally, and permanently."

The president faced still other political problems because of a backlash against his social programs. After midterm Democratic congressional losses in 1966, a more independent-minded and stronger opposition confronted him. Funds for some of his projects, such as the war on poverty, dwindled. Yet Johnson continued to advocate reform, if only to hold the sympathy of his liberal constituency.

AN AMERICAN IN VIETNAM. Why were these boys dying? It was a question the politicians were unable to answer persuasively. This U.S. soldier was photographed during the Tet offensive in 1968, a battle so overwhelming that many Americans were convinced of the need for their country to withdraw.

CHRONOLOGY

1958	John Birch Society founded
1960	"Impeach Earl Warren" campaign launched
1962	Students for a Democratic Society founded
1963(Nov.)	President Kennedy assassinated;
(Nov.)	Lyndon Johnson becomes president
1964(Mar.)	President Johnson addresses Congress on civil rights;
	Economic Opportunity Act passed;
	Berkeley Free Speech movement organized;
	Supreme Court decides *Reynolds* v. *Sims* case;
	George Wallace campaigns for presidency;
	First major northern ghetto riot, in Harlem;
(Aug.)	Gulf of Tonkin Resolution passed by Congress;
(Nov.)	Johnson reelected president over Barry Goldwater
1965	181,000 American troops committed to South Vietnam;
	Johnson orders bombing of North Vietnam;
	Malcolm X assassinated in New York City;
	Watts riot in Los Angeles
(Aug.)	Voting Rights Act passed by Congress
1965–1966	"Great Society" programs passed
1966	Black Panther party founded;
	Supreme Court decides *Miranda* v. *State of Arizona*

1967	Martin Luther King, Jr., speaks out against war in Vietnam;
(summer)	Seventy cities experience riots
1968	536,000 American troops in South Vietnam;
	Youth International party (Yippies) founded;
	New civil rights act bars discrimination in housing;
	National Advisory Commission on Disorders (Kerner Commission) reports;
(Jan.)	Tet offensive begins in South Vietnam;
(Mar. 12)	Senator Eugene McCarthy challenges Johnson in New Hampshire primary;
(Mar. 31)	Johnson renounces plans for reelection;
(June 5)	Robert Kennedy assassinated;
(July)	Republicans nominate Richard Nixon for president;
(Aug. 28)	Chicago Democratic convention riots erupt;
(Aug. 28)	Democratic party nominates Hubert Humphrey for president;
(Nov.)	Nixon elected president over Humphrey and George Wallace
1969	Senator George McGovern appointed chair of Democratic party reform commission;
	Several youth leaders indicted for inciting Chicago convention riot
1970	Judge Julius Hoffman sentences Chicago defendants to prison
1972	Judge Hoffman's sentences reversed by appeals court

JOHNSON BOWS OUT

A disastrous turn of events in Vietnam during early 1968 effectively ended Johnson's presidency. Beginning in January and extending for more than a month, the Viet Cong challenged American and South Vietnamese forces everywhere: in defended hamlets, in the countryside, in the cities, even in front of the American embassy in Saigon. This Tet offensive (so named because it coincided with Tet, the lunar new year) marked a turning point in the war. Although the Viet Cong eventually lost most of their gains and, in fact, suffered enormous losses of personnel, the gruesome battle convinced many Americans that the war could not be won.

This growing doubt registered in Johnson's disappointing showing in the New Hampshire Democratic primary. Young people by the hundreds flocked to the state to organize support for Senator Eugene McCarthy, who had declared his opposition to the war. Their efforts led to a near-defeat of the president. Johnson realized that even if he won renomination, his candidacy would rip apart the Democratic party. Thus on March 31, he surprised the nation by announcing his withdrawal from the race.

Yet Johnson's withdrawal could not stop the escalation of either the war or the dissension at home. Nor did it prevent the president from intervening in the convention to ensure that his policies would be defended by the party platform and by the candidate it chose. The expectations that he had helped to arouse had now soured. His administration, as versatile and innovative as any in the twentieth century, was about to be condemned on the overriding issue of the war. Civil rights, economic progress, the peace of American society—all seemed to hang in the balance of a struggle thousands of miles away. That struggle and the war came home in the summer of 1968. The stage was set for its reenactment as Yippie theater in the streets of Chicago.

SUGGESTIONS FOR FURTHER READING

SOCIAL UPHEAVALS

Even if the promise of the Kennedy-Johnson years remained unfulfilled, the 1960s was nonetheless a decade of fascinating social changes. One of the most important documents of that change and an influential book in its own right is Betty Friedan, *The Feminine Mystique* (1963). Another such influential work is Michael Harrington, *The Other America: Poverty in the United States* (1963). This work by a leading American socialist helped inspire the antipoverty programs of the 1960s. Explanations for such reforms have abounded. One of the most challenging interpretations is by William G. McLoughlin, in *Revivals, Awakenings, and Reform* (1978), which places the 1960s in the context of other periods of intense moral reform in American history. Charles A. Reich, in *The Greening of America* (1970), argues that Americans developed a wholly new consciousness of themselves, their environment, and their society. David Farber, *Chicago '68* (1988), traces in rich detail the events of the convention riot from several points of view. Kirkpatrick Sale, *SDS* (1973), is an indispensable guide to the largest student radical group of the decade. In *The Sixties: Years of Hope; Days of Rage* (1988), Todd Gitlin adds personal experience to his fascinating narrative of the events of that decade. At the other end of the political spectrum, George H.

Nash, in *The Conservative Intellectual Movement in America Since 1945* (1976), explores the decade's growing conservative challenge to American liberalism. One of the most persistently discussed issues of these years is the assassination of President Kennedy. A good summary and conclusion is contained in Gerald L. Posner's, *Case Closed: Lee Harvey Oswald and the Assassination of JFK* (1994).

KENNEDY AND JOHNSON

During the 1960s, American presidents inspired both admiration and profound disillusionment. Consequently, the evaluation of Kennedy and Johnson has been marked by controversy. In the first of several incisive books on American elections, Theodore White, *The Making of the President, 1960* (1961), provides a very readable account of the issues and personalities in the election that brought John Kennedy to the White House. Several memoirs by Kennedy aides have offered insights into Kennedy's style of governing. Among the best is Pierre Salinger, *With Kennedy* (1966). A much more critical account, which stresses the failures of the administration, is Henry Fairlie, *The Kennedy Promise: The Politics of Expectation* (1973). A more recent appraisal is by Herbert S. Parmet, *JFK: The Presidency of*

John F. Kennedy (1983). Lyndon Johnson's presidency was, if anything, more controversial. Doris Kearn, *Lyndon Johnson and the American Dream* (1976), is a loving portrait of an unlovely man. Jim F. Heath, *Decade of Disillusionment: The Kennedy-Johnson Years* (1975), is a readable critical history of the 1960s. Robert Caro, *The Years of Lyndon Johnson*, 2 vols. (1982, 1990), is an unfriendly but fascinating account of Johnson's early life. A more dispassionate and balanced biography is by Robert Dalleck, *Lone Star Rising: Lyndon Johnson and His Times*, Vol. 1 (1991).

THE WAR IN VIETNAM

Of all the issues that divided Americans during the 1960s, the Vietnam War was probably the most important. George C. Herring, *America's Longest War: The United States and Vietnam, 1950–1975* (1979), is a thorough history of the struggle. David Halberstam's brilliant *The Best and the Brightest* (1972) recounts the ultimate failure of the generation of promising political advisers who counseled involvement in Vietnam. Godfrey Hodgson, *America in Our Time* (1976), is a delightful general history of the era in which Vietnam became the single most important issue. A splendid and provocative collection of essays on Vietnam is John Schlight, ed., *The Second Indochina War: Proceedings of a Symposium* (1986). Also see the fascinating *American Myths and the Legacy of Vietnam* by John Hellman (1986). A gripping story of Vietnam is the book by Neil Sheehan, *A Bright Shining Lie: John Paul Vann and America in Vietnam* (1988). David Levy in *The Debate over Vietnam* (1991) explores the issue as it split the nation.

Questions of Credibility

Episode: Three Mile Island—An Accident Waiting to Happen

THE EPISODE: *In the early spring of 1979, in the peaceful countryside outside Harrisburg, Pennsylvania, a nuclear accident occurred at the Three Mile Island electrical generating plant. Despite the efforts of the operators, the company management, the manufacturers of the equipment, and local, state, and national officials, the situation deteriorated, risking a complete meltdown and the release of massive amounts of radioactive contaminants. The public around the plant and throughout the nation watched in grim expectation until operators finally tamed the reactor. Here was a technology full of promise. It was promoted as safe, cheap, and efficient. Yet for a few perilous days, no one could be sure, neither experts nor ordinary citizens. Nor did most Americans understand the complex technology of nuclear generating plants. Even government actions were confused and contradictory. In the end the accident revealed poor emergency planning, incautious management, and a fragile technology.*

THE HISTORICAL SETTING: *The Three Mile Island accident came at the end of a chain of dispiriting events. First was the long, drawn-out defeat in Southeast Asia and the ignominious fall of America's ally South Vietnam to North Vietnamese armies in 1973. Despite the expenditure of billions of dollars, the deployment of hundreds of thousands of American soldiers, and the in-*vestment of political capital by several administrations, the United States hastily withdrew from the war and watched an ally disappear. At the same time, the American government itself was reeling from the disgrace of President Richard Nixon's resignation. The shabby political intrigue known as the Watergate affair had slowly, gradually tightened around the president. The American public were spectators to what seemed a slowly advancing but inevitable end. Watergate not only consumed one of the nation's most skilled politicians, it brought disrepute to all government.*

Into this atmosphere of recrimination and shock stepped a relative political novice from Georgia, Governor Jimmy Carter. Elected president in 1976 to restore confidence and morality to government, Carter, despite strenuous efforts, succeeded only in making the problem worse and intensifying distrust in government.

The decline of political leadership in the mid- and late 1970s reflected serious changes in American life. The vocabulary of experts suddenly expanded with new words like constraints and limitations. The United States, it seemed, had run up against the far margin of possibility. Economic security and world leadership in politics seemed to be seriously compromised. In this atmosphere of diminished expectations, the accident at Three Mile Island exposed the roots of the problem: a decline in the credibility of American institutions.

Three Mile Island—An Accident Waiting to Happen

Several miles down the muddy Susquehanna River from Harrisburg, Pennsylvania, the Three Mile Island nuclear generating plant quietly pulsed electricity into the grids of the Metropolitan Edison Company. In the damp, predawn hours of March 28, 1979, a skeleton maintenance crew was operating Unit 2 of the installation. Unit 1 was still "cold" while undergoing its annual shutdown for inspection and refueling.

Unit 2 was a new reactor designed by Babcock and Wilcox Corporation of Lynchburg, Virginia. It was part of a family of reactor systems that used pressurized water to convey heat from the atomic core to steam turbines. The generation of electricity in this plant derived from the interaction of two closed systems. The primary system, containing the nuclear reactor, consisted of a circuit of pipes that pumped pressurized water over the atomic core, picking up heat and then carrying it through the heat exchanger. The secondary system led from the heat exchanger to turbines that generated electricity. The heat exchanger was partly filled with water. As superheated water in pipes from the reactor flowed through it, the water turned to steam, rushed out of the exchanger, and turned the turbine generators. Then the steam lost its heat, condensed into water, and flowed back into the exchanger.

Neither system was readily visible from the exterior, so control depended entirely on the accuracy of gauges and alarms. Furthermore, the danger always existed that the reactor system would lose pressure or water or both, causing the atomic pile to uncover and heat uncontrollably.

Unit 2 had been completed for almost a year, but frequent problems, such as faulty valves and quirks in the operation, had kept it shut down for most of the year. On this morning, however, it was operating at almost 100 percent capacity.

Quiet, almost serene-looking in its stark modern exterior, the Three Mile Island reactor system was, in fact, seething with energy and motion. Miles of pipes throbbed with the rapid flow of pressurized water and steam. In the control room, away from the reactor and the turbine, operators had to monitor scores of electrical commands registered by lights in the panels. These were attached to alarms. The plant's computer system recorded the various changes in the operation of the systems.

Shortly before 4 A.M., two technicians were working to clear the polishers (filters) of the feedwater pipes in the turbine system. This was a normal procedure, something regularly done while the plant was in operation. Unable to unclog the pipe, the engineers decided to blow the residues out with air, somewhat like expelling a pea from a pea shooter. Forcing air through the pipe and into the system, however, caused a sud-

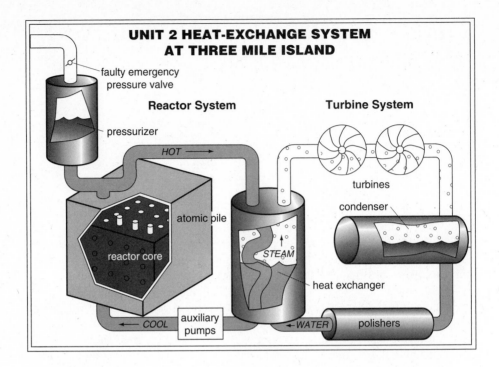

**UNIT 2 HEAT-EXCHANGE SYSTEM
AT THREE MILE ISLAND**

faulty emergency
pressure valve

Reactor System

pressurizer

Turbine System

HOT →

turbines

condenser

atomic pile

STEAM

reactor core

heat exchanger

← COOL   auxiliary
pumps

← WATER   polishers

den shutdown of all water intakes. "All of a sudden," Frederick Scheimann, the Unit 2 foreman, said, "I started hearing loud, thunderous noises, like a couple of freight trains."

What Scheimann heard in the next half minute was the automatic working of the plant's first-line emergency equipment slamming into place. Starved of fresh, cooled water, the turbine system heated too rapidly and the turbines shut off automatically. Pressurized, superheated water from the reactor continued to flow through the heat transfer area, but because little heat was being extracted, this system also overheated rapidly. As temperatures rose in the reactor, pressure also built. Then a special emergency relief valve on the pressurizer opened. Thus far only six seconds had elapsed.

The reactor continued to function because of a delay mechanism built into its shutdown procedures. Then, as pressure and heat built, the reactor system tripped. Damping rods fell into the core, shutting off most of the nuclear reaction. Heat and pressure began to fall in the reactor system. About ten seconds later, auxiliary pumps in the turbine system began to operate. The incident should have been over.

Except for two mechanical problems. In the reactor system, the emergency relief valve did not spring shut as it should have when pressure fell. Superheated steam continued to spurt out of the valve, further lowering pressure in the system. In the turbine system nothing happened. The three emergency pumps churned furiously, but no water flowed through the pipes. During a previous maintenance operation, the emergency pump valves had been shut, and left shut by mistake. In effect, phase one of the accident had already passed before anyone had had time to react. The first set of safety devices failed. Now the second line of defense went into operation.

Although the accident had begun in the turbine system, the emergency shifted to the reactor unit. As pressure fell there, two auxiliary pumps kicked on, pushing hundreds of gallons of water into the core. This was sufficient to keep the core covered and cool until the open emergency relief valve was discovered.

In the control room, lights on the horseshoe panel began flashing and several of the plant's alarms sounded. The overnight operators, Craig Faust and Edward Frederick, and supervisor William Zewe knew the company procedures handbook well. They paid special attention to the warning "Never take the plant solid." What that meant, simply, was not to let the reactor system get too much water in it. If it did, then any shock to the system might break it open. Protection against this sort of accident was maintained by keeping air in the pressurizer chamber below the emergency relief valve. Without this pillow of air to absorb changes in pressure, the reactor system would be in danger.

From the information available in the control room, this is precisely what appeared to be happening. The water level in the pressurizer moved up, indicating that the whole system was becoming superflooded. Thus the operators shut down the flow of emergency water into the reactor. At eight minutes into the incident, Faust discovered that the valves of the turbine system were closed. He turned them on and water began to flow back into that system. Once again the plant seemed to stabilize. The operators had followed instructions exactly.

But the operators had gravely misinterpreted the problem. Instead of being awash with coolant, the core system was still rapidly leaking through the broken relief valve. Water had risen in the pressure tank, but it had been forced there by steam now forming over the reactor and throughout the system. As pressure inside the system fell, the water began to boil, bubbling steam to the top of the reactor and then into the pipes that ran in and out of the core, blocking them and preventing cooling water from flowing through. The water level in the core began to drop dangerously. If the atomic pile uncovered, it would start to melt.

THREE MILE ISLAND. This photograph shows the nuclear power plant, with its large cooling towers, on Three Mile Island in the Susquehanna River, before the partial meltdown.

In the control room, the crew began to realize that a serious malfunction had occurred. Lights flashed and new alarms sounded. The computer reported problems throughout the plant, but in helter-skelter fashion. It was hours before it finally recorded the malfunction in the broken pressurizer valve. The third and last system of defense was about to be called into operation.

This system, unlike the first two, was designed to contain a nuclear accident. Should radioactivity escape from the plant, it could seriously endanger the lives of millions of people in its wake. However, the Three Mile Island containment building, which held the reactor system, was designed to prevent such an occurrence. This twenty-story-high, two-foot-thick, concrete-and-steel enclosure was built to withstand the force of a jet airliner crashing into it at full speed. More important, it could tolerate large increases in the pressure of gases that might build up inside. The only possible leakage from the containment building was through the sump pump system that took water off the floor of the building and into a storage tank in the unshielded auxiliary building. But the sump pumps were protected by a cutoff that stopped them if radioactivity was detected in the water.

At about twenty minutes into the accident, operators called Gary Miller, the station emergency director, who arrived at Unit 2 about an hour later. Operating crews believed that they had the plant under control. They knew that overflow water was gushing onto the floor of the containment building and then moving through the sump pump system into tanks in the auxiliary building. But they believed this was turbine water. As Frederick said, "We decided it was a nonradioactive leak, therefore it must be the steam system and not the reactor coolant system. The symptoms are identical except for the radiation alarm." That alarm had malfunctioned, however, and did not sound until 6:50 A.M. By that time, hundreds of gallons of radioactive waste had poured into the auxiliary building, some of it spilling out and venting small amounts of radioactive gas into the building and out into the atmosphere.

In the control room, operators followed accident procedures precisely, but they were puzzled by new alarms and flashing lights. Since they could not see inside the reactor system, they did not realize that their emergency responses had actually intensified the accident. The atomic core in shutdown position was still creating considerable decay heat. This, in turn, was increasing the steam trapped at the top of the reactor core and pushing more steam into the intake and outflow pipes. Steam bubbles shot through the system and the regular cooling pumps began to shudder and vibrate. At about 5:20 A.M., one set of pumps had to be shut off. At 5:41 A.M., a second pair shut down automatically. This further diminished the flow of water over the reactor. With the pressure emergency valve still trapped open, the system continued to leak. The nuclear core was about to be uncovered and no one knew it.

As the core water level fell, it exposed the nuclear fuel, causing three serious reactions. Radioactive discharges from the system increased rapidly, contaminating the coolant water and, eventually, the containment building. The very high temperatures, together with the continuing chain reaction, caused some of the oxygen in the water to combine with metals in the core, giving off highly flammable hydrogen gas as a byproduct. Most dangerous, the exposed fuel heated rapidly, melting the tubes that held it, and increasing the reaction. The 100 tons of uranium fuel, arranged in stacked pellets, began to fuse together, touching off a larger chain reaction. The plant now clearly risked a meltdown, in which fuel would fall into a searing radioactive heap at the bottom of the reactor. The intense heat, over 5,000°F, would melt through the twelve-inch steel encasement of the reactor, and uranium would tumble onto the floor of the containment building. Then it might melt through the cement base, cracking the building open and allowing the deadly release of gases and radioactive sludge.

However, neither the officials from Metropolitan Edison nor the plant operators worried about this risk because they did not realize that the core was uncovered. Their only measurements of water in the system were indirect, and these indicated, falsely, that the reactor was brimming with water. Shortly after 6 A.M., Brian Mehler, the Metropolitan Edison shift supervisor, arrived. At 6:22 A.M., after checking through other systems, he recognized that the emergency relief valve above the pressurizer had jammed open. He immediately ordered it shut. The leak in the reactor finally stopped, but no one started the emergency pumps. The core remained uncovered.

Starved of coolant, the reactor smoldered and crumbled. The damping rods overheated, swelled, and ruptured. Tubes containing the uranium pellets melted. Over the next sixteen hours or so, about one-third of the core fell into a superheated, poisonous mass. Hundreds of gallons of radioactive water flowed into the auxiliary building and gases escaped into the air.

Finally, at 6:50 A.M., radiation alarms in the auxiliary building sounded. Miller, the emergency director, declared a "site emergency" and began notifying authorities of a "slight problem at Three Mile Island." He also called the Pennsylvania Emergency Management Agency, the Bureau of Radiation Protection, and the regional headquarters of the U.S. Nuclear Regulatory Commission (NRC). Shortly thereafter, he declared a general emergency. The public was about to receive its first news of a nuclear accident that experts at the plant had yet to understand.

For the next several days, misleading statements, misinformation, confusion, and rumor clouded public understanding of what had happened. This is not surprising. Confusion had always surrounded the atomic power industry and issues of regulation and safety. In part, this came from the extraordinary complexity of the technology. The public understood very little of how this complicated plant worked, yet they had to make decisions that deeply affected their lives on the basis of what they expected to happen. There could be no more dramatic proof of the distance between modern science and the population at large. The accident also revealed an astounding inability to communicate: a panicky press, and government agencies and private corporations that distorted or misinterpreted what had happened. In the rush to protect groups that had an important stake in atomic energy, truthfulness and genuine accountability were lost.

In large industrial accidents, it is sometimes possible to assemble paper trails—that is, memos, letters, and reports that warn of weaknesses in a system that eventually fails. In the case of Three Mile Island, there were several of these trails, but none had led to any action. Each warning about the reactor system was sidetracked by bureaucracy, special interests, and communications breakdowns. Ignorance, ineptitude, and fear of upsetting the economically precarious nuclear industry combined to block warnings of impending problems before the accident.

One reason for the breakdown of Unit 2 lay in the design of the reactor-heat transfer system, its installation, and its operation. All these areas concerned the manufacturer and designer of the reactor, Babcock and Wilcox. Metropolitan Edison, the generating company, operated the equipment according to B & W instructions. Modifications in procedures continually flowed from B & W headquarters as the company monitored the operations at the generating plants it designed.

Just such a monitoring process led Joe Kelly, a B & W engineer, to ask the company in November 1977 to change its instructions for dealing with a depressurization incident (like the one at Three Mile Island). The company worried most about too much coolant entering the reactor system and so instructed operators to shut down emergency pumps if the system suddenly lost pressure. But Kelly argued that instructions should be changed to read that emergency pumps should never be turned off except during a normal shutdown. If operators had received this advice, the Three Mile Island accident would have ended without danger.

Kelly reached his conclusions after investigating an incident at the Davis-Besse generating plant near Toledo, Ohio. Using a B & W system, the Davis-Besse plant was operating at about 9 percent capacity in September 1977 when a loss-of-coolant accident occurred. With safety and measurement equipment giving confused signals, the plant operators responded according to B & W instructions and shut off the emergency cooling system. Had the reactor been operating at full capacity, Kelly reasoned, these actions might have caused major fuel damage and a dangerous meltdown.

In November 1977 Kelly collected his suggestions and submitted them in a memo to B & W executives concerned with safety procedures and customer relations. He enlisted others in the emergency-safety management service division. New guidelines were drawn up, but the department failed to send them out to B & W equipment operators. Kelly, however, did not realize this.

The company also had warnings from another source. In September 1977 Carlyle Michelson, a Tennessee Valley Authority engineer and consultant for the Nuclear Regulatory Commission, submitted a report on B & W equipment. He concluded that in a loss-of-coolant accident, the pressurizer gauge would mislead operators as to the amount of water in the system. Michelson submitted his report to the NRC. Nothing happened. So several months later, he shook the bureaucratic tree again to stimulate action. No decisions were taken. Babcock and Wilcox also received a copy of the report, but the company merely filed it away. Michelson sent two letters to B & W headquarters; the second arrived in February 1979, but the company did not respond or warn its customers.

The Nuclear Regulatory Commission was aware of these warnings about B & W equipment. The Michelson report had been pushed into the agency paper flow in 1977. More important, however, the NRC had done its own investigation of the Davis-Besse incident, and their investigator agreed with Kelly and Michelson.

James S. Cresswell, an NRC reactor inspector, worried about the Davis-Besse incident. After studying the problem there, he concluded that all B & W systems were susceptible to such incidents, and he tried to spur the NRC to action. He talked to a number of NRC officials, who generally rejected his conclusions. Finally, on January 8, 1979, he issued a formal memorandum on Babcock and Wilcox plants, in effect leapfrogging the immediate bureaucracy and making his findings public. But the company continued to reassure the NRC that their systems were safely insulated against accidents and that their instructions were appropriate.

Frustrated in his efforts, Cresswell went to the top of the agency in the spring of 1979 and finally got a meeting with two NRC commissioners. Both were impressed with his evidence, and one of them sent a request to the agency to act on the information. The commissioner's request arrived at the agency March 29, one day after the Three Mile Island accident began.

The company and the NRC acted slowly on these warnings for several reasons. For one thing, NRC "nugget" files (records of operating problems) showed hundreds of incidents in the operation of nuclear plants. It was not immediately clear that this particular problem with B & W equipment was any more dangerous than scores of others. Also, changes in equipment and operating procedures were expensive. Caught in a serious price squeeze, the nuclear industry was trying to save itself, and the NRC wanted to help.

Furthermore, the history of regulating nuclear electrical generation was an ambiguous one. The industry began in 1953 with the announcement of President Eisenhower's Atoms for Peace program. Atomic power plant construction began a year later, and the first generating unit was completed in 1958. From the beginning, the federal government subsidized the industry by allocating funds for research and development. The Atomic Energy Commission acted both as advocate for the industry and as regulator—a contradictory mission. In addition, Congress passed the Price-Anderson Act of 1957, which limited to $560 million the total liability of a nuclear generating plant in the case of accident. In effect, the government declared that victims of a serious accident would have to pay for most damages themselves.

Protected, encouraged, and screened by the government, the nuclear industry boomed during the 1960s. Low costs for uranium fuel (below seven million dollars a ton in 1970), rapid rises in demand for electrical power (about 7 percent a year), and increasing unreliability of oil and gas supplies, plus pollution and accident problems associated with coal burning and mining, made nuclear energy seem a perfect replacement. Over seventy plants had been constructed by 1979, and they produced about 13 percent of the nation's electrical energy.

Nonetheless, by the mid-1970s the industry was facing hard times. Uranium ore prices had shot up. Construction costs in plants had risen astronomically, due in part to stricter regulation. Some government directives were as thick as a telephone book. General inflation had also pushed construction costs upward, so that nuclear-generated electricity cost about ten times as much in 1979 as it had in 1970. Cost overruns in plants like Three Mile Island were huge. The original expense was projected to be about $130 million, but Unit 2 cost $700 million when completed.

The 1970s also raised problems because of a sudden drop in energy requirements. The huge increase in oil prices after 1973–1974 did not result in a switch to nuclear alternatives. Instead, sluggish economic growth and conservation cut demands for electricity. Optimistic predictions about a 50 percent nuclear future proved to be very wide of the mark. As *Business Week* commented in December 1978, "One by one, the lights are going out for the U.S. nuclear power industry. Reactor orders have plummeted from a high of 41 in 1973 to zero this year."

The federal government in 1974 had tried to reorganize the industry through better regulation. Recognizing the contradiction between advocacy and regulation, Congress abolished the Atomic Energy Commission and created the Nuclear Regulatory Agency. Nonetheless, many AEC employees, most of them nuclear enthusiasts, transferred to the new agency.

The NRC proved unwilling to tighten regulations at a time when the industry was beginning to nosedive. Expensive safety retrofitting of reactors was not ordered. The NRC hesitated to issue instructions that would make operations more costly. And it had to contend with opponents of nuclear power plants. With the industry in crisis and with growing public clamor to shut down plants, the NRC was reluctant to interfere with the operation of new plants such as Three Mile Island.

Another paper trail to the accident in Pennsylvania existed in consumer opposition to nuclear energy. Headed by consumer advocate Ralph Nader, antinuclear forces significantly slowed the licensing process of plants at hearings and through lawsuits. Nader's objections rested on several grounds. He cited evidence that any increase in radiation was a health and genetic danger to plant workers and nearby residents. Since all nuclear plants emitted some radiation, he concluded that this constituted technological victimization. Nader also worried about possible theft of radioactive fuels, sabotage, unresolved waste disposal problems, and the credibility of the government and the nuclear industry.

In his book *The Menace of Atomic Energy*, published in 1977, Nader cited AEC tests of 1970 and 1971 that showed the malfunctioning of emergency systems in a loss-of-coolant accident. These tests, he concluded, demonstrated that water pumped into the system at low pressure would turn to steam and block the intake and outlet pipes to the reactor. The core would then become exposed and melt. In such an event, the containment floor would also fail, and the China Syndrome would occur: the molten mass of uranium fuel would burn through the building, into the ground, and downward toward the earth's core, polluting groundwater as it went.

Nader's use of the term China Syndrome to describe a meltdown accident was nothing more than the adoption of industry slang, a kind of preposterous joke, that the molten mass would pass through the earth and come to rest in China on the opposite side of the globe. But the seriousness of such an accident was no joke. A secret AEC report, pried out of the agency in 1973, predicted that in the worst possible accident, 45,000 people would die, 100,000 would sustain injury, and an area that "might be equal to that of the state of Pennsylvania" would be devastated.

This same reference to Pennsylvania occurred in the film *The China Syndrome*, produced by Michael Douglas and released in March 1979, about two weeks before the accident at Three Mile Island. This was no mere coincidence; but only another paper trail based on a prediction that came true.

RALPH NADER. Beginning with his exposé of unsafe automobiles in the 1960s, consumer advocate Ralph Nader and his Raiders investigated other potentially hazardous industries. Nuclear-powered electrical energy plants were among their chief targets.

In 1976 Mike Gray, a documentary filmmaker, approached Douglas with a completed film script about a near-accident at a nuclear generating plant. Gray had studied AEC reports and investigated minor incidents at plants near Detroit and Chicago. The results of his study went into the script. Douglas liked the idea and approached actress Jane Fonda about joining the venture. She agreed but changed the script, writing in a character for herself to play as a television news commentator trying to find out about and then report honestly on a dangerous incident at a nuclear plant. Douglas hired nuclear engineers to provide expertise on plant operations. The film also incorporated testimony from hearings on nuclear plants.

Melodramatic though it was, the film accurately portrayed the sequence of events in a near-meltdown accident. And the drama confronted the larger issue of credibility. The action begins when Kimberly Wells [Fonda], a commentator on the evening news, accidentally films a serious incident at the Ventura, California, power plant while doing a feature story. After showing the film to a nuclear engineer, she becomes convinced that she has witnessed a near-accident. The engineer explains:

LOWELL: If that's true, then we came very close to the China Syndrome.

KIMBERLY: The what?

LOWELL: If the core is exposed for whatever reason, the fuel heats beyond core heat tolerance in a matter of minutes. Nothing can stop it. And it melts right down through the bottom of the plant, theoretically to China, but, of course, as soon as it hits groundwater it blasts into the atmosphere and sends out clouds of radioactivity. The number of people killed would depend on which way the wind is blowing and render an area the size of Pennsylvania permanently uninhabitable.

A plant engineer named Godell (played by Jack Lemmon) recognizes that the welds supporting cooling pumps are faulty, and he tries to prevent the plant from going back into operation. Holding the control room at gunpoint, he demands a live interview on television. Kimberly, eager to get the story, rushes to the plant with her crew. But when Godell tries to explain, he fails completely:

> GODELL: I mean, that happened, but that's not why I'm here. It's—I'm not making any sense.
>
> KIMBERLY: No, it's all right.
>
> GODELL: It's so complicated, but there . . . there's something else. There's this—see, it's so complicated . . . yet so simple . . . simple . . . it's terribly complex . . . and it's very difficult.

Action piles on action: Godell is shot by a special police squad; the plant shuts down safely; and Kimberly files her story. As Godell realized, nuclear technology is too complicated to explain to the public, which must depend on the credibility of government and industry. When that fails, only a feature reporter's chance persistence saves California from disaster.

Predictably, the nuclear industry attacked the film. In a public letter dated nine days before the opening of the film and two weeks before Three Mile Island, Southern California Edison charged that the movie had "no scientific credibility and is in fact ridiculous." But if anything, the film underplayed the danger.

One final trail led to the accident. This was the short but troubled history of Unit 2 operations. After a long and expensive construction period, the second reactor at Three Mile Island "went critical" (began operation) on March 28, 1978. At ceremonies in September, Metropolitan Edison representatives, the lieutenant governor of Pennsylvania, and U.S. Deputy Secretary of Energy John F. O'Leary dedicated the new facility. O'Leary addressed the assembly and called for keeping "the nuclear option open." He urged even more: "Our goal is to achieve a balance of 50 percent coal and 50 percent nuclear." The facility, he concluded, "was a sort of a miracle in many ways."

Residents of the area generally accepted this view. The plant pumped thousands of dollars in construction jobs into the region and employment for the "nukes," as permanent employees called themselves. But there was scattered opposition, centered primarily in a small group, the Three Mile Island Alert, which published a small underground tabloid, the *Harrisburg*.

The utility company replied to all adverse publicity with soothing words about safety, stressing the nuclear industry's exemplary record. They cited the industry motto: "Defense in depth—backup systems to back up backup systems." They noted that half the investment in Unit 2 was for safety devices. As a Metropolitan Edison flyer, called "Your Personal Radiation Inventory," explained: "If the worst conceivable accident were to occur at the Three Mile Island nuclear station, because of safeguards, a man could remain at a spot less than a half-mile from the reactor for 24 hours a day for an entire year and be exposed to only 2 mrems of radiation." (mrem stands for millirem, or one thousandth of a rem. Exposure of 600 rems is generally a fatal dose.) This was a negligible amount compared to the 100 mrems that all Americans received each year from natural causes.

Although utility officials exuded public confidence, Unit 2 proved unreliable and accident-prone. The emergency relief valve stuck open more than once, and operators installed an indirect gauge to determine its position, but even this gauge sometimes malfunctioned. The valve also leaked slightly. Other problems flared up in the complicated cooling and heat transfer systems. Employees complained that the alarm system was too complex and hence meaningless in an emergency. Nonetheless, Metropolitan Edison put the plant on line on December 30, 1978. They did so for two reasons. The company wanted to take advantage of tax breaks for 1978. They were also seeking a rate increase to help cover operating expenses. This was granted in March 1979. However, the flawed system remained out of operation for much of the time.

Plant operators, the utility company, and the NRC did not suspect the gravity of the Three Mile Island accident in its early stages. Communications between the plant and the NRC in Bethesda, Maryland, near Washington, were confused and difficult. When the utility did begin to realize the problem of a partial meltdown, it refused to admit so publicly. At first, the NRC accepted Metropolitan Edison assurances. As a result, the credibility of information flowing through the media from the plant and from the NRC degenerated. The local population was restrained by meaningless assurances and then panicked by rumors.

At 7:30 Wednesday morning, once the general emergency had been declared, the most immediate problem was whether or not to evacuate the nearby residents. This decision depended on accurate information. With the coolant system out of control (it remained so for about twelve more hours) the risk of total meltdown and radiation discharge increased. Plant operators, utility experts, B & W scientists, and the NRC only gradually realized the extent of the damage. But they could not advise state officials about evacuation until they knew what was happening on-site.

At the plant, emergency director Gary Miller tried to establish control of the reactor and also coordinate public communications. But he recalled, "I was constantly pulled to the phone by senior persons in the state government, the NRC, and my own management. . . . The phone, the pressure, the fact that the plant was in a state that I had never been schooled in combined to make it almost intolerable."

Those in charge of evacuation had even less information. The Pennsylvania Emergency Management Agency (PEMA), headed by Lieutenant Governor William Scranton, was charged with directing emergency procedures. Evacuation plans existed, but they had not been made public for fear of arousing anxiety. PEMA, located in a radiation-proof building in Harrisburg, prepared to act, but it had to have facts. The man who would instruct it to begin, Governor Richard Thornburgh, had received contradictory advice from Metropolitan Edison and the NRC.

The public first heard of the accident at about 8 A.M. A local broadcaster discovered that local civil defense authorities had ordered fire equipment on alert. He called Metropolitan Edison, and the company reported a "minor problem" at Three Mile Island. Later in the morning, the company released its first public statement:

The nuclear reactor at Three Mile Island Unit 2 was shut down as prescribed when a malfunction related to a feedwater pump occurred about four A.M. Wednesday. The entire

THREE MILE ISLAND REACTOR. The top portion of nuclear reactor Unit 1 at Three Mile Island. Had a complete meltdown of Unit 2 occurred, the blistering hot radioactive pile would have fallen through the reactor floor (not visible here).

unit was systematically shut down and will be out of service for about a week while equipment is checked and repairs made.

Against all evidence, Metropolitan Edison continued to maintain for several days that less than 1 percent of the fuel in the reactor core had been damaged. By underestimating the problem, the company quickly lost credibility with government officials and the public. While company experts worked to correct what they knew was an increasingly dangerous situation, they continued to reassure the public that no danger existed. By Wednesday afternoon, Lieutenant Governor Scranton publicly criticized the company for misrepresenting the extent of the accident. The company had "given you and us conflicting information."

Communications between the plant and the NRC offices were difficult to establish. Although NRC inspectors arrived at Three Mile Island at 10 A.M., phone lines to headquarters did not function well. Accurate information about the accident remained sparse in Washington. President Carter had been notified at 9:00, but he let the NRC monitor the problem.

At about 11:30 A.M., plant operators tried to reestablish the blocked flow of coolant into the reactor by depressuring the system, bleeding more steam out through the pressurizer. Their strategy failed. Indeed, it may have uncovered the core even further. Then at 1:50 P.M., the computer recorded an unnoticed pressure spike (a sudden rise in pressure in the containment building). Almost simultaneously, containment spray turned on and emergency liquid shot into the building to neutralize radioactive iodine. Operators shut off the spray. They did not realize, until later, that a bubble of escaped hydrogen, produced in the core, had exploded. This event, when recognized, became the source of fear that hydrogen might explode inside the reactor, creating the worst devastation imaginable and a total meltdown.

Finally, in late afternoon, plant operators attempted to repressurize the system. Gradually, they succeeded. Steam began to dissipate, and by 7:50 that evening, coolant water again began to flow through the system. The core was re-covered. It was now time to assess the damage.

To do this, a sample of core coolant water had to be taken and analyzed for radioactive discharges that would indicate fuel damage. Results of this test became available at 6 P.M. the next day. At last, officials understood the seriousness of an accident they could not see or measure directly. On Wednesday evening, however, the most immediate problem was how to eliminate the radioactive water and gas trapped in the containment and the auxiliary building. Whether they wanted to or not, company officials decided they had to discharge some of this into the air and into the Susquehanna River.

On Thursday morning, plant officials decided to dump mildly radioactive water into the river. If they did not, it would spill out anyway because storage tanks were completely filled. At about 2:45 P.M., technicians started to empty this pollutant into the Susquehanna. State officials strenuously objected, and at 6 P.M., the NRC ordered a halt to the dumping. But by midnight, all parties had agreed to resume the discharge. All day, conflicting stories reached the news media about releases of gas and water. Joseph Hendry, chairman of the NRC, briefed Congress, reporting that there might be some minor cracks in "perhaps about 1 percent" of the fuel rods, but he assured Washington that there was no serious risk.

Reporters and television crews began to flood the Harrisburg area. But unlike other sorts of accidents, this one attracted no spectators. The possibility of a deadly release of radiation kept bystanders at home. All of the media attention did little to improve the flow of information or restore credibility. The technological and scientific aspects of the accident were difficult to understand, and scientists themselves disagreed sharply about the accident. News reaching the governor remained contradictory. But by 11 P.M., he knew how serious the incident was: core samples confirmed a partial meltdown.

Friday was the most confused day yet. Communications among civil authorities concerning evacuation became scrambled. The public believed less and less of what it heard. Serious amounts of radioactive gas still had to be vented. Technicians also realized that a large hydrogen bubble was building in the reactor. It seemed only a matter of time before a fatal explosion.

The population around Harrisburg was obviously jittery. A quick telephone survey revealed that most area residents feared another nuclear accident even if this one ended uneventfully. Other residents confided their deep-seated fears about radiation to reporters. Paul Holowka, a dog breeder living near the reactor, claimed: "Last year I lost twelve dogs. They died of cancer. That never used to happen."

By the end of the day, the area was in turmoil. Phone circuits were jammed, schools had closed, and lines had formed in front of gasoline stations. Toll booth operators on the Pennsylvania Turnpike noted a sudden spurt of heavy traffic, with most cars filled with families. A general exodus that eventually reached almost 140,000 people had begun. One of those fleeing said frankly: "The main reason we're leaving is I don't trust the information they are giving us. No one really knows what happened Wednesday morning."

Even Governor Thornburgh admitted as much. "I am very skeptical of any one set of facts," he told a sweltering news conference in the capitol building (the air conditioning had been shut off to prevent circulation of radiation). At 12:30 P.M., Thornburgh ordered a partial evacuation. Radio broadcasts throughout the morning had warned of such an eventuality. After NRC officials received news that vented radioactivity had reached 1,200 mrems per hour, they phoned the state and suggested a general evacuation. Then they rescinded the suggestion. But Thornburgh advised all pregnant women and preschool children within five miles of the plant to leave. Other residents were asked to stay indoors.

Thornburgh, the NRC, and President Carter (more involved now in watching the crisis) grew increasingly worried about the hydrogen bubble. Operators realized that the earlier pressure spike represented a small hydrogen explosion. If, as many scientists warned was possible, the bubble continued to grow and if oxygen in the core reached sufficient levels, the reactor and the entire containment might explode. Metropolitan Edison officials declared that there was little danger of this, but no one listened. Instead, newspapers and television blared the news. Areas close to the Three Mile Island plant, such as the King River Haven mobile home park, became ghost towns.

Imagining a hydrogen explosion translated the accident into an occasion for venting people's worst fears. Some residents recalled stories of the terrible, fiery crash of the German dirigible, the *Hindenburg*, in New Jersey in 1937. A child told reporters of a dream she had had: "It was a big ball, and you know the way things glow? It glowed just like that. And then there was a witch and the big ball killed everybody. And all the cats and dogs and rabbits were all dead." To some residents, the hydrogen bubble represented the beginning of the end of the world, the first stage in a chain reaction leading to the Last Judgment. Yet there were some local residents who knew almost nothing about the accident or the danger. These were the Amish, the "plain people," who lived on nearby farms, not using automobiles, tractors, modern plumbing—or electricity.

After the confusion over evacuation, and because of scrambled stories coming from the facility, President Carter designated Harold Denton as chief and sole spokesman on the accident site. His first task was to restore the public's faith in the information it was receiving. Denton arrived at Three Mile Island about 2:30 Friday afternoon and quickly took charge. He also stepped into what seemed like the most critical moment of the accident.

During the next day, Denton worked to keep control of news coming from the plant. He warned Governor Thornburgh of a possible general evacuation of the area. For the next harrowing hours, he oversaw attempts to determine the danger of a hydrogen explosion. In Washington, Secretary of Health, Education, and Welfare Joseph Califano advised Carter to order a general evacuation. But the president insisted that Denton make such decisions. Nonetheless, the federal government took precautions to order massive amounts of potassium iodide shipped to the area. This drug, if taken before exposure to severe nuclear radiation, saturates the thyroid gland to prevent any absorption of radioactive iodine.

By late Saturday evening, Denton and experts working on the accident realized that the danger had passed. The bubble had begun to shrink. The site would be safe enough for President Carter to visit the next day. Quite clearly a publicity gesture, the

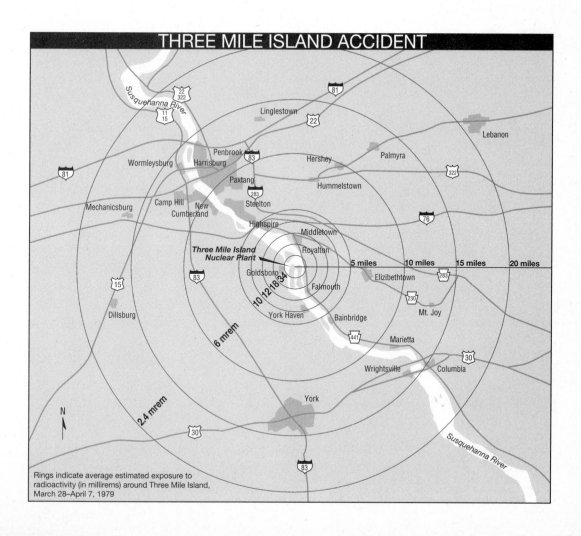

THREE MILE ISLAND ACCIDENT

Rings indicate average estimated exposure to radioactivity (in millirems) around Three Mile Island, March 28–April 7, 1979

visit would signal that the crisis had passed. Denton informed the media: the president would visit the plant the next afternoon.

On Sunday the president flew to Harrisburg and then went to the plant for an inspection. Mrs. Carter stopped to visit local residents. Shortly after the visit, scientists at Three Mile Island recognized that they had miscalculated the quantities of hydrogen and oxygen in the reactor. Late that night they confirmed that the bubble was disappearing. By midday on Monday, April 2, it had all but dissipated. The most dangerous phase of the accident had ended.

The Three Mile Island accident ended when operators recovered complete control over the reactor at 7:50 p.m. on April 4, but the radioactive pollution it released will probably outlast civilization. The reactor came, perhaps, within a half hour of complete meltdown. Although eventually contained, the event had serious and lasting effects on the utility company, the industry, the federal and state regulatory agencies, the local population, and on the credibility of government and the scientific establishment.

Gradually, the Three Mile Island plant was cleaned up. During the operation to extract the radioactive poisons and permanently remove the nuclear core, the core remained covered by cooling liquids. Worker safety, locating a dump site for wastes, and constant monitoring of the plant presented difficult problems. Over the four years of decontaminating the site, about 1,000 workers were employed and close to 1 billion had to be spent. If the costs of Metropolitan Edison's purchase of replacement electricity are added in, the total price is about $3 billion, bringing it to over three times the initial cost of Unit 2 and almost twenty-five times the original estimated cost of the unit.

In the years following the accident, local residents continued to worry about periodic radioactive releases into the air and into the Susquehanna. In March 1980, for example, a citizen living three miles from the plant told the NRC:

> Met Ed's alleged concern for my safety insults me. . . . I have been blitzed by their PR campaigns and their charts and their fancy numbers and their smiling assurances that the levels of radiation to be vented are within federal safety limits. But who knows if the federal safety limits are safe?

Bruce Smith, chairman of the board of supervisors in Newberry Township near the site, declared: "I am so angry about Three Mile that I have become one of the leaders in the movement to close TMI forever as a nuclear plant."

Plant workers received far higher doses of radiation during the accident than most area residents. Many of them absorbed the maximum safe yearly amount in a few moments. Measured in millirems, a level of 500,000 causes immediate death in 50 percent of a population; 100,000 mrems causes radiation sickness in most. Standard yearly maximums for plant employees had been set at 8,000 mrems. As Joe Hipple, a health physicist, told the press during the accident: "I was the hottest I've been in a long time. I hit the frisker [the radiation counter] and it went boing! I probably got half my year's exposure in a day, probably in four minutes."

This exposure to high radiation caused a shortage of technicians. To fill the gap and attract new employees, Metropolitan Edison ran a want ad in *The New York Times*:

NO-NUKES RALLY, 1979. Following the accident at Three Mile Island, sentiment against nuclear power plants mounted. At this rally in Washington on May 6, 1979, Tom Hayden (former leader of SDS and coordinator of the demonstrations at the 1968 Democratic convention in Chicago) and Jane Fonda, star of *The China Syndrome*, addressed the crowd.

"Immediate ground floor opportunities for dedicated scientists and engineering personnel who want to be in the forefront of emerging technologies."

Public reaction in the United States and the rest of the world to the accident was strong. Antinuclear sentiment mounted in the United States, as evidenced by a large rally in Washington on May 6, 1979. Local opposition to bringing new plants on line, or to planning for the future expansion of facilities, stiffened. In Europe, antinuclear opinion emerged as a strong force in countries like West Germany. During the accident, 35,000 West Germans marched, chanting, "We all live in Pennsylvania." Added to hugely mounting costs, delays, and new regulations, this growing skepticism hurt an already crippled industry.

The accident and the ensuing communications failure at Three Mile Island also undercut the faith of many Americans in their political, scientific, and economic institutions. Several congressional investigations faulted the NRC for its lack of leadership and candor. A separate presidential report criticized information provided to the public by the NRC and Metropolitan Edison. Exaggeration, ignorance, and rumor had dominated reporting of the event, at least until Harold Denton took control of communications. When the accident was at its most dangerous stage, the public received the advice that nothing was wrong. After the crisis had passed, the media and even state safety officials exaggerated the danger and incited a mass exodus.

Revelation of the existence of paper trails leading to the accident fueled public suspicion that the government and the nuclear industry had conspired to conceal atomic power plant dangers. Regulators did not regulate sufficiently, and companies cut corners to sustain a sick industry. Publication in 1979 of a report on a nuclear disaster in the Soviet Union added to the controversy. A Russian émigré scientist described an accident that had occurred in 1957 in the Ural Mountains at a nuclear dump site. He maintained that it had caused devastation of thousands of square miles and killed hundreds of people and that U.S. government officials had known about the accident for two decades. They had not reported it to the public for security reasons and, he speculated, to protect America's nuclear industry from public criticism. Even when the terrible meltdown occurred at Chernobyl in the Soviet Union in April 1986, public officials in the United States and in European countries with heavy commitments to nuclear power played down the incident.

The accident at Three Mile Island was, in the final analysis, a disaster that did not really happen. The worst predictions did not come true. The third line of defense in the containment building held. The core did not melt down completely, and the China Syndrome was avoided. Yet the accident had a profound effect. It spread a further cloud of doubt over American society at a time when many Americans were asking agonizing questions about social, economic, and political institutions that also did not function as they were designed.

The Credibility Crisis

The accident at Three Mile Island and its aftershocks of disbelief and doubt epitomized the growing problem of accountability in American society during the 1970s. As the economy, technology, government bureaucracy, and social issues became more complex, Americans wanted to know who was responsible. Often, it was impossible to find a straightforward answer to this question. In the case of Three Mile Island, the war in Vietnam, Watergate, the Iranian hostage crisis, and other major events of the decade, it was difficult to find a person, an agency, or an institution that would take responsibility. Increasingly, companies, government bureaucrats, and officials of all sorts masked their activities behind public relations, the object of which was to convince and persuade the public, but not necessarily to inform it.

AMERICAN SOCIETY AT A CROSSROADS

This reliance on establishing credibility and persuasiveness came at a time when private and public institutions were growing ever larger and more complex. The world of computers, nuclear plants, and space travel could not be translated into simple explanations. The technology of nuclear power plants performed remarkable tasks: in silence, out of sight, and beyond the comprehension of most Americans. There were no familiar spinning gears, whirling belts, or clanging machines in such new industries. They performed marvels of production, but they also sometimes released deadly and invisible pollutants. Their operation in the public interest demanded knowledge, skill, and honesty. The public had no other choice but to trust its experts.

Trust was also crucial for the success of government. During the 1970s the federal government took up difficult, perhaps impossible, tasks. Special-interest groups increasingly demanded that government redress grievances and balance old inequalities in social relations. Rising expectations about what government could do to solve problems transformed complex social, economic, and even personal and family issues into political issues. The federal government also had to confront new and contradictory economic crises such as rising inflation, low productivity, and energy shortages.

In this complicated and difficult world, institutions and bureaucracies often used public relations and the mass media to maintain their credibility. Indeed, *credibility* became a widely used political word in this decade, although the problem was certainly older. It meant the ability to inspire confidence in a government official, a company spokesperson, a labor union representative, a consumer advocate. But it did not necessarily mean truthfulness. Inevitably during the 1970s, times of crisis were also credibility crises. The accident at Three Mile Island became a credibility crisis because the public began to doubt official statements and reports, to distrust experts, and to question the intentions of elected representatives. More than ever, Americans wanted government to solve problems, and more than ever, they criticized it when it could not.

The 1970s were also years of limitation and readjustment. Many of the institutions whose stability a generation of Americans had taken for granted suddenly appeared weak and ineffectual. The period from 1945 to about 1968 had been exceptional in American history because of its sustained economic growth and dramatic social progress. Americans had come to accept such successes as normal. But prior to World War II, the nation had experienced prolonged depressions as well as booms, bitter social struggles, and political crises. The 1970s served to remind Americans that economic progress is erratic. This was not a welcome lesson to a nation that had come to expect uninterrupted expansion.

ECONOMIC PROBLEMS

Economic problems in the 1970s were complex and interrelated. The delayed impact of expenditures for the war in Vietnam pushed inflation higher. Small rises in productivity rates after 1966 indicated that many American industries were falling behind Japanese and Western European competitors in adopting modern technology. Profligate use of cheap energy made energy shortages and steep price hikes painful to absorb. In time, the energy crisis fueled inflation and slowed economic growth. The shrinking margin of competitiveness of American goods destabi-

lized the dollar and turned the international balance of payments against the United States. Large budget deficits, high interest rates, and inaction often compounded these problems. The economy did grow during this period, and real wages for most workers did increase, but not at the rapid pace set in the 1960s.

Social change, too, tested the resilience and credibility of American institutions. Political demonstrations and violence occurred sporadically in the early 1970s. As reported by the U.S. government, crime rates seemed to rise relentlessly: between 1968 and 1978, aggravated assaults increased by about 60 percent. Larceny and theft rates increased at about the same rate. Heavily concentrated in cities, these crimes were well publicized and visible. In fact there seemed to be a natural link between the size and congestion of a city and its crime rate.

While the 1950s had been an exceptionally stable, even unusual period, for many

VIOLENT CRIME RATES IN FOURTEEN AMERICAN CITIES, 1977

	Rate per 100,000 Population
Detroit	1,829
Baltimore	1,726
New York	1,629
Washington	1,427
San Francisco	1,409
Los Angles	1,209
Dallas	1,019
Chicago	935
Memphis	784
Indianapolis	744
Philadelphia	635
Phoenix	630
San Diego	560
San Antonio	491

Source: U.S. Federal Bureau of Investigation, Crime in the United States, annual, 1986.

Americans it became the benchmark of normality with all subsequent developments seen as a decline. By the 1970s, statistics suggested a transformation in the family, once the most stable of institutions, and now split by divorce and altered by changing relationships between men and women in American society. After a low point in the mid-1950s, divorce rates almost tripled by the end of the 1970s. The size of American families shrank as the postwar baby boom ended. This in turn affected the age structure of the population. America was growing older, and this older population was becoming increasingly active politically.

WOMEN

Perhaps most important in terms of lifestyles was the change in women's roles. Masked by the domestic ideology of the late 1940s and 1950s, rapid change had in fact deeply affected women's lives after World War II. Most significant was the increased participation of women in the workforce. In 1947 only about 27 percent of workers in the labor force were women. In 1981, women constituted about 43 percent of the labor force. Put another way, in 1947 about 30 percent of women worked. In 1981 almost 50 percent worked. Many of them joined the labor force to maintain their family's standard of living.

Together with increasing recognition of their past treatment as second-class citizens, this new economic power convinced many women to challenge the customs of family and society that had restricted their roles. Women demanded equality, respect, and an end to formal and informal restrictions on opportunities and careers. Many of their endeavors were highly visible: more women elected to public office, increased interest in women's sports, and perhaps equally important, the discovery of a hidden history of past achievements.

However, a change of this magnitude could not occur without challenges. Increasingly during the 1970s, disputes over women's roles focused on the proposed Equal Rights Amendment (ERA) to the Constitution. Pushed by such groups as the National Organization for Women (NOW), the ERA passed Congress on March 22, 1972. Little more, in fact, than a ratification of the rights to equal treatment that many women already enjoyed and that most Americans supported, the ERA came to symbolize those changes in modern society that more conservative Americans opposed. In this dispute, both sides viewed the government as the ultimate arbitrator. Although ratification of the amendment failed in 1982,

WOMEN'S PARTICIPATION IN THE LABOR FORCE

Married, with Children under 6		With Children under Age 1	
1950	11.9%	1976	31.0%
1955	16.2	1978	25.3
1960	18.6	1980	38.0
1965	23.3	1982	43.9
1970	30.3	1983	43.1
1975	36.6	1984	46.7
1980	41.5	1985	48.4
1985	53.4	1986	49.8
1987	56.8	1987	50.8

Source: The New York Times

MARRIAGE AND DIVORCE RATES IN THE UNITED STATES

Year	Total Divorces	Divorce Rate per 1,000	Marriage Rate per 1,000
1965	479,000	2.5	9.3
1970	708,000	3.5	10.6
1975	1,036,000	4.9	10.0
1980	1,182,000	5.3	10.6

Source: U.S. Department of Commerce, Bureau of the Census, Statistical Abstract of the United States, 1981 (Washington, D.C.: Government Printing Office, 1981), p. 56

public opinion supporting it did not diminish, nor did the struggle for women's rights decline. Opponents were quick to point out that women might lose special protective legislation or be drafted for combat. But even this did not deter most supporters. An even more contentious right was granted in 1973 when the Supreme Court in *Roe* v. *Wade* guaranteed the right of women to secure abortions, reversing decades of policy and practice. This decision effectively eliminated most state and local ordinances that regulated or outlawed the procedure.

MINORITIES

Much of the same sort of struggle prevailed in questions of race relations. Increasing ethnic and racial self-confidence in the late 1960s gave rise to strong pressure groups, but it also fed resentment and controversy over the gains of minorities through legislation and court mandate. Many Americans came to believe that the federal government operated in favor of special-interest groups, whether racial minorities, the poor, and women, or the oil companies and the nuclear industry.

This kind of thinking fed a general tendency toward less political participation that began in the mid-1960s. Percentages of eligible voters who cast ballots declined, despite the increased ease of registering and voting. Political scandals, corruption, and favoritism disillusioned and alienated voters, convincing many that their votes did not count.

A deep crisis of faith in government surfaced in an abrupt way during 1973 in the unlikely rendezvous of Native Americans and federal forces at Wounded Knee. The civil rights movement had promised to redress old wrongs. Not unexpectedly, its energies touched Native Americans, who by the 1970s lived for the most part in terrible poverty and dependence. A third of the population on reservations survived on welfare; life expectancy was only forty-six years; and rates of alcoholism and suicide were as-

REPRESENTATIVE SHIRLEY CHISHOLM.   During the 1960s and 1970s, an increasing number of African Americans and women were elected to local, state, and federal office. Shirley Chisholm of New York City was a pioneer. The first African-American woman elected to Congress, she served in the House of Representatives from 1969 to 1982.

toundingly high. Years of Indian policy designed to suppress Native American culture had, contrary to expectations, not created a population willing or able to assimilate.

Almost inevitably, this policy of neglect and cultural aggression created an explosion. With no little irony was it focused at Wounded Knee in the Pine Ridge Reservation in South Dakota. There in the late winter and spring of 1973, the American Indian Movement and the Oglala Sioux, protesting the terrible conditions on the reservation, violence by whites against Native Americans, and the hostile and inept leadership of the designated tribal chief, took over the town. Surrounded by FBI agents and local vigilantes, the group held out until May. Few of their demands were met; several were killed in gun battles; and other leaders became enmeshed in lengthy, dispiriting court battles.

Publicity about the plight of Native Americans did, however, result in increased federal funding for education and housing, at least up to the Reagan administration. A far more important result, however, came after various lawsuits before the Indian Claims Commission, in which Native Americans sued for compensation for tribal lands illegally seized by white settlers. Created to compensate tribes for lost territory, the commission and its rulings often engendered more controversy than it settled as tribes realized that accepting cash payments would lose them their territory forever. This prompted some groups to demand return of their ancient lands.

The general transformation of political and social change into stalemates such as these was partly generated by a new individualist ethic. This new morality of unlimited self-expression prompted satirist Tom Wolfe to dub the 1970s "the Me decade." The term refers to a decline of belief in community, of working together to solve problems, and an emphasis on the private individual. In some cases, this celebration of the self led to an increasing frankness about sexuality and lifestyles that would have been unthinkable ten years earlier. Movements of personal liberation included such groups as the handicapped, gay men and women, and children's rights advocates. Whether or not this development benefited society, however, became an increasingly disputed question.

Above all else, the war in Vietnam was the catalyst in creating the tone of political and institutional crisis in the 1970s. President Johnson's decision not to seek reelection in 1968 and Richard Nixon's defeat of Hubert Humphrey for the presidency reflected public opposition to continuing the war. But paradoxically, Americans did not wish to lose in Vietnam. Thus it took five more painful years before the United States finally extricated itself from the war.

NIXON AND SOUTHEAST ASIA

The career of Richard M. Nixon was marked by recurrent controversy, triumph, and defeat, or as he put it, crises. Born into a Quaker family in 1913 in Yorba Linda, California, Nixon earned a law degree at Duke University. He set up a law practice in Whittier, California, shortly before the beginning of World War II. During the war he served as a naval supply officer in the Pacific. Afterward, he returned home to California and began his rapid rise in national politics from representative to senator to vice president. From the first, his campaigns, if not actually dishonest, were marred by political smears and innuendos about the patriotism of his opponents. He served in Congress and achieved prominence for his pursuit of Alger Hiss while a member of the House Un-American Activities Committee. Loyal to the party and hardworking, by 1952 Nixon represented the best compromise candidate for the vice presidency.

During his eight-year tenure in Eisenhower's shadow, Nixon worked hard to build his leadership of the Republican party. In 1960 he was an easy winner of the presidential nomination and only a narrow loser in the election. Back after defeat in a race for governor of California, Nixon won the Republican nomination in 1968, again by occupying the center of his party. In the campaign, he benefited from growing dismay over the war and the social strife that it was causing at home. He promised to resolve the Vietnam conflict but refused to say how.

Nixon's attitude toward government was a curious blend of admiration, suspicion, and hostility. He was one of the most creative politicans to hold the office after 1945 and yet he undercut his greatest achievements in the tawdry Watergate affair. He enjoyed the power and pomp of office. But because of long-standing enmities with the press and the Democratic party, he saw himself as an outsider and a representative of those who distrusted government. This sort of division showed up in his political appointments. Most members of his cabinet were men with Washington connections, or they were well-known in Republican circles, like Henry Kissinger, his special assistant for national security. The White House inner circle was ruled by H. R. (Bob) Haldeman, the chief of staff, and, to a lesser extent, John D. Ehrlichman, Domestic Council chief.

VIETNAMIZATION

Promising an open government, Nixon in fact shut many of his most important decisions away from public scrutiny. He and Henry Kissinger were both convinced that the United States had to maintain credibility in opposing the Soviet Union and still end American participation in the Vietnam War. To achieve this contradictory purpose, the president decided to withdraw American forces from combat and yet deny victory to the Viet Cong and North Vietnam through air power. This tactic was called "Vietnamization." Over the next two years, he withdrew almost 500,000 American troops until only 50,000 remained in late 1972. American soldiers straggled back to their lives in the United States, neither heroes nor victors. Many of them were victims of low morale, drug dependency, and bitterness because of a lack of support from the American public. At the same time, Nixon stepped up air raids and approved the invasion of Cambodia and Laos to cut off enemy supply lines.

By bombing Cambodia early in his administration, Nixon altered the rules of the war. The president had ordered an attack on a nation that was officially neutral. He tried to keep the intervention a secret, especially from the American public. When news of the raids leaked to *The New York Times*, Nixon and Kissinger were furious and resorted to illegal counterattacks. The White House ordered wiretaps on the telephones of five newsmen to find out who had told the press. In effect, Nixon's crisis of credibility had begun.

FIGHTING THE WAR PROTESTERS

The president's anger at the press and television did not prevent him from using the media to try to defuse protests against his Vietnamization policy. During the summer of 1969 he attacked demonstrators in speeches and news conferences. But his efforts proved only partially effective. On October 15 thousands of Americans demonstrated against the war in several cities. An even larger coalition, supported now by important members of Congress and newspapers, began to solidify around the peace issue.

Nixon and his aides concluded that if the American public believed the criticisms of the administration appearing in the media, then it was time to attack the integrity and objectivity of the media. Consequently the president approved Vice President Spiro Agnew's accusations of biased reporting against the press and the major television networks. The president also approved Agnew's bitter denunciation of student protesters as an "effete corps of impudent snobs who characterized themselves as intellectuals." Both tactics, the administration hoped, would split the nation and polarize opinion. If antiwar opinion could be isolated, it might also be quieted. As Agnew put it, "it is time for a positive polarization."

Nixon's policy of diverting war casualties to the Vietnamese and deflecting criticism at home had achieved some success by early 1970. On April 4 a large group of prowar demonstrators congregated in Washington. The overthrow of neutral Prince Sihanouk of Cambodia and his replacement by the pro-American Lon Nol made it possible to take more drastic action to cut off supplies reaching the Viet Cong through that country. In late April, Nixon authorized an invasion of Cambodia. But he miscalculated the domestic effects of this incursion. The antiwar movement suddenly sprang to life with demonstrations and strikes on college campuses throughout the nation. Police and the National Guard were called out to restore order in a number of places. At Kent State University in Ohio, students organized to oppose the war. National Guard

THIS HUGE MARCH FOR PEACE IN VIETNAM, November 15, 1969, expressed the desire of millions of Americans for an end to the war. Because the American electorate was deeply divided, however, in the short run such demonstrations only increased the bitterness of political debate. The war ruined the careers of two eminent Democratic leaders, Lyndon Johnson and Hubert Humphrey, and deeply compromised the presidency of Richard Nixon.

troops were called out to repress the demonstrations. When a crowd of students gathered on May 4, troops suddenly opened fire, killing four of them. Shortly afterward, at Jackson State University in Mississippi, two black civil rights protesters were shot and killed. In his angry comments on such incidents, the president appeared to link all demonstrations and protests whatever their cause: they incited anarchy. Worse, he appeared to blame the demonstrators for their fate. In Cambodia the result was a civil war with hundreds of thousands of casualties that continued for twenty-five years.

With pressure mounting for an end to the war, Nixon tried to enlist the country's "silent majority" to turn back war opponents. His chance came during the fall congressional elec-

tions, but the results were inconclusive. The Republicans gained two Senate seats, but lost nine places in the House and eleven governorships. Rather than isolating war critics, the president had begun to isolate himself.

In early 1971, Nixon showed a more conciliatory mood, but this dissolved in the wake of further serious opposition to the war. A South Vietnamese invasion of Laos with American air support brought little vocal opposition. But two events riveted national attention on war critics. The first was a large, disruptive demonstration in Washington on May 2 and 3 by the "Mayday Tribe," which resulted in 10,000 arrests. Much more serious was publication of the "Pentagon Papers," beginning June 13 in *The New York Times*. This documentary history of U.S. involvement in Vietnam, culled from secret government files by Daniel Ellsberg, a former Kissinger aide, showed the extent of covert American involvement in Southeast Asia and exposed the intrigue and deception of three administrations.

Nixon tried to stop publication of these damning government records, but the Supreme Court ruled in favor of the public's right to know. No documents implicated the Nixon administration, but the history of America's secret and growing involvement in Southeast Asia undercut the reputations of three previous presidents. Nixon did not dispute the truthfulness of the history. His charge was that publication of the Pentagon Papers would undermine the credibility of government.

DÉTENTE

As the war in Vietnam continued its bloody course, Nixon and Kissinger pursued another, different goal in foreign policy. Both leaders were convinced that the United States must recognize the rising power of other nations. Europe, Japan, the Soviet Union, and China all represented separate poles of power. With Europe taking a more independent course, the president believed the time was ripe to upgrade relations with China. He also wished to reach a limited arms control agreement with the Soviet Union. Whatever their motives, Nixon and Kissinger began a process that eventually reversed decades of policy and initiated a successful strategy that all of their successors followed.

The president launched his policy secretly, in part because he did not wish to stir criticism from the right wing of his own party, which vigorously opposed détente (conciliation) with the Chinese Communists and the Russians. Nonetheless, signs of a thaw with the Chinese were unmistakable. In April 1971 a U.S. table tennis team traveled to mainland China for a series of matches. In July the president announced to a surprised nation that he would visit China, a result of clandestine negotiations carried out by Henry Kissinger.

Inevitably, these moves seriously compromised support for America's staunch ally Nationalist China, which still occupied Taiwan. On October 12 Nixon announced a similar trip to the Soviet Union. Both these initiatives represented major changes in American policy because they softened U.S. opposition toward an accommodation with the two major communist powers. After the president's dramatic weeklong visit to China in February 1972, the United States began to normalize relations with that nation. Warmer relations with the Chinese, in turn, convinced the Soviet Union to seek closer ties with the United States.

This bargaining with the Russians bore fruit in the spring and summer of 1972. When Nixon returned from the Soviet Union in late May, he had cemented two major agreements. The first was a Strategic Arms Limitation Treaty (SALT I), signed with Soviet leader Leonid Brezhnev on May 26 and limiting U.S. and Soviet deployment of antiballistic missile systems. The second was a large Russian purchase of American grain, announced in July.

THE END OF THE WAR

But the president failed to persuade either China or the USSR to abandon North Vietnam. Indeed, the Vietnam crisis worsened. The South Vietnamese government made no real advance in winning the support of its population. Militarily, the situation remained bleak. With diminished numbers of American troops in the country, U.S. policy relied more on air strikes. But time obviously favored the insurgents. Domestic support for the war continued to crumble. In a symbolic but momentous act in 1971, the Senate rescinded the Gulf of Tonkin Resolution. During the spring and summer and into the fall of 1972, the United States and North Vietnam conducted peace negotiations in Paris. To influence the 1972 presidential election, Kissinger announced during the fall that a peace treaty was imminent. But negotiations faltered, and the president ordered new saturation

NIXON IN CHINA. Richard Nixon, his wife Pat, Chinese Deputy Premier Li Hsien-nien and his wife, and Secretary of State William Rogers at the Great Wall of China in February 1972. Customary visits by politicians to this enigmatic boundary suggest the two extremes of Chinese policy—excluding foreigners or welcoming them in.

bombing of the north. Finally, in January 1973 a treaty was signed. American prisoners of war were to be released, and the South Vietnamese regime was to remain in power. But North Vietnam was allowed to keep troops in the south. In effect, the United States had abandoned the south, for which it had fought so long.

Although it ratified a military reverse of major proportions, the treaty was in one sense a positive accomplishment. Nixon had ended the war and yet had avoided the right-wing backlash that had paralyzed two presidents before him. Added to the rapprochement with the Chinese and the Russians, ending the war represented a significant turning point in American foreign relations and a major accomplishment for the president. He had also manipulated foreign policy to win a landslide reelection against Democrat George McGovern in 1972.

NIXON'S CREDIBILITY AT HOME

In domestic policy, President Nixon faced two obstacles: a Congress dominated by the Democratic party and a government bureaucracy unresponsive and unsympathetic to his policies. These stumbling blocks constituted a major impediment to the conduct of his administration. The president focused on four issues, but each of them proved highly resistant to change: He attempted to strengthen legal weapons against crime and political violence. He sought a major overhaul of social welfare policy. He attempted to cope with a serious bout of economic stagnation, inflation, and energy shortages. He tried to reorganize the executive branch of the government.

Elected partly because he had promised decisive action against social disorder, Nixon secured a tough new criminal justice law in the District of Columbia. His attorney general, John Mitchell, sought to isolate student and radical groups by infiltrating their ranks with agents and prosecuting them under an antiriot law passed in 1968. Since many administration members as well as voters believed that civil rights was a major source of social unrest, he also tried to slow federal desegregation actions. Attorney General Mitchell testified against extending the Voting Rights Act, due to expire in August 1970. But Congress renewed the act anyway.

Striking at another institution that had loosened social restraints, Nixon tried to transform the Supreme Court. Early in his administration, the president had his first opportunity to make a change when the position of chief justice fell open. Nixon appointed Judge Warren Burger to the post. The next vacancy occurred in 1971. In this case the president nominated first one, then another, undistinguished, conservative southern appeals court judge. The Senate rejected both. Stung by these defeats, Nixon appointed Judge Harry Andrew Blackmun. His final appointment did lay the groundwork for a conservative court when he appointed William Hubbs Rehnquist as Justice. Nixon had hoped to affect the complexion of the Court immediately, but it still continued to advance integration, and in 1973, in the *Roe* v. *Wade* decision, declared constitutional a woman's right to have an abortion.

The issue of welfare payments to nonworking mothers and children was part of the larger question of providing social services and income maintenance to the poor and elderly. Some Americans believed that the poor should suffer the consequences of their fate and that the federal government should provide only minimal assistance. The president did not share this harsh view, but he did oppose the tangle of agencies and programs left over from the Great Society. His first plan to correct this confusion was the Family Assistance Plan, a radical plan to provide a guaranteed income of $1,600 for a family of four (plus $820 in food stamps). Twice passed by the House, the act failed in the Senate, and Nixon abandoned it in 1971.

Taking a different tack, the administration did succeed in shifting some federal social programs to the states in the 1972 State and Local Fiscal Assistance Act. This law created "revenue sharing" for the states. In effect, it provided block grants to state authorities, with general standards set but wide discretion left to local administration as to how the money should be spent. This serious experiment in federalism allowed governments to fund programs according to local priorities.

THE ECONOMY

Some of the president's difficulties in passing new social legislation lay in the sluggish economy. As the leader of a political party that ritualistically proclaimed its faith in the private sector, Nixon used federal fiscal and monetary instruments to fight economic problems. To explain this economic activism, at one point he even declared himself a follower of Keynesian economics. But his administration lacked an overall, consistent policy.

Shortly after entering the White House, Nixon had promised to nudge the lethargic economy with increased federal expenditures. But by mid-1971, fighting inflation took top priority. In the summer the president acted on several fronts. Calling this Phase I of his economic program, he froze wages and prices for ninety days, slapped a 10 percent surcharge on imports, and devalued the American dollar.

A second phase began in the summer of 1973, when the president reimposed a price freeze for sixty days. After these controls were relaxed, prices soared again. One reason for this sudden, uncontrollable inflation was the steep increase in imported oil prices. By 1973 the United States was importing about one-third of its total crude oil. More than one-half of that total came from OPEC (the Organization of Petroleum Exporting Countries). These nations, among them Saudi Arabia, Kuwait, Libya, Iran, Iraq, Nigeria, and Venezuela, had jointly raised oil prices about 400 percent above 1970 prices. In addition, during the winter of 1973–1974, Arab members of OPEC embargoed all shipments of oil to the United States and other Western nations that supported Israel during the 1973 Yom Kippur War against Egypt and Syria. Spot shortages appeared in the United States, with long lines of automobiles snaking around filling stations.

DOMESTIC SPYING

Unable to develop a consistent and effective economic program, Nixon also discovered enormous inertia in government itself. Of all the problems he faced, none frustrated the president as much as his lack of control over the federal bureaucracy. Twice, Nixon and his advisers tried to reorganize the executive branch. But both efforts, in 1970 and in 1973, failed. In particular, his attempts to subordinate cabinet heads to the White House staff met spirited opposition.

Finding himself stalemated in several directions, and feeling besieged by the press and Congress, the president tried to undermine the institutions that blocked him. In doing so, he created a submerged, secret branch of government that depended on intrigue, conspiracy, and illegal measures. The first such instance was the phone taps used after the bombing of Cambodia. He took a more serious step in the fall of 1970. Tom Huston, a White House aide, prepared a program of domestic spying to be implemented by the president's staff. J. Edgar Hoover, head of the FBI, refused to agree, in part because it would undercut his own agency. When this proposal failed, the administration created the White House investigation unit known as "the plumbers," whose job it was to plug information leaks.

Losses in the election of 1970 and continued criticism of his Vietnam policy convinced the president to act. After publication of the Pentagon Papers, the White House approved plans to break into Daniel Ellsberg's psychiatrist's office to search for material that might discredit him. The operation was financed with money received in a secret donation from the milk industry, given in return for administration support of higher milk price supports.

WATERGATE

In 1972 the administration plunged deeper into illegal activities. Many of these originated in the Committee for the Reelection of the President (CREEP). CREEP hoped to shape the election of 1972 to Nixon's advantage. It willfully misinformed the public and broke the law. Using secret contributions solicited from corporate donors, the group employed "dirty tricks" that injected false issues into Democratic party primaries. CREEP also broke into Democratic party headquarters in May 1972 to install wiretaps and to photograph documents. When the group returned in mid-June to obtain more material, a night watchman alerted the Washington, D.C., police. They arrived quickly at the Watergate complex that housed the headquarters and arrested several of the burglars. A few were Cuban refugees, but two were ex-employees of CREEP.

The Democratic party denounced the break-in, but administration spokesmen dismissed it as a "third-rate burglary attempt." Watergate never emerged as an election issue. The Democratic candidate, George McGovern, tried to galvanize his party around opposition to the Vietnam War and promises of social reform. But his own credibility was compromised when he supported Senator Thomas Eagleton of Missouri for vice president and then dropped him after information about the senator's history of mental illness surfaced. This was less important, however, than his inability to rally the Democratic party. Much of McGovern's early support fell away, and traditional sources of Democratic power in urban political machines and in the labor movement refused to work for him. Nixon's campaign stressed his accomplishments: dramatic changes in foreign policy and a revived economy. Evidently, the voters believed him. He won every state but Massachusetts and the District of Columbia. Still, the Democrats retained their majority in Congress.

In his second inaugural address, the president spoke words that came to have a bitter irony for his next years:

> From this day forward let each of us make a solemn commitment in his own heart: to bear his responsibility, to do his part, to live his ideals.

At the beginning of 1973, Nixon moved to assert firmer control of the executive branch and to dismantle the Great Society. Even though he impounded funds (refused to spend appropriated money), he made little headway. Instead, he found himself increasingly mired in explanations of the Watergate break-in and other campaign irregularities.

The Watergate scandal hinged on the question of credibility. For Nixon and all his advisers, the problem of truthfulness was rarely the issue. Rather, the Watergate defendants tried again and again to create credible explanations for their behavior, willfully mixing truth with invention and

WATERGATE ROSTER

	Position	Role in Watergate	Sentence	Amount of Sentence Served
Richard M. Nixon	President of the United States	Unindicted coconspirator	Pardoned	
Dwight L. Chapin	Presidential appointments secretary	Convicted of lying to a grand jury	10 to 30 months	8 months
Charles W. Colson	Special counsel to the president	Pleaded guilty to obstruction of justice	1 to 3 years; fined $5,000	7 months
John W. Dean III	Counsel to the president	Pleaded guilty to conspiracy	1 to 4 years	4 months
John D. Ehrlichman	Domestic Council chief	Convicted of conspiracy to obstruct justice, conspiracy, and perjury	Concurrent terms of 20 months to 8 years	18 months
H. R. Haldeman	Chief of the White House staff	Convicted of conspiracy and perjury	30 months to 8 years	18 months
E. Howard Hunt	White House aide	Pleaded guilty to conspiracy, burglary, and wiretapping	30 months to 8 years; fined $10,000	33 months
Herbert W. Kalmbach	Personal attorney to the president	Pleaded guilty to violation of Federal Corrupt Practices Act and promising federal employment as a reward for political activity	6 to 18 months; fined $10,000	6 months
Richard G. Kleindienst	Attorney General of the United States	Pleaded guilty to refusal to answer pertinent questions before a Senate committee	30 days; fined $100	Sentence suspended

(continued)

WATERGATE ROSTER (*CONT.*)

	Position	Role in Watergate	Sentence	Amount of Sentence Served
Egil Krogh, Jr.	White House aide	Pleaded guilty to conspiracy	2 to 6 years (all but 6 months suspended)	4½ months
Frederick C. LaRue	Assistant to John Mitchell	Pleaded guilty to conspiracy	1 to 3 years (all but 6 months suspended)	5½ months
G. Gordon Liddy	White House aide	Convicted of conspiracy, burglary, and wiretapping	6 years and 8 months to 20 years; fined $40,000	52 months
Jeb S. Magruder	White House aide	Pleaded guilty to conspiracy, wiretapping and fraud	10 months to 4 years	7 months
John N. Mitchell	Attorney General of the United States	Convicted of conspiracy and perjury	30 months to 8 years	19 months
Donald H. Segretti	"Dirty tricks" specialist	Pleaded guilty to campaign violations and conspiracy	6 months	4½ months
Maurice H. Stans	Finance Director of Committee for the Reelection of the President	Pleaded guilty to misdemeanor violations of the Federal Elections Campaign Act	Fined $5,000	
Bernard L. Barker	Watergate burglar	Pleaded guilty to conspiracy, burglary, wiretapping, and unlawful possession of intercepting devices	18 months to 6 years	12 months
Virgilio R. Gonzalez	Watergate burglar	Pleaded guilty to conspiracy, burglary, wiretapping, and unlawful possession of intercepting devices	1 to 4 years	15 months
James W. McCord, Jr.	Watergate burglar	Convicted of conspiracy, burglary, wiretapping, and unlawful possession of intercepting devices	1 to 5 years	4 months
Eugenio R. Martinez	Watergate burglar	Pleaded guilty to conspiracy, burglary, wiretapping, and unlawful possession of intercepting devices	1 to 4 years	15 months
Frank A. Sturgis	Watergate burglar	Pleaded guilty to conspiracy, burglary, wiretapping, and unlawful possession of intercepting devices	1 to 4 years	13 months

misinformation. As they retreated, more and more of the real story emerged from the paper trail they left behind them.

The administration's problems began when Judge John Sirica, presiding over the trial of the burglars in Washington in early 1973, pressed the defendants. One of them, James McCord, implicated high administration figures in the planning of election espionage. He accused John Mitchell and White House staff members Jeb Magruder and John Dean. *Washington Post* reporters picked up loose ends of evidence that emerged in the trial and began weaving together the story of a painstaking plot to cover up ties between the Watergate burglars and the White House.

When John Dean testified during June hearings before the Presidential Campaign Committee, set up in the Senate, he used this forum to escape what he believed was a White House decision to make him a scapegoat for Watergate. He even implicated the president in the cover-up. With this new evidence, the investigation intensified. A grand jury began to weigh evidence against a mounting list of accused conspirators. Other material surfaced through efforts of a special prosecutor, Archibald Cox, appointed to oversee the investigation in the attorney general's office. Surrounded, and with his own defenses crumbling, the president worked publicly with the investigation while he privately tried to impede it. As he instructed John Mitchell:

> I want you all to stonewall it, let them plead the Fifth Amendment, cover-up or anything else, if it'll save it—save the plan.

AN AMERICAN DISGRACED. The first chief executive driven from office by scandal and the threat of impeachment, Richard Nixon succumbed to this last, largely self-inflicted crisis of his political career. Americans, although relieved, were stunned by the magnitude of the crisis; their faith in the presidency as an institution might never be the same.

One by one the president's close advisers resigned. In October 1973 Vice President Agnew left office, pleading no contest to charges of income tax fraud after a grand jury discovered that he had accepted bribes and payoffs while governor of Maryland. The most startling discovery, however, came when a White House aide told of hundreds of tapes of recorded conversations between Nixon and his advisers made secretly over the previous two years. These could establish the president's guilt or innocence.

Nixon's refusal to submit any of the tapes to Cox, the grand jury, or the Senate committee further damaged his credibility. He tried every means to keep the material secret, invoking "executive privilege," and fighting with lawsuits and delays. He even fired prosecutor Cox on October 20, 1973, in the infamous "Saturday Night Massacre" when Attorney General Elliot Richardson and Deputy William Ruckelshaus resigned rather than do the president's bidding. But Cox's replacement, Leon Jaworski, persisted in demanding the evidence. Finally, in April 1974, Nixon released edited versions of the tapes. Even in abridged form, the documents revealed that the president was deeply involved in the Watergate cover-up. They also uncovered the private Nixon, a man who was as ruthless and vulgar in private as he was cautious and well-spoken in public. The House Judiciary Committee began hearings on impeachment.

As Nixon was forced to release more tapes, impressions of his guilt became firmer. Two new groups of tapes released over the summer disclosed the president's direct participation in the cover-up of the Watergate burglary. On August 8, after his administration had almost ceased to govern—and facing impeachment—the president resigned. But he would admit no wrongdoing, only bad judgment. As Nixon boarded a plane for California, Gerald Ford, Vice President Agnew's replacement, became president.

The turmoil of Watergate and the dramatic exposures of corruption in government convinced many Americans that most politicians were either inept or immoral. True, the system

had worked to replace a government that had subverted some of the most important institutions of democracy. But the process was so wrenching that it undercut faith in government itself. New revelations in the media about kickbacks and other scandals and stories of CIA and FBI illegal activities added to the growing credibility gap.

CONSUMERS LOSE FAITH

The reputations of private institutions were also tarnished in the early 1970s. The consumer movement carried on a spirited attack on private corporations for their shoddy and dangerous practices. Consumerism had had an active history in the early decades of the twentieth century and was reborn in the mid-1960s. Critics such as Ralph Nader and Barry Commoner wrote exposés of dangerous flaws in automobile design, adulteration of foods, pollution, and, especially, nuclear hazards. They helped stimulate a wave of consumer protection legislation, such as the Consumer Product Safety Act of 1972, which established a five-member regulatory agency. These laws aided the removal of dangerous products from the market.

Nader's efforts coincided with an important social movement of the early 1970s that grew out of the counterculture. Many Americans began to lead what they believed was a less artificial life, stressing vegetarian diet, natural childbirth, communal and rural living, a more natural sexuality, less differentiated sex roles, and the use of solar energy. Many of the thousands of participants in this movement rejected competitive, urban living. They were wary of the great technological feats of the era, such as the U.S. moon landing in July 1969 and the generation of nuclear power. They viewed industrial and scientific progress with deep suspicion.

Perhaps most symbolic of this new mood was a change in automobile design. To increase fuel efficiency and compete with Japanese and European imports, American auto makers shortened and lightened their cars. They lopped off the titanic fins, chrome strips, and long hoods and trunks that had added weight, horsepower, and expense. The dream of owning a shiny new car did not end, of course, but it did take a more practical bent.

GERALD FORD AND THE FAILURE OF LEADERSHIP

Gerald Ford, the new president-by-appointment, had the difficult task of restoring belief in American institutions in a moment of deep crisis. A well-liked congressman from Michigan, Ford had almost no national reputation and little experience with the difficult administrative tasks of his new office. He faced a leadership crisis that was intensified by a serious recession, continuing energy shortages, and the final, bleak days before the fall of the South Vietnamese government. Out of his inherited administration, he retained Henry Kissinger, but he replaced most of the White House staff. To fill the vacant vice presidency, he appointed Nelson Rockefeller, who was governor of New York. The choice proved politically damaging. Rockefeller was without a significant following in the Republican party. Dis-

ASTRONAUT EDWIN E. ALDRIN, JR., photographed by Neil Armstrong on July 20, 1969, while both men stood on the surface of the moon. Aldrin's sharp shadow falls across footprints left by the two moon-walkers. Although it occurred decades ago, this endeavor represents the most spectacular success of the American space program to date.

liked by the large and growing right wing, he had little vocal support from moderates.

Soon after taking office, Ford made his most controversial move. He granted a general pardon to ex-President Nixon. As he said, "My conscience tells me that only I, as president, have the constitutional power to firmly shut and seal this book." But his act sealed only the lips of Richard Nixon, who did not reveal or admit the extent of his involvement in Watergate. Many Americans believed that Ford had struck a deal for the presidency with Nixon, although there was no evidence to support this suspicion.

Despite the damage of the pardon, Ford benefited from his reputation for honesty and openness. His wife, Betty, strengthened this impression of candor by speaking openly of a breast cancer operation she underwent in late 1974 and by supporting her own political causes, such as the Equal Rights Amendment. But Gerald Ford also had a reputation as a bumbler and a man not up to the intellectual rigors of the office. This impression of ineptness continued for the next two years, fed by the merciless satire of the popular television program *Saturday Night Live*.

The new president inherited the final debacle of Vietnam. Now prevented by law from committing any American forces to this Asian conflict, Ford could do nothing when the North Vietnamese army routed the forces of the south and drove toward Saigon in the spring of 1975. An emergency airlift rescued remaining Americans and thousands of South Vietnamese officials linked to the United States. The longest war in American history ended in scenes of hasty and confused retreat.

However, there were few domestic recriminations. America's reputation for decisive action was partly restored when Ford achieved the rescue of an American merchant ship, the *Mayaguez*, seized by Cambodians in May. Ford ordered ships, planes, and men into action. Although the expedition was costly in terms of lives lost, the thirty-nine-man crew was freed. Congress and much of the press applauded the president's at-

tempt to restore credibility, although they realized the action might have been unnecessary.

On the domestic front, Ford had few successes. His antirecession plans failed to pass Congress. Infighting and indecision in the administration convinced the public that weak leadership persisted. On questions of energy, conservation, and the environment, Ford relinquished leadership to Congress. Increasingly, he vetoed measures, only to see them passed again over his objections.

THE ELECTION OF 1976

In early 1976, Ford announced that he would seek election to a full term as president. He possessed the significant advantage of incumbency, but he had few concrete accomplishments. His party split into two factions, with the most vocal and highly organized portion supporting former governor of California Ronald Reagan. Reagan challenged Ford in primaries across the country, attacking his foreign policy, détente with the Russians, and the continued influence of Henry Kissinger. He filled his speeches with old-fashioned homilies and invited nostalgia for a vaguely remembered American past. This strategy almost succeeded. In a closely divided convention, Ford had to accept a "morality in foreign policy" plank that, in effect, criticized his own foreign policy. Nonetheless, Ford narrowly won the nomination.

The Democratic party in 1976 was, if anything, more deeply divided than the Republican. The multiple leadership of the party and the new rules for delegate selection made it difficult for any one candidate to emerge. The most obvious choice was Senator Edward Kennedy of Massachusetts. But Kennedy's chances remained seriously compromised by an accident that had occurred on Chappaquiddick Island, Massachusetts, on July 18, 1969. A woman companion riding in his car had been killed, and Kennedy could never satisfactorily explain the circumstances of the accident. Other candidates lacked national support. As a result, the most persistent candidate, James (Jimmy) Carter, former governor of Georgia, won the nomination.

Carter won a narrow victory in November after a campaign highlighted by televised debates. Carter's margin was provided by an exaggerated turnout of two traditional Democratic constituencies: the South (proud of its native son) and black voters. But beneath the surface, this coalition was shaky. African Americans and blue-collar whites could be split apart, as George Wallace's campaigns over several years had proven. Labor unions, once the backbone of the Democratic party, had declined in membership and prestige during the 1970s. They had also lost power in the party as a result of the new rules that gave proportional representation to women and minorities.

The South might have been solid in electoral votes for Carter, but the region had become increasingly diverse and Republican. While the Voting Rights Act had enfranchised large numbers of black voters, industrialization, large population increases, and traditional conservatism had brought a strong resurgence of Republicanism. Other, traditionally strong Republican areas also gained representation during the 1970s, particularly the Southwest and the West. The census of 1980 confirmed a massive trend in population flow after World War II, out of the North and East to the South and West. For the first time, the population center of the nation crossed the Mississippi River.

The election of 1976 demonstrated another long-term trend in American voting patterns, away from voter participation. Registration was easier, and whole new populations were enfranchised, but the percentage of persons voting continued to decline. So did party identification. The effect of this nonparticipation was to increase the power of special-interest groups and small, well-organized segments of the population. Furthermore, the mass media exercised an increased power in the campaign, with advertising and pollsters largely determining the issues and answers for candidates.

The only substantial exception to this trend appeared among America's growing elderly population. During the 1970s the average life expectancy in the United States increased by more than two and a half years, continuing a tendency to longevity that added millions to the number of retirees. Among older Americans, issues of cuts in Social Security or medical benefit programs were a matter of life and death. So not only did the elderly vote in large numbers, they also organized effective pressure groups such as the Gray Panthers.

Jimmy Carter appealed to many disaffected voters. His campaign criticized the Washington establishment and the lingering problems of Watergate. He promised never to deceive the American public. He stressed traditional values and honesty in government. He made character the issue of the campaign. This strenuous and persistent campaigning paid off.

Born into a Georgia farm family, Carter attended the U.S. Naval Academy and, after World War II, worked in the new nuclear submarine fleet. Retiring from the navy, he returned to Plains, Georgia, and started a successful peanut warehouse and distributing business. He entered Georgia state politics in 1962 and won the governorship in 1970. Widely known as a representative of the "new South," that is, a South that accepted racial integration, Carter in 1976 also had strong ties to the old South, with its tradition of evangelical Protestantism. The tone of his campaign stressed the personal virtues he could bring to the office: truthfulness, family values, decency, and principle. He promised nuclear disarmament, open and competent government, and a restoration of faith in America.

JIMMY CARTER AND THE CREDIBILITY CRISIS

The new president appointed several Washington professionals to his cabinet, including Cyrus Vance as secretary of state and Joseph Califano as secretary of health, education, and welfare. He named Patricia Harris, a black woman, as secretary of housing and urban development. Large numbers of lower-level administrative appointments went to women and African Americans. By appointing

ENERGY SOURCE BY TYPE (IN QUADRILLIONS OF BTUs)

	1960	1970	1980	1984
Refined petroleum	19.9	29.5	34.3	31.0
Natural gas	12.4	21.8	20.4	18.0
Coal	10.1	12.7	15.7	17.2
Nuclear	–	.2	2.7	3.5
Hydroelectric	1.7	2.7	3.1	3.5
Other	–	–	.1	.2
Total	44.1	66.9	76.3	77.5

Source: U.S. Department of Commerce, Bureau of the Census, Statistical Abstract of the United States, 1986 (Washington D.C.: Government Printing Office, 1985), p. 557.

two women, he had almost as many women in his cabinet as all previous presidents combined. Nonetheless, Carter's White House staff was headed by his campaign manager Hamilton Jordan, with other Georgians occupying leading roles. Among them were Bert Lance as head of the Office of Management and Budget and Andrew Young as U.S. ambassador to the United Nations. This group was known as the "Georgia Mafia."

Almost from the beginning, Carter's inexperience in national politics and his indecisiveness (perhaps reflecting the conflicts in his electoral majority) hurt his relations with the Democratic-controlled Congress. In a sense, Carter's personality and politics reflected each other. He was both liberal and conservative, a southerner with important ties and dependencies in the North, a born-again Christian with sophisticated views of moral and social problems. This was also the nature of his coalition and political support, and it was an inherently unstable one.

ENERGY POLICY

Energy took priority with the new president. Personally rejecting the extravagant style sometimes associated with the presidency, Carter urged all Americans to conserve energy and live simpler lives. His major energy legislation, introduced in April 1977, was designed to ease American de-

pendence on OPEC oil and induce domestic conservation. Sections of the proposed program encouraged a return to coal use and mandated energy savings in automobile design.

By August 1977 the energy bill had sailed through the House, practically intact. But it stalled in the Senate, primarily over the issue of deregulating natural gas. Although a new Department of Energy began operating in October 1977, Carter's principal energy legislation did not pass until a year later. In five linked acts, Congress approved measures to encourage home energy conservation, to enforce the use of coal in electrical generating, to encourage auto efficiency, and to allow increases in natural gas prices. Several key questions remained unanswered, however, such as the timing and extent of oil price deregulation and the fate of the nuclear industry.

Carter called the energy crisis the "moral equivalent of war." For his presidency, at least, this slogan proved to be apt. The president recognized that because of recurrent gasoline shortages, many Americans did not trust the oil companies. Were they withholding gasoline from the market in order to raise prices as many suspected? The president declared that this might be the case. Yet he did not act. A long, bitter coal strike over the winter of 1977–1978, in which the president did not intervene quickly, also added to the impression of his inability to show leadership on the issue of energy.

IMPORTED ENERGY BY TYPE (IN QUADRILLIONS OF BTUs)

	1960	1970	1980	1984
Crude oil	2.2	2.8	11.1	7.3
Refined petroleum	1.8	4.7	3.4	4.1
Natural gas	.2	.9	1.0	.9
Percentage of supply imported	9.2%	12.1%	19.8%	16.4%

Source: U.S. Department of Commerce, Bureau of the Census, Statistical Abstract of the United States, 1986 (Washington D.C.: Government Printing Office, 1985), p. 557.

SADAT, CARTER, AND BEGIN.   This portrait, taken at the beginning of the ceremony marking the signing of the Camp David accords, symbolized the achievement of President Jimmy Carter (center) in negotiating a peace treaty between President Anwar Sadat of Egypt (left) and Israeli Prime Minister Menachem Begin in March 1979.

Energy policy reached an impasse in the spring of 1979. Political turmoil in Iran in late 1978 and 1979 cut that country's oil production to almost nothing. Although Iran supplied only about 5 percent of U.S. needs, the cutoff was significant. Rapid price hikes and serious shortages resulted by spring. Particularly in California and in Washington, DC, long lines formed around filling stations. Many Americans believed the oil shortage to have been deliberately engineered, but there was little conclusive evidence, and the government failed to confirm or deny this speculation. Carter's response was a limited decontrol of oil prices and a windfall oil profits tax passed in 1980.

The Three Mile Island catastrophe in early spring 1979 compounded Carter's energy worries. Although, after the incident, he spoke enthusiastically about preserving the U.S. commitment to nuclear power, the nuclear industry did not recover. Alternative energy sources, such as gasohol, solar, wind, and geothermal, did not

prove as promising as originally hoped. The conservation that did occur in this period came from increased auto efficiency and a lower use of energy dictated by rapidly rising costs.

THE ECONOMY AND MALAISE

Carter's energy problems were matched by difficulties elsewhere. Fueled by expensive oil, large budget deficits, administered prices (prices not determined by the market), and high wage demands, inflation shot upward in 1978, to 7.7 percent per year. The stock market registered its lack of confidence in the president's economic program by declining sharply in the spring. The economy was hit by stagflation, the double bind of inflation and slow growth.

Carter's leadership faltered in the face of these circumstances. His difficulties with Congress, bickering among his staff, and allegations of improper campaign and banking practices by

Bert Lance, which led to his resignation in late 1977, compounded the president's problems. The implications of growing national frustration with government and with mounting taxes became apparent in California, where voters approved Proposition 13, cutting property taxes by more than 50 percent. Carter's reaction to this mood of disenchantment was to reorganize his cabinet and try to work more closely with Congress. Yet part of his response was quixotic as he mused in public about "a national malaise" that he should have recognized as partly attributable to his own lack of leadership.

FOREIGN AFFAIRS

Foreign relations questions provided the president with several accomplishments and also his final undoing. In part, his troubles stemmed from appointing two competing advisers: Cyrus Vance, a traditional, cautious diplomat, as secretary of state, and Zbigniew Brzezinski, a more aggressive anticommunist, as head of the National Security Council. At first, Carter tried to listen to both sides, to receive conflicting advice and then exercise his best judgment. It seemed as if this strategy would open a much-needed debate over foreign policy. But after some initial successes Carter relinquished some of his caution and pursued a more confrontational policy.

The weakness of the dollar, huge energy price increases, and controversial problems forced the president to make unpopular choices. His innovative foreign policy of emphasizing human rights, while commendable, was very difficult to pursue. It proved disruptive to American alliances to insist that friendly nations respect an internal climate of political freedom in order to receive American aid. But on the question of disarmament, Carter negotiated a new agreement with the Soviet Union—SALT II, limiting weapons systems—on June 18, 1979. The Senate, however, refused to ratify it. Passage of the Panama Canal treaties, although bitterly opposed in Congress, returned the Canal Zone and eventual control of the American-built canal to the government of Panama. The United States

also established formal ties with the People's Republic of China in 1979.

The president's most lasting achievement was a negotiated settlement between Egypt and Israel in March 1979. Intense negotiations between President Anwar Sadat of Egypt and Prime Minister Menachem Begin of Israel, urged on by Carter, took place in late 1978 at Camp David, Maryland, the presidential vacation retreat. For eleven days, Begin and Sadat and Carter debated the outstanding issues between Israel and Egypt. When the conference finally ended, Egypt and Israel, after years of hatred and intermittent war, were at peace. The Camp David agreement cemented the gradual peacemaking process that had begun in the aftermath of the Yom Kippur War of 1973. It increased hopes for a final settlement of the explosive antagonism in the Middle East between Israel and its neighbors.

Relations with the Soviet Union, despite SALT, cooled. Expansion of Soviet power and influence in Africa, especially in Angola and Ethiopia, and even more significantly, the Russian invasion and occupation of its neighbor Afghanistan, brought American-Soviet relations to a low point. Many Americans also believed that the Russians were near to achieving military superiority over the United States. Pressure built for increased defense expenditures, and Carter responded in 1979 with a larger defense budget and plans to install the complex MX missile system and to develop a neutron bomb. By this time, Carter had ceased to waver between his two major policy experts; Brzezinski had won the war of advisers.

Frustration over foreign policy intensified in November 1979, after angry Iranians stormed the U.S. embassy in Tehran and held the American staff hostage. (The hostages were not released until January 1981.) Early in 1979, the Ayatollah Khomeini had returned from exile to lead a Muslim fundamentalist revolution against the American-supported shah of Iran. The hostage crisis was precipitated when the deposed shah, then in exile, was granted entry into the United States to receive cancer treatment. Carter believed that an old friend of the nation must be welcomed to the United States despite the risks. The hostages' student captors, with the support of the Iranian revolutionary government, demanded the return of the shah to Iran. President Carter refused this demand and froze Iranian assets. He did, however, persuade Panama to allow the shah to settle there, although this act did nothing to soften the anger of the Iranians. Then Carter cut off imports of Iranian oil into the United States. But there was little else he could do to force the Iranians to release the hostages short of war. An ill-planned and ill-executed rescue attempt in April 1980 only increased the public's sense of the president's impotence. Cyrus Vance, who had opposed the raid as well as much of Carter's recent foreign policy, resigned. Nightly news broadcasts, which amounted to some of the most persistent coverage of any event in American history, cut away Carter's support and credibility.

THE ELECTION OF 1980

By the spring of 1980 the president's popularity had sunk. Senator Kennedy challenged Carter in presidential primaries. The president pursued a "Rose Garden strategy," refusing to campaign away from the White House (and hence its Rose Garden) so long as the hostages remained in Iran. While this worked to focus attention on Kennedy's weaknesses, it also increased public attention to the imprisoned Americans, who had become almost an obsession for the administration. After months of acrimonious and inconclusive campaigning, Carter won the nomination. But the damage of this skirmish was enormous. The president was unable to create a workable electoral coalition around the programs he supported, such as the Equal Rights Amendment, or around his accomplishments in foreign policy.

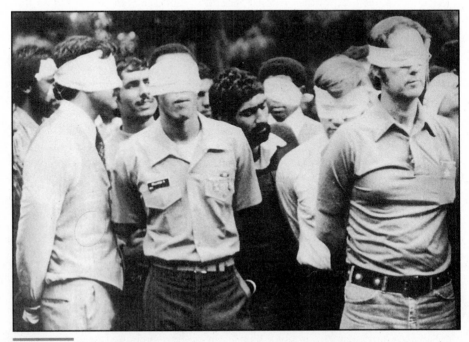

AMERICAN HOSTAGES IN IRAN. In early November 1979, Iranian militants seized the American embassy in Tehran and took its occupants hostage. Photographs such as this one infuriated the American public and increased their frustration with Jimmy Carter's foreign policy.

CHRONOLOGY

1960	Jimmy Carter elected governor of Georgia
1968	Richard Nixon elected president
1969	Chappaquiddick accident involving Senator Edward Kennedy;
(July 20)	U.S. astronaut Neil Armstrong becomes first human to walk on the moon;
(April)	Nixon authorizes invasion of Cambodia;
(May 4)	Four students killed by Ohio National Guard at Kent State University
1970–1972	Nixon adopts Vietnamization
1971	Gulf of Tonkin Resolution rescinded by Congress;
(Apr.)	U.S. table tennis team visits mainland China;
(June)	*The New York Times* begins publishing the Pentagon Papers
1972	Nixon drops Family Assistance Plan;
	Nixon administration begins revenue sharing;
	CREEP organized to ensure Nixon's reelection;
(Feb.)	Nixon visits mainland China;
(May)	Nixon visits Soviet Union;
	SALT I treaty signed;
(May–June)	Break-ins at Democratic headquarters in Watergate building;
	Nixon reelected over Democrat George McGovern
1973	Yom Kippur War of Israel vs. Egypt and Syria;
	Successive disclosures about Watergate cover-up;
	The Supreme Court legalizes abortion with *Roe* v. *Wade* decision;
(Jan.)	Treaty ends American military intervention in Vietnam;
(May)	Senate begins hearings on the Watergate scandal;
(June)	John Dean testifies before Senate committee;

1973 (Cont'd)	
(Oct. 10)	Spiro Agnew resigns as vice president
1973–1974	OPEC embargoes all oil shipments to the United States
1974 (Mar.)	Grand jury indicts seven people in Watergate cover-up;
(Apr.)	Nixon releases edited version of Watergate tapes;
(May)	House Judiciary Committee begins hearing evidence toward impeachment of the president;
(July 27)	House Judiciary Committee votes to recommend impeachment of Richard Nixon;
(Aug. 9)	Nixon resigns; Gerald Ford becomes president;
(Sept. 8)	Ford grants full pardon to Nixon
1975	
(Spring)	Last American forces evacuated from South Vietnam;
(May)	U.S. Marines rescue U.S. merchant ship *Mayaguez* seized by Cambodia
1976 (Nov.)	Democrat Jimmy Carter elected president over Ford
1977 (Oct.)	Department of Energy begins operations
1979	United States and China establish formal relations;
(Mar.)	Camp David Accords between Egypt and Israel signed;
(Mar. 28)	Problem develops in Unit 2 at Three Mile Island;
(June)	Carter administration negotiates SALT II;
(Nov.)	Iran seizes American hostages
1980 (Apr.)	Failed effort to rescue Iranian hostages;
(Nov.)	Ronald Reagan elected president over Jimmy Carter

PRESIDENT RONALD REAGAN. Ronald Reagan's successful campaigns for the presidency and his achievements in office partly depended on his ability to evoke patriotic feelings in the American public. Many of his speeches conspicuously appealed to such symbols as the American flag. George Bush recreated this strategy in the 1988 election.

Indeed, many of these accomplishments were turned against him by Ronald Reagan, who captured the Republican nomination. Reagan, a former movie star, a favorite of the Republican party right wing, and a longtime presidential aspirant, ran a remarkably well-focused and well-financed campaign. He capitalized on the antagonism to Carter and to government in general. Among a minority of voters, he inspired fervent support with his promises of a huge tax cut, a balanced budget, sharp increases in defense spending, and a much reduced federal commitment to social legislation. To a number of other voters, he simply represented the possibility of change and of leadership. Despite the third-party candidacy of Republican moderate John Anderson of Illinois, Reagan won a decisive victory in November 1980. More significant, the Republicans gained control of the Senate and, with the help of conservative southern Democrats, achieved an effective majority in the House.

By the late months of 1980, Ronald Reagan prepared to assume office, heading a conservative reaction to the political and social liberalism that had dominated much of American life since World War II. He promised to restore faith in institutions by reaffirming traditional American values and ideals and by releasing the energy of individualism and private enterprise.

SUGGESTIONS FOR FURTHER READING

THREE MILE ISLAND, ECONOMICS, AND ENERGY

Some of the specific economic and energy problems that contributed to the political instability of the United States during the 1970s are explained in Lester C. Thurow, *The Zero-Sum Society: Distribution and the Possibilities for Economic Change* (1981). Tad Szulc, *The Energy Crisis* (rev. ed., 1978), is a useful explanation of the oil shortages of the mid–1970s. The consumer movement, which cast doubt on the quality of American production, began with Ralph Nader's exposé of

the auto industry, *Unsafe at Any Speed* (1965). An excellent and thorough description of the bureaucratic tangles that aggravated the crisis at Three Mile Island is Daniel Ford, *Three Mile Island* (1982).

THE SEVENTIES

The 1970s was a complex period in which economic issues, problems of political leadership, and foreign relations assumed critical importance. An excellent account of the interrelationship of these problems is Richard Kirkendall, *A Global Power: America Since the Age of Roo-*

sevelt (2d ed., 1980). Gaddis Smith, *Morality, Reason, and Power: American Diplomacy in the Carter Years* (1986), is a very good description of this complex foreign policy. Richard J. Barnet, in his essay *The Lean Years: Politics in the Age of Scarcity* (1980), examines the impact of diminished productivity and scarcity of resources on the politics of the 1970s. Jonathan Schell's very readable *The Time of Illusion* (1976) stresses the impact of the Vietnam War on American society.

THREE PRESIDENTS

As in the previous decade, there was a rapid turnover of presidents and administrations during the 1970s. Nonetheless, the central figure of the decade was Richard M. Nixon. An excellent place to begin further reading about Nixon is his own *Memoirs of Richard Nixon* (1978). Patrick J. Buchanan, in *The New Majority: President Nixon at Mid-Passage* (1973), outlines the basis of a new conservative electoral majority inspired by Nixon. Stephen E. Ambrose, *Nixon* (1987–1991), is a fascinating, major biography of the former president.

Of several books on Watergate, the most intriguing remains the account by the two *Washington Post* reporters who uncovered much of the story: Carl Bernstein and Bob Woodward, *All the President's Men* (1974). Stanley Kutler's *The Wars of Watergate* (1992) illuminates the larger political issues of the event. The publication of H. R. Haldeman's *Diaries: Inside the Nixon White House* (1994) provides an unvarnished view of Nixon and his presidency. On the interim presidency of Gerald Ford, John Osborne, *White House Watch: The Ford Years* (1977), is one of the best works. Henry Kissinger, secretary of state under Nixon and Ford, offers interesting insights in *Years of Upheaval* (1982). Jimmy Carter, *Keeping Faith* (1982), is a readable, if self-justifying, appraisal of his one-term presidency. Carter's last hectic year of administration is well documented in the very readable *Crisis: The Last Year of the Carter Presidency* (1982) by administration insider Hamilton Jordan.

An Era of Ideologies

THE EPISODE: Early in 1986 a baby was born in New Jersey. Before she was a year old she had become famous, under a name given her by a judge. "Baby M" was the daughter of a married man and a woman who had been hired to conceive the man's child by artificial insemination and then to turn it over to him and his wife after delivery. But the man and the "surrogate mother" came to fight over who really was entitled to the baby, and their dispute achieved national attention that divided and disturbed the American people.

Public opinion hinged on the way people saw the nature of the contract that brought Baby M into being. The key questions were these: Had her natural mother sold her services? Or was she selling the baby itself? At the beginning of the trial, most people probably framed the issue in terms of the first question, and for that reason a majority were ready to accept the legality of the contract. But by the trial's end, many people had come to sense that the second answer might be the true one, and they found this prospect disturbing.

THE HISTORICAL SETTING: The fight over Baby M occurred on a stage of intense moral and political drama in the 1980s. A personal, intimate story became, for a time, the property of politicians and the mass media. The expansion of the mass media into a larger place in daily life was one of the significant marks of the postwar world. Television and tabloid journals dared, with little hesitation, intrude where historically they had once feared to tread.

More important, a broad shift in the style and content of American politics gained strength from such events. Some observers claimed that America was being swept by a wave of Puritanism. But the pivotal place of moral issues in politics had a more complex explanation. During the 1980s, centered on, but not confined to, the presidency of Ronald Reagan, a new political coalition emerged. Traditional Republican conservatives were joined by millions of Americans reacting to very troubling events. To them, moral issues appeared more important than the continuation of politics as usual. Many of these voters were troubled by threatened or real status changes among such groups as African Americans or women.

The American family was also changing. With increases in divorce and remarriage, illegitimate children, single-parent families, and nonmarital cohabitation arrangements, as well as legalized abortions, many Americans concluded that social morality was rapidly declining. Finally, there was a growing fear that American economic policy was inadequate.

The major conservative political movements of the day, led by Ronald Reagan, appealed to this constituency by promising a return to unregulated capitalism and a much more regulated moral and social order.

THE CASE OF BABY M—PRIVATE LIVES AND PUBLIC MORALS

Dear Friends:

We welcome you to The Infertility Center of New York. We know this is an emotional step for you—but one that is filled with new hope. The Center provides professional assistance for prospective parents who are seeking a realistic alternative to being childless . . . . No one who hasn't had the experience can presume to understand the agony of the long and frustrating search for fertility.

We believe it is every couple's right to experience the fulfillment, joy and challenge of parenthood. The Infertility Center offers childless couples a practical alternative—surrogate parenting. The advantages are clear: the husband is the biological father, the couple is involved in selecting the surrogate mother-to-be, and there is no prolonged waiting period.

We are anxious to help you. Please contact us.

These were the reassuring opening words of an advertising brochure issued by The Infertility Center of New York. But the actual process of surrogate parenting was rather something that many people would find a little disturbing, even to picture: sex without sexual intercourse, sex for money—but not for pleasure. Sex not in a bed or on some bearskin rug, but at a sperm bank, performed by a man and a woman who did not even meet for the act.

This is how it was done: In a small room, alone, the man masturbated, ejaculating into a receptacle provided for the purpose. His semen was stored. Later, when the woman ovulated, it was her turn to visit the sperm bank. She lay down on a table, her feet in a pair of stirrups. Using a medical instrument, a physician released a small portion of the stored sperm into the woman's vagina. The woman went home and waited to see if she had become pregnant. If not, she came back to the sperm bank each month until the procedure worked.

The crucial link between the advertisement and the act was a legal contract, arranged through a surrogacy center. The man and the woman would have signed a contract in which the woman agreed to bear the man's child but to give it up immediately after birth and to surrender all parental rights. In return for her services, she would receive a fee from the man—typically $10,000 plus expenses. The agency would also receive a fee for its services—typically an additional $10,000. All in all, counting expenses, the arrangement would cost the man about $25,000.

Surrogate motherhood was a sign of changing times. Unknown in America before the mid-1970s, by the mid-1980s at least 500 contracts had been fulfilled, with the number steadily increasing. There were several reasons. One couple in ten was not able to have children at all. More and more married couples were choosing to delay having children, only to discover that they had waited too long and could not produce offspring. Traditionally, such couples had only one recourse: adopting someone else's child. But adoption was itself becoming more difficult, and the waiting period was often as long as five years. At the very time that demand was rising, fewer and fewer children appeared to be available for adoption, because of other changes during the 1970s and 1980s. These included women's access to birth control and legal abortion, and a moral climate that was making it much easier for unmarried mothers to choose to keep their babies.

So in the 1980s, surrogacy agencies were set up, and by 1985 the largest of them, The Infertility Center of New York, was arranging about six conceptions each month. As the brochure noted, surrogacy was much faster than adoption, and also closer to "real" genetic parenthood. And it seemed to pose few ethical problems. If it was legitimate for a man to sell his sperm, then why should not a woman be allowed to "rent" her womb? Anyway, if the practice was banned, most people thought, it would simply move underground, or else to places like Puerto Rico, where women had once gone to have abortions before they became legal in 1973.

And so by 1984, surrogate childbearing had quietly taken its place among the publicly acknowledged sexual practices of Americans. In some ways, it was just a small part of an astonishing revolution in which millions of people suddenly came into the open with things that had once been hidden behind clothing, behind closed doors, underground, or "in the closet": nonmarital sex, abortion, homosexuality, pornography, birth control.

This was the setting for surrogacy. And this was the setting for the conception and birth of the little girl who became known as "Baby M." Eventually, this child became the center of a remarkable trial that riveted the attention of many millions of people. But when she was conceived, nothing seemed unusual. After all, as the man who arranged for the birth of Baby M put it, "You are not going to stop the drive of an infertile couple to have a genetically related child."

William Stern and his wife Elizabeth were a couple with this strong drive. Bill Stern was a child of the Holocaust, a Jew born in Berlin, the capital of Hitler's Third Reich, only a year after the end of World War II. His father had once been a banker but had been forced to go into hiding from the Nazis. Somehow, he and his wife managed to survive, the only members of either of their families to live through the war. Soon after Bill's birth in 1946, the family migrated to the United States. They settled in Pittsburgh, where his parents found menial jobs—his father as a short-order cook and his mother working in a window factory. Bill was their only child. Genetically speaking, he was the end of the family's line. He would later say that he felt "compelled" to see his "genes" continued.

Education came first, though—and a lot of it. Stern stayed in school until he was twenty-eight. Then, in 1974, he received his Ph.D. in biochemistry. He married the woman he had been dating for five years. She also received a Ph.D. the same year, in human genetics. But Betsy Stern soon decided that she wanted to become a physician, not a geneticist. The Sterns were a caring couple, supportive of each other's needs, and so, like many couples in their position, they decided to delay having a baby until Betsy had completed her medical training, seven years later. She would be thirty-five years old.

Then health intervened. At about the time Betsy Stern was finishing medical school, she began to experience some worrisome symptoms—blurred vision and a numbness in her toes and legs. She diagnosed these symptoms as the early signs of a dread disease, multiple sclerosis. And while the symptoms soon faded and did not re-cur, she was fearful, and her concerns intensified when she learned that getting preg-nant might bring her symptoms back. However much they had looked forward to hav-ing a baby, the Sterns now decided that pregnancy was simply not worth the risk. Adoption was one alternative, but the Sterns rejected it, since an adopted baby would not carry on Bill's genes, and it was likely to take four or five years, anyway. Surrogacy seemed the perfect solution. It would be fast, and it would continue *his* family line without risking *her* life.

In the fall of 1984 the Sterns sent for a brochure from The Infertility Center of New York. By December they had signed an agreement with the center giving them the right to look through the files of the women who had offered their services as surro-gates. They soon decided on a likely prospect, a twenty-eight-year-old married woman with two children of her own. The woman's name was Mary Beth Whitehead, and like the Sterns, she lived in New Jersey, within easy driving distance of their own house.

First, the Sterns wanted to see what the Whiteheads were like. In January 1985 the two couples arranged to meet at a restaurant halfway between their two houses. The meeting went well, and Mary Beth Whitehead seemed eager to come to terms on the spot. But the Sterns needed to be sure she would not change her mind and decide she wanted to keep the baby. Whitehead assured the Sterns on that point: "She had no interest in keeping a baby. . . . She said she would not come to our doorstep. All she wanted from us was a photograph each year and a little letter on what transpired that year." The Sterns were delighted. As William Stern later recalled: "We got back to the car, kissed each other, and said, 'This is perfect.' She was the perfect person. We didn't want to give her up. She was too good to be true."

That February, Mary Beth Whitehead signed a contract agreeing to be insemi-nated by William Stern, and to give up her rights to the baby she would deliver. It took Whitehead four months, four trips to the sperm bank, to get pregnant; she conceived in late June. The pregnancy went well. Tests revealed that the fetus seemed healthy, and that it would be a girl. The two couples sometimes got together socially, joined by the Whiteheads' own children, Ryan and Tuesday, and were soon on a first-name basis. Meanwhile, the Sterns prepared their house for the new arrival: The baby would have a second-floor bedroom, newly decorated in wallpaper with teddy bear patterns. The Sterns even had the baby's name picked out. They would call her Melissa. On March 27, 1986, in a hospital in Long Branch, New Jersey, she was born.

It is hard to know just when Mary Beth Whitehead began to have second thoughts. Almost a year before she met the Sterns, a psychological profile prepared by the Infertility Center reported that she was likely to have "strong feelings against giving up" a baby. (The Sterns were not shown this profile.) Richard Whitehead, Mary Beth's husband, said he knew that "toward the end of the pregnancy, she was getting very attached. I knew she

THE STERNS.   William and Elizabeth Stern were photographed walking arm in arm as they arrived at the Bergen County, NJ, courthouse for the first day of testimony, January 6, 1987. Despite the tension they must have been experiencing, both the Sterns managed to flash engaging smiles for this waiting newspaper photographer.

was getting torn." But Mary Beth Whitehead herself insisted that it was only after she delivered the baby that she changed her mind: "At the end, something took over. It overpowered me. I had no control." Moments after the birth, the obstetrician placed the baby on Whitehead's stomach. Within five minutes she was breast-feeding. The doctor would remember that "she was crying a lot," and that "she felt the baby looked exactly like her." He did not know that Mary Beth Whitehead had arranged to give up the baby. In fact, on the birth certificate she had given it a name of her own choosing, Sara Elizabeth. The birth certificate also said that the baby's father was her own husband, Richard Whitehead.

The Sterns quickly sensed that there was trouble, but the baby was two days old before Mary Beth Whitehead confirmed their fears: "She said she didn't know if 'I could go through with it,'" Elizabeth Stern later remembered; "I felt this pit in my stomach." A day later, the Whiteheads took the baby home with them. The situation was utterly confused.

The next day, March 30, was Easter Sunday. The Sterns drove to the Whitehead house in Brick Township to get their baby. They knew that Mary Beth had not actually reneged on the deal; she had only said she was having second thoughts. Whitehead was uncertain of her own intentions: "I didn't want to give her to them, but I felt an obligation to them also." She was sobbing when the Sterns arrived at her house.

William Stern recalled: "It was an unbelievable situation. I really didn't know what to do. I don't think anybody would have known what to do." But after about two hours, the Sterns prevailed and took the baby home with them. It was late afternoon. As soon as they had left, Richard Whitehead later said, his wife "broke down. She was crying hysterically. She couldn't believe what she had done. She said, 'Oh, my God, what have I done?'" Mary Beth Whitehead herself put it this way: "I just sobbed for hours and hours and hours. It was like somebody had cut off my arm."

A few hours later, Whitehead phoned the Sterns and told them "she didn't know if she could live anymore." That night, according to her husband, she kept waking up "crying and screaming." Things got so bad that Richard Whitehead talked about leaving the house. But eventually, in desperation, he said simply: "Let's go get the baby."

At 7:30 the next morning Mary Beth Whitehead again phoned the Sterns. She asked to come by. She and Rick arrived sometime before noon at the Sterns' house in Tenafly. Her behavior during this visit was something the Sterns would soon come to recognize. First, she told them how she had "woken up screaming in the middle of the

THE WHITEHEADS. Mary Beth and Richard Whitehead are pictured here with their daughter Tuesday (age 10) and son Ryan (age 11, wearing a New York Mets baseball cap and a shirt with an alligator logo). Mary Beth Whitehead was proud that she chose the clothing that her children would wear each day. To complete this portrait of her family, Whitehead holds the hospital photograph of newborn Baby M (her Sara).

night," and added that her husband was threatening to leave her. Then she repeated her suicide threat, how she had considered "taking a bottle of Valium." But over and over, what Mary Beth Whitehead kept telling the Sterns was that only one thing would help: Let her take the baby. Not forever, she added quickly—just for a few days. "I just want her for a week and I'll be out of your lives forever."

The Sterns did their best to calm her down, but they were also moved. Elizabeth Stern said later: "Bill was crying, I was crying, Mary Beth was crying." Finally, the Sterns gave in and let the Whiteheads leave with the baby. William Stern explained the decision this way: "We thought she was suicidal. She said she couldn't live without the baby." Elizabeth Stern put it like this: "She'd done this wonderful thing for us, and we couldn't have lived with ourselves if she went home and did something to herself."

As the Whiteheads left, Betsy gave Mary Beth some of the baby's things to take along, and Bill spoke to her with sympathy as she got to the front door: "He told me something nice I had done," Mary Beth Whitehead recalled. "He shared with me the death of his father and his mother. He told me I would get over the feeling of loss and that if I gave it time I'd be OK."

What Mary Beth Whitehead actually did with the baby was to go into hiding. She took a plane to Florida, staying with her parents. The days wore on. Every time Bill Stern phoned for news, it was Rick Whitehead who answered the phone, and it was plain that he was stalling. Finally, after almost two weeks, Mary Beth came back to New Jersey and gave the Sterns the news they had come to dread. She would not let them have the baby—not then, not ever.

Feeling manipulated and betrayed, William Stern finally took action. He consulted a lawyer, and within a few weeks he and his wife received a judge's order granting them temporary custody. On Monday, May 5—the baby was now five weeks old—the Sterns arrived at the Whitehead house. This time their compassion for Mary Beth had withered. They were accompanied by five policemen, who handed the Whiteheads an official document ordering that Melissa be handed over to the Sterns. But Mary Beth was prepared. She insisted that there was no baby named Melissa in the house. Standing in the living room, Richard Whitehead showed the police the birth certificate, on which the baby was listed not as "Melissa" at all but as "Sara"—the name Mary Beth had given her in the hospital. The policemen did not know what to do. In the confusion, Mary Beth went to a rear bedroom and passed the baby through the window to her husband, who was waiting outside. Eventually, the policemen went away.

The next day Mary Beth Whitehead once again fled to Florida with the baby, this time accompanied by her husband and the two other children. She was now a fugitive, in violation of a court order, and she was prepared to hide as long as necessary. Some of the time she stayed at her parents' house, but she knew that it was one of the first places the authorities would come looking. So she was mostly on the road with the baby, moving from one motel to another, never telling anybody who she was or why she was there, always trying to avoid the police or the detectives she knew would be coming for her and her child.

By July, after two months as a fugitive, Mary Beth Whitehead was getting desperate. She was out of money. Her husband had left his job when the family went to Florida. Even more serious, she had lost control of her remaining financial resources. In the effort to force her out of hiding, the Sterns had managed to get all her assets legally frozen. That meant she could not sell her house, or even withdraw money from her New Jersey bank account.

On Monday, July 15, Mary Beth Whitehead made a risky and dramatic gesture. She phoned Bill Stern at his office. Her purpose was to persuade him to give up his pursuit of her—or at the very least to call off the freeze on her assets. They talked for forty-five emotional minutes. What she did not know was that he was recording every word, and that the conversation would eventually be published in newspapers and magazines around the country.

Her tactics included a plea—and a threat. The plea was simple. The baby was now more than three and one-half months old, and she had come to know and to need the mother with whom she had spent almost all her life:

> Who do you think she's going to want more? Her own mother? And I've been breast-feeding her for four months. Don't you think she's bonded to me? . . . . Bill, she knows my smell, she knows who I am. You cannot deny that. . . . She's bonded to me, Bill. She won't even sleep by herself. You tell me, what are you going to do when you get this kid screaming and carrying on for her mother?

The threat was simple, too. It was of suicide—and murder. Yes, Whitehead told Stern, he had been able to take away her property: "You took my house. I mean, we don't even have a car anymore. I can't even afford the car payments. You took everything away from me." It was true, too, that Stern had the law on his side, and that she herself was a fugitive. "I'm telling you right now, Bill, you think you got all the cards. You think you could do this to people." But there was one card Stern did not hold: he did not have the baby. It was Whitehead who had her, and as long as she did, she could do whatever she wanted. First, she asked him ambiguously whether "me and Sara should just vanish off the face of the earth." When Stern said, "I want my daughter back," Whitehead responded with ominous words: "Well, Bill, how about if there's no daughter to get back?" And a little late she said simply: "I'd rather see me and her dead before you get her."

Later came this exchange:

> WHITEHEAD: I gave her life, I can take it away. If that's what you want, that's what I'll do.
> STERN: [frantic]: Mary Beth, no! Mary Beth, wait!
> WHITEHEAD: That's what I'm going to do, Bill.
> STERN: Please . . .
> WHITEHEAD: You've pushed me.

Stern did not panic at this threat, but he did concede one point. When he told Whitehead, "I don't want to see my daughter hurt," she rejoined: "My daughter, too. Why don't you quit doing that, Bill, OK?"

STERN: OK, OK. All right.

WHITEHEAD: It's *our* daughter. Why don't you say it, *our* daughter?

STERN: All right, our daughter. OK, Mary Beth, our daughter.

WHITEHEAD: That's right.

STERN: OK, Mary Beth, our daughter. . .

WHITEHEAD: Why do you keep on saying 'my, my, my, my'? She's mine, too.

STERN: OK, Mary Beth, OK. She's our daughter.

The next day, Whitehead called Stern again. (Once again, he recorded the call.) This time she made a different threat, even more bizarre than the first: She would tell the judge in New Jersey about an occasion—in the happier days when the two families got together socially—when Stern had tried to sexually molest the Whiteheads' eleven-year-old daughter. (Whitehead was simply making up this episode. Months later, she would admit as much. She made the threat because, as she put it flatly, "It was the last low blow I could think of.")

Actually, Mary Beth Whitehead was at the end of her rope. Less than two weeks after making the threatening pair of phone calls, suffering from exhaustion and a urinary tract infection, she entered a Florida hospital, leaving the baby behind at her parents' house. So it was there, on the last day of July, that the Sterns' private detectives found the baby and took her back to New Jersey. "Baby M," as she was now officially called, was four months old. Whitehead would not see her for another five weeks—and then for only a few hours each week, under strictly supervised conditions that resembled prison visits: The visits were held in a home for "wayward youths," and in the presence of an armed guard. The rest of the time, the baby stayed with the Sterns.

By the time the case of Baby M came to trial early the following January, her plight was becoming well-known to the public through coverage in the press and on television. As a "human interest" story, the case was irresistible. The only problem lay in how to interpret it. The dilemma was this: Who was trying to take whose baby?

Many people found it easy to identify with the Sterns, and to think that the couple had behaved reasonably and even generously. Mary Beth Whitehead, on the other hand, had lied about her intentions, kidnapped the baby, and even threatened to kill her. Above all, from a legal point of view, she had broken a *contract.* Whitehead had agreed in writing that she was not the real mother, but only a substitute (or "surrogate") for the real mother. (As one expert would put it at the trial, she was a "surrogate uterus.") The people who held this position argued, in effect, that Whitehead had rented the use of her womb to the Sterns, just as a man might sell his sperm to a woman who wished to conceive by means of artificial insemination. If Whitehead could now claim that the baby was really hers, then what was to prevent a sperm donor from demanding parental rights over an artificially conceived child?

For people who were sympathetic to the Sterns' position, the implications of this argument reached even further. What was to prevent a group of workers in an automobile factory, for example, from claiming ownership of a car they had been hired to produce on the assembly line—and then driving off with it? After all, in both the case of the auto worker and that of the surrogate mother, one party to the contract had provided the raw materials, while the other party had actually performed the "labor." Yet most Americans deeply respected such free labor contracts and believed them to be at the heart of the system of free enterprise. Few would have felt that the auto worker was entitled to drive off with the manufacturer's car. What, they could ask, entitled Mary Beth Whitehead to keep the Sterns' baby? For those people who believed that Whitehead had signed a normal contract to perform a "service," there could be only one answer: the baby was not hers.

But there *was* one thing that seemed to make a difference between Whitehead and the auto worker. Auto workers generally did not fall in love with the cars they made—but mothers did fall in love with their babies, contract or no contract.

One way of understanding the fascination generated by the Baby M case is to see how it brought into conflict two of the most deeply held values in American culture: the special sanctity of contracts and the special sanctity of family life. The two concepts had rarely come into such direct conflict before. Contracts had belonged to a public realm of business and paid work that involved mostly men. Family life had belonged to a private realm of unpaid work in which women played the central role. But all this was changing in the 1970s and 1980s. More and more women were entering the public world of paid work, and men were taking a more and more active part in the private world of the family. And now, it seemed, even motherhood might become a business. The story of Baby M seemed to bring to the surface the deep contradictions involved in that change. As one commentator put it, women who "fall in love with their babies" have "no business" becoming surrogates—"no business at all."

One way to avoid at least some of these contradictions was to try to maintain at all costs the old distinction between contract and family life, between business and motherhood. The attempt to maintain these traditional distinctions took several forms. Some people—especially conservative Roman Catholics and Orthodox Jews—argued that *any* "artificial" interference with "natural" sexual reproduction was wrong: surrogacy, artificial insemination, abortion, or even most forms of birth control.

Other people (and also many Catholics as well) took another tack. They argued that because surrogate mothers received money for giving up the babies they bore, surrogacy amounted to nothing less than baby selling. As one psychiatrist put it, "You can't sell babies." Responding to this argument, surrogacy advocates insisted that the surrogates were not selling babies, but only the *services* they provided by carrying the babies—a womb rental fee, in effect. The lawyer who had arranged the birth of Baby M made an additional claim: "I can say that most of the volunteers who want to be surrogates don't do it for the money aspect but because they wish to share the gift of a child with a childless couple." (Whitehead's own actions seemed to confirm the lawyer's point: She had refused to accept a penny of her $10,000 fee. But the lawyer was wrong. Almost all the women who had agreed to be surrogate mothers said they would not have done it without receiving their payment.)

The argument that surrogacy amounted to baby selling was a powerful one to many people. As word of the Baby M case spread through the United States, politicians in many state legislatures introduced bills that would effectively ban surrogacy by prohibiting would-be surrogates from receiving any significant payment for their services.

The sponsor of one such bill defended it by saying, "This [bill] recognizes that surrogate parenthood is not a business deal. I don't think we should be doing things that encourage surrogate motherhood as the newest cottage industry."

But underlying this argument lay an even deeper concern. It was the fear that if surrogacy was left unchecked, many couples would soon come to use it for the sake of *convenience* rather than *necessity*—not because they were incapable of having their own children, but because, for one reason or another, they did not wish to do so. For the people who had such fears, it was one thing for truly infertile couples to employ surrogate mothers, but it would be quite another for women who feared that pregnancy would interrupt their careers or spoil their "looks."

This anxiety was rarely expressed in public, but it had deep roots among tradition-minded Americans who were distressed at the new freedom many women suddenly seemed to be exercising—the freedom not to marry, or to combine marriage with an ongoing commitment to a career, or to retain their "single-girl" sexual identity after marriage (by not having children at all, or by looking and acting as if they had none). It was the power to control the reproductive use of their own bodies that permitted women to exercise this freedom. For many people who would have called themselves conservatives, the prospect of surrogacy for the sake of convenience—much like the prospect of abortion for convenience—seemed to symbolize and encourage everything that was going wrong with American society.

Nobody was willing to suggest in public that the Sterns themselves had acted out of convenience. The fact that William Stern's family had been killed off in the Nazi genocide made it easy to appreciate his special desire for a biologically related child. Similarly, his wife's fear that she was suffering from multiple sclerosis made it easy to understand her reluctance to become pregnant.

But there were some things that could cause anyone who was suspicious of surrogacy to be suspicious of the Sterns. It came out that the Sterns had decided not to have a child years earlier—well before Elizabeth Stern had her self-diagnosis confirmed by another physician. (In fact, the disease—a mild case in any event—was not diagnosed by anyone except Betsy Stern herself until after the beginning of the dispute over Baby M.) Also, there was no clear medical evidence that pregnancy would have aggravated the illness.

To those who feared that surrogacy might become a matter of mere convenience, these small points were unsettling. What if Betsy Stern's real concern had been only that a pregnancy might damage her career? How, a critic of surrogacy could ask, did *that* square with William Stern's professed wish to reproduce his genes?

To someone already inclined to be skeptical, there was an obvious and disturbing explanation. It would have run this way: The Sterns had postponed having a child in order to allow Betsy Stern to establish herself in a career. To begin with, there had been a long, five-year engagement while she earned her Ph.D. Then had come another seven-year delay while she completed medical training. The multiple sclerosis seemed to have had no serious effect on her life. It had not prevented her from completing her medical studies, or from winning and working at a coveted full-time position as professor of pediatrics at the Albert Einstein College of Medicine in New York. By the time Baby M was born, Betsy Stern was earning $48,000 a year. If she had gotten pregnant, she would have had to take at least a short maternity leave from her professorship. And even after she returned to work, the memory of her pregnancy would cause her colleagues to think of her as a mother instead of as a professional colleague. So, at least, a skeptical critic might reason.

From Betsy Stern's point of view—a point of view many other people shared—such suspicions were misguided and irrelevant. It was true that she cared about her career—she planned to continue working full-time after the child's birth. But what was wrong with that? Was it really fair for women to surrender their professional aspirations simply because they had children? Men were not obliged to do that. And what did it matter if William Stern had always wanted a child and Elizabeth Stern was unwilling to bear it? Was not surrogacy an ideal strategy—one that resolved their dilemma and satisfied the primary wishes of each of them?

As matters turned out, Betsy Stern did not continue working full-time. After Mary Beth Whitehead began to fight for custody of Baby M, Betsy Stern reduced her workload to twenty hours a week. As she explained this decision during the trial, "I didn't realize how much time is required to raise a child."

Mary Beth Whitehead was the kind of woman who thought that mothers should not hold full-time jobs. When she learned, seven months into her pregnancy, about Betsy Stern's plans, she got upset: "I didn't like the idea of Sara in the care of a baby-sitter. I thought Betsy wanted to be a *mother*."

This disagreement about whether mothers ought to "work" was only one of the many things that divided Mary Beth Whitehead and Elizabeth Stern, and the Whiteheads and the Sterns as couples. In 1972, when the Sterns were in their mid-twenties and still in graduate school, fifteen-year-old Mary Beth Messer decided to drop out of high school at the end of her sophomore year. Her father was a schoolteacher himself, and he was angry about her decision. But Mary Beth never enjoyed school, and she wanted to earn some money for herself.

She got a job working at a delicatessen owned by her brother, and, later on, another job at a local pizzeria. Early in 1973 she met a young man eight years her senior, and in December of that year, when she was sixteen, the two were married. Rick Whitehead was a policeman's son, who had been drafted soon after graduating from high school and sent to Vietnam, where he saw combat in the Mekong Delta. He was a pleasant and unaggressive young man, but without any of the skills that would allow him to get ahead in 1970s America. And after his return to the United States, he was injured in an accident that blinded him in one eye. Furthermore, like many other Vietnam veterans, Rick Whitehead developed a drinking problem.

Shortly after her marriage, Mary Beth got pregnant, and the year after her son was born she got pregnant again. Before her nineteenth birthday, she was the mother of two young children and had quit her job in order to be with them. (Betsy Stern was thirty at the same time, and still near the beginning of her medical studies.) Rick Whitehead was eking out enough money in his job driving a truck for a local construction company to keep the young family afloat.

The Whiteheads' precarious life took an ominous turn at the end of 1978. Rick's drinking problem had gotten worse. One day he fell asleep while driving and his car crashed into three telephone poles. He was convicted of drunk driving and lost his license, and, with it, his job. Mary Beth was now forced to be the sole support of the family. Once again she looked for a job, and found one as a barroom dancer and bartender. (The bar was owned by one of her sisters, just as the delicatessen in which she had worked years earlier was owned by her brother. She had six siblings in all, and most lived in the general area.) Speaking afterward about this job, Mary Beth White-head insisted: "I never did anything to embarrass my husband or my children."

Rick Whitehead joined Alcoholics Anonymous and abstained from alcohol for about a year. But when Mary Beth found him drinking again, she was furious. The couple had a shoving match, and she even had him arrested. Then Rick was convicted a second time of drunk driving. The marriage was on the rocks, and the couple separated for about half a year. But they had a reconciliation and moved back together again. Mary Beth Whitehead was twenty-two years old.

During these years the Whiteheads were living on the edge of poverty. They had never been able to buy a house of their own. Because the late 1970s and early 1980s was a period of high inflation, they were forced to move from one rented house to another, from one blue-collar town to another along the New Jersey shore, as rents went up faster than their ability to pay. By 1981 they had moved at least twelve times, sometimes living in the houses of other family members.

Rick Whitehead held seven different jobs in the course of the marriage, and he was sometimes unemployed. Mary Beth supplemented the family's meager income by working in a series of temporary, part-time jobs: cleaning houses, working at coat-check counters in restaurants, selling ski equipment during the Christmas season in a department store. Through it all, she was unwilling to take a full-time job, even though that would have brought in substantially more money. Doing so would have taken her away from her two children when they came home from school each day. "I wanted to be home with them," she insisted. "I felt that was more important than making money."

Mary Beth Whitehead's priorities, combined with the economic recession of the early 1980s and with her husband's ongoing difficulty with alcohol, proved too much for the family's precarious finances. The Whiteheads had gone deeply into debt. In 1983 they filed for bankruptcy.

⊶⟹◎⟸⊷

One day late that winter, as Mary Beth Whitehead was scanning the classified ads in a local newspaper, trying as always to find some new source of additional money, she read the following notice:

> SURROGATE MOTHER WANTED. Couple unable to have child willing to pay $10,000.00 fee and expenses to woman to carry husband's child. Conception by artificial insemination. All replies strictly confidential.

Ten thousand dollars! It seemed like some television game show. For years, Mary Beth Whitehead had been constantly buffeted by the conflict between money and motherhood, between her urgent need for cash and her cherished belief that mothers should not hold full-time jobs. Now, suddenly, she might be able to get the cash—lots of it—without "working" at all. She could get paid for doing the one thing she knew well: having babies. As she said of herself, "I don't have an education. I don't have a skill. The only skill that I know I do well is being a mother." If surrogacy seemed a good solution to the Sterns' problem, for Mary Beth Whitehead it was perfect.

Within a week she had answered the advertisement. (It had not actually been placed by a "couple unable to have a child," but by The Infertility Center of New York.) In April 1984, after submitting to a series of interviews and tests, Whitehead was accepted as a candidate for surrogacy. The very next month she was contacted by a married couple who wished to engage her services. Over the next eight months, she was inseminated regularly with the man's sperm, but each time, she failed to conceive, and the couple finally gave up on her in December 1984. Several weeks later, she was contacted by William and Elizabeth Stern. This time things went better.

Her luck had turned. If all went well with the pregnancy, the Whiteheads could count on receiving a check for $10,000 the following March. With this prospect, they might finally be able to settle down in a house of their own. Once again, Mary Beth's siblings came to her assistance. One of her sisters was planning to move out of her own house, and now she and her husband agreed to sell the house to the Whiteheads for $65,000, a price well below its market value. They even offered to lend the Whiteheads $33,000 to help them finance the purchase. As one of the terms of the arrangement, the Whiteheads would repay $8,000 of the loan at the end of March 1986. That was when the baby was due, along with the Sterns' check for $10,000.

Late in 1985 the Whiteheads moved into their new house. It was in a decent neighborhood, a ranch-style house with three bedrooms. All the Whiteheads had to do now was wait for the baby. Then the most elusive piece in the puzzle of their lives—money—would fall into place. They were on their way to security.

There is a simple term that describes many of the differences between the Whiteheads and the Sterns. The term is *class*. When Baby M was born, William Stern was working as a biochemist at a salary of $43,500 a year; Richard Whitehead was a garbage collector, earning $28,500—when he worked. Elizabeth Stern earned $48,000 as a professor of pediatrics; Mary Beth Whitehead was a full-time wife and mother who had no regular income at all. The Sterns were together making $91,500—more than three times the Whiteheads' income.

Closely related to this disparity were differences in education and family structure. Bill Stern was his parents' only child; Mary Beth Whitehead was the sixth of eight children. Both the Sterns continued their schooling into their thirties and received advanced degrees; both the Whiteheads ended theirs in their mid-teens, and only Rick graduated from high school. The Sterns delayed having children until they were forty; Mary Beth Whitehead was the mother of two when she was eighteen.

That is not to say that the Sterns were rich, or that the Whiteheads were impoverished members of some alienated American underclass. Ninety thousand dollars is not all that much money for a couple living in the suburbs of New York City, and the Whiteheads' house in Brick Township did not look all that different from the Sterns' house in Tenafly. For her part, Mary Beth drove a new Honda; for theirs, the Sterns were no doubt paying off medical school debts and a large mortgage. It was possible for the two couples to meet in the restaurant in New Brunswick, to socialize, and to be on a first-name basis—even (as they once did) to cry together. If Mary Beth Whitehead had been a true member of the American underclass, she would almost certainly have been screened out of the surrogate process—if she had ever thought to apply. It might be fair to say that the Sterns were living on the margins of wealth, where they could hope for an even better life, and that the Whiteheads were living on the margins of poverty, always fearful that they would fall through some invisible line that somehow

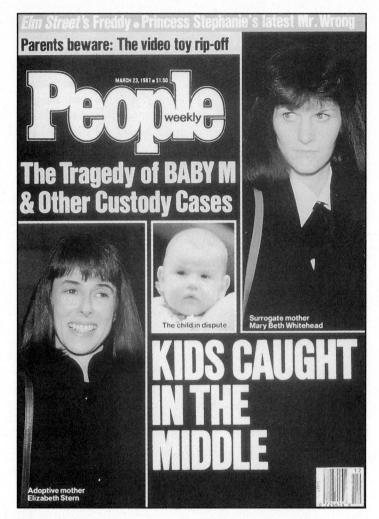

MEDIA COVERAGE. This is how the cover of *People,* a popular magazine, chose to represent the two women contending for possession of Baby M. Mary Beth Whitehead looks suspicious and vindictive, perhaps even somewhat out of control. (Because of the placement of the individual pictures on the magazine cover, she appears to be eyeing Elizabeth Stern and Baby M.) In contrast, Elizabeth Stern appears to be smiling at the baby with radiant good will. The photographer almost certainly took many pictures of these two women, and in some of these other pictures Whitehead almost certainly was smiling and Stern looking grim. The editors of *People* decided to use these particular pictures, placing them where they appear on the cover. The editors also chose the language of the captions: Whitehead is labeled the surrogate mother (she could as accurately have been dubbed the natural mother or the biological mother). Media coverage like this helped persuade many people to sympathize with the Sterns.

seemed reassuringly to connect them to the world of William and Elizabeth Stern. In truth, both couples (like most Americans) would no doubt have thought of themselves as members of the "middle class." But it was a class with two broad frontiers, one facing toward true wealth and the other toward true poverty. The Sterns lived on one of these frontiers, the Whiteheads on the other.

It was therefore no coincidence that it was William Stern who hired Mary Beth Whitehead as a surrogate, and not Richard Whitehead who hired Elizabeth Stern. Only the Sterns had the financial means with which to pay for a surrogate mother, and only the Whiteheads badly needed the money.

But the class difference between the Whiteheads and the Sterns involved something more than money, or jobs, or education. It also involved power. For example, even though Bill Stern and Mary Beth Whitehead each approached The Infertility Center of New York freely, and as legal equals, it was Stern who had the power to look through the files of surrogate volunteers containing Mary Beth Whitehead's name and telephone number, her personal history, and her photograph. It did not work the other way around. (The Infertility Center's promotional brochure promised that "surrogacy files tell you so much about the women who want to help you. You can see their pictures and read their own descriptions of their lives.") And it was Stern who held the power to select Whitehead from the files and contact her—just as he could have contacted any of the other would-be surrogates whose files he had read. The only thing any of these women could do was to sit and wait for a phone call from whichever stranger decided he liked what he had learned about her background, her attitude, or her looks.

Mary Beth Whitehead was used to being excluded from this kind of power, just as Bill Stern was used to having access to it. From her early years, she had come to feel alienated from the professional people who controlled the institutions she came in contact with. Her characteristic reaction was to fight for her independence by staying away from them. There was the school system, for example. Whitehead had dropped out of school at fifteen, and even when she was herself a parent, she chose to remove her own son from school rather than to follow his teacher's insistence that he be held back in the previous grade. After the birth of Baby M, when the Sterns won temporary custody of the infant, Whitehead responded by simply "kidnapping" her and running to Florida.

It is difficult to imagine William Stern doing what Mary Beth Whitehead did. That is partly because his personal style was so different from hers: calm and methodical rather than high-strung and risk-taking. But it is also because he expected to win the *cooperation* of the same authorities that she saw as her adversaries. That is a difference in class as well as personality. It was experience that helped make Stern personable and easygoing, and helped make Whitehead rebellious and abrasive. He had learned to achieve his goals through understatement; she had learned to assert hers through overstatement. *She* acted impulsively and by manipulating other people's emotions; *he* acted cautiously and by manipulating the structures of American power.

So it was the difference in their social class that had brought the Sterns and the Whiteheads together in the first place. The same class difference had shown itself clearly in the way the conflict between the two families took shape. Now it was another aspect of class—the difference in their expectations and styles of behavior—that would determine the course and outcome of the conflict over Baby M.

The class differences between the Sterns and the Whiteheads had already begun to play an important role in legal matters as early as April 1986, when Mary Beth Whitehead had refused to give up her "Sara." The Sterns' response had been to turn at once to the institutions of power. They made a series of telephone calls, trying to identify the *best* lawyer for their case. They used their professional connections in making these calls: one was to a high official of a national organization, Planned Parenthood Federation of America. The lawyer they had settled on was Gary Skoloff, known in New Jersey legal circles as "Mr. Family Law."

Skoloff accepted their case and went right to work. His first move was to take the case to a judge. What Skoloff needed from the judge was an order granting temporary custody of the baby to the Sterns. Up to now, Mary Beth Whitehead had just as much legal right to the baby as William Stern did (perhaps even a greater right, since Richard Whitehead, not Stern, was listed on the birth certificate as the baby's father). If Stern tried to take the baby from the Whiteheads against their will, *he* could be charged with a crime. But an official custody order would place the power of the state on the Sterns' side. Once presented with such an order, it was Mary Beth Whitehead who would become a criminal if she refused to turn the baby over to the Sterns. The word of a judge, and not the mere actions of the principals, would determine who was a criminal and who was a good citizen.

The judge readily granted Skoloff's request and signed the temporary custody order. Ordinarily, there would be a five-day waiting period before such an order went into effect. But Skoloff persuaded the judge to take the unusual step of waiving this waiting period and allowing the order to take effect immediately. It was not for nothing that Gary Skoloff was known as "Mr. Family Law."

When Whitehead violated that court order by taking her baby to Florida, she was acting the way people do for whom lawyers and courts always mean trouble and costs. She had not even consulted a lawyer. And when she telephoned Stern two months later and threatened to kill the baby, she still had no lawyer.

One legal scholar underlined the importance of this difference:

> The Sterns achieved a major legal advantage in the case by getting [temporary] custody in the beginning. They painted her [Whitehead] as unstable. If she had been a middle-class person, she could have gotten a lawyer to call up [before the Sterns arrived on May 5 with the police and a court order] and say, "Don't do anything until I show up."

Stern was fully aware of how he had gained his advantage. In the middle of the dramatic July 15 phone conversation, he even *asked* Whitehead why she had not relied on a lawyer's advice instead of impulsively taking the baby to Florida. In her tearful reply, she showed poignantly that she was more conscious than he of the real social and economic differences between them.

> STERN: You know, you just had to get a lawyer [all you needed to do was to get one], and he would have said to the judge, hey—
>
> WHITEHEAD: [crying hysterically]: With what, Bill? With what, Bill? . . . You hold all the cards, Bill.

In fact, Mary Beth Whitehead *had* tried to hire a lawyer while she was on the run in Florida, but none was willing to take her case without a cash advance. She had no cash to offer, because Stern had frozen all her assets. Under the circumstances, Stern's comment about her getting a lawyer was at best naive. And Whitehead's pained reply came from a true understanding of her plight. The "cards" of power that William Stern held were made of money, and the social habits it supported.

After she returned from Florida, Whitehead finally did manage to hire a lawyer. But he dropped the case after asking for a $5,000 lien on her house. Then she retained a second lawyer, but he, too, dropped the case. Finally, when Baby M had become a national celebrity, a third lawyer entered the case. His name was Harold Cassidy. When

Cassidy took the case in December 1986, the trial was scheduled to begin in a mere three weeks. He would have very little time to prepare.

Neither New Jersey nor any other state had laws pertaining to surrogate motherhood. On the one hand, that meant the original contract between the Whiteheads and the Sterns was not *illegal*. But it also meant that the contract was not necessarily *enforceable*. It was not even clear just what kind of law should apply to the case. Was it a matter of contract law? Or a matter of family law? And if it was family law, what kinds of rules should apply? Was it like a contested divorce in which the two "parents" argued over which one received custody of the children? Or was it closer to an adoption case in which the biological mother changed her mind and felt like keeping the child after all? Those were questions that would soon be decided by legislation in many states, but the judge in the Baby M case was on his own. (The case would be heard by the judge alone, without a jury.)

Judge Harvey Sorkow was in charge of the Bergen County branch of the State Superior Court's Family Division. It was Judge Sorkow who had originally granted the Sterns temporary custody back in May. The fact that the case was being tried in family court probably determined the answer to the first question: The case of Baby M would be treated primarily as a family dispute; the contract issue would be secondary.

The answer to the other question—was this like a contested divorce or an adoption that had gone awry?—would go a long way toward determining the outcome of the trial. In one way, it resembled a divorce case: Baby M was the biological child of both William Stern and Mary Beth Whitehead, and the two parents knew each other (though only in a limited way). But it resembled an adoption case even more. The biological mother, after all, had decided before the baby's birth not to keep her baby, and she had arranged the exchange through a special agency. Then, immediately after the baby's birth, she had changed her mind. But if it was adoption law that applied to this case, then permanent custody of Baby M would almost certainly be awarded to Whitehead. The reason was simple: In New Jersey (and almost every other state), the biological mother was entitled to a grace period after the baby's birth in which she could decide to keep her baby after all.

Judge Sorkow ruled that adoption law did *not* apply. The case would be tried like a divorce. Custody of Baby M would be awarded to whichever couple was likely to do the best job of raising her. The sole criterion was the baby's own "best interests." The judge added that "all other concerns . . . constitute commentary."[1]

Gary Skoloff—"Mr. Family Law"—specialized in winning just this sort of case, and he knew very well what his strategy had to be. Skoloff bluntly described the strategy to reporters: "It is my intention to show instability in the Whitehead family. That's what custody litigation is all about."

---

[1]*The "Best interests" doctrine was relatively new. Until the mid-1970s, mothers generally received custody under the doctrine of "tender years," which presumed that mothers were best suited to raise young children. But as custody rulings became more gender-neutral, "tender years" was gradually replaced by the doctrine of "best interests."*

For his part, Whitehead's lawyer, Harold Cassidy, chose not to pursue such a strategy. His decision may have been based on very practical considerations: Cassidy had only three weeks to prepare his case, not enough time for private detectives to investigate the past lives of the Sterns. But his decision may also have been based on Whitehead's own reluctance to win custody by attacking the Sterns. Whitehead insisted throughout the trial that she did not want her lawyer to use such tactics. As far as Whitehead was concerned, she was entitled to custody for just one, compelling reason: *She was the baby's mother.* When a reporter covering the trial asked her if she could give any reason why Betsy Stern would be an unfit mother, Whitehead replied, "No—other than she's not her mother."

But Whitehead and her lawyer were on shaky ground here. For one thing, by 1987, custody disputes were no longer routinely settled in favor of mothers. The feminist movement had persuaded many courts that such routine settlements only reinforced the traditional sex roles that kept women in the home, tied to their children. In any event, the baby herself had now been living with the Sterns for half a year—more than half of her ten months of life. When Whitehead had phoned Stern back in July, she had pleaded with him that the baby needed *her* ("She's bonded to me, Bill!"), but now the tables were turned. It was the Sterns who could, and did, argue that Baby M was now bonded to *them.* William Stern touchingly described the relationship:

> When I come home . . . she starts crawling across the floor as soon as I come in. If I don't pick her up right away, she starts crying . . . . You know, I never understood when friends talked on and on about their kids. It's hard to describe that feeling, but I know now. . . . She looks at every little thing I do. That's the really amazing thing. When I measure out her cereal in the morning—four tablespoons—she watches. When I open the refrigerator door, she tries to stick her head in. If there's a single thing in the middle of the room, she crawls to it. . . . When she grabs my shirt, I feel so special. When she smiles, I see her beaming. It makes me feel very happy. It makes me feel worthwhile. [Going on, in tears and scarcely audible] I always hope people will forget there's a Baby M, and she can be normal like other children.

Betsy Stern made the same point:

> She's the cutest thing around. She's always pulling at the clothes in Bloomingdale's [a fashionable New York department store], trying to get them off the rack. I feel I am Melissa's mother. I've been with her the past six months. I feed her. I bathe her. And I take care of her. Psychologically, I *am* the mother.

Attorney Cassidy was in a bind. He could not attack the Sterns. He could not argue that Baby M was "bonded" to Whitehead. So he was left with only one strategy, and it was defensive. He had to try to convince the judge that the Whitehead household was a good place for a child to grow up. He had Mary Beth describe the family's social activities: sledding, swimming, fishing, digging for shellfish at an ocean beach near their house. Mary Beth and Rick Whitehead always attended their kids' soccer games, and she was enthusiastic when describing how good her husband was with children: "This Halloween he had twenty-five kids trailing behind him. He does all the corny things kids like. I love him with all my heart." Other witnesses testified that the Whitehead children were unfailingly polite and well-groomed. (Mary Beth chose their clothing every day and even blow-dried their hair herself.) One of the Whiteheads' neighbors, a policeman, was apparently expressing the general opinion of people like those who lived in the neighborhood when he said of her, simply, "She's as good a mother as anyone can be."

But on point after point, the Sterns' lawyer was able to cast suspicion on the Whitehead family. For example, when one member of Cassidy's legal team tried to argue that the large Whitehead clan functioned as a "warm" and supportive "extended family," Skoloff was prepared with a rebuttal: His private investigators had discovered that one of Mary Beth's sisters had once been arrested on a bad check charge, and that her brother had pulled a shotgun on his wife during a marital fight. Skoloff also revealed that the sister who had so generously arranged for the Whiteheads to buy their house was now foreclosing the mortgage because the Whiteheads had not paid their debt on schedule.

Skoloff even tried to discredit Whitehead's treatment of her own older children. He brought up the episode in which she removed her son from school, and he disclosed that her daughter had once contracted frostbite when there was no heat in a small house the Whiteheads were renting. And over and over, he brought up the impulsive and even illegal way she had acted in the dispute over Baby M.

Skoloff had prepared his case thoroughly and presented it effectively. But it may have been Judge Harvey Sorkow himself who did the most damage to Whitehead's cause. Back in August, soon after Baby M had been "found" in Florida, the judge had appointed a lawyer, Lorraine Abraham, to represent the baby's own interests. To help her determine Baby M's best interests, Abraham consulted three mental-health experts whose assessments were expected to provide unbiased testimony. All three experts agreed that Mary Beth Whitehead displayed symptoms of emotional "instability" so serious that she should be denied all access to Baby M for at least five years.

SUPPORT FOR MARY BETH WHITEHEAD. By March 1987, as the Baby M trial approached its end, Whitehead had gained the sympathy of many feminist women (although other feminist women supported the Sterns). In this photograph Whitehead is shown with these supporters, holding placards in front of the courthouse. (Sara was the name Whitehead had given to Baby M.) As was so often the case, this photographer chose to capture an image of Whitehead looking grim and unmotherly.

One of the experts, Dr. David Brodzinsky, testified that Whitehead suffered from an "immature personality structure." The second expert, Dr. Judith Greif, spoke of "serious deficits" in Whitehead's parental ability. The third expert, Dr. Marshall Schechter (a distinguished professor emeritus of child psychiatry), presented the most damning diagnosis of all. Dr. Schechter had observed Whitehead during one of her two-hour visits with Baby M. As he looked on, the two played a game of "pattycake." When the baby clapped her hands together, Whitehead had responded by calling out "Hooray!" That was inappropriate, Dr. Schechter testified. The proper response would have been the word "pattycake." Schechter also criticized Whitehead for giving Baby M a stuffed panda, when a bowl, a spoon, or some other kitchen utensil would have been more suitable for a child her age.

A careful examination of Whitehead's history, Schechter argued, confirmed that these small mistakes were part of a larger pattern of inadequacy—a pattern of impulsive and self-destructive behavior, unstable personal relationships, suicidal and homicidal gestures, lack of empathy for people, a preoccupation with grooming, a constant craving for novelty, and chronic feelings of "victimization." The doctor concluded that Whitehead was suffering from a mental illness known to psychiatrists as "mixed personality disorder," and he stated that there was "clear and convincing proof that the mental disability which I have described . . . will continue indefinitely regardless of medical treatment."

In an effort to refute this bleak assessment, Harold Cassidy brought to the stand Dr. Donald Klein, the psychiatrist who had actually *written* the textbook chapter about "mixed personality disorders" on which Dr. Schechter had based his diagnosis. Dr. Klein pointed out that "Mrs. Whitehead is in a real fix right now," and he insisted that no diagnosis of personality disorder should ever be made on the basis of the way someone behaves in a time of intense conflict. If she was *feeling* victimized, it was because she was *being* victimized.

When the time came for Judge Sorkow to issue his decision, few people had much doubt what it would be. He had sustained almost every one of Skoloff's objections, and overruled almost every one of Cassidy's. He had refused to permit Cassidy to introduce important witnesses, and even chided him for being unprepared. On March 31, 1987, Sorkow issued the decision. It held few surprises.

Sorkow determined that living with the Sterns would be in the best interests of Baby M. He granted them permanent custody and denied Mary Beth Whitehead all further rights of visitation.

In explaining his decision, the judge berated Whitehead for the way she had coped with the difficult events of her life. He attributed her behavior to some great personal failing, a flaw in her character. Never did he recognize the possibility that her problems were not of her own making, or that she had dealt with them as well as most people in her position might have done. Over and over, Judge Sorkow used a curiously familiar set of adjectives to describe Mary Beth Whitehead: "*dominating*," "*impulsive*," "*manipulative*," "*exploitative*," and "*self-centered*." The adjectives were familiar because they were the clichés that men had used so often, for so many years, to describe women they did not like.

First, Sorkow concluded that Whitehead was too *dominating*: "Mrs. Whitehead dominates the family. Mr. Whitehead is clearly in a subordinate role . . . [and] permits his wife to make most of the important decisions in their family." She was "the controlling parent" of her older children, and she would be likely to dominate Baby M as well. (The judge seemed to be assuming that there was something repugnant about the role Mary Beth Whitehead played in her family, and he never asked what would have happened to it if she had *not* made the "important decisions.")

Second, Whitehead was *impulsive*:

> Mrs. Whitehead is . . . impulsive, especially in crisis circumstances. . . . She doesn't think of the consequences: at age fifteen and a half she drops out of school, she withdraws her son from second grade for what she perceives to be an affront to him without first inquiring of the teacher or principal, she elopes to Florida in direct violation of a court order, without considering the economic and emotional consequences.

(The judge did not ask whether dropping out of school, or having trouble with the authorities, might just be an understandable reaction for people who could expect only second-class jobs and had no hope of getting ahead.)

Third, "clear and convincing proof" had shown her to be *manipulative* and *exploitative*. The proof consisted of the murder threat she had made during her phone call to William Stern. If this threat was not a real one, it showed that Whitehead was "certainly manipulative." She was even willing to use her children for her own ends:

> Witness the bringing of her older daughter to court, where the child was terrorized by the crush of media, by her fawning use of the media to her own narcissistic ends.

(The judge raised no question about the way quite normal people behave when they are convinced that all the cards are stacked against them.)

Fourth, Whitehead was *self-centered*. She mistook her own needs for those of her children:

> She exhibits an emotional overinvestment. It was argued . . . that Mrs. Whitehead loved her children too much. This is not necessarily a strength. Too much love can smother a child's independence. Even an infant needs her own space.

Even her love for Baby M was a sign of Whitehead's selfishness:

> Mrs. Whitehead has been found too enmeshed with this infant child and unable to separate her own needs from those of the child. She tends to smother the child with her presence. The court doubts Mrs. Whitehead could or would subordinate herself for the child's benefit.

(The judge never mentioned the fact that he himself had forbidden Whitehead from seeing the child except for a few intense hours each week, nor did he acknowledge how common it was in many American working-class and ethnic families for mothers to "enmesh" themselves in the lives of their children.)

On only one issue did Judge Sorkow treat the difference between the Sterns and the Whiteheads as a difference between the social groups they belonged to. That issue was education, and the judge attributed this contrast to what he called the Whiteheads' *milieu*—a word taken from the French that means, roughly, "surroundings," or social "place":

The Sterns have demonstrated the strong role that education has played in their lives. They both hold doctoral degrees in the sciences. Mrs. Stern is a medical doctor. Mrs. Whitehead dropped out of the tenth grade in high school. Mr. Whitehead graduated high school doing enough, as he said, "to get by." . . . Education plays a subordinate role in the Whiteheads' milieu.

The judge did not even believe Whitehead when she assured him of her willingness to provide Baby M with the good education she herself had failed to get:

Mrs. Whitehead has interposed herself in her son's education, denying the finding of a professional child study team and rejecting their recommendations. . . . Dr. Metnick, the school psychologist, testified that in seven years only ten parents out of hundreds of students tested have rejected the child study team recommendations.

Finally, Sorkow pointed to the Whiteheads' difficult marriage, "plagued with separations, domestic violence, and severe financial difficulties requiring numerous house moves." (Once more, the judge seemed to assume that the Whiteheads' difficulties were caused by the personal failings of Mary Beth and Richard Whitehead, and not by a "milieu" that would have made millions of women "unfit" to be mothers.) He contrasted the Whitehead marriage with the Sterns' "strong and mutually supportive" relationship, "their private, quiet and unremarkable life, which augurs well for a stable household environment."

They have shown an ability to make rational judgments in the face of the most trying emotional circumstances. They have obeyed the law. . . . They have shown no difficulty coping with crisis.

The Sterns themselves had presented their case sympathetically in the courtroom and in interviews with the media. Bill Stern always said the judicious and generous thing. "I feel very bad for *all* of us that what started out as a beautiful experience should end like this." Stern even promised that if the judge awarded custody of Baby M to Whitehead, he would accept the decision so that the baby herself would not become a "ping-pong ball":

I'd prefer she just not know about me. I'd be an outside force in her life. For her to see me once a month and be told I'm her biological father—I don't think that's doing her any good. I just don't want to be in a position to start wondering, "Who's daddy? Who's mommy?" If I found she wanted to see me, that would be OK. But I don't want to come knocking at her door. I just don't want to intrude on her life.

And when Betsy Stern was asked whether she had been concerned about the ethics of "taking" the baby from Whitehead, she responded by using Judge Sorkow's favorite phrase: "Yes. In a sense I knew it would be very painful, but I was thinking in Melissa's best interests."

Responding to the same question, Mary Beth Whitehead spoke defiantly: "I don't care what they do. I will not surrender my child." She even denied that Stern should be regarded as the baby's father, dismissing him contemptuously as "Mr. Sperm."

It was clear that Judge Sorkow disliked Whitehead and felt comfortable with the Sterns. But his decision was based on something more than a personal reaction. At the heart of his legal logic lay his fundamental belief that everyone had the right to have children, and that this right was so basic that it must be protected from government interference, as an aspect of a general constitutional right to privacy in sexual matters. Sorkow quoted from a 1972 decision of the U.S. Supreme Court that had guaranteed Americans the right to use birth control:

> "If the right of privacy means anything, it is the right of the individual, married or single, to be free of unwarranted governmental intrusion into matters so fundamental affecting a person as the decision whether to bear or beget a child."

The judge went on:

> It must be reasoned that if one has a right to procreate coitally [through sexual intercourse], then one has the right to procreate noncoitally. If it is the reproduction that is protected, then the means of reproduction are also to be protected. The value and interests underlying the creation of family are the same by whatever means obtained.

The traditional recourse of childless couples who wanted to create a family was that of adoption. But Judge Sorkow pointed to the acute "shortage" of what he called "adoptable children." It was this dearth of adoptable children that had led to the need for surrogate mothers. To restrict or outlaw surrogacy "would constitute an unconstitutional interference with procreative liberty, since it would prevent childless couples from obtaining the means with which to have families."

Judge Sorkow also addressed another antisurrogacy argument: that surrogacy entailed the exploitation of poor people by more prosperous ones. He acknowledged that some people were arguing that "an elite upper economic group of people will use the lower economic group of woman [sic] 'to make their babies.'" But he found that argument to be "insensitive and offensive to the intense drive to procreate naturally and when that is impossible, to use what lawful means as [sic] possible to gain a child." He pointedly added: "This intense desire to propagate the species is fundamental. It is within the soul of all men and women regardless of economic status."

But Sorkow also used a second argument to deny that surrogacy constituted class exploitation. It was that William Stern and Mary Beth Whitehead had dealt with each other as equals in a free marketplace:

> Here neither party has a superior bargaining position. Each had what the other wanted. A price for the service each was to perform was struck and a bargain reached. One did not force the other. Neither had expertise that left the other at a disadvantage. Neither had disproportionate bargaining power. . . . The bargain here was for totally personal service. It was a very scarce service that Mrs. Whitehead was providing. Indeed, it might even be said she had the dominant bargaining position, for without her Mr. Stern had no other immediate source available. Each party sought the other to fulfill their needs.

Judge Sorkow did not even see surrogacy as a matter of "baby selling" but as the "gift of life" to an infertile couple:

> The Whiteheads have two children. They did not want any more. Theirs was the perfect family, Mrs. Whitehead testified. . . . Mr. Stern wanted progeny, a child. Mrs. Whitehead

AFTER THE VERDICT. Here Mary Beth and Richard Whitehead were photographed with their daughter Tuesday as they left the Bergen County courthouse soon after the verdict was announced by Judge Harvey Sorkow. In explaining his verdict, Judge Sorkow criticized Mary Beth Whitehead for exposing the girl to the fawning use of the media.

wanted to give the child she would bear to a childless couple. His sperm fertilized her egg. A child was born.

It was that simple.

⊷⇒⫯⇐⊷

Just before Sorkow issued his decision, a public opinion poll indicated that Americans would agree with him by a large margin—three to one. But their opinions varied with their income and education. People without a high school diploma were more likely to favor giving custody to Mary Beth Whitehead than people who had attended college. Those with annual incomes under $15,000 favored Whitehead in far greater proportion than did those with incomes over $50,000.

The case also caused many middle-class Americans who were originally prepared to side with the Sterns to reconsider their views. For some, it was a question of the way the Sterns had handled the problem. If the Sterns were really concerned with the "best interests" of Baby M, why had they put her in a situation in which, *whatever* the outcome, she would inevitably go through childhood under a public spotlight? After all, the Sterns *could* have backed off when Whitehead first let them know she had changed her mind. What William Stern wanted was a genetically related child—but only Mary Beth Whitehead had fallen in love with an actual newborn baby. The Sterns could have returned to the Infertility Center, looked through its files again, and hired another surrogate. Giving in to Whitehead would not have been easy—but perhaps it would have served the baby's best interests.

For other people, there was an even more troubling aspect to Judge Sorkow's decision. At several points he had referred to an "adoptable child shortage," to a "dearth of adoptable children." Everybody knew what he was talking about. But he was incorrect. There were, around the world and in the United States itself, thousands of babies who were available for adoption, babies who otherwise faced lives of extreme poverty, hunger, and disease. Most of these babies, however, were not white babies: they were black or yellow, brown or red. But few white American couples wanted to adopt these babies. Judge Sorkow knew that. When he spoke of a "dearth of adoptable children," what he surely meant was a dearth of adoptable *white* children.[2] If the judge had given the question a moment's thought, he would as surely have realized that his statement— an assumption, really—was, in the most literal sense of the word, racist. And he would have realized that if surrogacy could be justified only on the grounds that adoption was not a practical option for infertile couples, then surrogacy could be justified only with a racist assumption.

In July 1987 two groups filed separate but similar briefs opposing surrogate motherhood with the New Jersey Supreme Court, to which the Baby M case was being appealed. There was nothing surprising about the group filing the first brief: it consisted of the Roman Catholic bishops of New Jersey. In their brief, the bishops argued that surrogacy "promotes the exploitation of women and infertile couples and the dehumanization of babies. . . . In short, it traffics for profit in human lives. . . . To put it bluntly but truthfully, were it not for the fee, Baby M could not have existed at all." Surrogacy puts pressure on poor women to support themselves by selling the use of their bodies. It constitutes "a new form of prostitution."

The second brief was filed by a very different group, a group containing many of the best-known feminist women in the United States. The feminists and the bishops were bitter opponents on many controversial questions (the right to abortion, for instance, against which the Catholic Church was waging an aggressive political campaign, but which was a centerpiece of most feminists' ideology). Yet, on *this* issue of reproductive technology, the feminists' position was remarkably similar to that of the bishops. The feminists, too, argued that surrogacy involves "trafficking in human lives, particularly the buying and selling of infants and children." And they argued as well that it leads to the exploitation of poor women. What might have looked like freedom

---

[2] *For their part, many minority people in the United States were reluctant to see children of color raised in white households.*

to Mary Beth Whitehead actually amounted to the very degradation identified by the bishops: "She has been dehumanized and has been reduced to a mere 'commodity' in the reproductive marketplace."

There were differences between the two briefs. For example, the bishops emphasized that it was the *babies* who were dehumanized by surrogacy, whereas for the feminists it was the surrogate mothers themselves. And the bishops had reached their position easily; they had been insisting on it all along. For the feminists, on the other hand, the brief was the result of a real struggle. As one admitted, "It was difficult, because for years we have been saying it's wrong to tell women what they can or can't do with their bodies." Before the Baby M case, most of the opposition to surrogacy had come from conservative people who feared women's new sexual and economic freedom. But now many feminists were beginning to look with suspicion on the new reproductive technologies, and even to defend some of the values associated with traditional family life— for example, the right of a biological mother to her child. The convergence of feminists and conservatives over the Baby M case may have represented an important new development of the mid-1980s.[3]

By the beginning of 1988 the antisurrogacy movement had taken the political offensive. Bills intended to ban or restrict surrogacy had been introduced in the legislatures of nearly half the states as well as in Congress. By the middle of the year, four states had passed laws that prohibited surrogate-mother contracts from being legally enforced, and two others (Michigan and Florida) had actually made it a felony, punishable by years in prison, to arrange a surrogate-mother contract that involved money.

Back in New Jersey, the state supreme court acted in February 1988 on Mary Beth Whitehead's appeal of the Baby M decision. The court decided unanimously that surrogacy contracts were illegal in the state, and that Whitehead's contract with the Sterns was null and void. The court restored Whitehead's legal status as Baby M's mother and granted her extensive rights to visit with her child. But at the same time the court also allowed the Sterns to retain permanent custody of Baby M. The ambiguity of the court's decision indicates how difficult it was—and continues to be—to bridge the gap between the public world of contract, work, and business and the private world of sex, motherhood, and family.

But by this time, Mary Beth Whitehead had made some important changes in her own life, changes that made her new "victory" (like her original defeat) less urgent. Late in 1987 Whitehead publicly announced that she was divorcing her husband and that she was planning to get married again. Her prospective husband, Dean R. Gould, was a twenty-six-year-old accountant who worked in New York City, a professional man who belonged more to the world of William Stern than to that of Richard Whitehead, and who promised to offer his new wife the solid middle-class comfort and security that Rick Whitehead had never provided. Even before the divorce was made final, she had become pregnant again, by Dean Gould. A year later the Goulds had a second child together.

Mary Beth Whitehead-Gould (as she would henceforth be known) had changed in another way as well. The battle over Baby M had made her a well-known national

---

[3]*Some Catholics and feminists had come together before in the early 1980s, in joint opposition to the sale of pornography.*

figure. And it had given her a new sense of purpose. She was becoming a prominent representative of the emerging antisurrogacy movement, a public woman who was speaking out about her views at press conferences and rallies. She even testified before Congress.

By 1989 she had written a book about the Baby M case and the surrogacy question, and to publicize it she traveled across the country in high style. Here was a mission that promised to be as important, perhaps as time-consuming, as motherhood itself. At the age of thirty-one, Mary Beth Whitehead-Gould finally held within her grasp something that many other American women would have envied—the prospect of both private security and public acclaim. If she was lucky, the future might be hers.

The Eighties and Beyond

Like a handful of sensational public trials in this century and the last, the Baby M case bore the burden of contemporary political problems. It reflected a growing confusion in America between public and private spheres of life. Although the U.S. Supreme Court had greatly expanded the legal content of the word *privacy* during the 1970s and 1980s, in a contradictory sense, many of the most intimate questions facing any individual or family became grist for politics or the mass media.

The Baby M case also suggested some momentous consequences of new medical technologies that redefined sexual life, birth, and even death. The trial pointed up some of the implications of privilege and social class in America. And it expanded the national debate over the roles of women, men, and marriage. It evoked questions about the uses and abuses of mass media. But more fundamentally, the case also pitted two notions against each other, notions that as much as anything else during the 1980s defined much of American thinking about society and politics. The first was faith in the primacy of economic values and the private marketplace. Just as strong was the faith that society's highest values were family, religion, and individualism, in other words, non-materialist values. In the Baby M case, the judge and the public were forced to choose between a contract transacted between two adults and an age-old idea about motherhood. The judge was obliged to honor one of these ideals in a situation where, perhaps, neither was really appropriate.

Like previous court cases—the Dred Scott decision, the Lizzie Borden case, the Scopes trial, the trial of the Rosenbergs, and Watergate—that pitted conflicting interpretations of fundamental American institutions against each other, the Baby M case brought problems to the surface that seemed too complex or too explosive to be settled by political debate. Thus a small custody case, of limited impact, provides a glimpse into the polarized heart of contemporary history.

NEW LIFESTYLES

As the Baby M case suggests, much of the visible social change during the late 1970s and 1980s affected the American family. Whatever the persistent strength of the old ideal of a working father, a housewife mother, and two or three children, reality became infinitely more complex. Perhaps the most striking trend was the rapid evolution of living arrangements. As an illustration, divorce and remarriage figures increased slightly during this time, but the greatest growth was in the number of unmarried couples who lived together, rising from 523,000 in 1970 to 1,983,000 in 1985. Added to increased numbers of other nonfamily types of households, nonmarried groups made up 30 percent of all living arrangements in 1985. Put another way, this meant that the proportion of Americans over eighteen who were married in 1985 had declined by 10 percent from 1970.

By themselves, these statistics explain little, but journalists, sociologists, and even politicians worried about an apparently growing reluctance to marry. Indeed, marriage during the 1980s, although still predominant, was only one of several possible and acceptable social relationships in which men and women, adults and children, and single-sex couples or groups could live. As always, confirmation of the acceptability of these arrangements could be found in the mass media, which quickly recognized, mirrored, and focused on these groups as potential new markets. In part, this explains the rash of TV situation comedies in which an unusual living arrangement was the situation: "Kate and Allie" (two divorced women and their children), "The Golden Girls" (four older women), and "The Cosby Show" (remarkable because it featured a mother, father, and children).

Attention to evolving social relationships could scarcely overlook the yuppies (young urban professionals). This group—including men and women, whites, blacks, and Hispanics—was perhaps more an advertiser's dream than a reality, but it expressed an aspiration that immediately became a popular stereotype. Fresh from law or business school, these middle-class strivers purportedly stepped into $35,000-a-year professions, bought prestigious imported cars, and viewed human relationships as secondary to career. While the press and moralists treated such stereotypes with amusement or scorn, others celebrated their new materialism as a welcome relief from the angry and politically tumultuous 1960s and 1970s, a refreshing change from the counterculture that took everything seriously, from popular music to diet. Of course, yuppies and even most Americans were profoundly changed by that earlier age. For example, job opportunities for middle-class women certainly owed much to

the women's movement of the 1970s. Experimental lifestyles, so much a part of the expectations of the 1980s, had evolved during the embattled previous decades. Freer sexual practices owed much to the postwar period, and especially to the invention and acceptance of new contraceptive devices.

Other groups with more controversial lifestyles believed themselves now free of the heavy hand of social disapproval and repression. They too declared their presence and independence. This was especially true for homosexual men and women who made a visible and sometimes public move "out of the closet." Men and women from all walks of life openly declared their sexual preferences; many organized politically to encourage local officials to rescind sodomy laws and outlaw discrimination in hiring and housing. Gay groups achieved some initial successes, but encountered strong opposition, led particularly by the hierarchy of the Catholic Church and evangelical Protestant groups.

THE NEW POOR

Freer lifestyles and more fluid family arrangements inevitably had a negative side. The rise in divorce rates, decline in marriage rates, and increase of children born out of wedlock became more and more the burden of single women. The income of these female householders in 1986 was less than half that for married couples. With African-American and Hispanic families earning only 60 and 67 percent of white household income, respectively, poverty was concentrated especially among black and Hispanic women and children. Thus 45 percent of black children in America were born into poverty and one in five of all children lived in poverty in 1986. Undoubtedly, the decline of structure and stability in family life was a major cause for an accompanying sharp rise in reported cases of child abuse and neglect. Between 1978 and 1985, these dreary figures more than doubled, although some of the increase was undoubtedly due to better statistics.

The concentration of poverty among women and children represented, in some sense, the negative side of a striking success story: declining poverty among older Americans. In 1970 about one-quarter of Americans over the age of 65 lived in poverty. By 1987 this figure shrank by more than half, to 12.2 percent. This remarkable change vividly highlighted a shift in national priorities and confirmed a transfer of national resources and social welfare funds from one group to another, from one generation to another, from one increasingly disorganized and dispirited underclass to an increasingly visible and politically astute interest group of retired Americans.

As the number and percentage of poorer Americans slowly increased during the 1970s and then accelerated in the 1980s, the political clout of this population shrank. Participation in presidential elections by people living in urban poverty centers declined by one-half over the period. By 1984 three-quarters of the immense group of Americans who did not vote were from the blue collar and service workforce. This spiral of poverty and marginalization increasingly meant that the poor were viewed as objects of charity, not a potentially strong political bloc of organized voters. Victim to its own powerlessness, this growing population lost dignity as well as a sense of participation in society.

SURGING SUBCULTURES

Shifting opportunities and rewards did not always follow the fault lines of race and ethnicity. Despite the bleak and despairing black slums in American cities, a new African-American middle class became particularly evident in and around such cities as Atlanta, Georgia, Washington, Chicago, and Los Angeles. Resulting in part from freer access to government employment and better-paying service jobs, this important group acquired both economic and political visibility.

Moreover, the explosive growth and maturity of newer immigrant groups such as Hispanics and Asians profoundly affected the shape of the in-

come structure. Like the 1890s, the last two decades of American history have seen a fundamental shift in the sources of immigration. Although the flow to the United States from Asia and Latin America is not new, vastly increasing numbers precipitated visible changes in this period. Like immigrants before them, these newcomers entered for a variety of reasons: pushed by political repression and poverty and pulled by opportunity. As before, they also brought strikingly different skills, education, and status, which helped or hindered their adjustment to American life.

ASIAN AMERICANS

In particular, education was a vital badge of success. By the mid-1980s, whereas 16 percent of all native-born Americans had graduated from college, Asian groups—including Filipinos, Koreans, Chinese, Japanese, Indians, and Taiwanese—had substantially higher education levels. Only the Vietnamese had lower than average education levels. Their education and professional experience, which they either brought with them or acquired here, translated directly into earnings as Asian immigrants, except the Vietnamese, earned wages higher than or equal to those of the native born.

Given the significance of education to these groups, it is not surprising to find a nationwide movement of second- and third-generation Asian Americans into higher education. The impact has been striking. At the University of California at Berkeley, about one-third of the enrollment in 1989 was Asian American (based on a state population of 7 percent), while the native-born white contingency fell to less than half. As a consequence of such scholastic skills and ambitions, charges were leveled at several elite institutions of maintaining discriminatory quotas against Asian Americans.

HISPANICS

The same factors of class and education also influenced the lives of millions of Latin Americans who came to the United States in this period. Of foreign-born Hispanic Americans, only Argentinians had a significantly higher education level and average income than the United States norm. Cuban Americans tended to approximate both American education and income levels, but many other nationalities, especially the largest group, Mexican Americans, had low education and income.

Concentrated especially in Florida, Arizona, New Mexico, Texas, and California, but with large offshoot populations in cities such as Chicago and New York, Hispanics played an increasingly significant role, transforming some cities into bicultural and bilingual centers. With a huge population growth in neighboring Mexico, and revolutionary wars in Central America from which thousands sought refuge in the United States, legal and illegal immigration expanded rapidly. By 1985 over 17 million people of Hispanic origin lived in the United States, making this the fastest-growing population group in the nation. Like previous immigrant groups, Hispanic Americans tended to congregate in lower-paying service, manufacturing, and agriculture jobs.

As so often had happened with other immigrant groups, Hispanics were welcomed by employers who wanted cheap labor but resented by other elements of the population. In 1986 this sentiment spilled out into movements in sixteen states to declare English the official language. Some states, such as California, passed such ordinances, ending the use of Spanish in courts, on legal documents, and on ballots. To curb illegal immigration, particularly from Mexico, Congress passed the Immigration Reform and Control Act of 1986. This act granted amnesty to immigrants who had been living illegally in the United States since 1982. But to close off further illegal immigration, the act criminalized hiring workers who lacked official documents and imposed fines of $250 to $10,000 on employers for doing so.

This bitterly contested legislation made audible a problem of growing intensity: opposition to increasing Hispanic immigration into the United States, particularly across the lengthy and porous U.S.-Mexico border. The fight over language in various state legislatures, in turn, gave testimony to increasing debate over the effectiveness of bilingual education. Encouraged by federal government grants since 1968, bilingual education proposed to ease the transition of Spanish-speaking students into English by beginning instruction in their native language. But the programs were costly and, to critics, ineffective.

Both of these outbreaks of political controversy revealed, in turn, a major shift in the nature and impact of Hispanic immigration. Before the 1970s the relatively open borders of the American Southwest brought a steady source of labor for farms and ranches. Some of these temporary immigrants remained in the United States, but their numbers were relatively slight. With the weakening of the Mexican economy and the chronic violence, poverty, and civil war in Central America during the 1970s and 1980s, refugees who had no intention of returning home began to pour across the Mexican border, many from El Salvador, Guatemala, and Nicaragua. As these groups spread out across the United States, they congregated, as a century of immigrants had before them, in cities where they found relatives, compatriots, or the hope of employment.

Like other immigrants before them, Hispanic Americans lived in two cultures, their adopted North American world and the strong remnant of the cultural inheritance they brought with them. Divided by national cultures and strong rivalries, Hispanic Americans were torn between old loyalties and new identities. Like other immigrants, their transition to becoming an American meant giving up the extreme parochialism of loyalty to town and province in the old country, and even their identity as Mexicans, Salvadorans, or Cubans. Ironically, they became Hispanic Americans in part because other Americans, in dealing with them, disregarded complex questions about national origins. A Hispanic was someone who came from a Spanish-speaking culture.

As the numbers of Hispanics increased, this culture became more visible. With millions of potential buyers, the Hispanic community attracted

UNA CAFETERIA EN MIAMI LATINO.   This small coffee shop typified businesses that sprang up in major American cities with large Latino populations. Its bill of fare, although primarily Cuban, features typical American food—that is, food brought to the United States by other immigrants.

specialized advertising in Spanish. Radio and television stations sprang up to cater to these large groups of consumers. Among the favorite programs were broadcasts of Latin American soccer matches and *novelas* (Latin American soap operas).

A more controversial impact of Hispanics was on the American Catholic Church. A hierarchy dominated by Irish and other older immigrant groups, the church seemed cold, formal, and inhospitable to the huge numbers of Hispanic Catholics. With their emphasis on cults of the Virgin Mary, festivals, and other locally important traditions, Hispanics often found themselves either clashing with or avoiding the American Catholic Church. For example, when the union leader Cesar Chavez organized Mexican farm workers and marched behind the banner of the Virgin of Guadelupe, he found little support initially from the established Catholic Church in California.

This distance underscores two important trends in Hispanic-American religion. One is the significant inroads made by Protestant evangelicals like the Jehovah's Witnesses and Baptists, who offer a service and religious culture sometimes more compatible with Hispanics' desires. The second trend will bring Hispanic membership in the American Catholic Church to a dominant position sometime before the year 2000. By that time, about one-half of all American Catholics will be of Hispanic origin.

With enormous numbers of immigrants, refreshed by new recruits, and a culture made tenacious by the Spanish language and a host of specially created media, merchandising, and business institutions, the question that the immigration act and the fight over bilingualism posed was whether this new immigrant culture, unlike so many others, might resist melting into the great, confusing sea of American ethnic groups. Since there is no way to know, the argument and its manifestations ensure that the controversy will remain.

HOMELESS IN AMERICA. Homelessness affected poor people in every segment of American society in the 1980s. This growing population, with nowhere else to go, shared public spaces with residents and commuters in the city, making them visible to everyone.

THE EIGHTIES ECONOMY

In their complex and multiple effects, these changes in family and demography reflected a deep but slow change in the American economy that first became visible in the early 1970s. This was a slight increase in the inequality of American income distribution. In a book with the ominous-sounding title, *The Great Depression of 1990*, Ravi Batra, an economist at Southern Methodist University, noted the growing disparity in income between the top one-fifth of the population and the bottom one-fifth. Other economists contended that changes in income distribution were not unusual or permanent; there had always been cycles of greater or lesser equality. But many of them conceded that from the 1970s onward, the opportunities for social mobility were fewer. With a shrinking industrial sector that still paid high wages, and a burgeoning low-skilled service sector, the economy during this period generated a great many new jobs. Some of these were in high-paying finance and high-technology fields.

But many of them (close to half of those created from 1980 to 1985) paid at or less than the minimum wage of $3.35 per hour and $7,000 per year. Just this sort of difference in income and social class emerged as one of the most telling distinctions between the Whiteheads and the Sterns in the Baby M trial.

Despite greater optimism among middle-class Americans, particularly after 1980, this group also faced somewhat diminished opportunities. The median income of all American families fell slightly after the 1970s and would have turned down more precipitously except for the new earnings of millions of women who entered the labor force during those years.

These were slight but significant economic changes, and they had immediate effects. One was the rise of homeless people in American cities, numbering perhaps three million in 1988. Additional factors, of course, helped thrust these people onto the streets. Thousands of mental patients were released from hospitals and found nowhere else to go; there was a rapid increase in various drug addict populations. But a growing

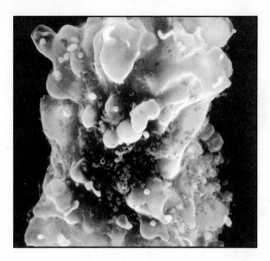

This human immune system cell is pictured under attack by much smaller HIV viruses responsible for Acquired Immune Deficiency Syndrome (AIDS). The infected cells reproduce the HIV virus and no longer function normally.

share of the homeless lived over heating grates or in makeshift city shelters simply because housing cost too much and social welfare programs were inadequate. Some of the homeless even had full-time jobs.

Homelessness in America became a national cause in the 1980s, particularly after Americans became aware of terrible famines in East Africa. In June 1985, an international rock concert, "Live Aid," raised funds to feed famine victims and focused attention on the terrible plight of starving families in eastern Africa. In 1986 a project modeled after this event, "Hands Across America," solicited money for the homeless in America. It momentarily raised national consciousness of the problem, but failed to deliver significant funds to ameliorate it.

THE GLOBAL ECONOMY

In linking the cause of the homeless in the United States to starvation in the Third World, Americans were only underscoring a fact of postwar life: the interconnection of the economies and societies of the whole world. Economic development throughout the world exhibited some of the same tendencies appearing in America. The dominant few economies of the industrialized world—including the European Economic Community, Japan, and newly expansive Taiwan, Hong Kong, South Korea, and Singapore, as well as the United States—continued to grow, although competition dramatically shifted the relative shares of production within this group. For the undeveloped and developing world, there were fewer success stories. In some cases, countries with strong initial growth—such as Mexico, Brazil, and Nigeria—fell into debt and stagnation. The very indebtedness of these nations gave them a kind of reverse power over the most prosperous lenders, for the threat to default on loans from private American and European banks became a way to squeeze out new loans or reduce the interest paid on old ones.

OTHER SOCIAL CHANGES

AIDS

Another area of internationalization was health. One of the greatest accomplishments of modern medicine was achieved during the 1980s, when the disease smallpox, one of history's deadliest killers, disappeared from the human community. At almost the same time, however, a new and equally frightening infectious disease was discovered, AIDS (acquired immune deficiency syndrome). A viral disease diagnosed in the early 1980s, but common before that time in certain parts of Africa, AIDS spread rapidly in America, particularly among male homosexuals and intravenous drug users. By the late 1980s the disease, with no known cure or vaccine, appeared to have jumped beyond these two groups to spread generally, although very slowly, among other sectors of the population. Increasingly, AIDS became concentrated among poorer occupants of American cities.

By 1987, AIDS had become one of the leading infectious diseases, certainly the most deadly. Like surrogate motherhood, abortion, and contraception, AIDS became a political issue tangled in moralism, with positions sometimes taken based on disapproval of the victims. Because homosexuals and drug users—groups traditionally shunned by the majority—formed the greatest percentage of patients, the United States declined, at first, to take fighting the disease seriously. Prevention programs were often stymied because of fears that contraceptive devices and sex and drug education designed to prevent transmission of the disease would, in fact, encourage promiscuity.

THE MEDIA EXPLOSION

The problems and possibilities of these complicated social changes of the 1980s formed a vast source of material for commentary and dramatization in American culture. For example, the Baby M case, homelessness, and AIDS became the subjects of made-for-TV movies and countless newspaper and magazine stories.

In part, the acceleration of change had to do with media technology itself. For example, the manufacture and sale of videocassette recorders spiked in the mid-1980s. Only 1 percent of American households owned a VCR in 1980; almost 40 percent had purchased one only five years later. Feeding the enormous and diverse appetite for home viewing were films rented through video outlets, special children's presentations, and rock videos. Cable television, available in millions of homes, also featured multiple entertainments aimed at special population segments. Even commercial television began to feature rock videos.

The vast increase in the number of programs available through cable television and the home rental of films and specially made videos opened a wider window on the world for most American households. The proliferation of television talk shows and radio call-in programs no doubt increased a sense of connectedness and even intimacy between audiences and celebrities. The other side of this development, however, may well have been a decline of public participation and an increase in rootlessness in American society. Consequently, soap operas, idiosyncratic confessions on talk shows, celebrity quirks, and prolonged media dramas such as the Baby M trial appeared to replace older networks of family and community.

More important, all of these media began to incorporate whatever was new in the cinematic and cultural values of each form, erasing distinctions between types of entertainments. For example, the television program *Miami Vice* adapted many of the values of other media: rock videos, fashion, and changing architectural tastes. The long-running program, shot in subtle hues of pink and blue against the striking art deco architecture of Miami, Florida, moved along skimpy plots punctuated by violence, drug busts, and sentimentality. Most interesting, however, was the studied ambiguity of the actors' racial and ethnic identities.

This ambiguity was also typical of rock videos. Shot in hostile-looking urban settings, pulsating with montages of images and dancers, these videos produced a new crossover culture, a visual blending of white, African-American, and Hispanic elements that became as various and eclectic as the music itself. Of all modern performers, perhaps Michael Jackson exemplified this trend best, as he strutted his sexual and racial ambiguities, appealing to millions of American youth.

To describe this new culture of ambiguous styles, multiple sources, and fractured meanings,

FORMER AT&T BUILDING, NEW YORK. This brilliant example of postmodern architecture self-consciously borrowed styles from other eras and forms. The result is a good-natured, witty facade that challenges the monotony of glass and steel boxes so familiar in urban areas.

social commentators borrowed a word already used in architecture: postmodernism. The term seemed to fit a great many developments in high culture. Among them were movements in art and literature that borrowed freely from previous styles and even from cinematic practices. But it was in architecture that the term had its most visual, obvious implications. A famous example is the brilliant and influential architect Philip Johnson, who discarded his own earlier designs to upstage the dominant minimalist styles and functionalism of the 1960s. Rejecting the cold but clean lines of functionalism, his buildings began to sport columns, arcades, atriums, balconies,

and arches, while new materials and pastel colors replaced glass boxes for a softer and more fanciful look. One of his most controversial skyscrapers, the former AT&T building in New York, was built to resemble a Chippendale cabinet, a witty act of borrowing that eliminated some of the design distinctions between art forms and blurred the history of architecture.

MATERIALISM

In this eclectic cultural context, mass culture celebrated some peculiar forms of individualism, materialism, and celebrity. In the mid-1980s, the popular singer Madonna recorded a song, "Material Girl," whose lyrics, whether satiric or serious, were a hymn to the newly approved materialism of the era, a paean "to living in a material world," where "the boy with the cold, hard cash is always Mr. Right." Another hero created by the new materialism was Wall Street *arbitrageur* Ivan Boesky. Riding a wave of publicity in 1985 generated by his breathtaking gains in the corporate takeover frenzy sweeping Wall Street, Boesky instructed an audience of business students: "Greed is all right, by the way. I think greed is healthy. You can be greedy and still feel good about yourself." Boesky's speech became a model for the amoral entrepreneur played by Oscar winner Michael Douglas in the film *Wall Street*.

This raw materialism did not pass without condemnation. In a thoughtful and disturbing book, *Habits of the Heart*, published in 1985, five prominent sociologists and philosophers explored the cultural resources that Americans brought to their world of the 1980s. Their conclusions were sobering. The American ideal of freedom had stimulated initiative and creativity, even toleration. But it had left "Americans with a stubborn fear of acknowledging structures of power and interdependence in a technologically complex society dominated by giant corporations and an increasingly powerful state. The ideal of freedom makes Americans nostalgic for their past, but provides few resources for talking about their collective future."

VIGILANTISM

What these sociologists feared seemed to come true in an ominous event in the closing days of 1984. Terrified by the experience of a previous mugging, a middle-class white man, Bernhard Goetz, shot four black youths in a New York City subway when one of them asked him for five dollars. Admitting his guilt and unrepentant for having paralyzed one of the group, Goetz became both a hero and a villain: the "subway vigilante." By his old-fashioned act of taking the law into his own hands, he symbolized the failure of efforts to end urban crime and the resulting frustration of citizens driven to protect themselves. Yet Goetz was an inappropriate symbol and a reluctant hero, undeserving either of the praise or animosity directed to him. Acquitted by a jury of attempted murder, he sought to retreat from public scrutiny and return to a normal life.

EVANGELISM

Unsettling and extreme reactions of the sort that flared up in the Goetz case symbolized the desire of many Americans to reaffirm old-fashioned

CRIME RATES IN THE UNITED STATES, 1957–1986

	Murder	Rape	Robbery	Burglary
(Rates per 100,000 Inhabitants)				
1957	5	8	39	355
1960	5	10	60	502
1965	5	12	71	653
1970	8	19	171	1,071
1975	10	26	218	1,526
1980	10	37	251	1,684
1985	8	37	209	1,287
1986	9	38	225	1,345

Source: Federal Bureau of Investigation figures.

notions of heroism, to revive "traditional values." An important minority of Americans found this aspiration best expressed among evangelical Protestant television ministers who crusaded for a restoration of conservative lifestyles. Although in the period from 1960 onward church membership by percentage actually fell slightly in America, the nature of religious experience changed dramatically. The number of Americans who considered themselves "born again," with a profound experience of religious conversion in their lives, almost doubled to about 40 percent of the population.

While individual religious experience was significant, its cultural expressions proved more important. Television evangelists such as Oral Roberts, Jim and Tammy Bakker, Jerry Falwell, Pat Robertson, and Jimmy Swaggart used the mass media with astounding skill to spread their message, raise money, and organize politically. They gathered a far-flung congregation of worshipers and consumers who bought books and pamphlets, purchased a huge variety of goods produced by affiliated companies, or traveled to the Bakkers' Heritage Park USA, a combination amusement park and didactic display that in the mid-1980s outdrew all other American theme parks except Disney World and Disneyland. Designing their programs to resemble talk shows, variety shows, dramas, and political and news events, television evangelists persuaded millions of Americans that they could live in the modern world, use the most advanced communications devices and consumer items, and yet cling to traditional values.

The politics of this movement also had an immense impact. Although not all television evangelists or born-again Christians belonged to the political right, and certainly not all were Protestant or white, the majority impulse cherished a vision of America that was Protestant and conservative. Using a nostalgic conservatism to judge the culture and politics of the 1980s, evangelical political groups blamed government for stimulating dangerous social change. Yet the same groups demanded government action to re-

store the paternalistic family and prayer in public schools, and to end abortion and other forms of sexual and social liberation. Jerry Falwell, founder of the Moral Majority, and Pat Robertson hoped to harness these sentiments as a permanent force inside the Republican party. Robertson ran in Republican presidential primaries in 1988 with considerable success. More important, evangelical groups made significant gains within the party structure, organizing around anti-abortion and other lifestyle issues.

CONSERVATISM

Although liberals continued to publish and even to dominate the academic world, conservatives of various persuasions increasingly defined public policy debates. This about-face has many explanations: for example, lucrative appointments in right-wing think tanks located in Washington, DC, and other key cities across the country. Several influential opinion journals such as *The New Republic* modified their enthusiasm for liberalism. The most audible defection sounded when an important group of New York liberals embraced neoconservatism, a philosophy that had been developing for several decades but now received brilliant statement by old masters of polemics such as Norman Podhoretz of *Commentary* magazine. Aggressively anticommunist, deeply discouraged by perceived failures of President Johnson's Great Society, and totally opposed to schemes of engineered egalitarianism like affirmative action, school busing, and racial and gender hiring quotas, they turned against the welfare state to celebrate the old ideal of individual social mobility.

Important books such as Charles A. Murray's *Losing Ground*, published in 1984, dissected postwar welfare programs and concluded that government subsidies, food stamps, and other forms of transfer payments actually increased poverty, broke up families, and encouraged forms of behavior that deepened dependency. Only if the poor faced the consequences of their failures, he reasoned, would they become strong enough to resist the calamity of poverty.

Developing alongside this movement was a different sort of conservatism, represented by Congressman Jack Kemp of New York and economists Arthur Laffer, George Gilder, and Milton Friedman, and articulated most persuasively by governor and presidential candidate Ronald Reagan of California. While this group of thinkers and politicians developed different strategies for releasing the energy of the American economy, all united behind another major idea of the 1980s: an almost mystical faith in the restorative power of the marketplace. Several corollaries followed from this belief. The first was that economic growth, and no other force, could end poverty and create a good society. The only true engine of economic growth was the private market. Its liberation from regulation and consequent freedom of individuals from excessive taxation would propel the American economy out of the doldrums of the 1970s. Of course, government had to intervene in the economy in profound ways: defense spending, regulation of banking and money, and so on. So some taxes and expenditures were acceptable. But this market philosophy demanded dismantling the welfare state, from Head Start programs to Social Security, from cradle to grave.

Creating a new right-wing politics, however, was no simple task. Two distinct impulses had to be blended: traditional moralism and the ideology of a marketplace test for economic, social, and cultural ideals. Before 1980, this was only a potential coalition with a very divided constituency. As the Baby M case so poignantly demonstrated, the free market could be a destructive enemy of traditional ideas about family and marriage. The validity of a contract in this case deeply undercut strong beliefs about motherhood. Indeed, throughout American history, economic change and market values have consistently challenged tradition. The force of capitalist enterprise transformed men, women, children, races, and ethnic groups as it embedded their destinies in the fate of an even larger and more complex world.

Yet one political appeal did seem to work: a call to a return to the past, when market and morality appeared to operate in tandem. It was the genius of Ronald Reagan to articulate this vision and provide a platform that combined the desires of born-again, poor, and middle-class populists with the interests of some of the wealthiest corporate leaders in America behind a program that could appeal to a majority of voters now convinced that government regulation sapped the strength of American enterprise. He was also fortunate to follow one of the most unpopular presidents of the twentieth century, Jimmy Carter.

THE ELECTION OF 1980

The election of 1980 was momentous, not because it initiated a sharp realignment of regions, races, ethnic groups, and social classes but because it brought profound political change without any radical transformation of the electorate. In the long run, this inertia acted to retard and then stop conservative attempts to dismantle the welfare state, exposing the contradictions inherent in the Reagan alliance. Yet in January 1981, when Ronald Reagan assumed the presidency, the Democratic party, the dominant political force in the postwar period, hung its head in stunned silence. The new president, whatever the depth or clarity of his mandate, moved quickly to translate his ideas into action.

In 1980 the bruising fight for the Democratic nomination between President Carter and Senator Edward Kennedy was matched by splits among Republicans. Before the Republican convention in Detroit in the summer of 1980, Reagan had defeated all his opponents, although George Bush, former head of the CIA, gamely contested the nomination. Liberal Republican congressman John Anderson of Illinois declared he would run as an independent. This defection of Republican liberalism clinched the victory of conservatives in the Republican party. They declared a far-reaching program of change.

RONALD REAGAN

Although no newcomer to electoral office—he had served as governor of California for two terms, from 1967 to 1975—Reagan represented a fresh force in politics. Despite his advanced age of 70 in 1981, he symbolized much that was contemporary in American life. He was the first president to have been divorced, and he shared with many other Americans the problems of two families and two generations of children. Practically his whole life had been spent working in the entertainment industry, first as a sportscaster, then as a film actor, and finally as a professional lecturer. He fulfilled the revised myth of American social mobility, based not on hard work but on celebrity, achieving his success in the most mythic place in America, Hollywood. Rising from an impoverished Illinois family, he made his way with force of personality rather than diligence. His career in films was solid if not distinguished; he had two glamorous marriages to actresses. Completely at home in the world of celebrities, Ronald Reagan promised a Hollywood ending for the problems of the American economy and foreign policy.

Along the path of this ascent, Reagan gradually relinquished a once strong allegiance to the Democratic party, although he never outgrew his deep admiration for President Franklin Roosevelt. Looking for milestones in his conversion to conservatism, journalists Rowland Evans and Robert Novak argue in their book *The Reagan Revolution* that the future president was jolted by the high income taxes he suddenly had to pay in 1939. Others cite the influence of his militantly conservative second father-in-law, Loyal Davis. Unfriendly critics point to a movie career that never really advanced and consequent scapegoating of Hollywood liberals and communist sympathizers. Reagan himself emphasized his struggle inside the Screen Actors Guild against communist influence in the 1940s.

None of these explanations, however, quite captures the emotional quality of Reagan's conversion to conservatism. For one thing, it did not take the form of the dour first principles of fiscal conservatism and isolationist foreign policy advanced by Ohio senator Robert Taft in the 1950s. Instead, Reagan's conservatism had a more theatrical flourish. He found sources of belief, for instance, in the film heroes he played, such as George Gipp, the legendary Notre Dame halfback, or the amputee hero from *King's Row*. Both these figures triumphed over enormous odds. Both provided inspiring examples of the modern American success story. Both illustrated the myth-making power of Hollywood's melodramas.

This same anecdotal approach to American individualism defined Reagan's political success story. The achievements of an individual, like that of a nation, he believed, depended on each person striving, without the interference of government. His repertoire included not just laudatory anecdotes and film heroes, but shocking ones: stories of "welfare queens" chauffeured in Cadillacs to pick up government checks or young men who used food stamps to buy liquor. These riveting parables illustrated Reagan's beliefs and provided a simple, plausible explanation for distressing social problems. They offered a smooth transition between contradictory ideas. They gave flesh to complex economic and social ideas.

Ronald Reagan actively sought the presidency between 1968 and 1976, but finally won the Republican nomination in 1980. He did so partly by persistence and partly with an upsurge of conservative voters in the party. But only in 1980 did he finally develop a program that appealed beyond his limited ideological base to a generally frustrated and disillusioned electorate.

The greatest cause of that disillusionment was President Carter's reaction to the cold, hard facts of America's relative decline in world economic and political status. From almost any perspective—from trade, manufacturing, finance, to military power—the United States was a less potent world force in 1980 than in 1945 or even 1960. One index illustrates it all: In 1945 the United States' share of world manufacturing was 60 percent. By 1985 this had fallen to 30 percent. Weak economic growth, sluggish productivity, slack investment, low savings rates, and inattention to human resource problems like education and training explained half this decline. The other

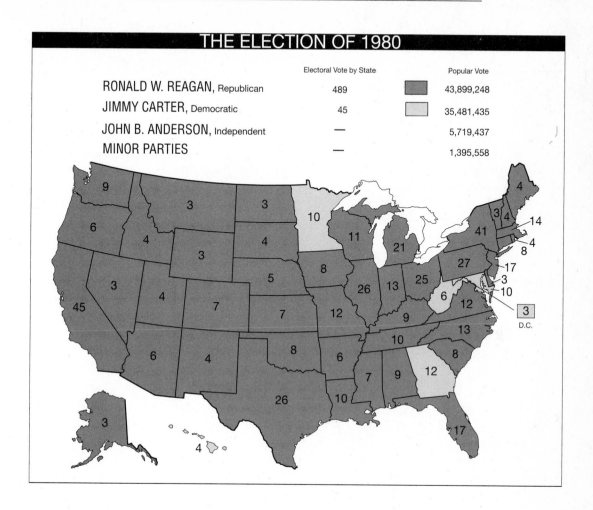

THE ELECTION OF 1980

	Electoral Vote by State		Popular Vote
RONALD W. REAGAN, Republican	489	▓	43,899,248
JIMMY CARTER, Democratic	45	░	35,481,435
JOHN B. ANDERSON, Independent	—		5,719,437
MINOR PARTIES	—		1,395,558

half was competition from the bustling economies of Western Europe, Japan, and the industrialized Pacific Rim nations like Taiwan and South Korea.

Over these long-term developments lay the immediate crisis of the terrible inflation rate of 12 percent. In a famous speech in July 1979, Carter warned Americans that they courted a deep spiritual crisis. But searching inwardly for solutions sounded like retreat and only intensified the growing sense that American leaders cowered helplessly before a hostile world. In 1978 the Soviet Union engineered a coup in neighboring Afghanistan, and throughout 1979 stepped up military aid to fight opponents of the new regime. In response, President Carter canceled American participation in the 1980 Moscow Olympic Games and imposed an embargo on sales of grain to the Soviet Union. Whatever the intent of these moves, many Americans believed that Carter suffered foreign policy problems much like a penitent, welcoming adversity, rather than as a tough leader. During the Iran hostage crisis of 1980, the president seemed to lose direction and self-confidence.

Ronald Reagan restored the nation's confidence, and began a program to rejuvenate the American economy. In some respects, his program was a seamless web of contradictions, woven together only by the candidate's political energy and charisma. In economics, Reagan urged a tight monetary policy (already begun under Carter) to squeeze inflation out of the economy.

At the same time, he was a convert to "supply-side" economics. This theory, called, in an unusual moment of candor, the "trickle-down" strategy by his budget director David Stockman, proposed large tax cuts especially for affluent Americans to encourage savings and investment. This would, theoretically, stimulate economic growth and, therefore, tax revenues. Another aspect of the program was to severely pare down social programs and pour huge amounts into defense spending. As further measures to liberate individual initiative, Reagan proposed abolishing or curtailing environmental, work-related, and other business regulations. This would be accompanied by the privatization, wherever possible, of all government services.

Yet while promising to get government "off our backs" in economic matters and let the values of the marketplace prevail, Reagan proposed a contradictory program of moral activism, using the office of the presidency and the federal government to restore traditional values to American society. He opposed the Equal Rights Amendment to the Constitution; he opposed abortion; he favored prayer in public schools and public funding of religious and private schools; he opposed affirmative action and quota systems of hiring. Most important, he denied the validity of "entitlement politics," wherein groups of Americans, bound by some common interest, sought permanent funding or programs from the government. Reagan denounced this as a subversion of the interests of democracy.

Thus Reagan's program promised that less could be more. By curbing the welfare state, restoring national moral standards, and a firm foreign policy, and liberating the private market, the United States could reassert its claim to a unique and special destiny. By November the 1980 election had become no contest at all. A series of debates showed Reagan a confident, witty, and congenial man. Reagan and vice presidential candidate George Bush won 489 electoral votes. Carter and Walter Mondale took only 49, and John Anderson none. In popular votes cast, Reagan garnered 51 percent, but this far exceeded Carter's 41 percent. As important as the size of the presidential victory was the Republican triumph in the Senate where, for the first time since 1952, the party won a majority. Significant gains in the House of Representatives meant that with expected support from conservative southern Democrats, the Republican party could pass its program.

On January 20, 1981, Ronald Reagan promised a new beginning, to preserve "this last and greatest bastion of freedom." Even by the standards of most inaugural addresses, this one promised more. With a sweeping declaration that "government is not the solution to our problem; government is the problem," Reagan proposed to use his office, Congress, and the courts to restore America to the pinnacle of power and self-confidence.

If there were sharp contradictions in promising to strengthen the positive power of government by limiting its size, collect more revenues by lowering taxes, balance the budget by decreasing revenues, and end government interference in individual lives by pressing for morals legislation, the contradictions only reflected the different priorities of the Reagan coalition. Not organized around political compromises, Reagan voters existed as independent groups: traditional Republicans; conservative, evangelical Christians; members of the new right; and working- and middle-class Americans opposed to various Democratic party social programs. They were ready to marshal media support, campaign funds, and votes for a specific cause. With their broad, even utopian aims, these groups did not operate as a traditional political party. By running against Congress and the bureaucrats of Washington, DC, Reagan promised not to play traditional interest-group politics. He would, he noted, go over the heads of politicians to appeal to the American people.

REAGANOMICS

The new president and his advisers quickly moved to institute their economic program while postponing serious and potentially unpopular attempts to achieve the moral reform so fervently demanded by their evangelical constituencies. Appointing conservatives to cabinet posts—such as James Watt, an anticonservation activist, to Interior and Caspar Weinberger to Defense—Reagan instructed David Stockman of the Office of Management and Budget to scrutinize and trim funds from each federal agency except Defense. Hoping to achieve large cuts in bureaucracy and regulations before cabinet officers became advocates for their agencies, Stockman, with Reagan's blessing, tried to eliminate the departments of education and energy and to slash funds from programs targeted at health, education, housing, agriculture, income maintenance, and unemployment. As Stockman later noted, "My blueprint for sweeping, wrenching change in national economic governance would have hurt millions of people in the short run." Stockman even proposed to squeeze the fat out of defense budgets, but the president remained adamant about a rapid and expensive arms buildup.

Alongside budget cutting blossomed a far more important and achievable goal: the promised tax cut. The president repeatedly accused the Democrats of a demoralizing policy of tax and spend. He proposed to prune federal income taxes by as much as 30 percent across the board. In justification, the president promised that a tax cut "would provide incentive and stimulate productivity, thus reducing inflation and providing jobs for the unemployed." This pledge prompted substantial popular support, in part because of the growing hostility to the way some federal funds were spent and to the recipients. Moreover, "bracket creep" up the rate ladder of the progressive income tax tables meant that every income earner in America, in this time of fast-rising prices and wages, became more and more alert to escalating income taxes.

Although liberals in the House of Representatives resisted a major tax cut, a group of southern Democrats, dubbed the "Boll Weevils," offered hope for decisive action. Just as pressure mounted to pass the legislation, on March 30, 1981, the president was leaving a Washington hotel following a speech when he was suddenly shot by a single gunman, John Hinckley. Pushed into his limousine and rushed to George Washington University Hospital, he survived the assassination attempt. Just as important, his joking manner and irrepressible good humor in a terrifying situation gained him enormous public sympathy. This he skillfully turned into support for his economic program.

Facing an inevitable defeat, the Democrats offered up an alternative plan, but Reagan won his battle. The bill passed Congress and became law on August 13, 1981. Graduated rates were lowered in three stages: 5 percent the first year and 10 percent in each of two succeeding years, making for a total reduction of 25 percent. In simplest terms, this meant that a taxpayer who owed $2,000 in federal income taxes in 1981 would eventually save $500 a year. For the taxpayer who owed $20,000 in 1981, the annual savings would be $5,000. Some economists deplored the unbalanced impact of this equal treatment; a few warned of an abrupt decline in federal revenues. Coupled with new tax savings for corporations, the income tax reduction eliminated $41 billion in revenues during the first year alone.

The president, however, had a compelling answer: He would balance the federal budget by reducing federal expenditures; tax revenues would rise with economic expansion. This promise, however, turned into an annual ritual of evasion. Despite Stockman's dogged attacks on a whole range of government beneficiaries, from Amtrak to farm subsidies, Medicare to science and health projects, not nearly enough was cut to offset either increases in defense spending or declining revenues. In negotiations with Congress over the budget, pet local projects inevitably crept in. Moreover, recognizing a growing public sensitivity, Congress balked at cutting Social Security benefits. Areas of the budget without strong constituencies lost more than those with powerful lobbies.

This significant shift in priorities had the greatest impact on the poor, who were growing in number over this entire period. Thus a decreasing share of funds fell to an increasingly

INCREASES AND DECREASES IN PERCENT OF FEDERAL BUDGET ALLOCATIONS, 1980–1986

Increases	1980	1986	Decreases	1980	1986
Defense	22.68	27.13	International affairs	2.15	1.75
Social Security	25.49	27.43	Income security	14.64	12.05
Agriculture	1.49	2.64	Health	3.93	3.64
Interest on federal debt	8.8	14.56	Veterans	3.59	2.71
			Education & training	5.38	3.13
			Commerce	1.59	.39
			Transport	3.69	2.77
			Environment	2.35	1.32
			Energy conservation	1.73	.45
			Commercial development	1.91	.81
			Science	.98	.91
			Justice	.78	.69
			Government expenses miscellaneous	.74	.64

Source: U.S. Department of Commerce, Bureau of the Census, Statistical Abstract of the United States, 1987 (Washington, D.C.: Government Printing Office, 1986), pp. 293–294.

large group of needy people. At the same time, some forms of entitlements shared by the middle class, such as Social Security, actually increased. Thus the income redistribution inherent in the Reagan administration budget and taxation programs marginally accelerated inequality in the United States. Ironically, the attempt to cut the budget across the board solidified support for some social programs, with most real cuts made only in those aimed at the bottom of society.

Because the 1981 tax act and the annual budgets worked at cross purposes, a huge increase in the federal deficit threatened. It became inevitable when tight money strategies to fight inflation touched off a recession. By mid-1982 the United States found itself in the midst of the most severe downturn since the 1930s. As production declined, revenues shrank. The deficit increased rapidly from around $60 billion in 1980 to over $200 billion a year in 1986.

To fund this massive debt, the government borrowed money from its citizens and from foreigners attracted by an overvalued dollar and high interest rates. In turn, the high dollar and a wave of consumer optimism after the end of the 1982 recession fueled a huge imbalance of trade that rose to over $170 billion a year in 1987. Over the seven years of the Reagan presidency, the United States fell from being the greatest creditor to the greatest debtor nation in the world.

By 1982, David Stockman, Treasury Secretary James Baker, and other cabinet members recognized that the push-me, pull-you economic program of stimulus and restraints demanded quick repair. Their solution, with the acquiescence of Congress, was a new tax act in 1984, the largest single increase in revenue yet in history. But this only slowed the growth of the deficit. President Reagan refused to lower defense spending or raise further taxes, and the administration, recognizing public sentiment against cuts to Social Security and veterans' payments, withdrew from the battlefield of the budget. The only rainbow among the deficit clouds was the supply-side theory that economic growth would solve all problems.

The election of 1984 proved to be something of a referendum on economics. With inflation down, consumption up, and the deficit having no visible impact, the administration won handily. The Democrats, led by former Vice President Mondale and Representative Geraldine Ferraro (the first woman nominated for such a position by a major party), advocated higher taxes and more social programs with restraint in defense spending. Reagan and Bush confidently defended their record. Their landslide victory confirmed that a majority of the Americans who voted approved of the policy of borrow and spend over the Democrats' tax and spend.

Returned to power with a somewhat diminished hold over the Senate and fewer representatives in the House, the Republicans (with the support of key Democrats) nonetheless won a further tax reform in October 1986, which all but ended the progressive income tax. While abolishing most tax shelters and deductions used by wealthier people, it lowered tax rates for 1988 to 15 percent on incomes below $29,750 and 28 percent on incomes above that figure. Billed as a fairer, simpler system, it was not immediately clear how its provisions would affect the average American family.

Although the growing deficit carried no political liabilities and provoked few hesitations in the consumer shopping spree of the mid-1980s, it lay like a terrorist bomb inside the economy. On October 19, 1987, the stock market registered a huge shock: values sank almost 500 points in a day. The giddy rise of prices and paper fortunes of the previous years were dashed by a decline as severe as the first days of the 1929 crash. Belated efforts to wean America off dependency on foreign borrowing and purchase of imports by lowering the value and foreign purchasing power of the dollar had failed. Foreign investors and governments quickly blamed U.S. economic policy for what became a world-encircling wave of stock declines and currency fluctuations.

Until 1987 this underlying distortion had a marginal impact on the president's popularity, although economic experts remained dubious. Despite an overall slowdown in economic growth since the 1970s and no substantial reversal of the relative decline of America's world economic standing, the administration maintained its popularity. In spite of strident words about budget cutting, after 1982 Reagan was stymied by entrenched interests and a gradually diminishing power base in Congress. Still, immediate benefits outweighed the intangible threat of future problems. Tax cuts put money into the pockets of wage earners. Inflation fell sharply, and the spending binge of the government merely validated the buying binge of consumers. Finally, the various Reagan policies had differential effects on Americans. If the poorest fell through wide tears in the "safety net" of social services, they were a constituency that rarely voted and possessed little power. Those who gained in these flush years had ample reason to celebrate fewer regulations and lower taxes.

REAGAN AND SOCIAL ISSUES

The strategy of flourish and postponement that the president pursued on the budget also framed his actions on social issues. In this area he disappointed many of his fervent admirers, who proposed a menu of moral demands including an end to legal abortions, reinstating school prayer, and funding private schools with public money. What the president could accomplish by speaking at evangelical conferences and before right-wing think tanks, he did. What he could accomplish by appointing conservative judges and revising government guidelines, he did. Several of his cabinet members—for example, William Bennett, secretary of education in 1985—urged a revival of "family values," and blasted sex education in the schools. In civil rights cases, Attorney General Edwin Meese and Assistant Attorney General for Civil Rights William Bradford Reynolds often entered court cases as friends of those accused of civil rights violations. Reagan also appointed a Civil Rights Commission with several members openly hostile to previous federal attempts to reverse patterns of discrimination.

But in this area, too, Reagan recognized the pitfalls of radical change. For one thing, as the Baby M case revealed, some of the most fundamental beliefs of the Reagan coalition could sharply contradict each other. The path of least political resistance, therefore, seemed to be through the Supreme Court. Having denounced the activist Court of Justice Earl Warren and the Burger Court that followed it, the president tried to use appointments to the Court to reverse decisions on abortion, privacy, affirmative action, and separation of church and state. His first appointment, of Sandra Day O'Connor in 1981, had little immediate impact. In fact, his appointment of the first woman to the Supreme Court was hailed as a breakthrough in women's rights. With his next opportunity, he elevated William Rehnquist to chief justice and filled his vacant position with Antonin Scalia, another conservative. But in 1987, when a further vacancy occurred, one that might have drastically shifted the Court, the president blundered in proposing Judge Robert Bork. Given his eccentric theories and controversial writings, Bork attracted the bitter opposition of civil rights and women's groups. He was also opposed by a sizable segment of the judicial and legal professions. The Senate soundly defeated his appointment.

This rebuke came partly because the Democrats had seized control of the Senate in the 1986 elections. But a second nominee, Judge Douglas Ginsburg, fared no better. Ginsburg also professed highly controversial beliefs about the functions of the Court and the meaning of the Constitution. But before battle lines could be drawn, he withdrew his candidacy after revelations that he had smoked marijuana some years before. Reagan's third (and successful) candidate was Anthony M. Kennedy, a conservative jurist with apparent orthodox views of the Court. He was no overt advocate of the president's social agenda and his appointment failed to shift the Court to the right.

SANDRA DAY O'CONNOR appointed to the Supreme Court by President Reagan in 1981, was the first woman to hold this position. Her tenure was more important for creating a conservative majority than in providing any special or distinct representation for women's issues.

In fact, by 1987 the president's most conservative supporters were in disarray, torn by warfare over succession, growing dislike for his foreign policy, and split by scandals that ripped the television evangelical ministry, the mainstay of the constituency crusading to restore traditional values.

The enormous growth in sophistication by the evangelical right during the 1980s had a seismic impact on American politics. Sending delegates to nominating conventions, winning concessions in party platforms, and altering the tone and language of campaigns, the evangelical right forced its issues onto the national agenda. Ronald Reagan encouraged this development. He visited the PTL Club of Jim and Tammy Bakker and addressed the National Association of Evangelicals and other such religious organizations. On March 8, 1982, before the NAE, he dramatically denounced the Soviet Union as an "evil empire." The struggle with the Soviet Union, he warned, was between "right and wrong and good and evil."

Despite this crusading rhetoric, the president kept his distance from the religious right. This policy proved wise when in 1987, an evangelical schism opened between the Bakkers, Jimmy Swaggert, Jerry Falwell, and others. The falling-out involved charges of misappropriation of funds and sexual philandering by Bakker. When Bakker confessed to serious misdeeds and a lurid sexual affair, his financial and religious empire collapsed with a crash that resounded throughout the evangelical world.

But the evangelical right was dismayed by Reagan's subsequent about-face in foreign policy. In this arena, his conservative following found both its greatest victories and worst defeats. As the president wavered between ideology and compromise and realism, he provoked hope and controversy.

⤙⟦◉⟧⤚

FOREIGN POLICY

From the beginning, Ronald Reagan never left doubts about his basic foreign policy values. In countless speeches during the 1970s, he had hammered away at American defense weakness and Soviet aggression. He had fervently supported the war in Vietnam and scorned detente with the Russians. Speaking in 1982, he recalled with approval the words of a fellow actor: "I would rather see my little girls die now, still believing in God, than have them grow up under communism and one day die no longer believing in God." In such moments, he imagined the final titanic struggle between the superpowers as the beginning of Armageddon, the fiery end of the world described in the Bible. Accommodation with the Soviet Union, as he told the Foreign Policy Association in 1977, meant retreat: "Détente to the Soviet Union became not a sign of compromise, but a victory for the U.S.S.R. and a growing sign of Western weakness caused by the internal contradictions of capitalism."

This searing anticommunism balanced another deeply held belief in the moral superiority of American society. "In a world wreaked [sic] by hatred, economic crisis, and political tension," he said in late 1982, "America remains mankind's best hope." A theme gilding all of his speeches, this faith in America as a morally redeemed society revived the strong nationalism characteristic of the cold war period. This nationalism had been muted in the 1970s by the loss of the war in Vietnam, by Soviet achievement of nuclear arms parity, and by the increasingly competitive world market. Haunted by fears that the nation might not maintain its military, political, and economic preeminence in this complex world, some Americans found Reagan's nostalgic vision comforting. If the exercise of power provoked warlike metaphors, better to talk of risks than accept decline without a struggle.

THE ARMS BUILDUP

Bolstered by accelerating defense expenditures and tough-minded advisers such as Secretary of State Alexander Haig, CIA director William Casey, and national security adviser Richard V. Allen, Reagan began to implement his foreign policy. The cornerstone was arms superiority over the Soviet Union—negotiating from strength, as the president called it. Claiming that the Soviets led in nuclear strike forces, the president pushed a huge nuclear arms buildup and then announced a revolutionary new defense strategy. In part a response to a growing antinuclear peace movement in the United States and Western Europe and continued deployment of missiles in Eastern Europe, the Strategic Defense Initiative (SDI) aimed through exotic outer space weapons such as laser beams to cripple any attacking rocket force. Portrayed as a shield against nuclear war, this "Star Wars" scheme promised survival from a nuclear attack and the ability to retaliate. But the Soviet Union claimed that its purpose was to allow the United States to launch a first strike and then survive any retaliation.

The SDI assured two benefits for America. Huge government investment in computer, laser, and other weaponry guaranteed new inventions and technological breakthroughs for industry. Given American technological superiority, it would force the Soviet Union to direct even larger funds into an already bloated defense budget, thus intensifying the severe economic problems of that nation.

Finally, Reagan assembled an able group of arms negotiators that was wary of making any agreement with the Soviets. Backed by defense secretary Caspar Weinberger, such men as Richard Perle, assistant secretary of defense and a leading arms control expert, made it clear that the Reagan administration was reluctant to sign any treaty at all.

The Reagan administration's anticommunism also led it into active attempts to roll back Soviet influence in the Third World. Thus the United States supported antigovernment forces in Afghanistan, Cambodia, Angola, Ethiopia, and Nicaragua, countries either dependent on or directly influenced by the Soviet Union.

To justify this policy, the administration accepted United Nations ambassador Jeane Kirkpatrick's distinction between authoritarian and totalitarian states. While certainly reprehensible, the former type, she declared, deserved qualified U.S. support because such governments could evolve in democratic directions. Translated into policy, this implied toleration for the apartheid regime of South Africa and dictatorships in the Philippines and South America. But in the world of political realities, this distinction proved elusive. Bitter opposition inside the United States prevented any closer ties with South Africa. In fact, college students forced universities to divest themselves of South African stock holdings. When dictator Ferdinand Marcos finally fled the Philippines after losing an election to Corazon Aquino in early 1986, the United States could even take some credit for this outcome.

TERRORISM

Terrorism was another matter that evoked deep political consequences. Terrorism had several definitions, depending on the context. It meant kidnapping and hostage taking, as when Iranians seized the American embassy in 1979. It applied to the tactics of the Libyan government, which encouraged clandestine attacks on American officials, soldiers, and tourists in the Middle East. It applied to Palestine Liberation Organization assaults on Israeli soldiers and civilians. In general, it described the tactics of indirect military confrontation practiced by states or groups hostile to the United States but far too weak to risk a direct confrontation.

Some of the president's advisers encouraged the belief that the Soviet Union and its allies secretly sponsored terrorism. This theory received an inconclusive test in the long trial of several Bulgarians in Italy for their alleged participation in a plot to assassinate Pope John Paul II. An Italian court eventually acquitted them in 1986. But some members of the administration continued to implicate Russians, Cubans, and eastern Europeans in the training of terrorists for hit-and-run warfare against American allies.

But terrorism was no imaginary issue. Standing tall in the Middle East unfortunately made Americans a target precisely because of the unorthodox tactics of guerrilla warfare in the region. When Lebanon erupted into civil war and threatened to disintegrate under pressure from neighbors Israel and Syria, the Reagan administration sent a peacekeeping force of marines to Beirut. In October 1983 a truck filled with explosives slammed into an American bivouac at the Beirut airport, killing 241 marines. Despite the folly of placing American troops at such risk, there were few recriminations. The administration quickly withdrew remaining troops to offshore ships.

INTERVENTION

The administration did win applause for its invasion of the Caribbean island of Grenada in October 1983. Beset by internal struggles and growing Cuban influence, Grenada seemed a perfect place to pursue the Reagan doctrine of turning back Soviet influence in the Third World. The brief skirmish between 10,000 American troops and a ragtag collection of Cuban militia advisers was hailed by Reagan as a major turning point in American policy. Many Americans were sure he was right.

A much more intractable problem was Nicaragua. Its history, like that of much of Central America, was written in economic misery, instability, dictatorship, and periodic United States interventions. When rebel forces known as the Sandinistas overthrew the ruthless Somoza regime in 1979, there was optimism for Nicaragua. But as the new regime swerved left politically, it aroused internal opposition and American hostility. Support for revolutionary groups in neighboring countries convinced some American policy makers to oppose the new Nicaraguan government and even finance its overthrow. Others, however, were willing to tolerate a nation friendly to the Soviet Union, provided it did not try to export revolution.

After the Reagan administration took office in 1981, however, it gave secret military assistance to the Contras, an army of old Somoza loyalists aided by Nicaraguans disenchanted with the Sandinistas. But CIA implication in mining the Nicaraguan harbor of Managua in 1983, and, in particular, a CIA training manual advising rebels "to neutralize" Nicaraguan officials with "selective use of violence" exposed the operation. In the same year, Congress passed the Boland Amendment, forbidding the administration to supply funds to the Contras.

THE IRAN-CONTRA AFFAIR

It was the genius and folly of President Reagan's leading advisers, William Casey, Robert McFarlane (head of the National Security Council), and Admiral John Poindexter (McFarlane's replacement), and Poindexter's assistant Lieutenant-Colonel Oliver North, to compound problems in the Middle East and Nicaragua by linking them together. In the process, they helped rescue two American hostages held by pro-Iranians in Lebanon, but the events shattered confidence in the president's leadership and competence.

WHO IS SWEARING IN WHOM? Witness Colonel Oliver North is sworn in by Senator Daniel Inouye at the Iran-Contra hearings during the summer of 1987. North's testimony was so successful that it seemed to place the Senate itself on trial.

The complicated intrigue known as the Iran-Contra affair began in the context of a long and bitter war between Iran and Iraq. Fought around the periphery of the world's richest oil reserves, the war was intensified by superpower interference. Iraq received arms from the Soviet Union and several Western countries. Because of Iran's extreme hostility to its pro-American neighbors and bitterness to the United States, it had difficulty securing arms.

Catching the ear of North and McFarlane, several shadowy Iranian and Israeli arms dealers proposed a complicated transaction. If the United States agreed to sell arms to Iran, the Iranians would help secure the freedom of several American hostages held in Lebanon. In their defense, it is possible that North, McFarlane, Reagan, and other administration officials convinced themselves that they were, in fact, also encouraging opponents of the militantly hostile Iranian leader, the Ayatollah Khomeini.

To execute this arrangement required presidential approval, particularly since it represented a dramatic contradiction of stated refusals to deal with terrorists. Hoping to keep the affair a secret, in early 1986 the president signed a finding, or a document legitimizing this policy change. Congress and the American people were not informed, and Secretary of State George Shultz and defense secretary Weinberger distanced themselves from a policy they disapproved of but declined to fight.

The second phase of the affair emerged when North, Casey, and others determined to send profits from arms sales as secret aid for the Contras. Although such transactions clearly violated the Boland Amendment, the administration had already waded deeply into operations in the gray areas of this prohibition. North and others also used their contacts with wealthy conservative supporters to solicit private funds for the Contras.

Unfortunately for these secret operations, a small Beirut weekly, *Al Shirra*, acting on a tip from the Iranians, published a story on November 3, 1986, disclosing the Iranian leg of the operation. Two days later, the story splashed across American newspapers, and the administration moved quickly to control political damage. At first, the president issued denials that the United States had swapped arms for hostages. On November 13, 1986, Reagan declared, "We did not—repeat—did not trade weapons or anything else for hostages—nor will we." Whatever the administration called the deal, however, after the Reverend Lawrence Jenco was freed on July 26, 1986, the United States had delivered Hawk missile spare parts to the Iranians on August 3. When David Jacobsen was released November 2, 1986, the Iranians received 500 TOW missiles.

But there was more. On November 15, 1986, Attorney General Meese revealed that funds from the arms sales had been secretly credited to Nicaraguan Contra bank accounts. Moving to protect the president, the administration fired North and replaced Poindexter. Since October, however, North had been using his office paper shredder to destroy incriminating documents.

Eventually, four investigating bodies sprang up to explore the enormously complex events: two congressional committees, a special commission headed by former senator John Tower of Texas to explore the workings of the National Security Council, and a special prosecutor, Lawrence Walsh, to prepare whatever criminal indictments might be warranted.

As evidence accumulated over the spring and summer of 1987, it became clear that the Iran-Contra affair was both comic opera and a miserable misjudgment. Tales of escapades ranging from U.S. officials carrying a chocolate cake and a Bible inscribed by President Reagan on a secret trip to Iran, to deals with shady arms merchants revealed an administration drawn into plotting with men craftier than they. American foreign policy was being conducted in secret, by private citizens, sleazy gun runners, and fake experts and profiteers. Still, Colonel North defended his actions before Congress in the summer of 1987: "I saw the idea of using the Ayatollah Khomeini's money to support the Nicaraguan freedom fighters as a good one. I still do. I don't think it was wrong. I think it was a neat idea."

It was also an idea that threatened the presidency itself. The Tower commission, when it reported in February 1987, criticized Reagan's "personal management style" and faulted Casey, Shultz, and Weinberger, as well as Poindexter and North. Finding no firm evidence that the president knew about the secret funding of the Contras, it chided him for *not* knowing, for not exercising more control over foreign policy.

Senate and House hearings over the summer exposed even more dreary details. But they also provided Poindexter, North, and others with a forum to preach their pro-Contra cause. North in particular proved to be a difficult witness. Claiming a higher purpose to justify his actions, he disarmed the legislators, becoming a momentary television celebrity. This success dampened the enthusiasm of Congress for the investigation. There were no answers to what everyone wanted to know: What did the president know and when did he know it? Even the trial and conviction of Oliver North on three felony counts in early 1989 only provided tantalizing hints that the president and Vice President Bush had known far more than they admitted.

SUMMIT WITH GORBACHEV

As several presidents before him had, Reagan gained immensely from successful negotiations with the Soviet Union. A summit conference, held in December 1987, brought Mikhail Gorbachev, general secretary of the Soviet Communist party, to Washington to sign the Intermediate Nuclear Forces Agreement (INF treaty) reducing mid-range nuclear missiles. Both Gorbachev and Reagan used this meeting to reinforce their shaky personal power. For different reasons, both needed a foreign policy success. But the compromise also meant reversal of long-standing policies. The Soviets dropped their opposition to on-site arms inspections enforcing the treaty. They agreed to destroy many more missiles than the United States. They dampened their strong opposition to SDI research and deployment. Reagan paid the price of cutting his ties to the extreme right wing, replacing a large number of

AFTER THE AMERICAN ELECTION OF 1988, General Secretary Gorbachev of the Soviet Union, President Reagan, and President-elect Bush met in New York. In the last years of his second term, Reagan established a close relationship with Gorbachev. Bush, in the photograph, still seems the outsider.

very conservative members of his administration with moderates.

This ideological winnowing had already begun shortly after the Iran-Contra affair. The day after the Tower commission released its report in February 1987, White House Chief of Staff Donald Regan resigned, and former Republican senator Howard Baker, a moderate, replaced him. William Casey also quit the CIA in February, and in early March the acerbic and combative Patrick J. Buchanan resigned as communications director. Shortly before the Washington summit, other advocates of a rigid line toward Soviet negotiations, including Weinberger and arms expert Richard Perle, left the administration. Their departure and the summit aroused an acrimonious split on the Republican right, with such former allies as political commentator Howard Phillips calling Reagan a "useful idiot" of Soviet propaganda.

Reagan's new, more moderate attitude to the Soviet Union seemed to betray his crusading anti-communist career. But the summit could also be considered a success of that stubborn position. Faced with the impossible predicament of increased arms competition with the United States, severe economic problems, and a desire to liberalize their society, the Soviet Union under Gorbachev wanted a compromise. They found a president willing to change.

There were other foreign policy successes. In May 1988 the Soviet Union, under immense pressure, finally agreed to withdraw its troops from Afghanistan. Rising casualties, drooping troop morale, and persistent, deadly attacks by guerrillas supplied with American weapons persuaded the Soviet Union to call its soldiers home. In southern Africa, a fragile peace was negotiated between Angola and South Africa in a very complex war. In April 1988 the Sandinistas of Nicaragua agreed to negotiate with the rebel Contras. Although the Reagan administration opposed some of the terms of this slippery cease-fire, it remained bound by congressional purse strings to uphold them. Finally, in the summer of 1988, Iran and Iraq signed a cease-fire to end their bloody eight-year war. Again,

the United States had at least an indirect hand in this settlement.

--==◉==--

THE REAGAN RECORD

Whatever the immediate reasons, the president's flexibility was entirely in character, for he often compromised in the face of difficulties. Determined in 1980 to dismantle the welfare state, he only chipped away at its weakest points and probably even strengthened support for certain programs like Social Security. Pledged to revolutionize the American economy, to make it freer and more competitive, he contained inflation but presided over the worst budget and trade deficits in American history. Promising to restore morality and traditional family values, he shrank from the serious political battles that might have advanced the program of the evangelical right. Determined to fight communism, he recognized the great-power stature of the Soviet Union.

Hoping for a major political realignment, the president built no great new coalition. Unlike Roosevelt and Eisenhower, two previous popular presidents, his elections did not bring out increasing numbers of voters. Participation in national elections hovered at around 50 percent of eligible voters in 1980 and 1984. In effect, this confirmed a growing trend in American politics for potential voters to drop out and for the electorate to consist of special groups, tied to a candidate but not a party. In a curious way, the electorate had become like an audience and the old parties operated more and more according to the dictates of the mass media.

Finally, the president did nothing to lower the expectations of Americans for their national government. By succeeding with intangibles, by allowing Americans to feel better about themselves and their national stature, without substantial reasons, Reagan continued and even exaggerated the affirmative bluster of his boyhood hero, Franklin Roosevelt, with his promises to awaken the American spirit. Yet difficult problems remained: the economy, the arms race, global com-

THE VIETNAM MEMORIAL in Washington, D.C., captured here on Memorial Day, 1987, evoked strong emotions and tearful reunions of veterans grieving for lost comrades.

petition, and the poor fit between morality and social change, poverty, problems of race and class. Scandal after scandal washed over the administration, the most serious and persistent involving the attorney general, Edwin Meese, and his lax behavior toward friends seeking special favors.

As the case of Baby M demonstrated in microcosm, the changing possibilities of technology and evolving sexual and social mores undercut tradition. Aggravated by the discrepancy between unequal power of individuals and abstract equal rights, this case tested the ability of Americans to come to terms with a new world of possibilities and risks. Was belief in the marketplace or traditional morality adequate to cope with the emerging world of the 1980s? In fact, neither helped very much in deciding this complex contest between two very different families, the Whiteheads and the Sterns. Such questions remained for the newly elected president, George Bush, to face.

⋆╼◉╾⋆

CHRONOLOGY

1981 (Jan.) Iran hostage crisis ends;

Ronald Reagan assumes presidency;

(Mar. 30) Assassination attempt against Reagan;

(Aug. 14) Tax reform act cuts income taxes by 25 percent

1983 Strategic Defense Initiative announced;

Boland Amendment prohibiting military aid to Contras passed;

(Oct.) Attack on marines in Beirut;

(Oct.) Invasion of island of Grenada

1984(June) Tax act raising $50 billion in revenues;

(Dec.) Bernhard Goetz shoots four black youths in New York subway

1985(June) Live Aid concert

1986 President Reagan authorizes secret arms shipments to Iran;

1986
(Cont'd)

(Mar. 27) Baby M is born;

(May) Hands Across America;

(Oct.) Tax reform act of 1986;

Immigration Reform and Control Act;

(Nov.) Iran-Contra affair disclosed

1987 AIDS recognized as a leading infectious disease worldwide;

(Mar. 31) Baby M decision grants sole custody of Melissa to the Sterns;

(Summer) Iran-Contra hearings in Congress;

(Oct. 19) Stock market crash;

(Dec.) Washington summit; INF treaty signed

1987–1988 Scandals rock televangelist ministries;

(Nov.) George Bush elected president

⋆╼◉╾⋆

SUGGESTIONS FOR FURTHER READING

BABY M

Mary Beth Whitehead tells her story in *Mother's Story* (1989). A feminist critique of surrogate motherhood is Phyllis Chesler, *Sacred Bond: The Legacy of Baby M* (1988); see also Rochelle Sharp, *The Case of Baby M: And the Facts of Life* (1989). For a defense of surrogate motherhood, see Carmel Shalev, *Birth Power: the Case for Surrogacy* (New Haven: Yale University Press, 1989). In the aftermath of the Baby M case, other surrogate mothers have published books about their experiences: Patricia Adair, *A Surrogate Mother's Story* (1987), and Elizabeth Kane, *Birth Mother: The Story of America's First Legal Surrogate Mother* (1988). Five years before Baby M was born, the broker who owned the company that arranged her birth (The Infertility Center of New York) published a book promoting surrogate motherhood: Noel P. Keane with Dennis L. Breo, *The Surrogate Mother* (1981); see also Lori B. Andrews, *New Conceptions: A Consumer's Guide to the Newest Infertil-* *ity Treatments* (1984). The general issues raised by the Baby M case are discussed in Martha A. Field, *Surrogate Motherhood* (1988); Thomas A. Shannon, *Surrogate Motherhood: the Ethics of Using Human Beings* (1988); Michael and Heather Humphrey, *Families with a Difference: Varieties of Surrogate Parenthood* (1988); Scott B. Rae, *The Ethics of Commercial Surrogate Motherhood: Brave New Families?* (1994); and Larry Gostin, ed., *Surrogate Motherhood: Politics and Privacy* (1990).

THE EIGHTIES AND BEYOND

Inevitably, the literature for the 1980s, particularly the social and cultural history of the decade, is incomplete. One book that touches all the aspects of this period, William Chafe, *The Unfinished Journey: America Since World War II* (1986), provides a beginning. *Habits of the Heart: Individualism and Commitment in American Life* (1985) by Robert N. Bellah and others is a fascinating exploration of the moral resources of Americans in the 1980s.

RONALD REAGAN

Two books on Ronald Reagan offer particularly interesting discussions of culture and politics in contemporary society. They are Michael Rogin, *Ronald Reagan, the Movie, and Other Episodes in Political Demonology* (1987), and George Will, *The Morning After: American Success and Excess, 1981–1986* (1986). Of two older biographies of Ronald Reagan, the best is Lou Cannon, *Reagan* (1982). Robert Dallek in *Ronald Reagan: The Politics of Symbolism* (1984) explores the relationship of the president with political symbolism. Perhaps the best and most persuasive inside story of Reagan's early successes is Rowland Evans and Robert Novak, *The Reagan Revolution* (1981). To catch a flavor of the president's words, it is instructive to read collections of his speeches. One such is *The Triumph of the American Spirit* (1984), edited by Emil Area and Gregory J. Pamel. A fine analysis of the crucial election of 1984 in an interesting collection of essays is Theodore Lowi, "An Aligning Election, a Presidential Plebiscite," in Michael Nelson, ed., *The Elections of 1984* (1985). Two liberal appraisals of the Reagan years are Joel Krieger, *Reagan, Thatcher, and the Politics of Decline* (1986), and Robert Lekachman, *Visions and Nightmares: America After Reagan* (1987). An excellent, critical book is Sidney Blumenthal's, *Our Long National Daydream: A Political Pageant of the Reagan Era* (1988). Gary Wills in *Reagan's America* (1988) outlines some of the broader ramifications of the 1980s. Finally, Haynes Johnson's *Sleepwalking Through History: America in the Reagan Years* (1992) sketches the political and social implications of the Reagan presidency.

Undoubtedly there will be more books from former aides and administration officials. Several of these kiss-and-tell memoirs have painted a curious, often acrimonious White House. So far the best of these is David A. Stockman's very self-serving, very interesting *The Triumph of Politics: How the Reagan Revolution Failed* (1986). Presidential assistant Michael K. Deaver in *Behind the Scenes* (1987) and former chief of staff Donald T. Regan, *For the Record: From Wall Street to Washington* (1988), reveal a good deal of the infighting in the administration from their perspective. Ronald Reagan's own story is disappointing, *An American Life* (1990).

American Diversity

THE EPISODE: Late on a spring night in Los Angeles in 1991, a young black man was apprehended for dangerous and drunk driving. While being taken into custody he was beaten by several police officers. Unbeknownst to them, almost the entire event was captured by an amateur photographer with a videocassette recorder. The next night, television audiences in Los Angeles saw in the grainy, shadowy light, the gruesome beating. The following evening, the video was broadcast over the national television networks. All of America itself had become a witness.

About a year later, the four Los Angeles Police Department officers involved in the arrest were tried in a California state court. The verdict was not guilty. When this result was announced, pandemonium and riot engulfed Los Angeles. Thousands of black and Hispanic Angelenos took to the streets to denounce the courts and the police, to loot and burn stores and businesses. Their anger and violence uncovered deep and abiding deformities in American society.

THE HISTORICAL SETTING: Despite the political success of Ronald Reagan's presidency, the years that followed were unsettling and contentious. Historians and politicians have agreed that the promise of those years was undermined by economic failing: a severe recession at the beginning of the 1990s and the continued inability of large numbers of poor people to rise above the inadequate and unpromising future they faced. Neither decades of reform nor an era of conservatism had succeeded. By 1989 and the beginning of the presidency of George Bush, division and inequality had intensified and deepened across America.

When tolerance faded and intolerance became politically fashionable and effective, the stage was set for inaction. Issues based on gender, race, and class erupted into political campaigns and became the subject of television dramas and films. Within a setting of increasing violence on city streets and in schools, with rising fears of crime, politics became edgy and quick to decline into name calling and recrimination. For the four years of George Bush's presidency, the Democratic Congress fought the Republican presidency to a standstill and neither side established a clear, consistent program. Of course, not all Americans lived on the frayed edges of uncertainty. But there were moments when the America that seemed to be emerging from the new immigration, from transformed cities and suburbs, from the behavior and culture of young people, was incomprehensible and even threatening. The rapid division of nations and alliances around the world into acrimonious and contending parts only underscored this feeling.

It was into this social and political world that Bill Clinton brought his buoyant but flawed presidency. Deeply committed to change, to making his government "look like America" in terms of ethnicity and gender, he found that goodwill, ideas, and enthusiasm did not necessarily move a lethargic bureaucracy, a divided Congress, and an uncertain nation.

WITNESSING

With two other companions, Rodney King drove his 1988 Korean-made Hyundai erratically down the Hillside Freeway in Northeast San Fernando Valley in the early morning of Sunday, March 3, 1991. He had had far too much to drink, and his foot was heavy on the gas pedal. A patrol car noticed his speed and accelerated after him with siren blaring. King saw the car, but didn't stop; if he was arrested now it would violate his parole for armed robbery. He would have to return to jail just when he had finally landed a job. There was no alternative. He shot off the freeway trying to elude the police, and raced along Hillside Boulevard. In the meantime, the patrol car radioed for backup: more officers and an LAPD (Los Angeles Police Department) helicopter. King plunged on, running several red lights and obviously speeding dangerously. Finally, a patrol car pulled alongside him and an officer shouted through a loud speaker ordering him to pull over. He complied.

As the car and its entourage of ten pursuing vehicles drew up outside the Lake View Terrace apartments, the commotion, sirens, headlights, and the aggressive chop of the helicopter hovering above woke several residents of the apartment building. George Holliday went to the window, looked at the scene under him, and then, reaching for his new Sonycam hand video camera, stepped out onto the balcony. He could clearly see a single black man, crouching on the ground and encircled by several officers who appeared to be striking him with police batons.

At first, King had refused to step out of the car, although his companions did. When he pulled himself out, several officers had their metal batons ready. What happened in the next moments is unclear. The police officers contended that he made a threatening gesture as if to pull a weapon or lunge at them, although none of the several witnesses watching the fracas from their apartments confirmed this. George Holliday's camera was not yet running. But King appeared to be resisting arrest and so the officers began to swing their batons, one stroke after another. At this moment, George Holliday turned on his video camera.

One of the officers moved close to King with a Taser—a stun gun capable of focusing a jolt of 50,000 volts. He shot King once in the chest. King was now desperate and tried to regain his feet. More blows rained down on him: on his legs, his body and his face. He was shot a second time with the Taser, kicked, clubbed, and finally handcuffed. Officer Laurence Powell delivered most of the blows, aided by Officer Timothy Wind. Officer Ted Briseno struck King once and then tried, hesitantly, to get his fellow officers to stop. Sergeant Stacey Koon, the officer in command, did not interfere.

Pushing King into a squad car, the officers began their drive back to police headquarters. They also phoned in their whereabouts and activities to the dispatcher. When they arrived, they booked King and filed their report. An aggressive, drunken driver had resisted arrest and had to be subdued. They then drove King to the hospital and explained to the doctor that he had been high on PCPs (hallucinogenic drugs). The doctor found no evidence of drugs, although he noted that King's blood alcohol level was high. But King was obviously seriously hurt. He had a broken leg, a fractured skull and fractured right eye socket, which gave him blurred vision, and partial paralysis of his face due to neurological damage. As King later told a grand jury, one officer at the hospital asked him what he remembered. King remained silent. "Well," the officer explained, "we played a little ball tonight, and guess who won? We did."

In custody and recovering, King was as unaware as the LAPD police officers that much of what happened had been captured on film. George Holliday, realizing the news value of what he had recorded, took the video the next day to a local TV station, KTLA, and sold it to them for $500. The first airing of the film was on Monday, March 4. By the next evening, CNN and the major national networks had played the film. What it showed was clear enough: a man lying on the ground was being beaten repeatedly by police officers.

To say that a great many Americans were shocked by the brutality of what they saw is certainly true. But it is also true that responses were shaped and shaded by other feelings, beliefs, and agendas. Clearly, different portions of the population saw the event differently. To black leaders, the beating and arrest of Rodney King was incontrovertible evidence of the disheartening prejudice that every African American confronted: the unwarranted assumption that all black men were potential criminals, that one had to prove one's innocence and good intentions to gain toleration by white Americans. To other black Americans, the filmed scenes repeated what they had seen or heard about: police brutality, false arrest, and disrespect that was a constant fact of life. Other groups such as Latinos or gay men also recognized a similarity in their confrontations with police. But from first to last, the Rodney King incident was construed as an issue of race, however much other groups were drawn in later.

To politicians preparing for the nomination and run-up to the presidential and congressional election of 1992, outrage was a political emotion that had to be tempered by some larger message and placed within a context that would attract potential voters. It had to confirm and support the position taken by the candidate on related issues of law enforcement. With a majority of American voters deeply distressed by crime and violence and a building drive for harsher punishment of criminals, there was substantial support for tough police reaction. That sentiment was captured in the powerful metaphor of "the thin blue line." This simply meant the line of police standing between the innocent majority and the violent, criminal minority. It was thin because it was fragile, a defense of last resort. Yet the graphic film of Rodney King seemed to contradict the positive impressions that many Americans had about the police.

In Los Angeles, the Holliday film played as a finale to a long-running confrontation between the two most powerful political leaders in the city: Daryl Gates, the white chief of police, and Tom Bradley, the black mayor. Both were long-entrenched political figures. Bradley had become mayor in 1973 after a career in the city council and, before that, in the police force. Gates, born and raised in Glendale, had joined the force in 1949 and worked his way through the ranks to the top position in 1978. Both were powerful men, and comfortable with their power. Increasingly, each saw the other as a bitter and uncompromising rival.

In this instance, however, they seemed to agree. Even Gates blamed the officers for the beating, and especially Stacey Koon for not halting it. He promised a swift internal investigation and prosecution for any wrongdoing. But he also carefully tried to isolate the event from the police force as a whole and from himself. "This is an aberration. This is something that should never have happened," he argued. With a history of thoughtless remarks about ethnic groups in the city, Gates intended to accept no blame for what many were calling the blatant racism of the LAPD. Mayor Bradley also placed his shock inside a political agenda. "There is a need for all of us," he said, "to recognize that the city draws its strength from its diversity, and that we will not let an incident of this kind divide us or cause us problems based on our neighborhoods or backgrounds." Understandably, Bradley wished to maintain peace among the very different ethnic elements of the city who had elected him. Behind the cameras and news releases, however, Gates and Bradley were furious at each other, and their long feud became sharper and more focused. Bradley was determined to force Gates to resign and Gates was just as determined to remain.

For many Americans there was another sort of reaction, mixed with shock. This was disbelief that Los Angeles could be a city of such open brutality. For years there had been an undercurrent of cynicism about Los Angeles, pictured in novels like the brooding detective mysteries of Raymond Chandler. More recently the cult film *Blade Runner* (1982) portrayed a futuristic Los Angeles overwhelmed by ecological and social disaster and presided over by ruthless and predatory corporations. But to most Americans, Los Angeles was still the city of bright futures: of two cars, a stucco house, a lawn, and Hollywood—an achievable American dream—shaped in Walt Disney's "imageering" studios and available to the hard-working and the fortunate.

The Los Angeles that produced both the images of success and wish fulfillment as well as the Rodney King beating was nothing if not paradoxical. A small town until the twentieth century in a state dominated by San Francisco, Los Angeles lacked water. It had no natural port like those at San Francisco or San Diego. It had no navigable rivers. It sat astride no extensive transportation system. It tapped only a sparse rural population. All of these basic elements of infrastructure had to be invented and constructed. Los Angeles, because of timing and location, also missed the large influx of early twentieth century immigration from eastern and southern Europe. Its initial population was Hispanic, mixed with white immigrants from the Midwest. Later a sizable number of African Americans moved to the area to work in the heavy industries attracted to the city in the 1930s and 1940s.

By World War II, Los Angeles had transformed its deficiencies into resources. It constructed an artificial port; it diverted huge amounts of water from northern California; it developed an extensive and efficient internal electric rail system; it built a vibrant downtown with commercial and cultural institutions. It also attracted a significant manufacturing base in rubber tires, aeronautics, steel, and other basic industries. Its climate, job opportunities, and location as the hub of Western economic vitality, led to a huge population boom. If not a typical American city, it became, nonetheless, a successful variant on the model.

After the war, Los Angeles benefited extensively from a variety of federal subsidies and income transfers. The G.I. bill made low-cost housing affordable to large numbers of newcomers to the city, sparking a housing and real estate boom whose momentum carried all the way through into the 1990s. Federal and state aid, sought by city boosters, built the extensive network of freeways that tied the identity of the city, even more than elsewhere, to the automobile. Its first-rate public transportation system was allowed to collapse, and Angelenos led the nation in experimenting with the use of automobiles for shopping, leisure, and entertainment—indeed, almost every activity of life at one time or another had its "drive-in" variant born in Los Angeles. A further great subsidy was for military production. The cold war federal budgets brought thousands of jobs to the area in terms of military bases, aircraft factories, and later, high-tech computer and information industries. Paid for in large measure by skimming tax revenues elsewhere, this federal largesse contributed hugely to the boom, making the city one of the most attractive places for industry and people to locate. As a result the original city of Los Angeles spilled out and blanketed the surrounding valleys with developments, housing projects, and mini-urban centers, creating a confusing patchwork of communities and industrial zones. Gradually, the old center of the city declined, as it did in all American cities, and the thrust of economic activity shifted to peripheral areas, to suburban light manufacturing and service industries. Tract housing and "freeway" industrial parks moved north, east and south. Orange County, in particular, on the southern edge of the city, attracted thriving new information-oriented industries and a highly skilled, affluent population.

By the time of the Watts riots in 1965 [see Chapter 25], Los Angeles had achieved a profile of economic and demographic specialization that concentrated the city's relatively small African-American population in the South Central and downtown areas around declining manufacturing enterprises and a decayed retail and commercial center that businesses abandoned in favor of suburban locations. Among the consequences of the Watts riots was an acceleration of this spatial differentiation as more affluent (and usually white) residents fled what they considered dangerous and declining urban areas. At the same time the city elected Tom Bradley mayor in 1973, the first African American to hold that position.

Bradley's promise to unite the population of the city in an endeavor of progress inspired many citizens. But so did tough, law-and-order, career policeman Daryl Gates, who assumed leadership of the police department in 1978. Because of singular restrictions in the Los Angeles City code, the police chief had unusual powers and protection from political interference. As a civil servant, Gates was practically immune to removal from office. Increasingly, his strong words and controversial acts as police chief placed him at odds with Bradley and helped polarize city government between two strong-willed, politically astute men.

Reorganizing the city police force, Gates emphasized mobile striking units, response speed, airborne surveillance, and SWAT teams. In a freeway city, with few sidewalks and a dispersed population, this strategy of law enforcement made some sense. So too did Gates's various initiatives against drug distribution and gang warfare. Black and Latino—and to a lesser extent—Anglo and Asian gangs, were responsible for an increasing amount of crime and violence in the city, and Gates targeted them for police attention.

Yet Gates did little to end the antipathy between the police and the black and Latino communities that often made law enforcement difficult or impossible. Cited as major causes of the 1965 riots, police brutality and disrespect were repeatedly mentioned by the black population, rich and poor, as aggravating factors in the riots. According to one survey taken in 1965, almost one-third of African Americans had been stopped and searched without provocation, and about half had seen it happen to someone else. About 15 percent reported seeing someone beaten during an arrest. The police chief's tough words only exacerbated the difficult situation. For example when the city council outlawed the controversial carotid throat hold practiced by police to subdue suspects, Gates thoughtlessly provoked hostile reaction in the city with his remarks: "We may be finding that in some blacks when (the carotid hold) is applied the veins or arteries do not open up as fast as they do on normal people." Many black Angelenos perceived that the police and much of the white population treated them as criminal suspects first and citizens second, and Gates provided the proof.

After the Rodney King beating, a joint commission with members appointed by Gates and Bradley and headed by Warren Christopher (later President Clinton's secretary of state), studied the LAPD. The Christopher Report, issued in July 1991, sharply criticized the police department and especially Gates, calling for less emphasis on high-tech equipment and more sensitivity to the feelings of minorities. It also advised a change in strategy to employ community policing, which was used elsewhere to bring police officers into daily contact with citizens. Most important, the report suggested that Gates retire. In unmistakable terms, the commission placed heavy blame on the police department for its troubled relations with blacks and Latinos in the city. "The commission also found that the problem of excessive force is aggravated by racism and bias." Impotent to follow this advice and remove Gates, Bradley stopped speaking to the chief, even in private.

THE RIOTS IN LOS ANGELES pockmarked the glittering international reputation of the city and created extraordinary vistas of contrast.

Elected in part to maintain social peace in Los Angeles, Mayor Bradley could do little to stop or even divert the strong economic and demographic forces that were transforming Los Angeles once more—this time into a global city of immense power and importance. Bradley did assist some of the economic groups seeking to revitalize the downtown area. When this was accomplished during the 1980s, Los Angeles could boast of a gleaming new center of corporate headquarters, commerce, and culture, and the new service jobs that went with it. The mayor also successfully pushed for a new light rail and subway system to restore public rapid transit. But there were costs to this strategy of urban renewal. State limits on real estate taxation rates and the continued disintegration of the local tax base severely limited expenditures for schools, libraries, and recreational institutions—the traditional, low-key community institutions of culture that bolstered social order and opportunity. In fact, despite Bradley's commitment to a diverse and equal society, Los Angeles by 1991 was far more a city of contrasts, of poverty and wealth, divided populations and divided spaces, than it had been in 1973 when he took office.

As Los Angeles assumed its new identity in the 1970s and 1980s as a global city, it was exposed to the benefits as well as the defaults of economic competition on the Pacific Rim. Japanese capital flowed into the city, particularly in real estate, banking, and the entertainment industry. About 20 percent of all Japanese real estate investment pouring into the United States concentrated in the Los Angeles area. By 1988, almost 70 percent of downtown real estate was held by foreigners. Perhaps more striking symbolically than economically was the purchase in 1989 by the Japanese Sony corporation of Columbia Pictures, with its vast holdings of old film and television shows.

This inflow of capital was only one noteworthy force reshaping the Los Angeles economy. Another came from competition with very efficient sectors of Japanese, Korean, and Southeast Asian economies. Basic industries declined abruptly and good-paying industrial and union jobs evaporated. Work became increasingly concentrated in high-paying managerial and technical employment located in suburban areas and low-wage service and sweatshop jobs in the central city. By the end of the 1980s the reduction in defense spending had cut further into the industrial base. At the same time, income became less equitably distributed. Those earning $50,000 per year or more rose to 26 percent of the population; the middle class, earning between $16,000 and $49,000, fell to around 32 percent; and the poor, receiving $15,000 or less, reached almost 40 percent of families. The severe recession of the early 1990s exaggerated these divisions. The result, for South Central Los Angeles and several other areas of the city, was very high unemployment, high percentages of female-headed, single-income families, and impoverished children.

In his autobiographical self-defense, *Chief: My Life in the LAPD*, Gates noted, "Driving to work in 1992, I pass through a Los Angeles that my parents would hardly recognize." He explained: "The influx of Hispanics and Asians continues. Many of my condominium neighbors are Asian; other parts of Highland Park are predominately Hispanic." Gates's comments acknowledged the most striking, visual transformation of Los Angeles in its new guise as a world city. By 1990, 40 percent of the city was foreign-born and almost half of its citizens did not speak English at home. In that year

General Ethnic Group Makeup of Los Angeles, 1990

Ethnic Group	Percent of Population
Latino	40%
Anglo	37%
Black	13%
Asian	10%

Source: United States Census, 1990.

the United States Census[1] revealed that Latinos were the largest portion of the population, with the number of Asians growing rapidly. Surrounding Los Angeles county showed much the same demographic profile, with the most dynamic growth in the Latino and Asian populations.

While there was considerable ethnic mixing in many parts of the city and county communities, most Asians, blacks, and Latinos were concentrated in limited areas. But even in these areas change piled upon change. South Central, which had been primarily black, now had a majority of Latino residents. Slightly north of this section was Koreatown, an area with a high concentration of recent Korean immigrants. This dynamic group of fresh arrivals to the United States, using family capital and loans from fellow countrymen, had established an extensive network of small groceries and other retail stores, including "swap-meets" (indoor flea markets) throughout South Central Los Angeles and in other less affluent areas. They provided minimal goods and services to areas that lacked the national chain-store outlets and competition of the suburbs. The result was some limited shopping opportunities, but with significantly higher prices—perhaps 30 percent for groceries—and less choice. Perhaps inevitably, there was a revival of traditional tension between poor residents and marginal shopkeepers—the sort of antipathy that had resulted in widespread looting and arson of hundreds of businesses owned by whites during the 1965 riots.

The concentration of population by ethnicity and income was pulled by the lure of newer, ever more handsome or affordable housing, shopping centers, and freeways, but also pushed by the desire of affluent whites to escape the city, crime, and integrated public schools. Sometimes the extremes of flight and exclusivity resulted in gated municipalities such as Rolling Hills, where only residents, their guests, or delivery men could enter. Blockaded streets, surveillance machines, and private, armed patrols came into increasing use in other communities. A few houses even sported alarm systems and signs that promised "Armed Response!" While these examples are uncommon, they point to the very real separation of residential spaces in the city. Public spaces in the poorer sections of the city where people congregated continued to be the city streets, parks, and small stores and mini-malls. Space in the suburbs and more affluent areas

---

[1]*The Census demographic categories make no sense upon close examination. For example, they group an Argentinian of Italian background and a Mexican of Mayan heritage together as Hispanic. They define the child of a mixed race, white and black couple as African American.*

THIS MOCK ASSYRIAN FORTRESS was built in 1929 for the Samson Tyre Co. during the great manufacturing boom in Los Angeles. In 1986, it was redeveloped as a modern mixed-use convention center and outlet store mall. As project designer Fernando Vazquez said "It's about movies, fantasy, about celebrating the outdoors. . . . Here manufacturing meets entertainment."

tended to be semipublic: enclosed shopping centers and malls with private or restricted recreation centers. Although Los Angeles city and county were immensely diverse in population and culture, these cultures were often separated rather than overlapping.

When Rodney King was beaten by three LAPD officers, a great many Angelenos of all backgrounds expressed shock and amazement. The question quickly became how to dispense justice to right a perceived wrong. By a slim plurality, city residents surveyed in a poll believed that Chief Gates should resign. This lack of confidence in the LAPD suggested that whatever else happened, there would be reform of the police force. But more immediate questions were: Would Rodney King receive justice? What was justice in this case?

On March 14, 1991, the state of California filed formal charges against police officers Laurence Powell, Timothy Wind, and Ted Briseno in Superior Court. The charges were using excessive force "under color of police authority," assault with a deadly weapon, and filing a false police report. Sergeant Stacey Koon was charged with acting as an accessory.

In preliminary hearings before the California Second District Court of Appeals, lawyers for the four officers successfully argued that they could not receive a fair trial in the Los Angeles area. The court agreed and changed the venue of the trial to Simi Valley in Ventura County, north and west of the city. The jury would be drawn from a population that reflected little of the ethnic diversity of Los Angeles County. But even considering the well-known fact that Simi Valley was a favored residence of retired police and military men, Terry L. White, the Deputy District Attorney, who led the prosecution, was confident. He had the 81-second tape; he had witnesses; he had the police report; he even had one of the accused officers willing to testify against his fellows.

When the trial opened on March 5, 1992, White played the incriminating tape. He presented testimony from Highway Patrol officer Melanie Singer. She told the court that Powell had struck King at least six times unnecessarily with his metal baton. Officer Briseno testified that both Powell and Wind were "out of control." King, he said, was not threatening. The prosecution also introduced evidence of a police report made by Powell twenty minutes before the incident at Lake View Terrace. Responding to a call to intervene in a domestic quarrel in the black community, Powell reported that the experience was "right out of '*Gorillas in the Mist*'"—referring to the well-known movie about Diane Fossey's studies of gorillas. All of this seemed to make an airtight case: motive, witness, and a videotape to convey the jurors to the very moment.

The defense attorneys, however, pursued an unusual strategy. They too played the tape, repeatedly, as if to diminish its emotional shock value through familiarity. They also slowed it down for a frame-by-frame analysis. In each case, they argued, King was acting in a hostile manner. As Michael P. Stone, attorney for Powell, argued, "We do not see an example of unprovoked police brutality. We see, rather, a controlled application of baton strikes, for the very obvious reason of getting this man in custody." In other words, Rodney King controlled the situation and provoked the police response.

THE SHADOWY, DIGITALIZED VIDEO OF THE RODNEY KING BEATING and arrest caused a sensation when shown on television. Despite what seemed to be firm visual evidence, a Simi Valley jury determined that King was in control.

If this reasoning provided an alternative way to see the videotaped evidence, the defense attorneys added a compelling argument to exonerate the defendants when they spoke repeatedly of the "thin blue line." This was the essential force of civilization dividing the citizen from the chaos of crime and violence. With the spread of gang and drug violence and random crime throughout the city—and with a growing fear of crime shaped and exploited by politicians and the media—this made considerable sense to jurors. As one reported after the trial, "They're policemen; they're not angels. They're out there to do a low-down, dirty job."

After several days of deliberation, the jury returned its verdict on April 29, 1992. The ten Anglos, one Hispanic, and one Filipino refused to convict the officers on any of the counts. There only remained disagreement over one officer and on one count. Consequently, Judge Stanley M. Weisberg ruled that officer Laurence Powell should be retried for "using excessive force under the color of police authority." The other defendants were released.

The twenty-nine-day trial ended with no convictions. There was scarcely time for official reaction to the verdict. It was early in the afternoon. Within 90 minutes, the worst riot in Los Angeles history would envelop the city. The second shock from the Rodney King beating was about to grip the attention of the nation.

Trouble began almost immediately when residents of South Central Los Angeles poured into the streets to cry their outrage. The largest demonstration occurred at the intersection of Normandie and Florence avenues. There, a number of young black men gathered, shouting, stopping cars, smashing windshields, and pulling drivers out of their cars to beat them. A small force of police rushed to the site, but was unable to contain the violence, and so withdrew. Looting and fires sputtered and flared in other parts of South Central, but the focus of attention was temporarily on Florence Avenue. A news helicopter flew over the area and began sending pictures back to the station for immediate broadcast. Just at that moment, thirty-six-year-old Reginald Denny drove his eighteen-wheel gravel delivery truck up to the blocked intersection. As he stopped, several youths rushed the cab and dragged him out. Grabbing bottles and bricks, they beat him repeatedly. One man did a fancy-step dance around him as he delivered a blow. Another removed Denny's wallet. The victim lay on the ground, blood streaming from facial and head wounds.

Above the scene, the news helicopter transmitted images and commentary back to the station, which immediately rebroadcast it. Throughout Los Angeles, viewers watching television rushed to the telephone to call 911, but the police did not respond. A black couple, living close by the trouble in South Central, however, hurried to the spot. They picked Denny up and pushed him back into the cab of the truck. With two other bystanders, they slowly eased the rig out of danger and drove toward Daniel Freeman Memorial Hospital nearby. As they approached, Denny went into convulsions, shaking and spitting up blood. Quickly wheeled into the operating room, Denny underwent three hours of emergency surgery to remove two blood clots on his brain. The good Samaritans who had saved his life drove his rig back to the gravel company shipping center and left.

Chief Daryl Gates had received reports of the escalating violence, looting and fires, but he saw no reason to remain at downtown police headquarters. He left, as planned, for a trek to the northern part of the city for a fund-raising meeting in opposition to a ballot initiative granting the city government closer supervision over the police department. In fact, however, the police department was in disarray. Little contingency

Looking straight down from a television news helicopter, the camera captures Reginald Denny sprawled on the cement with one of his attackers.

planning had been done to counter a possible riot after the Simi Valley verdict. Emergency calls poured in but the department lacked any overall strategy to contain the violence. At fire departments across the city telephones were jammed. Ordinarily one or two fires were reported in an hour for the entire city. In the early evening of April 30, alarms came in at the rate of one per minute. When firemen descended on one area, another burst into flames. Frequently they attracted sniper fire. Quickly, a thick blanket of smoke rose over the city, blocking the sun. It became so dense that Los Angeles International Airport shut temporarily, with traffic rerouted elsewhere.

Violence and disorder spread through the city, along avenues like Sunset, toward Hollywood and Beverly Hills and other affluent areas. Broken glass, shattered storefronts, stripped-down shops, and businesses gutted by fire were stark markers along the path of the conflagration. Increasingly residents joined in the frenzy: African Americans, Latinos, small numbers of Anglo and Asian youth. Gathering in front of the Parker Center, police headquarters downtown, a group of demonstrators suddenly began to hurl objects at the windows, smashing the glass and burning a parking kiosk. They then moved toward the *Los Angeles Times* building, where they smashed out the first floor windows, and then on to City Hall, the city Courthouse, federal and state buildings, and business offices. This assault on the monuments and centers of political and economic power was matched by other symbolic attacks. Angry groups also gathered at Lake View Terrace, where King had been apprehended. A mob at 71st and Normandie rocked cars that ventured into the neighborhood, occasionally pulling light-skinned or white drivers and passengers out to beat them. In Hollywood, the Sears store was looted; theaters were burned in downtown. Clearly there was no effective law enforcement in the city. Neither Mayor Bradley nor Chief Gates, who now returned to command headquarters, could stop it. Looting and violence were random and opportunistic. By nine o'clock that evening, the mayor had declared a state of emergency and curfew, but this was a sign of desperation, not an assertion of control.

Despite the chance assaults on people and property, certain distinct patterns quickly began to emerge from the confusion. Some of the violence had a racial and ethnic motivation: blacks against whites and sometimes Latinos. Yet a substantial number of Latinos joined in the looting and destruction, so extensively that their total arrests and deaths almost matched those of African Americans. One group in particular received the brunt of the assaults. Korean merchants who owned small shops and businesses throughout South Central and the periphery were repeatedly attacked, looted, and burned out. In Koreatown, word of the violence spread rapidly and some merchants mounted the rooftops of their businesses with guns and rifles to ward off attackers. Others patrolled the nearby streets in cars looking for suspicious characters.

While this animosity reflected deep interethnic competition and bigotry between blacks, Koreans, and Latinos, a recent event had focused anger on Koreans. In March, 1991, a Korean shop owner killed Latasha Harlins, a fifteen-year-old black girl. Convicted of manslaughter, the shop owner, Soon Ja Du, was given a sentence of only five years on probation. By the end of the riots, the pent-up anger over this case and general hostility and bigotry against Koreans resulted in 300 businesses burned and looted in Koreatown.

While much of the destruction in Los Angeles was inspired by anger and resentment, a considerable amount of looting happened in an almost carnival atmosphere. Some looters returned again and again to fill shopping carts at gutted stores. The *Los Angeles Times* reported a fairly typical example in this way:

> A Vons (chain store) and a Thrifty drugstore at the intersection were stormed shortly after noon to a chorus of war whoops and cheers. A trash can went through a window and within minutes a woman emerged with eight bottles of champagne, several cartons of cigarettes and a boom box.

By the end of the first day, the ineffective police response convinced Chief Gates that the situation was out of control. He welcomed the order by Governor Pete Wilson sending in 750 highway patrolmen and 2,000 California national guardsmen. Neither of these forces was quickly or efficiently deployed and during the second day of the riots and fires and looting, arrests and death continued to spread. In parts of the county, untouched by the riots, groups of homeowners organized vigilante groups to patrol the streets and warn off "suspicious-looking" people. Throughout the city handgun sales boomed as men and women sought to protect themselves and their families against spreading, random violence. Perhaps feeling some responsibility for the terrible events, a shaken and emotional Rodney King appeared on television that night. "People," he said, "I just want to say, you know. Can we get along? I mean we're all stuck here for a while. Let's try to work it out." It was too late.

Most of the deaths did, indeed, appear to be random. A driver or passenger shot; a store owner or looter killed; someone trapped in a fire; a bystander killed by a stray

AFTERMATH: A CITY IN CRISIS

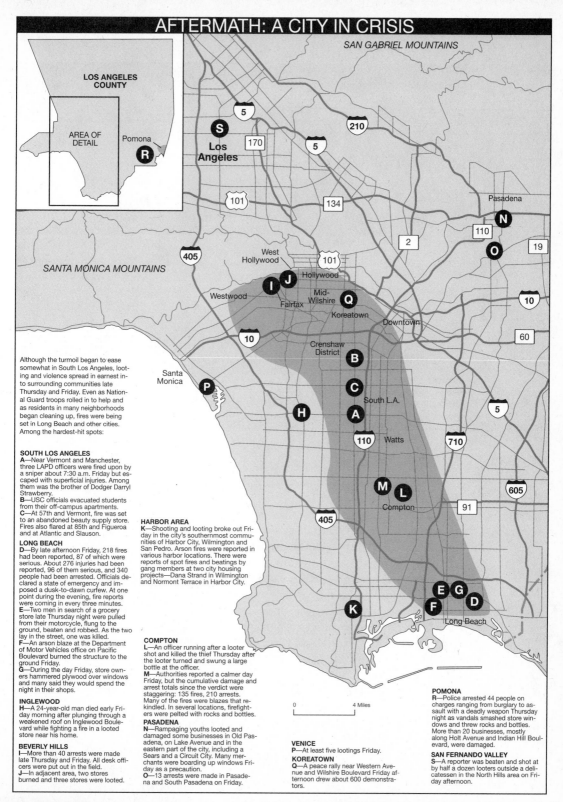

SAN GABRIEL MOUNTAINS

LOS ANGELES COUNTY

AREA OF DETAIL

Pomona

Los Angeles

SANTA MONICA MOUNTAINS

Pasadena

West Hollywood

Hollywood

Westwood

Fairfax

Mid-Wilshire

Koreatown

Downtown

Crenshaw District

Santa Monica

South L.A.

Watts

Compton

Long Beach

Although the turmoil began to ease somewhat in South Los Angeles, looting and violence spread in earnest into surrounding communities late Thursday and Friday. Even as National Guard troops rolled in to help and as residents in many neighborhoods began cleaning up, fires were being set in Long Beach and other cities. Among the hardest-hit spots:

SOUTH LOS ANGELES
A—Near Vermont and Manchester, three LAPD officers were fired upon by a sniper about 7:30 a.m. Friday but escaped with superficial injuries. Among them was the brother of Dodger Darryl Strawberry.
B—USC officials evacuated students from their off-campus apartments.
C—At 57th and Vermont, fire was set to an abandoned beauty supply store. Fires also flared at 85th and Figueroa and at Atlantic and Slauson.

LONG BEACH
D—By late afternoon Friday, 218 fires had been reported, 87 of which were serious. About 276 injuries had been reported, 96 of them serious, and 340 people had been arrested. Officials declared a state of emergency and imposed a dusk-to-dawn curfew. At one point during the evening, fire reports were coming in every three minutes.
E—Two men in search of a grocery store late Thursday night were pulled from their motorcycle, flung to the ground, beaten and robbed. As the two lay in the street, one was killed.
F—An arson blaze at the Department of Motor Vehicles office on Pacific Boulevard burned the structure to the ground Friday.
G—During the day Friday, store owners hammered plywood over windows and many said they would spend the night in their shops.

INGLEWOOD
H—A 24-year-old man died early Friday morning after plunging through a weakened roof on Inglewood Boulevard while fighting a fire in a looted store near his home.

BEVERLY HILLS
I—More than 40 arrests were made late Thursday and Friday. All desk officers were put out in the field.
J—In adjacent area, two stores burned and three stores were looted.

HARBOR AREA
K—Shooting and looting broke out Friday in the city's southernmost communities of Harbor City, Wilmington and San Pedro. Arson fires were reported in various harbor locations. There were reports of spot fires and beatings by gang members at two city housing projects—Dana Strand in Wilmington and Normont Terrace in Harbor City.

COMPTON
L—An officer running after a looter shot and killed the thief Thursday after the looter turned and swung a large bottle at the officer.
M—Authorities reported a calmer day Friday, but the cumulative damage and arrest totals since the verdict were staggering: 135 fires, 210 arrests. Many of the fires were blazes that rekindled. In several locations, firefighters were pelted with rocks and bottles.

PASADENA
N—Rampaging youths looted and damaged some businesses in Old Pasadena, on Lake Avenue and in the eastern part of the city, including a Sears and a Circuit City. Many merchants were boarding up windows Friday as a precaution.
O—13 arrests were made in Pasadena and South Pasadena on Friday.

VENICE
P—At least five lootings Friday.
KOREATOWN
Q—A peace rally near Western Avenue and Wilshire Boulevard Friday afternoon drew about 600 demonstrators.

POMONA
R—Police arrested 44 people on charges ranging from burglary to assault with a deadly weapon Thursday night as vandals smashed store windows and threw rocks and bottles. More than 20 businesses, mostly along Holt Avenue and Indian Hill Boulevard, were damaged.

SAN FERNANDO VALLEY
S—A reporter was beaten and shot at by half a dozen looters outside a delicatessen in the North Hills area on Friday afternoon.

0   4 Miles

THIS MAP OF LOS ANGELES shows some of the major places where riots broke out after the first trial of the police who beat Rodney King.

LOOTING DURING THE LOS ANGELES RIOTS. Despite such visual evidence as this photograph, Hispanic Americans were relatively unnoticed among those who participated in the riots.

bullet: these casualties occurred without premeditation. Yet it also appears that there were some vengeance killings carried out by gangs. In all, there were at least fifty-eight dead.

The surprising aspect of these figures is the high number of Latinos killed. This proportion matches the percentage of about one-third of the total 12,000 arrests for assault, looting, and curfew violations made during the four days of riots. But this large and very visible presence on the streets was practically invisible in the reasoning that observers voiced in interpreting the riots and in proposing resolutions to the long-standing problems of Los Angeles. Cast by the newspapers and television media, by commentators and public officials as a black/white issue, as an aggravated outbreak in the long, painful history of segregation and racism, the riots had other strong elements. One of these was the black and Korean antipathy, but a more important one was the contradictory role of Latinos. Sometimes victims, but much more often, participants, Latinos were a practically unmentioned element who played a critical role. When observers forced the events into a single polarity, they greatly oversimplified what had happened and misconstrued its causes.

National reaction to the Los Angeles riots first took the form of incredulity and surprise. The uncontained violence convinced President George Bush to send in federal troops on May 1. "What is going on in L.A. must and will stop," he sternly announced. "As your President, I guarantee you. This violence will end." Other cities braced for trouble. Police leaves were cancelled and special duty rosters organized. Nonetheless, trouble did strike elsewhere. In San Francisco, a number of elegant shops and depart-

DEATHS ATTRIBUTABLE TO THE LOS ANGELES RIOTS

	Men	Women	Total
African American	20	5	25
Latinos	18	1	19
Anglos	9	1	10
Asians	2	—	2
Unknown	2	—	2

Source: Los Angeles Times, *May 5, 1992.*

ment stores like Macy's were looted. Small but severe riots struck Atlanta, Georgia, and Madison, Wisconsin. Nonetheless, by May 2 the violence was rapidly receding, and by May 3 a semblance of order had returned to Los Angeles. On Sunday, thousands of curious residents drove through shattered areas of the city to look at the empty, twisted, and blackened stores and businesses. Hundreds of volunteers came to help sweep up the carpet of broken glass and debris that lay on streets, sidewalks, and parking lots in the stricken areas. A few of these brigades were led by Hollywood stars—most notable was James Olmos, the Hispanic actor known for his television role in *Miami Vice* during the 1980s.

Such local gestures of reconciliation were obscured by the accusatory positions taken by major political figures. Mayor Bradley and Chief Gates continued their bitter skirmishes about culpability, although both were deeply damaged by the riots. Gates had already resigned as of April 1992, and was waiting for his replacement, Willie L. Williams, to step in as chief. An October report—commissioned by the Los Angeles Police Commission, which was headed by William H. Webster, former director of the FBI and CIA—faulted the city and the police department for lax, disorderly, and confused responses to the riot. Mayor Bradley had also been slow to respond and ineffective in offering leadership. The commission saved much of its fire for Chief Gates. His "paramilitary model" was inappropriate and inflammatory. The slow and ineffective response to the riot was due "first and foremost to the performance of the chief of police and his command staff." In hindsight, the confused and failed attempt to control the initial violence was blamed for the much worse second wave that followed.

On the national level, the President and contenders for his office used the riots to weave another strand into the set patterns of their campaigns. Continuing the partisan and contentious blaming begun by Bradley and Gates, President Bush, Vice President Dan Quayle, and Democratic party front-runner Bill Clinton converted the Los Angeles riots into an event that proved their opponents' failures.

After a visit to the city on May 4, Bill Clinton blamed the withdrawal of federal programs and funds from inner cities prompted by budgets cuts of presidents Ronald Reagan and George Bush. Clinton promised to refocus resources on such areas. He also suggested welfare reform and the extension of enterprise zones with tax incentives to lure businesses into impoverished areas. Right after the King incident Clinton had aligned himself, emotionally, with the outrage expressed by Bradley and other black leaders. "It is obvious," he said, "that lurking beneath that verdict there is this huge feeling that the system is broke and unresponsive and unfair."

On the same day, President Bush read the event slightly differently. Expressing dismay about the King decision, he stressed law and order. "To Americans of all races who are shocked by this verdict, let me say this: You must understand that our system of justice provides for the peaceful, orderly means of addressing this frustration. We must respect the process of law, whether or not we agree with the outcome."

While Clinton hoped to cement support for his candidacy in the African-American community during this time, he did so cautiously, keeping alive a public breach with black leader Jesse Jackson. His purpose was to prevent too close an association with the civil rights movement and the liberal wing of the Democratic party. On June 13, he criticized the black singer Sister Souljah for justifying the riots, saying bluntly that her reasoning sounded like the excuses given by the Ku Klux Klan for taking the law into their own hands.

The Republicans gave a different interpretation to the riots, blaming federal welfare programs for fraying the social fabric. Welfare subsidies and government programs had undercut traditional values of family and community. Children raised by single women without adequate financial support or the psychological benefit of knowing a father, had turned into rootless criminals. The only way to revive the family was to restore respect for authority, the work ethic, religion, and traditional roles of parenting.

Vice President Quayle carried such notions into the realm of the fictitious. During a speech on May 19 in San Francisco, he blamed television for glamorizing single parenting. The worst example was the comedy series character Murphy Brown, who had in a recent incident decided to bear a child even though she was unmarried. As Quayle noted, "It doesn't help matters when prime time TV has Murphy Brown—a character who supposedly epitomizes today's intelligent, highly paid professional woman—mocking the importance of fathers, by bearing a child alone, and calling it in her words just another 'lifestyle choice.'"

This tilt with imaginary characters shifted both the Republican and Democratic explanations of the riots off solid ground and made Quayle himself the issue. Whatever the virtue of his larger argument about values and culture, he had badly missed the satiric point of the TV series: Murphy Brown's flip remark was, as she discovered in later shows, exactly the opposite of the real implications of parenthood. Unfortunately with such frivolous diversions and the short attention span of the public, the Los Angeles riots did not spark a thoughtful discussion of the causes and consequences of the event. The serious, long-term cultural and economic issues that impinged upon Los Angeles, and all American cities to some degree, reappeared as campaign sound bites and opportunistic political accusations.

Congress did rush through an emergency urban program on June 21, granting about a billion dollars in aid to cities for summer jobs, disaster relief, and small business loans for Los Angeles. Yet the riots themselves had probably caused a billion dollars in immediate damage. Perhaps 40,000 people were thrown out of work and 3,500 businesses destroyed. Residents in hard-hit areas had no banks in which to cash their checks, few jobs, and nowhere to shop. Local initiatives were focused on rebuilding. A Rebuild Los Angeles organization was set up, headed by Peter Ueberroth, former commissioner of major league baseball. His task was to persuade businesses to locate in riot-torn areas. But there were no quick fixes and very little money for special initiatives.

As for the charges of police brutality, something could still be done to achieve a measure of justice for Rodney King. In the spring of 1992, the federal government decided to retry the case, to start over again, as it were. This attempt at justice revisited began in federal court. The four officers were tried for depriving Rodney King of his civil rights. This time, the venue was Los Angeles County and the jury reflected a somewhat more representative sampling of the demographics of the area: eight men and four women—nine Anglos, two blacks, and one Latino.

The trial began in February 1993 and lasted several weeks. Unlike the first hearing, the prosecution put King on the stand, where he now testified that the police officers had shouted racial taunts at him during the arrest. Officer Briseno, however, changed his testimony, denying that he had expertise enough to be sure that Officer Powell had used excessive force. As before, the 81-second Holliday tape played a central role.

Prior to the verdict in April, the city gritted its teeth, armed itself, and prepared to face another riot. But on April 17, the jury convicted Laurence Powell of violating King's right to be free from an arrest made with "unreasonable force." Sergeant Stacey Koon was convicted of permitting the civil rights violation to occur. The two other officers were acquitted on all counts. Mayor Bradley's reaction was consoling: "Today a measure of simple justice has been delivered to our community." His unvoiced sigh of relief was widely shared; there would be no further riots. In August, Powell and Koon were given relatively light sentences by presiding judge John G. Davies, who noted that King had "contributed significantly" to his own fate. Moreover, the tape had been only "a partial, ambiguous and incomplete documentation."

The television video of the beating of Reginald Denny played a significant role in the final effort to close the accounts of the riot. On July 14, 1993, the trial of Denny's attackers began in Los Angeles. Henry Watson and Damian Williams were charged with the attempted murder of Denny during the first explosive day of the riots. Much of the trial revolved around the supposed effect of mob psychology as an instigating factor in the violence. Once again, a graphic video became the source of confusion and doubt. In mid-October the jury of four blacks, four Latinos, two Asians, and two whites delivered its verdict. Williams was guilty on one count of simple mayhem (willfully maiming or crippling) and four counts of simple assault in other attacks. He was not guilty of robbery, aggravated mayhem, and eight counts of assault with a deadly weapon. Watson was acquitted of attempted murder and several counts of assault and robbery. The jury remained deadlocked on another charge of assault. Two weeks later Watson pleaded guilty to felony assault in attacking another trucker, Larry Tarvin. A third defendant, Antoine Miller, pleaded guilty to two misdemeanors and one felony.

If nothing else, this exhausting consideration of multiple charges and the delivery of complicated decisions helped drain the city's anxiety and brought a closure to a situation that could never be ended to everyone's satisfaction. Neither the officers who beat King nor the rioters who attacked Denny received harsh sentences. The police department was restructured and reformed under its new chief, Willie Williams, who took office in June 1992. But the larger, national debate over the deep issues roughly uncovered by the violence and anger of the four-day riot never occurred. Like the initially clear and shocking videotapes of the King and Denny beatings, the initial, clear understanding of the riots and the simple cry for action that they demanded also became obscured as the events receded from the nation's first clear and certain impressions.

The Politics of Diversity

On September 9, 1990, boats ferrying passengers resumed regular runs to Ellis Island in New York harbor. Unlike the sixty-two years when it was the port of entry for millions of newcomers to America, however, the island was receiving no new immigrants. Its doors opened instead to tourists, many of them from among the 100 million Americans descended from parents or grandparents who had passed through its portals. Others were merely curious. Ellis Island, once the principal entry point for the "new" immigrants from eastern and southern Europe, had become a museum to commemorate a multi-cultural past. This huge wave of newcomers that rose in the 1880s and fell back in the late 1920s, for which the facility had been built, permanently changed the nation. Once controversial because of their differences from older immigrant groups, these "new immigrants" were now an accepted, even celebrated part of the American past.

The buildings of the new national park were careful restorations of the huge complex where immigrants had been processed and accepted, or in some cases, returned. Obvious disease, or mental impairment, or physical deformities, or political opinions like anarchism might disqualify an entrant. But in most cases, inspectors asked perfunctory questions: general health, name, birth date, place of origin, and prospects for work. In this way, America had greeted its newcomers and sent them on their way to reunions with relatives and compatriots, and to work in the labor-hungry mills and sweatshops of a booming industrial economy.

In 1990, the buildings were clean and quiet—no children, men, or women clamoring in Italian, Polish, Yiddish, or Russian; no adults weighted down carrying the family's belongings on their shoulders; just tourists asking questions. As had happened so often in the past, the United States received millions of immigrants who looked, acted, and spoke in dramatically different ways. Yet the force of Americanization overwhelmed cultural distinctions that once seemed indelible. Wave after wave of people had passed through generation after generation of transformation.

Yet the suspicion was regularly renewed that each time some new group arrived, America would be changed dramatically; consequently, it could no longer hold open its doors. Ellis Island National Park commemorated a multicultural past. But it was not the sort of ethnic pluralism that typified the new immigration of the 1980s and 1990s and that transformed Los Angeles (and New York itself) into a particularly striking example of the new world metropolis. Similar revolutionary urban agglomerations like London, Berlin, Miami, and Singapore in Malaysia represented something distinct in modern history: cities that had as much in common with other world cities as they did with the nation where

FORTRESSLIKE ON ITS OWN ISLAND, the immigration reception center at Ellis Island greeted huge numbers of European immigrants. It was reopened in 1990 as a monument to the successful assimilation of those who passed through it.

they were situated. Absorbing large, shifting populations of newcomers, such places bear the stresses of mass migration and the character of an international mass culture. They also exhibit the opportunities and difficulties of new forms of cultural pluralism.

THE NEW IMMIGRATION

The Los Angeles that exploded after the first verdict in the Rodney King case visibly exaggerates the nature of the new immigration that has swept through the United States in the last fifteen years and that is transforming American society and culture. However, nothing like Ellis Island exists to focus the entry of newcomers. American boundaries today are porous by land, open to the sea, and easily accessible by air. Thousands of Eu-

ropeans are still attracted by the promise of work, wealth, and political and religious liberty, but Asians and Latin Americans now make up the majority of newcomers seeking fortune and freedom.

RECENT CHANGES IN IMMIGRATION

Recent changes in immigration became possible because of revisions in law. After World War II there were temporary amendments to the Immigration Act of 1924 that made it possible for some refugees from the devastation of Europe to enter the country. Up through the 1950s Europeans still represented more than half of all immigrants, but their percentages quickly declined thereafter. In 1965, a new Immigration Act greatly altered policy, reversing decades of priorities granted to newcomers from northern Europe and putting in place a complex system of priorities that applied to every applicant. It also placed a maximum general quota on immigrants from both the Eastern and Western Hemispheres. The unforeseen result of this legislation was an increasing number of newcomers from developing nations—often highly educated and skilled. By the mid-1970s, Mexico, the Philippines, Cuba, Korea, China, India, and the Dominican Republic were sending the largest share of persons to the United States. Most of these congregated in six states: California, New York, Florida, Texas, Illinois, and New Jersey. By 1985 New York, Los Angeles, and Miami all had populations more than 25 percent foreign born. To the undifferentiating eye, these immigrants were either Europeans, Asians, or Hispanics. In actuality, they represented an extraordinary variety of distinct religions, cultures, and languages.

If legal immigration (around 269,000 per year) brought dramatic changes, illegal (undocumented) immigration magnified these trends. In the 1980s, for example, about 1,600,000 Mexicans entered the United States legally. When illegals are added, the number practically doubles. A great many in this hidden surge lacked the skills, education, or opportunities of Asians or Europeans. Consequently, they found themselves concentrated in poorer districts of cities, relegated to the worst-paying jobs, and often living outside the social services and economic possibilities open to others. Much the same was true of populations from the West Indies (Jamaica, Haiti, and the Dominican Republic) and the Caribbean (Trinidad, Guyana).

Another large category of immigrants were political refugees fleeing communism in Eastern Europe, Vietnam, and Cuba. After the 1965 act, 875,000 Cubans, 750,000 Indochinese, and about 600,000 Eastern Europeans arrived. Those escaping the political repression of totalitarian governments friendly to the United States—for example, Chile and Haiti—were, however, generally turned away on grounds that they were economic, not political, refugees.

The immigration laws of the 1980s hardly deterred large numbers of people wishing to enter the United States. A further law passed and

THIS SIGN IS A SERIOUS WARNING to motorists to avoid striking illegal immigrants who fled up the median strips of highways leading from the Mexican–U.S. border.

signed by President Bush on October 30, 1990, raised the ceiling of total immigration and greatly increased slots open to skilled workers. Illegal immigration, however, remained serious as unscrupulous entrepreneurs shipped illegals from China, Latin America, and Europe. Hundreds of thousands more made their way on their own.

The impact of this continuing wave of newcomers is difficult to measure. Americans remain ambiguous about new arrivals, sometimes forgetting their own origins. Yet the United States has been a success among nations in creating a multicultural society. Changes in recent immigration will, like other new developments, test this flexibility. Whatever the outcome, the present percentage of immigrants in the population remains far lower than in the past: in 1910, 15 percent of

Americans were foreign born, as opposed to half that number in 1990.

WORLDWIDE IMMIGRATION

Immigration into the United States is only part of a worldwide dispersal of populations. In July 1993, the United Nations reported that 100 million persons lived outside the country of their birth. Of these, 17 million were refugees from war or political oppression and 20 million had fled violence or environmental disaster like drought. In 1989, these migrants sent $66 billion home to families, thus transacting the second largest international economic exchange, behind oil sales. World immigrants were widely scattered: 35 million in sub-Saharan Africa and 15 million each in Western Europe, North America, and Asia and the Middle East. Adding to the turmoil of populations was a vast movement of people into urban areas. The result was huge agglomerations like Mexico City with 20 million inhabitants.

This movement of peoples shook Western Europe. Former colonial powers such as England and France have been inundated with migrants from former colonies and "guest" workers hired to perform jobs that ordinary citizens refuse. These immigrants generally have some knowledge of English or French, but their culture and religions are distinct. Muslim Algerians in France have encountered severe difficulties in assimilating. Racist political parties committed to ending immigration have gained significant voter support. In Germany the problems of guest workers

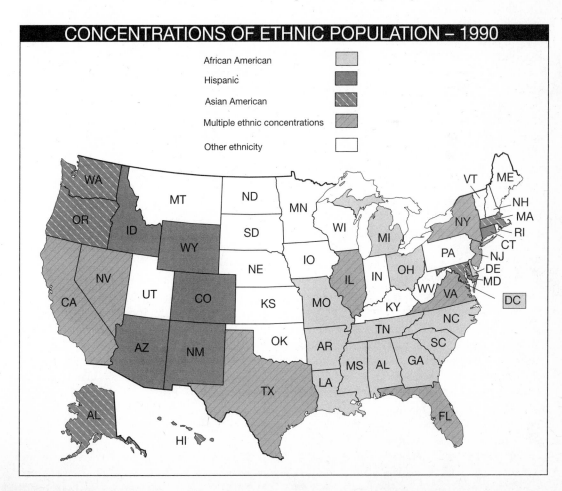

CONCENTRATIONS OF ETHNIC POPULATION – 1990

from Turkey have been compounded by refugees from the formerly Communist parts of Germany, streaming westward together with immigrants from collapsing nearby countries like Yugoslavia. During 1992 and 1993, gangs of German youths murdered a number of immigrants and refugees, seriously challenging that nation's texture of toleration and reviving memories of its Nazi past.

The new immigration intensified the anxiety of many Americans about multiculturalism. If, as many demographers predict, the United States will have a majority of non-European inhabitants in two generations, that reality has already begun to appear in the nation's schools. Local school boards have tried to accommodate this new trend. Should they offer bilingual education such as English/Spanish or English/Vietnamese? Can learning take place if only traditional American and Western cultures were taught? Should other approaches prevail: Afro-centrism, which stresses the priority of African achievements and heritage, for example? How could schools create an environment in which the contending national and social groups could be integrated, especially if there were several? Could the classroom simultaneously privilege traditional American Protestant and Catholic cultures, African-American, Asian, Hispanic, women's, or gay identities and still educate citizens for a integrated society with shared goals? Was the relevant history to learn still the story of the Puritans, the Civil War, progressivism, and the Industrial Revolution?

-•=◉●=•-

THE END OF
THE REAGAN ERA

Such questions exerted considerable force after 1988 and the end of the nostalgic political holiday of the Reagan years. The broken graph of achievement by African Americans, Hispanics, and women during the 1980s measured problems that returned with renewed intensity at the end of the decade. The politics of equal opportunity had, in fact, exacerbated inequality. The presidency of Ronald Reagan did not create homelessness, poverty, or racial discrimination, but it did foster a

shift in income shares that increased America's dubious leadership among all industrialized nations in economic inequality. The increasing stalemate between Congress and the presidency; the continuing impoverishment of cities that housed the poor, the homeless and the least assimilable immigrants; and the growing distrust of traditional institutions gave rise to the sentiment that America had succumbed to the moral disorder of greed and self-interest. This sentiment had a tangible, depressing side. During the 1980s, only one-half of American families maintained or improved their standard of living; others slipped lower.

At the same time, significant groups of Americans had grown to distrust institutions that once made pluralism the defining character of politics. Loss of faith in Congress, repeated scandals in the executive branch, and the political controversies surrounding the Supreme Court made government seem to be, as the Republican slogan maintained, the problem not the solution. Persistent high unemployment and worries about Japanese and German manufacturing competition aggravated doubts about the economy. The failure of scores of savings and loan institutions at the end of the 1980s, worries about the reliability of Social Security and private pension systems and medical insurance costs added to the sense that the American dream might end. Other traditional elements of social order such as churches became highly politicized over issues of abortion, women's rights, and gay rights. Revelation of scandals and corruption among some Evangelical ministries and sexual abuses by Catholic priests compromised trust in religious institutions. Institutions of information and learning—such as newspapers, television networks, universities and colleges—became embroiled in disheartening accusations of bias and privilege. Add to this discouraging mix the despair over crime and drug use and the scourge of AIDS, and the political agenda of 1988 suffered from an overload of divisive issues.

CONTINUITIES

To win the presidential election of 1988, one candidate had to exploit these issues and turn them into a problem for his opponent. The person best poised to accomplish this was George Bush, eight years the vice president of Ronald Reagan. It was the odd fact of politics in 1988 that while Reagan and Bush were partly responsible for governmental corruption, the savings and loan scandal, the swiftly mounting national debt, and the upward redistribution of American incomes, conservatism still defined political discourse. The anger and resentment of many Americans could still be directed at liberal programs of welfare and social reform, a Congress controlled by Democrats, and some of the constituencies identified as Democrat, such as African Americans.

Victory in such a volatile political world required either the popularity of a Ronald Reagan or perhaps some tough-minded new conservative program. George Bush had neither. The son of Senator Prescott Bush (Connecticut, 1952–1963), he grew up during the depression of the 1930s in upper-class luxury. He attended Phillips Academy of Andover, Massachusetts, and Yale University, where he joined the exclusive Skull and Bones club. World War II intervened and Bush joined the navy, serving with distinction as a torpedo bomber pilot in the Pacific war against Japan. After being mustered out of the service, he moved to Texas. This was an extraordinary time for a young man with good connections, a pleasant personality, a good business sense, and financial backing to plunge into Texas oil. Bush did remarkably well as a transplanted easterner, founding the successful Zapata Petroleum Co. He and his wife, the former Barbara Pierce of New York, began a family in their adopted state.

Early on, Bush showed a keen interest in politics, especially admiring the young and ambitious Richard Nixon from California. Bush ran for Congress from his Houston district, pushing a program of moderate Republican conservatism and staunch anticommunism, and won in 1966 and 1968. At a time of rapid social change and a general extension of the welfare state, Bush's idea of government was routine and cautious. He did not stand for change or new policies but rather for administrative competence with a decidedly pro-business bias. Whatever encouraged profits and investment was beneficial whereas, he believed, rules and government regulations and initiatives could only impede the system. There was nothing in this mix of ideas to set him apart from many other Republican or, for that matter, Democratic congressmen.

Election in Houston, Texas, meant a difficult negotiation between factions and especially the need to appease a growing conservative bloc among Republicans. Bush was repeatedly put to the test, for an outsider with natural inclinations to the center of the party was not a man this group trusted. To accommodate this element, the future president became a reborn conservative. It was not enough, however, to win a Senate seat in 1970, when he lost to Democrat Lloyd Bentsen.

Even in defeat, loyal service to the party and friendships with important figures like Nixon earned him important new entries on his political resumé. Serving first as United Nations Ambassador from 1971 to 1973, envoy to China, 1974–1975, and then as CIA director from 1975 to 1976, Bush gained an unusually clear and informed sense of American foreign policy. Together with his business experience and congressional service, he was well prepared for the office of vice president and then president. But he ran with a severe handicap in 1988. As a figure following in the long shadow of Ronald Reagan, he could scarcely take credit for the President's accomplishments; yet he might incur blame for Republican failures and for the growing sense of indirection in the nation. Without a strong program of his own to reproduce the impelling vision of Reagan, with a strong right wing of the Republican party suspicious of his eastern and Ivy League background, Bush's best tactic inevitably became to attack his opponent. He had, after all, once been an advocate of population control and abortion rights, until his nomination for vice president in 1980. He needed to keep the Democratic party on the defensive and turn the positive, warm feelings that Reagan still generated into fear and anger against his opponents. Any discussion of the growing federal debt crisis or the enormous failure of the savings and loan in-

JESSE JACKSON CAMPAIGNS during the Iowa presidential primary of 1988. Attempting to assemble a Rainbow Coalition—reflecting a union of genders, races, ethnic groups, and social classes—the candidate dons a farm cap and jacket to court rural voters.

dustry, any direct confrontation with the serious problems plaguing the American economy would not be broached. Bush could not allow the scandals trailing like another long shadow from Reagan's last years to cast doubt upon him: No mention of doubts about the scruples of Attorney General Edwin Meese or the growing Iran-Contra

scandal, or some misappropriation of funds in the Pentagon.

With the nomination securely in hand after dispatching his competitors, Senator Robert Dole of Kansas and television evangelist Pat Robertson, Bush crafted a campaign strategy in 1988 around cultural issues designed to split up the Democratic electorate into warring factions. Although their relationship to economic problems remained abstract at best, these issues motivated millions of Americans. Bush concentrated on issues designed to cement working-class voters to the Republican party. He took a strong stand against gun controls. He denounced his opponent Michael Dukakis as a "card-carrying" member of the American Civil Liberties Union (an aggressive lobbying group for legal rights). He portrayed his opponent as a liberal opposed to the Pledge of Allegiance. He effectively linked the Democratic candidate to a prison furlough program in Massachusetts under which a parolee, Willie Horton, a black man, raped and murdered a white woman. These tough images played well to a white working-class audience that was deeply suspicious and even angry at the Democratic party and its large contingent of African-American voters.

MULTICULTURALISM AT THE TOP. In this picture, President George Bush (center), the premier of Japan, Toshiki Kaifu (right), and, partly visible, the prime minister of England, Margaret Thatcher, attend a rodeo in Houston.

Although Bush willingly played the race and cultural cards in his campaign, he trumped his own strategy with a contradictory promise aimed at another audience to create a "kinder, gentler" America. This language aimed to attract Republican suburban voters who disliked raw, partisan politics or racial slurs. To unite all these groups, Bush made a clear and unmistakable pledge never to renege on the Reagan tax and income redistribution of the 1980s. "Read my lips. No new taxes," he promised.

Against this canny and flexible strategy, the Democrats were no match. After a long primary season in which major Democratic leaders either failed to run or dropped out, the candidate who emerged, almost by default, was a minor party figure, Michael Dukakis of Massachusetts. Governor of that state during the 1980s, when it was the beneficiary of a defense-spending boom and a demand for information technology based on its universities (especially Harvard and Massachusetts Institute of Technology), Dukakis claimed a large measure of credit for the "Massachusetts miracle." Something of a moderate technocrat with few ties to traditional constituencies in the party, Dukakis stood on an anti-Reagan platform that promised a fairer tax and economic system. Despite his vice presidential choice of Senator Lloyd Bentsen of Texas, a conservative Democrat with considerable standing and reputation, Dukakis never shook the accusation that he was a clandestine liberal. Bush made only one major misstep. He chose Senator Dan Quayle of Indiana to be his vice presidential running mate. While Quayle was well-known and admired in the right wing of the Republican party, his nomination seemed too obviously designed to attract younger voters. Quayle's adolescent gaffs and malapropisms during the campaign did nothing to quiet this criticism. Nor could he quiet charges that he had avoided military service in Vietnam. But Democratic strategists who believed it sufficient to expose the dubious tactics of the Republicans gravely underestimated the power of negativism in American politics and the impact of continuing prosperity. They miscalculated the secure hold of Ronald Reagan's presence upon the

WILLIE HORTON, a Massachusetts prisoner who committed a rape while on a weekend pass, became a potent symbol during the 1988 presidential election. Republicans attacked Michael Dukakis, governor of Massachusetts, for being soft on crime.

electorate. The result was a landslide for Bush and Quayle, who won the South, West, Midwest, and the Rocky Mountain States with 54 percent of the vote. Dukakis was competitive only in the East. But there were two contradictory trends. The Democrats maintained a large majority in the Senate (56 to 44) and the House of Representatives (262 to 173). The electorate had decidedly voted against change in the presidency and the Congress. What they got was a stalemate.

BUSH AS PRESIDENT

Although George Bush ran and won on cultural issues, his ambition was to manage the federal government in a prudent manner. He appointed a number of competent conservatives: Brent Scowcroft as national security advisor, and, in the cabinet, James A. Baker as secretary of state, Nicholas

Brady as treasury secretary, and Richard Darman as budget director. His White House chief of staff was the pugnacious and short-tempered former governor of New Hampshire, John Sununu.

If these appointments revealed the new president's indifference to far-reaching domestic initiatives, he still needed to reward party conservatives who demanded action in economic and social areas. This group gained representation through Vice President Quayle; former Congressman Jack Kemp as head of housing and urban development, William Bennett, who became "Drug Czar"; and various midlevel advisors sprinkled though the administration. During his four years, Bush spoke fervently for conservative causes, but he took few of the radical initiatives proposed by Kemp to create tax-sheltered enterprise zones in urban slums. He paid little attention to radical plans to restructure and privatize public education. As Reagan before him, Bush avoided legislative fights over controversial social issues. Instead, he attempted to use administration, relaxed regulations, and court appointments to fulfill this divisive agenda.

Bush had ample opportunity to choose conservatives for the Supreme Court. The last Democratic appointment to the Court had been in the 1960s. By 1989 the Court was moving toward a conservative majority on such issues as criminal rights, labor unions, and social and religious issues like abortion and church/state separation. The most divisive issue was abortion, and the Republican platform promised to end its legality and to promote Supreme Court appointments to that end. This had proven difficult in 1987, when Reagan failed to secure the nomination of outspoken conservative Robert Bork. The successful appointee, Anthony Kennedy, proved cautious about overturning important decisions. The Democratic Senate, while inclined to agree to most presidential appointments, heeded its labor, African-American, and women's group constituencies on such matters. Nonetheless, the right to abortion seemed very close to extinction. Very early in the Bush administration the Court narrowly (5 to 4) upheld a Missouri law that restricted abortions, allowing the state to prohibit public employees from performing the procedure unless the mother's life was endangered and barring the procedure from public buildings and requiring medical tests to determine if a fetus could survive after twenty weeks. If this was a signal, the majority on the court had begun to shift.

Bush's first chance to consolidate this majority came in July 1990, after one of the two leading liberals on the Court, Justice William Brennan, retired. Three days later, the president nominated New Hampshire Superior Court Judge David Hackett Souter. During confirmation hearings, the candidate revealed very little of his attitudes toward such issues as abortion and he was confirmed without difficulty.

Bush's next appointment was anything but easy. When Justice Thurgood Marshall—the leading civil rights advocate on the bench—announced his retirement in June 1991, the president chose another African American to replace him. The nominee, Justice Clarence Thomas of the U.S. Appeals Court of Washington, D.C. was cut from a different cloth. A conservative who opposed affirmative action or any other government or business program designed to accelerate the hiring and promotion of racial and ethnic minorities and women, Thomas had served an acrimonious stint on the Equal Employment Opportunity Commission (EEOC) under Reagan. Once there, Thomas reversed the commission's practice of class action intervention, vowing action only in cases of obvious individual discrimination. This stance earned him the bitter opposition of organizations such as the National Organization for Women (NOW) and the NAACP. A popular ideological stand among conservatives, however, was not sufficient to earn him respect in the legal profession. The American Bar Association gave him its low ranking of "qualified" rather than "well-qualified."

The president divided his opponents, playing on the unstable Democratic party alliance between women, African Americans, and other ethnic groups. To oppose the appointment of a black man would entail considerable risk for Democratic party senators. Yet to approve an opponent of prominent establishment leaders in the NAACP, to add a conservative vote on abortion, labor law, and other issues, was equally damaging. In September after extensive hearings, the Senate Judiciary Committee voted a noncommittal tie to report the nomination to the Senate. In that larger body the nomination appeared to be safe.

This smooth course was suddenly derailed on October 6 when National Public Radio and *Newsday* reported accusations by a former EEOC employee, Anita Hill, that Justice Thomas had sexually harassed her on the job. Suddenly the appointment was in jeopardy. The Senate Judiciary Committee—12 male Senators—rushed back into session to hear details of the accusation. Telecast to the nation, the hearings contained high drama and sordid detail. They also demonstrated how the issues of race, social class, and gender deeply divided Americans.

Hill, a conservative black lawyer herself, graphically described unwanted encounters with Thomas, her supervisor at the EEOC. "He talked about pornographic materials depicting individuals with large penises or large breasts involved in various sex acts," she calmly told the senators. "On several occasions," she continued, "Thomas told me graphically of his own sexual prowess." Hill also confirmed that she had informed several people of the incidents, although never mentioning Thomas's name. Hill remained at her job, asking Thomas for recommendations after the incident.

In his defense, Thomas simply denied everything and then angrily denounced the hearings and the senators. "You have robbed me of something that can never be restored," he said

ANITA HILL testifying before the Senate Judiciary Committee at the confirmation hearings for Clarence Thomas. Thomas was confirmed, but Hill's testimony opened a national discussion on sexual harassment.

with visible fury. "From my standpoint as a black American it is a high-tech lynching for uppity blacks who in any way deign [sic] to think for themselves, to do for themselves. . . . No horror in my life has been so debilitating." This brilliant counterattack befuddled the Democratic senators, who could only gasp apologetic questions. It also gave the Republicans on the committee the opening to pour accusations of perjury and fantasizing on Hill. In the court of instant public opinion, Hill seemed erratic to many Americans, who believed that she should have reported Thomas when the first incident occurred. The final vote in the Senate was close but positive: Thomas was confirmed 52 to 48. Bush's strategy worked. He also obtained a Supreme Court justice who consistently voted with the most conservative bloc of the bench.

The unexpected outcome of this painful hearing revolutionized the discussion of sexual harassment in the United States and began a movement that disclosed rampant sexual exploitation on the job, at universities and schools, in the government, and everywhere. Immediate polls revealed suspicion of Hill and sympathy for Thomas. But within a year this public judgment had reversed. The event also had serious political consequences for the 1992 election. Illinois voters tossed out Senator Alan Dixon, a Democrat who voted to confirm Thomas, in favor of a black woman who skillfully capitalized on the anger of women voters. Around the country, women entered politics in unprecedented numbers, promising never again to allow an all-male Senate committee to decide questions they so clearly misunderstood. If 1992 became the electoral "Year of the Woman," it was partly because of the Hill-Thomas hearings.

Still, nothing was settled on the Court by this wrenching experience. The issue of abortion rights further divided Americans, some of whom took to the streets. Over the summer of 1991, Operation Rescue, a group that blocked abortion clinics and harassed doctors and patients, tried to shut down all the abortion clinics in Wichita, Kansas. By August more than 2,000 demonstrators had been arrested, although the clinics remained open. Whether such tactics worked in the sense of persuading the public to oppose abortion is doubtful. Polls consistently and increasingly showed a majority of voters approving this right—although often with a variety of restrictions. Yet the public rancor and danger created by such groups discouraged doctors from entering the specialty. In two instances in Florida in 1993 and 1994, doctors who performed abortions were murdered by right-to-life extremists. The lack of available clinics in many states made legal abortion something only for the most persistent or well off able to travel to distant facilities. A further complication was the fulfillment of the nightmare of anti-abortion groups. The development of an oral abortive drug, RU 486, in France made the procedure easy, cheap, and private. President Bush, listening to Protestant Evangelical and Catholic groups, denied permission for any drug company to test the new pill. But the development promised to revolutionize and even end the debate.

THE NEW WORLD ORDER

If George Bush faced a United States that was deeply divided on ethnic, racial, and gender issues, he also confronted a world in which similar forces were upending old verities and redrawing national boundaries. From a stable division into cold war blocs, the world of the late 1980s and early 1990s dissolved into competing nations and ethnic groups. The most significant event—the decline and fall of communism—occurred by increments. There were moments of great symbolism: the destruction of the Berlin Wall on November 9, 1989, and the reunion of West and East Germany. But the disintegration of the Soviet Union and the emergence or reemergence of independent states throughout Eastern Europe and the Balkans and around Russia was a change that, once begun, neither the old Communist apparatus in Moscow could halt nor the United States exploit.

In the pages of spy novels, the predictions of political pundits, and the espionage reports of the CIA, this spontaneous degeneration of com-

munism was unforeseen and disquieting. Historians will forever debate the cause of the sudden Soviet collapse—the "evil empire" that was in reality fragile and incompetent. Something can be attributed to Ronald Reagan's huge military buildup, which the Soviets recognized would either bankrupt their nation to match or render them a second-rate power. The Soviet leaders fully realized this dilemma. There were other factors: the war in neighboring Afghanistan, where the Soviet army tried to prop up an unpopular leader against a rising tide of Islamic fundamentalists armed and aided by the United States and other nations. Like Vietnam for the United States, Afghanistan posed unanswered questions: What had soldiers returning in body bags given their lives for? Why was the war unwinnable? Other failures, such as the nuclear accident at Chernobyl (see Chapter 26), uncovered incompetence and inexcusable technological inadequacies in the most advanced sectors of Soviet industry. More than anything perhaps, the earnest reforms of Mikhail Gorbachev and the group supporting him set off an irreversible chain reaction. Believing that the communist system could be reformed from within, Gorbachev sought limited reforms: *glasnost*, or increased personal freedom for individuals, and *peristroika*, or reform of the bureaucratic, corrupt, and incompetent command system of central economic planning. But when Gorbachev nudged the tottering system, it collapsed of its own weight. The hatred of Soviet citizens for political repression, scarce consumer goods, the glaring inequalities of station, and the privileges assumed by Communist party members, the repression of religious and ethnic aspirations all suddenly erupted. The genius of Gorbachev was to control this flood, to preside with some grace over the collapse of the world he helped to build and wanted to maintain. When he failed, he stepped aside.

No profound political revolution is ever easy, quick, or bloodless or without outside interference of some sort, but President Bush quickly perceived in the early winter of 1988–1989 there was little he could or should do. He established a policy of verbal support for Gorbachev and his reforms and spoke warmly of democratization and market capitalism. But he did little to interfere, nor did he lead a cheering section of cold warriors to celebrate the extraordinary victory of the United States and its allies.

Bush's inauguration in January 1989 coincided with the intensifying expressions of nationalism within the staggering Soviet Union, as historically independent nations and aspiring ethnic groups within its borders demanded self-determination. The president encouraged Gorbachev to allow these expressions, particularly in the Baltic republics of Lithuania, Latvia, and Estonia, which had been incorporated into the USSR by force. Bush also encouraged the Soviets to relax control and influence over their neighbors and allies: Poland, Czechoslovakia, Hungary, East Germany, Bulgaria, and Romania. During the first two years of the administration this policy succeeded, but it blinded the administration to the swift changes in Eastern Europe, causing some to wonder if the United States actually feared what it had diligently sought since 1917: the collapse of communism.

In early 1989 reforms in Poland accelerated. Fighting in ethnically contested areas of the Soviet Union erupted. By December 1989, communists had been voted out of office in Czechoslovakia, and a sudden coup d'etat overthrew the despised Romanian communist dictator, Nicolai Ceausescu. In March 1990, Lithuania declared its independence, which Soviet military maneuvers and threats did little to prevent. It was evident that the Soviet Union was collapsing and that Gorbachev had decided not to resist this decline with force. Then in June 1991 Boris Yeltsin, a popular rival of Gorbachev, was elected president of the Russian Republic. Latvia and Estonia declared their independence. Bush continued to support Gorbachev, the premier of a nation (the USSR) that was decomposing and the head of a political party (the Communist party) that represented, at best, only itself, its vast numbers of bureaucratic retainers, and its sorry history.

In August 1991, while Gorbachev vacationed at a Black Sea resort, several government ministers bitterly opposed to his reformist policies declared themselves a new government of the Soviet Union. Held prisoner by soldiers at the resort, Gorbachev could do little, but Yeltsin in Moscow defied the reactionaries, calling out demonstrators to defend the nation against this extreme step backwards. For three tense days the people of Moscow and Leningrad (now St. Petersburg) stood their ground. The coup collapsed, the final casualty of a system of mammoth incompetence and political cynicism. Gorbachev returned to Moscow, but greatly weakened. Gradually Yeltsin accumulated power in his own hands. In December 1991, Gorbachev resigned as president of the Soviet Union, which had, in effect, ceased to exist anyway. Now the most powerful leader was Boris Yeltsin, president of Russia—one nation out of the twelve—now independent associated republics that had once constituted the largest nation on earth.

President Bush and many Americans watched Gorbachev fail with uneasiness because this sophisticated and urbane man had up to then controlled the political process. Gorbachev had also reversed Soviet foreign policy by supporting American initiatives around the world. This is what President Bush meant when he invoked the term, "New World Order."

Indications of a new cooperative role of the Soviet Union came almost at the beginning of Bush's tenure. Gorbachev did little to oppose the United States invasion of Panama on December 20, 1989 (Operation "Just Cause") to overthrow the government of Manuel Noriega. Noriega had fallen from friend, ally, and recipient of U.S. financing to an accused drug runner and threat to the Panama Canal. The Bush administration seized the occasion of a deadly confrontation between off-duty American soldiers, stationed in the Panama Canal Zone, and Panamanian troops, during which one American was killed. Bush ordered in twelve thousand army, navy, air force, and marine personnel to join the 20,000 U.S. service personnel already there. The short war ended abruptly when Noriega sought sanctuary in the Vatican embassy. On January 3 he surrendered to U.S. forces, who promptly dispatched him to Florida for trial on drug smuggling charges. Given the new balance of power in the world, the United States ignored a United Nations vote on December 29 deploring the invasion.

ETHNIC AND RELIGIOUS TURMOIL

Of the many areas of the world bedeviled by religious and ethnic hostility, the Middle East was perhaps the most important because of its huge underground sea of oil. Swept by centuries of conquest, imperialism, and colonialism, and religious wars, the area maintained an armed peace during the cold war, interrupted by occasional indecisive but bloody warfare. The collapse of the Soviet Union withdrew a stable influence from the area. In several countries, Islamic fundamentalism demanded strict observance of the laws of the Qur'an (the Islamic holy book) and the cleansing of European and American social and cultural influences from their societies. The intermittent warfare against the existence of Israel also threatened to erupt again.

The Reagan administration had been burned in its dealings with Iran, when efforts to release hostages resulted in the intrigues of the Iran-Contra debacle. The United States had also cautiously supported Iran's bitter enemy, Saddam Hussein of Iraq, during the late 1980s, when Soviet power began to wane in the area. During the brutal and inconclusive war between Iran and Iraq, the United States hoped for the best—the defeat of Islamic fundamentalism in Iran—and so supplied Iraq with moderate amounts of weapons and materiel. When the war finally ended in August 1988, Iraq turned on another rival, Kuwait to the south. The hostility between Kuwait and Iraq was partly historic, partly personal, but primarily a question of disputed real estate and oil resources. The kingdom of Kuwait, a nation of sand, millionaires, and migrant workers from Palestine, India, and other poor countries, sat atop one of the largest pools of oil in the world. Should Saddam Hussein possess these reserves,

he could control enough of the world's known oil resources to affect prices and supplies.

Why Hussein believed he could seize and absorb his important neighbor without serious reprisal is something of a mystery. It may rest on the ties he believed he still maintained with the United States. It may have reflected his sense of the chaos of the post–cold war world and the traditional reluctance of the United States to intervene outside the Western Hemisphere—as the mild United States reaction to the 1989 Tiananmen Square massacre of students in China illustrated. Whatever his reasoning, Hussein demanded that Kuwait return oil it had pumped from territories Iraq claimed. In fact, this was a ruse, for on August 2, 1990, Iraqi armies swept through the tiny kingdom. On August 8, Kuwait disappeared, as Iraq reorganized it as one of its provinces.

On August 2, the day of the invasion, President Bush denounced Iraq's action, demanding an immediate cease-fire and withdrawal. On August 3, the Soviet Union joined the U.S. in calling for an immediate end to the war. With the USSR in concert, Egypt and Saudi Arabia (now threatened by Hussein's troops) and Western Europe in agreement, President Bush worked skillfully to build support for action through the United Nations. On August 6 the United Nations Security Council condemned the invasion and initiated an economic blockade of Iraq. On the same day, King Fahd of Saudi Arabia granted permission to the United States to station troops in his nation. This was an extraordinary reversal of policy. Since the bitter end of French and British colonialism after World War II, the Arab Middle East had jealously guarded its independence. Saudi Arabia especially had sought to protect itself from Western cultural influences it judged corrupt and irreligious.

President Bush, after organizing a coalition of forces ranged against Iraq, turned to convert a more stubborn and difficult audience: American voters. Although it was something of a contrived slogan, Bush's declaration of purpose had a memorable ring to it: "This will not stand. This will

The public relations war in the Middle East.   Here General Norman Schwartzkopf, with pointer and map, explains to the assembled press corps and the world television viewing community watching over CNN, the progress of the United Nations (and United States) victory.

not stand, this aggression against Kuwait." Secretary of State James Baker, in a less eloquent but more convincing phrase, summed up the reasons for America to mobilize: because of "one word . . . jobs." While the reasoning was far-fetched, few missed his point. Hussein's monopoly of oil could lead to high prices for petroleum and thus a deep recession in the United States. Thousands of jobs might be at risk.

On November 29, the United Nations sent an ultimatum to Iraq: leave Kuwait by January 15, 1991, or face the military consequences. As the New Year began, the American military contingent in Saudi Arabia had swollen to include 527,000 personnel, 110 naval vessels, 2,000 tanks, 2,200 armored personnel carriers, 1,800

fixed-wing aircraft, and 1,700 helicopters. Egypt, France, Britain, and other nations contributed troops and aircraft. Only the assent of Congress was needed to dislodge Iraq. After a sharp and unusually intelligent debate, the Senate and the House both approved the military option, but by narrow margins: 52 to 47 in the Senate; 250 to 183 in the House.

When last-minute negotiations failed to budge Hussein, war began on January 16, 1991. The UN plan—Operation Desert Storm—was methodical and incremental. Combat began first in the air when a massive United Nations flying armada neutralized the Iraqi air force and silenced much of that nation's anti-aircraft protection. Next, bombers attacked communications, military centers, and supply lines. Some of this was accomplished by "smart bombs," electronically guided to hit selected targets. These weapons were widely noted and displayed for television audiences, who watched nose-cone cameras record direct hits on military targets. Residual doubts about the safety of civilian populations were calmed by this reassuring video, although after the war it was revealed that these weapons were less effective than initially claimed.

Control of communications crippled the Iraqi armies and gave a monopoly of information to the United Nations forces, who controlled the images and news flowing from the front. Frequent military briefings by the American commander, General Norman Schwartzkopf, and interviews with Colin Powell, chairman of the Joint Chiefs of Staff for the United States, plus announcements and interviews with spokespersons, designated representatives, and experts, made this a closely controlled war of ideas broadcast to the United States and the rest of the world over CNN (the cable news network) The military was more vigilant about regulating the news than they were during the Vietnam War. Few pictures of destruction inside Iraq or accounts of "collateral" civilian casualties appeared. The most graphic images of destruction and suffering among civilians came after Iraq fired crude SCUD missiles at Israel to provoke that nation into retaliation and hence force neutral or pro–United Nations Arab countries to change sides. Even here, the story became the efficiency of American "Patriot" antimissile missiles that appeared to prevent SCUDs from finding their targets. Again, after the war, the claim suffered a rude revision; the Patriots were not nearly as dependable as depicted.

Air supremacy achieved, 200,000 United Nations troops attacked the Iraqi army in Kuwait on February 24. One hundred hours later, Iraq had been routed and its armies fled in terror before the onslaught of tanks and aircraft. When a cease-fire was signed on February 27, Kuwait had been swept clean of Iraqi invaders. Compared to a very slight loss of about 300 dead on the United

Nation's side, Iraq's casualties were devastating: 100,000 soldiers killed and 175,000 captured.

REPUBLICANS AND RECESSION

Public euphoria over the victory in the Middle East, the celebration of American technology, and George Bush's skillful nurture of an alliance against Iraq earned him little permanent public affection. Nor could he focus attention on a much larger accomplishment: his successful Soviet/ Russian policy that effectively ended the cold war. The Reagan economic boom ended during the middle of Bush's administration. Excess investment in real estate, corporate restructuring, and dubious financial transactions, celebrated during the 1980s for their audacity, pushed major corporations into bankruptcy. As economic optimism began to fade in the early 1991, the wobbly foundations of a decade's economic prosperity were exposed to the further corrosion of a deepening international recession. The huge national debt grew like a malignancy, reaching around four trillion dollars in 1992.

MANAGING THE ECONOMY

President Bush brought two unfortunate liabilities to managing the problems of the economy. The Republican party controlled only a minority of votes in Congress. On occasion, Democrats might join with Republicans to pass legislation, but to begin any major initiative required substantial support and input from the opposition party. The second barrier was higher: the president had no real plan to alleviate economic problems nor did he believe, philosophically, in an interventionist federal role in the economy. At the same time, he showed little enthusiasm for the ideologically stringent plans of his party's conservative wing. He did not support radical proposals to return the nation to the gold standard (causing severe deflation) or another broad tax cut like Reagan had achieved, nor the serious dismantling of the welfare and Social Security programs. He did propose a major capital gains tax cut from 28 percent to as low as 15.4 percent for property held a considerable length of time. This would reduce federal tax revenues in the short run, but it was predicted that such an increase in investment and turnover of assets would result that tax revenues would eventually increase. While this proposal fit the tax-less-for-more-revenue ideology of Reagan's income tax cut in 1981, it generated little popular support. Nor did Bush have a consistent plan to reduce the federal budget deficit, which consumed more tax dollars to pay interest, pumping inflated money into the economy, weakening the American dollar abroad, and maintaining higher interest rates.

Inevitably, stalemated ideology and politics developed their own curiously ritualized pattern of pseudo solutions. Each year, a major confrontation developed around the federal budget. In January, the president would propose a budget whose numbers depended upon a "rosy" (unrealistic) estimate of growth and income. On this basis, the administration would seek higher defense spending, and farm subsidies, while maintaining such programs as Social Security. The budget would also call for severe cuts in social programs and welfare subsidies. This selective conservative agenda never stood much chance of passage, but it allowed both conservatives and liberals to speak to their special constituencies on issues about which they were not often called to account. Ideological escalation became a predominant part of the relationship between Democrats in the Congress and the president. Increasingly President Bush used his veto to block legislation passed by the Democrats, who lacked the majorities in either House or Senate to overrule him. Each side could then condemn the results: to Democrats the president was obstructionist; for Republicans, the Democratic Congress was corrupt and lethargic. To the American public, the confrontations in Washington appeared to resemble "gridlock," a word aptly borrowed from traffic jams so serious that no cars could move in any direction.

If the two parties believed they could gain advantage from deadlock, there was considerable evidence that the voting public became increasingly frustrated and angry. This rising fury fed the sentiment, expressed by many Republicans during the 1980s, that government was the problem, not the solution. They had hoped to slim the welfare state, continue high defense expenditures, and pass occasional social legislation designed to bolster "family values." But they seriously miscalculated on two counts. A great many Americans supported the welfare state, at least as it affected them, and any plans to prune it back threatened powerful interest groups. The disappearance of the cold war made defense spending considerably less compelling. In fact the problem of stalemate lay as much with voter indecision as with their representatives, for serious reform divided group against group. Neither political party commanded the loyalty of sufficiently large numbers of divergent voters to pass anything so threatening.

Economic growth in the United States slowed at the beginning of President Bush's first year in office, falling from a healthy 4.4 percent in 1988 to a weaker 3 percent in 1989. By the autumn of 1990, it was an anemic 1.7 percent. This economic bad news dashed the reputations of investment celebrities who had reaped fortunes during the booming 1980s. One of the highest flyers in the junk bond market, the Drexel Burnham Lambert Co., declared bankruptcy in February. Then, several months later in November, 1990, Michael Milken, an investment wizard, was sentenced to ten years in prison for fraud and fined $600 million. More dismaying was the implication of leading Democratic senators in a savings and loan scandal of disheartening proportions. When the sharp dealings of Charles Keating bankrupted the Lincoln Savings and Loan Corporation of California, $2 billion in assets was lost. Four Democratic senators: Alan Cranston of California, Dennis DiConcini of Arizona, Donald Riegle of Michigan, and John Glenn of Ohio—plus Republican John McCain of Arizona as a minor player—were accused of helping ward off industry regulators in exchange for campaign contributions from Keating. Investigated by the Democratic-controlled Senate Ethics Committee, only Cranston was reprimanded for misconduct, while the other three received rebukes but no penalties. Nevertheless, the reputation of Congress was compromised by the implication that some of its members had personally contributed to the nation's economic problems.

Most discouraging of all were the economic bruises endured by individual voters themselves. During the early 1990s, large manufacturing firms like General Motors and International Harvester lost markets, sales, and profits. They laid off thousands of workers and sought benefit and wage concessions from those who remained. Some large establishments like Ford moved crucial plants and employment to border areas of Mexico where wages were low and environmental regulations rarely, if ever, enforced. Other large manufacturing outfits—again like auto makers—slapped labels on their products designating them as American-made when many of their parts and designs were produced abroad. Even so, in 1992, Chrysler lost $795 million, Ford $2.26 Billion, and General Motors $4.45 billion. Not even information industries were spared. IBM, for decades the standard of America' advantage in computer technology, felt the shock of international competition and recession. Swamped by cheap clones of its products and innovative technology from companies like Apple, IBM closed factories and laid off workers. From a peak employment of 406,000 in 1986, it retained only 250,000 on its payroll by the end of 1993. Other giants in the computer industry like Wang were less fortunate and closed entirely. The miracle miles of defense and computer industries and consulting firms that clustered around Boston and in Silicon Valley in northern California suffered serious unemployment. By the middle of the recession, the victims of bankruptcy and reorganization included the rich and famous. Old, respectable firms like Pan American World Air-

ways, the pioneer in air travel before World War II, folded.

"THE ECONOMY, STUPID"

By January 1991, the recession had worsened considerably. In 1990 a million payroll jobs disappeared even though inflation remained relatively high. In the spring of 1991, unemployment jumped to 6.8 percent of the active workforce, and economic growth had fallen over to the minus side of the graph. Over the summer, unemployment continued to rise and pressure mounted for federal action. But when the Congress passed a new jobless benefits bill, extending eligibility for unemployment insurance, the president vetoed the measure, arguing that there was no serious recession. The economy would correct itself. His action was upheld by the Senate.

Still the economy did not improve and Bush's fortunes sank in tandem with its declining figures. As the Democrats scrambled to find candidates to oppose Bush in the election of 1992, those in the Republican party who neither liked nor trusted the president, began a harsh, ideological challenge in Presidential primaries. The two leading challengers included Patrick Buchanan, former advisor to Richard Nixon, a speech writer, journalist, and political commentator. The other was, briefly, David Duke, unsuccessful candidate for governor of Louisiana and a former Grand Wizard of the Ku Klux Klan and a Nazi admirer. Duke quickly withered, but the stern and righteous Buchanan attracted large numbers of anti-Bush voters. The results of the February 1992 New Hampshire primary were the first and gravest. The president won 53 percent of the votes and the delegates, but Buchanan gained 37 percent. Never a serious challenge to the nomination itself, Buchanan's run was more symbolic than real. In response the president made gestures to the right wing of the party, which Buchanan represented. He fired John Frohnmayer as chair of the National Endowment of the Arts for defending controversial grants. Buchanan had excoriated the government agency as "the upholstered playpen of the arts and crafts auxiliary of the Eastern liberal establishment." But Bush's action was too late and too transparent.

In fact the president could never escape his broken promise never to raise taxes. His defiant pose at the Dallas nominating convention in 1988 had greatly aided his election. Under no circumstances would he ever raise taxes, he said, striking the stance of a movie tough guy. But new taxes were exactly what he did approve midway into his term. In October 1990 he worked out an agreement for higher levies on upper incomes and increased excise taxes on gasoline, cigarettes, and beer. It was a fatal step but characteristic of the four years of his administration. To govern, the president had to work with the Democratic party. Consequently, on many important pieces of legislation such as this tax measure, the Republican party voted against him. This alienating process, in turn, made the president appear weak and unprincipled.

A THREE-WAY RACE

This extremely difficult and contradictory situation opened the door to an unwanted guest who intruded into the two-way race. This was as serious a challenge as Theodore Roosevelt had mounted in 1912 [see Chapter 19]. The diffuse anger of the electorate at corruption and stalemate in Washington opened the door for a third-party candidate. A man with a keen eye and a penetrating voice, Ross Perot of Texas used his huge fortune and unusual charisma to revolutionize the political discourse. Studiously antipolitical, Perot promised to clean out Washington by substituting good business practices for the prevailing system of deals, influence-peddling, and compromise. Beneath the folksy patter and Texas accent, Perot was a hardboiled autocrat, who quickly assembled a large group of volunteers and paid employees to push his candidacy. He also made two promises: he would offer a general plan to eliminate the bloated federal debt and he would reorganize government from top to bottom. This would require severe budget cuts as well as new taxes. But the candidate snared the admiration and confidence of many voters. The proof of his ability was his great wealth and the success it symbolized. A graduate of the U.S. Naval Academy, he had founded Electronic Data Systems in 1962 and made a fortune on government contracts. He was a businessman with visible success and supreme self-confidence.

Yet, he also possessed character quirks that often undermined his purpose. His quick temper and defensiveness caused him to insult groups of voters on occasion. Some were suspicious of his tax and budget plans. Others sensed in his disdain for politics a rigid and uncompromising attitude that would disrupt, not reform government. Perot's constituency was divided, if not contradictory. Much of his appeal aroused conservative, swing-vote independents or Republicans. This constituency was middle-aged, white, and suburban, and they might be expected to rally to George Bush.

But 1992 was no normal year and nothing reflected this so much as the Democratic party free-for-all primaries. A field of dark horses gathered at the gate, including Senators Robert Kerrey of Nebraska and Tom Harkin of Iowa; ex-governor of California Jerry Brown; and Bill Clinton, governor of Arkansas. Perhaps the least known nationally, Clinton lasted through a process guaranteed to expose candidates to the worst hazards of strange rules and unrepresentative constituencies. To emerge successful from this process was anything but a test of any ability to govern. But Clinton showed himself to be persistent, intelligent, and canny, with the outlines, at least, of a comprehensive plan to reform the economy and end the recession.

He also displayed potentially crippling handicaps. He was governor of a small, unrepresentative state. His inclinations were decidedly liberal, and his wife, Hillary Rodham Clinton, was an aggressive and competent lawyer and administrator. A history of marital difficulties and charges of extramarital affairs dogged the candidate. Even more troubling was his military ser-

IN THE 1992 ELECTION, Ross Perot (center) held center stage with his blunt language and simple solutions. While he took votes from both candidates, George Bush (on the left) and Bill Clinton (on the right), it is uncertain whether he greatly affected the outcome.

vice record—or lack of it. During the war in Vietnam in the 1960s, which he opposed, Clinton had signed up with the ROTC and then received an educational deferment. The full details of this story became public in February 1992, when former colonel Eugene Holmes of Arkansas told *The Wall Street Journal* that Clinton had evaded the draft. On February 12, Clinton released a letter he had written twenty-five years earlier to Holmes. In it he despaired at the choices he confronted: serve in a war he hated and opposed or defy the draft and face long imprisonment or exile. The choice he made—to put off making any choice—was certainly an attempt to avoid military service.

Many voters, urged on by the Republican party, interpreted this as simple draft evasion. Republicans were delighted to escape from charges that Vice President Dan Quayle had engineered

an assignment in the Indiana National Guard, thus avoiding combat service in Vietnam, a war he had vociferously supported. But Clinton shrugged off these charges and won the nomination, concentrating on the economy and promising to end politics as usual in Washington.

By the time of the Republican convention in August 1992, President Bush remained down in the political polls. The convention did not help him. There was little beyond Desert Storm to flag as an outstanding success, and so the president and the vice president and even their wives joined in a personal attack on Clinton and his wife. Setting the tone of this negative crusade was Pat Buchanan, whose keynote address threatened a cultural war against those (unnamed) groups who were corrupting American culture. This divisive attack on multiculturalism missed its mark because it appeared to disparage so many groups

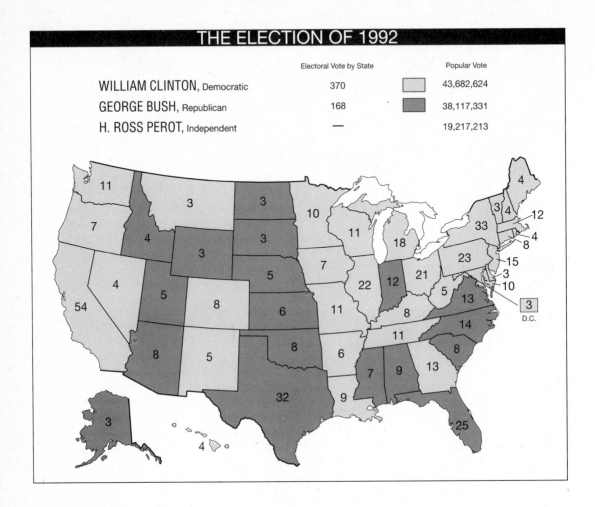

THE ELECTION OF 1992

	Electoral Vote by State	Popular Vote
WILLIAM CLINTON, Democratic	370	43,682,624
GEORGE BUSH, Republican	168	38,117,331
H. ROSS PEROT, Independent	—	19,217,213

while failing to consider the economic problems that troubled most voters. The strategy of dividing Americans by race, religion, gender, and ethnicity had worked once in 1989. But some of the consequences of division had lit the fires of the Los Angeles riots. And in 1992, Bush was unable to emerge from the shroud of negativism that deadened any attention to his accomplishments or plans for the future.

After a season of indecision, Ross Perot entered the race in October, but the least important of his purposes was victory. Perot's personal dislike for Bush was visible and vocal and his contempt for Clinton unrepressed. He was ambi-

tious. He had personal funds to finance a campaign his way, largely through television lectures and talk-show appearances. As a populist with no party, no debts, and no hope of winning, he could speak his mind or at least give the impression of complete candor. It was an extraordinary performance. He accomplished, in a few weeks, the transformation of the dialogue, away from Clinton's draft record and "character" issues like sexual misconduct and onto economics and the federal deficit—issues that seriously hurt the Republicans. When the votes were tallied, Clinton had swept 370 electoral votes to 168 for Bush and a comfortable plurality of the popular vote.

Perot came in third, with almost 20 million ballots but no electoral votes. Twelve years of Republican administrations ended. But the new Democrat had not won a majority of votes, and the political landscape remained both confused and crowded.

-→=◦=←-

MULTICULTURAL CULTURE

If an unstable chemistry of economics, political chance, and personality determined the immediate results of the election, there were immense cultural forces at work, changing American society in remarkable ways, often beyond the attention or grasp of politicians. These often occurred first among special cultural, age, gender, and ethnic communities and then spread quickly through the mass cultural phenomenon of crossover. This leap of cultural innovation from a more homogeneous group to the larger, more differentiated audience, had become the most significant phenomenon of twentieth-century mass culture. Jazz, for example, grew out of black musical traditions of the Deep South, particularly in New Orleans before World War I. It was then transformed by northern urban traditions of music, by reinterpretations of new artists, and even touched by the modern chords and chromatics of classical European music. It attracted a white audience in the 1920s and 1930s and, following World War II, even found influence in elite, intellectual circles in New York and Paris, where devotees listened to tinny old recordings of Bessie Smith and other "classics." Ethnic foods followed a similar trajectory. Pizza, created in Naples, Italy, in the seventeenth century, began to appear at Italian festivals in New York by the 1920s. By the 1950s, however, it became ubiquitous. The pizza "parlor" of the day (so-named to give elegance to simple food) became the drive-in and fast food staple of teenagers and then the rest of their families by the 1970s. Finally, it appeared in health-food versions with whole-wheat crusts and organic vegetables in the late 1980s.

The map of American cultural communities in the 1980s and 1990s and the borders and bridges between them were no less complicated. The process of integration and crossover continued with even greater speed and intensity. Rap music typified this hyperactive process. Created by African-American young people in the South Bronx and Harlem, New York, in the late 1970s, the music quickly attracted notoriety and criticism. "Rapper's Delight," recorded by Sugarhill Records in 1979, gained some national popularity. But it took the emergence of small groups or stars like Queen Latifah, Ice Cube, 2 Live Crew, and Public Enemy to establish the standard for the art and its recording style. Using street slang, the spoken song expressed hostility and alienation. It also explored the limits of public discourse on sexuality and racism. By the mid-1980s not only had rap spread to a far larger audience than the black urban community, but concerts and records were big business with racially mixed audiences and purchasers.

This music seized American young people as well as similar groups across the world, especially in the new international cities of Europe and Asia, because of its energy and accessibility. Against a background of detached video images, with a penetrating beat—a wall of sound and sights—the rap artist uttered a poetry of protest, anger, and refusal. While the words were not always crucial for foreign listeners, they certainly touched Americans. These were sometimes sharp rebukes of other ethnic groups or bitter and sexist views of women, attacks on government—an angry, rhythmic defiance drawn from America's dying cities. Even the titles of songs—"I Want Your Sex"—and the aggressive names of groups (Public Enemy, and Hoes wit' Attitudes) expressed this anger and resentment.

Words to "The Message" in 1982 by Grand Master Flash and the Furious Five were typical of the more philosophic side:

It's like a jungle
Sometimes it makes me wonder
how I keep from going under.

Much more controversial was the anti-Semitic, anti-Japanese and Korean–anti-cop and woman—piece by Ice Cube, "Now I Gotta Wat'cha." This became known to some as "gangsta rap" and expressed some of the bitterest and most hopeless thoughts squeezed out of the broken-down ghettos of New York, Los Angeles, and Miami. But it suggested a curious paradox. Not only did Chuck D, 2 Live Crew, and other groups make money, they inevitably drifted away from the sources of their music. The intense and original creations of this new music contradicted the hopeless lyrics and the anger expressed by this new genre. Like so much culture of this period, rap music ingeniously and unselfconsciously played upon the very essence of the artistic principles of the day: dissonance in sound and discontinuity of images. Whether it would succumb to crossover and commercialization was not obvious, although some groups used rap to present a positive message about drugs, crime, violence, and the treatment of women.

CULTURAL CONTENTION

This belligerent deconstruction of tradition was the opposite in content and politics from the ambitions expressed by a very different American community. Conservatives and European-centered scholars hoped to defend traditional learning and preserve the canon of great authors, by which they meant the great male theologians, writers, artists, and philosophers of Western Europe and America. With a sense of urgency and aura of gloom, this group of academics and conservative political essayists wanted to instruct a generation of American college students in the disappearing values of established culture. The most challenging articulation of these ideas came in University of Chicago professor Allan Bloom's, *The Closing of the American Mind: How Higher Education Has Failed Democracy and Impoverished the Souls of Today's Students*, published in 1987. This stirring defense of conservative literature initiated a feverish discussion in newspaper columns, opinion journals, and book reviews. Bloom's

ideas divided university professors, writers, and intellectuals. But his book gave subtlety to political clichés of conservatism. It lent credibility to the conservative movement as perhaps no other document of the era, defining clearly what, in effect, "traditional values" could be.

Bloom's focus on education was not accidental. He purposely chose the most contested American institution to pillory. Since the *Brown v. Board of Education* decision of 1954, American schools had been swept by demands for reform and for projects of social engineering that they were clearly unprepared to fulfill. Resistance to demands for integration and secularism in public education led from southern opposition to integration, to the founding of Christian private schools, to demands for home education, and, finally, during the Reagan and Bush presidencies, to a voucher system that might have privatized the best public schools.

Conservative demands to instill traditional values and observe religious forms, like public prayer, were matched in the schools by groups with different agendas like sex education, consumer literacy, and driver's education. Behind this spirited tug-of-war lay the questionable assumption that the classroom represented the most effective place to stimulate modern civic virtues.

By the early 1990s, this debate had become highly political and disjointed. In some areas, the issue was Afro-centric education. In other cases, the problem was social control. Absent strong families in many communities, schools were asked to intervene in sexual practices of students by teaching sex education and distributing condoms to lessen the risk of spreading the HIV virus. In still others, the issue became the multicultural classroom and the problem of creating an environment where any group—Latino, Asian, African-American, or women, gays, the handicapped—might feel completely at ease.

To achieve this complex compromise was undoubtedly utopian and, increasingly, controversial. Opposing this plan for controlling discourse was an older concept of the marketplace of free speech. Its defenders asserted that a unified American culture would emerge from the free competition of ideas. But opponents wished to know whether free speech included the right to insult and degrade other individuals. Incorporated around the phrase "political correctness"— an ironic term for multicultural sensitivity—debate over this question echoed from schoolyard to university quadrangle, from television studios to Congress.

Some Americans found community elsewhere, not in political or social institutions, but in the new technology of computers and computer-generated reality. The new public/private world of *cyberspace* was their preoccupation. Literally referring to the imaginary "space" created by the interlacing telephone cables, communications satellites, and computer modems, cyberspace became part of the new vocabulary of computer culture, anticipating the fusion of human and machine. It rested on an extraordinary linkage of individual computers via the Internet in what was undoubtedly the most important innovation in communications during the era. Popular novels such as William Gibson's *Neuromancer* and films such as *Blade Runner*, *Robocop*, *Terminator 2*, and *Lawnmower Man*, visualized a futuristic world of human-like robots and virtual reality. The latter experience, created by donning a special computer helmet and wearing a data glove, made it theoretically possible to design programs in which the individual might wander in an interactive computer-generated world, responding to computer-generated sensory stimuli.

Linked together by electronic networks, the "console cowboys" of this group created "virtual communities"—again dependent on modern information technology. Despite the unfamiliar terminology and science-fiction imaginings of such communities, their experiments only exaggerated the ordinary—what already existed in family rooms and offices around the country. From Nintendo games to integrated fax, phone, E-mail, television, and desktop publishing work stations, more and more Americans worked watching a computer monitor—and spent their leisure doing what they did at work.

NEW ETHNIC COMMUNITIES

Perhaps the most significant new community only just began to emerge from the ignorance of inattention and prejudice in this period. Suddenly in the 1980s and 1990s, it became obvious that Spanish-speaking immigrants were revolutionizing American demographics. Like so many ethnic groups before them, the immense new numbers of Latinos experienced stereotyping from many other Americans and suffered invisibility in terms of political and economic power— as evident, for example, in their underrepresentation in descriptions of the Los Angeles riots. Always a major presence in the history of America from the settlement of the Southwest to the twentieth century, Hispanics were a minority whose large numbers and concentration within a few states and cities created a strong presence. Yet recognition was feeble compared to the importance of this group. Despite the inadequacies of the US Census and the problems of underestimation of populations, it is projected that with its continued rate of differential growth, the Hispanic population will surpass the African-American population sometime around 2005, perhaps earlier.

The largest part of this population is of Mexican origin (around 60 percent) with much smaller percentages of Puerto Ricans and Cubans. Concentrated in border cities in Arizona, New Mexico, and Texas, as well as in Miami, Chicago, and New York, Hispanics have made considerable political inroads and promise to make far more. For example, there were around 3,360 elected officials of Hispanic origin in 1990. At the same time, the Spanish language emerged as the second language of choice for English-speaking students in schools and is increasingly spoken on radio and television. Like every other major ethnic group, its culture, in terms of food and music, has made a significant crossover into the US mainstream. For example, the religious impact of this varied community has also been broadly felt, both within the Catholic Church, the traditional religion of Spanish-speaking America, and within evangelical Protestant groups that have successfully recruited converts from this population both within the United States and in such countries as Peru and Guatemala.

In other areas like Hollywood films, actors of Hispanic origin are still perhaps less important than in the 1930s and 1940s, when exoticism, a foreign accent, and a romantic setting were far more frequent. To some degree this inattention began to change as numbers of actors and celebrities grew during the 1980s. Probably the most important Latino film of this era was *La Bamba* (1987), which became a crossover hit throughout the country. As with traditional European groups of immigrants, Hispanic Americans were pulled in two directions: toward preserving the heritage of the countries, provinces, and villages of their origin and adopting the powerful culture of the new country where they reside.

MULTICULTURAL POLITICS

In 1992, economics provided an issue that prevented the contentious issues of multiculturalism from deciding the presidential election. Nevertheless, Democrats and Republicans more or less followed the faultlines of groups and arguments that articulated this deep division in American society. Republicans were avidly supported by religious conservatives and traditionalists, among them Protestants, Catholics, and some Jews. Their vote was lopsidedly male and they lost the majority of African-American and Hispanic voters. Democrats, on the other hand, attracted a majority of Hispanic, African-American, Jewish, woman, and gay voters. This division of the voting population initially defined the actions of the Clinton administration once it took office in 1993.

The new president found he had to proceed on three fronts simultaneously to satisfy his constituencies and fulfill his broad campaign promises. In searching for early appointments, he made a strong and successful effort to make his government "look like America," in other words to be representative of its population in terms of ethnicity and gender. This meant several cabinet appointments for Hispanics, blacks, and women. Two were Hispanics from the Southwest. A former mayor of Denver, Federico F. Peña, became transportation secretary; and Henry G. Cisneros, former mayor of San Antonio, took over housing and urban development. There were also two African Americans: Ronald H. Brown became secretary of commerce and Mike Espy became secretary of agriculture. Former president of the University of Wisconsin, Donna E. Shalala, became secretary of health and human services. On occasion, however, Clinton faltered and either

RACE AND ETHNICITY IN AMERICA, 1980–1990

Race	1980	1990	%1980	%1990
White	188,371,622	199,686,070	83.1	80.3
Black	26,495,025	29,986,060	11.7	12.1
Native American	1,364,033	1,878,285	0.6	0.8
Asian	3,500,439	7,273,622	1.5	2.9
Hispanic	14,608,673	22,354,059	6.4	9.0

Source: World Almanac, 1993 *(New York, 1993), p. 388.*

made appointments that failed or had to be withdrawn. The most controversial of these occurred in the search for an attorney general. Two women had to withdraw from consideration because they had neglected to pay Social Security taxes for their domestic help. A third candidate, Janet Reno of Miami, Florida, was easily confirmed. Again after hesitating, Clinton made a safe Supreme Court choice in Judge Ruth Bader Ginsberg, confirmed in the summer of 1993, and then another in 1994—Judge Stephen Breyer. Neither of these appointees could be considered liberal, but they nonetheless solidified the Supreme Court as a centrist institution, unwilling to intrude seriously on individual rights.

Delivering on the promise to end discrimination against gays and lesbians in the armed services was far more difficult, although this was an important issue to an important constituency. Gay men and lesbians had increasingly organized politically. Since the Stonewall riots in New York City almost twenty-five years earlier (1969), when gay men fought back against a police raid at a Greenwich Village bar, issues of gay and lesbian rights had emerged into the public arena. The AIDS epidemic only intensified the crisis of blatant discrimination in housing and medical care. Perhaps most important were issues of simple dignity: the desire to be open and accepted. Yet such demands were extraordinarily controversial, as were the more fringe issues of gay and lesbian marriage.

When Clinton proposed a new policy of allowing openly gay and lesbian recruits, the armed services, their allies in Congress, and a sizable portion of the American population reacted with considerable alarm. Such a policy would destroy morale, they argued, and expose heterosexual males to harassment in barracks and close quarters of ships. A compromise policy allowed both sides to claim victory. The new policy of "don't ask," "don't tell," and "don't investigate," in July 1993, allowed the military to maintain the fiction that gays and lesbians did not exist in the services. The president could claim he had advanced the civil liberties of this group—but not by much.

Two other campaign promises proved contradictory. Part of Clinton's appeal to voters was his determination to end the recession, stimulate the economy through tax relief for the middle class, and induce job creation. Yet Ross Perot's intervention in the election, and his watchdog role afterwards, forced Clinton to accept a different economic agenda that made reduction of the national debt the higher priority. When Clinton and his congressional allies crafted a long-term budget bill in 1993 it significantly cut future federal budgets but it also raised taxes. As such it garnered little Republican support. Yet, compared to previous attempts, it represented progress. It was estimated that by 1998 $496 billion would be saved through new taxes and spending cuts. This was accomplished by raising gasoline taxes and corporate taxes and by increasing the top percentage of taxes paid by the affluent. An individual would pay 36 percent on income over $115,000, as opposed to a previous 31 percent, and a couple would experience the same increase for any income over $140,000. Spending cuts limited Medicare payments and federal pension cost-of-living adjustments and froze discretionary spending.

Another significant economic program that Clinton pushed through Congress was the North American Free Trade Agreement (NAFTA), passed after considerable bargaining in late November 1993. This treaty with Mexico and Canada significantly lowered trade barriers among the three nations and promised almost free trade in most goods. Whether it was the promise of these programs or the cyclical upturn after a long recession, the economy began to grow briskly after the second quarter of 1993.

CRIME

The issue that emerged most strongly after the election was crime and violence. Clinton's centrist Democratic administration took several small if significant steps to combat it. On November 30, 1993, after considerable lobbying, Congress passed the "Brady Bill" (named after the aide wounded in the assassination attempt on Ronald Reagan). This bill imposed a five-day waiting period as a condition of purchasing a handgun. Later, in the spring of 1994, Clinton succeeded in getting passed a limited bill banning the sale of certain forms of assault weapons.

Yet the sort of crime that frightened citizens of Los Angeles and other cities seemed almost impossible to control. The nationwide resumption of the death penalty after 1976 in increasing numbers of states appeared to have no appreciable effect on crime statistics. The number of persons in American prisons doubled in the 1980s. In 1990, expenditures for crime prevention and detection rose to almost 20 percent of the total spent on education in the United States. The result was the highest incarceration rate of any industrial power and the promise of more huge new expenditures, but very little effect on public fears. If anything, the opposite was true.

Explanations faulted drugs, single-parent families, a breakdown of morality, and a culture awash with images of glamorized violence. Television programs loaded with violence, computer games, films than ran from the ghoulish *Friday the 13th* series to the sophisticated *Silence of the Lambs* (1991), and a reading public that seemed enthralled with mysteries and courtroom dramas, convinced some critics to try to limit violence in the media. Senator Paul Simon of Illinois held hearings in May and June 1993 and persuaded networks to issue prior warnings about the violent content of some of their programs. Educators estimated that the average child had seen 8,000 killings and 100,000 acts of violence on television by the age of eleven or twelve. If this was a cause of real violence, the network warning was ineffective and narrow. And it sounded curiously like Dan Quayle's interpretation of the Los Angeles riots, an interpretation that most media critics surely rejected.

If the Clinton administration seemed intensely preoccupied with domestic affairs, with lobbying on health care, crime, gun control, and economic issues, it appeared to drift on foreign affairs. Part of the reason may well have been the serious and considerable influence of Hillary Rodham Clinton, the president's wife. Unlike other presidential wives in the postwar period, Hillary Clinton was a public activist, a persuasive and effective lobbyist, and a source of ideas and initiatives in the administration. She was not, however, deeply concerned with foreign policy. For her, the difficult and complex problem of a national health insurance providing universal coverage was the major focus. On this issue, she worked as an informal advisor, practically a cabinet member, with the president.

CRIME IN THE UNITED STATES, 1982–1991

	1982	1991
Total Crime	12,974,000	14,873,000
Violent Crimes	1,322,000	1,912,000
Murder	21,000	24,000
Rape	78,000	106,600
Property Crimes	11,652,000	12,961,000
Burglary	3,447,000	3,157,000

Source: Statistical Abstracts of the United States, 1993, *United States, 1994.*

A MULTIETHNIC WORLD

There were some successes in foreign policy that came to fruition because of long-range American policy. The peaceful transition of government from the racist Afrikaner regime in South Africa to a multiracial government in 1994 was an extraordinary achievement, although the United States was only a minor player in what was a brilliantly negotiated agreement by the South Africans themselves. The United States played a much more activist role in the peace treaty signed by the Palestinians and the Israelis that ended Is-

THE PRESIDENT'S WIFE, Hillary Rodham Clinton, made no effort to disguise her public role—with the support of Bill Clinton.

rael's occupation of the West Bank territory and provided for reversion of that territory to the Palestinians in 1994. The Clinton administration intervened quietly to help persuade the British government to negociate with Catholics in Northern Ireland to end the bitter terrorist civil strife there.

These were positive moments in an otherwise bleak and intractable world, however. A vicious civil war in the former multiethnic society of Yugoslavia seemed as interminable as it was bloody. Clinton seemed to vacillate between a desire to intervene and fear of doing so. In Haiti, indecision also ruled policy. Jean-Bertrand Aristide, the lawfully elected president of that impoverished nation, determined to return after a coup d'etat. Clinton supported him, but shifted between plans to invade the island, to blockade it economically, and to seek multilateral policies. Finally, on September 18, with an American invasion force en route to the island, its military

rulers backed down and allowed U.S. troops to land unopposed. The ruling generals fled in October and Aristide returned on October 15, his triumph assured by American force.

In one other area, the Clinton presidency appeared to founder. In late 1993, the scent of a scandal began to emerge around the Whitewater real estate development corporation, in which Bill and Hillary Clinton had made investments a decade before. By January 20, 1994, Republican pressure had forced the appointment of a Justice Department special counsel, Robert B. Fiske, Jr., to investigate their dealings with Whitewater and with a failed business, the Madison Guarantee Savings and Loan Association in Arkansas. This diversion meant that the president's personal political problems began to interfere with, and threatened to overwhelm, the reform agenda he had declared during the election. The promise to represent what was best about the diversity and social activism in America was submerged in political bickering and stridency. As mid-term elections approached, the United States appeared, once again, on the edge of a serious political reorientation.

THE "CONTRACT WITH AMERICA"

The health care debate of 1994 suggests why the Democratic majority in Congress was vulnerable and the president weak. Bill Clinton first presented his program for universal health insurance in September 1993. The result of long meetings and political compromises presided over by Hillary Rodham Clinton, the program was complex, expensive, aand difficult to explain. Whatever its merits, it quickly became a stereotype for bloated federal bureaucracy, and many Republicans and Democratics, as well as special interests like medical insurance companies attacked it. A variety of alternative plans emerged throughout 1994, but none could generate sufficient support. On September 26, the Democratic majority leader of the Senate, George Mitchell of Maine, declared the reform dead. Coming so close to the 1994 mid-term election this important defeat was instructive, for Clinton could neither persuade the American people nor hold his majority party together. The flustered and divided Democrats faced a united and aggressive challenge from Republicans.

Because of the results, the issues raised during the election of 1994 loomed even larger after November 8 than they had appeared before. By gaining 50 seats in the House of Representatives and 9 in the Senate, Republicans swept into control for the first time in 40 years. They also unseated some of the most important Democratic Governors: Mario Cuomo of New York and Ann Richards of Texas. The new congressional leaders, Senator Robert Dole of Kansas and Representative Newt Gingrich of Georgia, were unequivocal in this purpose: they intended to implement the Republican Party's "Contract with America." For many Americans, including those who voted for Republican candidates, the outlines of the "Contract" were vague at best, although many supported what they understood to be its spirit.

The Contract consisted of two parts: the first focused on congressional rule changes with the second promising legislation. Rule reforms in Congress were quickly adopted when the new Congress met in early 1995. All laws passed would henceforth apply also to Congress itself; committees were consolidated, staff cut back, and voting procedures clarified.

Legislative projects were slower to move. Although the House pushed through wide-ranging changes including a constitutional amendment to balance the federal budget, the Senate defeated this and slowed other measures. Yet profound reform of the federal welfare system and federal spending priorities seemed inevitable. For several months after the election, President Clinton appeared as much part of the audience to this political activity as a leader.

In a way, the election was also about another contract—the promises of the welfare state. Particularly since the 1960s, one of the purposes of welfare spending had been to achieve social equilibrium, order, and peace in America's troubled cities. Yet the leading indicator of success or failure, the crime rate, seemed to grow alarmingly. Welfare spending and countless federal and state programs did not end poverty, illegitimate births, broken families, drug consumption, or crime. They even appeared, to some people, to stoke the energy of irresponsible behavior. The middle class (to which most working Americans said they belonged) blanched at paying continued welfare subsidies.

There were other related issues including affirmative action programs, high taxes, government regluation, and certainly, the health care failure. Many of these issues swirled around a renewed politics of ethnic, racial, and class identity. When the votes were scanned, it was revealed that white males voted 63 percent to 37 percent for Republican candidates. Gender considered alone also made a considerable difference, as 54 percent of men voted Republican and 54 percent of women voted Democrat. If this amounted to the resurgence of a minority population—white men—it was, nevertheless, the most powerful minority group in America that demanded it and won a right to determine policy.

One of the most powerful issues of the 1994 campaign refocused the nation's attention on the racial and ethnic struggle which had erupted in the Los Angeles riots. California voters passed a tough initiative known as Proposition 187, curbing the rights of illegal immigrants. Aimed primarily at the large flow of Mexican nationals into that state, the referendum cut immigrants off from state services such as education, welfare, and nonemergency health services. It also required teachers, doctors, and law-enforcement officers to inform on illegal immigrants. Almost immediately, the law was tied up by lawsuits, but it inspired other states to propose similar measures.

Although the 1994 election empowered a familiar minority—white males—in American politics, it was because this group was sufficiently organized and energized to turn an election and, in the process, change the tone and content of national political debates. Despite the growing demographic complexity of the United States, the most traditional of political forces, the Republican party, emerged self-confident and sure of itself. Just how, after this victory, it might extend itself through political alliances or ideological persuasion, to become a true majority, is a problem that every political group in American society has faced. Played out increasingly in the public eye, nothing could be more of a challenge.

CHRONOLOGY

1965	Immigration act alters priorities of immigration
1969	Stonewall riots in New York City
1973	Tom Bradley elected mayor of Los Angeles
1978	Daryl Gates becomes chief of Los Angeles Police Department
1980	George Bush elected vice president of the United States
1987	Allan Bloom publishes *Closing of the American Mind;*
	Film *La Bamba* released
1988 (Nov.)	George Bush wins US presidency
1989	
(Nov. 9)	Berlin Wall breached;
(Dec. 20)	Operation "Just Cause" begins
1990	Ellis Island opens as a national park;
(Aug. 8)	Iraq completes conquest of Kuwait;
(Oct.)	President Bush signs bill raising taxes
1990–1992	Economic recession in the United States
1991	
(Feb. 27)	United Nations defeats Iraq and liberates Kuwait;
(Mar. 3)	Rodney King beaten and arrested;
(Aug.)	Attempted coup against Mikhail Gorbachev;
(Oct.)	Clarence Thomas–Anita Hill hearings

1992	
(Apr. 29)	Jury acquits Timothy Wind, Ted Briseno, and Stacey Koon in King beating case;
(Apr. 29–May 2)	Los Angeles riots;
(Apr. 29)	Truck driver Reginald Denny assaulted in Los Angeles;
(Nov.)	Bill Clinton wins presidency of the United States
1993	Clinton tax and budget bill passes Congress;
	North American Free Trade Agreement with Mexico and Canada approved;
(Feb.)	Federal trial of Ted Briseno, Stacey Koon, Timony Wind, and Laurence Powell begins;
(Apr)	Stacey Koon and Laurence Powell convicted in King case;
(July 14)	Trial of Henry Watson and Damian Williams begins for assault on Reginald Denny;
(July)	"Don't ask, don't tell" policy begins in Armed Services";
(Oct.)	Verdict in Denny case
1994	Free elections in South Africa end apartheid;
	Israel and Palestine negotiate partial end to Israeli occupation of West Bank

-►==◉==◄-

SUGGESTIONS FOR FURTHER READING

THE LOS ANGELES RIOTS

Rioting is certainly an old tradition in America, although the issues tend to be different for different eras. For an interesting, early account see David Grimsted, "Rioting in Its Jacksonian Setting," *American Historical Review*, 1971. A good background to the Los Angeles riots is knowledge of the widespread disturbances in the mid-1960s in American cities. For an influential assessment of their meaning see National Advisory Commission on Civil Disorders, *The Kerner Report* (1968). Two quite different books review the nature of multiculturalism. They are Ronald Takaki, *A Different Mirror: A History of Multicultural America* (1993) and Arthur M. Schlesinger, Jr., *The Disuniting of America* (1991). There have been a number of instant and unacceptable histories of the Rodney King beating, trial, and aftermath. The best place to study this event is in news journals and in the especially wide coverage given the issue by the *Los Angeles Times* in 1991 and 1992. A defensive but informative autobiography is Daryl Gates's *Chief: My Life in the LAPD* (1993).

There are a number of excellent works discussing the history of Los Angeles and its peculiar place in American life. The best of these is by Mike Davis, *City of Quartz: Excavating the Future in Los Angeles* (1990). An important earlier work (now updated) is by Robert M. Fogelson, *The Fragmented Metropolis, 1850–1930* (1993). A good general exploration of the phenomenon of world cities is in Peter Hall's book, *The World Cities*, 2d ed. (1984).

PRESIDENTS

A few studies have begun to appear on the Bush presidency. Among them are Kim Holmes, *George Bush's New World Order: Two Assessments* (1991), and Michael Duffy, *Marching in Place: The Status Quo Presidency of George Bush* (1992). Inside stories are initially interesting but usually disappointing. See, for example, John Podhoretz's, *Hell of a Ride: Backstage at the White House Follies, 1989–1993* (1993). There are, of course, a number of "kiss and tell" books about the Bush administration, written by insiders, ex-officials, and even members of the president's household. One of these is Barbara Bush's, *Barbara Bush: A Memoir* (1994). It is impossible yet to assess the Clinton presidency, nor has there been time to evaluate the meaning of his various successes and failures. A reading of such journals of opinion as *The New Republic, The Nation* and *The National Review* and others suggests varieties of interpretations.

A number of recent historical works try to assess the state of contemporary American politics and culture. A good beginning is Paul Boyer's *Promises to Keep: The United States Since World War II* (1995). A second book that makes a broad appraisal is John Judis, *Grand Illusion: Critics and Champions of the American Century* (1992). William Chafe discusses the history of American women in *The Road to Equality: American Women Since 1962* (1995). An interesting work on the bitter cultural disagreements in contemporary society is James Hunter Davison's, *Culture Wars: The Struggle to Define America* (1991). One of the most interesting interpreters of contemporary life is Christopher Lasch, *The Revolt of the Elites: and the Betrayal of Democracy* (1995).

The Declaration of Independence

In Congress, July 4, 1776. The unanimous Declaration of the thirteen United States of America.

When in the Course of human events, it becomes necessary for one people to dissolve the political bands which have connected them with another, and to assume among the powers of the earth, the separate and equal station to which the Laws of Nature and of Nature's God entitle them, a decent respect to the opinions of mankind requires that they should declare the causes which impel them to the separation.

We hold these truths to be self-evident, that all men are created equal, that they are endowed by their Creator with certain unalienable Rights, that among these are Life, Liberty and the pursuit of Happiness.

That to secure these rights, Governments are instituted among Men, deriving their just powers from the consent of the governed,

That whenever any Form of Government becomes destructive of these ends, it is the Right of the People to alter or to abolish it, and to institute new Government, laying its foundation on such principles and organizing its powers in such form, as to them shall seem most likely to effect their Safety and Happiness. Prudence, indeed, will dictate that Governments long established should not be changed for light and transient causes; and accordingly all experience hath shown, that mankind are more disposed to suffer, while evils are sufferable, than to right themselves by abolishing the forms to which they are accustomed. But when a long train of abuses and usurpations, pursuing invariably the same Object evinces a design to reduce them under absolute Despotism, it is their right, it is their duty, to throw off such Government, and to provide new Guards for their future security.

Such has been the patient sufferance of these Colonies; and such is now the necessity which constrains them to alter their former Systems of Government. The history of the present King of Great Britain is a history of repeated injuries and usurpations, all having in direct object the establishment of an absolute Tyranny over these States. To prove this, let Facts be submitted to a candid world.

He has refused his Assent to Laws, the most wholesome and necessary for the public good.

He has forbidden his Governors to pass Laws of immediate and pressing importance, unless suspended in their operation till his Assent should be obtained; and when so suspended, he has utterly neglected to attend to them.

He has refused to pass other Laws for the accommodation of large districts of people, unless those people would relinquish the right of Representation in the Legislature, a right inestimable to them and formidable to tyrants only.

He has called together legislative bodies at places unusual, uncomfortable, and distant from the depository of their public Records, for the sole purpose of fatiguing them into compliance with his measures.

He has dissolved Representative Houses repeatedly, for opposing with manly firmness his invasions on the rights of the people.

He has refused for a long time, after such dissolutions, to cause others to be elected; whereby the Legislative powers, incapable of Annihilation, have returned to the People at large for their exercise; the State remaining in the mean time exposed to all the dangers of invasion from without, and convulsions within.

He has endeavored to prevent the population of these States; for that purpose obstructing the Laws for Naturalization of Foreigners; refusing to pass others to encourage their migrations hither, and raising the conditions of new Appropriations of Lands.

He has obstructed the Administration of Justice, by refusing his Assent to Laws for establishing Judiciary powers.

He has made Judges dependent on his Will alone, for the tenure of their offices, and the amount and payment of their salaries.

He has erected a multitude of New Offices, and sent hither swarms of Officers to harrass our people, and eat out their substance.

He has kept among us, in times of peace, Standing Armies without the Consent of our legislatures.

He has affected to render the Military independent of and superior to the Civil power.

He has combined with others to subject us to a jurisdiction foreign to our constitution, and unacknowledged by our laws; giving his Assent to their Acts of pretended Legislation:

For quartering large bodies of armed troops among us:

For protecting them, by a mock Trial, from punishment for any Murders which they should commit on the Inhabitants of these States:

For cutting off our Trade with all parts of the world:

For imposing Taxes on us without our Consent:

For depriving us in many cases, of the benefits of Trial by Jury:

For transporting us beyond Seas to be tried for pretended offences:

For abolishing the free System of English Laws in a neighbouring Province, establishing therein an Arbitrary government, and enlarging its Boundaries so as to render it at once an example and fit instrument for introducing the same absolute rule into these Colonies:

For taking away our Charters, abolishing our most valuable Laws, and altering fundamentally the Forms of our Government:

For suspending our own Legislatures, and declaring themselves invested with power to legislate for us in all cases whatsoever.

He has abdicated Government here, by declaring us out of his Protection and waging War against us.

He has plundered our seas, ravaged our Coasts, burnt our towns, and destroyed the lives of our people.

He is at this time transporting large Armies of foreign Mercenaries to compleat the works of death, desolation and tyranny, already begun with circumstances of Cruelty & perfidy scarcely paralleled in the most barbarous ages, and totally unworthy the Head of a civilized nation.

He has constrained our fellow Citizens taken Captive on the high Seas to bear Arms against their Country, to become the executioners of their friends and Brethren, or to fall themselves by their Hands.

He has excited domestic insurrections amongst us, and has endeavoured to bring on the inhabitants of our frontiers, the merciless Indian Savages, whose known rule of warfare, is an undistinguished destruction of all ages, sexes and conditions.

In every stage of these Oppressions We have Petitioned for Redress in the most humble terms: Our repeated Petitions have been answered only by repeated injury. A Prince, whose character is thus marked by every act which may define a Tyrant, is unfit to be the ruler of a free people.

Nor have We been wanting in our attentions to our British brethren. We have warned them from time to time of attempts by their legislature to extend an unwarrantable jurisdiction over us. We have reminded them of the circumstances of our emigration and settlement here. We have appealed to their native justice and magnanimity, and we have conjured them by the ties of our common kindred to disavow these usurpations, which, would inevitably interrupt our connections and correspondence. They too have been deaf to the voice of justice and of consanguinity. We must, therefore, acquiesce in the necessity, which denounces our Separation, and hold them, as we hold the rest of mankind, Enemies in War, in Peace Friends.

We, Therefore, the Representatives of the United States of America, in General Congress, Assembled, appealing to the Supreme Judge of the world for the rectitude of our intentions, do, in the Name, and by the Authority of the good People of these Colonies, solemnly publish and declare, That these United Colonies are, and of Right ought to be, Free and Independent States; that they are Absolved from all Allegiance to the British Crown, and that all political connection between them and the State of Great Britain, is and ought to be totally dissolved; and that as Free and Independent States, they have full Power to levy War, conclude Peace, contract Alliances, establish Commerce, and to do all other Acts and Things which Independent States may of right do.

And for the support of this Declaration, with a firm reliance on the protection of divine Providence, we mutually pledge to each other our Lives, our Fortunes, and our sacred Honor.

John Hancock
(MASSACHUSETTS)

New Hampshire
Josiah Barlett
William Whipple
Matthew Thornton

Massachusetts
Samuel Adams
John Adams
Robert Treat Paine
Elbridge Gerry

Delaware
Caeser Rodney
George Read
Thomas McKean

New York
William Floyd
Philip Livingston
Francis Lewis
Lewis Morris

New Jersey
Richard Stockton
John Witherspoon
Francis Hopkinson
John Hart
Abraham Clark

North Carolina
William Hooper
Joseph Hewes
John Penn

Maryland
Samuel Chase
William Paca
Thomas Stone
Charles Carroll of
*   Carrollton*

South Carolina
Edward Rutledge
Thomas Heywood, Jr.
Thomas Lynch, Jr.
Arthur Middleton

Rhode Island
Stephen Hopkins
William Ellery

Connecticut
Roger Sherman
Samuel Huntington
William Williams
Oliver Wolcott

Pennsylvania
Robert Morris
Benjamin Rush
Benjamin Franklin
John Morton
George Clymer
James Smith
George Taylor
James Wilson
George Ross

Virginia
George Wythe
Richard Henry Lee
Thomas Jefferson
Benjamin Harrison
Thomas Nelson, Jr.
Francis Lightfoot Lee
Carter Braxton

Georgia
Bulton Gwinnett
Lyman Hall
George Walton

The Constitution of the United States of America

The preamble establishes the principle of government by the people and lists the six basic purposes of the Constitution.

We the People of the United States, in Order to form a more perfect Union, establish Justice, insure domestic Tranquility, provide for the common defence, promote the general Welfare, and secure the Blessings of Liberty to ourselves and our Posterity, do ordain and establish this Constitution for the United States of America.

ARTICLE I LEGISLATIVE DEPARTMENT

Section 1. All legislative Powers herein granted shall be vested in a Congress of the United States, which shall consist of a Senate and House of Representatives.

Section 2. The House of Representatives shall be composed of Members chosen every second Year by the People of the several States, and the Electors in each State shall have the Qualifications requisite for Electors of the most numerous Branch of the State Legislature.

Representatives serve two-year terms. They are chosen by those electors (that is, voters) who are qualified to vote for members of the lower house of their own state legislature.

No Person shall be a Representative who shall not have attained to the Age of twenty-five Years, and have been seven Years a Citizen of the United States, and who shall not, when elected, be an Inhabitant of that State in which he shall be chosen.

The number of representatives allotted to a state is determined by the size of its population. The 14th Amendment has made obsolete the reference to "all other persons"—that is, slaves.

A census must be taken every ten years to determine the number of representatives to which each state is entitled. There is now one representative for about every 470,000 persons.

Representatives and direct Taxes shall be apportioned among the several States which may be included within this Union, according to their respective Numbers, which shall be determined by adding to the whole Number of free Persons, including those bound to Service for a Term of Years, and excluding Indians not taxed, three-fifths of all other Persons. The actual Enumeration shall be made within three Years after the first Meeting of the Congress of the United States, and within every subsequent Term of ten Years, in such Manner as they shall by Law direct. The Number of Representatives shall not exceed one for every thirty Thousand, but each State shall have at Least one Representative; and until such enumeration shall be made, the State of New Hampshire shall be entitled to chuse three, Massachusetts eight, Rhode Island and Providence Plantations one, Connecticut five, New York six, New Jersey four,

Source: *House Document #529. U.S. Government Printing Office, 1967.*
Note: *The Constitution and the amendments are reprinted here in their original form. Portions that have been amended or superseded are underlined. The words printed in the margins explain some of the more difficult passages.*

Pennsylvania eight, Delaware one, Maryland six, Virginia ten, North Carolina five, South Carolina five, and Georgia three.

When vacancies happen in the Representation from any State, the Executive Authority thereof shall issue Writs of Election to fill such Vacancies.

The House of Representatives shall chuse their Speaker and other Officers; and shall have the sole Power of Impeachment.

Section 3. The Senate of the United States shall be composed of two Senators from each State, chosen by the Legislature thereof, for six Years; and each Senator shall have one Vote.

Immediately after they shall be assembled in Consequence of the first Election, they shall be divided as equally as may be into three Classes. The Seats of the Senators of the first Class shall be vacated at the Expiration of the second Year, of the second Class at the expiration of the fourth Year, and of the third Class at the Expiration of the sixth Year, so that one third may be chosen every second Year; and if Vacancies happen by Resignation, or otherwise, during the Recess of the Legislature of any State, the Executive thereof may make temporary Appointments until the next Meeting of the Legislature, which shall then fill such Vacancies.

No Person shall be a Senator who shall not have attained to the Age of thirty Years, and been nine Years a Citizen of the United States, and who shall not, when elected, be an Inhabitant of that State for which he shall be chosen.

The Vice President of the United States shall be President of the Senate, but shall have no Vote, unless they be equally divided.

The Senate shall chuse their other Officers, and also a President pro tempore, in the absence of the Vice President, or when he shall exercise the Office of President of the United States.

The Senate shall have the sole Power to try all Impeachments. When sitting for that Purpose, they shall be on Oath or Affirmation. When the President of the United States is tried, the Chief Justice shall preside: And no Person shall be convicted without the Concurrence of two thirds of the Members present.

Judgment in Cases of Impeachment shall not extend further than to removal from Office, and disqualification to hold and enjoy any Office of Honor, Trust or Profit under the United States: but the Party convicted shall nevertheless be liable and subject to Indictment, Trial, Judgment and Punishment, according to Law.

Section 4. The Times, Places and Manner of holding Elections for Senators and Representatives, shall be prescribed in each State by the Legislature thereof; but the Congress may at any time by Law make or alter such Regulations, except as to the Place of chusing Senators.

The Congress shall assemble at least once in every Year, and such Meeting shall be on the first Monday in December, unless they shall by Law appoint a different Day.

Executive authority refers to the governor of a state. The Speaker, chosen by and from the majority party, presides over the House. Impeachment is the act of bringing formal charges against an official. (See also Section 3.)

The 17th Amendment changed this method to direct election.

The 17th Amendment also provides that a state governor shall appoint a successor to fill a vacant Senate seat until a direct election is held.

The Vice President may cast a vote in the Senate only to break a tie.

The president *pro tempore* of the Senate is a temporary officer; the Latin words mean "for the time being."

No President has ever been convicted on charges of impeachment. In 1868 the Senate fell one vote short of the two-thirds majority needed to convict Andrew Johnson. Thirteen other officials—eleven federal judges, one senator, and one secretary of war—have been impeached; five of the judges were convicted.

Elections for Congress are held on the first Tuesday after the First Monday in November in even-numbered years.

The 20th Amendment designates January 3 as the opening of the congressional session.

Each house of Congress decides whether a member has been elected properly and is qualified to be seated. (A quorum is the minimum number of persons required to be present in order to conduct business.) The House once refused admittance to an elected representative who had been guilty of a crime. The Senate did likewise in the case of a candidate whose election campaign lent itself to "fraud and corruption."

Section 5.   Each House shall be the Judge of the Elections, Returns and Qualifications of its own Members, and a Majority of each shall constitute a Quorum to do Business; but a smaller number may adjourn from day to day, and may be authorized to compel the Attendance of absent Members, in such Manner, and under such Penalties as each House may provide.

Each House may determine the Rules of its Proceedings, punish its Members for disorderly Behavior, and with the Concurrence of two thirds, expel a Member.

Each House shall keep a Journal of its Proceedings, and from time to time publish the same, excepting such Parts as may in their Judgment require Secrecy; and the Yeas and Nays of the Members of either House on any question shall, at the Desire of one fifth of those Present, be entered on the Journal.

Neither House, during the Session of Congress, shall, without the Consent of the other, adjourn for more than three days, nor to any other Place than that in which the two Houses shall be sitting.

Congressmen have the power to fix their own salaries. Under the principle of *congressional immunity,* they cannot be sued or arrested for anything they say in a congressional debate. This provision enables them to speak freely.

This clause reinforces the principle of separation of powers by stating that, during his term of office, a member of Congress may not be appointed to a position in another branch of government. Nor may he resign and accept a position created during his term.

The House initiates tax bills but the Senate may propose changes in them.

By returning a bill unsigned to the house in which it originated, the President exercises a *veto.* A two-thirds majority in both houses can override the veto. If the President receives a bill within the last ten days of a session and does not sign it, the measure dies by *pocket veto.* Merely by keeping the bill in his pocket, so to speak, the President effects a veto.

Section 6.   The Senators and Representatives shall receive a Compensation for their Services, to be ascertained by Law, and paid out of the Treasury of the United States. They shall in all Cases, except Treason, Felony and Breach of the Peace, be privileged from Arrest during their Attendance at the Session of their respective Houses, and in going to and returning from the same; and for any Speech or Debate in either House, they shall not be questioned in any other Place.

No Senator or Representative shall, during the Time for which he was elected, be appointed to any civil Office under the Authority of the United States, which shall have been created, or the Emoluments whereof shall have been encreased during such time; and no Person holding any Office under the United States, shall be a Member of either House during his Continuance in Office.

Section 7.   All Bills for raising Revenue shall originate in the House of Representatives; but the Senate may propose or concur with Amendments as on other Bills.

Every Bill which shall have passed the House of Representatives and the Senate, shall, before it become a Law, be presented to the President of the United States; If he approve he shall sign it, but if not he shall return it, with his Objections to that House in which it shall have originated, who shall enter the Objections at large on their Journal, and proceed to reconsider it. If after such Reconsideration two thirds of that House shall agree to pass the Bill, it shall be sent, together with the Objections, to the other House, by which it shall likewise be reconsidered, and if approved by two thirds of that House, it shall become a Law. But in all such Cases the Votes of both Houses shall be determined by Yeas and Nays, and the Names of the Persons voting for and against the Bill shall be entered on the Journal of each House respectively. If any Bill shall not be returned by the President within ten Days (Sundays excepted) after it shall have been presented to him, the Same shall be a Law, in like Manner as if he had signed it, unless the Congress by their Adjournment prevent its Return, in which Case it shall not be a Law.

The same process of approval or disapproval by the President is applied to resolutions and other matters passed by both houses (except adjournment).

Every Order, Resolution, or Vote to which the Concurrence of the Senate and House of Representatives may be necessary (except on a question of Adjournment) shall be presented to the President of the United States; and before the Same shall take Effect, shall be approved by him, or being disapproved by him, shall be repassed by two thirds of the Senate and House of Representatives, according to the Rules and Limitations prescribed in the Case of a Bill.

Section 8. The Congress shall have Power to lay and collect Taxes, Duties, Imposts and Excises, to pay the Debts and provide for the common Defence and general Welfare of the United States; but all Duties, Imposts and Excises shall be uniform throughout the United States;

To borrow money on the credit of the United States;

To regulate Commerce with foreign Nations, and among the several States, and with the Indian Tribes;

To establish an uniform Rule of Naturalization, and uniform Laws on the subject of Bankruptcies throughout the United States;

To coin Money, regulate the Value thereof, and of foreign Coin, and fix the Standard of Weights and Measures;

To provide for the Punishment of counterfeiting the Securities and current Coin of the United States;

To establish Post Offices and post Roads;

To promote the Progress of Science and useful Arts, by securing for limited Times to Authors and Inventors the exclusive Right to their respective Writings and Discoveries;

To constitute Tribunals inferior to the superior Court;

To define and punish Piracies and Felonies committed on the high Seas, and Offenses against the Law of Nations;

To declare War, grant Letters of Marque and Reprisal, and make Rules concerning Captures on Land and Water;

To raise and support Armies, but no Appropriation of Money to that Use shall be for a longer Term than two years;

To provide and maintain a Navy;

To make Rules for the Government and Regulation of the land and naval Forces;

To provide for calling forth the Militia to execute the Laws of the Union, suppress Insurrections and repel Invasions;

To provide for organizing, arming, and disciplining the Militia, and for governing such Part of them as may be employed in the Service of the United States, reserving to the States respectively, the Appointment of the Officers, and the Authority of training the Militia according to the discipline prescribed by Congress;

To exercise the exclusive Legislation in all Cases whatsoever, over such District (not exceeding ten Miles square) as may, by Cession of particular States, and the acceptance of Congress, become the Seat of the Government of the United States, and to exercise like Authority over all Places purchased by the Consent of the Legislature of the State in which the Same shall be, for the Erection of Forts, Magazines, Arsenals, dock-Yards, and other needful Buildings; And

To make all Laws which shall be necessary and proper for carrying into Execution the foregoing Powers, and all other Powers vested by this Constitution in the Government of the United States, or in any Department or Officer thereof.

Section 9. The Migration or Importation of such Persons as any of the States now existing shall think proper to admit, shall not be prohibited by the Congress prior to the Year one thousand eight hundred and eight, but a tax or duty may be imposed on such Importation, not exceeding ten dollars for each Person.

The privilege of the Writ of Habeas Corpus shall not be suspended unless when in Cases of Rebellion or Invasion the public Safety may require it.

These are the *delegated,* or *enumerated,* powers of Congress.

Duties are taxes on imported goods; *excises* are taxes on goods manufactured, sold, or consumed within the country. *Imposts* is a general term including both duties and excise taxes.

Naturalization is the process by which an alien becomes a citizen.

Government *securities* include savings bonds and other notes.

Authors' and inventors' rights are protected by copyright and patent laws. Congress may establish lower federal courts.

Only Congress may declare war. *Letters of marque and reprisal* grant merchant ships permission to attack enemy vessels.

Militia refers to national guard units, which may become part of the United States Army during an emergency. Congress aids the states in maintaining their national guard units.

This clause gives Congress the power to govern what became the District of Columbia, as well as other federal sites.

Known as the *elastic clause,* this provision enables Congress to exercise many powers not specifically granted to it by the Constitution.

This clause concerns the slave trade, which Congress did ban in 1808.

The writ of *habeas corpus* permits a prisoner to appear before a judge to inquire into the legality of his or her detention.

A *bill of attainder* is an act of legislation that declares a person guilty of a crime and punishes him or her without a trial. An ex post facto law punishes a person for an act that was legal when performed but later declared illegal.

The object of Clause 4 was to bar direct (per person) taxation of slaves for the purpose of abolishing slavery. The 16th Amendment modified this provision by giving Congress the power to tax personal income.

States are hereby forbidden to exercise certain powers. Some of these powers belong to Congress alone; others are considered undemocratic.

States cannot, without congressional authority, tax goods that enter or leave, except for a small inspection fee.

Federal officials are ineligible to serve as presidential electors.

No Bill of Attainder or ex post facto Law shall be passed.

No capitation, or other direct, Tax shall be laid, unless in Proportion to the Census of Enumeration herein before directed to be taken.

No Tax or Duty shall be laid on Articles exported from any State.

No Preference shall be given by any Regulation of Commerce or Revenue to the Ports of one State over those of another; nor shall Vessels bound to, or from, one State, be obliged to enter, clear, or pay Duties in another.

No Money shall be drawn from the Treasury, but in Consequence of Appropriations made by Law; and a regular Statement and Account of the Receipts and Expenditures of all public Money shall be published from time to time.

No Title of Nobility shall be granted by the United States: And no Person holding any Office of Profit or Trust under them, shall, without the Consent of the Congress, accept of any present, Emolument, Office, or Title, of any kind whatever, from any King, Prince, or foreign State.

Section 10.   No State shall enter into any Treaty, Alliance, or Confederation; grant Letters of Marque and Reprisal; coin Money; emit Bills of Credit; make any Thing but gold and silver Coin a Tender in Payment of Debts; pass any Bill of Attainder, ex post facto Law, or Law impairing the Obligation of Contracts, or grant any Title of Nobility.

No State shall, without the Consent of the Congress, lay any Imposts or Duties on Imports or Exports, except what may be absolutely necessary for executing its inspection Laws: and the net Produce of all Duties and Imposts, laid by any State on Imports or Exports, shall be for the Use of the Treasury of the United States; and all such Laws shall be subject to the Revision and Controul of the Congress.

No State shall, without the Consent of Congress, lay any duty of Tonnage, keep Troops, or Ships of War in time of Peace, enter into any Agreement or Compact with another State, or with a foreign Power, or engage in War, unless actually invaded, or in such imminent Danger as will not admit of delay.

ARTICLE II   EXECUTIVE DEPARTMENT

Section 1.   The executive Power shall be vested in a President of the United States of America. He shall hold his Office during the Term of four Years, and, together with the Vice President, chosen for the same Term, be elected, as follows.

Each State shall appoint, in such Manner as the Legislature thereof may direct, a Number of Electors, equal to the whole Number of Senators and Representatives to which the State may be entitled in the Congress: but no Senator or Representative, or Person holding an office of Trust or Profit under the United States, shall be appointed an Elector.

The Electors shall meet in their respective States, and vote by Ballot for two persons, of whom one at least shall not be an Inhabitant of the same State with themselves. And they shall make a List of all the Persons voted for, and of the Number of Votes for each; which List they shall sign and certify, and transmit sealed to the Seat of the Government of the United States, directed to the President of the Senate. The President of the Senate shall, in the Presence of the Senate and House of Representatives, open all the Certificates, and the Votes shall then be counted. The Person having the greatest

Number of Votes shall be the President, if such Number be a Majority of the whole Number of Electors appointed; and if there be more than one who have such Majority, and have an equal Number of Votes, then the House of Representatives shall immediately chuse by Ballot one of them for President; and if no Person have a Majority, then from the five highest on the List the said House shall in like Manner chuse the President. But in chusing the President, the Votes shall be taken by States, the Representation from each State having one Vote; a quorum for this Purpose shall consist of a Member or Members from two thirds of the States, and a Majority of all the States shall be necessary to a Choice. In every Case, after the Choice of the President, the Person having the Greatest Number of Votes of the Electors shall be the Vice President. But if there should remain two or more who have equal Votes, the Senate shall chuse from them by Ballot the Vice President.

> The 12th Amendment superseded this clause. The weakness of the original constitutional provision became apparent in the election of 1800, when Thomas Jefferson and Aaron Burr received the same number of electoral votes. The 12th Amendment avoids this possibility by requiring electors to cast separate ballots for President and Vice President.

The Congress may determine the Time of chusing the Electors, and the Day on which they shall give their Votes; which Day shall be the same throughout the United States.

No person except a natural born Citizen, or a Citizen of the United States, at the time of the Adoption of this Constitution, shall be eligible to the Office of President; neither shall any Person be eligible to that Office who shall not have attained to the Age of Thirty-five Years, and been fourteen Years a Resident within the United States.

> A naturalized citizen may not become President.

In a Case of the Removal of the President from Office, or of his Death, Resignation, or Inability to discharge the Powers and Duties of the said Office, the same shall devolve on the Vice-President, and the Congress may by Law provide for the Case of Removal, Death, Resignation or Inability, both of the President and the Vice President, declaring what Officer shall then act as President, and such Officer shall act accordingly, until the Disability be removed, or a President shall be elected.

> The Vice President is next in line for the presidency. A federal law passed in 1947 determined the order of presidential succession as follows: (1) Speaker of the House; (2) president *pro tempore* of the Senate; and (3) Cabinet officers in the order in which their departments were created. This clause has been amplified by the 25th Amendment.

The President shall, at stated Times, receive for his Services, a Compensation, which shall neither be encreased nor diminished during the Period for which he shall have been elected, and he shall not receive within that Period any other Emolument from the United States, or any of them.

Before he enter on the Execution of his Office, he shall take the following Oath or Affirmation:—I do solemnly swear (or affirm) that I will faithfully execute the Office of the President of the United States, and will to the best of my Ability, preserve, protect and defend the Constitution of the United States.

Section 2. The President shall be Commander in Chief of the Army and Navy of the United States, and of the Militia of the several States, when called into the actual Service of the United States; he may require the Opinion in writing, of the principal Officer in each of the executive Departments, upon any subject relating to the Duties of their respective Offices, and he shall have Power to Grant Reprieves and Pardons for Offenses against the United States, except in Cases of Impeachment.

> This clause suggests written communication between the President and the principal officer in each of the executive departments. As it developed, these officials comprise the Cabinet—whose members are chosen, and may be replaced, by the President.

He shall have Power, by and with the Advice and Consent of the Senate, to make Treaties, provided two thirds of the Senators present concur; and he shall nominate, and by and with the Advice and Consent of the Senate, shall appoint Ambassadors, other public Ministers and Consuls, Judges of the supreme Court, and all other Officers of the United States, whose Appointments are not herein otherwise provided for, and which shall be established by Law: but the Congress may by Law vest the Appointment of such inferior Officers, as they think proper, in the President alone, in the Courts of Law, or in the Heads of Departments.

> Senate approval is required for treaties and presidential appointments.

Without the consent of the Senate, the President may appoint officials only on a temporary basis.

The President delivers a State of the Union message at the opening of each session of Congress. Woodrow Wilson was the first President since John Adams to read his messages in person. Franklin D. Roosevelt and his successors followed Wilson's example.

The President shall have Power to fill up all Vacancies that may happen during the Recess of the Senate, by granting commissions which shall expire at the End of their next Session.

Section 3.   He shall from time to time give to the Congress Information of the State of the Union, and recommend to their Consideration such Measures as he shall judge necessary and expedient; he may, on extraordinary Occasions, convene both Houses, or either of them, and in Case of Disagreement between them, with Respect to the Time of Adjournment, he may adjourn them to such Time as he shall think proper; he shall receive Ambassadors and other public Ministers; he shall take Care that the Laws be faithfully executed, and shall Commission all the Officers of the United States.

Section 4.   The President, Vice-President and all civil Officers of the United States, shall be removed from Office on Impeachment for, and Conviction of, Treason, Bribery, or other high Crimes and Misdemeanors.

ARTICLE III   JUDICIAL DEPARTMENT

Federal judges hold office for life and may not have their salaries lowered while in office. These provisions are intended to keep the federal bench independent of political pressure.

Section 1.   The judicial Power of the United States, shall be vested in one supreme Court, and in such inferior Courts as the Congress may from time to time ordain and establish. The Judges, both of the supreme and inferior Courts, shall hold their Offices during good Behaviour, and shall, at stated Times, receive for their services, a Compensation, which shall not be diminished during their Continuance in Office.

This clause describes the types of cases that may be heard in federal courts.

The 11th Amendment prevents a citizen from suing a state in a federal court.

Section 2.   The judicial Power shall extend to all Cases, in Law and Equity, arising under this Constitution, the Laws of the United States, and Treaties made, or which shall be made, under their Authority;—to all Cases affecting Ambassadors, other public Ministers and Consuls;—to all Cases of admiralty and maritime Jurisdiction;—to Controversies to which the United States shall be a Party; to Controversies between two or more States;—between a State and Citizens of another state;—between Citizens of different states;—between Citizens of the same State claiming Lands under Grants of different States, and between a State, or the Citizens thereof, and foreign States, Citizens or Subjects.

The Supreme Court handles certain cases directly. It may also review cases handled by lower courts, but Congress in some cases may withhold the right to appeal to the highest court or limit appeal by setting various conditions.

The 6th Amendment strengthens this clause on trial procedure.

In all Cases affecting Ambassadors, other public Ministers and Consuls, and those in which a State shall be Party, the supreme Court shall have original Jurisdiction. In all the other Cases before mentioned, the supreme Court shall have appellate Jurisdiction, both as to Law and Fact, with such Exceptions, and under such Regulations as the Congress shall make.

The trial of all Crimes, except in Cases of Impeachment, shall be by Jury; and such Trial shall be held in the State where the said Crimes shall have been committed; but when not committed within any State, the Trial shall be at such Place or Places as the Congress may by Law have directed.

Treason is rigorously defined. A person can be convicted only if two witnesses testify to the same obvious act or if he or she confesses in court.

Section 3.   Treason against the United States, shall consist only in levying War against them, or in adhering to their Enemies, giving them Aid and Comfort. No Person shall be convicted of Treason unless on the Testimony of two Witnesses to the same overt Act, or on Confession in open Court.

The Congress shall have Power to declare the Punishment of Treason, but no Attainder of Treason shall work Corruption of Blood, or Forfeiture except during the Life of the Person attained.

ARTICLE IV RELATIONS AMONG THE STATES

Section 1. Full Faith and Credit shall be given in each State to the public Acts, Records, and judicial Proceedings of every other State. And the Congress may by general Laws prescribe the Manner in which such Acts, Records and Proceedings shall be proved, and the Effect thereof.

Section 2. The Citizens of each State shall be entitled to all Privileges and Immunities of Citizens in the several States.

A Person charged in any State with Treason, Felony, or other Crime, who shall flee from Justice, and be found in another State, shall on demand of the executive Authority of the State from which he fled, be delivered up, to be removed to the State having Jurisdiction of the Crime.

No Person held in Service or Labour in one State, under the laws thereof, escaping into another, shall, in Consequence of any Law or Regulation therein, be discharged from such Service or Labour, but shall be delivered up on Claim of the Party to whom such Service or Labour may be due.

Section 3. New States may be admitted by the Congress into this Union; but no new State shall be formed or erected within the Jurisdiction of any other State; nor any State be formed by the Junction of two or more States, or parts of States, without the Consent of the Legislatures of the States concerned as well as of the Congress.

The Congress shall have Power to dispose of and make all needful Rules and Regulations respecting the Territory or other Property belonging to the United States; and nothing in this Constitution shall be so construed as to Prejudice any Claims of the United States, or of any particular State.

Section 4. The United States shall guarantee to every State in this Union a Republican Form of Government, and shall protect each of them against Invasion; and on Application of the Legislature, or of the Executive (when the Legislature cannot be convened) against domestic Violence.

ARTICLE V AMENDING THE CONSTITUTION

The Congress, whenever two thirds of both Houses shall deem it necessary, shall propose Amendments to this Constitution, or, on the Application of the Legislatures of two thirds of the several States, shall call a Convention for proposing Amendments, which, in either Case, shall be valid to all Intents and Purposes, as part of this Constitution, when ratified by the Legislatures of three fourths of the several States, or by Conventions in three fourths thereof, as the one or the other Mode of Ratification may be proposed by the Congress: Provided that no Amendment which may be made prior to the Year One thousand eight hundred and eight shall in any Manner affect the first and fourth Clauses in the Ninth Section of the first Article; and that no State, without its Consent, shall be deprived of its equal Suffrage in the Senate.

ARTICLE VI GENERAL PROVISIONS

All Debts contracted and Engagements entered into, before the Adoption of this Constitution, shall be as valid against the United States under this Constitution, as under the Confederation.

Punishment for treason extends only to the person convicted, not to his or her descendants. (Corruption of blood means that the heirs of a convicted person are deprived of certain rights.)

States must honor each other's laws, court decisions, and records (for example, birth, marriage, and death certificates).

Each state must respect the rights of citizens of other states.

The process of returning a person accused of a crime to the governmental authority (in this case a state) from which he or she has fled is called *extradition*.

The 13th Amendment, which abolished slavery, makes this clause obsolete.

A new state may not be created by dividing or joining existing states unless approved by the legislatures of the states affected and by Congress. An exception to the provision forbidding the division of a state occurred during the Civil War. In 1863 West Virginia was formed out of the western region of Virginia.

A *republican* form of government is one in which citizens choose representatives to govern them. The federal government must protect a state against invasion and, if state authorities request it, against violence within a state.

An amendment to the Constitution can be proposed (a) by Congress, with a two-thirds vote of both houses, or (b) by a convention called by Congress when two-thirds of the state legislatures request it. An amendment is ratified (a) by three-fourths of the state legislatures or (b) by conventions in three-fourths of the states. The twofold procedure of proposal and ratification reflects the seriousness with which the framers of the Constitution regarded amendments. Over 7,000 amendments have been proposed; only 26 have been ratified.

The *supremacy clause* means that if a federal and a state law conflict, the federal law prevails.

This Constitution, and the Laws of the United States which shall be made in Pursuance thereof; and all Treaties made, or which shall be made, under the Authority of the United States, shall be the supreme Law of the Land; and the Judges in every State shall be bound thereby, any Thing in the Constitution or Laws of any State to the Contrary notwithstanding.

Religion may not be a condition for holding public office.

The Senators and Representatives before mentioned, and the Members of the several State Legislatures, and all executive and judicial Officers, both of the United States and of the several States, shall be bound by Oath or Affirmation, to support this Constitution; but no religious Test shall ever be required as a Qualification to any Office or public Trust under the United States.

ARTICLE VII   RATIFICATION

The Constitution would become the law of the land upon the approval of nine states.

The Ratification of the Conventions of nine States shall be sufficient for the Establishment of this Constitution between the States so ratifying the Same.

DONE in Convention by the Unanimous Consent of the States present the Seventeenth Day of September in the Year of our Lord one thousand seven hundred and eighty-seven and of the Independence of the United States of America the Twelfth. In Witness whereof We have hereunto subscribed our Names.

G° WASHINGTON
Presid^t and deputy from
VIRGINIA

Attest: *William Jackson,* Secretary

Delaware
Geo: Read
Gunning Bedford, jun
John Dickinson
Richard Bassett
Jaco: Broom

Maryland
James McHenry
Dan: of St Thos Jenifer
Danl Carroll

Virginia
John Blair
James Madison Jr.

North Carolina
Wm Blount
Richd Dobbs Spaight
Hu Williamson

South Carolina
J. Rutledge
Charles Cotesworth
  Pinckney
Charles Pinckney
Pierce Butler

Georgia
William Few
Abr Baldwin

New Hampshire
John Langdon
Nicholas Gilman

Massachusetts
Nathaniel Gorham
Rufus King

Connecticut
Wm Saml Johnson
Roger Sherman

New York
Alexander Hamilton

New Jersey
Wil: Livingston
David Brearley
Wm Paterson
Jona: Dayton

Pennsylvania
B Franklin
Thomas Mifflin
Robt. Morris
Geo. Clymer
Thos. FitzSimons
Jared Ingersoll
James Wilson
Gouv Morris

Amendments to the Constitution

[The date following each amendment number is the year of ratification.]

AMENDMENT 1   (1791)

Congress shall make no law respecting an establishment of religion, or prohibiting the free exercise thereof: or abridging the freedom of speech, or of the press; or the right of the people peaceably to assemble, and to petition the Government for a redress of grievances.

Establishes freedom of religion, speech, and the press; gives citizens the rights of assembly and petition.

AMENDMENT II   (1791)

A well regulated Militia, being necessary to the security of a free State, the right of the people to keep and bear Arms, shall not be infringed.

States have the right to maintain a militia.

AMENDMENT III   (1791)

No Soldier shall, in time of peace, be quartered in any house, without the consent of the Owner, nor in time of war, but in a manner to be prescribed by law.

Limits the army's right to quarter soldiers in private homes.

AMENDMENT IV   (1791)

The right of the people to be secure in their persons, houses, papers, and effects, against unreasonable searches and seizures, shall not be violated, and no Warrants shall issue, but upon probable cause, supported by Oath or affirmation, and particularly describing the place to be searched, and the persons or things to be seized.

Search warrants are required as a guarantee of a citizen's right to privacy.

AMENDMENT V   (1791)

No person shall be held to answer for a capital, or otherwise infamous crime, unless on a presentment or indictment of a Grand Jury, except in cases arising in the land or naval forces, or in the Militia, when in actual service in time of War or public danger; nor shall any person be subject for the same offence to be twice put in jeopardy of life or limb; nor shall be compelled in any criminal case to be a witness against himself, nor be deprived of life, liberty, or property, without due process of law; nor shall private property be taken for public use, without just compensation.

To be prosecuted for a serious crime, a person must first be accused (*indicted*) by a grand jury. No one can be tried twice for the same crime (*double jeopardy*). Nor can a person be forced into self-incrimination by testifying against him- or herself.

AMENDMENT VI   (1791)

Guarantees a defendant's right to be tried without delay and to face witnesses testifying for the other side.

In all criminal prosecutions, the accused shall enjoy the right to a speedy and public trial, by an impartial jury of the State and district wherein the crime shall have been committed, which district shall have been previously ascertained by law, and to be informed of the nature and cause of the accusation; to be confronted with the witnesses against him; to have compulsory process for obtaining witnesses in his favor, and to have the Assistance of Counsel for his defense.

AMENDMENT VII   (1791)

A jury trial is guaranteed in federal civil suits involving more than twenty dollars.

In suits at common law, where the value in controversy shall exceed twenty dollars, the right of trial by jury shall be preserved, and no fact tried by a jury, shall be otherwise reexamined in any court of the United States, than according to rules of the common law.

AMENDMENT VIII   (1791)

Excessive bail shall not be required, nor excessive fines imposed, nor cruel and unusual punishments inflicted.

AMENDMENT IX   (1791)

The listing of specific rights in the Constitution does not mean that others are not protected.

The enumeration in the Constitution, of certain rights, shall not be construed to deny or disparage others retained by the people.

AMENDMENT X   (1791)

Limits the federal government to its specific powers. Powers not prohibited the states by the Constitution may be exercised by them.

The powers not delegated to the United States by the Constitution, nor prohibited by it to the States, are reserved to the States respectively, or to the people.

AMENDMENT XI   (1798)

A state cannot be sued by a citizen or another state in a federal court. Such a case can be tried only in the courts of the state being sued.

The Judicial power of the United States shall not be construed to extend to any suit in law or equity, commenced or prosecuted against one of the United States by Citizens of another State, or by Citizens or Subjects of any Foreign State.

AMENDMENT XII   (1804)

The Electors shall meet in their respective states and vote by ballot for President and Vice-President, one of whom, at least, shall not be an inhabitant of the same state with themselves; they shall name in their ballots the person voted for as President, and in distinct ballots the person voted for as Vice-President, and they shall make distinct lists of all persons voted for as President, and of all persons voted for as Vice-President, and of the number of votes for each, which lists they shall sign and certify, and transmit sealed to the seat of the government of the United States, directed to the President of the Senate;—The President of the Senate shall, in presence of the Senate and House of Representatives, open all the certificates and the votes shall then be counted;—The person having the greatest number of votes for President, shall be the President, if such number be a majority of the whole number of Electors appointed; and if no person have such majority, then from the persons having the highest numbers not exceeding three on the list of those voted for as President, the House of Representatives shall choose immediately, by ballot, the President. But in choosing the President, the votes shall be taken by states, the representation from each state having one vote; a quorum for this purpose shall consist of a member or members from two-thirds of the states, and a majority of all the states shall be necessary to a choice. And if the House of Representatives shall not choose a President whenever the right of choice shall devolve upon them, before the fourth day of March next following, then the Vice-President shall act as President, as in the case of the death or other constitutional disability of the President:—The person having the greatest number of votes as Vice-President, shall be the Vice-President, if such number be a majority of the whole number of Electors appointed, and if no person have a majority, then from the two highest numbers on the list, the Senate shall choose the Vice-President; a quorum for the purpose shall consist of two-thirds of the whole number of Senators, and a majority of the whole number shall be necessary to a choice. But no person constitutionally ineligible to the office of President shall be eligible to that of Vice-President of the United States.

> Revises the process by which the President and Vice President were elected (see Article II, Section 1, Clause 3). The major change requires electors to cast separate ballots for President and Vice President. If none of the presidential candidates obtains a majority vote, the House of Representatives—with each state having one vote—chooses a President from the three candidates having the highest number of votes. If no vice presidential candidate wins a majority, the Senate chooses from the two candidates having the highest number of votes. The underlined portion was superseded by Section 3 of the 20th Amendment.

AMENDMENT XIII   (1865)

Section 1.   Neither slavery nor involuntary servitude, except as a punishment for crime whereof the party shall have been duly convicted, shall exist within the United States, or any place subject to their jurisdiction.

> Abolishes slavery.

Section 2.   Congress shall have power to enforce this article by appropriate legislation.

AMENDMENT XIV   (1868)

Section 1.   All persons born or naturalized in the United States, and subject to the jurisdiction thereof, are citizens of the United States and of the State wherein they reside. No state shall make or enforce any law which shall abridge the privileges or immunities of citizens of the United States; nor shall any State deprive any person of life, liberty, or property, without due process of law; nor deny any person within its jurisdiction the equal protection of the laws.

> This section confers full civil rights on former slaves. Supreme Court decisions have interpreted the language of Section 1 to mean that the states, as well as the federal government, are bound by the Bill of Rights.

A penalty of a reduction in congressional representation shall be applied to any state that refuses to give all adult male citizens the right to vote in federal elections. This section has never been applied. The underlined portion was superseded by Section 1 of the 26th Amendment. (This section has also been amplified by the 19th Amendment.)

Section 2.   Representatives shall be apportioned among the several States according to their respective numbers, counting the whole number of persons in each State, excluding Indians not taxed. But when the right to vote at any election for the choice of electors for President and Vice-President of the United States, Representatives in Congress, the Executive and Judicial officers of a State, or the members of the Legislature thereof, is denied to any of the male inhabitants of such State, being <u>twenty-one</u> years of age, and citizens of the United States, or in any way abridged, except for participation in rebellion, or other crime, the basis of representation therein shall be reduced in the proportion which the number of such male citizens shall bear to the whole number of male citizens twenty-one years of age in such state.

Any former federal or state official who served the Confederacy during the Civil War could not become a federal official again unless Congress voted otherwise.

Section 3.   No person shall be a Senator or Representative in Congress, or elector of President and Vice-President, or hold any office, civil or military, under the United States, or under any State, who, having previously taken an oath, as a member of Congress, or as an officer of the United States, or as a member of any State legislature, or as an executive or judicial officer of any State, to support the Constitution of the United States, shall have engaged in insurrection or rebellion against the same, or given aid or comfort to the enemies thereof. But Congress may by a vote of two-thirds of each House, remove such disability.

Makes legal the federal Civil War debt, but at the same time voids all Confederate debts incurred in the war.

Section 4.   The validity of the public debt of the United States, authorized by law, including debts incurred for payment of pensions and bounties for services in suppressing insurrection or rebellion, shall not be questioned. But neither the United States nor any State shall assume or pay any debt or obligation incurred in aid of insurrection or rebellion against the United States, or any claim for the loss or emancipation of any slave; but all such debts, obligations and claims shall be held illegal and void.

Section 5.   The Congress shall have power to enforce, by appropriate legislation, the provisions of this article.

AMENDMENT XV   (1870)

Gives ex-slaves the right to vote.

Section 1.   The right of citizens of the United States to vote shall not be denied or abridged by the United States or by any State on account of race, color, or previous condition of servitude.

Section 2.   The Congress shall have power to enforce this article by appropriate legislation.

AMENDMENT XVI   (1913)

Allows Congress to levy direct taxes on incomes.

The Congress shall have power to lay and collect taxes on incomes, from whatever source derived, without apportionment among the several States, and without regard to any census or enumeration.

AMENDMENT XVII   (1913)

Provides for election of senators by the people of a state, rather than the state legislature.

The Senate of the United States shall be composed of two Senators from each State, elected by the people thereof, for six years; and each Senator shall have one vote. The electors in each State shall have the qualifications requisite for electors of the most numerous branch of the State legislature.

When vacancies happen in the representation of any State in the Senate, the Executive authority of such State shall issue writs of election to fill such vacancies: Provided, That the legislature of any State may empower the executive thereof to make temporary appointments until the people fill the vacancies by election as the legislature may direct.

This amendment shall not be so construed as to affect the election or term of any Senator chosen before it becomes valid as part of the Constitution.

AMENDMENT XVIII (1919)

Section 1. After one year from the ratification of this article, the manufacture, sale, or transportation of intoxicating liquors within, the importation thereof into, or the exportation thereof from the United States and all territory subject to the jurisdiction thereof for beverage purposes is hereby prohibited.

Section 2. The Congress and the several States shall have concurrent power to enforce this article by appropriate legislation.

Section 3. This article shall be inoperative unless it shall have been ratified as an amendment to the Constitution by the legislatures of the several States, as provided in the Constitution, within seven years from the date of the submission hereof to the States by the Congress.

Legalizes *prohibition*—that is, forbidding the making, selling, or transporting of intoxicating beverages. Superseded by the 21st Amendment.

AMENDMENT XIX (1920)

The right of citizens of the United States to vote shall not be denied or abridged by the United States or by any State on account of sex.

Congress shall have power to enforce this article by appropriate legislation.

Gives women the right to vote.

AMENDMENT XX (1933)

Section 1. The terms of the President and Vice-President shall end at noon on the 20th day of January, and the terms of Senators and Representatives at noon on the 3d day of January, of the years in which such terms would have ended if this article had not been ratified; and the terms of their successors shall then begin.

Section 2. The Congress shall assemble at least once in every year, and such meeting shall begin at noon on the 3d day of January, unless they shall by law appoint a different day.

Section 3. If, at the time fixed for the beginning of the term of the President, the President elect shall have died, the Vice-President elect shall become President. If a President shall not have been chosen before the time fixed for the beginning of his term, or if the President elect shall have failed to qualify, then the Vice-President elect shall act as President until a President shall have qualified; and the Congress may by law provide for the case wherein neither a President elect nor a Vice-President elect shall have qualified, declaring who shall then act as President, or the manner in which one who is to act shall be selected, and such person shall act accordingly until a President or Vice-President shall have qualified.

The "lame duck" amendment allows the President to take office on January 20, and members of Congress on January 3. The purpose of the amendment is to reduce the term in office of defeated incumbents known as "lame ducks."

Section 4. The Congress may by law provide for the case of the death of any of the persons from whom the House of Representatives may choose a President whenever the right of choice shall have devolved upon them, and for the case of the death of any of the persons from whom the Senate may choose a Vice-President whenever the right of choice shall have devolved upon them.

Section 5. Sections 1 and 2 shall take effect on the 15th day of October following the ratification of this article.

Section 6. This article shall be inoperative unless it shall have been ratified as an amendment to the Constitution by the legislatures of three-fourths of the several States within seven years from the date of its submission.

AMENDMENT XXI (1933)

Repeals the 18th Amendment.

Section 1. The eighteenth article of amendment to the Constitution of the United States is hereby repealed.

States may pass prohibition laws.

Section 2. The transportation or importation into any State, Territory, or possession of the United States for delivery or use therein of intoxicating liquors, in violation of the laws thereof, is hereby prohibited.

Section 3. This article shall be inoperative unless it shall have been ratified as an amendment to the Constitution by conventions in the several States, as provided in the Constitution, within seven years from the date of the submission hereof to the States by the Congress.

AMENDMENT XXII (1951)

Limits a President to two full terms or one term plus two years of a previous President's term.

Section 1. No person shall be elected to the office of the President more than twice, and no person who has held the office of President, or acted as President, for more than two years of a term to which some other person was elected President shall be elected to the office of the President more than once. But this Article shall not apply to any person holding the office of President when this Article was proposed by the Congress, and shall not prevent any person who may be holding the office of President, or acting as President, during the term within which this Article becomes operative from holding the office of President or acting as President during the remainder of such term.

Section 2. This article shall be inoperative unless it shall have been ratified as an amendment to the Constitution by the legislature of three-fourths of the several States within seven years from the date of its submission to the States by the Congress.

AMENDMENT XXIII (1961)

By giving the District of Columbia three electoral votes, Congress enabled its residents to vote for President and Vice President.

Section 1. The District constituting the seat of Government of the United States shall appoint in such manner as the Congress may direct:

A number of electors of President and Vice-President equal to the whole number of Senators and Representatives in Congress to which the District would be entitled if it were a State, but in no event more than the least populous State; they shall be in addition to those appointed by the State, but they shall be considered, for the purposes of the election of President and Vice-President, to be electors appointed by a State; and they shall meet in the District and perform such duties as provided by the twelfth article of amendment.

Section 2.   The Congress shall have power to enforce this article by appropriate legislation.

AMENDMENT XXIV   (1964)

Section 1.   The right of citizens of the United States to vote in any primary or other election for President or Vice-President, for electors for President or Vice-President, or for Senator or Representative in Congress, shall not be denied or abridged by the United States or any State by reason of failure to pay any poll tax or other tax.

Section 2.   The Congress shall have power to enforce this article by appropriate legislation.

Forbids the use of a poll tax as a requirement for voting in federal elections.

AMENDMENT XXV   (1967)

Section 1.   In case of the removal of the President from office or of his death or resignation, the Vice-President shall become President.

Section 2.   Whenever there is a vacancy in the office of the Vice-President, the President shall nominate a Vice-President who shall take office upon confirmation by a majority vote of both Houses of Congress.

Section 3.   Whenever the President transmits to the President pro tempore of the Senate and the Speaker of the House of Representatives his written declaration that he is unable to discharge the powers and duties of his office, and until he transmits to them a written declaration to the contrary, such powers and duties shall be discharged by the Vice-President as Acting President.

Section 4.   Whenever the Vice-President and a majority of either the principal officers of the executive departments or of such other body as Congress may by law provide, transmit to the President pro tempore of the Senate and the Speaker of the House of Representatives their written declaration that the President is unable to discharge the powers and duties of his office, the Vice-President shall immediately assume the powers and duties of the office as Acting President.

Thereafter, when the President transmits to the President pro tempore of the Senate and the Speaker of the House of Representatives his written declaration that no inability exists, he shall resume the powers and duties of his office unless the Vice-President and a majority of either the principal officers of the executive department or of such other body as Congress may by law provide, transmit within four days to the President pro tempore of the Senate and the Speaker of the House of Representatives their written declaration that the President is unable to discharge the powers and duties of his office. Thereupon Congress shall decide the issue, assembling within forty-eight hours for that purpose if not in session. If the Congress, within twenty-one days after receipt of the latter written declaration, or, if Congress is not in session, within twenty-one days after

Outlines the procedure to be followed in case of presidential disability.

Congress is required to assemble, determines by two-thirds vote of both Houses that the President is unable to discharge the powers and duties of his office, the Vice-President shall continue to discharge the same as Acting President; otherwise, the President shall resume the powers and duties of his office.

AMENDMENT XXVI (1971)

Lowers the voting age to eighteen.

Section 1. The right of citizens of the United States, who are eighteen years of age or older, to vote shall not be denied or abridged by the United States or any state on account of age.

Section 2. The Congress shall have the power to enforce this article by appropriate legislation.

Credits

Unless otherwise acknowledged, all photographs are the property of Scott, Foresman and Company. Page abbreviations are as follow: (T) top, (C) center, (B) bottom, (R) right.

Index

Page numbers in italic refer to art.